'The ... en Mother was a le... ... example of the type that scarcely exists today – a highly intelligent, well-connected woman . . . Such women were often well educated by governesses and well-read . . . they wrote with modesty, precision, spontaneity and with kindness and wit . . . Queen Elizabeth spots small things . . . She can move from the big to the small in a way that illuminates both'   Charles Moore, *Daily Telegraph*

'We get her take on two world wars, the abdication, the premature death of her husband and the marriages of her daughters and grandchildren . . . there is something to be said for reading the Queen Mother in her own words, which are embellished with copious capitals, exclamation marks and underlinings'   Peter Conradi, *Sunday Times*

'Has any previous collection of letters spanned Queen Mary, Eleanor Roosevelt, Benjamin Britten and Norwich City Football Club? . . . Here is a fluent narrator who, despite frequent grumbles about journalists, would have made a very good one with her natural eye for the telling detail . . . There are countless fresh insights . . . an enchanting, often moving and sometimes hilarious canter from the Great War to the new millennium with a rider who refuses to slow down'

Robert Hardman, *Daily Mail*

'This book will revive you from any recession blues'   *Readers Digest*

'These expertly edited collected letters show she was an intelligent, thinking Tory who understood the importance of the culture wars and was almost always on the right side of the great issues of her day . . . superb editing [by Shawcross] . . . choosing from the several thousand letters the Queen Mother wrote those couple of hundred which best illustrate her charm, wit, steeliness, interest in the world'

Andrew Roberts, *New Criterion*

'How one warms to her! . . . Precocious historian; shrewd literary critic; discerning gastronome: so much more than a nice old doll in a hat'

... ening Standard

04089079

WILLIAM SHAWCROSS became a writer after leaving University College, Oxford in 1968. He was in Czechoslovakia during the Soviet occupation; this inspired his first book, a biography of Alexander Dubček, the Czechoslovak leader, which was published in 1970. Since then he has written and travelled widely. In 1995 he wrote the BBC Television series *Monarchy*. In 2002 his BBC Television series and book, *Queen and Country* celebrated the Queen's Golden Jubilee and examined the changing face of Britain during her reign. His official biography of the Queen Mother was published to acclaim in 2009. He lives in England.

Also by William Shawcross

DUBČEK

CRIME AND COMPROMISE

SIDESHOW

THE QUALITY OF MERCY

THE SHAH'S LAST RIDE

MURDOCH

DELIVER US FROM EVIL

QUEEN AND COUNTRY

ALLIES

QUEEN ELIZABETH, THE QUEEN MOTHER,
THE OFFICIAL BIOGRAPHY

JUSTICE AND THE ENEMY

COUNTING ONE'S BLESSINGS

The Selected Letters of
Queen Elizabeth The Queen Mother

EDITED AND WITH A PREFACE BY
WILLIAM SHAWCROSS

PAN BOOKS

First published 2012 by Macmillan

First published in paperback 2013 by Pan Books
an imprint of Pan Macmillan, a division of Macmillan Publishers Limited
Pan Macmillan, 20 New Wharf Road, London N1 9RR
Basingstoke and Oxford
Associated companies throughout the world
www.panmacmillan.com

ISBN 978-0-330-53577-9

The letters of Queen Elizabeth the Queen Mother by courtesy of
The Royal Archives copyright © Her Majesty Queen Elizabeth II
Selection, preface and commentary copyright © William Shawcross 2012

The right of William Shawcross to be identified as the
editor of this work has been asserted by him in accordance
with the Copyright, Designs and Patents Act 1988.

The list of illustrations on pages xi–xiii and the acknowledgements on pages xv–xxii
constitute an extension of this copyright page.

Every effort has been made to contact all copyright holders of material in this book.
If any have been inadvertently overlooked, the publishers will be pleased to
make the necessary arrangement at the earliest opportunity.

All rights reserved. No part of this publication may be reproduced,
stored in or introduced into a retrieval system, or transmitted, in any form,
or by any means (electronic, mechanical, photocopying, recording or otherwise)
without the prior written permission of the publisher. Any person who does
any unauthorized act in relation to this publication may be liable to
criminal prosecution and civil claims for damages.

1 3 5 7 9 8 6 4 2

A CIP catalogue record for this book is available from the British Library.

Typeset by SetSystems Ltd, Saffron Walden, Essex
Printed and bound by CPI Group (UK) Ltd, Croydon CR0 4YY

This book is sold subject to the condition that it shall not, by way
of trade or otherwise, be lent, re-sold, hired out, or otherwise circulated
without the publisher's prior consent in any form of binding or cover other than
that in which it is published and without a similar condition including
this condition being imposed on the subsequent purchaser.

Visit **www.panmacmillan.com** to read more about all our books
and to buy them. You will also find features, author interviews and
news of any author events, and you can sign up for e-newsletters
so that you're always first to hear about our new releases.

'Letters are like wine; if they are sound they ripen with keeping'

SAMUEL BUTLER

'Sometimes, one's heart quails at the thought of
the things that lie ahead, and then one counts one's blessings
– and things don't seem so bad!'

THE QUEEN,
5 May 1939 to the Archbishop of Canterbury

CONTENTS

Illustrations

PREFACE

HER MAJESTY THE QUEEN graciously permitted me to compile and edit this collection of letters of Queen Elizabeth the Queen Mother. I am deeply indebted to her. As a result of her generosity, I was allowed unrestricted access to the Royal Archives, where I had worked on the official biography of Queen Elizabeth, published in 2009, and to all other sources which I had used for that book.

As well as to Her Majesty the Queen, I am very grateful to other members of the Royal Family who have helped me, in particular the Duke of Edinburgh, the Prince of Wales, the Duchess of Cornwall, the Duke of York, the Earl of Wessex, the Princess Royal, the Duke of Gloucester, the Duke of Kent, Princess Alexandra, Viscount Linley, Lady Sarah Chatto and the Earl of Snowdon for their assistance.

I thank Her Majesty for permission to quote material from the Royal Archives, as well as from all other letters subject to her copyright. Anyone who has worked in these archives knows what a pleasure that is. Once again, I was assisted in the most efficient and supportive way by the Registrar, Pam Clark, and her staff, including Jill Kelsey, Allison Derrett and Lynne Beech. Felicity Murdo-Smith kindly assisted in transcribing letters in the Archives. The Curator of the Royal Photograph Collection, Sophie Gordon, the Assistant Curator, Lisa Heighway, and Shruti Patel and her staff at the Royal Collection Photographic Services were all immensely helpful in providing photographs to illustrate this book.

At Glamis Castle, the ancestral home of the Bowes Lyon family, I must thank the Earl of Strathmore for permission to quote papers within the family's possession. The Archivist at Glamis, Ingrid Thomson, helped me in every way, tracing names and dates and letters. Among other members of the Queen Mother's family, Sir Simon and Lady Bowes Lyon again allowed me access to their papers at St Paul's Walden, one of the Bowes Lyon family homes, and I must thank Queen Elizabeth's nieces, Lady Mary Clayton, Lady Mary Colman and the Hon. Mrs Rhodes (née Margaret Elphinstone) for their assistance. I have also been generously assisted by Queen Elizabeth's nephew the Hon. Albemarle Bowes Lyon and her great-nephew James Joicey-Cecil, by her cousin John Bowes Lyon and by her great-nieces Rosemary Leschallas, Lady Elizabeth Shakerley and Rosie Stancer, and by Jenny Gordon-Lennox.

I am much indebted to everyone who allowed me to quote from their own letters and who gave me access to letters from Queen Elizabeth which they held. These include Sir Antony Acland, Sir Edward Cazalet, Mrs Alan Clark, Lady Katharine Farrell, the Hon. George Fergusson, Canon Dendle French, the Earl of Halifax, Mrs Anthony Harbottle, Sally Hudson, Carol Hughes, Joanna Johnston, Henrietta Knight, Mark Logue, David Micklethwait, John Murray, the Hon. Lady Murray, Susan Crawford Phipps, Lady Penn, Anthony Russell-Roberts, the Marquess of Salisbury, Alexandra Sitwell, Susanna Sitwell and the Osbert Sitwell Estate, Sir Jock Slater, Earl Spencer, Lord Tweedsmuir, Violet Vyner, Cath Walwyn, Diana Way, Robert Woods, Lady Wyatt.

I have received help from the staff of many archives and libraries as well as from the archivists of private collections. They include Dr Nicholas Clark, Librarian at the Britten–Pears Foundation; Tanya Chebotarev, curator of the Bakhmeteff Archive, Columbia University; Helen Langley, Curator, Modern Political Papers, Department of Special Collections and Western Manuscripts, Bodleian Library; Michael Meredith, Librarian at Eton College; Susan Worrall, Cadbury Research Library: Special Collections, University of Birmingham; Allen Packwood, Director, and Madelin Terrazas, Archives Assistant, at the Churchill Archives Centre, Churchill College, Cambridge; Giles Mandelbrote, Librarian, and the Trustees of Lambeth Palace Library; Kathryn McKee at St John's College, Cambridge; Alison Metcalfe at the National Library of Scotland; Vicki Perry, Head of Archives and Historic Collections at Hatfield House; Bruce Bailey, archivist at Althorp; staff at the Harry Ransom Center, University of Texas at Austin; staff at the Franklin D. Roosevelt Presidential Library and Museum, Hyde Park, New York. I am grateful to them all.

I have been helped by many members of the Royal Household, as I was with my official biography of Queen Elizabeth. They include Sir Christopher Geidt, The Queen's Private Secretary, and Samantha Cohen, her Assistant Private Secretary. Sir Christopher has a superb understanding of the monarchy's place in British life and I am grateful to him for approving this collection. Miss Cohen oversaw the publication of my biography of Queen Elizabeth with consummate talent and grace, and was especially generous with her time on this work also.

I am indebted to the Royal Librarian, the Hon. Lady Roberts, and to

Sir Hugh Roberts, former Director of the Royal Collection, and to his successor Jonathan Marsden. All of them gave me the benefit of their knowledge and insights. So too did Lady Susan Hussey and the Hon. Mary Morrison, each of whom has served the Queen for over fifty years.

In the office of the Duke of Edinburgh, Dame Anne Griffiths was extremely helpful and at Clarence House I was assisted by Sir Michael Peat, Private Secretary to the Prince of Wales, and his successor William Nye, as well as by David Hutson, Virginia Carington and Paddy Harverson.

I thank Ailsa Anderson, Press Secretary to The Queen, always a fount of impeccable and witty advice, Zaki Cooper and other members of the Palace press office. As always, the Buckingham Palace switchboard under Michelle Redpath was marvellously efficient.

Many of the Queen Mother's Household and friends provided me with great help. They include Dame Frances Campbell-Preston, Martin and Catriona Leslie, Jamie Lowther-Pinkerton, Lucy Murphy, Leslie Mitchell and Jacqui Meakin. Ashe Windham, former equerry and friend of Queen Elizabeth, and Lady Penn, former lady in waiting to Queen Elizabeth, gave me particular friendship and assistance.

There are many others to whom I am grateful for different forms of help. They include Sir Eric and Lady Anderson, Fiona Bruce, Sir Edward and Lady Cazalet, Miss Pamela Fleetwood, Dame Drue Heinz, Nigel Jaques, Lady Rupert Nevill, Patty Palmer Tomkinson, Brigadier Andrew Parker Bowles, Simon Parker Bowles, Major Johnny Perkins, Lord and Lady Sainsbury, the Dowager Countess of Strathmore, Colin Thubron, the Duchess of Westminster.

As with my biography of Queen Elizabeth, I owe debts to other writers, particularly to Hugo Vickers, author of many books on the monarchy, including *Queen Elizabeth* (2005), who gave me generous access to letters in his own archives.

Above all I am indebted to those who helped me most closely, in particular Lady Elizabeth Leeming, a skilled editor in her own right, great-niece of Queen Elizabeth and sister of the Earl of Strathmore, the head of the Bowes Lyon family. She tirelessly worked through many drafts of this book and, through her careful research, discovered not only family facts but also many others. She and her husband Antony were also very hospitable to me, allowing me to work and stay in their house in Cumbria. I am once again very grateful to Sheila de Bellaigue, former Registrar of the Royal Archives, who was my peerless scholarly companion on this book, as on the official biography. Without her meticulous scholarship and erudition I could never have completed either book.

My literary agents, Carol Heaton in London and Lynn Nesbit in New York, were supportive and helpful as always. In New York I was happy to be published by Jonathan Galassi of Farrar Strauss and in London I was fortunate that once again Georgina Morley of Macmillan was my editor. It was not a simple book to create but she accomplished it with patience, charm and skill. Peter James copyedited the book with precision, Jacqui Graham arranged publicity with skill, Tania Wilde was coolheaded and managed all the final details of publication with dexterity. As before, I was privileged to have Douglas Matthews create the index.

Finally, I am grateful to my family, especially my wife Olga, and Conrad, Ellie, Alex and Charlie for their patience while I had the joy of assembling these letters.

~

LETTERS HAVE ALWAYS been treasured, sometimes revered. Archives and museums all over the world cosset them. So do people, in the drawers of their desks, in bundles hidden in boxes, in attics or in wardrobes. Letters are history, public and personal. They can evoke times, characters, hopes and fears like almost nothing else. And, above all, they can evoke love. There is almost nothing so exquisite as a letter bearing, describing, offering love. The crackle of paper drawn out of envelopes has a mystery, if not a magic, that evokes an age gone by. The letters of many prominent people – statesmen, politicians, writers, artists, lovers, kings and queens – can command both awe and high prices.

Throughout the ages, letter writing has flourished. In the nineteenth and early twentieth centuries, pen and paper were almost as natural and frequent a means of communication as word of mouth for those with money and time. In central London and other great cities, the postal services were superb and swift – letters written and posted in Mayfair would be delivered in Belgravia an hour or so later. Mornings in many households, both grand and less so, were given over to letter writing, certainly by the lady of the house.

But today letters sometimes seem of another time, almost as ancient as calligraphy. In this digital age into which the world has been thrust, almost without warning, the art of letter writing is already being swamped by emails, text messages and tweets and many more means of communication that only recently could hardly be imagined. How will historians of the future manage without the glorious primary source of private thoughts in private letters?

Of course, lamenting the death of letter writing long predates the current revolution in technology. Roger Fulford, the editor of an earlier collection of royal letters, pointed out in 1964 that phrases such as 'Nobody writes letters nowadays' and 'The art of letter writing is dead' were already constant lamentations in the middle of the twentieth century.

Fulford was introducing the first of what became five volumes of correspondence between Queen Victoria and her daughter Victoria, the Princess Royal and later Crown Princess of Prussia and mother of the last Kaiser of Germany. He ruminated about how such mid-nineteenth-century letters should be presented to readers of the 1960s. Should they be to and fro, or is a one-sided correspondence enough? Should they deal with a specific period of a life, or with the whole life? He did not lack for material – for over forty years, the Queen wrote to her daughter at least twice a week and the Princess replied almost as often. All those letters have survived. The Queen alone wrote half a million words to this one daughter.

Roger Fulford had to decide whether to publish a selection of the most interesting letters from four decades in a single volume, or to concentrate on a shorter period in order to be able to show 'the interests and occupations of the Queen'. He chose the latter and his first volume, *Dearest Child*, covers only four years, ending with the death of the Queen's husband and the Princess's father, Prince Albert, in December 1861.

In this book, by contrast, I have chosen letters from all ten decades of Queen Elizabeth's life. I hope nevertheless to have avoided the 'distracting' effect of a selection which 'jumps the reader from decade to decade', in Fulford's words.[1] And I hope also that the wide variety of those to whom the letters are addressed reflects the breadth of this Queen's interests and occupations.

~

WHEN I BEGAN RESEARCH in the Royal Archives on the official biography of Queen Elizabeth, box after box of material was brought to my desk and I was immediately struck by the wonderful letters she wrote.

Unlike Queen Victoria, she had beautiful clear handwriting from the age of ten to the age of a hundred. From childhood onwards, her words danced on the page, teeming with vitality, ebullience and optimism. Although by today's standards her formal education was limited, her letters showed a relish for language, and sparkled with the sheer joy of living.

I quoted from many such letters in the biography. But there were far more which I was not able to include even in part, let alone in whole, for simple reasons of space. And so I must repeat my gratitude to Her Majesty The Queen for granting me the huge pleasure, and responsibility, of delving again into Queen Elizabeth's letters to make the selection in this book.

The structure is simple. I have followed the path of her life and have written short passages and notes to provide context and information about those to whom she was writing and those whom she mentions. I have kept her childhood spelling but corrected her rare mistakes as an adult. In addition, I have included extracts from diaries that she kept in her early years and quotations from her remarkable recorded conversations in the 1990s with Eric Anderson, then Provost of Eton College, in which she recalled many incidents and relationships throughout her life.*

The letters span the entire twentieth century, as did her life. They are drawn from the thousands that Queen Elizabeth wrote to family and friends. Naturally, not all of these have survived. In all families, letters are thrown away, letters are put somewhere safe and forgotten, letters are lost. Sometimes letters are deliberately destroyed.

When I made my first trip to Glamis Castle I was astonished to be handed a box containing hundreds of letters written during the First World War by the adolescent Elizabeth to Beryl Poignand, her governess and friend. Many of these letters are ten or more pages long and some are filled with girlish enthusiasms, even nonsense, but almost all of them are fun – except, of course, those that deal with sombre matters of war and death. Many of them discuss the soldiers who came to convalesce at Glamis during the war, and with whom Elizabeth and Beryl made friends and played games. They show the spontaneous, joyous side of her character which she later had to control as the wife of a prince – in public at least.

Prince Albert, the second son of King George V and Queen Mary, fell in love with her in 1920 and the letters between them during their

---

* *Conversations with Eric Anderson 1994–5* (RA QEQM/ADD/MISC) and throughout. Quotations from these conversations appear in italics.

courtship – he did most of the courting – are at times almost unbearably poignant, testament to his dedication and to her hesitancy. After their marriage in April 1923, letters between them are much rarer, probably because they spent very little time apart.

There are almost no letters from Elizabeth to her father; sadder still, many of those to her mother are missing. They had an extraordinarily close, affectionate relationship, and as a child Elizabeth confided completely in her mother. The day after her wedding to the Prince, now Duke of York, Elizabeth wrote to her, 'I could not say anything to you about how utterly miserable I was at leaving you and Mike & David & father. I could not <u>ever</u> have said it to you – but you know I love you more than anybody in the world mother, and you do know it, don't you?'² Lady Strathmore replied at once, 'I won't say what it means to me to give you up to Bertie – but I think you know that you are <u>by far</u> the most precious of all my children, & always will be.'³

As soon as she entered the Royal Family, the Duchess of York made it a rule never to talk (let alone write) about her new relations, even to her Strathmore family. This discretion was wise and she maintained it for the rest of her life. Nevertheless, her letters to her mother would probably have included more accurate reflections of her thoughts and hopes and fears than any others. Unfortunately few of these letters have been found.

It is important to remember that for the first twenty-two years of her life Elizabeth Bowes Lyon was a private individual with no expectation of becoming a public figure, let alone a prominent member of the Royal Family. And after she became Duchess of York and then Queen, she continued to write private letters to friends and family with little thought that they would one day be published. Indeed, one or two of the recipients of her letters said to me, quite understandably, that they regarded their missives from Queen Elizabeth as private and not for publication.

Princess Margaret felt strongly about this; she made little secret of the fact that in the 1990s she 'tidied' her mother's papers and consigned many of them to black bin-bags for burning. These bags, she said, included letters from the Princess of Wales to the Queen Mother. After the Princess's death in 1997, her mother, Frances Shand Kydd, shredded the correspondence she found in her daughter's home.

Everyone is entitled to privacy, especially in a world where far too much becomes too public too fast. In letters, each of us sometimes writes things in haste which, on consideration, we might have phrased differently – and would not wish to see published. Sometimes letters are too long, or too repetitive. I have tried to edit these letters with these concerns in mind.

The vagaries of life have already made their selection of Queen Elizabeth's letters. Yet so many have survived that the hardest task has been to decide what to discard from the pen of this prolific and talented letter-writer. I can only hope that this book truly displays the great loves – for God, for family, for Britain and for life – which, from first to last, inspired Queen Elizabeth and her writing.

PART ONE

ELIZABETH

'A flashing smile of appreciative delight'

LORD GORELL

ELIZABETH ANGELA MARGUERITE BOWES LYON, born on 4 August 1900, was the ninth child of Lord and Lady Glamis, Claude and Cecilia. She was followed in 1902 by her brother David, to whom she became exceptionally close. Cecilia Glamis called these last two children 'My two Benjamins'. They had eight siblings: Violet, born in 1882, was followed by Mary Frances (May), Patrick, John (Jock), Alexander (Alec), Fergus, Rose and Michael. (Violet died of diphtheria in 1893 at the age of eleven, just two weeks before the birth of Michael.) In 1904 Claude Glamis's father, the thirteenth Earl of Strathmore and Kinghorne, died and he succeeded to the title.

Life for these children was as contented and secure as any childhood could be. In the first decade of the twentieth century, visitors to St Paul's Walden Bury, their handsome Queen Anne house of rose-red brick in the fields of Hertfordshire, found a bustling, happy household, full of laughter, kindness and a wish to do good in the community.

Elizabeth's first biographer, Cynthia Asquith, later wrote, 'Its atmosphere of a happy English home recalls to one's memory so many of the familiar delights of childhood – charades, schoolroom tea, homemade toffee, Christmas Eve, hide-and-seek. Nowhere in this well-worn house, one feels, can there ever have been very strict rules as to the shutting of doors, the wiping of boots, or the putting away of toys.'[1]

Throughout Elizabeth's childhood, country-house life continued with little change. White tablecloths were still spread for tea on spacious lawns; field sports, especially shooting, were immensely popular among the aristocracy and their friends.

Years later, in conversation with Eric Anderson, Queen Elizabeth remembered her childhood years:

> We were a very big family, you see. I had six brothers. I was nearly the youngest. It's so nice being brought up by elder

brothers. They kept a good eye you know. I was the youngest practically except for one little brother and so we were cherished and also disciplined, which is a very good thing. We all liked each other tremendously, I think. My very elder sister was at the very beginning of the family. She was a long way up. My middle sister was an absolute angel. Everybody loved her. In a way, my generation was very lucky – you feel very safe in a big family. It was a great thing to be loved.[2]

Cecilia Strathmore was the greatest influence on the household. She was a woman of both gaiety and religious conviction who brought up her children in love of God, love of family and love of country. 'Noblesse oblige' may not have been a term she used, but Lady Strathmore certainly impressed on her children that they had been born very lucky and that their responsibility, indeed their duty (an important word to her), lay in being generous to others, especially those less fortunate. 'Work is the rent you pay for life,' she would tell her children.

Elizabeth was from infancy vivacious, loving the company of adults as well as of her siblings. One of her governesses later recalled that she had 'a small dainty figure, a narrow, finely shaped rather pale little face, dark hair and lovely violet-blue eyes'.[3]

An admirer, Lord Gorell,* later recalled that she had even as a child 'that blend of kindliness and dignity that is the peculiar character-istic of her family. She was small for her age, responsive as a harp, wistful and appealing one moment, bright eyed and eager the next, with a flashing smile of appreciative delight.'[4]

Her brothers were all sent to Eton, but Elizabeth was educated at home by governesses. After lessons, she and David would play together in the outbuildings around the house, and explore the vegetable garden. One governess observed, 'Lady Elizabeth was adept at crawling under the netting and filling herself with strawberries while lying on her stomach.'[5] Elizabeth herself recalled the 'absolute bliss' of being in the stable surrounded by the smell of horses and leather, bits of which the groom allowed her to polish.

Every August, the family travelled to the Strathmores' Scottish home, Glamis Castle. They would go up by train, with some of their

---

* Ronald Gorell Barnes, third Baron Gorell (1884–1963), Liberal peer and author.

servants, for the opening of the grouse season on 12 August. It was a great adventure for a child – Glamis was a thrilling place, with its tower, its turrets, its history and its myths.

The Castle was lit by hundreds of candles – electric light did not come until 1929 – and there were immense fires in many rooms. Two pipers marched around the table at the end of dinner, and then there were games or songs in the drawing room, led by Cecilia at the piano. Lord Gorell wrote later that the family was without any stiffness or formality. 'It was all so friendly and kind . . . No wonder little Elizabeth came up to me once as my visit was nearing its end and demanded "But why don't you beg to stay?" '[6]

Both houses employed many of the local people. At Glamis, the Castle provided employment for inhabitants of the village near by; in Elizabeth's memory all those who worked there – housemaids, kitchen maids, grooms – were friends of the family.

The new century into which Elizabeth was born was seen at the time as a moment of great optimism. Nineteenth-century industrialization had enriched Europe and North America as never before. Railways, steamships, motor cars and even bicycles had created an almost unprecedented revolution in transport. Aged ten, Elizabeth wrote an essay entitled 'A recent invention, Aeroplanes': 'An aeroplane is usually shaped like a cigar, and has a propellor at one end, and on each side the great white wings, which makes it look like a bird [. . .] They are not quite safe, yet, and many, many axidents have happened.'[7]

Among her happiest childhood memories were the trips she made to Italy with her mother to visit her maternal grandmother in her various homes in Florence, San Remo and Bordighera.* Two affectionate letters to her father from Italy survive and one of them opens this collection.

At Christmas 1909 she was given a diary and for a few weeks thereafter she kept it diligently – 'Jan 1 1910 – I had my first nevew – great exitment.'[8] This was John, Master of Glamis, first son of her eldest brother Patrick, Lord Glamis, who had married Lady Dorothy Osborne, daughter of the Duke of Leeds, in 1908.

---

* Lady Strathmore's father, Charles Cavendish-Bentinck, had died, aged only forty-seven, in 1865. Her mother, Caroline, married again in 1870, becoming Mrs Harry Scott of Ancrum; she was widowed again in 1889.

In July 1910, only weeks after the death of King Edward VII and the accession of his son, King George V, Elizabeth's older sister May got married. By now Elizabeth had developed her happy letter-writing habit and wrote to May, 'Darling May-Di-kin', several times on her honeymoon. And whenever her mother was away, Elizabeth wrote her affectionate letters.

Elizabeth was dismayed when David was sent to preparatory school and then to Eton, but she wrote to him constantly. She remained at home whether in the country or at their rented house in London, in St James's Square, with a succession of governesses, while making short forays to small schools including that of the Misses Birtwhistle in Sloane Street. She said later that she did not think she learned anything there – 'A little bit of poetry I certainly remember. So I'm afraid I'm uneducated on the whole.'[9] In fact her school reports, preserved in the archive at Glamis, show her doing well in English, scripture and history, not so well in mathematics.

Probably the most effective governess was a young German woman, Käthe Kübler, who arrived in 1913. She was struck by Elizabeth's love of her mother and their shared devotion to the Bible, which they read together every day. But she was shocked by how disorganized Elizabeth's education had been. 'With true German thoroughness I drew up a timetable for her lessons and a plan of study, both of which were approved by Lady Strathmore.'[10] Fräulein Kübler's work was brought to an end by the outbreak of war on Elizabeth's fourteenth birthday, 4 August 1914. On that day, everyone's world changed for ever.

Elizabeth's brothers Patrick, Jock, Fergus and Michael all marched off at once to war, with hundreds of thousands of young men from all over Europe. Like many great country houses, Glamis and St Paul's Walden Bury were converted into convalescent homes for wounded soldiers. Elizabeth was told by her mother that her task – her duty indeed – was to make the soldiers feel at home, visiting the wards, talking, running errands, playing cards with them. She did it all with grace and ease. One soldier said later, 'She was always the same, asking, "How is your shoulder? Do you sleep well? Does it pain you? Why are you not smoking your pipe? Have you no tobacco? You must tell me if you haven't and I'll get some for you." For her fifteen years she was very womanly, kind hearted and sympathetic.' Everyone in the Castle 'worshipped' her.[11]

Her closest companion throughout the war was Beryl Poignand, whom Lady Strathmore engaged as her governess and companion in November 1914. Thirteen years older than Elizabeth, Beryl became her best friend and co-conspirator, and Elizabeth's extraordinary letters to her were full of the joy, excitement and fears of adolescence. Beryl ceased to be Elizabeth's governess in 1917 but remained a close friend thereafter.

Like so many families, the Strathmores tasted tragedy in the First World War. Fergus, serving as an officer with the Black Watch, was killed at the Battle of Loos in September 1915. Elizabeth and her family, particularly her mother, were devastated. When her brother Michael was reported missing in 1917, the family went through more agony until he was discovered to have been taken prisoner, at which moment she wrote one of her typically exuberant letters to Beryl to declare that she was '!!MAD WITH JOY!!'[12]

Her share of wartime suffering did not end with the Armistice of November 1918. Nine months later, one of her closest friends was killed in August 1919, fighting for the White Russian cause. She was inconsolable.

By this time Elizabeth was no longer a carefree girl but a mature young woman. She was beautiful, charming, even coquettish, and attracted the attention of many young men. But there was much more to her. She had always displayed great sensitivity, and as a result of the sufferings of her own family and of the wider circle in which she had moved during the war, she had acquired an understanding of human problems, strengths and frailties which was to stand her in good stead in later life.

10 February 1909 to Lord Strathmore

Poggio Ponente
Bordighera
Italy

My darling Father, Thank you very much for the interesting letter
you sent me. Yesterday I went down to the sea shore and enjoyed
myself very much on the rocks. I could not go far because of the sea,
it was lovly? Mother and Auntie Vava* went to Florance on Sunday
evening at 7 oclock. There is a dear little donky here called
Marguarita and we put it in a little carrage and I drive it is so quiet
have got nothing more to say exept it is a lovly garden my best love
to yourself good by from your very loving Elizabeth
   Xxxxxxxxxxxxx
   Ooooooooooo

~

Cecilia Strathmore's mother, Mrs Harry Scott, spent a good deal of
time in Florence and in Bordighera, on the Italian Riviera. Elizabeth
and her mother made several visits there. When in England, she lived
at Forbes House, Ham.

~

Diary: 1 January 1910

I had my first nevew great exitment. Same day went to Lady Littens
Fancy dress party and had great fun. Jan 2 Sunday – did nothing went
to church. Jan 3 lessons in the morning – in the afternoon I went to a
party at Kings Walden there was a Xmas tree. Jan 4 had lessons in the

---

* Violet Cavendish-Bentinck (1864–1932), known as 'Vava', Cecilia Strathmore's younger
sister and twin of Hyacinth. She never married and lived with her mother, Mrs Scott, at Ham,
and later at Dawlish in Devon.

morning. At 7 in the evning May, Rosie, David and I went to Lady Verhner in Fancy dress it was great fun, there were proggrams too and supper at half past nine. We went away at ten. It was from 7 to 12.

~

Elizabeth began her diary on 1 January 1910. Her handwriting was strong and even, but her interest in recording her life waned – as so often happens.

~

16 July 1910 to May Elphinstone

20 St James's Square*
S.W.1

Darling May-Di-kin,

This letter will reach you just after the one I wrote last night, perhaps you will think it funny me writing so soon, but I have got such a lot more to ask and tell you, that I am writing before I forget it. Aslin has been a donkey, she has been looking in all your draws (I don't mean what you wear) and was going to send you those fans (you know the ones you told me you were going to leav behind) and all sorts of things, but Mama told her not to touch a thing, except the trousseau dresses and things.

David and I are going down to Ham in an hour for Sunday and on Tuesday we go to P.W. [St Paul's Walden].

wasn't it funny when they showered Sidney and you with rice,[†] how far did you go with the shoes fastened on the motor, the boys told Charles May to stand in front of them so you would not see.

Good bye Darling May

From your loving E.A.M.B.L.

PS Please tell me if I am to call Sidney Darling or Dear.

~

---

* The Strathmores rented 20 St James's Square, designed by Robert Adam for Sir Watkin Williams-Wynn in the 1770s, from late 1906 to 1920.

† Elizabeth's elder sister, May (1883–1961), married Sidney Herbert, sixteenth Baron Elphinstone, at St Margaret's Westminster on 14 July 1910. Elizabeth was a bridesmaid at the wedding. Lord Elphinstone had been a big-game hunter and explorer. In 1900 he had travelled to the Tian Shan Mountains on the Sino-Russian border. He lived at Carberry Tower outside Edinburgh.

'We always had cricket week at Glamis. A good many Eton people came and played . . . it was great fun, it really was. We played the neighbours, my father bowled. We played the Airlies* from next door. Then there was a very good team called the Dundee Drapers.† It was easier then. People stayed in the house. I don't suppose you could do that nowadays. What used to be so good was that lovely weekend in London at Lord's in the old days when Eton played Harrow. That died didn't it after the last war?'

~

Sunday 20 November 1910 to Lady Strathmore

St Paul's Walden Bury
Welwyn

Darling Darling Lovie

I am writing to tell you Alec‡ is much much better. In fact he feels nearly quite well.

Yesterday afternoon, Furgus made a big oven in the Yew Roundabout. We took down a frying pan, and roasted chesnuts and potatoes. Darling, Mother I do hope that the visit wasn't <u>very</u> dull. Jockie got up early this morning and went to Holy Communion, he is going with Fergie and us again at 11. Everybody sends there love to You, Father, and Rosie. Please give mine too from your <u>very</u> loving Elizabeth

~

---

*   The Earl and Countess of Airlie lived near by at Cortachy Castle.

†   One newspaper described a typical match: 'This year the Glamis team includes the Earl of Strathmore (captain), the Earl of Airlie, Lord Carnegie, Lord Coke, and two of the young Lyons. It puts on no aristocratic airs however, it plays with the local Forfarshire clubs, one of them being the Dundee Drapers.' (*Singapore Free Press and Mercantile Advertiser*, 10 September 1910)

‡   Alec, the Strathmores' third son, had been injured at Eton when he was hit on the head by a cricket ball. This appears to have caused a tumour and he suffered from headaches thereafter. He died in his sleep on 19 October 1911, aged twenty-four. His humour and bravery under suffering were mentioned in many letters after his death.

Tuesday 13 December 1910 to Lady Strathmore

St Paul's Walden Bury

Darling Sweetie Lovie Mother

I hope Alec is <u>much</u> better. <u>Please</u> <u>please</u> don't worry <u>too</u> much about him. We <u>do</u> miss you so! Hester Astly has got a party on the 17th of this month, it is a sort of meeting to explain the Childrens Union. If we are not to go please tell Lady Hastings. Outside your bedroom door here there is a long parcel which has the smell and touch of Umbrella's! May is here and this afternoon we went into the wood with Ferges and her and we got some wild hyacinth bulbs in a place where they will not show. Poor Juno's right leg is very lame! and her shouldour. I hope you won't mind lovie, dovie but I took your rain umbrella to church with me on Sunday because it was raining so hard. [. . .] Miss Wilkie has not been here yet, but she sent me a letter to say what she would like David and me to do she said – essays, music, geografy, and sums. Good-bye darling lovie dovie from your <u>very</u> loving Elizabeth

PS David's love and May's and Furges's, my love to Alec, Father and Rose.

~

16 December 1910 to Fenella Trefusis

St Paul's Walden Bury

My Dear Neva,*

Thank you <u>very</u> very much for the <u>delicious</u> box of chocolates. You did not put who it was from, but two or three day's later Rosie wrote and told me it was you. Is'nt it awful perhaps we are going to have Xmas in London!!!! Think of it <u>Xmas</u> in London. Yours was the first present I have recieved. It was most awfully kind of you to think of us. I have'nt the slitest notion of where you are staying so I am going to look in the Red Book. I am afraid you will hardly be able to read my writing as it is nearly tea-time and the lamps have not come yet. It has been raining and blowing for the last three days.

---

* Hon. Fenella Hepburn-Stuart-Forbes-Trefusis (1889–1966), known in the Strathmore family as 'Neva', younger daughter of the twenty-first Baron Clinton. She married Hon. John Bowes Lyon, 'Jock', on 29 September 1914.

David send's his love and wants me to thank you for his chocolates.

Good-bye with much love from
Elizabeth

~

17 February 1911 to Miss Ela Collins

St Paul's Walden Bury

Dear Miss Ela Collins*

I hope you are feeling quite well. We are at St Pauls Walden, and it is a lovely day. This morning David and I got up at 6 o clock.

We first went and let out – Peter, Agiratem, Bumble-bee, Lion-mouse, Beauty and Delicate, our six silver-blue Persian kitten-cats. After that we went to see the ponies, then we fed the chickens, there are over three hundred. Then we went to get Judy, Juno, her four puppies, and Major. Then we went to look for eggs for breakfast. After that we had breakfast, then went for a ride. After that lessons till lunch-time. Then lessons till half past four, then we took our tea into the wood and when we came home I began to write this letter. Good-bye Miss. Ela & with

Love from
Elizabeth A. M. B. Lyon

~

'I spent half my life in the stables when I was a child. And of course the groom was one's best friend who allowed one to sit and polish bits of leather. Absolute bliss.'

~

Wednesday 11 October 1911 to Lady Strathmore

Carberry Tower
Musselburgh

Darling Precious, I must just write a line to say goodnight and to tell you about the journey. Well about three miles from Perth we heard sssssssss, and we found a tyre had burst. Charles only took ten minutes

---

*   Unknown.

putting on the other one, so we only just caught the train. We had a very nice journey, but it was very foggy when we got to Edinburgh. [. . .]

Do give Rosie, Father and Alec my love, and a lot of kisses.

Good night darling precious lovie duck from your more than loving Elizabeth.

~

26 December 1911 to the Hon. Clarence Bruce*

St Paul's Walden Bury

Dear 'Rotton Tomato'

Thank you very <u>very</u> much for the dee-licious peppermints. Its awfully kind of you to think of me. I hope you have had a <u>very</u> happy Xmas, and I hope you will have a very nice New Year. You know in your letter you put 'from the Green Tomato'. Well it isn't 'Green' its 'Rotton'. I haven't forgotten you in the least. I am afraid I cant write you a very long letter, as I have got so many to write. I hope you are very well. Thank you again very much for the Peppermints.

Good-bye, Yours Affec Elizabeth Lyon

PS Please excuse my bad writing.

[With two small drawings of heads, one scowling, the other smiling. Also a Christmas card signed 'Elizabeth Lyon', with a piece of dried heather inside.]

~

Diary: Saturday 17 February 1912

At St Pauls Walden with Rosie, Father, David. Went out riding with Rosie from eleven o' clock, till three o' clock. <u>Great</u> fun. <u>Lovely</u> Day. Sunday Feb. 18 Went to Church with, Rosie, David & Father. Lovely day. Went for walk with R, D & F. [. . .]

~

---

* The Bruces of Aberdare, an influential Welsh coal and iron family. Hon. Clarence Bruce (1885–1957) became third Baron Aberdare on the death of his brother in 1929. He stayed at Glamis in October 1908 and 1909. Years later, after the announcement of her engagement, Elizabeth wrote to him: 'Thank you so very much for the tomato! How clever of you to remember our old joke . . .' (27 January 1923, reproduced courtesy of Glamorgan Archives DBR/176)

*'St Paul's and Glamis are both very much the same in one's mind. We
loved Glamis very much. Well, I think I stayed in them fifty fifty . . . St
Paul's is a dear old Queen Anne house – rather lovely gardens – and, of
course, in those days very, very villagey. Before buses the villages focused on
each other you know. It was very medieval in a way. We all adored my
mother who really ran everything. My father, as people were in those days,
was rather inclined not to take great part in running the family. He lived
more of his own life.'*

~

Diary: March 1912

<u>Wednesday</u> Not at all well. Took some Gregory Powder.* Grannie
and Auntie arrived in the afternoon was not allowed to see them in
case I had influenzer. [. . .] Dr Thomas came.† Felt quite well, a little
tired. He said it was just a chill. So I came downstairs and saw
Grannie. Michael arrived with his friend Lyonel Gibbs before lunch.
They played tennis in afternoon. [. . .] Grannie gave me a little cup.
Goodnight.

~

Friday 10 May 1912 to Lady Strathmore

St Paul's Walden Bury

Darling Preacious Love

I hope you had a good journey to Glamis (kiss kiss kiss). This
morning Lady Kinnaird sent me a beautiful little snuff-box of
~~tortashell~~ tortoisshell inlaid with mother-of-peal and gold. I think I
have got a little chill today because my head is aching and I cant
write properly. We read the bible this morning about Samson. We
have got to do lessons in a minute so my writing will be very bad.
David's bycicle has come, I <u>cant</u> help envying him. It is <u>so</u> hot today
that its quite uncomfortable, one person in London has already died
of the heat. I am missing you dreadfully lovie. Please give Darling

---

* 'Gregory's Powder', the commonly used name for 'Rhubarb Compound Powder', a foul-
tasting brew that was nevertheless popular for its ability to settle the stomach without side-
effects; it was also used as a laxative for children.

† Dr Bernard Thomas, the family doctor from the surgery in Welwyn.

Mickie a lot of love and say to him from me 'Fie! Fie! who forgot the cigarettes'. I think it is the heat which has given me a headache because I <u>have</u> been to the <u>Ahem</u>. Please give Darling Father my love too. I simply must fly to lessons, but I will write you a longer letter tomorrow.

kiss.-kiss.-kiss.-kiss.-kiss.-kiss.-kiss.-kiss kisskisskisskisskiss for you. Ditto for Father & Mickie. Ditto trice for you lovie from your more than loving

Elizabeth

XoXoXoXoXoXoXoXoXoX

~

19 September 1912 to Lady Strathmore

Carberry Tower

My Darling Preacious Love

I hope you are having fun at Pauly. Is it nice weather. Yesterday here, it was gloriouse. We went to see Roslin Chapel.* I took some photographs of it.

I never in my life have seen such a beautiful thing the shape, the carving its too lovely. We also went to see some Prehistoricle caves, where Robert the Bruce is supposed to have hidden. I cannot remember the name of the place but I will tell you in my next letter Love. There are huge cliffs on each side of the river, running by the house, and they are finding new ones, and secret passages everywhere.

The Baby, Sidney and May are very well. I am writing this in bed, before I go and see May to have a cup of tea. I hope you are very well Lovie, and are having lots of fun. I believe we are going to see Nina Balfour† this afternoon, it is about forty miles there.

---

* Rosslyn Chapel, situated in fine landscape seven miles south-east of Edinburgh, founded in 1446 as the Collegiate Chapel of St Matthew by William St Clair. The architecture of the Chapel is richly beautiful and complex; its history has been turbulent. The building was seized by Protestant reformers in 1571, in 1592 the altars were demolished and it fell into disrepair. By the time Elizabeth visited, however, the Chapel was a consecrated church again. (The Earl of Rosslyn, *Rosslyn Chapel*, The Rosslyn Chapel Trust, 1997)

† Lady Helena Balfour (1865–1948), née McDonnell, daughter of fifth Earl of Antrim, married to Captain Charles Barrington Balfour of Newton Don near Kelso, and Balfour House,

Good-bye darling Preaciouse lovie duckie dodulums,
from your very loving
Elizabeth

~

'[My mother] would say, now darling you must look at these two houses, we
were passing. One was ugly and one was beautiful in her eyes. So we had to
learn. This is the beautiful one, you see, and bypass the ugly one.'

~

17 October 1912 to Lady Strathmore
Glamis Castle
Glamis
N.B.*

My Darling <u>very</u> Preasious LoveableLove
     I hope you had a very good journey. Please give every kind of
message to David.
     And <u>do</u> bring him up if you can. Lovie I was so sorry to have
cried when you went away. I couldnt help it though. Love if you
could get something for the dessert for our party do and put it down
to Father. I am writing just as I am getting into bed, your train is just
passing through Glamis Lovie darling.
     Good night Love, I hope David is all right.
     Your very very loving Elizabeth

~

David had started prep school at St Peter's Court in Broadstairs, Kent,
in September 1912. Elizabeth missed him greatly. Princes Henry and
George, two of King George V's younger sons, also attended this
school.

~

Balgonie, Fife. In the summer she lived at Bisham Abbey on the Thames. She was a great
friend of Cecilia Strathmore.

* 'North Britain' was often shortened to 'N.B.' in Scottish postal addresses in the nineteenth
century; the practice gradually died out but there was evidently still such writing paper at
Glamis.

Diary: 3–7 January 1913

January 1st
    Overeat myself.
    Thursday Jan 2nd
    Headache in the morning. very good tea. Christmas cake, Devonshire Cream, honey, jam, buns & tea. eat too much.
    Friday Jan 3rd
    Not quite the thing today Breakfast very good. Sausages, kedgeree, Brown Bread, Scones & honey. Excellent lunch – beefsteak – 3 helps – ham and roley poley. I eat a good deal.
    Sat Jan 4th
    I am putting on weight. My waist measurement today 43 inches. Appetite good.
    Sunday 5th
    Appetite still good, After healthy breakfast went to church. Came back very hungry for lunch. Roast beef, chicken, Yorkshire pudding, Plum pudding, cheese, cake & oranges. Oh, my poor tummy. Just going to have tea. Am very hungry.
    Monday Jan 6th
    Quite an ordinary breakfast. No jam today! Rode Wonder in the morning & came in simply ravenous for lunch. Omelette – two helps of roast chicken, finished up the bread sauce – five chocolate éclairs rium rium. Chocolate éclairs for tea – as no one else liked them, finished them up. Wish I was allowed more supper – always so hungry by the time I go to bed.
    Tuesday Jan 7th
    Barrel of apples arrived today – had one for breakfast. 10 am eat an apple. 11 am had an apple for 11 oclock lunch. 12. had an apple. Roast pigeons and chocolate pudding & apples for lunch! 3 pm eat an apple. 3.15 pm David and I fought and have got bruise on my leg because he said I was greedy. eat two apples for supper.*

~

---

* Elizabeth did not write this diary entry herself. The handwriting could be that of either Mike or Jock, teasing her, as her brothers often did, for the enthusiasm she showed for her food.

Diary: Tuesday 15 April 1913

At present we are at Poggio Ponente. This evening we are starting to Florence, Mother, Auntie, David & me, by the 7.30 from Bordighera. We are very busy packing. I have got 25 francs to spend, but I can always get some out of the Post Office Savings Bank if I see anything extra pretty. We are only staying till Friday evening.

~

Diary: Wednesday 16 April 1913

We have arrived in Florence at about 7 o'clock. We went straight to the Hotel Minerva. It is just next door to the Santa Maria Novella Church. Poor Mother was not feeling at all well, but she came with us all the same. First to the Duomo, then the Baptistry, the Singing Gallery, then we went and had lunch at 11.30 at a resterant. We also went to Cettepassi, and arranged about the pearls. I also bought an old cross, pearls & red stones, it was very pretty £6.0.0, but Mother paid half. In the afternoon we hired an open motor and drove right around Florence, up to Fiesole, where we saw the old roman remains and the Cathedral. It was lovely. 50 francs. In the evening Auntie & I did a little shopping.

~

Diary: Thursday 17 April 1913

Mother was quite well that day. In the morning Mrs Jefferson took David & I to see St Marco's Convent, where Savonorola was a long time, we saw a lot of Michael Angelo's pictures. On the way back I bought 4 very pretty old cups & saucers. Then Mother, Auntie [Vava], D & I went to see Meacci,* Auntie gave us each a picture by him.

Very pretty ones, she also gave Mother a lovely one. Then we went back to lunch. Directly after we went to the Pitti Gallery, and then to Canta Gali, David & I each bought 3 plates, & Mother gave

---

* Ricciardo Meacci (1856–[1938]), Florentine painter popular among the British community. Ten years later Meacci was commissioned by Aunt Vava to create an elaborate triptych as a wedding present for Elizabeth. He also painted another wedding present, a headboard incorporating the arms of the Strathmores and of the British Royal Family.

us each a pretty blue jar. Then Angelina took us to see Caponi, I love it. After that we met M & A at Jiacosa and had tea.

~

'When we were children both my grandmothers lived in Italy in the winter, and I just loved Italian things. I had a very clever Cavendish-Bentinck aunt, who took us to the Uffizi in Florence. She only allowed us to look at one picture . . . it was wonderful. Instead of poor little legs getting flabby with exhaustion, I remember looking at the Primavera. I can see it now. I suppose I was ten. I thought it was very clever of her really.'

~

18 July 1913 to David Bowes Lyon

St Paul's Walden Bury

My Darling David

I hope you are very well. We have come down here for good now, at least till you come home. Fraulein* goes to Germany on Tuesday 22nd next. Well, and 'ow are yer, Hay? Boo, you haint no good, you haint woggeling yer tooth. Oi ham. Dur. Whats the good o' not woggeling. Hay? Aint no good at all. Arthur Duff has given me a new pony. Its 16 years old, but awfully good still. Only 11 more days now [until the summer holidays].

    HOORAY,
    WHAT HO!
    PIP, PIP.

---

* Käthe Kübler, the daughter of a Prussian official living in Erlangen, came to the Strathmores in 1913, aged twenty-one, as a governess to Elizabeth. On 12 July 1914 she left to take her month's holiday. War began and she never returned; she volunteered for the German Red Cross in Erlangen and was sent to nurse in field hospitals in northern France, from where she continued to correspond with Elizabeth. Two wartime letters from her survive in the archives at Glamis. In 1933 Käthe Kübler wrote to her former pupil defending Hitler, something she may have come to regret. She came to see the Queen in 1937 and asked to dedicate her memoir *Meine Schülerin – die Königin von England* to her. Queen Elizabeth said many years later, in conversation with Eric Anderson: 'She was headmistress of a big school in Munich and then those horrible Nazis discovered she was a Jew and she was out in a day. She was sacked.'

Its a very short time. Everybody's well. Do write me a letter soon.
Please do Ducky.

Goodbye your very very very very very very loving Elizabeth
Xxxxxxxxxoooooooo

~

30 November 1913 to David Bowes Lyon

St Paul's Walden Bury

My darling David,

Thank you so much for your delightful pc. I'm afraid Ive been a
dreadfull long time writing but Ive been <u>horribly</u> busy, trying to knit
Xmas presents and doing lessons.

Only 18 days to the holidays. 2 weeks and 4 days. It's nice to
think about. Mother got two enormous stockings the other day. I do
look forward to us two opening them. I suppose next week you'll
write and wish Fergie a happy Christmas and a bright New Year. I
really don't know what to give him Its so awfully difficult to give a
man something which he really likes, except guns and motors. Good
thought. I might send him a motor. Shall we give it between us? Only
a few hundreds! [. . .]

Ta Ta young-feller-me-lad
From your respaactible E

~

Friday 26 June 1914 to Lady Strathmore

Glamis Castle

My Darling Mother

Most terrible goings-on here. At this present moment Fraulein is
crying and sobbing in her room, and David is doing lessons with Mr
Hewett. They had a dreadful quarrel just before tea, two at lunch, and
I really <u>don't</u> know what to do. For the last week I haven't had one
single moment of peace, even in my room, and its <u>too</u> awfull. I cant tell
you how I look forward to Thursday, oh it will be nice. I really cant help
just one tear now and then. But I do hope you will enjoy your weekend at Ham House, was Bisham fun? Only six more days! Hooray.
We are going to tea with Freda Robertson tomorrow Saturday, and

Gavin* is going to take us out in his motor, one day. Everybody is very well, I don't know about Fraulein, but I do pity her poor thing, and I'm afraid she'll go away for good, with a bad feeling against this family, though I believe she quite likes me. I had such a nice letter from Mikie this morning, <u>so</u> funny, I'm going to wait till I'm cheerfull again to reply to him. Good-bye lovie, from your very very loving Elizabeth

~

Saturday 27 June 1914 to Michael Bowes Lyon

Glamis Castle

My Darling Mike

Thank you most awfully for your delightful episal. I was glad to get it, and it made me laugh some, you bet. I suppose you'r moving around pretty slick just now, dinner, balls ect. I hope you are having plenty of champenge, clarit, 'oc, mosel, and baeer, Baaeer, Baaeer, wonderful baaer, fill yourself right up to here (neck). That was by Shakespeare. Oi ad an horful noice toime yesterday playing 'opscotch with Fairweather,[†] oi can taal you he got a talent for 'opscotch.

We are coming down on Thursday next, it will be nice seeing you all again. I'ts not very peaceful here! I am sorry to see by your picture that Spicer has'nt been shaving his nose lately, do tell him before I come down. Williams is playing the concertina most wonderfully, it's really a delight to hear him, he attracts <u>crowds</u> of people from all round. How's old Rosie. I hope your health is good. Been to 'Hullo Tango' lately? I went to the Alhambra last night, jolly good show. Waal, good-bye Mike old gump, (Mike Gump) Ha Ha I <u>do</u> call that funny. From your very loving and sweetly Elizabeth

~

'The war broke out on my birthday. We went to the theatre and two people in the box were called up and one was a [young man called] William who had been in the Eton Eleven. I can't remember who the other one was. The streets were full of people shouting, roaring, yelling their heads off – little

---

*   Gavin Ralston, factor (agent) at Glamis, 1913–49.

†   Several generations of the Fairweather family worked at Glamis in the first half of the twentieth century. This could have been William or George Fairweather, who in turn held the post of Head Keeper.

thinking what was going to happen.' Soon after this, Elizabeth went to
see her brother Mike off at the station, on his way to war: *'There was a
very young little officer going off, and his mother – I can see her now – was
weeping. And I remember my brother leaning out of the train and saying
"Don't worry, I'll look after him." And do you know, he was killed the next
day. It was so awful when one thinks about it.'*

~

20 October 1914 to Beryl Poignand

Glamis Castle

Dear Miss Poignand*
    Mother wishes me to write and tell you our address in Herts:
    St Pauls Walden Bury
    Welwyn
    Herts
    She is very busy as we have just heard this morning that my
brother Michael is starting for the front at any time, so I expect she
will fly down South to say good-bye.
    Please excuse my bad writing, as I'm in rather a hurry.
    Yours sincerely
    Elizabeth Lyon

~

9 August 1915 to Beryl Poignand

Glamis Castle

My Dear Miss Poignand
    Thank you very very much indeed for your long and amusing
letter, no news of you, comments on my letter, but all the same great

---

* Dorothy Irene Beryl Poignand (1887–1965), daughter of Colonel George and Catherine
Maud Poignand. Engaged by Cecilia Strathmore as governess to Elizabeth, 1914–17. She
quickly became, and remained for many years, Elizabeth's most intimate confidante outside
her family. During the Second World War she was temporarily employed by the Royal
Household in the Central Chancery of the Orders of Knighthood, and stayed on until 1949. In
1947 she helped organize the exhibition of Princess Elizabeth's wedding presents and compiled
the catalogue. Until her death in 1965 she remained in touch with Queen Elizabeth the Queen
Mother, whose letters to Beryl were subsequently returned by her cousin Mrs Leone Poignand
Hall.

fun talking or rather writing about our mutual friends. First I will try and answer one or two of your questions.

We sat in the stalls at the Hippodrome, right in the middle just under the gangway thing, so I got a lot of extra amusement, because you see the actors & actresses all walk along it.

2) Yes, we did have rather an exciting journey up to Glamis, in this way. Two _most_ beautiful sailors were also travelling in the same corridor. [. . .] We had long conversations in the corridor in the morning, David and I were travelling alonio. Rather amusing, what?

3) My hat is only a rotton little shiny rainproof one.

The soldiers are charming. My dear Miss Poignand you <u>are</u> missing something! One is a fisherman and a Naval Reserve, he has been shipwrecked five times. Blue eyes, black hair, <u>so</u> nice. Reminds me of Henry.* By the way it's getting awful. The vulgar and insulting telegrams on my birthday were about darling Henry's stomach, was it real or a cushion, he was just having his 25th anniversary on the stage & such insults. Really it's awful. Dear Beautiful One,† I do so miss him, it was great luck, before I went, he had to pass right under the window so I had a good look at him, he really, honestly (bar rot) is very good looking and <u>clean.</u> You know what I mean by clean, not like Fatty.‡ [. . .]

Wouldn't it be wonderful if Fenella succeeded in getting a photograph of Henry, he would go first place on my dressing table. But I'm afraid he's too modest to have any published. Father gave me a little horseshoe in pearls and diamonds for my birthday. [. . .] It's very pretty stones, tho' it would have been prettier <u>not</u> a horseshoe.

I must end now, haven't I written a lot of rot? Can you read my writing? David is yelling for me

au revoir, y l

Elizabeth

~

---

* Henry Ainley (1879–1945), a classical actor who starred in numerous theatre productions and many films over a forty-five-year career. Elizabeth had a crush on him in the early part of the war and frequently went to his performances.

† A chauffeur working with the Red Cross, whose headquarters was in St James's Square, close to the Strathmore home. Elizabeth and Beryl very much admired him.

‡ Another Red Cross chauffeur. Elizabeth pretended he was Beryl's heart-throb.

'Glamis became a sort of hospital and St Paul's Walden was a hospital and
we had ward jobs in the First World War, helping a bit in the hospital.
Rosie did proper nursing and I only went and played cards with them in the
evenings or perhaps wrote a letter or things like that. They all cheated like
anything. It was all right – we played one of those games when you can cheat
quite easily. There were about fifteen of them, mostly convalescent from the
big hospital and I think they were really happy there. Then all my brothers
went off. Everybody went. There was nobody left.'

~

26 August 1915 to Beryl Poignand

Glamis Castle

My dear Miss Poignand,

Perfectly wonderful, marvellous, absolutely indescribable news,
prepare yourself ---------.

Lavinia* has a first cousin
who --------------
KNOWS
darling
HENRY
VERY
WELL!!!!

He is 35 (Hahahoo, Rosie and Mike will be squashed!) & she is
going to write & find out the colour of his eyes, & everything, also –
get his signature. Isnt it absolutely unbelievable. Darling Henry. I am
so pleased. I feel that it was quite worth sticking up for him all this
time. Oh my sacred Aunt in pink tights, perhaps we shall even meet
him, help I shall die in a minute.

Yours, Elizabeth

Friday Aug 27 1915. Spare neither time nor money in procuring
a couple of photos of Basil Hallam.† T'is of great importance. The

---

* Lady Lavinia Spencer (1899–1955), second daughter of sixth Earl Spencer; married 1919
Hon. Luke White, later fourth Baron Annaly. Lady in waiting to the Duchess of York on the
East African tour, 1924–5.

† Basil Hallam (1889–1916), another actor whom Elizabeth admired. His most famous role
was as Gilbert the Filbert in the revue *The Passing Show*. He joined up in 1915 and was killed
in a parachute jump on the Western Front in 1916.

news of Henry is wonderful. I really do not despair of <u>meeting</u> or at least seeing him. Oh my sacred Aunt, you wait a few days. You just wait.

From the usual person

~

31 August 1915 to Beryl Poignand

Glamis Castle

My Dear Miss Poignand

I will now try to write you a letter with some news in it. (Not so much of the Darling.)

Fergus* has been home on leave, only 5 days. He went back on Saturday. Christian and the Baby are both here the baby is going to be called Rosemary.

I went to tea with Lady Jellicoe on Saturday last, she lives quite close. She had heard from Sir John who said he thought it wasn't true about the Moltke† being sunk, that it was only damaged, but that he wasn't yet sure.

Mademoiselle [Lachaise]‡ went away this morning. [. . .]

Isn't it quite too wonderful about Henry. <u>Please</u> try and get some pictures of Basil. You know that postcard shop in Regent St we both hunted for? Well, I know where it has now moved to!! Please try there for Basil. Photograph preferred to a P.card. I enclose a plan of

---

* Fergus Bowes Lyon (1889–1915), the fourth son of Lord and Lady Strathmore, was an officer in the Black Watch. In September 1914 he had married Lady Christian Dawson-Damer (1890–1959). Their daughter Rosemary was born on 18 July 1915. Two months later, on 27 September 1915, he was killed at the Battle of Loos.

His death plunged the whole household, particularly his mother, into grief. The soldiers at Glamis wrote to Lady Strathmore in sympathy. She thanked them and said that she hoped they would carry on using the Castle just as before. No letter from Elizabeth describing Fergus's death has been found, but her friend Lavinia Spencer to whom she wrote replied on 5 October 1915, 'your letter was so brave.' Glamis Archives (Box 270).

Rosemary married 1945 Edward Joicey-Cecil and had two children, James Joicey-Cecil (1946–) married 1975 Jane Adeley, and Anne (1950–) married 1971 Alastair Malcolm. Rosemary died in 1989.

† New type of German battlecruiser named after the nineteenth-century military strategist Field Marshal Helmuth von Moltke.

‡ Lydie Lachaise (1888/9–1982), holiday governess to Elizabeth and David for the Easter and summer of 1915. She never forgot the sadness in Lady Strathmore's face when Fergus left to return to the Front. (Information from Clare Elmquist, daughter of Lydie Lachaise)

where it is. In Piccadilly, same side as Piccadilly Hotel. Nearly opposite St James' Church. <u>The</u> only place. If they don't keep 'em they get 'em for you.

Goodbye Write soon,
Yours till the moon turns blue
Elizabeth

~

14 September 1915 to Lady Strathmore

Carberry Tower

My Darling Mother

I hope you had a very good journey down, & also David. I miss you both <u>very</u> much. I wonder if you could ask Catherine,* if she has time, to buy me some hair ribbon like the enclosed pattern as I have none at present? Darling Mother, don't forget, a little white fox neck thing, a really chic hat, the 'dernier cri' in shirts, & a warm winter coat, the newest mode!!!!!! There is nothing much to say, as everything goes on just the same. I am feeling much better. I shall write to David. Please give him lots of kisses from me, and to you. Love to Jock & Neva from your very very very loving Elizabeth

~

16 September 1915 to Beryl Poignand

Carberry Tower

My Dear Miss Poignand

Many thanks for your letters. I will first answer your questions. [. . .] Yes, the Zeppelins did a good deal of damage,† Wood St demolished as you say, and a Rubber Factory gutted, also, most of the casualties were from a bomb dropping on to a motor bus. They knew

---

* Catherine Maclean (c. 1890–1966), lady's maid and subsequently dresser to Elizabeth both before and after her marriage. She retired in 1952. In the 1950s and 1960s she and her two sisters ran the Dores Inn on Loch Ness, where Queen Elizabeth sometimes visited them.

† Zeppelins, the lighter-than-air machines, caused terror over England in the First World War. One historian wrote that the Zeppelin 'was the H-bomb of its day, an awesome sword of Damocles to be held over the cowering heads of Germany's enemies' (quoted in Martin Gilbert, *First World War*, Harper Collins, 1995, p. 42). Wood Street in the City of London was bombed on the night of 8–9 September 1915.

a whole day before that they were coming and yet made no
preparations. I hear we have captured a German aeroplane & pilot at
Wantage. That's good. Its quite true. London is full of dreadful
rumours. Dardanelles is going badly for us. But much the worst is
that Kitchener is going to resign. [. . .] But, Sidney, who wrote about
it, says that he does'nt think that this long suffering country would
stand that, for they have such faith in K of K.* I hear the Russians are
getting a much better supply of ammunition now, perhaps they will
pick up a bit. I am going back to Glamis this afternoon, Oh,oh,oh,
Miss Poignand old sport. How terribly you would have envied me.
I spent the whole afternoon on the shores of the Forth. So near
the ships that I could see people. And a conversation with a most
beautiful sailor, with blue eyes and black lashes and so good looking.
That was yesterday. He pointed out all the ships to me. First, nearest
the bridge, came the Lion, then Tiger, New Zealand, H.M.A.S.
Australia (to which he belonged), Indefatigable, Queen Mary and
many others. They looked too fine for words. I simply revelled in
'em. And simply hundreds of beautiful brown Lieutenants, Subs,
Snotters [midshipmen], Admirals and sailors. Oh my. They were all
most amorous! While I was watching the ships, they all turned round,
it looked so nice. Beatty's fleet I suppose.

Love Elizabeth

~

Sunday 26 December 1915 to Beryl Poignand

Glamis Castle

My Dear Silly Ass

Thank you very much for your letter. Always received with
grateful thanks. I wonder if you have left London, anyhow I shall
send this to Cheltenham.

---

* Field Marshal Horatio Herbert Kitchener, first Earl Kitchener KG KP GCB OM GCSI
GCMG GCIE ADC PC (1850–1916). In 1898 Kitchener won the Battle of Omdurman, after
which he was created Lord Kitchener of Khartoum. He was crucial to the British victories of
the Second Boer War and, in 1914, became Secretary of State for War. He was one of the few
men to foresee a long war and organized the largest volunteer army Britain had ever seen.
The recruiting posters bearing his image and the words 'Your Country Needs You' are potent
even today. He died in 1916 when the warship carrying him to Russia struck a German mine
and sank.

Well, I hope you had a very happy Christmas, and nice presents. Would you like to know what I had?

Father gave me a wrist watch, Mother a kettle, Rosie some handkies, David some chocolates, Nurse a box with patience cards, Catherine a hankie, Auntie Vava a picture, Grannie a bowl, May a pair of shoe buckles etc in fact rather nice useful presents. I hope you liked the book. [. . .]

The men liked the Tree very much I think, they each got an electric torch, a shirt & chocolate & crackers & things.

I believe the noise last night at 'lights out' was something appalling, trumpets & squeaky things going like mad etc. Abell said, 'It's a funny thing, I wanted a bloomin' cigarette case, and I wanted a blinkin' electric torch and I got 'em both'! So he ought to be quite pleased. Pegg asked me if you'd gone to Cheltenham. Ernest was simply delighted with his book. Of course we drank 'To Hell with the b— Kaiser' last night and good 'ealth to Henry and Larry!* Nurse gets passionate love letters from Ralph & Co, also from one who signs himself 'Prince William the Conqueror'. I think he must have got slightly mixed up! 'Ow h'are you my h'only h'adored one? Pretty bobbish??† [. . .]

Good-bye, farewell, fare ye well, Tarry not, so long, au revoir good bye farewell etc etc etc etc and so on for 2 pages.

~

6 February 1916 to Mrs Poignand

Glamis Castle

Dear Mrs Poignand‡

Thank you very much for the delightful cutting about Mr Ainley and your letter. We have now got a huge box of cuttings,

---

* Abell, Pegg, Pearce and Ralph were all convalescent soldiers. Ernest Pearce developed a lifelong relationship with Elizabeth. She described him as 'A most delightful Corporal, nice boy indeed', (Elizabeth to Beryl Poignand, 7 September 1915, Glamis Archives (CH)) and often played boisterous card games with him and other soldiers. He survived the war and then worked in a shipyard in Sunderland, until Elizabeth offered him a job as gardener at her home, Royal Lodge in Windsor Great Park. He stayed with her until he died in 1969; and his niece, Mary Ann Whitfield Pearce, worked at Royal Lodge also, becoming head cook.

† 'Bobbish' meant hearty and in good spirits. The word occurs in Charles Dickens's *Great Expectations*. Sadly it appears to have fallen into disuse.

‡ Catherine Maud Poignand, mother of Beryl.

photographs and 'poems' all about him and we always welcome any addition to the collection! It must be delightful the spring flowers out, we have none up here yet, only Christmas roses and daisies. We all went into Dundee to the theatre there the other evening. Miss Poignand behaved herself in a <u>disgraceful</u> manner, she very nearly got chucked out by the 'chucker out'! She sang <u>so so</u> loud that the manager came and asked her if she would kindly stop, whereupon, she sang <u>most</u> aggressively to him (the poor man had a red nose) 'Put a bit of powder on it', which is a vulgar song. To crown all that, she drank <u>three</u> cocktails on reaching home, and had to be carried up to bed by Barson,* who seemed to enjoy the job!!! I really felt quite ashamed of her! Thank you very much for your wishes about my exam. I don't really think I shall pass, you see I don't know much, and I'm most stupid. I think much the best plan would be for Miss Poignand to let her hair down, put on a short frock and do it for me. I should pass & get many distinctions! Don't you [think]? Yes, she looked too funny for words on the pony, with her legs flapping, & her arms wagging about, I laughed till I nearly cried. But she stuck on all right, which was the chief thing! When we get to London she & me are going to have a gay time, we're saving up for it. Thank you so much for your letter. Yours sincerely

    Elizabeth Lyon

~

* Arthur Barson (1879–1944) served the Strathmore family through several generations. In the 1901 census he is listed as 'footman' and in 1911 as 'valet', and he then became butler. No job title describes his important place in the family. 'Nothing would go on without him – he keeps everything going,' the young Elizabeth once said. He could turn his hand to everything and also acted as Lord Strathmore's loader – indeed 'Father and Barson' is a phrase that often appears in Elizabeth's letters. Anecdotal evidence suggests that his fondness for the grape and the grain in no way impaired his skills or the family's affection for him. He is included in a family portrait painted in 1909 by Alessandro Catani-Chiti, which hangs at St Paul's Walden Bury. When Lady Strathmore died in 1938, Barson was distraught. At her memorial service at St Martin-in-the-Fields, in the words of Arthur Penn, a close family friend, Barson 'advanced down the aisle with his battered old face full of grief, making apologetic & deprecatory noises at being given the place to which his long and ample service so amply entitled him' (Arthur Penn to Queen Elizabeth, 28 June 1938, RA QEQM/PRIV/DEATH/STRATH). When he died in 1944 as butler at St Paul's Walden, the house had been turned, once again, into a wartime convalescent home for soldiers.

17 March 1916 to Lady Strathmore

20 St James's Square

My Darling Mother

Just a little letter to tell you the news from here.

I began my examination today.* I started soon after 8 this morning, and got to Hackney about 9.30! Bus and tram, it's the only way. I did a 'memory drawing' paper, which ended 10.45, so I came back for lunch, & then went back again at 1.30! I did a 'model drawing' paper this afternoon and got home about 4.30. Altogether it took 4 hours on journeying from here to Hackney and back again! I'm what you might call 'slightly fatigued'. The exam place is about the last house on that side of London, green fields beyond, stupid sort of place I call it. My cold is much better, but staying in bed, even for only 2 days makes me feel 'pale' for a bit.

I am going down to Eton tomorrow, to see David, May and Sidney are coming. I am taking him an Angel cake, six plums, & one lb of grapes, is that right? I hope that you are quite well Lovie, also Father, Rosie & Mike. I got a letter from Father this morning, what beastly weather you must be having, it's fairly warm here just now. How are those horrible beastly, disgusting, food-gobbling, hideous, putrid, and above all USELESS chickens? I have never seen such supercilious and snobbish birds in all my life. I am going to see Henry next Friday when I've done my exam, you said I might, didn't you? I am saying 'Miserere' this Friday but next Friday I shall say 'jubilate'.

I've got to start at 8 tomorrow morning!

So goodbye darling Mother from your very, very loving Elizabeth ooooooxxxxxxxxx

~

25 March 1916 to Lady Strathmore

20 St James's Square

My Darling Mother Lovie,

Thank you very very much for your letter this morning. Yes, I am

---

* The junior examination of the Oxford Local Examinations Board took place at the Hackney Examination Centre. Elizabeth subsequently received a letter from the Examination Board stating, 'you do not appear to be entitled to a certificate'. (RA QEQM/PRIV/PERS/Education)

very happy to stay another week, and I <u>do so</u> hope you won't be lonely. I am going down to Slough with May this afternoon, to see her little house, with no roof, <u>or</u> drains <u>or</u> bath!

Then on to tea with David. I am staying the night with her. Lady Airlie* got on the telephone this morning, and said 'when are you coming to see me?' And I've got to go to tea with her on Monday.

I <u>am</u> so dreadfully frightened. I can't think why she asks me, it's <u>so</u> kind of her but I wish she would'nt. I wish I'd suggested Tuesday, because then Rosie would have been there. [. . .] May is giving me a mauve linen dress by a French dressmaker who was with <u>PAQUIN</u>,† aren't I smart?!!!

I got a letter from Father, and he said that I didn't tell him all the little bits of news that I told you, I didn't think that they would interest him, being a man, but I will write him a really 'chatty' one now. I hope he is quite well. I am afraid I've failed in my exam, the Geography and Arithmetic were <u>quite</u> hopeless, much too complicated for me! [. . .]

Goodbye darling Mother from yr very very loving Elizabeth

~

28 March 1916 to Lady Strathmore

20 St James's Square

My Darling Mother

Rosie arrived all right this morning, though her train was rather late. We went out shopping together before lunch, she seems very well. We tea'd with May, and had to wait over an hour for a taxi! A terrific gale blowing, sheets of snow and altogether beastly weather. It must be disgusting at Glamis. [. . .] My tea went off fairly well with Lady Airlie!! Only she and Mabel‡ were there. [. . .] Lavinia wants me

---

*   Blanche, widow of fifth Earl of Airlie (1826–1921).

†   Jeanne Paquin (1869–1936), innovative French dress designer who became, in 1891, the first woman to open her own fashion house. Her designs were vibrant and beautiful and she publicized them with élan.

‡   Mabell (1856–1956), widow of sixth Earl of Airlie, who had been killed in the Second Boer War on 11 June 1900 at the Battle of Diamond Hill, Pretoria, leading his regiment in a charge that saved the guns. She was a lady in waiting to Queen Mary from 1901 until the Queen's death in 1953.

to go to tea, to meet Princess Mary* and Prince Albert† next Sunday. They don't frighten me quite as much as Queens. I do hope that Father's cold is better. I sent Mike some papers today, and I'm bringing some songs with me too. Good bye darling Mother, don't you think I'm very good at writing?! From your very very loving Elizabeth

~

4 April 1916 to Lady Strathmore

20 St James's Square

My Darling Mother

I hope that you will get my telegram about David today. I wanted to go down and see him today, but he said that the doctor didn't want him to see anybody for a day or two, and he was feeling 'extraordinarily well'. Also he is leaving Eton Thursday or Friday, and, from his telegrams, sounded very cheerful, so I hope he's not bad. Rosie is going down tomorrow. I can't as I've got the dentist.

My tea on Sunday with Lavinia was rather frightening – in fact, very. She had to get a few people to meet them, Princess Mary & Prince Albert I mean. The Duchess of Sutherland (young)‡ was there, she's rather pretty is'nt she? Moucha Cecil,§ Lady Bury,¶ Maud Cavendish,‖ all the Spencers also a Mr Penn,** who asked after Lady 'Rosie', a Mr Robinson who was very nice, & a Mr Dill.

---

* Princess Mary (1897–1965), daughter of King George V and Queen Mary; married 1922 Viscount Lascelles, later sixth Earl of Harewood. Elizabeth was a bridesmaid.

† Prince Albert Frederick Arthur George (1895–1952), later King George VI, second son of King George V and Queen Mary. He married Elizabeth in 1923.

‡ Duchess of Sutherland (1891–1943), née Lady Eileen Butler, daughter of seventh Earl of Lanesborough, married 1912 fifth Duke of Sutherland.

§ Lady Mary ('Moucher') Alice Cecil (1895–1988), daughter of fourth Marquess of Salisbury, married 1917 Lord Hartington (later tenth Duke of Devonshire).

¶ Lady Bury (1889–1928), née Lady Judith Wynn-Carrington, daughter of first Marquess of Lincolnshire, married 1909 Viscount Bury (later ninth Earl of Albemarle).

‖ Lady Maud Cavendish (1896–1975), eldest daughter of ninth Duke of Devonshire, married 1917 Capt. Angus Mackintosh (d. 1918); 1923 Hon. George Baillie.

** Arthur Horace Penn (1886–1960), served in Grenadier Guards in the First World War (MC, mentioned in dispatches), practised as a barrister and worked in the City, appointed groom in waiting to King George VI, 1937. A friend of Jock Bowes Lyon at Eton. Elizabeth met him at

I had a table all to myself at tea, with Mr Robinson on one side,
& Mr Dill on the other, and I nearly <u>burst</u> trying to think of
something to say! Prince Albert was next door, he's rather nice.

I was photographed yesterday. I am so afraid that you will be
disappointed in them, the other photos there were all <u>so</u> hard but
they're coming tomorrow.

May took me to the matinée this afternoon. Henry did a most
weird and eerie sort of little play. The masks they wore were
designed by Dulac,* who hopped about in brown velveteen the whole
time. Henry has got <u>the</u> most <u>wonderful</u> voice, and he was universally
admired. He is so dreadfully shy, that it's quite painful I believe.
Thelma Cazalet[†] said that they'de often asked him to lunch and that
he was <u>so</u> shy that he'de accepted, and <u>always</u> telegraphed an excuse,
poor old Henry!!! I'm so glad as it shows that he is'nt a fast sort of
man. There was a delightful orchestra conducted by Sir Thomas
Beecham, who played some beautiful music. All the usual 'matinee'
people were there. The <u>beeeeautiful</u> siren, Lady Diana Manners,[‡]
Nancy Cunard (???!!!) Duchess of Rutland (white haggard face, red lips
and 'oh oh' eyes!)[§] Lady Lytton,[¶] quite pretty, Mrs Bonham Carter
(otherwise Miss Asquith),[|] a beautiful widow, unknown, fast, slightly
painted, but undeniably good looking, <u>all</u> the Duchesses, and the
Dowager Duchesses, Queen Alexandra & family, & last but not least
ME!!! <u>And</u> of course dear Henry.

I suppose I'de better wait and come with David on Saturday
night? Rosie dined with Marjorie Dalrymple Hamilton last night,

this time and found him entrancing. During the Second World War he served as her Private
Secretary and Treasurer, remaining in the latter role until his death.

*   Edmund Dulac (1882–1953), celebrated book illustrator, who also designed costumes and
sets for the theatre.

†   Thelma Cazalet (1899–1989), daughter of W. M. Cazalet; became an MP (1931–45), was
briefly a junior minister at the end of the Second World War and sat on many public
committees afterwards; married David Keir in 1939 and was known as Thelma Cazalet-Keir
after that. Sister of Peter Cazalet, the Queen's postwar racehorse trainer.

‡   Lady Diana Manners, later Lady Diana Cooper (1892–1986), daughter of eighth Duke of
Rutland, married 1919 Alfred Duff Cooper, later Viscount Norwich.

§   Duchess of Rutland (1856–1937), mother of Lady Diana Manners; married 1882 eighth
Duke of Rutland.

¶   Countess of Lytton, née Pamela Chichele-Plowden (d. 1971), married 1902 second Earl of
Lytton.

| (Helen) Violet Bonham Carter – see letter of 7 March 1944 (p. 359).

Freddy was up for the evening.* I lunched with May today. Two munitions men were there. The powder factory in Kent blew up, because somebody was walking about, smoking a cigarette, which was the stupidest thing that could possibly be done! Also the Zepps dropped 90 bombs round Waltham Abbey our biggest <u>cordite</u> place, and killed – three chickens! Which was extraordinarily good luck. The damage done by the gale last week is frightful. They say it will be <u>quite three months</u> before the train service is normal again, & every telegraph wire is down. Tell Father they'll want poles. All ours come from Russia.

Well, darling Mother, I do hope that you are not <u>very</u> dull at Glamis. Rosie & I got a few dress stuffs at Harvey & Nichols, I hope you will like them.

Goodbye darling Mother from your very very loving Elizabeth

~

19 April 1916 to Beryl Poignand

Glamis Castle

My dear Medusa†

[. . .] I shall have to start right now answering all your questions. Two records of Henry have arrived, 'Sing, Belgians sing'. Mike said, 'Yes, he <u>has</u> got a beautiful voice', which was a lot for him! Though of course it doesn't sound so good on the gramophone. I shall fly to the Haymarket directly I get to London. We must try and go together, because we are about the only two people who <u>really</u> appreciate the poor darling! Well, now I have got a bit of news for you. ROSIE is engaged to be married! Aren't you surprised? to Wisp Leveson Gower! She got engaged last Friday! I know you always want to know everything so I will give you his full address: Commander the Hon William Spencer Leveson-Gower

---

* Frederick Dalrymple Hamilton KCB (1890–1974), served in the navy throughout his life. While commanding HMS *Rodney* (1939–41) he took part in the destruction of the German battleship *Bismarck* in May 1941. A close friend of the Strathmore family, he met Elizabeth for the first time in 1911 and described her as a 'little angel!!'. His diaries revealed the fun of life with the Strathmores. Marjorie was Freddy's sister-in-law, born Lady Marjorie Coke, daughter of third Earl of Leicester, whom his brother, North, had married in 1910.

† From this time, Elizabeth often addressed Beryl as 'Medusa', presumably a reference to her hairstyle, which she sketched in this letter.

RN.* He's Lord Granville's next brother. He's been staying here the last few days, and he went down to London last night, and comes up again tomorrow for about 2 days. They wanted to be married in May, which is in less than three weeks, isn't it awful. Though as he's a sailor I hope she will be able to be a good deal with us, when Wisp's at sea. He's got a destroyer. [. . .]

Barson is very well thank you, he's <u>always</u> well! The Nurse is coming May 2nd, and Mother is going to re-open May 3rd. <u>All</u> our soldiers have now left Dundee. Tommy, the Sergeant, & Nicky have been discharged & gone. Pegg has been sent to a New Zealander's hospital, where I expect he will be happier than in Dundee, & poor little MacGilhuddyreeks goes to a consumptive hospital. I don't know about Freddy and Stevie, but I think they've all gone. [. . .]

Well, I must stop now. I will send you one of the dreadful photos of me when they arrive.

Gott strafe Miss Jemima Goodman.† Gott strafe Hackney. Gott strafe Dalston Junction, Gott strafe the tapioca pudding (most especially), Gott strafe the whole exam, <u>but</u> God bless Henry. God bless the shops with his photograph and all the nice things, we won't strafe them. Shall we say 'Gott strafe Medusa Poignand, the curse of the Poignands? <u>No</u>, we shall not. We shall say Gott <u>bless</u> Medusa Poignand, the source of continued worry & anxiety to Elizabeth Lyon, who makes eyes at Fatty & conducts herself in a most unseemly manner.

Yours forever
Elizabeth

~

---

* William Spencer Leveson-Gower KG GCVO CB DSO (1880–1953). He became fourth Earl of Granville in 1939 on the death of his brother. After a distinguished career in the Royal Navy, he was appointed Lieutenant Governor of the Isle of Man in 1937 and was Governor of Northern Ireland, 1945–52.

† Margaret Goodman, Secretary of the Local Examinations Board, whose name was on the notice informing Elizabeth that she had failed the examination she took in Hackney.

26 April 1916 to Beryl Poignand

The Little House
Clova
Forfarshire

My dear Medusa

Don't for one moment imagine that Glamis is burnt or blown up,
because it is'nt. We've only come up here for the day, to plant & tidy
etc. It is the <u>first fine day</u> that we've had since I came up from
London, the weather has been hopeless. David & I are coming down
next Monday if all's well. He goes back to Eton on Wednesday, & I
prophesy that Tuesday evening will be taken up. Most probably
'Stand & Deliver.'

Wisp thinks he won't be in for a refit anyhow before May 10th, so
the wedding can't be fixed. Rosie & he go down tomorrow. She's got
to get her trousseau, & he joins his ship. I didn't realise what a lot of
things have to be got for a trousseau. I should <u>never</u> be able to use <u>2</u>
dozen of everything, <u>lingerie</u> I mean, good heavens, I'm thankful to
say no. She and Wisp will be very poor. His destroyer is the Comet I
think, & he is in the Grand Fleet up North. [. . .]

All that I say is <u>DAMN THE EXAM</u>!! I always was good at poetry
wasn't I?!! I'm not going to tell <u>anyone</u> about it, anyhow till they ask
me!! Good heavings! What <u>was</u> the use of toiling to that er, place er
Hackney? None, I tell you, none. It makes me <u>boil</u> with rage to think
of that vile stuff, tapioca, eaten for – nothing? [. . .]

Rosie will probably be married between the 16th & 26th, some
time about then. [. . .] [She] gets all sorts of funny letters amongst her
<u>hundreds</u> of congratulations. Lord Curzon called her 'an unplucked
blossom' [. . .]

You remember that Friday (it's always Friday) the last one I mean,
after we'de been with Lavinia, & we had to go to tea with Mlle
Lachaise?

We went by tube, & there were two old gentlemen sitting
opposite, & they never took their eyes off me for <u>one</u> second, it was
<u>so</u> embarrassing. And a little foreigner who heard us speaking French
in the lift followed us all the way, & sat next to us, & absolutely
<u>dwelt</u> on our words, he simply loved us, & was <u>dreadfully</u>
disappointed when we got out!

To hell with all such people as the Oxford Examiners.
Good bye & behave yourself. A bientot Elizabeth

~

'It's a funny thing working for exams, it doesn't last very long, does it? I
remember working up a history bit or something. It's awfully easy to forget.
I think it's easier to go round Windsor Castle and learn from that. There's
the whole of history there. From William the Conqueror and the stones
coming up from Caen in Normandy.'

~

1 May 1916 to Beryl Poignand

20 St James's Square
[Addressed to 'Miss Medusa Pinpoint Poynard Poynment Poiggnand
Poignand'
'If NOT away please do NOT forward.']

My dear Medusa
    I wrote you a most beautiful letter yesterday, and now I've had to
tear it up & begin all over again, as I got one from you this morning!
Zut! I mean Phut or Fut or Futte. We arrived yesterday morning
from Glamis, quite safely, lots of sailors.
    We left father and Barson sorrowfully drinking cocktails. It was
9 o'clock when we left & the sun was setting. I've never seen it look
quite so lovely. You see it sets right behind the hills now, & it was
yellow & pink & gold, going gradually down to deeper & deeper
blue, with a few huge yellow stars. Lordy how pretty it was. [. . .]
    Father comes on Tuesday, I expect he will spend his days in the
Army & Navy Stores buying toothbrushes & sponges & campstools &
such things! [. . .]
    Yours till Henry is no longer our beloved
    Elizabeth

~

23 August 1916 to Beryl Poignand

Glamis Castle

My dear Medusa

Thank you many times for your charming & amusing letter. I am so glad that you are enjoying yourself at Ramsgate. Did you know I did <u>such</u> a silly thing! Before I left London I wrote a long & <u>very</u> good poem all about our adventures (very private) and then went and left it in the blotting book in the Morning Room! Fool that I am.

Mike left London for France yesterday. Damn. [. . .] Admiral Jellicoe* came over to tea last week. He's too nice, <u>so</u> silly, just like a sailor! We went over to tea with him and his spouse last Friday, that is, Rosie & I. [. . .]

Rosie went off yesterday to see Wisp. She will be about three weeks away. Mike went the day before, Rosie yesterday, my best soldier friend also yesterday, so I'm in a BAD temper! My 'best boy' being the Drummer boy as I don't know any of them very well. I went & played 'Donkey' with them the night before last, at the end there was a <u>wall</u> of faces standing round and watching! Oh it <u>was</u> embarrassing! One has the D.C.M. Most of the men won't believe him, tho' he has his ribbon. There are 15 men. [. . .]

We are often getting Zeppelin scares, at least about 9 o'clock they telephone that the Zepps are here or coming, and by 11 all's well. [. . .]

Mother is better thank you.

Well, good bye, I don't think it's at <u>all</u> proper you pushing soldiers about. I wish you'd met Ernest!! Well old thing <u>BE GOOD</u> & luck pursue you.

Yours
Elizabeth

~

* John Jellicoe, first Earl Jellicoe (1859–1935), commanded Britain's Grand Fleet at the Battle of Jutland, 1916. He later served as First Sea Lord, but was removed from that office in 1917 over differences of strategy. Governor General of New Zealand 1920–24.

17 September 1916 to Beryl Poignand

Glamis Castle

My dear Medusa

I don't know whether you've heard anything about the fire yet? It's a beastly nuisance. Yesterday, Saturday at 5.30, we saw smoke coming from the <u>very</u> top roofs. Nine soldiers & Sister had gone to the 'pictures', but the remaining 4 & <u>all</u> the maidservants rushed up and handed buckets like old Billy-o. The more water, the more smoke, we absolutely could <u>not</u> find the fire. We then telephoned for the Forfar and Dundee fire brigades.

Before they arrived the little flames were sort of creeping through the roofs, you know – where the tiles are. It was too awful. Before 10 minutes the whole village was down! The former was absolutely <u>no</u> use, having only a hand pump. The Dundee one heard at 6 o'clock, & was here in 26 minutes! Wonderful. They had powerful engines, and by midnight most of it was out. But the danger was great, & we <u>were</u> so thankful when the water started. From 6.30 till about 10 o'c I stood just outside the drawing room door, sweeping down the water. The cistern upstairs had burst and the flooding was dreadful. Four soldiers who were harvesting on the farm helped very well, also people from the village. <u>All</u> the furniture on the top two floors had to be carried down, & I had an awful job trying to find place. The drawing room was full, then King Malcolm's Room, then your room (Mdlle's) & the Strathmore Room! Only the very top rooms (where the empty turret is) were absolutely gutted, and the most awful amount of damage by water. It was pouring into the Drawing Room <u>all</u> night, and the Chapel is a wreck. All the pictures with <u>huge</u> smudges, it's beastly. The Blue Room & Crypt were flooded, & the water didn't stop till 5 this morning. Everybody was splendid, & my word I do ache!

You see there was none of us indoors, and I had to direct every man bringing down the furniture, also it began to get dark, & I had to get candles. Mrs Stewart commanded everybody, & Mrs Swann was <u>very</u> flurried, just like a little partridge!! I can't tell you all the little incidents, but it was <u>too</u> dreadful, we thought the whole place would be burnt. Captain Weir, the Chief of the Dundee F.B said that if the fire had been today (a <u>strong</u> wind is blowing) nothing on earth would have saved the castle. I can't tell you how unhappy we were, the flames were so awful. <u>Half an hour after it started</u>, Lady Airlie telephoned to say would we come over if it got too bad, then Hughie Munro to ask us, then the Douglas's telephoned, then the Fotheringhams, then Lady Dalhousie, all thought the Castle was burnt to the ground. The photographer, Dunn, (our old friend) was here last night, & presented me with postcards this morning. He took the charred remains today. I will send you one or two. Oh Lor, I've swept the big stairs the <u>whole</u> morning, I <u>am</u> so tired.

Yours till the firemen leave (they like this place!)

Elizabeth

PS Two firemen are staying. It broke out again this morning, and wants watching for a day or two.

~

When the fire broke out Elizabeth's father and brother David were shooting and many of the soldiers were at the pictures in Forfar. Elizabeth seized the initiative, calling the fire brigade and organizing the effort to save the pictures and other valuable contents of the Castle. The *Dundee Courier* reported that she was 'a veritable heroine'.* Her mother wrote to Beryl, 'Eliz'th was wonderful . . . Poor darling she was quite worn out after and ached all over for days.'†

~

20 October 1916 to Beryl Poignand

Glamis Castle

My dear Medusa

Thank you <u>so</u> much for all your charming letters! I hope you are enjoying Richmond. Nothing doing up here. I go to the Ward every evening now. They are very nice. I wrote a 'poem' for dear Sergeant Little's book‡ yesterday. <u>All</u> by myself. I did it when I woke up in the

---

* *My Darling Buffy, The Early Life of the Queen Mother*, Grania Forbes, Richard Cohen Books, 1997, p. 84.

† Lady Strathmore to Beryl Poignand, 22 September 1916, Glamis Archives (CH).

‡ Sergeant Little's poem to her was written in Elizabeth's autograph book:

> There is a young lady so charming and witty
> (I'm really not forced to tell you she's pretty)
> But she is

morning. Sister always teases him about his mental condition, because the poor man put a postal order in the fire by accident, and he does talk rather nonsense! Its rotten!

> His mental state, said Sister
> Gives me quite a fright
> He talks such dreadful nonsense
> Morning, noon and Night.
>
> [. . .]
>
> Though Sergeant Little's brain is weak
> His arm is very strong,
> He strafes the Bosche like anything
> Here's Luck to him life long!

They all thought it <u>too</u> wonderful! They really thought I had brains! Also I was given the Queen of Spades <u>11</u> times. I wondered what the terrific joy was about, & I found they'de been passing it under the table to give me! They are such babies! [. . .]

Good bye swine, write soon to Me

~

'When the soldiers came to be nursed or convalesce, were they fun?' asked Eric Anderson.

She replied: *'Oh, yes. And one kept up an enormous correspondence when they went back, you know . . . one used to hear what was going on, you know. Oh no, they were absolutely splendid.'*

~

> She wrote some nice verses about where the sense ended
> Of a Patient whom she thought would be rather offended
> But he isn't
>
> Needless to say that the patient was me
> But to think I'd been offended at a lady like she,
> Is all rot
>
> It will give me great pleasure to read those few lines,
> When the great war is over, if, in between times,
> I'm not shot.

Sergeant J. Little of the 8th E. Yorks Regt, October 1916 (RA QEQM/PRW/PERS)

25 October 1916 to Beryl Poignand

Glamis Castle

Mr Dear Medusa

Many thanks for your charming long letter. I was delighted to get it. I'm so sorry that you are cold, but you'll be nice and warm when you die, which must be a great consolation to you.

I'm feeling sick already. Tomorrow they've got one of those – whist drives (pardon me oh), but really my feelings are a bit too much for me! I of course have got to present the prizes, and I shall die. SIXTEEN huge men, all the Hoggs and Stewarts and oh it's too awful. And not even you to hold my hand. Damn. Ten men go on Friday. I know them quite well now. [. . .]

I wrote another poem and sent it back by Mother! It was to Harding, who delights in giving me the Queen of Spades! It goes thus – and is frightfully bad!

> I sometimes go into the Ward
> And play a game or two;
> And if I get the Queen of Spades
> Tis only due to you – Private Harding!
> [. . .]

Apparently he is delighted, and Sister said that he and Nix are very haughty now!!! Nix is angelic. I love him. You would too. He's very small and merry with a golden heart as you might say. Did I tell you that Mother & I were solemnly photographed with all the soldiers?! By Mr Dunn? They all dressed up yesterday evening, and looked too funny. The Glamis Band gave a selection! Twelve sit in a circle and one conducts. The gramaphone in the middle. The dinner horn is tooted, a bell is rung, the melodeon is squeaked, two penny whistles, a penny rattle rattled, a drum beaten, no tune at all, just only as much noise as they can possibly make! The noise is infernal! Poor Mrs Swann sits on a bed with an agonised expression on her face, stoping up her ears! Sister likes it! They are quite mad. Harding was the Queen of Spades!! That was a great joke! Nix was 'His Lordship's Jockey' and frightfully pleased with himself. I believe I'm

going to be confirmed on 5th November, and we come South the 7th
or the 9th. [. . .]

Goodbye from yours I like whist drives

Elizabeth.

~

26 October 1916 to Beryl Poignand

Glamis Castle

My dear Medusa

Just a line to tell you about the whist drive. I was <u>perfectly
terrified</u> all yesterday, but it wasn't so bad as last time, somehow. The
'Housekeepers Room' people had got it up, and Catherine arranged it
nearly all. [. . .] Wilson made a long speech, and then said that he
wouldn't keep them any longer as Lady Elizabeth had a long speech
to make!! My face and jaw fell down to the ground with horror!
However I didn't! Harding got the 1st prize, 6 handkerchiefs, Pat
Keeney an Irishman got 2nd, & McCleod got Booby. The two Booby
prizes were a chocolate Nurse & a chocolate kiltie [a Highland
soldier]. [. . .]

Then, we danced! Rosie & I led off with Sergeant Robinson &
Gordon. I with Gordon, who waltzed round & round and round, till
I nearly <u>died</u>, then thank the Lord his shoe came off, or else I should
have fallen down with giddiness! [. . .]

Ten of them went this morning, at eight o'clock. I've just
waved them off from the Ward window. They were all dreadfully
unhappy, and <u>too</u> darling. They say they are all coming back in
February.

The little Irishman wished me a merry Christmas & happy New
Year!! Williams said 'God bless you' and they all said, thank you, very
nicely. I do wonder if they caught their train! Because every two
steps, they stopped, threw their kit bags into the air, and waved
frantically, and of course <u>all</u> the kit bags fell down, so <u>that</u> took about
3 minutes to pick them all up. They all enjoyed themselves frightfully
last night. No other news at all. [. . .] Well, I hope I shall see you in a
couple of weeks. There is <u>no</u> excuse for you because there are
<u>hundreds</u> of trains to Richmond and it's only sixpence. The little tiny

funny Irishman said 'You'll get a letter from Ireland'. I don't expect I will!

> Good bye
> Yours till the moon turns blue
> Elizabeth

~

27 January 1917 [misdated 1916] to Beryl Poignand

St Paul's Walden Bury

My dear Medusa,

I was so sorry not to see you last week but we were only there for the dancing & Wednesday, & left Thursday. David went on Wed. Will you come to a play with me soon? [. . .]

We might be coming to London in February, I <u>hope</u> so. Rosie is going to be painted by P de Laszlo* with the money that the tenants gave her for her wedding. She went to see him to arrange about sitting, and he simply went into raptures about her! He pulled down her hair, & did it up again quite differently, he bent her best hat and ruined it, and said she was exactly like Lady Hamilton you know, [George] Romney's Lady H. <u>Too</u> funny.

Must fly goodbye. Oh, I had two letters from the front Nix and the Fish boy, both amusing.

Yours till the cows come home. E

~

Thursday 3 May 1917 to Beryl Poignand

Glamis Castle

My dear Medusa,

Just a line to tell you we had a telegram this morning to say that Mike is missing on April 28th.† I don't know what to say, you know

---

* Philip de Laszlo MVO PRBA (1869–1937), renowned Hungarian-born portrait painter who settled in England in 1907 and painted many royal and society portraits. In 1925 Lady Strathmore commissioned him to paint Elizabeth as Duchess of York; later he painted Elizabeth's sister May, both of her parents and her brother David. In 1931 he painted portrait sketches of the Duke and Duchess of York which were later hung in Clarence House.

† Michael, an officer in the 16th Battalion, the Royal Scots, had been leading his company in

how we love Mike, and it would be <u>so</u> terrible if he's killed. It's horrid & selfish of me to write you a miserable letter, but I'm so unhappy, & added to that I can't help worrying about Mother in London. I thank the Lord that Rosie is there.

It's dreadful, and somehow I never thought Mike could get killed. If he's all right, he <u>must</u> be, I'll tell you. Your loving Elizabeth

~

6 May 1917 to Beryl Poignand

Glamis Castle

My dear Medusa

Thank you <u>so</u> much for your letter, it was such a nice letter. It's so dreadful having to <u>wait</u>, I <u>do</u> wish we could hear something. Somehow I never thought anything could happen to Mike, everybody is so fond of him, but one forgets that doesn't count in a War, but you know I still have a hope that he is all right, because one simply <u>can't</u> tell, can one? I think you know, that Mike is the favourite of the whole family, Father's very favourite son, & you know how Mother adores him, & Pat & Jock too, Rosie & me, everybody. It would be <u>so</u> dreadful if he was killed.

I'm going down [to London] tomorrow night. I'm afraid Mother is in a terrible state, & Pat you know is at St James' Sq waiting for a [medical] board, & he is very bad too, I'm afraid. I'm <u>so</u> sorry writing such a depressed letter, and <u>how</u> I hope the next one will be mad & full of the usual rubbish.

He said in his last letter you know, 'If I'm pipped, I think little John* had better have my guns', and so he knew they were going to have a bad time I suppose. I'll tell you what Mother's found out so far. <u>Ten</u> officers of the 16th & <u>many</u> of the 15th are missing, and only <u>2</u> in his battn are wounded, none killed so far. Sidney went to the W.O. [War Office] & found that out. Then May [Elphinstone] asked old Princess Christian† if she'd write to the Crown Princess of

---

an attack at the village of Roeulx near Arras. The Germans counter-attacked and many of the British troops were listed as 'missing'.

* John, Master of Glamis (1910–41), son of Patrick Lord Glamis, see p. 317.

† Helena (1846–1923), third daughter of Queen Victoria. She married Prince Christian of Schleswig-Holstein and they made their home in England. The Crown Princess of Sweden was

Sweden who would find out quicker if he is a prisoner. Princess C cabled, so we ought to hear quite soon if he's a prisoner of war. That's all we could do. I'll let you know the very minute we hear anything, and thank you again for your letter so much.

Your loving
Elizabeth

~

Tuesday 22 May 1917 to Beryl Poignand

20 St James's Square

Ma Chere Medusa,

I'm quite and absolutely stark, staring, raving mad. Do you know why? Can'st thou e'en guess ? I don't believe you can!

AM I MAD WITH MISERY OR WITH JOY??

WITH

!

!! JOY !!

!

Mike is quite safe! Oh dear,

I nearly, nearly burst this morning, We had a telephone message from Cox's [Bank] to say they'd received a cheque from Mike this morning, so we rushed round, and it was in his own handwriting, & they think he's at Carlsruhe. Is'nt it too, too heavenly. I can't believe it, yes I can but you know what I mean, & how awful the last 3 weeks have been.

Yours madly, Elizabeth.

~

9 October 1917 to Beryl Poignand

Glamis Castle

My dear Medusa

Thank you so very much for your nice 'scrappy' letter. I was so glad to get it. How exciting about your War Office job, I am so glad it's near us, and I do hope you'll like it. How beastly the air raids must be.

---

her niece Margaret (daughter of Arthur, Duke of Connaught, third son of Queen Victoria), who had married Crown Prince Gustaf Adolf in 1905.

We've had <u>such</u> an excitement here! The Forfar 'boys' came to tea last Thursday, and ours gave them a concert! I got back from Carberry on the Wednesday, & was met at Tay Bridge Station by Wright & Morris, the two <u>angelic</u> & darling regulars. I do love them – you would too. Morris is a second Twinkley in a way. That evening we had the 'dress rehearsal' in the drawing room. Mother was accompanist, and the performers numbered 5. They came in at the door leading to the billiard room, & sang at that end of the room. Of course they were dressed up, & made up. It was <u>too</u> priceless & <u>really</u> excellent. About a dozen songs, including a frightfully funny thing of 'Annie Laurie'. They all five come on and sing Annie L. When they get to the middle, Wright goes wrong. 'Hi stop, stop, you're wrong.' Then to Holley, 'You're out of it'. ''Oo? Me?' 'Yes, you're out of it.' 'Alright, sing it yourself then'. And Holley departs. They start again. At the same place Wright goes wrong & the whole thing is done over again – till he is left alone to sing it. Then comes the <u>supreme</u> joke of the concert!! He goes wrong again, and this time it's <u>Mother</u> that's 'out of it'! <u>Yells</u> & <u>roars</u> of laughter. Mother also says – 'sing it yourself then' & goes 'off'. He sings again, & has just got started when Morris comes 'on'. 'The stage manager wants to see you' – & that's the end of the song. My goodness, <u>what</u> a success it was. [. . .]

We sing every evening nearly, even <u>me</u> too!!! Mother plays, & we go through <u>dozens</u> of songs. Last night was Wright's last night, he went this morning. We shall miss him <u>dreadfully</u>, he is <u>too</u> darling. When I was saying goodbye, he said 'I'll write'. So I remarked what a lot said that & <u>didn't</u>. So, <u>very</u> seriously he said, 'I take an oath I will'. We are all great friends – it's like old days! Waring has black eyes, 'ooo and they <u>do</u> glitter, it's quite awful! I amused them most immensely yesterday evening, by singing 'Wonderful Girl, Wonderful Boy, Wonderful Time'. I <u>cannot</u> make out the joke, I sang the ladies' part, & they sang the man's! I must find out what amused them so. [. . .]

I must stop, as the post is going – people seem to think Peace is nearer now. I <u>do</u> hope so.

Good bye my love, & keep safe from these air raids –
Yours very coldly
(we've had snow here)
Elizabeth

~

Sunday 21 October 1917 to Beryl Poignand

Glamis Castle

My dear Medusa

Thank you so very much for your delightful letter,
I was <u>so</u> pleased to get it. [. . .]

Chapel was well attended this morning, and the hymns went
very well. The men are very nice just now, only 10 of them.
Yesterday afternoon, Sister, Waring & I went in to Dundee to the
War Hospital to see Morris. It is a <u>horrid</u> place, dreary and smoky.
We found Morris simply miserable. He had lost <u>6lb</u> since leaving
Glamis one week ago, and was looking dreadfully thin and ill. He
was buried for 2 days & ½, his chest was crushed, and he can
breathe only very badly. He is simply longing to get away. You see
he'll be discharged, (he's had 13 years' service, enlisted at 14) & so
Mother has written to Major Young. Everybody likes Morris,* he's
<u>so</u> nice, and very upright & honest. He quite depressed us! We took
him eggs, butter etc. [. . .]

There is a terrific gale blowing today. There is nothing thrilling to
tell you. [. . .]

Your loving
Elizabeth

~

26 November 1917 to Beryl Poignand

Glamis Castle

My dear Medusa

[. . .]

Just back from a nerve racking and terrible experience – bidding
good-bye to <u>FOURTEEN</u> men! It really makes me weep & a lump in
my throat. I can't bear it ever. And there is such a nice dear Sergeant
whom I took a violent affection to yesterday evening, he is so nice
tho' dreadfully ugly. I begged Sister to push him downstairs or give
him a blister or something. I wish I didn't take violent affections too
late – it's <u>always</u> the day before they go!!! I always have to say
goodbye after dinner now, because firstly they go at 7 A.M. and

---

* The Strathmores took on Private C. Morris as a gardener at St Paul's Walden Bury.

secondly Sister likes to show me off in evening dress, because they never have seen evening dresses which embarrasses me <u>too</u> dreadfully. They invariably look at my shoes, except the ones that gaze rapturously into my eyes sighing deeply all the while, which are <u>nil</u>, nowadays that I have my hair up etc!! Some of them are charming, but oh! the difference from Dec. 1914! I was just remembering this evening, that night when Mr Brookes, Harold Ward, Teddy, David (in pyjamas) & I had a bun fight in the crypt, and David chased Nurse A round the Ward with cocoa & water to pour, & how it all got spilt on the floor, & her black fury!! It <u>was</u> fun – weren't they darlings? I have been thinking so much between these lines that it is now 10.15 & I must go to bed. [. . .]

It's so dreadful saying goodbye, because one knows that one will never see them again, and I <u>hate</u> doing it. Do you remember our goodbyes on the doorstep, & waving them all the way up the Avenue? [. . .]

We shall come down next week I expect, I'll let you know the date later. Goodbye from your loving but at the moment depressed –
    Elizabeth
    [. . .]

~

'I remember quite well thinking when I was seventeen I could never be happy again. I mean everybody was unhappy. Because one knew so many people. Every day somebody was killed, you see. It was a real holocaust. It was horrible. I remember that feeling quite well.'

~

5 January 1918 to Beryl Poignand

St Paul's Walden Bury

My Chere Medusie

How <u>splendid</u> about your brother's promotion. I <u>am</u> glad, thousands of congratters. He's very young isn't he? I expect you are deeeeeelighted, m'sure. Poor overworked thing.

You must come here for a Sunday soon to recuperate. The apple house is overflowing (at the moment), so there will be <u>something</u>.

Mother, David & I went up to London for the night on Tuesday, but I hadn't a moment to ring you up. It was a terrible rush. On the way from the station, we were dropped at the dressmaker, & I tried on my dress. [. . .]

The next day, D & I were <u>slightly</u> en retard for breakfast! Then I rushed & had my hair washed (!) (ze leetle naturrral currrls) & rushed all over London trying to get some shoes to go with my dress. Swallowed some lunch, & <u>just</u> caught the 1.35!! I was a white haired wreck on reaching here. [. . .]

Oh by the way, I had a lecture the other day from Mother & David! That I ought to be more flirtatious! I nearly died of surprise. You know I daresay I've got rather quiet from having all those Australians & NZ (!!!) at Glamis, as one simply <u>must</u> sit on them! Wasn't it funny? And the worst of it was, Major Metcalfe came here yesterday, & I <u>absolutely forgot</u> to try the 'appy 'optic on him!! It would have been such a chance! Never mind, Captain Jebb is coming this evening to stay, tho' I know I shall be just as mouse like when he's here!

I <u>did</u> laugh. Ha Ha.

What I remember of Mr Parker* was one evening at dinner, he asked me if my birthday was between August 1st & 10th or some such dates. I said 'yes', & he then remarked mysteriously 'ah, that accounts for it'. I asked him what he meant, but he refused to disclose the dread secret! However, next morning I made him tell me, and apparently he'd read some book in N.Z., about stars, & dates & calculations & things, <u>you</u> know the sort of book. It put all the ways of finding things, & apparently he'd worked out that 'THE' person for him's birthday had to be some time between August 1st & 10th!!! Somehow, you calculated between the two birthdays. I laughed, couldn't help it.

Well, I <u>hope</u> he's found a charming gurrrrl in N.Z.! That's the best thing for him. His Father was an Englishman. Everybody liked Mr Parker, I did too, & David did, which was a good thing. [. . .]

I am coming up on Monday, as my dance is on Tuesday (ugh), so if you get this in time, <u>do</u> come in, if you can get off after tea, & have supper with me. I shall be alone as Mother isn't coming till Tuesday. So <u>do</u> if you can on Monday. I <u>expect</u> I shall come up in the morning,

---

* Mr Parker, a New Zealand officer recuperating at Glamis. As Duchess of York, she met him again, in New Zealand while on her official tour in 1927. See letter to her sister May of 17 March 1927 (p. 157).

so do ring up if you have a moment, & perhaps you could come to lunch too.

 Must fly,
 V loving
 Elizabeth

~

9 January 1918 to Beryl Poignand

St Paul's Walden Bury

My dear Medusa

 I am writing in my bedroom to tell you about the dance, & also why I didn't ring you up this morning. Well, I trembled all yesterday afternoon! I arrived at Lady Dorothy Wood where I was dining for the dance at about 8.15. The ladies there were – Sybil Scott (Buccleuch), Vere Smith, Margaret Sutton (whose dance it was), a 'Wood' girl & Lady Dorothy.

 The men consisted of Mr Wood (our host),* Mr Johnson, Archie Balfour, Count de Grünne & Lord Halifax. I sat between Lord Halifax & Lord St Audries who didn't turn up. The dance was quite close, & we arrived at a little before 10. Michael Biddulph (Adèle's† brother) was there & I danced with him, Archie, Mr Johnson, a Mr Phillips, Mr Brocklehurst, Mr Ogilvy‡ & last but not least little Willy de Grünne.§ He dances too divinely, & is at the Embassy. I danced

---

* Hon. Edward Wood (1881–1959), later Lord Irwin, then third Viscount Halifax and first Earl of Halifax, uncle of Margaret Sutton. He and his wife Dorothy became good friends to Elizabeth as both Duchess of York and Queen. He was Foreign Secretary under Neville Chamberlain and Winston Churchill and subsequently British Ambassador in Washington. Dorothy Halifax was a lady in waiting to the Queen. The 'Lord Halifax' mentioned by Elizabeth here was Edward Wood's father, the second Viscount.

† The Hon. Adelaide Mary Biddulph (1901–85), daughter of second Baron Biddulph. Married 1929 Henry Vincent Yorke (the novelist Henry Green).

‡ The Hon. Bruce Ogilvy (1895–1976), son of sixth Earl of Airlie and neighbour of the Strathmores. He served in the 12th Royal Lancers, Life Guards and Irish Guards and was equerry to the Prince of Wales, 1921–30.

§ Count Willy de Grünne, Second Secretary at the Belgian Embassy. On 1 October 1978, Queen Elizabeth wrote to her Treasurer, Sir Ralph Anstruther, from Birkhall to say that 'dear old Willie de Grünne' had died, aged ninety. She asked Sir Ralph to write to Count de Grünne's daughter and added, 'perhaps you could say that he was the best waltzer in London

every single dance, & Mother came to fetch me, & we departed at about 1.30. [. . .] I enjoyed it <u>very</u> much. One could only dance with such few people tho' because the dances were <u>so</u> long, but I loved it, and enjoyed it fearfully. Do you know I think my dress really looked quite pretty. [. . .] I saw Lavinia at the dance, but she had an ugly dress on, & wasn't looking half as nice as I've seen her look, I <u>was</u> so sorry. And Delia* looked <u>so</u> old, but perhaps she was bored or something.

Oh! When I arrived here yesterday what do you think I found? A letter from – ! Yes it was! Mr Parker! He had left England about the middle of November, & so he must have sent that story thing off himself. His letter was dated Nov 29th. He said he had not been able to get off before. The two other New Zealanders who had been at Glamis, were also on board with him, rather curious, wasn't it? So he must have arrived in N.Z. by now. Ought I to thank him for his letter? Oh dear! it's so muddling! I expect we shall come up next week, but I'll let you know.

Your very loving & perplexed
Elizabeth

~

7 February 1918 to Beryl Poignand

20 St James's Square

My dear Medusa

Where are you? Why do you hide away? Why don't you ring up? Don't be shy dearie, nobody's looking & 'ere's the mistletoe.

Oh dear I <u>am</u> so worried. You remember I told you that we were having a tiny dance tonight, sort of to ask back people who'd asked me etc? Well, <u>millions</u> of people have proposed themselves & it's <u>grown</u> and <u>grown</u>, & nearly <u>everybody</u> is coming. I really had no idea that the Strathmore family was so popular, it's awful. And really, people <u>do</u> propose themselves rather too much I think. Well, I'm so mixed up. I can't write but I'll tell you all about it later. Lavinia is coming. I'll show you the sort of thing that happened. Mother asked

(in my youth) & I adored being waltzed around the ballroom – tho' I think we called it a valse in those days!' (RA QEQM/OUT/ANST)

* Lady Delia Spencer (1889–1981), daughter of sixth Earl Spencer, married 1914 Sidney Peel. After his death in 1938 she was appointed Woman of the Bedchamber to Queen Elizabeth.

Delia to bring a very few people, & she is bringing <u>ten</u>, lots of people are doing that, so it mounts up <u>dreadfully</u>

<u>Such</u> a funny thing happened!! You remember the little Lieut I told you about? (Naval of course.) Well, he rang me up on the phone last night, & we had a I-don't-know-how-to-describe-it talk. Poor little man, I <u>was</u> sorry for him. You know I've got a soft spot in my 'eart for a bhoy in blue, so 'ave you and he was so pathetic! I'll tell you about it, if it would amuse you, when I see you. And I've written four pages to Mr Parker, but I simply <u>can't</u> get the last bit in! I wish I could talk to him, it's so difficult writing, & I know it will just miss him in New Zealand! If you get this tomorrow <u>do</u> ring up – I <u>might</u> be here.

These young men <u>do</u> worry me so, I <u>wish</u> they wouldn't. Do come round & give me some more of your sage (?) advice!

David is <u>very</u> run down & weak, & it will be quite a long time before he goes back to Eton I expect. Dr Thomas examined me 'eart, & said it was enlarged!! I laughed! Couldn't help it! It sounds <u>so</u> funny, doesn't it? Anyhow I'm not to do much, & I suppose I oughtn't really to dance! Must stop, I'm all trembly inside me, oh oh – <u>do</u> ring up if you can. Yours full heartedly (!!) Elizabeth.

I haven't seen you for years – <u>do</u> come.

PS Mother wants me to ask you this. She has promised to have a small dance for Overseas Officers next Tuesday from 8–12!! Can you come? We could put you up for the k-night. You simply <u>must</u>, it would be such fun. You really must come, & if you have a friend – a young nice-looking one mind, send her along too. If you know anybody who could get home at night I mean. None of these <u>fast</u> people, my dear Medusa who are corrupting your poor mind, but anyhow <u>you</u> must come – Pip Pip!!

~

Wednesday 13 March 1918 to Beryl Poignand

20 St James's Square

My dear old thing

Thank you <u>so</u> for your amiable letter, ah, what joy! What <u>palps</u> the mere sight of that wonderful handwriting gives me! Etc etc.

Well, Mother & I came up yesterday, and Mother went back to St Paul's Walden this morning, & I am going this afternoon. The reason we are going back, is, that it is Father's birthday tomorrow, & we must be there for at least a portion of it! We are coming up again tomorrow afternoon, as Lady Portarlington's dance is in the evening, and I shall probably stay here till Monday. We went to Lady Hastings' dance last night, it was quite fun. [. . .] Katie was there,* looking supremely bored, till I took her up to the top of the house, & we giggled foolishly for a few minutes, then she cheered up!! We got home just before two.

The darling [Elphinstone] children came to tea yesterday. Elizabeth has lost her front teeth, otherwise they are just the same. They were so darling. I called Elizabeth 'Toothy' at tea, whereupon they all burst into yells of laughter, & food was sputtered all over the place! They've got extraordinary senses of humour, and see jokes in the most harmless things! I am going down to Pauly with them this afternoon. I foresee a riotous journey. 'Let's draw'. 'Draw me a cow Peter'.† 'No Peter, draw me a bow wow'. You know! I am writing in bed which is horribly lazy isn't it. It's 11.30 so I must get up.

12.30 Just as I wrote that Catherine came up to say that Lieut. Hamilton was here. I tumbled out of bed, and was dressed in 10 minutes. I always like seeing Freddy, he cheers one up so much, because he really is ridiculous! He's just gone, as he's only passing through London on his way to Dover, where he is joining a new ship called the 'Murray'.

I am going to lunch with May so I must 'urry. When shall I see you? Do ring up. I shall be here by tea time tomorrow probably. There is very little to tell you really, so I will now draw to a close hoping this finds you as it leaves me at present in the Pink. (Pretty good, that.)

Your very loving Elizabeth
I shall be late for lunch!!

~

---

* Lady Katharine Hamilton (1900–85), daughter of third Duke of Abercorn. She married, in 1930, Lieutenant Colonel (later Sir) Reginald Seymour, equerry to King George V, and became a lady in waiting to Queen Mary for some time before transferring to Queen Elizabeth's Household in 1937.

† Throughout their lives the Elphinstone children, Elizabeth, John, Jean, Andrew and Margaret, called their Aunt Elizabeth 'Peter', ever since one of them had been unable as a child to pronounce the name 'Elizabeth'.

Friday 22 March 1918 to Beryl Poignand

St Paul's Walden Bury

My dear Medusa

I don't know <u>why</u> I start writing letters to you at this hour! I am in bed, & feeling tired after 2 late nights, but not sleepy! I had great fun last night at the Harcourts'. Rather a terrifying dinner first, in which I sat between the Prince of Wales* & Count Michael Torby.[†] It was very nice tho'. As usual I danced the first dance with P.W., I don't know why, but I usually do! I danced three with him, & several with my faithful friend, Victor Cochrane Baillie.[‡] He is very nice, but extremely ugly poor thing. Also Gerard Brassey,[§] who is very nice, & all my old friends. It was the last dance for some time, so tho' I enjoyed it very much, I felt slightly depressed at moments. Such a lot of these boys are going out quite soon – in fact nearly everybody I know. I suppose they expect fearful casualties. They are <u>so</u> young, a great many only nineteen. [. . .]

Good night and <u>do</u> write soon, and cheer me up for losing my young men. I do hope your brother was well. Your loving Elizabeth

~

23 March 1918 to Lady Strathmore

St Paul's Walden Bury

My Darling Mother

I do hope you had a good journey up to Glamis, & arrived alright. It <u>was</u> a bore having to go off & I am <u>so</u> looking forward to your return. I expect you won't be back till Wednesday.

I got down here alright yesterday and found the children

---

*   Edward, Prince of Wales (1894–1972), the eldest son of, and heir to, King George V; later the Duke of Windsor. Known in his family as David, he took the name King Edward VIII on the death of George V in January 1936, and abdicated in order to marry Mrs Ernest Simpson in December that same year.

†   Count Michael Torby (1898–1959), son of Grand Duke Michael Mikhailovitch of Russia, whose family lived in exile in England and France after the Russian Revolution.

‡   Victor Cochrane Baillie (1896–1951), later third Baron Lamington.

§   Gerard Brassey (1898–1918), a lieutenant in the Coldstream Guards, was killed in action on 27 August, aged nineteen.

staying awake for me. Father is <u>very</u> well, & so far has eaten quite
well. I feel very flourishing, tho' a tiny bit tired, & have been out
all the afternoon. It has been <u>so</u> hot, I couldn't wear a coat or
gloves or flannel petticoat or anything warm! It is too delicious for
words.

I enjoyed Lady Harcourt's dance <u>so</u> much, tho' I felt a little
depressed, because it was the last dance, & I expect nearly everyone I
know will be gone by the next one. [. . .]

Please remember me to Sister and the Ralstons & everybody. I
am longing for you to come back Mother darling.

I must stop as it's post time. Good-bye darling Mother, from your
very very

loving Elizabeth

~

20 April 1918 to Beryl Poignand

St Paul's Walden Bury

My dear Medusa

[. . .]

We've just come back from Devonshire. It was deliciously warm
there, and very pretty. The cliffs are such a wonderful red colour
there, and <u>you'd</u> adore it because of the bathing! [. . .]

I won't write about the War – It's too awful. I heard from Nina
Balfour yesterday, that Lord Settrington* is reported wounded &
missing. I am so sorry, he is so nice, & I <u>hope</u> he'll turn up alright.
So very many are missing now aren't they? It was snowing hard last
night but it's warmer today! I wonder if Peace will <u>ever</u> come. I feel
as if I never want to go to a dance again, one only makes friends &
then they are killed. Don't you feel depressed lately! But the news is
better now, I hear that Foch† is quite pleased. I do hope you'll enjoy
yourself frightfully. V loving E

---

* Charles, Lord Settrington (1899–1919), eldest son of eighth Duke of Richmond and brother
of Doris Gordon-Lennox, with whom Elizabeth began a lifelong friendship at this time.
Charles Settrington had been taken prisoner. He was the first cousin of Gerard Brassey (see
p. 56).

† Maréchal Ferdinand Foch (1851–1929), French military commander, appointed Supreme
Commander of the Allied armies in April 1918.

PS Please forgive a deadly dull letter but I am cold, and depressed! Do write soon old thing. The children leave on Monday.

~

26 May 1918 to Beryl Poignand

Dutch House
Dovercourt
4 o'clock

My dear Medusa

Here is my promised letter. I am still waiting for yours! It is great fun here, tho' we did nothing till yesterday when we dined with Wisp. My first visit to a warship of any kind at all! We have just come back from lunching & will be shortly returning to dine!!! Well, I'll tell you all about it. You see we didn't go before as he was boiler cleaning. We take the train out to Parkeston (5 minutes) and there his motor launch meets us and we go alongside the 'Scott'.* Then there is a 'wavy ladder' (thank the Lord there are ropes each side) and when you get to the top a couple of sailors who salute, and one feels foolish and doesn't know if one ought to bow low and return their salutation! Then one falls heavily down the hatch (is it?) into the waiting arms of a Sub or (preferably) a Lieut! Wisp's cabins are most luxurious & beautifully fitted, as of course it is one of the very newest ships. He has his meals in lonely splendour, the Ward room is opposite. He's got three pipers & they always play during meals which is very nice. I haven't seen over the ship yet, but hope to soon. [. . .]

The station master (Syme) at Glamis' son is still with Wisp. He is a very good looking man, and excellent I believe. He bursts in at meals with Signals, he is Yeoman of Signals. The Sub also yells things in & says 'Aye Aye Sir' & altogether it's fearfully nautical!!! Mess traps. Hatch somethings. Port holes. Cocktails. Aft – Forrard! Etc Etc. [. . .]

Very loving Elizabeth

~

---

* HMS *Scott* was torpedoed a few months later, with the loss of twenty-six men. Wisp Leveson-Gower survived.

Thursday 13 June 1918 to Beryl Poignand

20 St James's Square

My dear Medusa

You <u>were</u> a swine in St James' St yesterday. You made me blush like anything! I knew what you were thinking – two couples walking out one behind the other!! We went and had lunch with Freddy at the Berkeley, a very riotous one I assure you! But it was great fun. In the evening I dined with Lord and Lady Powis, a huge dinner party and we danced afterwards till about 1 o'clock. I had several dances with a little American* from the Embassy with such nice eyes. He was so funny and asked me to come to the play with him. I said 'wouldn't that be fun' and he's coming to tea next week! Oh Lor I've gone and been and done it now! [. . .]

Lord Erskine would insist on walking home with me, and whenever I danced with the American he looked furious and whenever I danced with him the American was angry! It was awful. 'Oh Gawd' as the private soldier said when he was doing Macduff. I have suddenly taken to blushing again. I do hope it will go soon, it's such a bore. Oh dear, do write and let me know how you are enjoying yourself, you know I haven't seen you <u>properly</u> for some time now – I don't count our midnight conversation last week! Have a very good time. V loving Elizabeth

~

10pm Saturday 21 September 1918 to Beryl Poignand

Glamis Castle

Thank God – it's all over! I've made my speech, and now there are only the hymns to play in Chapel tomorrow, & I shall be at peace. I've really had an awful time these last few days – things <u>invariably</u> crop up when Mother goes away, and I've had <u>such</u> a lot to decide. [. . .]

---

*   Sam Dickson, Third Secretary at the US Embassy. He invited her to dinner but she said she could accept only if chaperoned by her mother. After the three of them had dined at the Berkeley, she talked to him at home in St James's Square. He told her all about his family life in America – 'it sounds exactly like what we imagine cowboys to be,' she wrote to Beryl later that month ([20 and 25] June, 5 July 1918, Glamis Archives (CH)). There is a charming postscript to this episode (see letter to Lady Johnston, 30 December 1989, p. 597).

I had this sale in Forfar today! I was so sick and frightened and can't remember anything about it except that I managed to get through my speech without a mistake! Adèle and I were greeted by Mr Tubey, then Adèle, Eupham Douglas & I went up on to the platform with a clergyman on each side of us!!! I was presented with a bouquet! 'Orrible. I am so glad it's over I feel weak and dithery this evening in consequence! [. . .]

Pip Pip! I feel so tired, must stop. Goodbye old darling do behave. Very loving Elizabeth

[. . .]

~

'I was brought up like that: "Well darling, it's your duty" and saying to one's mother "I can't". But you know that, aged seventeen, you've got to go and open the flower show: "It's your duty, darling."'

~

Tuesday 1 October 1918 to Beryl Poignand

Glamis Castle

My dearest Medusa

Many many thanks for your letter – I was beginning to wonder what had happened to you if you'd eloped with —— or some such 'orrible affair! You must be very very hard worked, I <u>do</u> wish you could come up here for a holiday. It <u>would</u> be so heavenly! [. . .]

Very nice men in the hospital now. We sing in the evenings a certain amount – they love it. [. . .]

Bulgarian news is good isn't it? I do hope Turkey will be reasonable. What about Peace next Spring?

Goodbye old thing, do write when you can, as I shall feel so lonely. R & Wisp also going today, oh why can't you come?

Elizabeth

PS We had Holy Communion on Sunday, & 4 soldiers came & Sister. I <u>do</u> wish you could have painted a picture of them kneeling before the Altar, in their hospital blue with Sister. It really was a beautiful sight, tho' it gave me a lump in my throat. I keep on thinking of it. Poor dear boys, it was <u>so</u> pathetic somehow. You can't imagine quite I daresay, but it would have made a heavenly picture.

The white & silver Altar, & the blue suits with Sister's white apron & cap etc.

~

22 October 1918 to Beryl Poignand

Glamis Castle

My dearest Medusa

Many many thanks indeed for thy charming letter – I am so glad you are having a nice quiet rest at Westgate – it will do you a lot of good.

I was just thinking how sad it would have been if I'd never met you! You are my best friend and adviser now – worse luck pour vous! I am writing at 11.30 p.m. and ought to be in bed. I'm in my dressing gown anyway and all ready for bed. The two Aussies are very nice. Mr Williamson is good-looking & very nice; Mr Rohan is tall, fat and merry and also nice. We have great jokes and they are always saying the most complimentary things to me which I take as a terrific joke; so we are great friends. Mr W is really a dear, I am very fond of him – poor boy, he has got a very badly smashed foot and has been very ill. I give them quinine twice a day and feed them up, so I am called 'Nurse'.

Yesterday we all drove into Forfar in the wagonette (Rosie is still here) and did lots of shopping. I went with Mr Williamson to try to get a pair of shoes, but he couldn't get one anywhere near on. I'm afraid he was dreadfully disappointed.

Well – on Saturday I got quite a good post – two letters and a parcel from France, and one from an Australian!! A very long and really quite interesting letter from my little Canadian,* with an iron cross in the parcel. I am so pleased with it – one from Victor Cochrane Baillie – he is coming on leave at the end of the month, and wonders whether I shall be in London – which I shall not. And some photos from this Aussie who had been staying with the Ralstons. [. . .]

Yes – what shall we do about Ernest?† It must be over 6 months

---

* Lieutenant J. S. Reynolds, who wrote to Elizabeth in September 1918 saying, 'if I get out of this mess alive will send you an iron cross if you think it will be OK.' (RA QEQM/PRIV/PAL)

† Ernest Pearce survived the war and, as already noted, the Duke and Duchess of York subsequently gave him a job as a gardener.

since we heard. Do you think he can be killed or anything? I cannot understand his not writing.

Here is the post coming – I hear Barson and a crackle of papers arriving? What for me? Nothing? [. . .]

Well, there isn't much to tell you, I must go and give my little boys their quinine and they will say some silly things!! I do wish you were here.

Good byeee old darling,
from your very loving
Elizabeth

~

At eleven o'clock in the morning of 11 November 1918, the Armistice was signed and the war ended. Elizabeth was at Glamis and years later would recall the soldiers from the Castle marching happily together to the pub. *'They went straight to the village to celebrate and I think they drank too much. Seats got broken up to make a bonfire and all that sort of thing. I can see them now, all going to enjoy this wonderful moment.'*

~

27 November 1918 to Beryl Poignand

20 St James's Square

My Thweet Medutha

Ithn't it thad? I've developed a lithp. Do you like lithpth? [. . .]

Mr Williamson, Mr Rohan & a friend of theirs came to tea with me today. They were very nice & so silly, & we yelled songs round the piano after tea. I did so hope you would come in, why didn't you? I would have liked you to have seen them.

I feel depressed now. Can't <u>think</u> why. No reason on earth. Everything is wonderful. <u>So</u> long waiting for Mike perhaps – see only 241 officers have arrived in a fortnight. <u>Do</u> ring up; Mr W has such a funny soft voice. Mr R just as fat & nice & jolly as ever.

Very loving
Elizabeth
PS Let's go to a play. Find out what's good pleeeeese.

~

5 January 1919 to Beryl Poignand

St Paul's Walden Bury

My dearest Medusa

I was so dreadfully sorry to fly off and leave you in that rude fashion on Friday! We simply dashed off to the station and arrived just as a train full of repatriated prisoners got in. However, [Mike] wasn't there and we watched five trains in and at last he came at about 7 o'clock. We waited with such amusing people from Kennington and Whitechapel!

Mike is fairly well and cheerful, it is so delicious having him. He and David are playing billiards at the moment and I am rushing between the gramophone and this here letter! Mike brought a friend with him to stay on Friday, a man called Lathom. He looked very ill and absolutely dazed. He merely sat and looked at the fire. Tho' he certainly looked much better after a good night's rest. Poor boys, they must have had a beastly time, they hate talking about it. It was so pathetic at the station, you ought to go and watch a special in from Ripon. Personally I rather loved 'The man from Toronto'. Did you? Do ring me up as we are coming up tomorrow for two days – must stop. Goodbye darling old thing.

Very loving Elizabeth

~

The Armistice had been greeted with joy across Britain but by the spring of 1919 the country was struggling with the enormity of the sacrifices that had been demanded of it. Three-quarters of a million British people had been killed. At the end of the war millions of people around the world were out of work and at least twenty million are thought to have been killed by the Spanish flu epidemic. Economic output had collapsed. Discontent grew and the siren calls of revolution were heard (and sometimes accepted) across Europe.

~

Saturday undated [22 March 1919] to Beryl Poignand

20 St James's Square

My dearest M

 Many <u>many</u> thanks for your note. [. . .]

 I went with Adèle & her mother today to see the Guards* from the Equitable Insurance Office, in front of the Mansion House, & we saw beautifully. I was so amused recognising all my partners looking so comic & stiff!! You see they had to give 'Eyeeeeees – right' for the Lord Mayor. But the awful thing was not a soul cheered. There were millions & millions of people absolutely silent. <u>Dreadful</u> feeling. I longed to say 'Cheer – damn you' or words to that effect – it was ghastly. But they always get a wonderful reception in the West End, so that might make up. The only time they cheered was for the Prince of Wales, and at the <u>very</u> end of the procession a Black Maria rumbled along. You should have heard the roars of laughter & cheers – Oh the Cockney sense of humour! They simply doubled up with mirth! After 2 hours of silence this really tickled them! It was too funny going home! We had an electric brougham, & they thought we were some kind of Royalty, & I bowed smilingly, & it <u>was</u> fun. (New hat.) And going across Berkeley Square we passed three American officers, I bowed beautifully to them with my best smile, & they saluted! To change the subject. Alas! The letter is from a far far worse person than Mr Reynolds or Mr Parker! Do guess. I never had such a shock in my life when I got it. It began by my Christian name & 'please forgive but what the heart feels, the tongue must speak or the hand write!!' Darling I loff you – will you be mine – sort of idea – isn't it orful? When shall I see you? Soon, pleeeeese <u>do</u>.

 Very loving Elizabeth

~

---

* The occasion was a Triumphal March of the Household Cavalry and the Brigade of Guards from Buckingham Palace to St Paul's Cathedral and Mansion House and back, with lorries following each battalion carrying the wounded who could not march.

Sunday night undated [6 April 1919] to Beryl Poignand

20 St James's Square

My dearest Medusa

How goes life with you? The usual beginning! I haven't seen you for ages – at least it seems like ages to me – I haven't written that letter to Mr Bagshawe* – 'My dear Vivian, thank you a thousand times – I'll come by the next boat – till then! Thine E.' – do you think that would do? Ha Ha!

Well, last night I gave a play party! We dined at the Ritz & went to 'Joybells' – George Robey† is too priceless. We must go – It was Neva, Emma Thynne & me, Mike, Captain Keenan & Charlie Settrington. I am writing in bed and am beginning to be sleepy. As a matter of fact I have taken a lot of exercise today! I went out for a joy ride with Charles – (as above). We went down to Walton & had lunch – then went to Box Hill, & went for a long walk – it was a delicious day, quite hot, & there is a most glorious view for miles & miles. Then we tootled along, & had tea at an extraordinary place, where the waiter winked, & said he also came from London! Then we went back to London, & I had a second tea with Katie. He's a dear is Chawles, & honestly, just a friend. One's family always thinks a man must be violently in love with one, which is so annoying if one is friends. Because there is nothing more pleasant than being friends, & the whole enjoyment would go at once, wouldn't it, if anything flirtatious came into it? It's a funny thing, but quite true!!

If you have nothing to do one Sunday or Sat – I should go down there, & climb Box Hill – the view is worth it. I should think the bus would go to Dorking for that. [. . .]

Goodbye old darling and do write soon, from your loving
Elizabeth

~

---

* Canadian officer convalescing at Glamis, one of the many men who proposed marriage to Elizabeth.

† Sir George Robey (1869–1954), much-loved music-hall comedian known as the 'Prime Minister of Mirth'. He raised £500,000 for war charities during the First World War and even larger sums during the Second World War.

'You weren't supposed to go out actually without somebody. I was never allowed to go to a ball unless I went to dinner with somebody, you know, first. An eye was kept. As for being asked out to lunch by a young gentleman, absolutely impossible. Funny how things have changed . . .

'But of course it made it frightfully exciting. I remember once creeping out of the house in St James's Square round the corner into Duke Street and going off to lunch with a very nice young gentleman in one of those horrible little low cars. You know, you whizzed off and had lunch at some pub down Portsmouth Road, came back again. You know you felt so wicked. We were so innocent.'

~

Thursday 17 April 1919 to Beryl Poignand

St Paul's Walden Bury

My dearest Medusa

Thank you so very much for your letter which I was more than pleased to receive – ah!! It's really simply years since I last saw you – I don't count Althorp, that was merely a glimpse. Wasn't it awful? I do hate weddings! I was so annoyed at being drawn into conversation just when I was talking to you and when I came down again you'd gone. And with you all the sunshine (Colonial touch). Little Elizabeth [Elphinstone] is here and I had to chide her! She said to me – 'Peter I know I am going to enjoy myself – Peter, I'm enjoying myself like the <u>devil</u>'. So I said, 'darling you must not say such things', 'but Papa says it <u>always</u>' she said. What can you say? She is such a darling.

No – no more drives to Box Hill with Chawles – he probably loathes me by now, people usually do when they get to know me! But it was great fun, & he's really very nice.

I've got a very sore arm from being inoculated! It's all swollen up and looks 'orrid.

I haven't answered Baggy yet. Isn't it awful? Oh dear!

How are you old darling? Very well I hope. I simply can't write as Mike, Jock & David are having a comic argument in Hertfordshire! Forgive dull letter. Goodbye old darling.

Very loving Elizabeth

~

Sunday undated [31 August 1919] to Beryl Poignand

Glamis Castle

My dearest M

Thank you a thousand times for your angelic letter. I have been very unhappy over poor Charlie* – he is my only <u>real</u> friend, & one feels one can never have another like him. He was a <u>real</u> friend, I wasn't shy of him, and he was <u>so</u> delightful. It's a dreadful thing, and his family simply <u>adored</u> him. He was quite unique, and always said what he thought, and altogether it's terrible. I think I must have been fonder of him than I realized, because now there seems a kind of a blank – if you understand what I mean? Captain Glasses, Bruces etc are nothing, Charlie was the only one I could just talk naturally to – he was a darling, and I miss him very much. I liked him specially because he <u>never</u> tried to flirt, or make love or anything like that – which always spoils friendships. Even that day we spent down at Box Hill. [. . .]

Thank you again a thousand times for your letter, Very loving Elizabeth

---

* Having survived the war, Lord Settrington went to fight for the White Russians against the Bolsheviks. He was wounded, and died on 24 August 1919.

PART TWO

DUCHESS OF YORK

'If she weren't late, she would be perfect'

KING GEORGE V

THE LONG WAR OVER, people tried to resume their lives despite the immense losses that had been suffered. The grand houses of the land closed their convalescent wards and gradually returned to family and social life. Elizabeth enjoyed her first Royal Ascot in summer 1919 and she was busy 'in a dissipated way', as she put it, with many dinners and dances throughout the year.[1]

In early 1920 she joined a house party with the Salisburys at Hatfield House. She remained friends of the family for life.

July 1920 was fateful for her. She was presented to the King and Queen, and on 8 July Albert, Duke of York, saw her across a crowded room at the RAF Ball and invited her to dance. He was reported to have said later that he fell in love with her that night, even if he did not know it at the time. For her the dance was at first less important.

Prince Albert was a sensitive young man who had always been overshadowed by his glamorous elder brother David, the Prince of Wales. Knock-kneed and left-handed, he suffered from serious digestive problems, fear of his father, a stammer and a temper. But he was also devout, sporting, kind and courageous – as he showed when serving on his ship, HMS *Collingwood*, in the Battle of Jutland in 1916.

By the end of the First World War, George V was concerned at the spread of revolution throughout Europe and was anxious to strengthen the ties between Crown and people. He created the Order of the British Empire to open up the Honours system to the mass of people, changed the Royal Family's dynastic name from Saxe-Coburg and Gotha to Windsor and encouraged his children to look for spouses at home rather than principally amongst foreign royal families.

In August 1920, only weeks after the RAF Ball, Prince Albert, who had just been created Duke of York, invited himself to Glamis. Elizabeth was nervous, she told Beryl. But the weekend went wonderfully; they played games, sang around the piano, went for walks and laughed a lot. The Prince was entranced by the happiness of all the family and friends whirling around Elizabeth, the free spirit at the centre of the house party. The contrast with the formality of his own family life was intoxicating, and the weekend appears to have persuaded him that Elizabeth was the only woman for him. For her part, she wrote to Beryl that the Prince's visit had 'kept us pretty busy! He was very nice, tho', and much improved in every way.'[2]

For more than two years Prince Albert paid devoted court to her. She was far from certain – the prospect of exchanging her carefree life, her friends and family for the golden cage of the Royal Family was not enticing to her. Some of the letters they exchanged throughout this long courtship were painful, showing his unrequited love and her concern, expressed always in the kindest way.

Finally, on the night of Sunday 14 January 1923, after a weekend together with her family at St Paul's Walden, she accepted him.

~

ELIZABETH'S ENTRY INTO the Royal Family and into public life was an immediate success. King George V, remote and stern with his own children, was at once captivated by her. Queen Mary told her son, 'You ask what Papa and I think of Elizabeth, well we are simply enchanted with her & think her too dear & attractive for words & you have made a wonderful choice.'[3]

The Duke thought so too and a few days after their engagement he wrote to her, 'My own little darling one . . . This is my first letter to you since you made me such a very happy person that Sunday at St Paul's Walden & you don't know what a wonderful difference it has made to me darling, in all ways. I think I must have always loved you darling but could never make you realize it without telling you actually that I did & thank God I told you at the right moment.'[4]

The weeks before the wedding at Westminster Abbey on 26 April 1923 became more and more hectic for her. The demands of her new family were considerable. So were those of the public. Newspapers were less voracious than they later became, but they were still insistent by the standards of the day and she found their attentions tiring. But the crowds were thrilled by her and she discovered she could respond to them with ease and with pleasure.

The adjustments she needed to make are reflected in her letters. When one of her closest friends, D'Arcy Osborne, wrote to ask how he should address her after she became Duchess of York, she replied,

'I really don't know! It might be <u>anything</u> – you might try "All Hail, Duchess", that is an Alice in Wonderland sort of Duchess, or just "Greetings" or "What Ho, Duchess" or "Say, Dutch" – in fact you can please yourself, as it will certainly please me.'[5]

The night before the wedding she spent at her parents' house, 17 Bruton Street in Mayfair. 'Felt terribly moved when I said goodnight to the darling boys & mother. I adore them,' she wrote in her diary.[6]

The wedding address was given by the Most Rev. Cosmo Lang, Archbishop of York, who said, 'You will have a great ambition to make this one life now given to you something rich and true and beautiful.'[7] Elizabeth Bowes Lyon left the Abbey as the Duchess of York, the fourth lady in the land. At the end of the day, from her honeymoon home, she telegraphed her mother, 'Arrived safely deliciously peaceful here hope you are not all too tired love Elizabeth.'[8]

~

FOR THE NEXT FOURTEEN YEARS the Duchess of York became an essential member of the Royal Family, in private and in public. Within the family she was an emollient presence, soothing relations between the King's children and their father. He was far more indulgent of her than he was of them. As a small example, the King was a stickler for punctuality, but that was not one of the Duchess's most obvious characteristics. On one occasion early in her marriage she arrived two minutes late for lunch. After she had apologized to him, he replied, 'You are not late, my dear, I think we must have sat down two minutes early.'[9]

One of the crucial roles of the monarchy is in the voluntary, charitable world – members of the family have long been associated with different charities, which enormously increases their visibility and fundraising capacity. Quickly the Duchess demonstrated her gift for raising funds and she built up her own long list of charities and other organizations, including regiments of which she was appointed Colonel-in-Chief by the King. She supported them all her life.

In July 1924 the Duke and Duchess made a difficult and important official visit to the most troubled part of the United Kingdom, Northern Ireland, riven with tensions between Catholics and Protestants. The trip went well, with the Duchess demonstrating her extraordinary ability to make contact with people. The Duke wrote to his father that she had been marvellous and people loved her. 'I am very lucky indeed to have her to help me as she knows exactly what to do & say to all the people we meet.'[10]

Visits to Scotland were no longer the purely pleasurable family holidays, surrounded with friends, that summers at Glamis had been. Now she had duties, both public and private – and had to spend a good deal of time with the King and Queen at Balmoral. The atmosphere there was formal and other guests were rarely young or enchanting. The Duke and Duchess were always relieved when they could leave for the more convivial atmosphere of Glamis.

In December 1924 they set off on a great adventure, a tour of East Africa. This visit had been recommended to them by Winston Churchill, who had told the Duchess at a dinner, 'You ought to go and have a look at the world. I should go to East Africa. It's got a great future.'[11] They left in December 1924; their families were nervous for them. The King warned them not to run unnecessary risks 'either from the climate or wild beasts';[12] Queen Mary wrote, 'God bless you both, my precious children.'[13] Lady Strathmore hated farewells and so her daughter promised not to come and say goodbye, writing, 'you won't worry about me will you darling, as I will take great care of myself in every way, I promise you.'[14]

Their journey through Kenya, Uganda and the Sudan was a revelation. The Duchess wrote to her mother that their first safari was 'simply wonderful. The country is quite unlike anything I expected and it is beautiful.'[15] To D'Arcy Osborne she wrote, 'I rise at 4.30 (I can hear you say "My God") & go walking with my spouse and the white hunter who is a <u>charming</u> man with an imagination, an accent and a sense of humour. He is exactly what I imagine the Scarlet Pimpernel to be, very slow & sleepy & long, and if he wasn't so brown he would be <u>rather</u> good looking.'[16]

Later another hunter, Roy Salmon, wrote home of the Duchess, 'She is awfully pleasant to look at & topping manners. He speaks very slowly but has practically no stammer as a rule though occasionally he does.'[17] He had no doubt that theirs was 'a love match'. They each adored the adventure and the release it gave them from the constraints, public and private, of life at home. Soon after they arrived back in England in April 1925 she wrote to D'Arcy Osborne, 'I am bubbling inside with Africa.'[18] Many years later she described the journey as 'Wonderful. Best bit of one's life.'[19]

On the morning of 21 April 1926 the Duke and Duchess's first child was born at 17 Bruton Street. They called her Elizabeth Alexandra Mary. Her birth caused great joy in the family and excitement throughout the land; one newspaper, the *Daily Graphic*, wrote that the family's happiness was shared by the nation and added, 'The possibility that in the little stranger to Bruton Street there may be a future Queen of Great Britain (perhaps even a second and resplendent Queen Elizabeth) is sufficiently intriguing; but let us not burden the bright hour of its arrival with speculation of its Royal destiny.'

The Princess was born at a moment of great industrial unrest, which some feared might tip Britain towards revolution. Both the King and the Duke were concerned by the danger of a general strike called by the Trades Union Congress. Dire consequences of social breakdown were forecast. In the event, the strike caused much less disruption than was feared and after only nine days the TUC called it off. The King was much relieved and thought that 'our old country can well be proud of itself.'[20] His official biographer, Harold Nicolson, later wrote that people of all sorts saw it as a common tragedy, not a purely class tragedy.[21]

The strike and its cancellation did nothing to alleviate the terrible economic crisis affecting much of the industrialized world through the 1920s and 1930s, but perhaps it showed that Britain could deal with industrial discontent reasonably and thus avoid the totalitarian solutions which were beginning to seem attractive to many across continental Europe.

That summer was a happy one for the family. For the Duchess, the only shadow over her delight in her new daughter was the prospect of a long trip to open the new federal Parliament in Australia in early 1927. The Duke was concerned about that but also about whether his stammer would ruin the many public speeches that he would have to make during the tour. In October 1926 the Duchess persuaded him to visit an Australian speech therapist called Lionel Logue, now practising in Harley Street.

Logue recorded his first impression of the Duke as 'a slim, quiet man, with tired eyes and all the outward symptoms of the man upon whom habitual speech defect had begun to set the sign. When he left at five o'clock, you could see that there was hope once more in his heart.'[22] In the next few weeks the Duke went many times to Logue, often with the Duchess, and the Australian's treatment had a superb effect upon his self-confidence; his fear of the trip diminished.

The Duchess's dread of it, by contrast, grew, as she contemplated parting from her baby. 'She is growing so big and is as sharp as a needle, & so well. She sleeps beautifully and has always got a smile ready.'[23] As the day of departure, 6 January 1927, loomed she became 'more and more miserable'.[24] That morning, when the nanny brought the baby Princess down to say goodbye, the Duchess was emotional and so she 'drank some champagne and tried not to weep'.[25]

The trip – the first time the Duke had been asked by his father to represent him on an imperial mission – was gruelling and long but the young couple learned a lot and the voyage was a personal success for both of them. They were impressed by the apparent strength of the Empire and the loyalty of its citizens to the Crown. Their travels gave the Duke confidence in his ability to confront the world and it showed the Duchess that she could support her husband in his public as well as his private life, abroad as well as at home. On their return to Britain, the Duke and Duchess, with Princess Elizabeth in her mother's arms, appeared on the balcony at Buckingham Palace, cheered by ecstatic crowds in the Mall. *The Times* reported, 'Twice the Duchess, her face radiant with smiles, brought the Princess forward.'

Both families were delighted to have their children back after a successful tour, and the Duke and Duchess were overjoyed to be with their daughter once more. The Duke told Lionel Logue that he could now talk to his father without any problem. And the King wrote to Queen Mary saying how pleased he was to have his second son back. He had spoken to him several times and found him 'most sensible, very different from David'.[26] The Prince of Wales was charming and charismatic, but the King considered him to be so careless of his responsibilities that he would not allow him access to confidential information. The King was also dismayed that, unlike the Duke of York, the Prince of Wales had shown no signs of wanting to marry and start a family.

On 21 August 1930, the Yorks' second daughter, whom they named Margaret Rose, was born at Glamis. The Duchess soon realized that she had a character very different from that of her elder sister. She wrote to Cosmo Lang, now Archbishop of Canterbury, 'She has got large blue eyes and a will of iron, which is all the equipment that a lady needs!'[27]

Through the 1920s and early 1930s the international economic crisis became chronic. Business failures abounded and unemployment grew almost everywhere. As the Depression bit deeper, charities and other organizations needed more and more help with fundraising. The Duchess's role in the life of the country grew ever more significant as she took on more and more charities, regiments and other public duties. She found it tragic that so many men would never work again and, calling herself an 'anti-feminist', she thought that women should give up jobs so that men could work.

In 1935, despite all that hardship, the people of Britain greeted King George V's Silver Jubilee with warm enthusiasm. The King and Queen Mary drew huge and happy crowds wherever they went, and so did the Yorks. But over all the celebrations hung still the domestic scourge of unemployment and the international shadow of Europe's dictators.

The Duchess was ill that Christmas with one of her frequent attacks of influenza. She and the Duke stayed at their home, Royal Lodge in Windsor Great Park. Their children were at Sandringham with their grandparents and the Duchess wrote to them often. To Princess Elizabeth she wrote, 'Mind you answer very nicely when you are asked questions, even though they may be silly ones!'[28]

It was King George V's last Christmas. Already weak, his condition worsened through the next few weeks, and on 21 January 1936 he died. It was the beginning of a terrible year for the monarchy and for the Yorks in particular.

The Prince of Wales acceded to the throne, taking the title Edward VIII. But it quickly became clear to those around him that he had little enthusiasm for the task. He was entirely preoccupied by the effect that his father's death would have on his relationship with Wallis Simpson, a divorced American woman with whom he was in love. During the course of that year, Mrs Simpson acquired her second divorce and the King informed his Prime Minister, Stanley Baldwin, that he intended to marry her. When Baldwin took soundings at home and throughout the Empire, it became evident that Mrs Simpson would be widely unacceptable as Queen and he so informed the King.

Edward VIII eventually decided to abdicate in favour of his brother Bertie; on 11 December 1936 he did so. To their horror the Duke and Duchess of York suddenly and unexpectedly became King and Queen. He took the name George VI. She wrote to her brother-in-law, the departing King, 'We are all overcome with misery and can only pray that you will find happiness in your new life.'[29]

In their own new lives much was demanded of them. They had to rescue the monarchy from crisis, and convince the British people that George VI would be an effective monarch. It was not easy; Edward VIII had been popular in the country, and there were rumours that the new King's stammer and shyness indicated his inability to reign. But by the force of their own personalities the King and Queen dispelled the doubts. To the Archbishop of Canterbury the Queen wrote that she could hardly believe the challenge they faced but 'the curious thing is that we are not afraid.'[30]

Friday undated [9 January 1920] to Beryl Poignand

St Paul's Walden Bury

My dearest M

How are you? Did you get the photograph alright? I have come back today from Hatfield* after a most wonderful party. It really was great fun, & I enjoyed it so much. The people there were the Cranbornes,† Monica Grenfell,‡ Helen Cecil,§ Mollie Cecil,¶ Bay Smith & me, Mr Arthur Penn, Lord Apsley,| Bruce [Ogilvy], Bobby Somerset,** Mr Rex Benson, Count de Grünne, Walter Dalkeith,†† & Mr Francis Manners.‡‡ One day we played tennis in the real tennis house, which was most amusing. Two afternoons we played hockey violently, which was great fun. On Tuesday evening we danced, and

---

* Hatfield House, the ancestral home of the Cecil family in Hertfordshire.

† Robert ('Bobbety'), Viscount Cranborne, later fifth Marquess of Salisbury KG PC (1893–1972), Conservative politician who resigned in February 1938 with Anthony Eden in protest at Chamberlain's foreign policy, member of wartime government, leader of the House of Lords 1942–5, Secretary of State for Commonwealth Relations, 1952. Elizabeth ('Betty', 1897–1982), daughter of Lord Richard Frederick Cavendish.

‡ Hon. Monica Grenfell (1893–1973), daughter of first Baron Desborough. She married in 1924 Marshal of the RAF Sir John Maitland Salmond.

§ Helen Cecil (1901–79), daughter of Lord Edward Cecil, married 1921 Hon. Alexander Hardinge, later second Baron Hardinge of Penshurst.

¶ Mary ('Mollie') Cecil (1900–94), twin daughter of Right Rev. Lord William Cecil, Bishop of Exeter, second son of third Marquess of Salisbury, married 1921 fourth Baron Manners.

| Allen Algernon Bathurst, Lord Apsley (1895–1942), eldest son of seventh Earl Bathurst. He served in the First World War, DSO and MC; he was killed on active service in the Second World War. His son succeeded as eighth Earl.

** Henry Robert Somers Fitzroy de Vere Somerset DSO (1898–1965), married 1922 Elizabeth's friend Bettine Malcolm (see footnote, p. 83).

†† Lord Dalkeith (1894–1973), succeeded as eighth Duke of Buccleuch in 1935.

‡‡ Hon. Francis Manners, later fourth Baron Manners (1897–1972). Married Mary ('Mollie') Cecil (see above).

ended up by a terrific game of follow-my-leader right round the
house, which is immense, under the dining room table & even across
the roof!! On Wednesday we went to a dance given by the Aclands,
but only stayed till 12, as the Hertford Ball was the next night. I met
an extraordinary American at it, and the awful thing was I couldn't
remember his name, & he asked me if I knew it. I guessed Johnson,
but it turned out to be Williams. I never can remember names! The
Hertford Ball last night was heavenly – bed 4 a.m. this morning!! I
had on my new white frock. Several people admired it, which pleased
me immensely!! Walter drove me here this morning in his car, & I
have never been in such danger before! Unluckily we passed all the
Brands who are his cousins, shooting, & he got thrilled & waved at
them, & each time we swerved wildly into the ditch, & out again.
We crashed into the gate here, & I wonder that I am alive. He has
hardly ever driven before!!

The Salisburys are a most delightful family, and I love David
[Cecil].* He is very clever, and most entertaining. Quite vague like
they all are. You must be getting dreadfully bored at hearing all this.
Have you been to any good dances? Do write and tell me. I received
a letter from an Australian, also a book of views of NZ from another
a box of chocs from Bruce & Capt Glass, but that is all amusing.

I hope I am coming to London next week & shall see you. David
is up at Glamis & Mother is returning tonight. Goodbye old pip,
much love from your loving Elizabeth

~

11 June 1920 to Beryl Poignand

20 St James's Square

My dearest M.

I must write you a last letter from this darling house, as we leave
it for ever next week.† I can't bear it – it is too dreadful. I was so

---

* Lord David Cecil CH (1902–86), son of fourth Marquess of Salisbury. Married 1932 Rachel
MacCarthy. Writer of elegant and witty biographies; Goldsmiths' Professor of English
Literature at Oxford 1948–69. Lifelong friend of Queen Elizabeth, who he said had captured
his heart as a child.

† The lease on 20 St James's Square had expired. The Strathmores moved first to a rented
house in Eaton Square and later to 17 Bruton Street in Mayfair.

disappointed you couldn't come last Thursday – it was all my fault I know – & after all D & P never came & there was only Katie & another girl. I wish you could have come – I waited anxiously by the front door but you never came. Oh alas perfidious one.

I suppose you are on your holiday now, I do hope you are really very happy. We are in an <u>awful</u> state here, moving everything, packing up, & thoroughly upset in every way. The terrible thing is, that we simply can't get another house, & so we are warehousing the furniture, & trying to find a small house just to live in for a month or so. I'm so depressed old darling, I love every corner of this house. All the funny things that have happened; the Australian dances, our schoolroom where I used to flatten my nose against the window & make eyes at the Beautiful One – (& <u>you</u> to Fatty) the stairs we used to race up, the spot where Capt Glass* proposed, the room I got Mr Bagshawe's letter in saying 'will you marry meh?', the place you looked over the banisters when your brother returned suddenly from France – our dinner when all the food was on the floor with Wellsie† & Lavinia, our heavenly repast of roast chicken after the first time we saw Henry (<u>was</u> it him or was he not there?), the glass Uncle Freddy rubbed when he came to tea, oh & thousands of others. Do you remember them all? This house has more old associations than nearly anywhere. I will write & let you know directly we get another house.

I am going to stay with Nina Balfour for Ascot next week, but I am not particularly looking forward to it! It rather frightens me. I do hope you are really enjoying yourself, do write & tell me how you are & what you are doing. Did you see that ghastly picture of me in the Sketch? Oh!

Must stop, I have been <u>so</u> busy lately, & I had to write & tell you the last news.

Very loving Elizabeth

~

---

* Elizabeth had become friendly with Captain Glass in 1918. In March 1920 he proposed to her, which caused her consternation.

† 'Wellsie', Miss Wells, governess to Lavinia Spencer.

Tuesday 13 July 1920 to Beryl Poignand

90 Eaton Square
S.W.1

My dearest M.

I have been trying to write to you for ages, but you can't imagine the busy time I've been having lately. Mostly gaiety I'm afraid! First of all, thank you very very much for your letter. I am so glad you have got another month [of holiday], I'm sure you needed it badly, and I do hope it will do you a lot of good. We have taken this house for a few months furnished, & it is very ugly but quite comfortable. I miss St J. Square terribly, & very nearly as much, I miss the locality. Isn't it funny? But the traffic & people are so deadly here, & one can't pop round to Mr Harris [chemist in St James's Street] or Mr Bottom [newsagent at 32A Duke Street] or anything nice like that.

I went down to Henley – stayed with the Hambledens* at Greenlands for it. It pelted the whole time, but it was quite fun. Then on Sunday we motored up to London with Geordie Haddington,† & Mother & I went up to Carberry that night for the King & Queen's visit to Holyrood.

May & Sidney had a large party, all over 60, including the Duchess of Roxburgh & also Montrose, Lord Mar & Kellie, Lord Balfour, & a few other rather Royal people! We dined with the K. & Queen at Holyrood on the Monday. It was really quite fun. I was taken in by the Lord Justice General! & had the Admiral Commanding at Rosyth on the other side!! They were very nice.

On Tuesday I was formally presented, & on Wednesday there was a garden party. We came down on Wednesday night! On Thursday [8 July] I went to the R.A.F. Ball at the Ritz. It was really most amusing, & there were some priceless people there. All the heroes of the Air too. I danced with Prince Albert who I hadn't known before, he is quite a nice youth. Then on Friday & Sat. the Eton v. Harrow.

---

* Second Viscount Hambleden (1868–1928), MP for Strand Division of Westminster, 1891–1910. He succeeded his mother, Viscountess Hambleden in her own right, in 1913. He married Lady Esther Gore, daughter of fifth Earl of Arran, in 1894 and their son, third Viscount Hambleden, married Lady Patricia Herbert (1904–94), a girlhood friend of Queen Elizabeth, who was later her lady in waiting for many years.

† George 'Geordie' Baillie-Hamilton, twelfth Earl of Haddington KT MC TD JP (1894–1986), succeeded his father 1917.

That was really <u>great</u> fun. I loved it, & it was so nice having David
back. He returned to Eton yesterday.

Rosie is still in Malta and can't get home. I believe she is very well
though. Mother and I are going to 'Mr Pim'* this evening. Have you
seen him? By the way, 'At the Villa Rose'† sounds rather
melodramatic! We must go. Do write again and tell me how you are
and if enjoying yourself goodly. Very loving Elizabeth

~

Tuesday undated [14 September 1920] to Beryl Poignand

Glamis Castle

My dearest M,

[. . .]

I am now completely exhausted from our Forfar ball party. It was
really great fun, & we were about 20 altogether, & I've never done
so much before in my life! We dressed up, & ragged about, & now
that the hard tennis court is finished, we played all day. The people
were Katie Hamilton, Doris Gordon Lennox,‡ Bettine Malcolm,§
Katharine McEwen,¶ Diamond Hardinge,‖ Grisell Cochrane
Baillie,** Hilda Blackburn†† & us. Also Lord Doune, James Stuart,‡‡

---

* *Mr Pim Passes By*, play by A. A. Milne written in 1919, a hit in London, with Leslie Howard
in the starring role.

† *At the Villa Rose*, British silent detective film starring Manora Thew and Langhorn Burton
made in 1920, based on the 1910 novel *At the Villa Rose* by A. E. W. Mason.

‡ Lady Doris Gordon-Lennox (1896–1980), daughter of eighth Duke of Richmond, married
1923 Clare Vyner.

§ Bettine Malcolm (1900–73), daughter of Major C. E. Malcolm, married 1922 Captain Robert
Somerset.

¶ Katharine McEwen (1899–1979), daughter of R. F. McEwen, married 1922 Roger Lumley,
later eleventh Earl of Scarbrough; Lady of the Bedchamber to Queen Elizabeth, 1947–53, Extra
Lady, 1953–79.

‖ The Hon. Diamond Hardinge (1900–27), daughter of Charles Hardinge, first Baron
Hardinge of Penshurst, married 1923 Major Robert Abercromby.

** The Hon. Grisell Cochrane Baillie (1898–1985), daughter of second Baron Lamington,
married 1922 Captain Edward Hastings.

†† Hilda Blackburn (1902–86), Elizabeth's cousin, daughter of Lord Strathmore's sister Lady
Constance Blackburn, married Archibald Pearson 1929.

‡‡ James Stuart (1897–1971), third son of seventeenth Earl of Moray. Equerry to the Duke of
York, 1920–1; MP for Moray and Nairn, 1923–59; Joint Parliamentary Secretary to the

Lord Gage,* Victor Cochrane Baillie, Jock McEwen,† Sir Richard Leighton,‡ Prince Paul of Serbia§ & David & Mike.

The most awful thing happened. Victor proposed to me the night we all dressed up! He looked <u>too</u> awful with great black smudges all over his face! I <u>did</u> hate it! Don't tell anybody.

Still a few people here, must fly & dress for dinner. [. . .]

Much love, & again a thousand thanks

Your very loving Elizabeth

~

'People were always popping the question. I remember somebody proposed to me at a fancy-dress ball at Glamis, and I remember his face was covered with black paint. He was sitting next to me and proposed and I remember saying "No, thank you very much." And when one turned them down, he'd say, "Oh, I thought you wouldn't." So that was all very nice and light-hearted, really, I think. Occasionally there was a very serious one. He used to go away to America or something, you know.' These last remarks referred to James Stuart.

~

Thursday undated [23 September 1920] to Beryl Poignand

Glamis Castle

My dearest M,

How is life treating you? I haven't heard from you for ages, do

<hr>

Treasury, 1941–5; Conservative Chief Whip, 1941–8; Secretary of State for Scotland, 1951–7. He was created Viscount Stuart of Findhorn in 1959. Before Prince Albert, he was Elizabeth's most serious suitor. Married 1923 Lady Rachel Cavendish. Lord Doune was his elder brother Francis, later eighteenth Earl of Moray (1892–1943).

* Henry Rainald ('George') Gage, sixth Viscount Gage (1895–1982), lord in waiting to King George V, King Edward VIII and King George VI; Parliamentary Private Secretary to the Secretary of State for India, 1924–9. Married 1931 Hon. (Alexandra) Imogen Grenfell. His family estate was Firle on the South Downs near Lewes in Sussex.

† Jock McEwen (1894–1962), brother of Katharine, later Sir John McEwen, first Baronet.

‡ Sir Richard Leighton, tenth Baronet (1893–1957).

§ Prince Paul of Serbia (1893–1976), son of Prince Arsene Karageorgevic (brother of King Peter I of Serbia) and his Russian wife Aurora Demidoff. After his parents separated he was taken in by King Peter, who brought him up with his own sons. He had been at Oxford, was popular in London society and shared a flat with Elizabeth's brother Michael. He admired her 'shining lively eyes and beautiful smile' and many thought he was keen to marry her. They remained friends throughout his life.

write soon. I don't believe either, that I've seen you for about 4 or 5 months! I hope you are feeling quite well again. I am writing in bed as I've got rather a cold, & am now utterly exhausted after 3 weeks of entertaining people! Last Saturday Prince Albert came to stay & that kept us pretty busy! He was very nice tho', & very much improved in every way.*

Princess Mary was staying at Airlie to review Girl Guides – she dined here on Saturday, and we danced afterwards till 12. Lady Airlie, Dit, & her Lady in Waiting, Lady Joan Mulholland came too. The people staying here, were Katie, Doris Gordon Lennox, Helen Cecil, Venetia James, Lord Carnegie, Lord Doune, Tom Bevan & James Stuart besides our family.

Albert proposed himself & seemed to enjoy it all! Princess Mary came to Chapel on Sunday & afterwards I showed her & the Duke round the Castle, & terrified them with ghost stories! We also played ridiculous games of hide and seek, they really are babies. She didn't leave till 6.30, & then we all played General Post and Flags etc till dinner time – I had played tennis all morning, so you can imagine how tired I was!! We sang all evening – & it was all quite fun. Poor P. Mary really did enjoy herself – she is most awfully nice.

So you see we have been very busy lately, & are at last going to have a little peace!! [. . .]

I must stop, do write soon. Have you been to any dances since your return?

Your very loving
Elizabeth

~

Thursday undated [?November 1920] to Beryl Poignand

90 Eaton Square

Why did'st thou not come this evening Medusa?

As a matter of fact our <u>Bert</u> stayed till 7, talking 100 to 20, or even 200 to a dozen.

---

* After this first visit to Glamis, the Duke of York wrote to Lady Strathmore: 'I did enjoy my time there so much, & I only wish I could have stayed there longer, I hope you will forgive me for the very abrupt way in which I proposed myself.' (Duke of York to Lady Strathmore, 21 September 1920, Glamis Archives (RA))

I am just off to a smart dance, & I <u>know</u> I shan't know a soul, & will be miserable. I <u>must</u> see you some time – when on earth can it be? I <u>do</u> wish he hadn't come this evening, but I simply couldn't stop him, & I am longing to see you.

Ever your loving Elizabeth

~

Monday undated [13 December 1920] to the Duke of York

St Paul's Walden Bury

Dear Prince Albert

Thank you so much for your letter. I am looking forward very much to Mrs Ronnie Greville's* party – though the thought of it <u>terrifies</u> me! I haven't been to a proper dinner party for months and months, and have quite forgotten how to behave! I expect it will be great fun though. Have you been very gay? Dancing every night I expect –

Only a short note, as Wednesday is so soon.

I am Sir, Yours sincerely

Elizabeth Lyon

~

23 December 1920 to the Duke of York

St Paul's Walden Bury

Dear Prince Albert

Thank you so <u>very</u> much for the lovely little box, which I simply love.

It <u>is</u> so nice of you to think of giving it to me, and <u>very</u> many thanks. It is <u>so</u> pretty, and will help to ornament my sitting room in Bruton Street next year. I was so sorry about the dance on Tuesday, but my mother has really been very ill, and I couldn't leave her.

---

* Hon. Mrs Ronald Greville, née Margaret McEwan (1863–1942), daughter of the Scottish brewer and philanthropist William McEwan MP, whose fortune she inherited in 1913. She was friendly with several members of the Royal Family and entertained with largesse both in Mayfair and at her Surrey mansion, Polesden Lacey. A forceful character, notorious for her acerbic wit, she had many critics, but she could also be kind and generous. During the First World War, like the Strathmores, she set up a convalescent home at her house. She was made a DBE in 1922. She proved a loyal friend to the Duke and to the Duchess of York.

She is a little better now, which is a great relief. Did you enjoy Lady Evelyn's* dance last week? I loved it, tho' I enjoyed 'your party' at Mrs Greville's even more. I feel I shall not be going to another one for months, which is dreadfully sad. I lead such a deadly existence here, that there is simply nothing to tell you – oh except that I have just fallen into a pond! The only event which happened for weeks!

I hope you will have a very merry Xmas, & I send you all my very best wishes for 1921. I hope it will be a very happy year for you. Thank you again a thousand times for the darling little box – I do love it.

I am Sir,
Yours sincerely,
Elizabeth Lyon

~

10 January 1921 to the Duke of York

St Paul's Walden Bury

Dear Prince Albert

Thank you so much for your letter, which I received on return from my 'round of gaieties'! I am so sorry to hear that you have been ill, and hope you are really feeling better.

I am a complete wreck still, as on Friday night I went to bed at 6 o'clock – an unearthly hour, after the Southdown Ball which was great fun. My brain refuses to work – hence a dull letter! About luncheon on the 17th. It would be delightful if you could come – the only thing is, would you mind having it alone? Not alone by yourself I don't mean (it sounds so funny that, as if you would have it in one room, and me in another!!). But you see my mother has been very ill, and she & I are really only having a sort of picnic down here by ourselves, and I am afraid you would be bored to tears. It would be delightful if you are sure you wouldn't mind not having a large luncheon party? Please do say if you think you might!

This is quite a small house, and no ghosts like at Glamis!

There is a signpost just before you reach a village called Codicote,

---

* Lady Evelyn Guinness (1883–1939), daughter of fourteenth Earl Buchan, married 1903 Walter Edward Guinness, later first Baron Moyne. The Prince dined with Lady Evelyn on 16 December; the dinner was followed by a dance.

beyond Hitchin, with St Pauls Walden on it, and then you keep to the right all the way, till you come to a tumbledown old gate on the left. Then you go up a bumpy road full of holes, and eventually reach an even more tumbledown old house, and a tumbledown little person waiting on the doorstep – which will be <u>ME</u>!!!

But do come if you <u>really</u> don't mind having luncheon with my mother and me, or would you rather put it off till we come to London? <u>Whichever</u> you like best.

I am Sir,

Yours sincerely, Elizabeth Lyon

~

28 February 1921 to the Duke of York

St Paul's Walden Bury

Dear Prince Bertie

I must write one line to say how <u>dreadfully</u> sorry I am about yesterday. It makes me miserable to think of it – you have been so <u>very</u> nice about it all – please do forgive me. Also <u>please</u> don't worry about it – I do understand so well what you feel, and sympathise so much, & I hate to think I am the cause of it. I honestly can't explain to you how terribly sorry I am –, it worries me <u>so</u> much to think you may be unhappy – I do hope you won't be. <u>Anyway</u> we can be good friends can't we? Please do look on me as one. I shall <u>never</u> say anything about our talks I promise you – and nobody need ever know.

I thought I must just write this short letter to try & tell you <u>how</u> sorry I am.

Yours very sincerely, Elizabeth

~

The Prince had invited himself to lunch with Elizabeth for a second time at St Paul's Walden Bury on 27 February. Evidently he had proposed to her but she had turned him down.

~

6 March 1921 to Jock Bowes Lyon

St Paul's Walden Bury

My Darling Jock

Thank you a thousand times for your letter which I loved. I will speak to Bragger about the cricket pitch, and being a young man of remarkable perseverance I feel something may come out of it!

It sounds too delicious at St Jean, it has also been too lovely here ever since you left, but today the weather broke up – alas!

I did not take what you might call a violent fancy to Sir P[hilip]. Sassoon;* he was merely rather amusing to talk to, and I like talking to people who have got quite different points of view to the usual run of men. Perhaps not very <u>elevating</u> ones, (points of view) but très moderne (French).

Now I have a momentous piece of news for you. Over the page now! Ha ha.

No, it isn't what you thought it was going to be – so Ha Ha again. It is, that I was IN MY BATH, by TEN MINUTES TO NINE this morning. <u>Can you beat it?</u>

I thank you in advance for your kind congratulations. Merci, and likewise danke schön.

The tennis lawn is a vision of beauty – green velvety turf – I <u>don't</u> think. But it really is rather good now, but you bet it rains all summer. I have just been immersed in the 'Saturday Evening Post', and consequently start all my sentences with 'Say, listen'! And very nice too.

Wasn't it nice Gee† getting in at East Woolwich, and Ramsay MacDonald‡ failing? I was really pleased. We are going up to Glamis

---

* Sir Philip Sassoon PC GBE CMG (1888–1939), British politician, aesthete and socialite. MP for Hythe from 1912, Private Secretary to General Douglas Haig, December 1915–18, Under-Secretary of State for Air, 1924–9; Trustee of the National Gallery, Wallace Collection and Tate Gallery. During the 1920s and '30s, he gave lavish parties at his country house, Trent Park, at which guests such as Winston Churchill, George Bernard Shaw, Rex Whistler and many other eminent men and women enjoyed wit and luxury.

† Captain Robert Gee VC MC (1876–1960), MP for East Woolwich, 1921–2, and for Bosworth Division of Leicester, 1924–7.

‡ James Ramsay MacDonald PC FRS (1866–1937), prominent Labour politician, MP for Leicester from 1906 to 1918. He then tried to enter Parliament again at several by-elections, including East Woolwich, 1921; after being elected MP for the Aberavon Division of

for Easter I believe, which falls fairly soon – I suppose you will still be abroad. Do you approve of the idea of me becoming a royalty? What ho!!

I write to the accompaniment of the squeaking of rats, melodious and soothing to a degree; and the patter of their little feet in the walls calm my troubled brain – the little darlings. Bless them.

Ah Jock! How seldom we remember the vast debt we owe to the rat – his winsome winning ways, and always fresh humour which helps us so in the daily battle of Life. Ah! how small the world is; As Virgil says 'Tempus fugit,' or as Homer aptly has it – 'Nil desperandum non lapsus linguae'.*

Well, so long Bro, guess I'm off to pound the pillow.

Your very loving Buffy†

~

12 April 1921 to Beryl Poignand

St Paul's Walden Bury

My dearest M,

I haven't heard from you for <u>years</u> fickle Beast. I am longing to hear, so take up your pen oh Medusa, & forthwith set down on paper all your doings & thoughts for the last month. [. . .]

Bad times my dear M, but I love the calm way the British people take it all! Nothing but talks of Revolution & Ruin,‡ & yet everybody moons along in the same old way, except that the 'Boys' join anything they can.

Mike has joined something, and goes to Hertford tomorrow. Very bored, but I suppose he's right. I do hope all that won't be needed, & that something will be arranged. [. . .]

Glamorganshire in the 1922 general election, when Labour replaced the Liberals as the main opposition to the Conservatives, he was the dominant figure of the Left. He was Prime Minister January–November 1924, and again after the 1929 election.

* Literally: 'Never despair no slip of the tongue.'

† 'Buffy' was her family nickname.

‡ Industrial unrest had grown throughout 1920. In the first quarter of 1921 unemployment almost doubled to 1,300,000. The miners declared a strike and railway and transport workers threatened to join them. King George V wrote to his mother saying, 'we are passing through as grave a crisis as this country has ever had.' (King George V to Queen Alexandra, 10 April 1921, RA GV/PRIV/AA38/20) The troops were called out into the streets. At the last minute, on Friday 15 April, the transport unions called off their strike, but times remained febrile.

Father dashed off to Glamis yesterday to raise volunteers – he &
Barson flew off with great celerity!

Mother & I have been here since Xmas now – isn't it
extraordinary? I am longing for '17' [Bruton Street] to be finished, and
then you must instantly come & see it. [. . .]

I simply can't write a decent letter. I feel just like I used to on
those hot days during lesson time, when I used to lie on the bed
upstairs – do you remember? And those delicious suppers of chicken,
green peas & strawbugs, when we used to cheer up considerably!
Good old days – I feel much older now, I suppose I am a few years
older!! Write From your very loving Elizabeth

Curse strikes.

~

Wednesday undated [18 May 1921] to Beryl Poignand

Bicton
East Budleigh
Devonshire

My dearest M

Thank you so much for your letter I was wondering what had
become of you! The party here has been great fun, and I am leaving
today. We played tennis & lazed about, & occasionally did a few
official Prince of Wales things and had great fun.*

[. . .] The Prince was away all day working hard, & only got back
at tea-time – he does have a hellish life – that's the only word for it.

It has been the most perfect weather here. I am going on to
Dawlish to see my aunt [Violet Cavendish-Bentinck], & returning to
London tomorrow – & then to Paris when Lord Hardinge† makes up
his mighty mind to go back! [. . .]

Au revoir, your very very loving Elizabeth

~

---

* The Prince of Wales stayed at Bicton, home of Lord and Lady Clinton, parents-in-law of
Jock Bowes Lyon, from Monday 16 to Wednesday 18 May.

† Charles Hardinge, first Baron Hardinge of Penshurst (1858–1944), Viceroy of India, 1910–16;
Permanent Under-Secretary of State at the Foreign Office, 1916–20, then Ambassador in Paris,
1920–2. He was the father of Alec (Assistant Private Secretary to King George V) and
Elizabeth's friend Diamond.

Saturday 28 May 1921 to the Duke of York

British Embassy
Paris

Dear Prince Bertie

Your letter has only just reached me here, and I telegraphed a
reply which I hope you will understand! It is so nice of you to ask me
to play tennis, and I would have adored it, but I am rather far away
unfortunately, in the land of 'ou la la wee wee'! So far the only
French I've had to use is 'oui oui' or 'non non', both quite useful. I
am having great fun here and last night escaped from the Embassy,
and went out to dine with Paul of Serbia; & Walter & Mollie
[Dalkeith],* who were spending two nights in Paris. It was such fun,
and delicious seeing Mollie again – also it felt very odd being
chaperoned by her! She & Walter were both very flourishing, and
they left this morning which was very sad. We danced at Ciro's† until
it shut, and then went on and danced at another place where Leonora
& Maurice‡ were dancing; and chucked little balls at everybody!! It
was all so funny.

I am going to stay here quite another week I think, as London is
so dull now, and this is amusing. Are you going to Ascot? I know you
love it!! I am going from Bisham, but don't think I can stand more
than two days of it – probably Tuesday & Thursday.

I do wish I could have come tomorrow, and again many thanks
for asking me,

Yours very sincerely,
Elizabeth

~

---

*   Walter Dalkeith had married Elizabeth's friend 'Mollie', Vreda Esther Mary Lascelles, in
April 1921.

†   Ciro's, a fashionable London nightclub.

‡   Leonora Hughes and Maurice Mouvet, professional dancers.

9 June 1921 to the Duke of York

British Embassy
Paris

Dear Prince Bertie

Thank you so much for your letter – I am so sorry to have been such ages answering – I was trying to find out about the Sunday 19th. My sister will not be down in Surrey that week-end, which rather knocks the 'strawberry feed' on the head! I do hope you have made other plans by now – it is unfortunate, that Sunday is no good, and I really am sorry to have been so long letting you know.

There was a tremendous ball here last night, and I am in the last stages of exhaustion!

They dance the Tango a great deal out here – rather an amusing dance I think. I danced it with a Russian called Constantine Somebody the other evening – I never found out his other name! It was so funny, one is suddenly hurled into the air, & then bounced on the floor till one is gaga, ooh la la! Very painful.

I expect I shall see you at Ascot some time – do you think there will be any dances in London? I hope there will be.

Yours v. sincerely
Elizabeth Lyon

~

Monday undated [18 July 1921] to the Duke of York

6 Upper Brook Street*
W.1

Dear Prince Bertie

I would love to play tennis on Thursday, tho' I find I am getting worse & worse! I am sure you will all be far too good for me.

I thought you were coming to tea tomorrow, and will continue to expect you unless I hear to the contrary. Is that alright?

After you left the Grahams' dance the other evening, my French friend got fearfully excited when they played 'Mon Homme', and

---

* The London home of Sidney and May Elphinstone.

threw me into the air, uttering short sharp cries! I think he was mad!

I remain –
Yours sincerely
Elizabeth Lyon

~

6 August 1921 to the Duke of York

Glamis Castle

Dear Prince Bertie

Thank you so very much for writing to me on my birthday – it was very nice of you to remember it. I love the book too, and they really are very amusing some of the verses, aren't they?

Welbeck* was great fun – an immense party of about 36 people, and we played tennis violently all day, & danced violently all night, so I'm now even more of a wreck than I was! They had a band from London in the house, and the party was very nice, so it was very amusing.

Have you been enjoying Cowes? It was as if it might be such fun, and I hope you are feeling quite well again now.

Your Boys Camp was a great success wasn't it? I hope so anyway, as it is such an excellent idea, and a wonderful thing for the boys.

Have you seen the Bisham photographs? Nina has just sent me a terrible one of myself sitting between you and Arthur [Penn]! I am simpering in the most awful way – I do hope it's only the sun.

It is rather cold up here, and the tennis court has been ruined – isn't it sad. 'ou la la oui oui', and likewise 'ci-ci'.

Yes, this summer has been great fun, and I'm so glad you enjoyed it, and that we are such friends after what happened. It was very hectic, & I feel tired out, don't you? You are coming on Sept. 24th, n'est-ce pas?

Yours sincerely
Elizabeth

~

* Welbeck Abbey, the home of the Portland family. The sixth Duke (1857–1943) was a first cousin of Cecilia Strathmore.

4 October 1921 to the Duke of York

Glamis Castle

Dear Prince Bertie

Thank you so very much for your delightful letter I got this morning. It was so nice of you to write like that about mother, and I can't tell you how touched I was.

The operation itself was very successful,* and the doctors are quite satisfied, but she has been terribly ill these last two days, and it has all been too awful.

However, she had a very good night last night, and I really think she is a little tiny bit better today. The only real worry is her intense weakness, but I am so grateful that the operation was successful, and have great hopes that she will improve today. Of course it was a terrible handicap her already being so weak when it was done.

I'm afraid this is a very depressed letter, but you know, it is such a relief to write about it, & does one so much good, that I hope you don't mind.

I'm afraid I must have made a lugubrious hostess last week, but I enjoyed having everybody here, and I only hope that it wasn't too depressing for you.

I shouldn't worry about your shooting, it was just bad luck that you happened to be 'off', and I'm sure next time you will be back in your old form. It must be infuriating when one is a good shot, to have off days like that, but I bet you will be shooting like a book the next time.

I hope you will have fun riding, and find that you like your new horses – aren't you longing for the hunting to start?

Shall I write a little later on, to let you know how my mother is? You are very sympathetic about it all – worry <u>is</u> awful isn't it? I am really much happier today tho', and I will write you a more cheerful letter soon & tell you how she gets on.

Thank you again for your letter, it is <u>such</u> a help to have the sympathy of one's friends on these occasions.

Yours sincerely
Elizabeth

~

---

* Her mother had had an operation to remove a gallstone, which was successful but left her very weak. Lady Strathmore relied greatly on Elizabeth at this time.

11 October 1921 to the Duke of York

Glamis Castle

Dear Prince Bertie

Many thanks for your letter – do you know my mother is <u>really</u> better today, isn't it wonderful? The doctors are quite satisfied, and I feel she makes good progress now. It has been a ghastly week, and now the relief is so intense, that I don't know what to do!

She is still of course terribly weak, but everything is going well, and I'm so pleased. It was nice of you to take so much interest.

What is London like at this time of year? Do you go to dozens of fast little parties, or just do nothing?

The heat sounds too depressing – it is cold, rainy, windy, foggy, misty, & everything that is beastly here – but <u>I</u> don't care! I'm so happy at the moment that nothing matters.

I'm not really in a fit state to write a letter – it can only be pure drivel, so I hope you won't mind. The grim and doleful Gomm is standing by me waiting for the letters. His baleful eye is fixed furiously on me, and I am beginning to feel quite nervous. The post ought to be going he says, so I must finish.

Mother will get well now I'm sure, & many thanks for your letter.

Yours

Elizabeth Lyon

Don't lead too fast a life in London, & above all don't have anything to do with 'FASTY'* – she's dangerous.†

~

16 December 1921 to the Duke of York

Glamis Castle

Dear Prince Bertie

I was just starting to write to you for your birthday, when I read in the Morning Post that it was on Wednesday. I am so annoyed, as I thought it was tomorrow, and now it is over, and I shall have to wish

---

* Nickname for Doris Gordon-Lennox.

† Prince Albert replied that he was glad of her mother's recovery and that he would keep her warning about 'Fasty' 'in mind!!!!'. (Glamis Archives (Box 270))

you many happy returns of the day before yesterday. It was very stupid of me, as I remembered your birthday several days ago, & had it firmly fixed in my mind that it was Dec: 17th! Anyway, I send you lots of good wishes, and a very happy and successful 26th year. This is an impossible place to buy presents in, otherwise I should have bought a large and magnificent offering. The only thing one <u>can</u> buy are bull's eyes – very sticky, and they won't travel!

All best wishes,
Yours sincerely
Elizabeth

~

Friday undated [December 1921] to the Duke of York

Glamis Castle

Dear Prince Bertie

Just a line to wish you a happy Xmas, and a wonderful New Year, full of everything delicious & joyful. I am not quite sure where you are, but will send this to York Cottage.* Please forgive pencil, but I am writing in bed with a chill or flu or something.

Your delightful present has <u>just</u> arrived as I write!

I simply cannot thank you enough, it is the most darling little clock, and I simply love it. Thank you a million times – you should not give me such a lovely present. It really is too pretty for words, and besides being pretty is useful too. I am <u>enchanted</u> with it. Also that is an excellent photograph of you – I wish I had got something to send you too.

All good wishes, & good luck
Yours v sincerely
Elizabeth

~

---

* The house at Sandringham in which the King and Queen lived while King Edward VII's widow Queen Alexandra was still alive and living in Sandringham House itself.

Wednesday undated [8 March 1922] to the Duke of York

17 Bruton Street
W.1

Dear Prince Bertie

I am so terribly sorry about what happened yesterday, & feel it is all my fault, as I ought to have known. You are one of my best & most faithful friends, & have always been so nice to me – that it makes it doubly worse. I am too miserable about it, & blame myself more than I can say. If you ever feel you want a talk about things in general – I hope you will come & see me, as I understand you know.

I do wish this hadn't happened.

Yours Elizabeth

~

The Duke of York had proposed to her for the second time. In his reply on the same day he asked her not to be miserable – 'I was entirely in the wrong to bring up the question in the way I did without giving you any warning as to my intentions . . . I am so so sorry.'*

~

Sunday undated [12 March 1922] to the Duke of York

17 Bruton Street

Dear Prince Bertie

Thank you so very much for your very nice letter – it relieved my mind tremendously in a way, and I do hope you are not worrying about it all any more.

I must return to Glamis tomorrow, and am hoping very much to get my mother south before so very long, so we shall not meet for several weeks I expect. Please do try & forget about this, as I hate to think that you worry over it – things are hard for you anyway, and I can't bear to think they are any harder through me.

I couldn't manage to go to Brixworth, as I was originally going tonight. I hope you had a good hunt. Au revoir – till I don't know when.

Yours Elizabeth

~

---

* RA QEQM/PRIV/RF.

On 16 March, the Duke of York wrote a 'very difficult' letter. 'I feel I must tell you that I have always cared for you and had the hope that you would one day care for me.'*

~

Saturday 18 March 1922 to the Duke of York

Glamis Castle

Dear Prince Bertie

Thank you so much for your letter. You write the nicest letters of anyone I know, and the one I got this morning was just as charming. Yes, I think it has been difficult for both of us, but especially for you, and thank you so much for being so nice about it. I do hope we can go on being friends, as it would be too sad if a happening like this should come between our friendship, and I don't see why it should, do you?

I shall always be glad to see you if you ever feel like dropping in to tea, & having a talk. As I <u>do</u> understand you know, and when people are as good friends as you and I are – there is always a lot to talk about. I wish I could put into words what I feel about it all, & I think it is wonderful of you to have gone on caring – oh <u>why</u> didn't I guess. How silly I've been, and, as you say in your letter, of course I shall look on you as more than an ordinary friend.

I found my mother much better, and I do hope to come south at the beginning of May. I had already told her before you wrote, but nobody else in the world, & never shall.

What are you going to do now? Shall you be in London – I wish I wasn't up here – it is <u>so</u> dull.

Thank you so very much for your letter.

Yours ever

Elizabeth

~

On 26 March Prince Albert replied, 'Thank you so much for your charming letter which has cheered me up a great deal. You wrote too nicely to me, & I do feel now that you are not angry with me for what happened.'† In early May Queen Mary wrote to Lady Strathmore

---

* RA QEQM/PRIV/RF.

† RA QEQM/PRIV/RF.

saying that she and the King were 'much disappointed that the little "romance" has come to an end as we should so much have liked the connection with your family'.*

~

3 October 1922 to the Duke of York

Glamis Castle

Dear Prince Bertie

Thank you ten million times for sending me all those gramophone records, which arrived in record time (oh! a joke, accident I promise). I can't tell you how much I have enjoyed playing them. When one is in the country far away from everything, it is too delicious getting new records. Thank you so much, it was very angelic of you to take the trouble to get them for me. I enclose some notes of enormous value, but I don't know quite how much I really owe you. I hope two crackly sovereigns is enough? Thank you also so much for the excellent photograph, it is a very good one I think, and I am so pleased to have it.

I am listening to 'Stumbling' as I write, it is so good, I love it, and also 'Limehouse Blues' and 'I'm Simply Mad about Harry'.

We all went into Perth races on Saturday to see Joe Airlie win his race – he did it quite easily, as one man fell off & lost his horse, & the other never got over the first jump! There were only three of them. Diamond† is here now, I think she looks so ill poor thing. [. . .]

I do hope your trip to Rumania will go off well, and that it will all be a great success.‡

James looks very thin, doesn't he? I suppose it is pretty dirty work too – he looks covered in oil & grease.§

Many thanks again for your photograph, which I have stuck up in my room, & the best of luck on your trip abroad.

Yours sincerely,

Elizabeth

~

---

*   Queen Mary to Lady Strathmore, 6 May 1922, Glamis Archives (RA).

†   Diamond Hardinge suffered from leukaemia.

‡   The Duke travelled to Romania for the marriage of King Alexander of Yugoslavia to Princess Marie of Romania.

§   Early in 1922 James Stuart had left for the United States to work in the oil business.

Thursday [26] October 1922 to D'Arcy Osborne

17 Bruton Street

Dear Mr Osborne*

I am so sorry to hear that you had to have chloroform, & do hope that you are really feeling better. It must be too horrible being operated upon, even though it's a small one.

You seem to have spent rather a pleasant autumn – I spent the time entirely at Glamis, entertaining a series of guests, some were nice and some were NOT. Some were funny; one person who amused me was a gentleman called Mr James K. Hackett, the American actor. I don't know quite why he came. I [have] never seen a man drink so much – little drops all day long, that's the road to ruin – ah well. I am coming to London the week after next I think, so perhaps you will come and have a small drink (to help you on the downward path) on your way home from work. I am here now as a matter of fact, but only for a day or so, & I've got to go to a ball at Wilton, which rather terrifies me, as I hear the party numbers 48. Isn't it AWFUL?

I feel so sorry for some people we know, don't you? Perhaps you don't know who I mean, but I feel sorry for the poor man. How <u>can</u> you know who I mean?!!

Yours sincerely,
Elizabeth Lyon

~

Friday undated [1922] to D'Arcy Osborne

Glamis Castle

Dear Mr Osborne

I must tell you that I have come across a most mysterious stone, which must be full of magic power I think. It is <u>PINK</u>, with one white circle and nearly round. The appearance is arresting, being a very

---

* Francis Godolphin D'Arcy Osborne (1884–1964), great-great-grandson of fifth Duke of Leeds and a cousin of the eleventh Duke. He was thus also a cousin of the eleventh Duke's sister Dorothy, wife of Elizabeth's brother Patrick, Lord Glamis. Elizabeth met him in 1919 or 1920 and they became lifelong friends, exchanging both whimsical and serious letters. His Foreign Office career took him to Washington DC, and from 1936 to 1947 he was Minister Plenipotentiary to the Holy See. In 1963 he became the twelfth and last Duke of Leeds.

pure pink, & most fairy like. I found it in a pinewood – Scotch firs
you know are full of sorcery, usually of a rather sad and sinister kind,
and I could not resist telling you about it. I don't think anyone else
<u>believes</u> in Magic Stones, do you?

I hope you are very well, & not too overworked. The East must
have been keeping you busy I expect.

Yours sincerely, Elizabeth Lyon.

~

Friday undated [1922] to D'Arcy Osborne

17 Bruton Street

Dear Mr Osborne,

This is just to tell you that I have to go away on Monday, so
perhaps you had better not come to visit us on Tuesday. I did not go
away today on a visit, as I have a slightly sore throat. I do believe I
<u>need</u> that MAGIC STONE. Life has not been quite so smooth since
I gave it to you, and if you have not felt any very violent benefit
from it so far, perhaps you would very kindly return it. There is <u>no</u>
hurry, but I have a FEELING (<u>you</u> know) that I must take it north
with me.

I hope you have enjoyed Thursday and Friday. I remember you
told me about the little boy.

Yours sincerely,

Elizabeth Lyon.

PS If you are not busy this weekend, do come here some time –
or perhaps you are going away? I think I am staying with my mother.
I am not going North for a week so no hurry about the Stone.

~

4 January 1923 to the Duke of York

17 Bruton Street

Dear Prince Bertie

I have just come back from seeing Lady Airlie and talked it all
over with her. She is most discreet, and I don't think she will say a
word. [. . .]

It is so angelic of you to allow me plenty of time to think it over
– I really do need it, as it takes so long to ponder these things, & this

is so <u>very</u> important for us both. If in the end I come to the
conclusion that it will be alright, well & good, but Prince Bertie, <u>if</u> I
feel that I can't (& I will not marry you unless I am quite certain, for
your own sake) then I shall go away and try not to see you again.
I feel there are only those two alternatives – either it will all come
right, which I hope it will, or the other. I do hope you understand my
feelings – I am more than grateful to you for not hurrying me, and I
am determined not to spoil your life by just drifting on like this. You
are so thoughtful for me always – oh I do want to do what is right for
you. I have thought of nothing else all today – last night seems like a
dream. Was it?

It seems so now.

Perhaps you had better not say anything just yet to <u>anybody</u> –
what do you think? Do as you think best.

I never thanked you last night for your delightful party. I really
enjoyed it very much, & many thanks.

I have just been persuaded to go down to the Lewes Hunt Ball
tomorrow night, & shall return here on Saturday. Then I shall go
down to St Paul's Walden the same day. I really am terribly sorry
about Pitsford, I would have so loved it, but somehow I feel I was
right not to come with you today.

Au revoir till next Thursday,

Yours Elizabeth

~

Mabell Airlie acted as a confidante for Prince Albert and Elizabeth and
a go-between for Queen Mary with the Strathmores. On 3 January 1923
the Prince and Elizabeth danced together at Claridge's and it seems he
again declared his wish to marry her. Many years later Eric Anderson
asked her, 'When it came to the serious proposal for you, did you take advice
from anybody or did you know at once?' She replied, 'It went on for a year or
two. You know you are not sure about anything and then one of my brothers
said to me, "Look here. You know you must either say yes or no. It's not
fair." I think he was right. Because one is rather inclined to dither along if
somebody's fond of you, you know. I suppose when one is young and busy
and things. No, he was quite right.'

~

Diary: Thursday 4 January 1923

Woke at 9.15. Letters from Doris, Mary Thynne & Ruby Smith. Talked to P.B. on the telephone. Said I could not go to Pitsford. Dressed by 12.15. Rushed off to try on my blue tweed. Walked home. George Gage came to lunch. [. . .] Ava* came, & we went to tea with the MacRaes. Very amusing. David & Stephen Tennant[†] there. Ava & I took taxi to Victoria. I went to see Lady Airlie – talked a long time & explained everything. She was so nice. I ma tsom dexelprep. Home 7. Wrote some letters. George bullied me into saying that I'll go down tomorrow for Ball. Dinner 8.30. Bed 11.

~

Elizabeth used mirror writing in her diaries when she wanted to conceal her thoughts.

~

Diary: Friday 5 January 1923

Woke at 9. Up by 12. Feel rather tired. Ma gnikniht oot hcum. I hsiw I wenk. Mother lunched with Nina. Catherine & I took the 3.20 to Lewes. George [Gage] met us there, & Imogen & Ivo Grenfell came by the same train. The Westmacotts & Chips[‡] came a little later, bringing evening papers saying that I was engaged to the Prince of Wales – not mentioning my name, but quite obvious enough. <u>Too</u> stupid & unfounded. Two Miss Gages & one fiancé. Dinner 8.15. Sat between George & Ivo. We went to the Lewes Hunt Ball. Great fun. Danced with some very nice old friends – John Bevan, Tom Bevan, Ian Melville, Mr Wethered, besides our party. Danced till nearly 4! Home 4.30. Ate biscuits & sherry. Bed 5.

~

Diary: Saturday 6 January 1923

Woke at 9.30. Breakfast 10.15. I took the 11.17 to London. [. . .] James & the Daimler to meet me. Home 1. Mother not feeling very well.

---

*   Ava Bodley (1896–1974), married 1941 Sir John Anderson, later first Viscount Waverley.

†   Hon. David and Hon. Stephen Tennant, third and fourth sons of first Baron Glenconner.

‡   Henry 'Chips' Channon (1897–1958), Conservative politician and diarist.

Letter from B. At 3 Mother, Father & I motored down to St P. W. Home 4.15. [. . .]

~

Diary: Sunday 7 January 1923

Woke at 9.30. Breakfast in bed. Up 11.30. Dr Thomas came to see Jock who has a bad cold. Read prayers with Father & Mother. Did not go out, horrid day. Read & knitted & talked. Dinner 8.30. Played the Grammy. Bed 11.

~

Monday undated [8 January 1923] to the Duke of York

St Paul's Walden Bury

Dear Prince Bertie

I am so sorry to have been such ages sending you back your handkerchief, which was most useful. Thank you so much for lending it to me.

Thank you also so very much for your angelic letter which I got on Saturday – it was such a nice one. Do you know, last Wednesday evening seems just like a dream to me now. I think the great thing is to be <u>with</u> the person, or it all seems too unreal – do you feel that at all?

I get back from Longleat* on Thursday, are you coming to tea on that day? I shall be in Bruton Street anyway, so if you are in London do look in. I do hope the Pytchley Ball was fun, and also Emma [Thynne]'s ball at Castle Ashby – did you enjoy them?

Did you see any of the papers on Friday? Some of them said I was engaged to the Prince of Wales – one or two of them mentioning my name and a few my photograph. It's too extraordinary, why can't they leave one alone? And in this case, it was so utterly absurd. I'm so sleepy, I must go to bed.

Thank you again <u>so</u> much for your letter,

God Bless you,

Yours Elizabeth

~

---

* Elizabeth was going to Longleat to the ball of Lady Mary Thynne, daughter of the Marquess of Bath, married 1927 third Baron Nunburnholme; Lady of the Bedchamber 1937–47; married 2nd 1947 Sir Ulick Alexander. Her sister Emma was married to the Marquess of Northampton and lived at Castle Ashby.

Diary: Monday 8 January 1923

Woke at 9. Breakfast 10.15. [. . .] Sheaf of cuttings about my
rumoured engagement to the Prince of Wales. Too silly. [. . .]

~

Diary: Thursday 11 January 1923

Doris came to lunch with me [in London]. [. . .] Talked till 3.30. [. . .]
Prince Bertie came to tea – we talked till 7.30. I am yrev deirrow oot.
[. . .]

~

Diary: Friday 12 January 1923

Woke at 9. Felt <u>very</u> tired. Up by 11. Doris came round & talked till
12.30. [. . .] I sat before the fire in a stupor till 1.30. Dashed off & was
photographed for Vogue. Home again – telephoned for father to
Prince Bertie – he was out, so left a message to bring guns. [. . .]
Prince Bertie called for me at 6 & we motored down to St Paul's
Walden. Arrived 7.30. Dinner 8.30. At 11 Fenella & I went to a dance
given by the Martin Smiths. Danced with John Bevan, Mr Fane, Mr
Gibbs, Christopher Barclay etc. Good supper. Home 1.30.

~

Diary: Saturday 13 January 1923

Woke at 9.30. Breakie 10.30. Talked to Prince Bertie, & went for
tiring walk before lunch. Mr Beck to lunch. I felt a bit tired. Went &
sawed wood with father in Michael's Hope. Prince Bertie sawed <u>hard</u>!
Talked after tea for hours – dediced ot tiaw a elttil – epoh I ma not
gnivaheb yl[d]ab. Dinner 8.30. Fenella had gone to London. Talked till
¼ to 12. Bed 12.30.

~

Diary: Sunday 14 January 1923

Woke at 9. Breakie 10.30. Sat & talked till 12.30, & then went for a
walk in the enchanted wood. Long walk after lunch & long talks after
tea & dinner.

~

Late on the evening of Sunday 14 January 1923 Elizabeth accepted Prince Albert. Her mother described it to her daughter May thus: 'He came down to St. P.W. suddenly on <u>Friday</u>, & proposed continuously until Sunday night, when she said Yes at 11.30!! My head is completely bewildered, as all those days E was hesitating and miserable, but now she is absolutely happy – and he is <u>radiant</u>.'*

In similar vein, on 17 January Lady Strathmore wrote to her daughter-in-law Lady Christian, widow of Fergus, who was now remarried to Captain William Martin:

'He has wanted to marry Elizth for nearly 3 years, & she had refused him quite steadfastly, but lately I noticed that she liked dancing & talking to him more than anyone else – so when he came suddenly to St Paul's Walden last week I felt pretty certain she wd say yes.

'She is <u>very</u> happy & he is radiant – & we are (at last) quite happy about it – I like him immensely.

'I don't know what I shall do, Christian, when she goes – I cannot tell you what she has been to me – never once a cross word in her whole life & such a sympathetic & loving help to me.'†

The following day the Prince set off to Sandringham to tell his parents. King George V recorded in his diary that 'we gladly gave our consent'. Queen Mary wrote, 'We are delighted and he looks beaming.'‡ The King and Queen invited Elizabeth and her parents to stay with them at Sandringham the following weekend.

~

Diary: Monday 15 January 1923

Woke at 8. Slept rather badly. Breakie 9. At ¼ to 10 P.B. motored me up to London. Dropped me at Bruton Street. Then I went to the dentist. Called on Fenella – told her news, & had a cocktail. Home 1. B. called for me & we lunched at Chesterfield House with Princess Mary & Lord Lascelles. The Prince of Wales came round to see me there. B. went off to Sandringham, & the P. of W dropped me home. Found mother. Wrote <u>lots</u> of letters. Went to see Nina & told her.

---

* RA QEQM/OUT/ELPHINSTONE.

† Joicey-Cecil Papers.

‡ RA GV/PRIV/GVD/1923: 15 January; RA QM/PRIV/QMD/1923: 15 January.

Also Lady Airlie. Jock came in. Wrote lots more letters. The
telephone rang the whole evening – hundreds of reporters
clamouring! Last day of peace I suppose! Bed 11.

~

16 January 1923 to Arthur Penn

17 Bruton Street

My dear Arthur,

Arthur, I must tell you, I am going to marry Prince Bertie – I <u>do</u>
hope you like him – I feel terrified now I've done it – in fact nobody
is more surprised than me. Arthur, you have been one of my best
friends for years – <u>please please</u> don't cast me off as one now, will
you?

I <u>do</u> hope you are pleased about this – I felt I must tell you
Yours, Elizabeth

~

Diary: Tuesday 16 January 1923

Woke at 8.30. The papers announce my engagement this morning.
Great headlines & lots of rot! Up by 11. Telegrams poured in all
day, letters & reporters tumbling over each other. Saw Aunt
Maudie.* Bertie came to lunch. There were hundreds of
photographers & a crowd when we came out. Awful! Went to
Buckingham Palace & chose the ring. The Prince of Wales came in
for some time, & sent for some rings from Boucheron! Had tea with
Bertie – then he brought me home. More telegrams, & saw two
Scotch reporters & [Victor] Gordon-Lennox. Quite exhausted! Bertie
dined – Father came up. Talked till 12 – & were photographed – not
a success! Bed 1.

~

---

* Lady Maud Agnes Bowes Lyon, third daughter of thirteenth Earl of Strathmore, sister of
fourteenth Earl. She died unmarried on 28 February 1941.

17 January 1923 to King George V

17 Bruton Street

Sir,

Thank you so much for your very kind letter, which Bertie gave me. I am so grateful to Your Majesty for welcoming me so kindly as a future member of your family and I only hope that I shall be able to help Bertie in all his many duties, and in many other ways also.

I shall look forward so much to coming to Sandringham on Saturday, and with many more thanks for your kindness,

I remain, Your Majesty's humble and obedient servant,

Elizabeth Lyon

~

17 January 1923 to Queen Mary

17 Bruton Street

Madam,

I must thank you so much for your most kind letter, welcoming me as your future daughter in law. I do hope I shall make Bertie very happy, as he so deserves to be, and my greatest wish is to be a <u>real</u> daughter to your Majesty.

I shall look forward intensely to my visit to Sandringham on Saturday, and I do hope you will think I shall make Bertie a good wife, we are both so happy, and it is all wonderful.

I remain, Your Majesty's humble & obedient servant,

Elizabeth Lyon

~

Wednesday 17 January 1923 to D'Arcy Osborne

17 Bruton Street

Dear Mr Osborne,

Thank you so <u>very</u> much for your charming letter. It was so nice of you to write. You must come round and ''ave one' soon. You have no idea how tiring it is being engaged! I am quite gaga already, & can only clutch my magic stone and hope for the best. Good 'ealth, Yours sincerely,

Elizabeth Lyon

~

Diary: Wednesday 17 January 1923

Woke 8.30. Great pile of letters, & papers still very full of it! Betty Cator* came to see me. So nice. Simply inundated by awful reporters & photographers. Too appalling. Bertie went off hunting today. Telegrams from Paul in Serbia, Mr Brown in Australia, Doubledays in America etc. Very busy writing. Louis Greig† brought a secretary round to help me. Doris came at 3.30. We crept out for a walk in the fog! Talked hard – she is so pleased. She left 5. Diamond came in, also Christopher [Glenconner] for a few minutes. Lots more letters & telegrams. Bertie came to dinner. Rosie arrived up for tea. We talked till 12! Bed 12.30.

~

19 January 1923 to Arthur Penn

17 Bruton Street

Dear dear Arthur,

You wrote me such an angelic letter – <u>far</u> the nicest I've had yet. Thank you <u>so</u> so much, I really loved it.

I <u>am</u> so glad you are pleased, Arthur. It was all so surprising and I am very pleased with being engaged! Except for this awful publicity. How beastly the papers are – nothing but lies! am completely exhausted, but I don't think this can last much longer. <u>Do</u> come in one evening soon.

Yours, Elizabeth

~

---

* Elizabeth Cator (1899–1959), Elizabeth's future sister-in-law. She married Michael Bowes Lyon on 2 February 1928. She was one of Elizabeth's best friends and was a bridesmaid at her wedding to Prince Albert.

† Group Captain Sir Louis Greig KBE CVO (1880–1953), whom Prince Albert met in 1909 at the Royal Naval College, Osborne, where Greig was a naval surgeon. They served in HMS *Malaya* together. Greig became a mentor and medical adviser to the Prince and was appointed his equerry in 1918. In 1919 both men joined the RAF. On 8 July 1920, the day when the Prince met Elizabeth Bowes Lyon at the RAF ball at the Ritz, he and Greig had won the RAF doubles tennis championship. When the Prince was made Duke of York in June 1920 Greig was appointed comptroller of his household, a post he held until 1924. Until his marriage the Prince was dependent upon him and Greig never let him down.

Diary: Friday 19 January 1923

Woke at 10! <u>Lots</u> of letters. Up by 11.30. Miss Chard [temporary secretary] came, & we got through dozens. Bertie to lunch. Afterwards, he & I motored down to Richmond,* where we went for a walk & looked at the garden of White Lodge. Then we called on Mrs Greig & had tea with her. Home again at six. More letters! Wrote several. Bertie gave me my engagement ring today, it is lovely. He came to dinner & we talked till nearly 12! Bed 12.30.

~

21 January 1923 to Beryl Poignand

York Cottage
Sandringham

My dearest M.

I did not have time to let you know I was engaged, before it was announced in the paper. I longed to tell you, but did not know where you were. It was all such a hurry – I got engaged on Sunday – Bertie dashed off here on Monday, & it came out Monday night. So I could not even let the family know.

I've had a ghastly time this week with reporters & photographers curse them, but hope they will very soon get tired of us.

We came down here yesterday, & it has been a bit of an ordeal meeting all the relations. They have all been so <u>very</u> kind & charming, but I'm feeling <u>utterly</u> exhausted. We go back to London tomorrow, I dread the pile of letters.

Oh, my dearest M – I've heard from Ernest [Pearce] & Norman Jepson† already – such <u>delicious</u> letters. I was so pleased.

I am so happy, & most surprised, as I never thought I'd marry him!!! You must come back in time for the wedding tho' that won't be just yet.

---

* White Lodge, Richmond Park, built by George II in 1727–9 'as a place of refreshment after the fatigues of the chace', was Queen Mary's family home before her marriage; she was eager for her son and daughter-in-law to live there too. They moved in but soon found it too far from central London. White Lodge subsequently became the Royal Ballet School and remains the site of its Lower School.

† Lance-Corporal Norman Jepson had written a sixteen-verse 'Ode to Glamis' in Elizabeth's autograph book, celebrating her as 'a maiden charming and rare'.

I am so tired already – I think I shall probably die <u>long</u> before I get married! How delighted the papers would be – after the ROMANCE the TRAGEDY! What ho.

Best love, I have got at least 500 letters to write.

Your very very loving

Elizabeth

~

25 January 1923 to Beryl Poignand

17 Bruton Street

My dearest M,

A thousand thanks for your angelic letter. I am most awfully happy my dear M – it is all wonderful except this publicity still – it's <u>ghastly</u>!!

Look here, <u>do</u> come back soon & take over control of my presents, will you?

I should be so grateful, & will make somebody or other (not me!) pay you an IMMENSE salary. Do, if you are coming home soon. If you don't, I shall have to get a stranger. I would love to see your ugly face about. Your loving E.

PS I've had to have a secretary lent to me! I'm completely exhausted already.

~

Undated [25 January 1923] to the Duke of York

17 Bruton Street

My dear Darling

I am just writing you a very little letter, which I hope you will get on Friday or Saturday. There won't be anything in it at all, except to say that I shall be thinking about you when you get this, & hoping that everything will go wonderfully well. I am quite sure it will. Also, I might add that I <u>do</u> love you Bertie, & feel certain that I shall <u>more</u> & <u>more</u>. I shall miss you terribly. You are such an Angel to me. Goodbye till Sunday – may it come quickly

from your always and forever loving E

~

4 February 1923 to Beryl Poignand

York Cottage

My dearest M

Of course you must not <u>dream</u> of coming home just to do presents! I thought you said you were coming almost at once in your last letter – that's why I wrote! I can <u>easily</u> do them, and May loves doing them too – so that's alright. Also nobody may send me anything. I was regretting very much that I haven't cultivated some very RICH people! All my friends are poor. We've had a delicious and restful week down here, & return to hard work in London tomorrow.

It is a bit of a strain staying with one's future in laws, whoever they are. Mine have all been too angelic to me I must say. Let me know when you are coming home.

Oh, Ernest wrote a <u>wonderful</u> letter and sent messages to you.

You must meet my fiancé soon. I hope you'll like him. He is a darling really – & very shy!

Au revoir, & <u>please</u> don't come home. I only suggested it because I thought you were anyway coming.

Your loving
Elizabeth

~

Diary: Tuesday 13 February 1923

Woke at 9.30. Up by 11.30. Mother & I went off to have my throat done.* Called at Upper Brook St & asked after Sidney. Operation went off well. Home 1. Bertie came at 3. Then the Queen & her brother Cambridge [Adolphus, Marquess of Cambridge] came. They looked at the presents, & the Queen stayed till 4.30. Lady Mary Trefusis called for her. Colonel & Mrs Erskine to tea. Bertie went to the House of Lords, & then came back. At 8.15 he, the Prince of Wales, & Prince George called for me, & we four dined at Claridge's. Very gay dinner. Then we went to 9 o'clock revue – very amusing. Giles & Anne†

---

* Elizabeth suffered from frequent throat and bronchial problems.

† Captain (later Lieutenant Colonel Sir) Giles Sebright (1896–1954), equerry to the Duke of York 1922–3 (in succession to James Stuart). Succeeded his uncle as thirteenth Baronet in 1933. Anne Cameron was his girlfriend at this time.

joined us there – also Bruce [Ogilvy]. We talked in the Manager's
room! The others went to a ball (charity) & we four supped & danced
at the Berkeley. Great fun. Bed 1.30.

~

Undated [February 1923] to the Duke of York

17 Bruton Street

Bertie darling, I am so terribly disappointed at not being able to
come with you today. I think I must have got a chill of sorts, as I
feel like death with a terrific headache. I did so want to come with
you today, it would have been heavenly – a day in the country
with you. I tried to get up, but I would have been a miserable
companion for you darling I know, so I shall probably stay in bed,
& I may feel alright tonight. I do hope you will have a delicious day,
don't worry about me. I do sometimes catch chills like this worse
luck, & I shall think of you in the country. I am so disappointed
Bertie you angel,

Your very and always loving E

~

Tuesday undated [13 March 1923] to the Duke of York

Glamis Castle

My Darling Bertie

I wish you were here – it is really too marvellous, and I know it
would do you good too. When I arrived this morning the sun was
just rising over the Sidlaw hills, and made the snow on the Grampians
look pink & heavenly. It was wonderful to be able to see about
twenty miles instead of down one London street! It would be more
delicious if you were here too. I hate to think of you in horrible
London all by yourself.

My cold is worse today, but I expect it will very soon go here – I
only hope you won't catch it.

I love Glamis.

Bertie, while I remember it, will it be approved do you think if I
ask Betty Cator to be my bridesmaid? She is such a darling, I would
like to have her.

Don't worry about White Lodge & furniture. I am quite certain
we shall make it enchanting – you & I; so please don't fuss yourself
little darling. You are such an angel to me always, and I hate to think
of you worrying about anything. 'Keep calm and don't be bullied –
rest if you can' is my advice!!

Forgive this scrawl, I want to catch the early post – au revoir till I
write again, & be good darling,

Your always loving Elizabeth.

PS I miss you very much. Do you miss me?

~

Wednesday undated [14 March 1923] to the Duke of York

Glamis Castle

Bertie darling

I hope you are well & happy – I am thank you – I haven't heard
from you yet, but the evening post comes late. I am writing this to
catch the night mail, & David Arthur the odd man (<u>very</u> odd) is
waiting to what he calls 'pop up' on his bicycle & post it!

Another marvellous day – blue sky & sun & a little cold.

I am just going off to see if there are any duck on the pond, &
Peter will chaperone me – it is light so late now, which is heavenly.
[. . .]

My guides have got a present for me, & are giving it tomorrow –
isn't it delicious of them.

I was photographed when out today by a low friend of Daddee's.
Most annoying, otherwise everybody has left me in peace which is
very tactful.

All the people here hope you'll be good to me! I hope so too!

Good bye darling – <u>why</u> aren't you here.

Till Saturday,

Your very loving

E

~

Diary: Monday 19 March 1923

Woke at 9. Breakie 10. [. . .] Bertie came round, & we went & looked
at furniture at Harris & also went to Carrington. [. . .] Then mother

& I went to Handley Seymour* & looked at hundreds of lovely
clothes. Chose my wedding dress.

~

Saturday undated [31 March 1923] to the Duke of York

St Paul's Walden Bury

Darlingest Bertie

   I was enchanted to get your delicious letter this morning – thank
you so much. A.F.A.G, those <u>are</u> your initials aren't they? I wonder
what you do all day? I read in the paper today that you walked to
Frogmore† & had tea. Having never seen Frogmore, I imagine it as a
large white Tomb full of frogs! I can't think why, but that is the
impression it gives me – isn't it silly?

   David and I walked down to church in the little Tin Chapel, but
no bird got in this time to amuse us. We stayed an hour and a
quarter, & by then Mr Whitehouse had only just finished the service
on the First Word, and we became rather depressed & left! At that
rate the service would last 6 hours.

   Father arrived today bringing darling Peter & Barson – it is
delicious having them back again.

   Bertie, do you know you have got a most changeable face? It is
too odd, sometimes you look a completely different person, always
nice though, but I must not flatter you because then your head will
swell, & you will have to buy new hats. That would be very sad,
wouldn't it? [. . .]

   I <u>wish</u> you were here. Why haven't you got a small aeroplane,
then you could fly over here for an hour or two, get thoroughly hurt
as usual, & return to Windsor, a scratched and bruised but let us
hope a happy wreck.

   What rot this is, & I have got about forty letters to write, curse it.

---

*   Madame Handley Seymour, London couturier and Elizabeth's choice to make both her
wedding dress and her Coronation robes.

†   Frogmore House in Windsor Home Park, purchased by Queen Charlotte in 1792 and later
home to various members of the Royal Family. The Duke and Duchess were to spend part of
their honeymoon there. The mausoleum which Queen Victoria built for Prince Albert and
herself is in the grounds.

Well, s'long Bertie, don't forget your Honey Lamb will you? Darling
B, you are an Angel. Your as ever loving E
    PS For Gawd's sake don't leave my letters lying about

~

Diary: Thursday 5 April 1923

[At Windsor] Woke at 8. Had breakie in bed. Up by 10. Bertie went
out riding at 11.30. I talked to the Prince of Wales for a bit. After
lunch the King showed me his room & played some gramophone
records. Then the Queen took me & Bertie all round the house –
marvellous things. At 4 B & I went out to tea with the King & Queen
to Sir Harry Legge. Very nice man. Home 6.30. Talked. The P. of W
& Prince George left this morning. Dinner 8.30. Lord A. Innes-Ker &
Lord —— to dine. Much chaff. Bed 12.

~

12 April 1923 to D'Arcy Osborne

17 Bruton Street

Dear Mr Osborne,
    Thank you so very <u>very</u> much for the two books. I really can't tell
you how much I love them, and I wish I could thank you sufficiently.
It is <u>delicious</u> of you and I could see at once that they were a
thought-out present, which gives me infinitely more pleasure than
eight ropes of pearls from a new oil Lord. They are divinely bound
and I am going to take them up with me to read in bed now, which I
hope you won't mind. Thank you a *thousand* times, it really is a
marvellous present, and just what I like. I haven't found any magic
stones lately – have you?
    It is nearly midnight and the only time I get for writing. There are
fifty people I must write to, but I <u>had</u> to thank you first, because I
love your present. I wish you would come in one evening if you can,
& drink a cocktail & exchange a few ideas on MAGIC and POLITICS
and SPIRITUALISM and RELIGION, and GEORGE ROBEY and
AMERICANS and all the terribly interesting things in this world. If
you will ring me up, I am always here after tea. Also I want to ask
you about a story you told me once, in the hot sun at Bicton – I

remember it because it sent a cold shiver from my head way down to my heels.

I hope you are well, and that thrilling things happen to you. And thank you.

Yours sincerely,
Elizabeth Lyon

~

Diary: Tuesday 24 April 1923

[. . .] Terribly busy. Bertie to lunch – he & I went to the Palace, & attended a servants' party. Had tea with the Queen & King. [. . .] Bertie & I dined with James at Claridge's. He is engaged to Rachel!* The party was him, Bertie, Mike, David, Arthur, Francis & Freddy, me, Rachel, Katie, Betty, Mary Thynne, Mary Cavendish & Hermione.† We dined [in] a private room – then went to Hippodrome then to the Berkeley & danced. I was in good form! Went home, & talked to Bertie. Then talked to Mike for ages. Bed 3.30.

~

Diary: Wednesday 25 April 1923

Woke at 10 feeling very ill! Miss Poignand came in. I talked on the telephone, & did a million things before lunch. Betty Cator came in. Bertie to lunch – he & I went off at 3.30 to B.P. Large crowd as usual! Mrs Lindsay Carnegie presented an address from Forfarshire – in B's room. Then we went downstairs, & attended an afternoon party. Shook hands with hundreds of people. Very tired. Had tea with the King & Queen & Duke of Connaught‡ & [the] Lascelles.§ Mother too. She & I got home 6. Very tired. Bruce came in – also Katie –

---

* James Stuart married Lady Rachel Cavendish (1902–77), daughter of ninth Duke of Devonshire, on 4 August 1923.

† Michael and David Bowes Lyon, Arthur Penn, Francis Doune, Freddy Dalrymple Hamilton, Rachel Cavendish, Katie Hamilton, Elizabeth Cator, Mary Cavendish (1903–94), daughter of Lord Richard Cavendish, married 1925 twenty-eighth Earl of Crawford and Lady Hermione Herbert (1900–95), daughter of fourth Earl of Powis, married 1924 Duca della Grazia.

‡ Prince Alfred, Duke of Connaught (1850–1942), third son of Queen Victoria.

§ Princess Mary and her husband Lord Lascelles.

Jock to dinner. Felt terribly moved when I said good-night to the darling boys [Mike and David] & mother. I adore them. Bed 11.

~

Diary: Thursday 26 April 1923

Woke at 8.30. Up by 10. Put on my wedding dress, aided by Suzanne & Catherine. It looked lovely. All the family went off early, also mother. Miss Chard came & talked to me. At 11.12 the carriage came, & father & I started off for the Abbey. Lots of people in B St., & crowds in the streets. Did not feel very nervous. Bertie smiled at me when I got up to him – & it all went off well. We had a long drive home to B.P. Crowds very kind. We were photographed, & also went out on the balcony. Then luncheon. Sat between Bertie & the King. After lunch talked & cut cake etc. Went to change about 3.40. Mother & Anne* came – then May & Rosie, Mike & David & father. Awful saying goodbye. B & I drove off at 4.15 & had a special to Bookham. Very tired & happy. Bed 12.

~

The Duke of York was married to Elizabeth Bowes Lyon on 26 April 1923 at Westminster Abbey. The ceremony was followed by a wedding breakfast at Buckingham Palace, after which the couple left for their honeymoon at Polesden Lacey, the Surrey home of Mrs Ronald Greville.

~

Friday undated [27 April 1923] to Lady Strathmore

Polesden Lacey
Dorking

My Darling Angel,

I do hope you weren't too terribly tired yesterday. I felt so worried about you, & after all these last three months you must be exhausted. I could not say anything to you about how utterly miserable I was at leaving you & Mike & David & father. I could not ever have said it to you – but you know I love you more than

---

* The new Duchess's five-year-old niece, daughter of Jock and Fenella Bowes Lyon.

anybody in the world, mother, and you do know it, don't you? Bertie adores you too, & he is being too marvellous to me, & so thoughtful. He really is a darling – I hope you all like him.

I stayed in bed all this morning to rest & read the papers, and am just going down to lunch in my old blue tweed! Poor Catherine is miserable because I won't wear anything new – I hate new things!

This is a delicious house, & the food is too marvellous, & it seems too funny not to be dashing about! I think the wedding went off alright, don't you? Do write, angel, from your very, very loving Elizabeth.

Do tell Mike & David that Billy Merson* sent us a telegram last night from the Hippodrome.

~

28 June 1923 to D'Arcy Osborne

White Lodge
Richmond Park

Dear Mr Osborne,

It was very nice of you to write, and I have quite given up whooping.† As to asking after my health, I am afraid I talked so hard, that you probably would not have been able to ask, even if you'd thought of it?

You must come down here one day if you have time. When it is hot in London (& people always look so nasty then, which I hate don't you?) it is quite cool & delicious here. So sometime you must throw the Eastern question firmly aside, turn your most magic stone three times from East to West, & start for Richmond.

As to what to call me – I really don't know! It might be anything – you might try 'All Hail, Duchess', that is an Alice in Wonderland sort of Duchess, or just 'Greetings' or 'What Ho, Duchess' or 'Say, Dutch' – in fact you can please yourself, as it will certainly please me. [. . .]

Yours very sincerely
Elizabeth

~

---

* Billy Merson (1879–1974), popular English music-hall actor and songwriter.

† The Duchess had developed whooping cough while on honeymoon.

19 September 1923 to Queen Mary

Invermark*
Edzell

My Darling Mama

I want to thank you so very very much for my delightful fortnight at Balmoral, and for having asked us there. It was the greatest fun, and I enjoyed every moment of it, and we were both very sad at leaving on Friday. Everybody was so kind and nice to me, and I was so happy with you.

After two lovely days on Saturday & Sunday, it is pouring with rain today! However, they have bravely gone out stalking, but I am afraid it does not look very hopeful. Even though I am the wife, daughter and sister of 'guns', I fail to see what pleasure there can be in walking about all day in an icy wind and driving rain!!

Thank you again so very much for my wonderful visit to Balmoral,
    With much love,
    I am, your very loving daughter-in-law
    Elizabeth

~

Undated [27 September 1923] to the Duke of York

Somewhere in England (on train from Darlington)

My Darling Darlington

I've just had luncheon and also my pencil has broken. So you probably won't be able to read this at all! I wish you were here, but I'm glad for you to be out on the 'mower' [moor] instead of in this stuffy beastly train. The waiter said 'May I have the pleasure of serving you' each time before he gave me any food, which made me long to laugh. I think we ought to train Seton [Steward at White Lodge] to say it too, don't you?

There was the usual crowd of slightly hysterical females at Darlington, who murmured 'Isn't she sweet', gazing fondly at Catherine. I think they thought Hay [the Yorks' detective] was you.

---

* The shooting lodge in Angus of the Dalhousie family.

The train is full of odd people. I hope you'll have a good journey to Glamis, little darling. I send you some kisses and a couple of hugs. I shall miss you horribly till Sunday

Yours forever and always E

~

This note was scribbled in blue pencil on the inside of the dust jacket of P. G. Wodehouse's novel *Psmith in the City*. Wodehouse was one of the Duchess's favourite authors throughout her life. Asked by Eric Anderson who had given her most pleasure as a writer, she replied, *'P.G. I suppose . . . I had older brothers who were at Eton, and of course at Oxford and I think P.G. was all the rage. I think I read them all . . . If you are feeling very tired or depressed, one page of P.G. and you feel better. You laugh and you're interested.'*

~

17 October 1923 to D'Arcy Osborne

White Lodge

Dear Mr Osborne

It is too delicious of you to send me two books for the journey to Belgrade.* It really *is* nice of you to think of it, and I am very grateful, as the prospect of three days in the train shocks me to a degree, & your books will make all the difference.

I am so glad you don't mind returning to London as much as you thought you would. Do you ever go to a musical comedy? I think there is nothing to beat them, & the worse, the better. I go occasionally to see the Astaires† dance in 'Stop Flirting'. Have you seen them – they are delicious, I think.

About Isabel [a young American friend of D'Arcy]. Is a bell

---

* On 18 October 1923 the Duke and Duchess set off by train to Belgrade for the christening of the son and heir of Alexander, King of the Serbs, Croats and Slovenes (the new Yugoslavia) and the wedding of their friend, and Alexander's cousin, Prince Paul of Yugoslavia (formerly of Serbia) to Princess Olga of Greece. The Duke of York was godfather (*koom*) and the Duchess godmother (*koomitsa*) to the baby.

† Fred Astaire (1899–1987), film and Broadway dancer, choreographer and singer – and one of the greatest stars of the early twentieth century. He had a successful dancing partnership with his sister Adele. Subsequently his most celebrated dance partner was Ginger Rogers.

1. Elizabeth Bowes Lyon with her mother, Lady Strathmore.

2. Elizabeth and David Bowes Lyon with their older brother, Jock.

3. Elizabeth, aged about five.

4. A letter written by Elizabeth aged six, with grown-up help.

5. Beryl Poignand in 1915.

6. A letter from Elizabeth to Beryl Poignand, her 'Dear Medusa'.

7. Jock, May (playing the piano) and Rose Bowes Lyon in the drawing room at Glamis.

Feb. 22. 1907

Darling Father
this is a most
lovely place and
there is an oran-
ge tree in the garden
and lots of flow-

ers I pick them
before breakfast.
I shall be with
you very soon
shall you be glad
to see me. your
darling Elizabeth

Thursday. Oct. 20th
1916.
CLAMIS CASTLE.
CLAMIS.
N.B.

My Dear Medusa

Thank you _so much_
for _all_ your charming letters!
I hope you are enjoying Richmond
Nothing doing up here. I go to
the Ward every evening now. They
are very nice. I wrote a "poem"
for dear Sergeant Little's book
yesterday. _All_ by myself. I did it
when I woke up in the morning.

8. Elizabeth with Prince Paul of Yugoslavia.

9. Elizabeth (third from left), with Doris Gordon-Lennox, Freddy Dalrymple Hamilton, Bruce Ogilvy, Geordie Haddington, Alix Cavendish and Diamond Hardinge.

10. Prince Albert in 1920.

11. Elizabeth in 1920.

12. At Bisham, Ascot week 1921. Back row, left to right: Jamie Balfour, James Stuart, the Duke of York, Lord Colum Stuart, Captain Coats, Charles Balfour. Middle row, left to right: Katherine McEwan, Elizabeth, Moyra Brodrick, Amy Coats, Mollie Cecil. Front row; left to right: Arthur Penn, Bay Smith, Doris Gordon-Lennox, Aurea Balfour.

13. Elizabeth with Princess Mary and Geordie Haddington.

14. Elizabeth at Glamis with her dogs, Peter and Biffin.

15. A house party, September 1921. Back row, left to right: Wisp Leveson-Gower, Michael Bowes Lyon, David Bowes Lyon, Lord Strathmore, James Stuart, Rose Leveson-Gower, Mrs Annand. Front row, left to right: Katie Hamilton, Doris Gordon-Lennox, the Duke of York, Elizabeth, Mida Scott.

16. The Duke and Duchess of York on the balcony
of Buckingham Palace after their wedding.

17. The bride and groom leaving for their honeymoon.

necessary on a bicycle. That's one point against her poor girl. Now let me see –

Against.	For.
1. Her name.	Sense of humour.
2. American.	
3. Eight millions.	
4. Indifferent features.	
5. No parents.	

Yes, I think you ought to marry her. The sense of humour balances everything. [. . .]

I must stop now, and turn over the clocks, wind up the piano, & generally prepare for Adventure in the Balkans. I feel it is going to be rather an ordeal, but amusing.

Thank you again so much for the books,

Yours sincerely,

Elizabeth

~

21[22] October [1923] to Lady Strathmore

Palais Royal
Belgrade

My Darling Mother,

Just a hurried line to tell you that we had a very good journey out here, & found a large party, all family. Everything is very funny here, just like a musical comedy! Everything is very unpunctual, & very pompous! Yesterday was a very long day, & tiring, today is Paul's wedding. I will tell you all about it later, as there is only a few minutes now. Alexander's wife is ill, so her mother, the Queen of Roumania* has taken the lead in everything, and enjoyed herself wildly! She is very nice though, & they all speak English always. The King of Roumania is too absurd, we get on so well, & he honestly is a pure Bateman.† Alexander gave me a lovely little watch & his order, which spoils all my clothes, as it's blue & white.

---

* Queen Marie (1875–1938), the former Princess Marie of Edinburgh, granddaughter of Queen Victoria and a flamboyant character. She married King Ferdinand of Romania (1865–1927).

† H. M. Bateman (1887–1970), prolific cartoonist and caricaturist, most famous in the 1920s and 1930s for his 'the man who . . .' series.

It has been <u>boiling</u>, <u>80</u> degrees today & shining sun.

I hope you will be coming to London soon darling, so au revoir, & please forgive this short scribble,

From your very loving

Elizabeth

~

26 October [1923] to Lady Strathmore

White Lodge

My Darling Mother

Thank you a <u>million</u> times for ringing up last night. We had an awful crossing, but luckily I didn't feel sick. Catherine was <u>VERY</u> sick!!

The Serbian visit was terribly funny. They all walk about all day in musical comedy uniforms. I will try & tell you a little about it.

We arrived at Zagreb at about 9 o'clock last Saturday, where we hitched our carriage onto Alexander's train which he had sent for us. It was once the Austrian Emperor's, & very rattly! There were several footmen dressed in beautiful liveries of pale blue, with trousers that went into spats, do you know the sort, and huge silver buttons. We travelled the whole day, through a completely flat plain, all cultivated, but no roads at all. We got to Belgrade at 7.30, where Alexander met us, and his sister, as his wife was ill. The band played God Save The King <u>very</u> quickly over & over again, & we got into tiny blue Victorias with white horses & rushed off to the Palace. The whole family were there, the King & Queen of Roumania, their eldest son & his wife, the other daughter who is Queen of Greece, Ileana, & all Paul's fiancée's family. They are all so nice, & very English.

The next day, the christening was at 11, & Bertie was simply terrified at having to carry the baby about! However, it went off very well, and the singing was too lovely. Afterwards, there was a tremendous luncheon party of about 300. At about 4, Bertie & I & Paul & Olga drove out & looked at Belgrade, & then went & had tea with the Roumanians on their yacht in the Danube. They nearly all lived there, as there is so little room in the Palace. There was a family dinner, & then a concert & reception after. I got so tired, that Bertie & I crept away.

The next day, was Paul's wedding. Olga looked lovely I thought,

& it went off very well, and Paul is <u>so</u> happy. He was enchanted at
having us there, & otherwise he had no real friends. A large
luncheon, & then I went off to see a hospital for children run by a
Scotch woman doctor. It is the <u>only one</u> in all Serbia, and does
marvellous work. Then I went down to the Danube, & joined Bertie
on the Glowworm which is a British monitor, & then we went off to
the Legation & met the British Colony. Very small, & all Scotch!
Then home, & I rested, whilst Bertie went down to see Paul off. After
dinner, we departed – I drove down to the station with Alexander,
and it was very funny, as we did not <u>really</u> go! You see the train went
very early the next morning, so we thought it would be less trouble
to sleep in our own 'wagon lits' carriage, & just get hitched on to the
train very early when we were asleep. So we went through all the
usual pomp, & a guard of honour, looking <u>exactly</u> like the male
chorus of a revue, & a band, & rows of ladies with bouquets, & kisses
all round, & then we steamed triumphantly out of the station, for
about 20 yards, where we stopped all night! It was so funny, because
it was all a sham, & they all knew it too!! You have no idea how odd
they are, & so nice!

I feel rather tired now, but am having a good rest. I got on very
well with them all, especially the King of Roumania, who is the silliest
& kindest old idiot – also Alexander, who is very shy. I <u>do</u> hope you
are coming south soon, you must be longing to see your polo ponies.

Au revoir, Angel, lots of love to Father, from your very loving
Elizabeth

~

Diary: Tuesday 8 January 1924

[. . .] At 7.30 drove up to St James's. Picked up David [the Prince of
Wales], & dined at Claridge's. [Prince] George came too. Then we
went to the Hippodrome & then on to the Winter Garden where we
went to see George Grossmith & Leslie Henson [in *The Beauty Prize*].
Then back to York House [the residence of the Prince of Wales], &
then to the Midnight Follies,* where we joined the Nortons & dance.
Home 3!

~

---

* Nightclub and cabaret at the Metropole Hotel.

Diary: Monday 14 January 1924

After dinner went through papers. Apparently na lufwa wor tuoba eht thgindim seillof. Bed 10.30.

~

14 January 1924 [misdated 1923] to King George V

The Old House
Guilsborough*

My dearest Papa
    Commander Greig tells me that you are angry with us for having been seen at the Midnight Follies. I am so sorry about this, as I hate to think of you being annoyed with us, or worried in any way.
    We went to have some supper before our drive back to Richmond, and it really is a most respectable place. I promise you we would not go anywhere that we ought not to, and this place is supposed to be quite all right for supper after the theatre. I thought I would just write you a short note to tell you about it, & hope you will not mind, as I know how terribly busy you are right now.
    It is very kind of you to ask us to luncheon tomorrow, and I only hope I shall not be under the influence of a drug!! As whilst you are opening Parliament, I shall be opening my jaw to the dentist, and he told me he was going to inject some 'dope' into my face, so I hope you will not mind if I am rather odd. The effect on one, is that of having received a stunning blow to the head!
    I do hope your cough is better, & that the little yellow Chinaman† is bringing the luck he is supposed to.
    I am, Your affectionate daughter in law,
    Elizabeth

~

Unlike his own children, the Duchess found it easy to communicate with the King. She later recalled, 'I was the first to marry into the family and I think the King rather enjoyed having somebody new and young. We got

---

*   Rented by the Duke and Duchess of York for winter weekends and to enable the Duke to hunt with the Pytchley and Whaddon Chase.

†   Probably the statue of Buddha in the grounds of Sandringham.

on; he was always very kind to me and I was very fond of him. He was a bit gruff, the old sailor, but essentially kind underneath, but alas he had rather Victorian ways. He didn't always get on with his children, especially his sons. It was more difficult for them. What was really rather sad was just at the end before he died, he was beginning to melt and he was having fun with them.'

~

17 March 1924 to D'Arcy Osborne

White Lodge

Dear Mr Osborne,

I have been meaning for ages to write to you. First to thank you so much for your last delightful letter, & secondly, just to please myself by putting down anything that comes into my head! I have had flu and tonsillitis & am still in bed. It's disgraceful really, as I've been in bed nearly ten days, but I am so tired. I have put off four engagements next week, so I consider that I am free for a fortnight.

I shall have to sit quietly here for a bit – would you ever have time to come & see me?

I am bubbling with talk at the moment, & would love to hear from you about the new regime at the FO [Foreign Office]. I am extremely anti-Labour. They are so far apart from fairies and owls and bluebells & Americans & all the things I like. If they agree with me, I know they are pretending – in fact I believe everything is a pretence to them.

I have got a dear little Scotch nurse whom I sent for from Dundee. She is deliciously enthusiastic about everything, & adored Hampton Court when I sent her there yesterday. <u>How</u> I love the little things of life. Thank God for two doctors consulting over one – also for puppies playing, & a good joke – anything can be amusing if it's not too pathetic.

Your sincerely,
Elizabeth

~

22 March 1924 to D'Arcy Osborne

White Lodge

Dear Mr Osborne

I <u>must</u> write & thank you for the flowers, because I love them so. They are <u>so</u> lovely, & it was so nice of you to bunch me – there is nothing I like more than being given flowers, & so I <u>must</u> say thank you. It is nice of you to say that it was not altruism that made you send them – that would have been so sad! 'The sacrifice of self in the interests of others' is what my dictionary says.

I am 'up' now, & planning a terrible summer. It is going to be so busy – the more you do, the more people expect you to do. One 'stunt' intrigues me. Mr [John D.] Rockefeller apparently has given one & a quarter millions towards 'medical research', & there is going to be a large dinner party in a huge room in May, with dozens of round tables. At each table a host or hostess who will entertain RICH SNOBS, & extract money in vast quantities from said RICH SNOBS. I hope to have a table. What fun it will be.

I would love to see your modelling – shall I pay you a visit one evening (anon) & inspect? I would love to. I <u>could not</u> recuperate in company with Mrs [Grace] Vanderbilt. She stuns me at every turn. I like Gracie* tho'. But then I like so many things – Gracie, fairy stories, fat butlers, porters, the smell of tangerines, suave Orientals, a good tune, lovely colours, French accents, puppies, bath salts, & a million more.

I dislike very few things, but I dislike those heartily. Tactlessness annoys me – also rudeness, & inability to understand, also crass stupidity, & people who are pleased with themselves. Also spiders, caterpillars, slugs, frogs, toads, loud voices & nasty coughs. And a few more including Mr Noel Buxton.† I must stop and fondle my dogs. Yours sincerely, Elizabeth

PS I think the Labour Party is narrow minded and snobbish.

~

---

* Probably Grace Vanderbilt (1899–1964), the daughter of Cornelius Vanderbilt III and his wife, Grace Graham Wilson.

† Noel Edward Buxton (1869–1948), MP for North Norfolk, Liberal 1910–18, Labour 1922–30; Minister of Agriculture and Fisheries, 1924 and 1929–30; created first Baron Noel-Buxton, 1930; advocate of temperance legislation, writer on Balkan affairs.

Diary: Saturday 26 April 1924

Woke at 8. Breakie in bed. This is the first anniversary of our wedding! I went up to London to see Mother & Mike. Talked for an hour and then rushed home. Lunch at 1. Colonel Wigram* came – at 2.15 we went off to Wembley, & saw the Cup Final. The King couldn't go, so we went. Enormous crowd. Sat between the Duke of Devonshire & Ramsay MacDonald [the Prime Minister]. The latter talked a lot. He & Ishbel go to Windsor today. Newcastle scored two goals in the last 5 minutes. Terrific excitement. Bertie gave the cup & medals. [. . .]

~

Diary: Tuesday 3 June 1924 Trooping the Colour

[. . .] Went to B.P. & drove to the Horse Guards with Mama. Bertie rode with the King. It was a very beautiful sight as usual. Went back to B.P. & watched from the Balcony. [. . .] Lunched B.P. Large family gathering. Slipped away 2.45. Went down to Home for Incurables† Putney, & opened their Sale & went round the place. [. . .] [After dinner] we had a small party. About 70. Great fun, & band good. The Astaires came. Stopped dancing 3.15. Bed 4.

~

Thursday 2 October 1924 to King George V

Glamis Castle

Dearest Papa

I have finished 'Sant Flavio', the book that you kindly said I might borrow from the library, and am sending it back to Bertie, who will replace it in its little nest. I enjoyed it so much, and got quite excited over it, and thank you so much for allowing me to take it away.

You will be pleased to hear that the stocking is getting on well – the heel is almost finished, and altho' it is rather lumpy, it is really very pretty. When I have finished this pair, I will make a beautiful

---

* Colonel Clive Wigram, later first Baron Wigram of Clewer PC GCB GCVO Royal Victorian Chain CSI (1873–1960), soldier, courtier, Assistant Private Secretary then Private Secretary to King George V 1910–36, Acting Private Secretary to King George VI 1936–7.

† Later the Royal Hospital for Neuro-Disability. Queen Elizabeth was Patron from 1923 until the end of her life.

pair for you, and if I work as fast as I do at present, I shall hope to have them finished in ten years or so. I am afraid that mine will never be as pretty as your pale grey and white ones, that I admired so the other day!

I enjoyed my fortnight very much indeed at Balmoral, & thank you a thousand times for having me.

The political situation seems very wobbly from the papers – I hope you will not have more worries soon.

Ever your affec: daughter in law, Elizabeth

~

Diary: Saturday 1 November 1924

Went to see David [the Prince of Wales] who got back yesterday from America. Very well. Then back to White Lodge. [. . .] Read etc & helped Bertie with a speech. After dinner same.

~

4 December 1924 to D'Arcy Osborne

From 60 bis Avenue d'Iéna, Paris, XVI, en route to Africa

Dear Mr Osborne,

It is very very nice of you to give me a belt, which I wanted terribly. It is so funny, but it was the one thing I forgot, and I was enchanted when I received it today. Thank you so much.

I was on the point of writing & making a date with you several times lately, but in the end I was so terribly busy that I saw nobody at all. There were all sorts of things that I wanted to speak with you about, & now I must put it off till April which is annoying.

I am feeling slightly mingled in my feelings about going to Africa, as I hate discomfort, and am so afraid that I shall not like the heat, or that mosquitoes will bite my eyelids & the tip of my nose, or that I shall not be able to have baths often enough, or that I shall hate the people. On the other hand, I think it is good for one to go away & see a little LIFE, and then think how pleased I shall be to get home again.

Do write me a letter or two from the Foreign Office (I like the paper) & if you ask at White Lodge, they will give my address, or I believe we shall be staying in Nairobi with the Governor for some time – anyway for letters.

What fun Paris is. Yesterday we went to Versailles and walked in the gardens, which looked so lovely & forlorn & empty, & in the evening went to the Casino de Paris, where for the first time in my life I saw ladies with <u>very</u> little on, & somehow it was not in the least indecent. Then we went to a dance hall full of doped Russians & Argentines, & then to a tiny place where we drank off a coffin, surrounded by skeletons & exchanging very vulgar badinage with a man carrying a huge Bone. Then to a Russian place where I enjoyed myself <u>so</u> much being very fast, & throwing balls at rather a nice American, & then to a tiny place with several Negroes with delicious voices who sang & <u>sang</u>.

Now I'm just off to Africa, so au revoir & a *thousand* thanks for the belt.

Yours sincerely,
Elizabeth

~

On 1 December 1924 the Duke and Duchess set off for Paris, the first leg of a journey to East Africa which had been inspired by a conversation the Duchess had had with Winston Churchill at dinner on 27 June 1924. Many years later, Queen Elizabeth recalled this moment: *'Winston was extraordinary. I remember sitting next to him at dinner just after we were married & he said, "Now look here, you're a young couple. You ought to go and have a look at the world. I should go to East Africa," he said. "It's got a great future, that country." So we did. We went off. We spent about five months. We walked in Kenya and Uganda, right down to the Nile. We went up the Nile into Sudan. And I have always been grateful to him, you know, because I don't think we would have thought of going. It was wonderful. Best bit of one's life.'*

~

Diary: Thursday 11 December 1924

Got up at 6.30 to see the Suez Canal. All desert on each side, & quite interesting. At about 8, we passed the Wryneck* who took us over to Belfast last July! They turned out & cheered us. It was quite a

---

* HMS *Wryneck* had taken the Duke and Duchess to and from Ulster on their successful official visit in July 1924.

homesick feeling! Stayed at Suez for an hour or so, and then sailed. It
is getting warmer quickly.

~

Friday 12 December 1924 to Lady Strathmore

SS Mulbera

My darling Sweet,

We get to Port Sudan tomorrow, so I will just send you a little
line. We reached Port Said on Wed. evening, and found the
Barham (a Battleship) there, & dined on board which was amusing.
All that night we went through the Suez Canal, & I got up at
6.30 yesterday morning to see it. It is quite narrow with desert on
either side, & the most marvellous light early. Just like all pictures
of Egypt!! Then we got to Suez, & yesterday went through the
Gulf of Suez, with Egypt on one side & Palestine I suppose on the
other – quite narrow – about ten miles. Quite early yesterday
morning we passed the destroyer Wryneck in the Canal. She took us
over to Ireland in July, and it was so funny passing her like that in
quite another part of the world! They all turned out & cheered us,
& it was all so friendly! Today we have been through the Red Sea, &
though it is hot enough to wear thin clothes, there is always a little
breeze & plenty of electric fans. The evenings are too lovely, with a
huge moon. I am not sure whether you will get this letter very long
before Xmas, so I will wish you a very merry one darling, and don't
worry about us, because we are simply surrounded with doctors
& people to look after us! We just lie about on chairs & are very
peaceful. Au revoir Angel,

Your very loving
Elizabeth

~

Diary: Tuesday 16 December 1924

Still pretty hot. We arrived at Aden at about 3.30. The Governor
came on board, General Scott,* and we went ashore with him. Large

---

* Sir Thomas Edwin Scott (1867–1937), eminent military and colonial service officer;
Governor of Aden, 1920–5.

crowds everywhere & most picturesque. We had tea at his house & met the Sultan of the Hedjaz – very beautifully dressed. Also staying there was Miss Ellis, the girl who saw her mother murdered, & was abducted by Afghans.* At about 4.30 we drove back, & went to the Crater – the old town, & saw the Tanks – very interesting. Then went to see the Air Force – very nice people. Then round by the golf course, with lots of cheering, & had a drink at the Club, & a dance too. Talked to lots of people. Then dined with the Gov. Very merry little dinner & had great fun. Back to ship at 9.45. Tired!

~

Monday 29 December 1924 to Lady Strathmore

From camp

My Darling Mother

We arrived at the camp two days ago, and it is simply wonderful. The country is quite unlike anything I expected, and it is <u>beautiful</u>. We took two days motoring here, and the camp is in the middle of a huge plain† exactly like an English Park, and on every side there are mountains. We have got very nice little huts, and each a black servant. Mine is so good, that I infinitely prefer him to Catherine! There are two professional white hunters, Major Anderson & a Mr Ayre – also the doctor – very nice, Colonel Llewellyn who runs the camp, and Captain Something who is always called K.P. and who is a sort of extra white hunter. He is one of the Governor's ADCs. There are masses of lions, who growl all night, but they don't appear much. I am feeling frightfully well; we get up at 6 & one wakes <u>at once</u>, and go to bed soon after 8. The climate is marvellous – the sun is hot in the morning, but it's quite cool all the time. I am wearing flannel trousers & a jumper & sun hat.

---

* In April 1923 Mollie Ellis, the daughter of Major A. J. Ellis DSO, was kidnapped and her mother was murdered in their military bungalow in Kohat in the Khyber region of Pakistan. The *New York Times* reported the story under the headline 'Captive English Girl is Seen with Savages' (*New York Times*, 18 April 1923). Mollie was freed ten days later thanks to a knowledgeable and brave Englishwoman, Lilian Starr, matron of the Peshawar Military Hospital. She rode into the Tribal Territories, found where Mollie was being held and, with the help of village elders, managed to persuade the kidnappers to hand her over (Roderick Martin, Tavistock District Local History Society, *West Devon Magazine*, August 2010).

† Siolo Plain, beyond Meru, near Mount Kenya.

This morning I went out to try & shoot something with Col. Llewellyn, and we dashed after some oryx (very pretty) but couldn't get near them. It is all great fun and no hardship at all. The flowers coming here were too <u>wonderful</u>. I saw great masses of Morning Glory & thought of you, also arum lilies, orchids, carpets of bright blue forget me nots, and wonderfully coloured daisies – big ones like marguerites.

Tuesday.

This morning we got up at 4 and went out to try & get a lion. It was <u>too</u> thrilling. They had left a rhino & a zebra out, & as it was getting light we crept up behind bushes & found two lions growling over the zebra. Before we saw them we heard the most blood curdling growls and grumbles, and all felt petrified with fear! We all shot together, but it was still too dark to see properly, and they were off like a streak of lightning. Then later on in the day Bertie & I & Major Anderson saw three lionesses and a big lion all lying out in the sun like big cats. They looked very bored when they saw us and stretched & yawned and went quietly into some bush. They are beautiful things and very difficult to get near. I saw about 12 giraffes too the other day – quite close. They are too funny. I enclose a little scribble of what I can see out of the door of my hut as I write. It is very bad, but might give you an idea of the country – it is an undulating plain with little trees right away to the hills – that is Mount Kenya, the peak.

Au revoir, angel, your very loving Elizabeth

PS Bertie has just got a lion and 2 buffaloes.

~

13 January 1925 to the Prince of Wales

[From Siolo Camp, while the Duke of York was away on safari]

Darling David,

I know now your feelings of relief and freedom when you get away from England on your own – away from all the petty little annoyances and restrictions that drive one crazy. It's marvellous, isn't it? I hate to think that you may have a real bad time in S. Africa, and it is terrible to think also that we shall all be nearly a year older before we meet again. At least, I already feel about two years older since December, having aged considerably on board the ship coming

out, but I am losing it out here again, and now feel ready for
anything.

It's a good life here, and you have no idea what it has done for
Bertie. He is a different being, quite calm and losing all his nerviness –
never turns a hair when he is being charged by a lion, and enjoying
every moment of safari life. He was charged by an infuriated lioness
with cubs the other day, and she was very close before she died – you
sure do get some sort of excitement every day.

I have shot 2 oryx (one quite good), 2 Grant's Gazelle and had a
shot at a lion, and am loving it! Don't tell your sweet Father that I
am shooting, but I hope to get something a bit bigger soon.

It is extraordinary how <u>very</u> brave one becomes when one is
hundreds of miles from anywhere – every day I marvel at my
courage, because I really am a loathsome little coward. [. . .]

I hate the thought of coming home – no, I love coming home,
but I hate being always under the eye of a narrow minded autocrat,
and it will be <u>awful</u> with the two human members of the family
away. Dear David, I hope your affairs are going well, and that neither
your heart or your staff are giving you cause to worry. Those two
seem to give you most trouble in life, and also of course you are <u>very</u>
<u>very</u> naughty, but delicious. [. . .]

There are four wild men here who take us out hunting – one is a
villainous young American from Texas – rather amusing, one a sleepy
looking man of some English nationality, who is really the most wide
awake charmer, & others; it's great fun, and I don't look <u>too</u> bad in
my trousers and shirt. It makes me look very <u>small</u> which annoys me,
but as thank God there are no tall women here, I don't really mind.
God bless you David, & best love
  Elizabeth

~

31 January 1925 to D'Arcy Osborne

From Kenya

Dear Mr Osborne,

I was so pleased to get your letter when I got back to camp last
night; it brought a little whiff of wet black London and it also made
me laugh, which I like. I am becoming very middle class out here,
but am terribly happy and <u>adore</u> this life. It really is marvellous,

and I find that I have taken wildly to shooting. I shot a rhinoceros
the other evening, and when I tried to have my photograph
taken standing sternly with one foot on the beast, I found this was
quite impossible, and had to be taken ignominiously peering over
its back. However I shall give you one, as I know you would
appreciate it. I rise at 4.30 (I can hear you say my God) & go walking
around with my spouse and the white hunter [Pat Ayre], who is a
charming man with an imagination, an accent & a sense of humour.
He is exactly like what I imagine the Scarlet Pimpernel to be, very
slow & sleepy & long, and if he wasn't so brown he would be rather
good looking. He is English South African and talks American.
Everyone talks American here and so do I. We usually hunt till ten
or eleven, and then join the camp which has moved after us like
magic, & drink and sleep till about 3.30, when we sally forth once
again.

I am so pleased, because I can walk *miles* here. I should say we
walk at least twelve or more per day and mule the rest. I have been
very lucky & seen quite a number of lions, and we hunt them wildly
which is lots of fun. The game is amazing, & it is such fun to watch
them. Rhino are very funny, very fussy like old gentlemen, & very
busy all the time, quite ridiculous, in fact. Giraffes I adore – they are
utterly prehistoric and very gentle. Also they move like a slow motion
movie.

I never knew that I could like this sort of life so much – out all
day long, and one never knows the day of the week. I feel it must be
good for one. England seems so small & full & petty and unhappy in
contrast to Africa.

The country up here is all plains & hills, mostly covered with
bush – all thorn trees and simply huge. The flowers are delicious –
this morning we went to try & find a lion which had been grumbling
away quite close and failing to find him, I collected seeds & dug up
roots, which both shocked and amazed our gun bearers! Yesterday we
had stopped by a river to have breakfast when we heard shrill
screams, and found a pretty little American lady stuck in her car in
the middle of it. We hauled her out, & it turned out to be Mr & Mrs
Martin Johnson,* who are doing the most marvellous cinema films of

---

* Martin (1884–1937) and Osa (1894–1953) Johnson, photographers, film-makers, explorers
and authors. The Johnsons came from Kansas and captured the American imagination with

animals, hundreds of miles further north. They were coming down
for mails, and we spent the day together, as they hadn't seen anyone
for months. He took a movie of us, and close ups of me, which will
be ghastly. I will show you when I get home. They are charming and
have certainly got the most wonderful photographs of elephant &
rhino & leopards that you could imagine.

I do hope you aren't bored to death with all this – everything is
out of proportion now, and I really am getting <u>so</u> common. I say 'Ta
awfully', instead of 'thank you', & WORSE. There is also a doctor
with the camp, a man called Capt. Caldwell who runs it and Lavinia
Annaly. We are all <u>so</u> pally (!), and talk gaily on the most intimate
subjects. Goodbye and may I come & see your modelling when I get
back? I have never yet seen your house & would love to.

Yours very sincerely,

Elizabeth

~

Undated [March 1925] to Rose Leveson-Gower

The *Nasir**
Sudan

My Darling Rosie

Thank you a thousand times for your letter which arrived a day
or two ago. We are now going down the Nile, having arrived in the
Sudan about five days ago, and it is <u>quite</u> delicious. We had a
marvellous time in Uganda, and I adored the shooting. It was very
hard work as we used to walk about twenty miles a day – at least
Bertie & I & the hunter did, and it was the greatest fun. I shot two
buffalo there, and several of the buck, and one day I spent walking
amongst elephants. It was simply wonderful, and made one feel such
a worm looking at those <u>enormous</u> creatures. One could watch for
<u>hours</u> – they are too amusing, and frightfully dangerous, but the man
we were with is a great elephant hunter, and we walked about
amongst the herds quite easily. We saw the source of the Nile at Jinja
on Lake Victoria Nyanza, & then we went right down Lake Albert &

---

films and books of their adventures around the world, including in Africa and the South
Pacific. When they met the Yorks they were on their second African safari.

*   The river paddle steamer in which the Duke and Duchess spent a month (5 March–6 April)
sailing down the Nile from Rejaf in Southern Sudan to Kosti.

went up the White Nile there till we got to Nimule which is the border of Uganda & the Sudan. There we were met by Captain Brocklehurst* & we came 90 miles by car, & joined this boat at Rejaf. It is very hot indeed here – in fact the first real heat that we've had – 100 in the dining place, and about 120 outside.

Uganda I thought lovely in parts – especially the Ruwenzori mountains – the ones called the Mountains of the Moon, & the Semliki Valley which we walked down. That is about 50 or 60 miles wide, or even 100, with the Congo hills on one side & the Uganda on the other, with Ruwenzori at the top. The birds here are very marvellous – every sort & colour & shape, and the duck & geese are innumerable. [. . .] The early mornings & evenings are <u>so</u> lovely, just like Scotland – tho' this is far more African than anything I've seen yet. We stayed a day or two with the Francis Scotts [in] Kenya – it was rather amusing finding quite an English atmosphere suddenly like that.

Well Rosie darling, I hope you are not going to desert Park Street altogether for that foul Chatham – you <u>mustn't</u>. [. . .]

This is a very comfortable boat, & it is rather nice to have a real bath & wc, after having neither for about 6 weeks – tho' personally I <u>love</u> a tent, and will you believe it – I get up with the greatest ease at 5! In fact I am always called at 6, even on ordinary days!! Jock would laugh. Some ridiculous things happen out here – our boys are very funny – the other day Lavinia wanted me & asked my boy where I was – & all he said was 'Memsahib Bumbum' pointing at the w.c. What he thought he meant I <u>don't</u> know. [. . .]

Lavinia is being very nice & a <u>fearful</u> flirt – she is very modern & I feel quite old fashioned! I wonder if Wisp has shot down here at all? I am longing to show you my heads – how bored you'll all be with them. Goodbye, darling, from your very loving, Elizabeth

~

* Captain Courtney Brocklehurst (1888–1942) was married to Lady Airlie's daughter Helen, and the Duchess had danced with him at her first ball in January 1918. He was Game Warden of the Sudan; Major R. H. Walsh was his assistant. They led the team that accompanied the Duke and Duchess through the Sudan.

30 March 1925 to Lady Strathmore

The *Nasir*
Sudan

My Darling Mother

I got three delightful letters from you by the last mail, and they made me laugh so much – especially about old Gilbey & Lord Wodehouse! How <u>dreadful</u> about Leslie Blackburn – I sent Aunt Conta* a cable at once – I <u>do</u> feel sorry for them all. [. . .]

We have had a very peaceful time going down the Nile on this very comfortable boat, and shooting a little here and there. It is certainly very hot, the temp. is 104 inside here! So what it must be outside I don't know!

The birds are very wonderful here – marvellous colours, & lovely crested cranes & storks & every sort of duck & geese. <u>Very</u> few flowers as it is the dry season, but I believe they are good. As a matter of fact we've missed the flowers everywhere, except in Kenya.

Captain Brocklehurst is being <u>so</u> nice. He has got charming manners, no temper so far! and has really been very pleasant, & I like him very much. The other man, Major Walsh, is also very nice, about 38, a pre-war soldier & very simple nice man. [. . .]

I wonder if the clothes have changed at all?! [. . .] I hear that James & Rachel are quite friendly towards each other now, which is excellent! [. . .]

One is called at 6 always here, and gets up almost at once, & breakfast about 7.30. It really is too hot later, and the sun rises punctually at 6 & goes down at 6 in the evening, when it is nice & cool and <u>lovely</u> stars.

We saw a very good native dance yesterday evening at a place called Kodok† done by Shilluks. They have a little leopard skin round

---

* Lady Constance Frances Bowes Lyon, daughter of thirteenth Earl of Strathmore (1865–1951), married 1893 Hon. Robert Francis Leslie Blackburn (1864–1944); he became Lord of Session as Lord Blackburn, 1918–35. Their son, Leslie, had just died of appendicitis.

† Kodok, formerly Fashoda, in the south Sudanese state of Upper Nile, the capital of what used to be known as the Shilluk kingdom. The Shilluks are a Nilotic people, the third-largest minority ethnic group in southern Sudan after the Dinka and the Nuer. They were led by a king and the society was strictly hierarchical. As today, their principal wealth lay in their herds of cattle, which were always used as currency as well as to provide their main food, milk.

their waists & huge bracelets & painted faces, & sing very well –
rather like a violoncello, & the dances are most amusing. They act all
the time, & have lion-hunts & sham battles. Further south where
we've come from the people are Dinka's, & wear nothing whatever.
They have huge herds of cattle which they live for. A man would
rather lose three wives than one cow! They live off nothing but
curdled milk & blood – it must be very sustaining! They are very wild
but quite friendly. The Uganda people are very civilised round the
capital, rather <u>too</u> civilised, and the wilder ones in the North look far
far healthier & better with nothing on & no religion.

The missions only teach them religion poor things, & don't
trouble about making them work or keeping themselves clean, so
consequently nobody will hire a Christian, as they are always dirty &
dishonest. Isn't it a pity? The Roman Catholics aren't so bad, I believe
they do teach them a few occupations.

Well, au revoir Angel, perhaps I shall get home before this!

Your very very loving

Elizabeth

~

Diary: Monday 6 April 1925

Got up in my blue crepe de chine, & said goodbye to my dear &
hideous trousers. Arrived at Kosti at 10.30 – flags etc. Joined the train,
& puffed off to Makwar, having bidden Capt. Flett* a fond farewell.
Very hot. Got to Makwar at 4, & went to see the Great Dam. Lots of
engineers & DCs [District Commissioners] & Governors. [. . .]

~

Diary: Thursday 9 April 1925

[In the evening the Duke and Duchess took the train to Port Sudan,
accompanied by Brocklehurst and Walsh.] They sent a lot of soldiers,
as somebody had put a bullet through the dining saloon the night
before when they thought we were on the train! Dinner 8. Bed 10.

~

Many Shilluks were converted to Christianity in the late nineteenth and early twentieth
centuries.

* Master of the *Nasir*.

Diary: Friday 10 April 1925

Woke at 6.30, no shots at the train yet! [. . .] We are all very sad it is all over – it has been <u>marvellous</u>. [. . .] We got out & stood outside the train just before the sun went down, & the Red Sea Hills looked very grim. [. . .] Arrived Port Sudan at 9.30. Met by Tebbits & went straight out to the Maloja* – 21,000 miles from Australia. Said goodbye & sailed at once. Goodbye Africa.

~

4 May 1925 to D'Arcy Osborne

White Lodge

Dear Mr Osborne,

I have suddenly thought that I would like to talk to you on the telephone! Will you ring me up one morning when you are feeling like telephoning. I am awake from 8 o'clock onwards. Somehow, when I ring somebody up myself it takes all the pleasure away from it, so if you would grapple with your instrument one morning, I'd be very glad to converse for, say, two minutes. Then perhaps we could make a date for a more magical conversation.

I loved your magic book. The witch was delicious, and I read it on the Nile and it seemed quite possible there.

I have just had tonsillitis and haven't been out for over a week so I have been lucky – perhaps you are still away? In that case you are still luckier. I am bubbling inside with Africa, but I promise you I'll keep it there, & won't tell you stories when I see you. [. . .] What about the Peace of Europe? I feel that E. P. Oppenheim† would solve any little difficulties at once. Have you read his last book?

Yours sincerely,

Elizabeth

~

---

* RMS *Maloja*, P&O liner built in Belfast and launched in 1923 to run between Sydney and London. In the Second World War she served first as an armed merchant carrier and then a troop ship.

† E. Phillips Oppenheim (1866–1946), prolific writer of forty-three novels and stories, many of which were filmed. Among his most famous titles were *Monte Carlo Knights*, *The Great Prince Shan* and *The Amazing Quest of Ernest Bliss*.

Diary: Saturday 9 May 1925

Woke at 7.30. Breakfast 8.30. Bertie went off to Wembley at 11.15 very downhearted. I got up & listened to his speech on the wireless. It was marvellously clear & no hesitations. I was <u>so</u> relieved.

It all went off very well, & he got back at 1.30. At 3.30 we went off to S.P.W. for a night. May & Andrew* were there, also Jock & Neva & Anne, David, Mother & Father. Looked at the Rockery after tea, & had a cocktail party. Bed 10.

~

This was the speech which was shown at the beginning of the film *The King's Speech* (2010, directed by Tom Hooper). The Duke was portrayed as being practically unable to speak because of his stammer. He had indeed been nervous in advance, and wrote to his father on 4 May,[†] five days before the speech was to be made:

> My dearest Papa
>
> I am enclosing a copy of my speech to you next Saturday, which I hope you will think is short enough. Several portions have been removed including the thanks to different people. I do hope I shall do it well but I shall be very frightened as you have never heard me speak & the loud speakers are apt to put me off as well. So I hope you will understand that I am bound to be more nervous than I usually am.
>
> > Best love to you [. . .]
> > Your very devoted son
> > Bertie

Family reactions to the speech were mixed. The Duchess's diary showed that she was pleased and so was the Duke. In a letter of 27 May 1925 to the Prince of Wales, who was abroad, the Duke himself wrote: 'At Wembley the opening of the B.E.E. went off very well, & thank God my speech was a success. In fact I thought it easily the best

---

* Andrew Elphinstone (1918–75), younger son of Sidney and May Elphinstone. A talented pianist; Rector at Worplesdon in Surrey, 1953–68. Married 1946 Jean, widow of Captain Hon. Vicary Paul Gibbs.

† Duke of York to King George V, 4 May 1925, RA GV/PRIV/AA61/250.

I have ever done. And in front of Papa too. I was only nervous in the
legs & not in my mouth or throat. It was an ordeal but I came out of it
all right. I spent several sleepless nights before it though as you may
imagine. Papa seemed pleased which was kind of him.'*

King George V may in fact have been less enthusiastic. In a letter
to Prince George (future Duke of Kent) dated 10 May 1925 he wrote:
'Bertie got through his speech all right, but there were some rather
long pauses.'†

~

10 September 1925 to the Duke of York

Carberry Tower

My Darling

Your letter arrived this morning, and I simply loved getting it.
The posts are very queer here, so I don't know when you will get
this.

Bertie, at this moment the gramophone is playing into my
ear, Andrew is talking to me, & Jean is reading aloud, so I really
don't know if this will read sense! I am so glad your Aberdeen thing
went off alright – my flower show only took an hour, fighting my
way round through silly hysterical old ladies, so that wasn't too bad.
[. . .]

May is really much better and is able to do quite a lot. Today we
are going to lunch with Arthur Balfour‡ which bores me very much,
as I really don't care for going to see people in the country, do you?

I am feeling much better now, tho' the sight of wine simply turns
me up! Isn't it extraordinary? It will be a tragedy if I never recover my
drinking powers.§ [. . .]

---

* RA EDW/PRIV/MAIN/A/2516.

† RA GV/PRIV/AA61/252.

‡ A. J. Balfour, first Earl of Balfour KG OM PC DL (1848–1930), Conservative politician and
statesman; Prime Minister, 1902–5; Foreign Secretary, 1916–19; author of the 1917 Balfour
Declaration, which supported the creation of a Jewish homeland in Palestine. His home was
Whitingehame House in East Lothian. In the Second World War it was converted into a
school for Jewish refugee children who came to Britain through the Kindertransport.

§ The Duchess was pregnant with her first child, Princess Elizabeth. The aversion to alcohol
passed.

I hope that the atmosphere at Balmoral is good. Tell Lord Esher*
that I am sorry to miss him! He is rather horrid, but rather amusing
too.

I miss you frightfully, and am looking forward <u>so so much</u> to next
week. Only to seeing <u>you</u> tho', nothing to do with Balmoral! It must
be dreadfully cold up there – don't catch a cold darling.

Do write again, I love to get a letter from you, bless you darling,
and stick up for yourself, remember that you are an elderly married
man, & don't let anyone patronise you. [. . .]

So long sweet, your very very loving ~~Bertie~~ <u>bother</u>! I mean
Elizabeth

~

28 October 1925 to Queen Mary

White Lodge

My Darling Mama

I was very disappointed at being unable to come to Sandringham
last Saturday, and I stayed here quietly and rested, which helped the
stupid neuralgia a great deal. The long day at Norwich would have
been unwise too I feel.

I think that Bertie has written & told you of our idea of taking
Curzon House for the next few months? It is rather an attractive old
house, and we can all squeeze in, which will make things much more
convenient. I am sure you will think this a good idea, as after October
it gets very foggy and lonely in the Park here.

Tomorrow we hope to see the Tattoo, as it rained the last time
we tried to go, and I am longing to see it. It is really very sad to think
that in two days that wonderful Exhibition† will be no more, and the
fairylike buildings empty and forlorn – I do hope they will be suitably
occupied soon, & not allowed to go forever.

I am really feeling very well; except for headaches, and probably

---

*   Reginald Baliol Brett, second Viscount Esher (1852–1930), politician and influential friend
and adviser of King Edward VII and King George V. A frequent guest at Balmoral.

†   The British Empire Exhibition at Wembley which had opened in May 1925 with the
ceremony at which the Duke of York had struggled to make his speech. The exhibition closed
on 31 October 1925.

soon they will go. Bertie & I are so pleased and excited about it all, & talk endlessly on the subject, which is perhaps a little previous!

With much love darling Mama

I am your loving

daughter in law

Elizabeth

~

8 January 1926 to Mrs Beevers

Curzon House

Curzon Street

W.1

Dear Mrs Beevers,*

I am so very glad that you are able to come to me in April, and shall feel very safe and happy in your hands I know.

My mother wants me to have a tonic of sorts, as I get rather tired (& irritable I fear!) and she thinks you would know of something. If you do, would you very kindly send it here?

If not, just let me know, and I'll ask the doctor for something.

Yours very sincerely,

Elizabeth

~

13 March 1926 to Lady Helen Graham†

Curzon House

My dear Nellie,

I can't tell you how delighted I am that you will take on the job of lady in waiting. It will be <u>so</u> so nice for me, and I do hope that you

---

* Anne Beevers (1862–1946). Following the death of her husband she trained as a midwife and became a private maternity or monthly nurse, cherished by many society mothers. She was engaged by the Duchess, who called her 'Nannie B', for both her confinements, and they remained in touch until Mrs Beevers's death.

† Lady Helen Graham (1879–1945), daughter of fifth Duke of Montrose, the Duchess's sole full-time lady in waiting from 1926 until 1933. She continued to serve her as Queen until shortly before her death. The Queen wrote of her, 'I loved & admired dear Nellie – she helped me through so much when I was young & silly. She was such fun too.' (Queen Elizabeth to Lady Delia Peel, 27 August 1945, Althorp Archive)

will like it. [. . .] There is no hurry <u>at all</u> about it; perhaps you will come & see me when you come to London, & we can arrange things. Engagements are made so far ahead nowadays, that you will be able to make your plans quite easily, and I really need very little – just a few letters to answer, & protection from certain determined old snobs!!

I really am <u>so</u> pleased that you have accepted, & now that I am writing to you, I would like to say how <u>terribly</u> sorry I was about your father's death. It is such a terrible break-up, I do feel so terribly sorry for you all, & send you my real sympathy.

Ever yours affec:
Elizabeth

~

12 April 1926 to Queen Mary

17 Bruton Street

My Darling Mama
The baby clothes have all arrived, and they really are quite exquisite. I do not feel that I can ever thank you enough for giving me such a lovely present, but at any rate, it is <u>very</u> much appreciated. The day frocks are too angelic, and the little sheets I examine all day! I do thank you so very much; you are far too kind and give me such divine things.

I am just sitting here waiting now, though I don't think it will make an appearance for another two or three weeks. It is very dull, but I haven't got very long to wait now, and Bertie is being angelic, and so understanding.

I expect Windsor must be looking delicious, and I hope you are having a rest after your more than strenuous winter, and all its anxiety.

With much love darling Mama, and again a <u>thousand</u> thanks from your loving daughter in law
Elizabeth

~

Princess Elizabeth was born at home in Bruton Street on 21 April 1926. The next day the Duke of York wrote to his mother, saying, 'You don't know what a tremendous joy it is to Elizabeth & me to have our little girl. We always wanted a child to make our happiness complete, & now that it has at last happened, it seems so wonderful & strange.'*

~

9 August 1926 to Lady Strathmore

Bruton Street

My Darling Sweet

I am so dreadfully ashamed, but I have just found a letter I wrote last week in my blotter, about plans, and so I have hurriedly sent you a telegram. I can't tell you how sorry I am, as you must have thought me so odd not writing. [. . .] I hope it's alright coming on Wednesday morning.

Bertie, and I, the baby, Alah[†] & nurserymaid, Catherine & Osborn!![‡] Isn't it a terrible party?

I simply can't tell you how much I am looking forward to a peaceful time at Glamis. I haven't really been properly in the country since last September, & I am longing for the country. [. . .]

Mother, Bertie's brother David is longing to come to Glamis for a night or two at the end of September, only he doesn't want to be a nuisance he says. I told him the Forfar Ball was on then, & he would love to come unless he's in the way. Do tell me when I come up. He is so frightfully modest, & is terrified of pushing in where he's not wanted. [. . .]

Goodbye darling, I am longing for Wednesday.
Your very loving
Elizabeth

~

---

* RA QM/PRIV/CC11/87.

[†] Clara Cooper Knight ('Alah'), employed by Lady Strathmore to look after Elizabeth soon after her birth in 1900. She stayed with the family thereafter, working first for Elizabeth's elder sister, May, and then for the Yorks when Princess Elizabeth was born. She died at Sandringham in 1946.

[‡] Catherine Maclean, the Duchess's dresser; Victor Osborn, the Duke's valet.

5 October 1926 to Mrs Beevers

Glamis Castle

Dearest Nannie B

Thank you a thousand times for the darling little boots & the little shoes which are <u>perfect</u>. She wears both pink & blue, so either colour would do if you were thinking of making another pair. I am longing for you to see her – she is growing so big and is as sharp as a needle, & <u>so</u> well.

She sleeps beautifully, and has always got a smile ready. You won't recognize her!

I am very well, and had a delicious long rest up here which I loved. I hope I shall see you in London – do come in when you can. We shall get to Bruton St on the 11th, and we shall be very busy preparing for this horrible trip.

Thank you again <u>so</u> much for the boots & shoes. It <u>is</u> so kind of you Nannie B.

Ever yours affect.

Elizabeth

PS I've just finished another Pilch [knitted baby garment]!

PS I shall send you some kodaks in a few days of the baby.

~

20 October 1926 to Major R. H. Walsh[*]

17 Bruton Street

My dear Walshie

Thank you so much for your letter. I am so glad that you were not bored at the tennis. I thought you simply <u>must</u> have been. I loathe it myself! Did you enjoy your leave? I was so sorry that we saw so little of you. Next year will be more normal I hope, though by next June I shall be old & worn & grey after our Australasian tour. You must prepare for a cynical & hardened old woman of the world by the time I've finished with the Aussies. [. . .] I'll bring my gramophone and my '275 [hunting rifle], & we'll vary the Charleston with a little letting off at crocs & other four-legged animals.

---

[*]   Assistant to the Game Warden of the Sudan, Captain Brocklehurst; accompanied the Duke and Duchess on their journey down the Nile in 1925.

Forgive this awful writing, I've been pretty busy, and I've found such a good new cocktail. Not strong enough for you I'm afraid, but you must sample it next summer. And after all you can always have two. Or three. Or four.

I saw Brock [Brocklehurst] in Scotland – he seemed in excellent form. A little prone to talking of death, but then one is used to that of course, & takes little notice.

Did you fall in love this summer? Sorry, that's very rude – forget it.

It was nice of you to write, do so again soon please, & tell me local news. I love hearing, it reminds me of that wonderful time nearly two years ago now – how I'd love to go shooting Boooshbuck once again.

Yours sincerely
Elizabeth

~

28 October 1926 to Lady Strathmore

Sandringham
Norfolk

My Darling Mother

Thank you a thousand times for your two last letters. I am so sorry that poor Father has got a cold, and I do hope he is better now. I wonder when you will be coming south? [. . .]

We leave here tomorrow, & return to B.[ruton] Street. I honestly don't know what we would have done without it.

The baby is very well, and now spends the whole day taking her shoes off & sucking her toes! She is going to be very wicked, and she is very quick I think.

It is a million times better here than at York Cottage.* Plenty of room, and a much better atmosphere. [. . .] I never had a moment to write in London – I was flying from Piccadilly to W. Lodge & back! Lord Lee is going to take it [White Lodge], so that's all right.†

---

* After the death in December 1925 of Queen Alexandra, who had lived in Sandringham House, the King and Queen had moved into the 'big house' from their less spacious quarters in York Cottage near by.

† The Duke and Duchess had found the drive to and from White Lodge in Richmond time-

The house is getting on slowly. I am going to spend my Marland Oil* (when it goes up) in doing several things to make it prettier. Two pilasters on either side of Bertie's fireplace, proper pillars in the hall, a new overdoor in my bedroom, etc etc which are small things but I hope will improve the house. Luckily Mr Parvin the head man of the decorators has got <u>very</u> good taste, & one can trust him not to do anything dreadful. Goodby darling, <u>do</u> come to Bruton St when you want, as your room is empty and also Father's downstairs.

Your very loving
Elizabeth

~

In January 1927 the Duke and Duchess set off on a long imperial tour focused on Australia and New Zealand. This had been agreed in the summer of 1926 and the Duchess had been dreading it because it meant that they would be parted from their daughter for at least six months.

Their other concern, shared by the King and Stanley Bruce,[†] the Prime Minister of Australia, was whether the Duke's stammer would prevent him delivering all the speeches that a formal tour required. Fortunately, help was at hand. In October 1926, encouraged by the Duchess, the Duke began consultations with Lionel Logue, the Australian speech therapist. Logue had an extraordinary gift and over the next few weeks his treatment, which involved breathing and other exercises, helped the Duke as nothing had before. The Duke wrote to thank him: 'I am full of confidence for this trip now.'[‡]

~

---

consuming. They were offered 145 Piccadilly to rent; while it was being renovated they stayed at the Strathmore home, 17 Bruton Street. No. 145 Piccadilly remained their London residence until the end of 1936.

* The Marland Oil Company was founded in Oklahoma in 1917 by an American oil explorer, E. W. Marland. Within a few years it was thought to represent 10 per cent of the world's oil production. In 1929 it merged with the Continental Oil Company.

† Stanley Melbourne Bruce CH MC FRS PC (1883–1967), Australian politician and diplomat and eighth Prime Minister of Australia, 1923–9. In 1947 he became first Viscount Bruce of Melbourne.

‡ Logue Papers.

Diary: Thursday 6 January 1927

Woke at 7.15. Up by 8.30. Feel very miserable at leaving the baby.
Went up & played with her & she was so sweet. Luckily she doesn't
realize anything. [Dr] Still came for a minute, & I explained about the
baby. Mother came in at 10 for a short time. I had on a grey lamb
coat with fox collar & grey everything else. I drank some champagne
& tried not to weep.

Said goodbye to the baby & Alah downstairs, & left at 10.40.
Large crowd, also near Victoria. Long leave taking & at last the
special train left. David, Harry & George* came down to see us off.
Huge crowds at Portsmouth, & the Renown† looked lovely. Lord
Cavan‡ was on board. We left at 1.40, & soon got into bad weather!

~

9 January 1927 to Queen Mary

HMS *Renown*

My Darling Mama

We shall have an opportunity to post some letters tomorrow, so
just a little line to tell you our sparse news.

We have settled down very comfortably, and after a horrible night
& day, the weather seems better – today was very pleasant and quite
warm. We had a very nice Church this morning, but that has been
our only diversion so far. [. . .]

The Captain is very nice, and they all take great trouble to make
us happy. I felt very much leaving on Thursday, and the baby was so
sweet playing with the buttons on Bertie's uniform that it quite broke
me up! David & George & Harry were all angelic, and cheered us up
for a bit. [. . .]

---

* The Prince of Wales, Prince Henry, later Duke of Gloucester, and Prince George, later
Duke of Kent.

† HMS *Renown* and her sister ship *Repulse* were the fastest capital ships ever built when
launched in 1916. *Renown* did not see action in the First World War but was in full service
during the Second World War. She covered Arctic convoys and took Winston Churchill to
meetings with other Allied leaders.

‡ Field Marshal Frederick Rudolph Lambart, tenth Earl of Cavan (1865–1946), Chief of the
Imperial General Staff, 1922–6. He was appointed by the King to be chief of staff for the tour,
and his wife Joan acted as lady in waiting to the Duchess.

With much love darling Mama, ever your very loving daughter in
law
Elizabeth

~

9 January 1927 to Lady Strathmore

HMS *Renown*

My Darling Mother
I believe a post goes tomorrow, so I thought I'd drop you a line,
tho' there is very little to say. We had one very rough day on Friday,
and it got better yesterday and was really very pleasant and warm.
This evening it is a little rougher, and we may not be able to land at
Las Palmas tomorrow which I don't mind as there is nothing to see
there! We cannot get closer than 2 miles of the island, & as the
Atlantic has a very big swell which doesn't notice in a big ship, one
cannot get a boat close enough to get into.

We are very comfortable, and the food is excellent. Today was
lovely with a warm sun.

Tortor* is very nice, and I only see Joan Cavan at meals as she
mostly stays down with poor Lord Cavan.†

You will go and see the baby, won't you darling, and when she is
at BP, just ring Alah up, & either run in and see her (same door as
we used Wed. night) or tell A to bring her to you. You will never see
the King or Queen, as they <u>never</u> use that door & are quite separate.
[. . .]

Well, au revoir darling, I will write again fairly soon, and give my
love to Father and everybody.

Your very very loving Elizabeth

~

---

* 'Tortor' was Victoria, Hon. Mrs Little-Gilmour, née Cadogan (1901–91). She acted as lady
in waiting on the tour and remained a lifelong friend.

† Lord Cavan had broken a bone in his foot.

Diary: Tuesday 11 January 1927

[. . .] Just before dinner heard that Diamond* had died this morning.
A blessed relief, but it seems so sad. She has suffered so much.

~

Diary: Saturday 5 February 1927

Woke very early, as we slept out. Not a breath of air. Read & talked
to Bertie etc. Sat out & read & slept a little on the triple gun deck.
After tea played some deck tennis. Felt depressed – I miss the baby all
the time, & am always wondering what she is doing. After dinner
four of the midshipmen came up & danced. Courtney very good
Tango & Charleston. Bed 11.

~

9 February 1927 to Queen Mary

HMS *Renown*
Nukuhiva, Marquesas Isles

My Darling Mama
      We have spent a very pleasant two days here in this lovely Island,
and quite regret leaving today. After nearly a fortnight at sea, it was
delicious to be able to stretch our legs again. We went on expeditions
and fished and bathed. It is very hot indeed and my cabin is 95 deg:,
but the evenings are fairly cool which is a help.
      The natives danced for us last night, and it was really most
remarkable, and very interesting. They are brown and the men quite
nice-looking, but very diseased and are rapidly dying out. Instead of
being strong healthy cannibals with strange religions and no clothes,
they are now weakly half hearted Roman Catholics with European
clothes. It seems all wrong, but that is what happens.
      We lead a very pleasant life in the ship – we dance sometimes
after dinner on the quarter deck, and the officers are all good, and
especially the midshipmen who dance quite beautifully. Tortor is
being a great success and such a help – I only hope that she will stand
N.Z. and Australia well.
      It is very difficult to write in this heat, so will you please forgive

---

* Diamond Hardinge, now Abercromby, who had been gravely ill for several years.

rather a stupid letter. There is so little as yet to tell you, as in all these five weeks we have only stopped at Las Palmas, Jamaica, Panama & Nukuhiva. Panama was very interesting indeed, and the Americans do run it in an amazingly efficient way. They really were very nice to us, and did not make themselves at all a nuisance. I don't know what their Press said though, and that is far the worst part of them. We feel so terribly cut off from home, and have heard no news beyond the usual wireless Bulletin, which only mentions China and football results.

I do hope that you like having the baby, and that she continues to be well and happy, and no colds. They do put a baby back so much, and I was always very particular that people with colds should not go near her. [. . .] I miss her quite terribly and the five weeks we have been away seem like five months.

I promised my father that she should go to him later on, and I thought that April would be a good time, and it will do her a great deal of good to be in the country for a bit, and especially when it gets warmer.

I will write again a little later, and hope to have more to tell you.

I do hope that you are well, and no horrid colds or influenza for you or Papa. With my very best love to you & Papa, I am darling Mama, your very loving daughter in law

Elizabeth

~

8 March 1927 to Queen Mary

Government House
Wellington
New Zealand

My Darling Mama

We are just finishing our visit to Wellington, and this evening we return to the Renown for the night, starting tomorrow on the tour of South Island.

The fortnight in the North Island seems to have been a success, though rather tiring and everybody has been very nice to us.

The marvellous loyalty of the people of N.Z. is quite amazing, and any mention of 'the King and Queen', 'the Mother Country', 'The Empire' or 'Home' or any other expression brings out such very genuine and whole hearted cheers that it gives one quite a lump in the throat. The children are so well looked after here – so different to England, in that they come first in <u>everything</u>. They are taught to be loyal to the Crown before anything, and then they are taught to be well & healthy & clean. Everywhere that we have been, we have been intensely struck by the appearance of the children. Apparently the teachers are very good, and they have to take most stupendous oaths of loyalty to the Crown before they are allowed to teach. Considering that it is the Crown that keeps the Empire together, I think it is a pity they are not more particular about teachers at home.

Rotorua was most interesting. I expect we saw much the same things that you did in 1901. I must say I hated walking round the geysers, although I was so interested, thinking that every moment we would all disappear through a thin crust into the unknown!

We both rather dread Australia, as politics there seem to govern everything, but I am sure it will be all right when we are once in the country.

I do hope that you are enjoying the baby, and that she is not too advanced for her age. I miss her more and more, but am happy to think that she is being so well looked after.

Yesterday I opened a Hospital for babies & mothers here, run by Sir Truby King,* who has done a most amazing work in lowering the death rate for babies. I hope that it will really spread in England, though of course his ideas will have to be adapted to suit conditions in England.

I find that clothes are a <u>great</u> problem here, especially when we are joggled about for days in motor cars, and the luggage is always going ahead or following after!

Already I long sometimes for a really quiet few days, and by the time we get home, we shall be pining for solitude.

I must fly to a Garden Party.

with very best love darling Mama

Ever your loving daughter in law

Elizabeth

~

* Sir Truby King (1858–1938), celebrated New Zealand physician and medical reformer, recognized particularly for his work on infant care.

The Duchess had another attack of tonsillitis and remained in
Auckland while the Duke went to South Island. She then rejoined the
Renown, which went to pick him up on their way to Australia.

~

Sunday 15 March 1927 to the Duke of York

HMS *Renown*
Wellington

My Darling Sweet

We have just arrived here, and I am feeling very lonely and
wishing I was with you, and that I could help you a little bit. It is so
much easier for two than one, and anyway when you tackle the
Mayor, I can tackle the Mayoress!

I think you are marvellous the way you keep it up, and so does
everybody else. I only hope you won't be too terribly 'done in', and
that you will get three fine days going to Australia. It is much too
short, and quite ridiculous to think that any human can do about
eight weeks at a stretch.

On studying the Aust. Programme it's really not so bad in a way,
as there are several 'free' mornings evenings etc, & here we've only
had 2 Sundays!

Darling when you are feeling very depressed and tired, remember
what wonderful work you are doing. They all loved you in N. Island,
and quite rightly. All the sentimental twaddle they write about me is
obviously absurd – they always like a bit of romance, & the baby too
helps the women to get silly – horribly silly.

I am using your cabin today as it's cooler, and am sitting in bed &
feeling very depressed – I always do from 4 to bedtime when I'm ill!

The poor old Town Clerk of Nelson fell into the sea yesterday
when he went to 'receive' the ship. Batters* clutched his behind just
as the waves closed over it, & plucked him out. It was very rough.

Everybody was so kind in Nelson. The baker sent me bread, the
bookseller books, the ladies cakes & flowers, the fruiterer pears and
grapes, Lady Rhodes also bunched me, and all I wanted really was a
nice comforting kiss from you. I never dreamt that I would be such a

---

* Sir Harry Batterbee GCMG KCVO (1880–1976), political secretary to the Duke for the
tour, served as UK High Commissioner to New Zealand 1939–45.

failure, but no doubt women are <u>not</u> made for the life we were leading, or men either if it comes to that. [. . .]

Well darling, I do pray that you will get through this nightmare of a programme and I shall <u>only</u> look forward to the moment when I shall see you again. I send you all my love and hundreds of kisses & several hugs.

Your very very loving
Elizabeth

~

17 March 1927 to May Elphinstone

Wellington
N.Z.

My Darling May

It was angelic of you to write. [. . .]

This is a lovely country, & <u>anything</u> grows. The climate really is divine, & quite hot. The children are marvellous – so strong & healthy & good looking the NZ children are. Not like your puny, pale, small delicate & hideous children. Poor May, what a trial it must be to you. I often wonder if you hear all the nasty things that people say about them. 'What lugubrious kids' I heard an elderly Peer exclaim, 'Have they melancholia?' I heard another time some nasty whispers about 'miserable little things – beaten all day & nothing to eat – can you wonder they're skeletons'. However – don't worry, dear May, I expect they'll grow out of it. I am so looking forward to June 27th. Shall you be in London? Oh do be.

I saw Mr Parker here!!* I danced with him. He proposed to me during the war, but I don't believe I ever answered him. It's too late now I suppose. Well, au revoir May old pip, Give my love & kiss to Sidney & the darlings.

Your very loving
Elizabeth

~

---

* See p. 51.

10 April 1927 to Lady Strathmore

Tamrookum
Beaudesert
Queensland

My Darling Mother

I am afraid I haven't written for ages, but there really hasn't been time, and soon you will see us before a letter can reach you.

We have come here for Sunday to stay with a Mrs Collins. It is most lovely country, and this is a comfortable one storey house. It is a large station – mostly cattle, & Bertie has been out all day mustering cattle and enjoying himself. The climate is marvellous – very hot sun and cool breezes, and we have both enjoyed ourselves up here in Queensland. The people are so nice & friendly, & the distances are so vast that it keeps them simple.

I am feeling so well, and hope to keep so. I do hope you have got the baby now, as I know you will enjoy her. I am so looking forward to June. The tour is going very well, and all the Scotch people are very glad to see me!! They are so nice & sentimental about each other.

I have seen Mr Dent, Mr McKillop, Nobby, Mr Brown & many others – also Emilie, Frank, & Cyril Cato!!* Frank looks exactly the same.

Though we are working very hard, & find some of it very boring, I have managed to keep well, & I really believe that it is all being a success. All the Governments are Labour, and the N.S.W. one is composed of very Red people. However, I got on very well with them, & the acting Premier here comes from Longforgan, so we get on like a house on fire. [. . .]

Well darling, I am longing to see you & the baby, from your very loving

Elizabeth

~

---

* Soldiers and acquaintances from wartime Glamis.

20 April 1927 to Queen Mary

HMS *Renown*
nearing Melbourne

My Darling Mama

I am afraid I have not written for a long time, but we have been so terribly busy, that letters are extremely difficult to write.

Everything seems to be going well. I think this sort of tour is far too strenuous for a woman, and I do get terribly tired – of course wireless, cars and the Press complicate things enormously, and one is expected to do the impossible, with never a moment's rest.

For instance in Tasmania, when you & Papa stayed at Hobart, we had to go off to Launceston their other town – merely because there is keen hatred & jealousy between the two towns, and if we had not gone there, the whole Island would have been furious. The jealousy in Australia is terrible – of course they are young, but it makes everything so 'suburban'.

Politics are very bad in N.S.W. The Premier who is cordially loathed by all classes, never appeared, except when we landed, & I expect he will very soon be thrown out.

Most of the Ministers are disgruntled Englishmen with a grievance, and none of the better class Australian will touch politics. It seems a great pity, but perhaps a sense of responsibility will grow in time.

We had a most delightful time in Queensland with wonderful weather. The people were so nice and friendly, even though they are called the Bolshie State. Everywhere they talk of yours and Papa's visit, and this loyalty is amazing. The children are so healthy to look at, but very spoilt, and completely without discipline – I don't believe they have any home life to speak of.

Please forgive me for setting out my opinions in this manner. They are probably completely wrong, but just what I think personally, and only after a glance really.

It will be delightful to get home and have some real peace, after these months of crowds and publicity. I shall be so excited at seeing the baby that I don't <u>dare</u> think about it.

Bertie has been wonderful, and is far less shy & more sure of himself. I expect this Tour will mean a great deal to him. Do you

remember you told me at Sandringham what a help such experience
would be to him?*

You have been so kind to the baby, and I do hope she will go on
being so well & merry.

With so much love, ever darling Mama, your loving daughter in
law

Elizabeth

~

They embarked in the *Renown* on the voyage home on 23 May. Three
days later a fire broke out in the engine room which could have
destroyed and sunk the ship. Years later Queen Elizabeth recalled: *'The
nearest ship was a thousand miles away. Totally empty sea. So we had to
prepare to leave. The deck got quite hot and I couldn't think of anything to
take in the boat except a bottle of Malvern Water and my [book of] prayers.
I couldn't leave them behind.'*

~

12 June 1927 to King George V

HMS *Renown*
In the Red Sea

My dearest Papa

I have not written to you before, as I know that Bertie writes
regularly & tells you our news, but I thought I must write a little line
to say how much we are looking forward to seeing you and Mama
again. It seems such a long time since we left you in January, and I
cannot believe that we are really getting home at last – older, and
I hope wiser!

_____

* Both the Queen and the Duchess were correct. The Duke wrote to his father at the end of
the tour: 'I was not very nervous when I made the Speech, because the one I made outside
went off without a hitch, & I did not hesitate once. I was so relieved as making speeches still
rather frightens me, though Logue's teaching has really done wonders for me as I now know
how to prevent & get over any difficulty. I have so much more confidence in myself now,
which I am sure comes from being able to speak properly at last [. . .] Elizabeth has done
wonders & though I know she is tired she never had a return of her tonsillitis & went about
with me every day. I could never have done the tour without her help; that I know, & I am
so thankful she came too.' (12 May, 12 June 1927, RA GV/PRIV/AA/62/30)

I hope you will not think me looking old and ugly, but a week in the Red Sea in June does not help the complexion to look its best! It has been very hot, and my cabin (sleeping) had been 105, which is most uncomfortable.

We had a bad time in the Bight, and I got washed out of bed at 3 A.M. by a huge sea which crashed suddenly over the ship, & had to spend an hour drying my hair at the radiator! I could not help laughing, but it was very annoying too.

I see that dear 'Rose Marie'* is finished, but that another good play is on with Edith Day† – I fear the music won't be as pretty, because the 'Rose Marie' tunes were quite out of the way.

I also read in the papers that Lily Elsie‡ has returned to the stage – I wonder if she is as pretty as she used to be. [. . .]

Mr Bruce [Prime Minister of Australia] was charming, & quite undaunted by having to deal with four very Labour State Governments. N. S. Wales has got the most revolting set of politicians that one could imagine – they are like men out of a nightmare, & seem to be well on the way to ruining the State.

I am looking forward more than I can say to the baby & a good rest. I have missed her all day & every day, but am so grateful to you & Mama for having been so kind to her. It will be wonderful to see her again.

With much love dearest Papa,

Ever your affec: daughter in law,

Elizabeth

~

22 September 1927 to Queen Mary

Glamis Castle

My darling Mama,

I am writing to thank you so very much for my delightful time at

---

* Broadway musical set in the Canadian Rockies.

† Edith Day (1896–1971), American performer who starred in many musicals and enjoyed many successes on the London stage. Her name graces a cocktail made with gin, grapefruit juice, sugar and an egg white.

‡ Lily Elsie (1886–1962), Edwardian actress and singer who enjoyed great success in *The Merry Widow*, 1907.

Balmoral. As usual it was the greatest fun, and I loved every moment of our visit. I was so sad at leaving both you & Papa as invalids on Monday, & am so glad to hear in Alah's letter today that Papa was able to go out.

Our visit to Glasgow went off very well I think – especially as it rained without ceasing from morning to night! I could have spent hours at the Exhibition,* it was so well arranged & so interesting, but as usual time was short, & we had to hurry round.

I visited a child welfare centre in Govan on Tuesday, & had a marvellous reception from every shade of socialist, crimson, red & pink!

I am so looking forward to coming back next week, it will be delightful to see you again, and I <u>hope</u> & <u>trust</u> that you will be able to dance by then, & that Miss Gordon has done good with the electric treatment.

I miss the baby horribly, but am so glad that you are enjoying her (how swelled headed I am about her).

With much love darling Mama, & so many thanks for such a heavenly fortnight at Balmoral.

Ever your loving daughter in law
Elizabeth

~

9 April 1928 to Queen Mary

Le Zoute
Belgium

My Darling Mama

We are having the most wonderful weather here, and are enjoying ourselves very much indeed. This is a most delightful place, and the air is marvellous, and we both feel very well & extremely healthy! We play golf every day, and do a little sightseeing also which has been very interesting. Yesterday, after church, we went to Ypres, and spent a very interesting few hours seeing some of the Flanders battle area. We went up to Hill 60 which is kept as it was in the War,

---

* The Duchess received the Freedom of the City of Glasgow in the morning and later opened the Housing and Health Exhibition.

saw the Menin Gate* which is <u>very</u> fine – really magnificent, also
Zonnebek & a lot of the famous villages of the War. It was very
tragic in a way, and perfectly amazing in the way that the Belgians
have effaced almost every sign of the War. Instead of a sea of mud &
shell holes, thousands of new houses, thriving farms and prosperity
everywhere. They are great workers & very willing ones. Also great
money makers – even the little children try to sell 'souvenirs' that
they have picked up – bayonets, bullets & cap-badges etc – which is
rather dreadful really! We also went to Bruges, and saw the pictures
and buildings, & Zeebrugge, where we went on the Mole, & went
through the War Museum, which is one of the best & most
interesting that I have seen.

The War is very near here, because of course the Germans
occupied all this country for years & how they hate them in these
parts.

We are staying here as Lord & Lady Inverness, and everybody has
been most kind, & allowed us to go everywhere incognito. [. . .]

With much love darling Mama, & please forgive this hurried letter
– we do so much there seems to be no time! Your very loving
Elizabeth

~

13 July 1928 to D'Arcy Osborne

145 Piccadilly

Dear Mr Osborne,

I have been meaning to write to you ever since you left,† and I
feel very badly about it, especially as I enjoyed your two letters
enormously. You gave me such a vivid picture of your life – I can
imagine it all quite well, & am so glad that it is pleasant. To have a
pleasing place to live in makes the whole difference, a house, I mean
& I am so glad for your sake that you have found something that you
like.

It amused me to hear that your sense of drama took you through

---

* Built at Ypres in Belgium as a memorial to the missing. It was completed in 1927 and
contains the names of 54,896 British and Commonwealth soldiers who were killed in the Ypres
salient in the First World War and whose bodies were never found.

† D'Arcy Osborne had recently been posted to the British Embassy in Lisbon.

any awkward moments of official entertaining! It sometimes helps me when I am faced with difficulties in that line. What a lot of our life we spend in acting. I expect that it is very lucky really, otherwise one would hardly ever be decently polite.

I have been very busy these last two months, and am looking forward <u>really</u> intensely to Glamis at the beginning of August. I <u>know</u> that I am happiest in the country.

Would you like some books or have you got a great many? Have you read,

A Lost Lady,

Uncle Tom Pudd,

The White Wallet (a soulful collection of poetry).*

If not, I will send them & some others, but I expect that you are well supplied.

Last night I dined with Venetia James, & a large dinner party of elderly couples, all Lords and Ladies, except one Baronet and his wife. All gossipy & a little dangerous, & with very little beauty. Then I left early & went to a cinema party given by the Mountbattens† at Brook House.

What a contrast. Lovely ladies with no very definite ideas in life beyond looking beautiful & having at least one young man; the King of Spain, making love to them, & altogether a very modern gathering.

I think that it is good to have some real butterflies flying about. They do very little harm, & they certainly decorate a room very well.

In the afternoon we went to Stoke Newington E[ast], a supposedly very Red part of London, where we were greeted by huge & frenzied crowds. How lucky that the throne is not included in their political views. I really do think that their politics makes very little difference to their loyalty. [. . .]

---

*   *A Lost Lady*, novel by Willa Cather (1923); *Uncle Tom Pudd*, novel by Laurence Housman, brother of A. E. Housman (1927); *The White Wallet*, poems by Pamela Glenconner (1912), one of the literary circle known as the 'Souls'.

†   Admiral of the Fleet Louis Mountbatten, first Earl Mountbatten of Burma KG PC GCB OM GCSI GCIE GCVO DSO FRS (1900–79), born Prince Louis Francis of Battenberg. Uncle of Prince Philip, Duke of Edinburgh. He had a distinguished naval career, serving in both world wars; in 1947 he was appointed Viceroy of India, and after independence served as its first Governor General in 1947–8. He then returned to the Navy, was largely responsible for creating the Ministry of Defence and became the first Chief of the Defence Staff. He married in 1922 the Hon. Edwina Ashley (1901–1960), daughter of the first Baron Mount Temple.

I have met Osbert Sitwell* lately, and I find him charming. He was a little restrained, but I believe that when he unbends, he can be most amusing. [. . .]

Life in London is always exactly the same, except that I miss you coming in for a talk & a drink of an evening. There is a chance that I may meet the McEwens at Lumley this weekend. I do hope so. I must quickly stop, & write to the Bishop of London, Lady Grey of Falloden & Sir Oliver Lodge before I go out. They have each sent me books written by themselves! The first an account of his journey round the world, the second a book of poetry, & the third a book on spiritualism. I shall write exactly the same letter to each.

I do hope that all goes well with you, & that the sun will shine on you.

Ever yours sincerely,
Elizabeth
PS I like the Godolphin

~

24 December 1928 to May Elphinstone

145 Piccadilly

My Darling May

Thank you both a thousand times for sending us that lovely cup. It was so kind of you to think of us, and we were delighted to have it. I am sending you a little tiny present, which I do hope you haven't already got one of. It's a pair of gardening scissors, & they are supposed to hold the flower when 'plucked', & thereby saving much labour!

We are still here, but hope very much to get away after Xmas for a day or two. All this long anxiety is very wearing to mind & body!

Darling May, will you forgive me if I say something to you? It's very interfering of me, but Bertie who has suffered so horribly himself, is terribly anxious that Andrew's stammer should not get worse and he did not think that he was any better when he came to

---

* Sir (Francis) Osbert Sacheverell Sitwell CBE CH (1892–1969), writer of many novels, poetry and a five-volume autobiography. The Duchess had met him through Mrs Ronnie Greville. She enjoyed his personality and his writing and they became good friends; he was one of her principal correspondents.

lunch here. It would be so horrid for the darling little boy if it became too much of a habit to get out of, and I expect <u>now</u>, that it's only that he is always thinking a few words ahead!

I <u>do</u> hope that you don't mind me saying this – it's only because I love you all that I dare, & one gets so used to it, that one hardly notices a little stammer like he has got.

Would reading aloud help at all do you think? It's really not serious enough to notice much, but now's the time to stop it.

What a letter! Do forgive me old sport, and deal a few kisses round the family not forgetting Sidney & yourself

from your very loving
Elizabeth

~

On 14 March 1929 the Duke and Duchess travelled to Oslo, via Berlin and Sweden, for the wedding of Crown Prince Olav of Norway to Princess Märtha of Sweden.

~

15 March 1929 to Queen Mary

British Embassy
Berlin

My Darling Mama

We arrived in Berlin early this morning, and came straight here to bathe & breakfast. Afterwards, we spent 2½ hours seeing over the Schloss, which was most interesting & rather sad. Especially the Kaiser's own rooms which they showed us, which of course have none of his own furniture left in them. Incidentally, in his dressing room which was filled with paintings & pictures, we found a charming picture of Frederick Duke of York by [John] Hoppner. I coveted it very much!

Then after luncheon here, we went out to Potsdam, & saw Sans Souci & its gardens & the Neues Palais. It is rather sad seeing all places public, but they are in such good order – gleaming furniture etc. I was especially taken with the many little Watteaus at Sans Souci.

Then, just to see a little of modern Germany, we had tea at a tea & dance place in Berlin. It was most amusing. I am writing this before dinner, & then we resume our journey to Oslo later this evening. The Rumbolds* have been most kind, and I have enjoyed my day here, tho' rather a tiring one as we have seen a lot in it!

I hope that Lilibet is well, and I am sure that she is enjoying Bognor very much.

With much love darling Mama,
Ever your loving daughter in law
Elizabeth

~

16 March 1929 to D'Arcy Osborne

Hotel Kramer
Malmö

My dear Mr Osborne,

Do you know where I am? I don't really, & can't find an atlas. We arrived here this morning from Berlin, & found that our train which arrived here at 10 am, did not leave until 9.30 pm. So we came to this hotel and I can't tell you how comfortable it is. Exquisitely clean, with magnificent bathrooms, & excellent food, and if I can ever discover where we are, I think that I shall come back some day.

The Governor of the Province arrived after lunch, & arranged a little sightseeing. Firstly we went to see a castle built in 1540, quite untouched, of delicious little pink bricks. It belongs to an old Baroness who is 70 years old today and we arrived with dozens of other guests all bearing flowers & clicking their heels. A birthday party! & such a deliciously old fashioned atmosphere of compliments and clicks, & tea handed in boiling hot rooms by Rectors of neighbouring Universities. I enjoyed it so much, and they all talked such good English.

Then we went to a town called Lund and looked at a Cathedral etc which was most exhausting.

I cannot think of more of a contrast than you in effete Portugal and me in more than efficient Sweden. So well educated & every cottage with electric light and telephone. We are going to Oslo for a wedding but our train, which started in such a businesslike way from Calais, every second being of importance, has now deteriorated into a

---

* Sir Horace Rumbold (1869–1941), the British Ambassador to Germany, 1928–33, and his wife Etheldred.

kind of Oriental timeless affair, & I feel that we may be days before
we reach our destination. We ought to be at a reception at the
French Embassy there tonight. Instead of which we are sitting in a
spotless room furnished with chairs of a hardness that I cannot
describe. The other 3 members of our party are reading E. Wallace.*
I am writing to you. [. . .]

I am delighted to hear that you are coming home soon, & I hope
also to get home, but I really don't know whether we shall. I feel
quite prepared to take weeks over the return journey. Are you an
unperturbed traveller? I am always very calm and rather annoying, &
I point out things I see out of the window, which is unforgivable.

We must dine soon, my pen rushes along these little lines leaving
sad drivel for you to read I fear.

Yours ever,
Elizabeth

~

21 August 1929 to King George V

Birkhall
Ballater

My dearest Papa

It was so very kind of you to send me that letter by Harry, and I
can't tell you how delighted I was to receive it. I am sure that we are
going to love being here,† in fact I already feel that I have lived here
most of my life. The garden is too lovely, real masses of flowers, and
the burn makes a lovely rushing noise, very soothing at night!

Bertie & I went down to Balmoral on Monday, and the garden is
looking perfect. There are some very good beds of pansies outside the

---

* Richard Horatio Edgar Wallace (1875–1932), prolific English crime writer, playwright and
novelist. He was the co-creator of King Kong and wrote 175 novels and 24 plays, including
The Four Just Men. He was one of the most popular writers of the time.

† Birkhall, a charming house on the Balmoral estate, was acquired by Queen Victoria and
Prince Albert in 1849 for the Prince of Wales (the future King Edward VII). Surrounded by
birch trees, with the River Muick running through the garden, it was a lovely, private spot. In
1856 it was lent to Florence Nightingale when she returned from the Crimea. It was a perfect
family home for the Yorks in the 1930s; in 1947 Princess Elizabeth and Prince Philip used it for
part of their honeymoon, and they lived there in the summer until the death of King George
VI in 1952. It was then enlarged and lent to Queen Elizabeth and, after her death, taken on by
her grandson, the Prince of Wales.

ballroom which are most effective. Everybody is so sad that you &
Mama are not coming up this year,* in fact old Arthur Grant† was
most emphatic that the air would really make you feel well again. But
I must admit that the air, though like wine, is <u>very</u> cold; and there has
been no sun yet. In fact it is colder than I have ever had it when I
stayed at Balmoral, but I expect that it will warm up soon. [. . .]

It is so kind of you to let us come here Papa, and we are so happy
in this heavenly place, and I only wish that you could be up in
Scotland too.

But I am sure that the bracing air of Norfolk will soon make you
feel better. It is too awful to think of the long & dreary time of illness
that you have had, and I <u>do</u> hope that you will soon begin to feel
really well again. [. . .]

Yes, aren't the Wee Frees‡ silly old things, we thought that it was
such a holy little occupation for Sunday!! They are dwindling fast
poor things.

With much love, dearest Papa, ever your
very loving daughter in law
Elizabeth

~

11 November 1929 to Osbert Sitwell

145 Piccadilly

My dear Mr Sitwell,
Thank you so much for sending me your book. It is so kind of
you to have thought of me, and I have enjoyed reading it more than
I can say. I am appalled at the horrible end of Edgar Poe – this seems
a trivial thing to mention, but I had no idea that his death was so
sordid.§ Elections are so horrible, & bring the worst out in everybody,
so perhaps it was an appropriate death. [. . .]

---

* The King was still convalescing after a serious chest infection from which he had nearly
died in 1928.

† Arthur Grant, son of Queen Victoria's stalker, entered royal service as a boy in 1865, and
was head stalker at Balmoral from 1902 until his retirement. He was a great favourite of King
George V, and died in 1937 aged eighty-seven.

‡ The 'Wee Frees', members of the Free Church of Scotland, had criticized the Duke and
Duchess for inspecting an ambulance on a Sunday.

§ Edgar Allan Poe (1809–49), American poet and writer of macabre stories, died at the age

I hope that we may meet again some time, perhaps in the house of your dedicatee* (if there is such a word). If not in her house, I hope that you will visit us here. I am longing to know whether you have

A) Arranged that the Foundling Hospital† become an 18th Century Museum

B) Managed to delay the erection of that menace to good health & good pictures in Battersea. That would indeed be good news, but I fear the worst.‡

With again so many thanks.

I am, yours very sincerely,

Elizabeth R

~

17 November 1929 to D'Arcy Osborne

145 Piccadilly

My dear Mr Osborne,

I have started so many letters to you since August, & each one has died a horrid death by fire or hatred. The reason is this. August and September were so wonderful in Scotland, that one rose eagerly at 8 am and came home at sundown, weary and <u>terribly</u> contented, and letters were almost impossible to write. The sun blazed all day (a Scottish blaze, not your Portuguese haze) and I felt so well at the end of the Autumn that I kept on saying to myself, 'My goodness, how well I feel.'

But I have often thought about you, & wondered whether you will be coming home for leave soon. We shall be delighted to see you when you do come and there will be a great deal to talk about, what

---

of forty in a Baltimore hospital after being found unconscious in a public house that was being used as a polling station. The cause of death was variously ascribed to alcoholism, drugs, rabies, suicide or even murder.

*   Sitwell's new book, *The Man Who Lost Himself*, was dedicated to Margaret Greville, 'in all affection and because she is so constant a friend'.

†   The Foundling Hospital in London, established by Thomas Coram in 1741. It became the first public art gallery, displaying works donated by Hogarth, Gainsborough, Reynolds and others to support the work of the hospital. The present Foundling Museum was created in 1998.

‡   Battersea Power Station, constructed on the south bank of the River Thames between 1929 and 1933.

with one thing and another. It is very foggy, and dark and cold here now, and I am just going off to Naseby* for a few days in the Midlands. [. . .]

Let me see, what news is there.

The Queen of Spain[†] is here and luncheon parties and dinner parties are given for her by all the snobs in London. And she is so extremely nice too, and very brave.

Have you read A High Wind in Jamaica and do you like it? Also The Man Within; the latter irritated me very much at moments.[‡]

The Labour government is spending a lot of money. I have spent too much money.

Thank you so much for your latest letter. I feel very ashamed of my long silence, and fear that this letter will really hardly be worth receiving. I have been doing a lot of stunting lately, but am going to have a blank week now – it is really very boring at times. One wonders how much good it all does. I think that half the good of a long slaving day in Birmingham or Manchester is undone by a few paragraphs in the Daily Sketch or Mirror describing my very frequent new dresses and my alterations to this house. Already this year I have done up my sitting room five times, and the number of dresses trimmed with diamonds would keep ten families going for ten years. It is very annoying isn't it? However, we must take the rough with the smooth & keep the old flag flying. Hooray.

With kindly & Christian thoughts to ALL, I remain yours sincerely, if a trifle sourly, Elizabeth

~

In December 1929 the Duchess realized she was expecting another baby.

~

---

* The Duke and Duchess had rented Naseby Hall in Northamptonshire for two seasons so that the Duke could enjoy the hunting.

[†] Princess Victoria Eugenie of Battenberg (1887–1969), Queen Consort of King Alfonso XIII of Spain and granddaughter of Queen Victoria. In 1931 the Spanish Royal Family was forced into exile when republicans came to power and declared the Second Spanish Republic. Known as 'Queen Ena', she was the grandmother of King Juan Carlos, King of Spain from 1978.

[‡] A High Wind in Jamaica by Richard Hughes, published 1929 to great acclaim. The Man Within, Graham Greene's first novel, also published 1929.

31 December 1929 to Mrs Beevers

St Paul's Walden Bury

Dearest Nannie B

I am writing to ask whether you can come to me in August! [. . .] I <u>do</u> hope that you are not engaged, because then it would be too dreadful. Also Simson* said perhaps it would be better to be ready at the end of July in <u>case</u>.

I have not told a soul yet, because people find out all too soon, and that makes life miserable, so would you please keep it quiet too, as long as you can? I hope to keep it a secret for a good bit yet.

Now, <u>if</u> you are engaged in August, you must ruthlessly chuck the poor woman. No, I don't really mean that, but I <u>do</u> hope that you will be free, as I couldn't bear it if you could not come to me. I do hope that you are well, and that the Weymouth baby† is better. You must have had a terrible time.

 With much love
 Elizabeth
I shall be back in London on Friday.

~

11 February 1930 to Queen Mary

Naseby Hall
Northampton

My Darling Mama

Thank you so very much for your most kind and sympathetic letter. It has been a great blow to us all, as Jock was a very dear brother,‡

---

* Sir Henry Simson (1872–1932), obstetric surgeon at the West London Hospital who had attended the Duchess at the birth of Princess Elizabeth in 1926.

† Thomas Timothy Thynne, second son of Viscount Weymouth, later sixth Marquess of Bath. Born 13 October 1929, died 14 September 1930.

‡ Jock's early death was a great blow, particularly as the youngest two of his four surviving daughters needed special care. (His eldest daughter, Patricia, had died aged eleven months in 1917.) Nerissa (1919–86) and Katherine (born in 1926) inherited a mental condition from which three of their cousins, on their mother's side, also suffered. All five of them were placed in a private care home in the late 1920s. Nerissa and Katherine's mother visited them regularly, but after her death family visits were discouraged by their carers. Lady Mary Clayton, Queen Elizabeth's niece, described the girls as 'lovely children . . . like easily frightened does'.

and we shall miss him so much. He was so clever, and wise too, and one could always depend on the very best of advice if one ever wanted it.

He had been very ill with pneumonia, and on the Wednesday before he died was really much better, & the doctors were very pleased. Then suddenly came another abscess on the lung, and he died on Friday morning, as by then he was too weak to operate. Nobody expected such a thing, and I can hardly believe that it has really happened.

Your letter was so understanding and comforting darling Mama, and I thank you with Papa and yourself from my heart for your sympathy.

With much love,

Always your loving daughter in law

Elizabeth

PS I have just returned here from St Paul's Walden where I went for the funeral.

~

11 March 1930 to D'Arcy Osborne

Naseby Hall

Dear Mr Osborne,

I was so pleased to receive your letter this morning, especially as you can have no idea how deeply depressing every aspect of life has been here, for months, and your letter was so deliciously and refreshingly <u>cheerful</u>.

I am delighted that you are so happy in Rome, and you certainly deserve to be, after your exile in Lisbon.* It all sounds quite perfect, I am sure that one must be surrounded with Beauty to be really happy, and you seem to be wallowing in it (if one may use such an unsuitable expression). I am glad to hear that you have escaped a wild Marchesa up till now, but in your present state of mind I much fear that shortly I shall hear rumours of an ENTANGLEMENT.

This morning I had two letters of interest. One from yourself, and

* In December 1929 D'Arcy Osborne had been transferred to Rome as Counsellor of Embassy, from Lisbon where he had been en poste since 1928.

one from Mr Thornton Wilder* sending me his last book 'The Woman of Andros'. In his letter he writes, 'This one was to have been, alas, a book in praise of Christianity. It was to have shown the frustration of some finer pagan minds, and their wistfulness, as they groped by intuition towards the handful of maxims that was soon to modify home-life, education, the theory of the state, and most of all, man's courage in regard to himself,' and several more pages.

How <u>can</u> one answer letters like that? I love authors sending one their books, but how difficult to thank them. Please <u>never</u> write a book. What <u>can</u> one say? Dear Mr Wilder, Thank you so much for your most delightful book. How interesting the story of the frustration of those pagan minds and their wistfulness as they groped by intuition towards the handful of maxims etc etc –

Do you not dislike intensely the word wistful? I do. At least, I have never thought about it before, but having written it twice on this page, I now loathe it with a great loathing.

I think that next year we must come to Rome incognito, and enjoy ourselves. I am sure that it must be very bad to stay too long in this country, and think only of Lord Beaverbrook,† and parrot disease, and debts (one's own) and the kitchenmaids going, and whether one should offer up a prayer for the Boiled Bishops of Russia.

I hope that you will get your apartment on the top of a palazzo. It sounds perfect in every way – in fact most delectable.

The toffee that you kindly sent Elizabeth is very much appreciated, and the second tin is now being eaten. It was very nice of you to remember, tho' I fear that there was not much chance of your forgetting after such a very pointed question!

Yes it was terrible about Jock, and I can't tell you how much we all miss him in the family. Though sometimes he was sarcastic & a little difficult to please, he was intensely affectionate, and a <u>really</u> good friend. If I needed good advice, I always asked Jock, because though it might not be as palatable as one could wish, it was always

---

* Thornton Wilder (1897–1975), American writer. In 1927 *The Bridge of San Luis Rey* won the Pulitzer Prize and was subsequently named by the American Modern Library as one of the hundred best novels of the twentieth century.

† Max Aitken, first Baron Beaverbrook PC ONB (1879–1964), controversial Canadian–British newspaper magnate and politician. A friend of Churchill, Beaverbrook was appointed Minister for Air Production and, later, Minister of Supply during the Second World War, roles in which he excelled.

right. He had a very strong sense of duty you remember & very high ideals, so advice from him was difficult to take but <u>right</u>.

I don't really think that he ever contemplated dying at all, and am certain that if he had, he would have gone to St Paul's Walden where he wished to be buried, and I think that as usual the doctors were much too late in finding out that he had pneumonia, and then could do nothing. Poor Fenella was absolutely broken up, you know she nursed him for nearly two months at Glamis, and that brings people very close together. I am sure that none of the male parts of my family ought to live in London. They all adore the soil, and Jock was really only happy in the country. It kills people in the end if they are parted from the land. It's too strong a thing to understand. But one cannot regret for <u>him</u> anyway, and I for one, have got a lot of delightful things to remember about him, which is lucky.

I must not ramble on any longer this is already a most disconnected letter.

The hunting is nearly over, and we return to London in April. I hope that you will continue to be happy & contented in Rome.

With much wistfulness,

Ever yours sincerely,

Elizabeth

~

14 April 1930 to Queen Mary

145 Piccadilly

My Darling Mama

We are so looking forward to coming to Windsor on Thursday, and we will arrive in time for tea, and bringing Lilibet with us.

I do hope that you will forgive my clothes, which I fear are not at all suitable to Windsor, but dressing properly in the evening is becoming difficult, and so please forgive any great shortcomings!

I have had to cancel three old engagements in May & June, so have had to say that I am not doing any more things this summer, which will come out in the papers I suppose. It is a bore, but there was no way out of it, and we thought that the simplest way was to make this short announcement. My <u>instinct</u> is to hide away in a corner when in this condition, which I know is silly, but I suppose it is a feeling handed down from many generations back. I should really like to live quietly in the country for the last few months, and then reappear afterwards as if nothing had happened! [. . .]

With much love darling Mama,

Ever your loving daughter in law

Elizabeth

~

Thursday undated [June 1930] to Lady Helen Graham

St Paul's Walden

My dearest Nellie,

There is nothing to return to London for, and I strongly advise you to stay away as long as possible! It is too lovely here, and the sun is really hot, & one can be out all day long.

I used to take such joys for granted not so very long ago, but I suppose the approach of middle age makes one appreciate weather much more, and I do love sitting out in the sun. The smells in the evening are marvellous. Last night it was honeysuckle & very sweet new mown hay – it went to my head and made me feel slightly intoxicated. [. . .]

Yours affec, E

~

31 July 1930 to Queen Mary

Glamis Castle

My Darling Mama

I am so delighted to have the miniature of Bertie, and I thank you a thousand times for sending it. I have so few relics of his childhood, and so am very pleased to have this charming miniature.

I do hope that you are not having horrible weather at Cowes, though it sounds as if all the South of England is windy & wet. Here it has rained a great deal the last week or so, after several months of complete dryness.

The last three weeks seem to have lasted for three months at least, and I am longing for the whole business to be over – the waiting gets on one's nerves rather, & I find myself becoming slightly irritable I fear! Sir Henry Simson is hovering anxiously about, and the more he hovers the slower it all seems! The next time, I shall make every effort to have a child in London during the winter, as it is much more agreeable for both of us I think, as when one is in the country one misses all the lovely flowers and cadeaux for the baby, & little excitements like that!!

I must thank you once more darling Mama for sending me the miniature – I really am so enchanted to have it.

With all my love to Papa & to yourself,

I am, always your loving daughter in law

Elizabeth

~

5 August 1930 to Queen Mary

Glamis Castle

My Darling Mama,

I cannot tell you how enchanted I am with the lovely little clock which arrived on my birthday. It is exactly what I love, and it fits so beautifully with my gilt dressing table things. Thank you so very very much. I am so pleased to have it, and it was so kind of you to send me yet another present.

I am so sorry to hear that you have had such stormy weather, and I do hope that by now it has improved, as it makes everything so miserable.

Mr Clynes* has arrived today to stay with kind Lady Airlie who is having him to stay. There are two doctors here, and why they are all so very previous I don't know, as I certainly do not expect anything to happen before the 10th. I suppose that I shall be given all sorts of horrid drinks, so as not to keep these foolish people waiting. I wish that Mr Clynes had waited until he was sent for, but he would not do that, and here they all are waiting & hovering like vultures! I shall be glad when they are gone.

---

* John Robert Clynes (1869–1949), trade union leader; Home Secretary, 1929–31. There was a convention that the Home Secretary should be present at the birth of a child in the direct royal succession to see that no substitution took place. King George VI thought the practice archaic and subsequently abolished it.

The little clock is such a joy, and I do think that it was kind of you darling Mama –

With much love, ever your loving daughter in law

Elizabeth

~

The Duchess's second daughter, Princess Margaret Rose, was born at Glamis on 21 August 1930.

~

27 August 1930 to Queen Mary

Glamis Castle

My Darling Mama

Thank you so very much for the two sweet little boxes, and for your most angelic letter of congratulation. I adore the boxes, and hope that I shall be ordered a pill to take after meals, and I shall keep it in the smallest box & flaunt it about! It <u>was</u> kind of you to think of my love of cadeaux, and I never expected to get any up here. I am feeling so much better than last time, and I expect that a recovery in the good Scotch air will be much more pleasant than one in London. The baby is nice & round & neat I am glad to say. I do hope you will be pleased with her. I am very anxious to call her Ann Margaret, as I think that Ann of York sounds pretty, & Elizabeth & Ann go so well together. I wonder what you think? Lots of people have suggested Margaret, but it has no family links really on either side, & besides she will always be getting mixed up with Margaret the nurserymaid.

It was such a wonderful surprise seeing Bertie yesterday, because I was missing him <u>terribly</u>. I am so glad though that he is having a change with you for a bit, as it is always a very trying time for husbands, and he will be all the better for his visit to Balmoral I am sure.

The papers have been so vulgar and stupid as usual, that it made it all the worse for him, and it is all a nerve-racking business at the best.

I am thrilled to hear that there is a suggestion that you may both come here soon – (I don't even dare write the day!) and I shall look forward so <u>very</u> much to seeing you, my first visitors.

With all my love and a million thanks for the boxes,
Ever darling Mama, your very loving daughter in law
Elizabeth

~

Undated [27 August 1930] to the Duke of York

Glamis Castle

My Darling Sweet

I must write you one line just to say how much I loved seeing you yesterday, and how much I miss you now. I do hope that everything is settling down at Balmoral, and that the Monarchical temper is improved. I wrote to Mama today, & I suggested Ann – I hope that they will be tactful about it.

Simson came back this morning to bring me a trout, & to say that he proposes coming here on <u>Friday</u> evening at about 6 to send out the last bulletin. Apparently the daily (& more decent papers) are terribly anxious that the Sunday press should not get it, & I rather agree that it would be better to have it out on Saturday. Do you? But don't trouble to return or anything, as there is nothing to say, and he only wanted you to know. I did not like to tell him that you were not returning until Sat. and perhaps he is better off out of the way!!

Goodbye Angel. P.T.O.

This is my last piece of paper, & am not supposed to be writing another letter!! A great many kisses, & I hope that Thursday & Friday will pass quickly.

Your <u>very</u> loving E

~

6 September 1930 to Queen Mary

Glamis Castle

My Darling Mama

I am sending you up Lilibet, and I must confess that I shall miss her very cheerful companionship very much. But I am sure that she will enjoy her visit enormously, and Bertie will bring her back next Saturday, which is a comfort, as I am always terrified of her travelling by road nowadays. I have asked that I might have a telephone message of safe arrival. This sounds like a fussy mother, but I do think that car travelling is dangerous!

I hope that you had a pleasant visit to May, and managed to do all that you wanted to do in Edinburgh. And I wonder so much whether you found any exciting things in the Curiosity shops?

Bertie & I have decided now to call our little daughter 'Margaret Rose', instead of M. Ann as Papa does not like Ann. I hope that you will like it. I think that it is very pretty together.

I am getting on well, and am having massage which is helping my flabby muscles back wonderfully. I expect that next week I shall start getting up, and that I always think is a bad moment, as one feels so weak out of bed.

I see that the Braemar Gathering* is next week. What a joy! If Lilibet asks to go too, which she is quite likely to do, I do hope that you won't take her Mama, as she is really much too little for that sort of thing, and would get very weary standing about in the pavilion.

I shall miss not seeing lovely Balmoral this year, and we often talk of the happy time we spent at Birkhall last autumn.

With much love darling Mama,

Ever your loving daughter in law

Elizabeth

PS Lilibet is unfortunately not <u>very</u> good on a long car journey now, but with plenty of air is fairly all right.

~

9 September 1930 to the Duke of York

Glamis Castle

My Darling Sweet

Thank you so very much for your letter which I was <u>so</u> pleased to get. I am delighted to think that you were politely received – quite right too, and don't you stand any rudeness. I am writing this sitting in a chair by the window, and the sun is shining on me! Isn't that grand? It's such a lovely day, I do wish you were here duckie. I have thought of a lovely way to exercise you when you get back.

---

* One of the most famous of the annual Games in the Highlands. Queen Victoria became the first royal patron of the Gathering in 1849 and the Royal Family has attended regularly since then.

And that is lugging me round the garden in a bath chair. Now what do you think of that? It is one o'clock, and I have had a very busy morning as usual, and this is my first opportunity of writing, so I thought I would continue sitting-up & writing to you. [. . .]

I shall long for Saturday. [. . .]

I had a very sweet and sugary letter from Mama, and I am glad that they realise what a sacrifice it is sending Lilibet away. The sun has now gone in and it's rather cold! I loved Lilibet's letter and please give her the enclosed from Margaret Rose – she held the pencil for the kisses specially for Lilibet. Will you give it to her & tell her this? Also do read her my letter.

Well darling, I will write again soon, and I do hope that your week will be pleasant. I miss you horribly, and get very bored at moments.

Kiss Lil for me, and a great many for yourself darling,

from your very loving Elizabeth

~

10 September 1930 to the Most Rev. Cosmo Lang, Archbishop of Canterbury

Glamis Castle

My dear Archbishop,

Thank you so very much for your most charming letter of congratulation. It was very kind of you to write, and I was so delighted to hear from you.

Daughter No. 2 is really very nice, and I am glad to say that she has got large blue eyes and a will of iron, which is all the equipment that a lady needs! And as long as she can disguise her will, & use her eyes, then all will be well.

I do hope that if you can find time you will christen her for us later on in London? I couldn't bear to have a child not christened by you, and we shall be so grateful if you will do this.

I was very disappointed as I was longing to ask you to stop here during your Scottish 'tour', & christen her in the Chapel here, but that idea was most firmly stamped on by Lord Stamfordham,* who assured

---

* Arthur John Bigge, first Baron Stamfordham (1849–1931), Private Secretary to Queen Victoria and to King George V. According to the *Dictionary of National Biography*, he 'showed

us that it was quite impossible for you to do this. I had no idea that the two Churches were so far apart, and I thought that not only would it have been delightful for me, but that it would have given pleasure in Scotland. However, this raised a storm in the vicinity of Balmoral and the King practically told me that you would be appalled at the very idea, so I regretfully said goodbye to that nice peaceful plan!

It is such a long time since I have seen you, but I know that my mother has asked you if you can stop here for a meal on your way from here to there, so that if you come I do hope that you will pay me a visit. It would indeed be a pleasure for me.

I shall think of you motoring to Dunecht & other beauty spots this week, & wish that I was there, to talk, but not to drive, for I hate long shut drives – don't you?

With many thanks for your kind letter, I am,

Yours very sincerely

Elizabeth

~

Friday undated [12 September 1930] to the Duke of York

Glamis Castle

My Darling Sweet

I do feel so sorry for you with all this disgusting weather – it must be so dull, & such a waste not being able to go out stalking or anything. I should absolutely refuse to go all the way to London for a banquet. I should say that you can't go dashing up & down, and we might be going south early I suppose. It all depends when I finish with the baby, and anyway I think it sounds about the most unnecessary thing that I've ever heard of! Well, you can always write & say that you can't go.

Isn't Oct 30th a bit late for the christening – the baby will be 10 weeks old, and still a pagan. But we can talk it over when we meet, as Papa & Mama need not be there. In fact it would be much nicer to have it whilst they are away at Sandringham. I am so looking forward to tomorrow, & mind you come down the Elbow in second, or whatever it is! I hope Lilibet won't be sick again.

---

persistent industry, tact, wisdom, sure grasp of affairs, and unswerving rectitude and impartiality, bearing delicate responsibilities with sagacity and resourcefulness'.

It's cold & damp still – ugh – I now drink Maggie's beer for lunch, it makes me feel very heavy in the head, but it does me good too.

Margaret Rose put on 8oz this week. Isn't that grand? [. . .]

Lots of love darling, from your very very loving

Elizabeth

~

1 October 1930 to Lady Helen Graham

Glamis

My dearest Nellie,

This seems quite passable in a twaddly way.* [. . .] The only thing that she [Beryl Poignand] might take out is a remark at the bottom of page 7 to the effect that I may one day rule this country. That is just too much, and she can easily omit the words, 'she may one day rule as Queen'. It always irritates me, this assumption that the Prince of Wales will not marry – he is quite young and it is rude to him in a way too. Otherwise it is all quite innocent. [. . .]

With much love,

Elizabeth

~

24 October 1930 to Lady Strathmore

145 Piccadilly

My Darling Sweet,

I can't tell you how miserable I was at having to leave Glamis. It was so delicious being there with you darling, and I can never never thank you enough for all your angelicness to me & Bertie & Lilibet & the baby. [. . .]

It is horrible getting back to London, and Lilibet at once got a very bad cold. [. . .]

The only good thing is that baby is very well, and has put on 8½ oz this week. She is so merry. It must be horrid not having any noisy little creature tramping in for 'just five minutes with Granny'.

---

* The Duchess had given Beryl Poignand permission to write a short book about Princess Elizabeth, to be published by John Murray. Beryl wrote under her pseudonym Anne Ring.

[. . .] I think you <u>must</u> come down darling & meet David. I think that after all you do for Father he should certainly pay your journey down.

I wish that I could pop up to Glamis, as I am sure you must be feeling rather dull after such a busy Autumn.

Goodbye darling, I really don't know what we would all do without you,

From your <u>very</u> loving
Elizabeth

~

17 December 1930 to Dr Varley

145 Piccadilly

Dear Doctor Varley

I am writing to ask you whether you would mind if Doctor Weir* came to see the leg whilst you are dressing it this evening.[†] My husband is a very nervy person (which I expect you have noticed), & he has great faith in his little homeopathic powders, & Dr Weir is a homeopathic doctor. My husband is so afraid of not keeping fit, and if you don't mind, I really believe that the <u>idea</u> even of these little doses will make him feel more cheerful! It is not the leg that worries him, it is his fitness. It seems almost a religion nowadays does it not? And if you have no objection to Dr Weir seeing the leg, then he can swallow his little powders down.

I am quite ignorant about etiquette, and I hope that it is alright suggesting this? Dr Weir is an old friend of my husband's, but he has not asked him to come in yet before asking you. If it is alright, my husband thought that he might look on whilst you are looking at the leg, and then he can swallow down his powders with joy.

I am, yours very sincerely, Elizabeth

~

---

* Sir John Weir (1879–1971), homeopathic doctor, physician to many members of the Royal Family. The Duchess later became convinced by homeopathy herself. After Sir John Weir's death Dr Marjorie Blackie and then Dr Anita Davies treated her with homeopathic remedies.

† The Duke of York had been kicked in the leg while out hunting.

26 January 1931 to Queen Mary

Thornby Grange*
Northampton

My Darling Mama

It is too kind of you to send me the 3 pretty little dresses for the baby, and I think the work is very good. I will certainly give them some work, and will start by giving them a dress of Lilibet's to copy. [. . .]

I had to leave the children behind in London as the baby had a very bad cold & cough, and then Alah & Bobo† had it – (a sort of flu) & so all our plans were upset, and I am now hoping very much to get them here this week.

I hope that you have been having nice sunny days at Sandringham – Lilibet & I miss our evening 'hops' very much, & often wish that we were marching or polka-ing in the ballroom with you.

The Government seem to be in rather a precarious position over the Trades Disputes Bill, but it looks as if those horrid Liberals are going to keep them in all the same. I wonder if there has ever been a more stupid & spendthrift Government than this one.‡

I wonder when you are going to visit the British Industries Fair this year? It opens about Feb. 16th I believe.

With much love darling Mama, & so many thanks for the little dresses –

Ever your loving daughter in law
Elizabeth

~

---

* The last of the houses the Duke and Duchess rented so that the Duke could hunt with the Pytchley. They took Thornby Grange from January to April 1931. In November that year the Duke sold his horses; the country was facing economic hardship, and the King had decided to reduce the Civil List by £50,000.

† Margaret 'Bobo' McDonald (1904–93), long-time nurse to the children in the Royal Family, principally to Princess Elizabeth, whose dresser she later became and to whom she remained close all her life.

‡ In early 1931 Ramsay MacDonald was Labour Prime Minister, leading a minority government. By August 1931 it was clear that this administration could no longer deal with the financial crisis of the Great Depression which was engulfing the world. Encouraged by King George V, MacDonald formed a 'National Government' with the Liberals and Conservatives, but most of his Labour colleagues refused to serve. In October 1931 the National Government secured an overwhelming electoral victory. MacDonald remained Prime Minister till the election of 1935 when the Conservatives returned to power.

16 March 1931 to Mrs Beevers

Thornby Grange

Dearest Nannie B

Thank you simply a thousand times for the darling little jumper for Lilibet – it fits her beautifully, and she thinks that the 'Brownies' are too lovely.

I do think that it is kind of you to think of her, especially when you have been having this horrible flu – I do hope that you are really feeling better – I wish that I had known a little sooner & you might have come down here for a few days' change. The air is wonderfully bracing, you ought to see the two children! Lilibet is so full of spirits, & as for Margaret Rose – she is simply bounding with energy. I am longing for you to see her again.

We shall be returning to London some time in April I think.

Such a lovely little jumper has arrived for the baby – please do thank your kind cousin very very much – she makes such perfect ones. And blue suits the baby so well – when she has her bonnet on with blue ribbons her eyes look like the blue sea.

With much love dearest Nannie B & many thanks.

Yours affect.

Elizabeth

~

20 March 1931 to Duff Cooper

Thornby Grange

My dear Mr Duff Cooper*

I feel that I must write and congratulate you on your most excellent victory over Lords Rothermere† & Beaverbrook.

---

*   Alfred Duff Cooper, first Viscount Norwich GCMG DSO PC (1890–1954). Known as Duff Cooper, he was a British Conservative politician, diplomat and author. Secretary of State for War, 1935–7; First Lord of the Admiralty, 1937–8; British Ambassador to France, 1944–7; an exuberant connoisseur of fine words, wine and women. In a March 1931 by-election he stood against Sir Ernest Petter, the Empire Free Trade candidate who was supported by Lords Rothermere and Beaverbrook. Duff Cooper's wife, Lady Diana, was one of the most beautiful women of the time, an accomplished writer and a vivid personality.

†   Harold Harmsworth, first Viscount Rothermere (1868–1940), newspaper proprietor and founder, with his brother, Lord Northcliffe, of the *Daily Mail*.

After what you told me at Lady Astor's party, I have taken a violent interest in your campaign, and was so very pleased at your courage in taking on St George's.

I dispatched a busload of servants up to London to vote for you – each clutching their Daily Mail, and the middle page of the Daily Telegraph thrust into their unwilling hands by myself!

I subsequently ascertained that they voted for you en masse.

Please do not trouble yourself to acknowledge this short letter, it is only to tell you how pleased I am at your victory.

I hope that Lady Diana and yourself are not too exhausted.

I received my papers and longed to use my vote, and also was furious to receive a communication from old Petter.

I placed it as obviously as possible in the waste paper basket.

I am,

Yours very sincerely,

Elizabeth

~

19 June 1931 to the Hon. Richard Molyneux*

Windsor Castle

To the Windsor Wets.†

Fellow Soakers!

I have received with gratification the invitation to become Patroness of your exclusive Club. It is with pride and pleasure that I accept this responsible position, and if the occasion arises, you may rest assured that your Patroness will be with you to the last glass. And so, from half pint to Jeroboam, let us go forward together, always

---

* Major Hon. Richard Molyneux (1873–1954), son of fourth Earl of Sefton, groom in waiting to King George V, c. 1919–36, and extra equerry to Queen Mary, 1936–53. He was appointed KCVO in 1935 and he became one of the Duchess of York's closest friends.

† A secret group created by the Duchess and a few like-minded friends at Court who enjoyed a glass of wine. 'Aqua vitae, non aqua pura' was their motto. She later said of the Wets, 'the great thing was, that being a SECRET SOCIETY we had to have a secret sign, & this was, to raise the glass to other members without being seen by the dis-approvers! It was a silly, but most enjoyable underground movement, & we laughed a lot. The only lady members were myself (Founder) and Magdalen Eldon, who was not only beautiful, but witty and loved by everyone, & Mary Beaufort.' (RA QEQM/OUT/MOLYNEUX/140)

remembering our watchword – 'Aqua Vitae <u>NON</u> aqua pura'. With kind regards and many hiccoughs,

I remain,

Yours in thirst, Elizabeth

~

24 July 1931 to King George V

145 Piccadilly

My dearest Papa,

Here is the cigarette box that I got for you in Paris. I thought that it might do to use in the yacht, and is of rather modern French workmanship. In case you do not notice the design, the little silver things are yachts floating across the lid! [. . .]

With much love, dearest Papa,

ever your very affectionate daughter-in-law

Elizabeth

~

3 August 1931 to D'Arcy Osborne

145 Piccadilly

My dear D'Arcy,

Thank you so very much for your letter from on board the Cunard RMS Aquitania.* I feel slightly abandoned at addressing you in this very familiar fashion, but dash it all, I have known you now for about twelve years, and as you are one of my few friends, I think that I may venture? Eh? You seemed to think that it was quite OK when I broached the subject at Ciro's, so I hope that it's all right. I quite agree with you that we did not discuss things half enough when you were here – I like to thrash every subject out – and next time you MUST take your leave in the winter when life is more peaceful and there is plenty of time for argument and tattle.

I do want to know one thing. Did your mind veer at all towards matrimony? I wondered so much one evening, and hoped that you rather liked a certain fair and intelligent young lady. Excuse an old pal

---

* D'Arcy Osborne had just been appointed Envoy Extraordinary and Minister Plenipotentiary at Washington DC.

butting in, but I would love to see you happy and affianced.
However, these things are nobody's business, and I daresay it never
entered your head. You know, I have <u>very</u> few friends, and there are
very few people that I write to like this – so you don't mind do you?
I don't mean that there are not a lot of people who I don't love
dearly, but I have only a mere half dozen of intimates, so you must
put up with this kind of letter.

Paris was great fun in the end, and Lord Tyrrell* I found
charming and quite without a soul. Everything seemed to go quite
well, and the French were most polite, and we exchanged
compliments and kissed hands without ceasing for four days. Old
[Marshal] Lyautey† was a dear old boy and rather liked me – he
<u>thought</u> he liked me, but he really liked my hats, which had sweeping
feathers & reminded him of his gay young days.‡

Tomorrow we go to Glamis. I long for Scotland, as we have had
a very busy summer & somehow I feel more connected and older this
year. I don't know how to describe it quite, but I am beginning to
feel that I am 'the good old Duchess' rather – I suppose the younger
generation has got used to me. I can't quite tell you what it is,
because I don't know myself, but I expect you can guess. You usually
know what I mean!

Goodbye for the moment,
Yours ever,
Elizabeth

~

* William George Tyrrell, first Baron Tyrrell GCB GCMG KCVO PC (1866–1947), diplomat,
Ambassador in Paris 1928–34; he was a firm Francophile, spoke fluent German and distrusted
the Nazis from the start.

† Louis Hubert Gonzalve Lyautey (1854–1934), French army general and from 1921 Marshal
of France. On the outbreak of the First World War he said, 'a war among Europeans is a Civil
War, it is the most monumental folly the world has ever committed.'

‡ The Duke and Duchess went to Paris 17–22 July to visit the Colonial Exhibition. The
French saw in it a renewal of Edward VII's Entente Cordiale.

16 September 1931 to Queen Mary

145 Piccadilly

My Darling Mama

Having just returned from our inspection of Royal Lodge,* I hasten to write and tell you our impressions. We thought it the most delightful place, & the garden quite enchanting, also the little wood. Of course, the bedroom accommodation is <u>very</u> limited for us with our large nursery, but I think that we can manage quite well if Bertie makes one of the 'reception' rooms on the ground floor into his dressing room. That means putting in a bathroom, but I think that would be quite easy. It would be wonderful for the children, and I am sure that they would be very happy there.

Most of the carpets & beds etc belong to Mrs Fether – but we have got one or two beds over, & I daresay that we can manage.

Everybody seems very depressed here, and very troubled about the future. [. . .]

My father is thinking of shutting up Glamis, which would be very sad, but I fear that the new super tax makes it almost inevitable.

I really feel rather worried about everything Mama. The world is in such a bad way, & we seem to be going from bad to worse here too. Everybody is hard hit by the new taxation, & everybody is feeling very unhappy!

To change to lighter subjects. We <u>did</u> so enjoy our time at Balmoral, and we both felt much better after our visit. The air is so bracing, & one got away from the usual melancholy conversation of 'how can one economize'!

With much love darling Mama, & I will write directly we have worked out the cost of Royal Lodge,

Ever your loving daughter in law
Elizabeth

~

---

* The Royal Lodge in Windsor Great Park had been the country home of King George IV. In 1931 the King offered it to the Yorks. Queen Elizabeth later recalled to Eric Anderson, 'we borrowed the money to build our little bit on. I think King George V was very strict about those sort of things. He wouldn't have thought it right to help.' The house remained a much-loved family home. Queen Elizabeth died there on 30 March 2002.

Undated [January 1932] to D'Arcy Osborne

Sandringham
[Written on two Post Office Telegraph forms]

This is not by any means the first letter that I have started to you during the last three months, but somehow it has been impossible to write you a letter of any kind. Somehow everything has been crumbling around one, & the written word is so hopelessly inadequate, I have <u>so</u> much to say!

I wish that you could be back & come & see me & talk & talk & talk. Last time somehow we didn't talk quite enough, and there were many things that I wanted to discuss. I have so enjoyed your letters & cuttings. Please go on. America thrills me & I love hearing about it from you.

Please forgive my writing in pencil, but I am in bed with influenza for the second time since Jan 1st, and now today I am feeling better, & somehow, in bed, ordinary writing paper seems so silly, so the telegraph forms just suit.

I read Shakespeare all yesterday. Hamlet – every word, & Twelfth Night & the Rape of Lucrece & some sonnets. He does get some lovely sounds – it is like music, <u>&</u> the drama – <u>&</u> the everything! I have suddenly begun to love him. In fact, I am only just beginning to know what I like, which is a sign of great age, & it is very exciting indeed.

I wrote you a long letter at the end of July, which I found in my despatch case the other day – I must show it to you some time, because I wrote in a fever of anxiety & ignorance, & it is rather odd & unhinged to read now.

Our visit to Paris was most amusing last summer – we never went to bed until 4.30, and we managed, God knows how, to return compliment for compliment & made many French friends. I thought that the Embassy seemed in rather a bad way – too much petty feeling & plotting. When are you coming home again?

This country seems to have settled down to being poor, & everybody is quite cheerful, but only because it is inevitable to change one's circumstances. I find a tremendous change in the last year – everything more simple, it is quite fashionable to be sentimental, you may like music – weaker cocktails, less food & a slight very slender streak of patriotism starting again. Rather shamefaced it is, but there, to be encouraged.

I spent most of Oct. Nov. & Dec. in London, and went out a lot – no parties, but little tiny dinners & cinemas & then back to somebody's house to talk – Oh yes – I forgot to tell you that conversation is becoming the fashion. Isn't it fun – conversation & beer & eggs instead of Embassy & champagne & twitter.

My hand is aching, & I am certain that you won't be able to read this scribble. You are one of my few real friends, and so I must allow myself the luxury of a Lodore* of words – how pleasant to have friends. Have you made any new or delightful ones in the U.S.? I quite agree, I should <u>love</u> a trip there, but only with a <u>very</u> good press agent, and also, how awful if they loathed one. It would be ghastly to be loathed in America, my Scottish blood would congeal.

Have you heard of Noël Coward's play Cavalcade?† It is marvellous, I think, as a Pageant & very moving.

Have you got pleasant people at the Embassy?

I <u>do</u> hope that your money troubles won't become too severe – it must be horribly difficult now, & I do feel for you.

I hope you got the photograph alright.

I <u>adored</u> that magazine you sent – Ballyhoo – & laughed a lot, & <u>do</u> send any more funny things that you can.

Hoping to have a few words with you before too long.

Yours ever

Elizabeth

~

30 April 1932 to Mrs Beevers

145 Piccadilly

Dearest Nannie B

Thank you a thousand times for the two scarves & for the telegram on Lilibet's birthday. She was so pleased, and so was I, and it was kind of you to think of us both. You must come & have a cup

---

* The Lodore Falls are situated at the southern end of Derwentwater in Cumbria. The waterfall was popular with Victorian visitors staying in nearby Keswick. Robert Southey (1774–1843) wrote an onomatopoeic poem about it in 1820 called 'The Cataract of Lodore'.

† Cavalcade had opened at the Theatre Royal, Drury Lane, in 1931. It was a magnificent variety show which evoked the patriotic and progressive values of the Victorian era. It was also a remarkable piece of stagecraft – a cast of 400 people was brought up on to the stage on six hydraulic lifts.

of tea & see the children. Do let me know when you are free – they come back today from Windsor, & any time would suit me – either tea time or after. Of course Margaret Rose sleeps in the morning – she is too wicked for words & most amusing.

I am longing to see you again, it is such ages since I last saw you, so do just let me know when you are free to come round.

With love,

Yours affect.

Elizabeth

~

14 June 1932 to the Hon. Richard Molyneux

[Telegram to Major Molyneux, Windsor Castle]

CLUB EXPECTS ITS SOLE REPRESENTATIVE TO DO HIS DUTY AND LIVE UP TO THE MOTTO. PATRONESS

~

5 August 1932 to King George V

145 Piccadilly

My dearest Papa

I am writing to thank you so very much for the most beautiful screen that you & Mama have given us. I cannot tell you how delighted I am to have such a really wonderful present, and it will look quite perfect at the Royal Lodge. I am so very grateful, and do thank you a thousand times for your great kindness.

I am beginning to feel pretty aged, & today I found TWO GREY HAIRS!! I suppose one must expect this at 32, or shall I pay a visit to my hairdresser, & come out a platinum blonde!

I do hope that the weather has improved for you, and I was so pleased to see that you had won some races. I felt very sad to think that I had missed some good racing, and last week I lay in bed thinking of Cowes & what I was missing. I do hope that you have enjoyed it, & that it has been a rest from the cares of these troubled times. It must be very rare for you to get away completely dearest Papa. You & Mama have always been so wonderful to me, and it has made such a difference in every way. I was very young & ignorant of the world when I married, & had no idea at all of what I would be plunged into – the pitfalls were many; but Bertie was so good, & you

& Mama so kind & forgiving of my mistakes that I shall always feel
very grateful to you for your understanding & affection. It means so
much to me, & it has helped me tremendously. I do hope that you
don't mind me saying this – it somehow just came as I wrote.

    With much love dearest Papa,

    Ever your loving daughter in law Elizabeth

~

10 October 1932 to D'Arcy Osborne

Birkhall

My dear D'Arcy,

    First of all, I must tell you that Scotland just around this house, is
looking too lovely & beautiful for words of mine to describe. The
birches are golden & silver, the river is an angry black & blue, every
other tree is scarlet & yellow, & I feel very satisfied every time that
I look out of my window. It really is delicious to be able to see so
much beauty, & I find it most helpful & calming.

    This little house is enchanting. It is very small, & lined with
caricatures of the 90s, with extremely comfortable & ugly beds of the
late Victorian era, & is badly lit with neo-Edwardian oil lamps, with
an ever present smell. I am so happy here. In fact I am certain that
I am a most simple creature and am most ill suited to my present
calling. I inherit a hermit complex from my Lyon family side, & the
older I get, the more exclusive I feel. Do you understand? I wish you
could be here more, because you are one of the very few people that
I can talk to. There are only about 3 people who I can be intimate
with, & I never see them, so I therefore never talk about myself. I
daresay that this is a very good thing.

    I was so interested in your letter of August 22nd, & I thank you for
it. I am deep in some volumes of a magazine of 1832 just now, & am
very comforted to read that almost all our problems now, were just as
vital then. The Tories were more Die-hard then, than even your
Republican party in the USA, & the Banks needed reorganising, so did
the Post Office, & Trade was dead, & in fact everything was much the
same a hundred years ago, as will be a hundred years hence.

    [The end of this letter is missing.]

~

30 November and 20 December 1932 to D'Arcy Osborne

145 Piccadilly

My dear D'Arcy,

First of all, I thank you very much for sending me your intensely interesting Memorandum to read. Please may I file it with my secret & confidential papers, because it is so thrilling to re-read, & it has given me a feeling of superiority when I meet Americans. It was kind of you to remember to send it, & I am most grateful.

Of course, you know, I have a weakness for nice Americans. I met an old man last night, a lawyer called Post, & I have made a date with him to dine with a dining club belonging to Harvard, & I am to receive from them, some candlesticks with the Bowes arms on them (when I visit the US). Weak, I suppose, but still, what fun!

I hate writing to you, because you are one of the few people that I can <u>talk</u> to, & as I cannot make my pen keep pace with my thoughts, I hope that you will forgive an unintelligible scribble.

I am feeling very thwarted at this moment. There is so much to be done in this country, things that I could easily do, but a combination of Press & Precedent make it impossible. And I am quite sure that it is not only useless, but almost dangerous to flout convention. Curse it!

I had a delicious two months in Scotland this autumn, & I am now feeling distinctly mellow & oh so full of conversation.

When are you returning? I did not talk to you half as much as I wanted to last summer but I was tired, & not myself, through that tiredness. Could you not return before high summer next year, when I have still a little zest left?

Trade seems to be looking up a little in this country, but the shipyards & steel works seem to be dead. I cannot think what we can do with our middle-aged unemployed. Perhaps the young men will now get employment, but I cannot see how the older men can ever work again. It is a tragedy, & unless the land can absorb some work & unless some women will give up their jobs, I fear that a lot of them will be workless all their lives.

Women can be idle quite happily – they can spend <u>hours</u> trying their hair in new ways, & making last year's black coat, into this year's jumper, & all this on 3 cups of tea and some buns. But a man must be seriously busy, & eat meat. Therefore, I think it a crime for women to take jobs that men can do as well. I am writing very wildly I am afraid, and could go on for ever with this chitchat, but will spare you. [. . .]

This piece of paper takes, in ink, my wishes for everything of the best for you in 1933.

Yours
Elizabeth

~

D'Arcy Osborne replied, somewhat tongue in cheek, on 26 January, 'I am sorry to hear that you are suffering from a frustration complex over unemployment & other national affairs. Perhaps one day you will be able to take things in hand and order the women of the country from the plough and the counting house to their proper place, the home . . . Anyway the winning of the vote symbolised the right to technological and other equality. And I don't think you'd ever get women to go back to dy[e]ing their hair and their jumpers and living on tea and buns . . .'*

~

20 February 1933 to Lady Helen Graham

145 Piccadilly

Dearest Nellie,

I wrote in such a hurry last night, that I quite forgot to thank you for all the trouble you took over the famous speech, which was really the reason for my writing to you.

It was so kind & <u>exactly</u> what I wanted. In fact 'the trying time is the time to try' has become quite famous – a leader in the Daily Telegraph, & many earnest salesmen & manufacturers repeating the phrase with sobs of emotion in their very British (or rather Lancashire) throats when I went round the Fair today.

I cannot thank you enough, & if you will write me more good speeches, I will take lessons in delivery & tour the country for Toc H.†

Yours affec Elizabeth

~

---

*   RA QEQM/PRIV/PAL/OSBORNE.

†   Toc H was founded in Belgium in 1915 by the Rev. Tubby Clayton as a place in which soldiers on the Ypres Front could find solace from battle and pray. After the war, Clayton

Monday 31 July 1933 to Lady Strathmore

HMY *Victoria & Albert**

My Darling Angel

Thank you so very much for your letter which I loved. Bertie & I have been here a week, & are returning to London today, & I shall hope to see you on Saturday morning.

I have been out three days racing in the 'Britannia', & it is the greatest fun in the world. You would love it darling, and I now feel most marvellously well! It is a most delightful way of spending a day, & the weather has been lovely too. Everybody is as old as the hills, but they all behave as if they were seventeen!

I am so looking forward to Saturday, & Lilibet is getting very excited too, and of course Margaret Rose is also excited!

Well darling, I must fly, so goodbye for the moment
from your very very loving
Elizabeth
PS I also thought May was looking so young & pretty.

~

1 August 1933 to Queen Mary

The Royal Lodge
The Great Park
Windsor

My Darling Mama

I was so sad at having to leave the Yacht yesterday after such a very delightful week, and I cannot tell you how much I enjoyed everything. It was all such fun, and I loved every moment of my visit.

---

expanded Toc H into an international movement of Christian fellowship; its aims were Friendship, Service, Fairmindedness and Love of God. The Duchess had become committed to Clayton and to Toc H, and she remained so all her life. On 18 February 1933 she made a speech about unemployment at the annual festival of the Toc H League of Women Helpers in the Kingsway Hall.

* Royal cruising yacht, launched in 1901. *Britannia* was the King's racing yacht. She was scuttled after his death in 1936 in accordance with his wishes.

It was so intensely interesting to see Osborne,* after having heard & read so much about it, and I was thrilled with all I saw. Thank you so very much for showing me so many interesting and amusing things on that most delightful Sunday expedition.

I was really miserable at having to leave yesterday, but I feel a different person after such an invigorating week, and am so grateful to you & Papa for all your kindness & thought for us.

We came down here today for two days' planning for the garden next autumn, and find the whole place quite dried up & yellow from lack of rain.

It must be great fun having Mary at Cowes, and I wish so much that I had not missed her – we never seem to hit off the same party nowadays & she is one of the most elusive people to meet that can be imagined!

I saw Lord Ebbisham this morning, and the new arrangement of the School of Needlework seems quite satisfactory. The only bother is, that after 15 years the College of Technology takes over the whole building and we have to find new accommodation; but of course we have plenty of time to discuss this, and probably it will be better to have a smaller building nowadays. I was pleased to hear that the shop that I suggested & started has proved a success, & I hope that it will long continue to be one.

When I was at Cowes with you, Papa one day mentioned to me that he had heard that a certain person† had been at the Fort‡ when Bertie & I had been there, & he said that he had a very good mind to speak to David about it. I never had a chance to reopen the subject, but I do hope that he won't do this, as I am sure that David would never forgive us for being drawn into anything like that. I do hope

---

* Osborne House, Isle of Wight, designed by Prince Albert in the style of an Italian Renaissance palazzo as a summer retreat for his family, was completed in 1851. Queen Victoria loved the house and died there in 1901.

† The Duchess was referring to Wallis Simpson, with whom the Prince of Wales had recently become infatuated. Queen Mary replied on 20 August: 'Darling Elizabeth, I am so sorry I quite forgot to answer yr letter to me to Cowes. Of course Papa never said a word to D. about Belvedere so all is well for I agree with you that it wld never do to start a quarrel, but I confess I hope it will not occur again for you ought not to meet D's lady in his own house, that is too much of a bad thing!!!' (RA QEQM/PRIV/RF)

‡ Fort Belvedere, a Georgian folly at the southern end of Windsor Great Park. It was the Prince of Wales's favourite home.

that you do not mind my mentioning this Mama, but relations are already a little difficult when naughty ladies are brought in, and up to now we have not met 'the lady' at all, & I would like to remain quite outside the whole affair. It really is very difficult sometimes, and I am sure that you & Papa can appreciate the difficulties of the position. I trust that you will forgive me for mentioning the subject, but I know that it would only make things more uncomfortable if David thought that I had been brought into it all. I would have said this to you at Cowes if I had had a chance, but there was always someone else present!

With again all my grateful and loving thanks darling Mama for all your kindness and sympathy which I appreciate more than I can <u>ever</u> say,

Ever your loving daughter in law
Elizabeth

~

24 October 1933 to Lady Strathmore

The Royal Lodge

My Darling Sweet

I have been wondering so much as to how you are feeling, and I do hope that you are <u>really</u> keeping quiet darling, as I am sure that is the only way to get stronger. You must have had more of a shock than you realized after your fall, and with that horrid bronchitis on top, please <u>please</u> do be careful and rest. Don't dream of going to Chapel for instance! And no more work parties! May would adore to do some for you I know, so do make her – it would give her such pleasure.

We came down here on Saturday, and Lilibet at once developed a bad cold. She had started Margaret's, and had a temperature, so is now looking rather white. It so often happens that they come back so well from the country, and at once catch something!

Darling, we did so <u>adore</u> our last week at Glamis. It was all so heavenly, and great fun having all the family once again. If only you hadn't been ill.

I do hope that Mikie was able to stay with you after Rosie had gone.

I have ordered my lilies. [. . .] I do so badly want some gardening advice. When you come South duckie, I do hope you will have time to

pop down & give me some. Do let me know how you are <u>truthfully</u>, as
I long to know.

   We go back to London tomorrow.

   Well darling, goodbye for the moment, and do take great care
from your very very loving
Elizabeth
Are you buzzing about in the Chair? Or is it too much for you?

~

Undated [1930–6] to the Duke of York

Hints to Bertie in case of anything happening to me.
   1. Be very careful not to ridicule your children or laugh at them.
      When they say funny things it is usually quite innocent, and if
      they are silly or 'show off' they should be quietly stopped, &
      told why afterwards if people are there.
   2. Always try & talk very quietly to children. Never shout or
      frighten them, as otherwise you lose their delightful trust in you.
   3. Remember how your father, by shouting at you, & making you
      feel uncomfortable lost all your real affection. None of his sons
      are his friends, because he is not understanding & helpful to
      them.

~

12 January 1934 to the Most Rev. Cosmo Lang, Archbishop of Canterbury

Sandringham

My dear Archbishop
   It was so very kind of you to write me such a charming letter for
Xmas, and I was indeed delighted to receive it. I love to have your
Benediction for ourselves & for our children for the coming year.
I hope that it will be a happier one for many people in this land,
and their happiness will certainly make us happier. One cannot help
worrying over the misery & hardship suffered by so many good people,
and their courage in facing hardship is the thing that I admire most in
them. It is a great example to all of us luxurious minded creatures – not
<u>you</u>, but us, I mean! Everything seems to be so much better
everywhere.

With every possible good wish for 1934, & with again so many thanks for your kind thought of us at Xmas.

I am

Yours always affec:

Elizabeth

~

31 January 1934 to Duff Cooper

145 Piccadilly

Dear Mr Duff Cooper

It was so kind of you to send me the essays of Max Beerbohm,* and I have read 'King George the Fourth' with great enjoyment, and much satisfaction. I read everything that I can lay hands on which has anything to say about that attractive old naughty, & it was a joy to realise that Mr Beerbohm was a cordial admirer of 'a swaying figure & a wine-red face.'

Thank you so very much.

Also I would wish to thank you for giving us supper after that most charming disappointment of a play that we saw last week.

I could have talked so much, but perhaps the E . . . . . y† is not an encouraging place for anything but light conversation! The little house in Windsor Park that we live in now, was the last 'favoured residence' of George IV, and although it was practically demolished by Queen Adelaide after old Naughty died, we still have one deliciously Gothic & expensive room left – the last one built by order of G.IV.

With again my grateful thanks for the Book.

I am, Yours very sincerely,

Elizabeth

~

---

* Sir Henry Maximilian Beerbohm (1872–1956), prolific English essayist, caricaturist and novelist. A man of extraordinary talent, Beerbohm is best remembered for his novel *Zuleika Dobson* (1911) and for his witty cartoons.

† 'The Embassy', one of the smartest nightclubs in London. The popular band leader, Bert Ambrose, played there through much of the 1920s.

28 July 1934 to D'Arcy Osborne

The Royal Lodge

My dear D'Arcy,

It is so sad that you were not able to come here this summer for your reunions, and all your friends have missed you sadly. It is the first time for many years that I have failed to mix you a White Lady, and I do hope that you will soon be with us again.

Don't come until October, because we shall all be out of London – though of course you could come & stay with us which would be nice, because then we could talk & talk – & talk.

London has been very gay these past few months – many balls every night, and a few very grand & much appreciated affairs.

The fact that people enjoy a 'show' once again is a very good sign I think, and tiaras are worn almost as a matter of course! A few years ago people were embarrassed and unhappy if they glimpsed a diamond or ate quails in company, which was a shame and a stupid feeling really – as it had no relation to one's misery at the poverty and sadness of the people of this country. And yet I suppose on second thoughts that this was the right feeling, & is perhaps one of the reasons for our triumph as the only civilised country in Europe today.

There was a lovely ball at Syon given by the Duchess of Northumberland. The house was floodlit & the garden looked quite perfect, & exactly like a Canaletto of London, with exquisite little figures strolling in front of an eighteenth century house. It was delicious to watch.

The opera went well, & the Russian Ballet is having a great success in Covent Garden. I do wish that you were here, because I would so like to go with you. I have been several times and it is beautifully done. I know that you would like it.

How is America? The only news lately has been of Dillinger* – all the papers (except the Times) had huge pictures of his dead body which filled all stolid Englishmen with horror, and today

---

* John Dillinger (1903–34), infamous American outlaw, shot in Chicago while trying to escape arrest on 22 July.

huge pictures of poor little Dollfuss* lying in state – that was a
tragedy.

I have been wishing to write to you for many moons and
because I cannot put pen to paper does not mean that I don't think
of you often & with affection. I have been very busy this last 3
months, and am looking forward to going to Scotland in about 10
days' time.

Next week I am going to Cowes to race with the King, which I
rather enjoy – I like the feel of yacht racing – it is very exciting and
very peaceful. No noise, except the creak of the sails & the water
rushing by – and a glow of health after a few days at sea!!

I must go, & do tell me when you are coming home again,

Yours very sincerely,

Elizabeth

~

The Duchess was a lover of the arts, especially ballet, giving her
support to the Camargo Society for the Production of Ballet from the
early 1930s. She would later tell Eric Anderson that *'going way back
I did see Pavlova.*† *I suppose I must have been nine or ten and luckily my
mother thought it was a good thing to go. And she was doing the Swan, I
think, and Karsavina.*‡ *I remember it so vividly, you know. This wonderfully
graceful little creature.'*

~

6 August 1934 to King George V

145 Piccadilly

My dearest Papa

I do so want to thank you for my perfect few days with you in
the Yacht. I enjoyed myself very much <u>indeed</u> last year, and this year

---

* Engelbert Dollfuss (1892–1934), Austrian Federal Chancellor and opponent of Hitler who
tried to keep Austria independent; he was assassinated by Austrian Nazis on 25 July.

† Anna Pavlova (1881–1931), Russian ballerina, one of the greatest dancers of the time. She is
best known for *The Dying Swan*, a solo created for her by Fokine.

‡ Tamara Karsavina (1885–1978), leading ballerina of Sergey Diaghilev's Ballets Russes. She
came to London in 1918 and, in 1920, helped to found the Royal Academy of Dancing.

I was just as happy. In fact it was all quite blissful, and I am so grateful to you for having me to stay and for giving me such a wonderful few days.

I was so sad that it was only possible to race one day, but I enjoyed that day madly, and was thrilled to hear of your marvellous win on my birthday. I only wish that I could have been there; I expect that I would have blown up with excitement! It is very odd, but nothing in the whole year gives me such pleasure as my few days at Cowes. I feel quite different, & so happy. Of course the fact of sailing is enough to explain this effect on me. The excitement, & the wonderful peace of a day in the Britannia – no noise, but the creaking of the sails, & the cooing voice of Sir Philip [Hunloke],* softly inviting the crew to Lee-o! And there is something so exhilarating about the elements, the sea & the wind & the sun, and one feels far away from the horrors of modern civilization with its noise and eternal hurry.

I had a very good passage to Portsmouth in the destroyer, & was chaperoned most beautifully by the Commander-in-Chief, who placed me in my train in a very successful manner.

London was too horrible, & I kept on thinking of you sailing in Britannia with deep envy.

I can never thank you enough dearest Papa for all your angelic goodness to me – & also I must send my grateful thanks for my lovely birthday presents. I am indeed a lucky creature.

With all my love, and 1000 thanks for my heavenly week at Cowes,

I am, dearest Papa,
Always your loving & dutiful daughter-in-law
Elizabeth

~

---

* Philip Hunloke (1868–1947), British yachtsman who competed in the 1908 Summer Olympics, held in London. He was Sailing Master to King George V and was regarded as one of the twentieth century's greatest helmsmen.

18 August 1934 to the Hon. Richard Molyneux

PRIVATE AND STRICTLY CONFIDENTIAL IF THAT IS
POSSIBLE FOR DICK
Gannochy*
Edzell
CLUB BUSINESS

My dear Dick
    As Treasurer of the Windsor Wets I think that you should know
that I have decided to make Lady [Magdalen] Eldon (spouse of our
valued Secretary) an honorary Lady Member of the Club. And no
interference from you please. It's quite time that I took the reins again
I can see.
    Well, aqua vitae non aqua pura still holds good, & I hope that
you will have a good week here & will live up to the motto of the
Club. Elizabeth (Patroness)

~

23 February 1935 to Duff Cooper

145 Piccadilly

Dear Mr Duff Cooper
    Thank you so very much for remembering to send me Mr
Belloc's† most touching 'Ballade of Illegal Ornaments' – The right
feeling of anger is in it, and it made me want to cry when I read it
this morning. What a good poet he is – it is wonderful to be able to

---

*   Shooting lodge owned by the Dalhousies. The Elphinstones ran it for the American banker
J. P. Morgan, who was the shooting tenant for many years. In 1929, the year of the Wall
Street Crash, the one telephone box in Edzell was said to have had a queue of his American
guests trying to call their brokers to see if they had any money left.

†   Joseph Hilaire Belloc (1875–1953), yachtsman, prolific poet, satirist and author, whose
devout Catholicism informed much of his work. He wrote this Ballade in indignation at a
report that an Anglican bishop had ordered a priest in his diocese to remove from his church
'all illegal ornaments, and especially a Female Figure with a Child'. The affecting poem ends:

> Prince Jesus in mine Agony,
> Permit me, broken and defiled,
> Through blurred and glazing eyes to see
> A female Figure with a Child.

know the fundamental things, and to be able to write about them so beautifully.

I have copied it, and so return to you the copy you kindly sent me, with my grateful thanks and a tear or two.

Yours v. sincerely

Elizabeth

~

1 April 1935 to Clare Vyner

The Royal Lodge

My dear Clare,

How nice of you to write and thank for dinner. It was angelic of you & Doris to come. [. . .]

I have been so worked up by your wonderful scheme for settling unemployed, that I have written to our friend the riveter in Sunderland & offered him a job here with us.* The man with children. I do think that it's up to people like us who can afford to dine at a restaurant & go to a night club to try & employ as many as we can. Oh dear – it makes one furious & despairing that one can't do more. Anyway, nobody has done more than you, and it is a real bright spot in life that you have done such a good work. I do hope that I shall be able to see your settlement soon. I would like to very much. [. . .]

If I ever meet a rich man, I am going to tactfully bring up the subject of the one good amateur scheme that I know – or perhaps not 'amateur' but non-government – most important. [. . .]

Goodbye and many thanks for your letter.

Yours,

E

~

---

* Ernest Pearce, the wounded soldier from the Durham Light Infantry whom she had met at Glamis in 1915. Clare Vyner had created a scheme whereby families of unemployed people from Tyneside were given an acre and a half on which to build a bungalow and a smallholding. A new community quickly grew up of former industrial workers, shipyard craftsmen and clerks.

27 June 1935 to Duff Cooper

145 Piccadilly

Dear Mr Duff Cooper

Forgive me please, for having been so long in writing to thank you for the most enchanting books that I have ever read, but I wished so much to have read a little before attempting to convey my gratitude to you in words.

And having now finished the first volume, I feel incapable of expressing what I feel – if <u>only</u> I could write you a little poem, 'as the wings of the dove beat softly in the air, so is my heart stirred by your offering' is lame – but indeed my heart is grateful and I do thank you for giving me such real pleasure.

I have been very busy lately, and unable to read much, but the first volume of the 'Tale of Genji'* is a joy, and I am now in the middle of the second book. It has been an eye-opener to me – the simplicity & beauty of Murasaki's language is wonderful. 'Her construction is in fact classical; elegance, symmetry, restraint' says the Introduction to 'The Sacred Tree,' and I am so pleased to think that I can look forward to four more volumes. Thank you a thousand times for such a lovely present.

Yours very sincerely,
Elizabeth

~

5 August 1935 to Queen Mary

The Royal Lodge

Darling Mama

We were both so sad at leaving yesterday, and I hadn't enjoyed myself so much since last Cowes! The whole week is such a perfect rest in every way, and I do so love sailing in the Britannia. Thank you a thousand times for all your kindness and angelicness – I adore being with you always, and this last week was perfect. It is such a complete change to get away from telephones, letters, & the eternal questions

---

* Japanese classic of the eleventh century, sometimes called the world's first novel, by 'Lady Murasaki'.

that ruin one's life in one's own home, and I feel ten times better than when we left London last Tuesday.

We got back here at 5 o'clock which made a very easy journey – left Portsmouth at 3.25, & got home in good time for tea, and found the children waiting with their presents, & little bouquets of flowers that they had picked themselves. They are looking so well after their week here – London is very trying towards the end of July, & they were looking rather white when I left last Tuesday.

Bertie & I are taking on a man from Sunderland in Durham to work in the wood & garden, & he arrived here this evening. He is a most excellent type of superior artisan, & he has been out of work for <u>seven</u> years. It is such a tragedy, & his gratitude is touching. We felt that it would be a useful act, & this man is an ex-soldier who was badly wounded in the arm – I wish that one could do more for the poor things.

Margaret Rose came up to me today, & after looking at me very affectionately, & giving me a sweet kiss said, 'Mummy darling, I really do believe that I love Papa much more than I do you'! I felt very small!

It was delicious seeing Mary Beaufort* for a minute yesterday, she is an angel & I wish that we met more often. This house is singing with mosquitoes and I am rather glad to be leaving tomorrow as the biting insects are very bad.

I must stop this letter, as I fear I am boring you with tittle-tattle.

Thank you again darling Mama for such a divine week, ever your devoted daughter in law

Elizabeth

~

---

* Duchess of Beaufort, née Lady Mary Cambridge, Queen Mary's niece, married to tenth Duke of Beaufort.

1 October 1935 to Duff Cooper

Birkhall

Dear Mr Duff Cooper

It was so kind of you to send me 'Haig',* and to write in it for me. I have been reading it with great interest and delight, and I think that it is very clever of you to make it so fascinating. It must have been a great work, and I cannot imagine how you did it in such a short time.

The few critics have been quite idiotic in writing about the book. Their only cry being 'why is it not more sensational,' which is too foolish to even speak about. The only people I have seen up here who have read it, are the King & one or two tough Scottish Majors & Captains (ex), & they are all enthusiastic. Being sane because they do not live too much in cities they are grateful to you for giving a true picture of Haig, & for writing a very difficult book so brilliantly. I do hope that you are pleased with its reception & great success. Are you calm about it, or are you a cauldron, seething and boiling?

I hope that you will forgive me for not writing before, but I wished to read anyway part of the book before sending you my grateful thanks for your kindness in sending it to me. I was so pleased to have it before it came out in the shops.

The Archbishop of Canterbury came to luncheon with me here, and instead of the comfortable heart to hearter that I had been looking forward to after luncheon, he pounced on your book with a cry of joy, & then there was silence only punctuated by 'ah those were the days' (he was at Oxford with Haig) & 'dear old so & so' & other old-time remarks – not at all the sort of thing that had been expected by his lonely and forgotten hostess.

I am still reading 'Genji' with great enjoyment, & lent the first volume to the local Minister here who gobbled it up and asked for more! I shall always be grateful to you for having given me so much pleasure with Talleyrand, Genji & Haig. What a nice party they would make.

'The desolate autumn hurries through the fields apace, to nodding

---

* Duff Cooper had just published the first volume of his biography of Field Marshal Douglas Haig, first Earl Haig, Commander of the British Expeditionary Force, 1915–18. This followed his life of the French statesman and diplomat Talleyrand (1754–1838), published in 1932.

flowers the wind's cold breath betrays' and soon we must leave this peaceful place & return to London. It is so lovely now, the birches are turning from silver to gold, the air is cold & the sun shines, so that I am sorry to go.

I hope that you have had a peaceful & happy time, & are feeling well.

With again my very grateful thanks.

I am, Yours very sincerely,

Elizabeth

~

The Duchess of York had another severe bout of influenza over Christmas 1935. She had to remain in bed at The Royal Lodge while her husband and daughters went to Sandringham for the Royal Family's traditional celebration. It was King George V's last Christmas.

~

29 December 1935 to Princess Elizabeth

The Royal Lodge

My Darling Lilibet

It seems such a long time since I last saw you and Margaret, and I do hope that I shall be allowed to get up in a day or two, and then I shall soon be with you.

I hope that you are having a lovely time at Sandringham, and being very polite to everybody. Mind you answer very nicely when you are asked questions, even though they may be silly ones!

Do you manage to practise the piano a little bit?

Dookie* is very well, and sends his love & a big lick. [. . .]

I have got a very nice Nurse, and she gives me a good wash every day in bed. I haven't been so clean for years! Please give Alah my love, I hope that she is being good. Give Margaret some GREAT BIG KISSES from me, and a great many to your darling self.

Goodbye angel, from your very loving Mummy

~

---

* The first in a long line of corgis cherished by the family.

29 December 1935 to the Hon. Sir Richard Molyneux

The Royal Lodge

My dear Dick

Thank you so much for your letter. I am so glad that you missed us at Xmas, tho' I daresay you all managed to be pretty gay & pretty tight all right. I say, what do you think of CHAMPAGNE stripes on a CLARET ground for the Club Tie?

Have you had to wear your long snow boots yet?

I am much better, but the doctor told me this morning that I can't get up just yet. It is too sickening, but apparently I've had that old fashioned flu that has pneumonia with it, and it's very slow to get rid of. I expect that when I <u>am</u> well again I shall be <u>VERY</u> well. Oh Boy. Well, be good if you can, which I doubt, and I should stay away from Abyssinia if I were you just for a bit. I know it's very tempting, but make it one of your New Year resolutions & <u>stick</u> to it. I couldn't give you better advice – remember what happened last time.

A very happy New Year to you from your suffering President Elizabeth.

PS Is it true that you have been sold with the house in Charles Street? Rather cunning of you Dick.

~

30 December 1935 to King George V

The Royal Lodge

My dearest Papa

I was so delighted to receive your lovely Xmas card this morning, with your kind message inside. It is quite the most charming card that I have seen, and will be a wonderful souvenir of that never-to-be-forgotten day in Westminster Hall. I thought it almost the most moving ceremony of the many Jubilee celebrations – in fact, it <u>was</u> the most moving, and I am so glad to have such a nice picture of a wonderful moment.*

---

* King George V celebrated his Silver Jubilee in 1935. He and Queen Mary were greatly touched by the enthusiasm shown by the people of Britain. The King said, 'I had no idea they felt like that about me . . . I am beginning to think they must really like me for myself.' (Harold Nicolson, *King George V: His Life and Reign*, Pan Books, 1967, p. 669)

I do hope that you are having better weather at Sandringham than we are here. It has <u>poured</u> with rain all today again, and last night there was a noise like a terrific crash of thunder, which turned out to be one of the best beeches falling down. It has spoilt another good beech, & I expect it is the heavy rain after a long drought which had loosened the roots. So sad to lose good trees.

I am feeling so much better the last two or three days, and it is sickening how slowly this lung business is 'clearing up'. I believe it is always very slow. I am longing to come & get well at Sandringham. I feel that the good bracing air will work wonders, and soon make me well. One gets so weak in bed, but I shall have some massage in a few days to try & coax some muscles to work!

I do hope that you have kept well, and are able to get some shooting. I am so glad that the children are being good. I am pining to see them again. [. . .]

Have you heard what the Abyssinian soldier said about Mussolini? 'He is my enema, the Douche'. Blackie* will appreciate that!

With so many thanks again for the card, and much love dearest Papa

from your very loving and
dutiful daughter in law
Elizabeth
PS May I wish you a very happy & peaceful New Year.

~

3 January 1936 to Princess Elizabeth

The Royal Lodge

My Darling Lilibet

Thank you so much for your darling letter. It made me laugh very much the idea of having to go upstairs whilst the water rushed about downstairs.

Fancy Dookie's disgust if he had to <u>paddle</u> to the door to go out! And how would Annie clean the carpet with her roaring machine under water! And Ainslie would have to swim round the dining room

---

*   Sister Catherine Black, of the London Hospital, had looked after the King since 1928.

offering food, and Papa & I would have to have a boat to go round the garden. Mr Stone & Cripps would have to wade about in the Chapel splash, splosh. & how would Owen exercise the horses! I think that it would be easier to build an ark like old Noah, and live in it until the rain stops! However luckily it has not rained today, so I hope the poor people in Windsor will be happier.

It is three weeks tomorrow since I went to bed. Isn't it a long time – much too long I think. But I am feeling much better today, my cough has practically gone, so I hope that the doctor will let me get up. After being in bed so long, one's legs feel a bit wibbly wobbly, so I shall have to get them strong.

Well my darling, I hope that you are quite happy & that your cold is gone. Give Alah & Margaret a kiss.

Goodbye my Angel from your
very loving Mummy

~

10 January 1936 to D'Arcy Osborne

The Royal Lodge

My dear D'Arcy,

It was kind of you to send me two such FUNNY books for Xmas, and I have enjoyed them both enormously. Thank you very much for thinking of such a nice present, I am extremely grateful. They arrived just at the right moment, when I was beginning to come back to life after having pneumonia. I never thought that I would be really ill. I suppose that is the optimism that one is born with! But it's really very pleasant, nothing matters; people, things, food & drink don't exist, in fact one becomes a NOTHING.

The only unpleasant thing is returning to Life & feelings. However, even that is made bearable when kind friends send one amusing books.

What do you think of everything? All that Sam Hoare & Laval & Baldwin business* was going on when I had a very high temperature.

---

* The Hoare–Laval Pact was a secret plan devised in December 1935 by the British Foreign Secretary Sir Samuel Hoare and the French Prime Minister Pierre Laval. It envisaged the partition of Abyssinia, making the major part of the country an Italian colony. The scheme

Consequently I am not sure whether it all really happened or not.
[. . .]

I have spoken to Mrs Greville on the telephone who, I may say,
takes the gravest view of everything. 'I can't tell you on the telephone
but Austen* told me' etc. I believe somebody heard her speaking of
her 'dear little brown shirts'.†

I have been in bed for a whole month, & the last week or so I
have been able suddenly to think clearly (for me) instead of being in a
fog. It is very interesting. Especially about people. One <u>realises</u> them if
you know what I mean. Silly people, who one forgave for being silly
& probably rather cruel because one liked them, become what they
are – cowardly, futile & unhappy. And nice dull people become
valuable, & one's real friends turn to gold, and become more
important than anything else in the world.

At the end of November we went to Paris for a St Andrew's Day
Scottish Dinner, & were worked very hard. We lunched with the
President,‡ when I sat between the old boy & Laval, who was very
pleasant of course, & a huge dinner party at the Embassy &
Reception, & French people at odd hours, M. Pietri§ twice running for
dinner, and an enormous man who said that he was Herriot's¶ chief
man, who practically sank to his knees beside me, & gurgled 'If <u>only</u>
we had people like you both in France' etc etc whilst I pretended that
it was quite O.K. to have a Huge Frenchman with a Légion
d'Honneur in his buttonhole kneeling violently beside one. They
don't mean a word they say, but they <u>are</u> so nice, & so nasty. I like

---

was partly intended to conciliate Mussolini in the hope of persuading him not to ally Italy
with Germany. But when news of it leaked, there was outrage and the British government
dissociated itself from the Pact; both Hoare and Laval had to resign.

* Sir Austen Chamberlain KG (1863–1937), British statesman, politician, winner of the Nobel
Peace Prize (1925). Having been in favour of appeasing Germany in the 1920s, in 1934 he
joined Winston Churchill in calling for British rearmament.

† Mrs Greville had been to Nuremberg in 1934 and met Hitler briefly at her own request.

‡ Albert LeBrun (1871–1950), President of the Third Republic, 1932–40.

§ François Pietri (1882–1966), French Naval Minister until 1936. He was later French
Ambassador to Spain under the Vichy regime, 1940–4.

¶ Edouard Herriot (1872–1957), three times Prime Minister of France between 1924 and 1932.
In the Second World War he refused to support Pétain; he was arrested and later deported to
Germany. In 1945 he was elected President of the National Assembly, a post which he held
until he retired in 1954.

their sense of humour – it's so delicious, & yet, how can one trust them? They are so unsentimental when it comes to politics & horribly straight seeing. What do you think of them?

I have been wondering what you are going to do about moving to Rome.* It all seems so unnecessary. I have always hated the League of Nations† – do you think that they will be stronger or weaker after this business? Do tell me what you think.

I gather that America is determined to keep out of any European trouble, before anything else. One can be sympathetic with that, but is the British Empire exactly an European country? It's all very complicated, and I am sure that you must be tired with this disjointed letter. Half the blame for its stupidity I put on this Fountain Pen that I am trying to write with. Only the most boring words come from its horrid nib, and I have the greatest difficulty stopping it writing words like 'dainty' and 'afternoon tea'. So you see I am labouring under a disadvantage.

Thank you so much again for the books
From
Yours gratefully
Elizabeth

~

18 January 1936 to Queen Mary

The Royal Lodge

My Darling Mama

I must send you one little line to tell you that I am thinking & praying for you & Papa all the time. I cannot think of anything else, my life has been so bound up with yours the last twelve years, and I cannot bear to think of your anxiety. I feel so cut off & far away from you here, & I do hope that you will let me come down to

---

* D'Arcy Osborne had recently been appointed Envoy Extraordinary and Minister Plenipotentiary to the Holy See, where he would remain throughout the Second World War.

† The League of Nations was created after the First World War to try to ensure that future wars would be prevented by collective security. It proved incapable of averting aggression by the fascist dictators in the 1930s; the outbreak of the Second World War in 1939 demonstrated the extent of its failure. It was replaced by the United Nations in 1945.

Sandringham if I can be of <u>any</u> use, I would like to. I won't write any
more darling Mama, but send all my love & devotion.

    Your very loving

    Elizabeth

    Please do not dream of an answer

~

King George V was growing weaker every day. The Duchess of York
was still recuperating from influenza at The Royal Lodge and was
unable to join the rest of the family around the King's bedside. He died
on the night of 20 January and his son David, Prince of Wales, became
King, taking the name Edward VIII.

~

11 March 1936 to Queen Mary

Compton Place,
Eastbourne

Darling Mama

    We have been here a week now, and so far have had very mixed
weather.

    Yesterday was divine, and in the morning we went down to the
little 'chalet' on the beach, and the sun was heavenly. The people
were rather a bore, and though they stared quite politely, they <u>stared</u>
& <u>STARED</u>. I do think it is such bad manners, especially in the type
of rather prosperous middle class people that they were! However, we
shall try again on the next fine day. In the afternoon we went to
Cooden Beach, & the children enjoyed themselves enormously. I am
feeling <u>so</u> much better, and feel sure that a fortnight or so more will
put me quite right.

    I do hope that you are feeling well, and not feeling the reaction
from all that terrible time too much. I find that from my own point
of view one misses Papa more & more, and I cannot imagine what it
must mean to you, darling Mama. You have been so wonderful all
this time, but the strain must have been terrific.

    Also I feel that the Family, as a family, will now revolve round
you. Thank God we have all got you as a central point, because
without that point it might easily disintegrate. And a united family is
the strongest thing in the world, & so important, don't you think?

Also it provides a check on all those little jealousies and backbitings that occur even in the best regulated of families!

This house, for me, is full of memories of you & Papa, & when we went to the nice service on Sunday, it was almost too much for Bertie & I.

With much love darling Mama, ever your loving daughter in law Elizabeth

~

3 August 1936 to Duff Cooper

The Royal Lodge

Dear Mr Duff Cooper

I write to thank you most gratefully for so kindly sending me the copy of your speech in Paris. I have read it again, & most cordially agree that in no part of it did you say anything that could have raised ire. In fact it's a dashed good speech.

Also, permit me to thank you for the translations of the three Japanese poems. They are so romantic & exquisite. I am sending you (this sounds so grand) a pair of porcelain vases!

But wait. They are only a couple of inches high, & were painted in the 18th century. The translation of the verse is as follows –

'The blossoms tipping the branches
of the trees flourish in the splendour,
And even the lower creation
makes virtue its chief concern.'

It's a rather disappointing little poem, but I thought that I would like to send you a little nothing with a verse, & these vases were the only suitable means of conveying my gratitude for having introduced to me so charming a person as Prince Genji.

Could you not arrange to accept into the Army men who are not quite fit, & <u>make</u> them fit? Say 'C' men, & after 6 months they will be 'B' men.

It seems such a pity nowadays that men who wish to join the Army should not have the chance through the horrible system under which they live. I mean the 'keep unfit' system so prevalent in our towns & villages nowadays.

Oh do.

I have just returned from some days spent in Durham,

Northumberland & Yorks. We went to Jarrow, which I regret very much, as it really made me unhappy. I always dread going up to Tyneside, because I admire the people there with all my heart, & it darkens my thoughts for months afterwards, to know how desperate they are. Thank God that they can still feel desperate, as they have not yet given way to that dreadful apathy that seems to follow on prolonged unemployment.

I went to see Palmers Shipyard,* Jarrow's sole means of employment – a horrible scene of desolation, & then out through the streets – driving through large crowds of emaciated, ragged, unhappy & <u>undaunted</u> people, who gave us a wonderful reception. It made me weep – their courage is so high. I hope that you do not think that I am carried away by just a glimpse of the tragedy up in the North. I often think about it all, it seems terrible that such good material should be wasted.

It is <u>such</u> a pity that the Trades Union officials etc are so foolishly anti-military – it would solve the problem of these young boys – if they would join the Army.

I did not mean to write at such length, but got carried away!

I really only wished to thank you very much for the speech, & to say that we shall hope to see you in the winter.

I am, Yours sincerely
Elizabeth

~

---

* The closure of Palmer's Shipyard in 1935 devastated the north-eastern town of Jarrow. In October 1936, some 200 Jarrow men marched 300 miles to London to bring their plight, and that of other industrial workers all across the north, to the attention of Parliament and people.

In his response to the Duchess of 14 August 1936, Duff Cooper (who was now Secretary of State for War) wrote, 'your suggestion that we should enlist recruits who are not quite fit with a view to improving them shall be acted on at once – and I will, if I may, keep you informed of the results. Do you remember what Maurepas used to say to Marie Antoinette? "Madam if what you desire is possible it is done – if it is impossible it shall be done."' He referred to a new scheme to give unemployed young people six months' military training to see if army life suited them. 'Myself I am convinced that no healthy young man who knew what life in the Army is like could possibly prefer the miserable existence on the dole.' Duff Cooper's views were close to those of the Duchess. She was increasingly worried about unemployment and since childhood she had admired the armed services. (RA QEQM/PRIV/PAL)

27 August 1936 to Lady Strathmore

Birkhall

My Darling Angel

[. . .]

We were <u>so</u> sad at leaving Glamis on Sunday, I always feel the same every year, but was so glad that you were feeling a little better darling. It was such bad luck getting ill again, and I would have been very unhappy to have left you feeling miserable & ill. <u>Do</u> promise not to do a little too much when you feel well! And <u>please</u> don't go to Chapel. I am sure that Father won't mind, because he really did get worried about you.

It has been <u>too</u> lovely up here the last three days, and yesterday was boiling on the hill. Where Bertie is shooting the views are too marvellous for words. You see over the Dee valley, and the hills are spread out for miles & miles, I do wish that you could see them.

Lilibet enjoys coming out very much, as you can imagine!

The garden is really looking lovely. I <u>do</u> wish that you could come up very soon & see it. The phloxes are perfect, and in great huge masses, and everything seems to have done well.

Do you remember you gave me some seed of a blue Columbine? It is very well & strong here, & I wondered whether you would like some seed in return, as I remember the old gardener at Glamis pulled up all your seedlings thinking they were weeds!

If you feel well enough for a motor drive on a lovely day, <u>do</u> come up here. But <u>only</u> when you are <u>quite</u> well.

I did love my time at Glamis darling, but I do wish that the time did not go so quickly there. [. . .]

Goodbye duckie, from

Your very loving

Elizabeth

~

19 September 1936 to Queen Mary

Birkhall

My Darling Mama

It is too kind of you to send us that charming picture of Birkhall, and it is exactly the right size for a little room too. Thank you a thousand times – it fits in most beautifully.

I went to Balmoral the other day and chose out the photographs that you wanted. I do hope that they will prove the ones that you wanted sent, as in one or two cases I was a little puzzled. However, the nice housemaid was a great help, as of course the housekeeper did not know very much.

The latter seemed a very nice woman, & most capable and intelligent, and very happy at Balmoral.

Next week we go to Aberdeen to open the new Hospital.* I do wish that David could have done it, as they have all worked so hard for so long, & it will be one of the best in Scotland, and it would have given such enormous pleasure to the countryside round here. But he won't, so there it is!

I am secretly rather dreading next week, but I haven't heard if a certain person is coming or not – I do hope not, as everything is so talked of up here. I suppose it is natural, the place being empty for eleven months, that the time it is occupied every detail is discussed with gusto! Mr Pierpont Morgan† is coming up to luncheon tomorrow, and David may come over too, which would be very nice of him, & it would give the old man such pleasure.

We went to the Gelder‡ for a picnic yesterday, it was too divine

---

* King Edward VIII was to have opened the new hospital. He then declined on grounds that he was still in official mourning for his father. However, on the day of the opening, he drove himself to Aberdeen to meet Mrs Simpson and other friends off the train from London. The *Aberdeen Evening Express* published a photograph of the King at the station with the headline 'His Majesty in Aberdeen. Surprise visit in car to meet guests'. Next to it was a photograph of the Yorks opening the hospital. The press had not yet disclosed Mrs Simpson's relationship with the King, but this incident was an indication of his priorities.

† John Pierpont 'Jack' Morgan, Jr (1867–1943), American banker and philanthropist who became a friend of the Duke and Duchess of York. He helped finance the First World War and after the Treaty of Versailles his bank, Morgan Guaranty, managed Germany's reparation payments.

† Geldershiel, a small shooting lodge built by Queen Victoria in the shadow of Balmoral's highest mountain, Lochnagar.

for words, the mountains heavenly, the sun hot, and the air like
champagne. In fact Scotland at its most lovely, & it is hard to beat
then. We have been round to see a few of the people, and the schools
– I could not remember how many people you used to visit beyond
the obvious ones like Abercromby & the Stirtons* & Arthur Grant etc
– are there any others that you would like us to do?

　　With so much love darling Mama,

　　Your very loving daughter in law

　　Elizabeth

　　PS I do hope that Marlborough H. is getting on well.

~

11 October 1936 to Queen Mary

Birkhall

Darling Mama

　　We have been thinking so much of you this last week, and are so
glad to hear that you are getting settled at Marlborough House. It
sounds as if you have made it quite lovely, and I am simply longing
to see it.

　　We are leaving here today, and spend a week at Glamis on our
way to London, and are looking forward so much to seeing you
again. It seems such ages since July. It has been so lovely up here this
year, the weather has been heavenly & the gardens blazing with
colour, but there has also been a great sadness & sense of loss both
for us & all the people. It will never be quite the same again for us.
You & Papa made such a <u>family</u> feeling by your great kindness &
thought for everybody, but David does not seem to possess the
faculty of making others feel <u>wanted</u>. It is very sad, and I feel that the
whole difficulty is a certain person. I do not feel that I <u>can</u> make
advances to her & ask her to our house, as I imagine would be liked,
& this fact is bound to make relations a little difficult. However,
luckily Bertie is quite outside all that, & I am sure that it is very
important for him to steer clear of those very difficult questions. The
whole situation is complicated & <u>horrible</u>,[†] and I feel so unhappy

---

*　Rev. Dr John Stirton (1871–1944), Minister at Crathie, and his wife.

†　The King had imposed sweeping and unpopular economies and staff changes at both

about it sometimes, so you must forgive me darling Mama for letting myself go so indiscreetly. There is nobody that I can talk to, as ever since I married I have made a strict rule never to discuss anything of Family matters with my own relations – nor would they wish it, but it leaves so few people to let off steam to occasionally!

It will be heavenly to see you again. Has anything transpired about Xmas? Can we all spend it together – do suggest it to David as he loves & admires you & I am sure would arrange what you wished.

With much love darling Mama, & I do pray that you will be blessed & happy at Marlborough House,

Ever your loving daughter in law
Elizabeth*

~

21 October 1936 to Queen Mary

145 Piccadilly

Darling Mama,

Tuesday December 3rd will suit me very well indeed, & I shall look forward so much to bringing the children. It was so wonderful to see you again today. In these anxious & depressing days you are indeed 'a rock of defence' darling Mama, & I feel sure that the whole country agrees. It was a great joy to us to be with you again.

Your always devoted daughter in law
Elizabeth

~

23 October 1936 to Lady Strathmore

The Royal Lodge

My Darling Angel

We were <u>miserable</u> at leaving Glamis & you on Tuesday, and each year I think that we all enjoy being there more & more. It was

---

Sandringham and Balmoral since the death of George V. He had never liked either property as much as his father or the Yorks did.

* In reply to this letter, Queen Mary thanked the Duchess for writing so fully 'on a subject which grieves me beyond words & which is a great worry to me, as well as to us all'. She had gathered that the King did not wish to go to Sandringham for Christmas and she had asked him to let her and the Yorks have their family party there. (QEQM/PRIV/RF)

heavenly this year and the only sadness was that you were not feeling well. I <u>do</u> hope that you won't have another attack just yet, & give it time to heal up. It is <u>horrible</u> for you darling, and worries me very much.

I don't think that there is anybody else who would make so little fuss as you do – you are very brave duckie.

We had a very good journey down, and found London looking very dirty & horrid, & all felt very sorry that we were not at Glamis! [...]

I have got Lilibet down here alone, & she is sleeping in my room which is very nice.

Goodbye darling, & please take great care of yourself, & a million thanks for all our delicious time at Glamis.

Your very loving
Elizabeth*

~

29 October 1936 to King Edward VIII

145 Piccadilly

Darling David

I do want to thank you most gratefully for lending us Birkhall this year. It is the most wonderful holiday for us, and I cannot tell you how much better we both feel after 6 weeks of complete peace. I honestly don't believe that I could cope with all the problems of modern life, if it wasn't for Birkhall, & it was ANGELIC and kind of you to let us have it. I do thank you from my heart – you are always so sweet & thoughtful for us, and I wish that I could thank you as I would wish.

Now please may I bother you with something? It really isn't my business at all, but I am implicated with the St John of Jerusalem as Commandant of the Nursing Divisions, and I know that the Order is very anxious for you to do some function for them next summer. I am wondering whether it would be possible for you to do such a thing as a Review or Inspection of the Brigade in Hyde Park some

---

* In this letter to her mother (and that of 27 August) the Duchess was typically discreet; she made no mention of her concerns about King Edward VIII, which she discussed freely with Queen Mary.

time? It would do an incredible amount of good, because you know the men are practically all working men who give up holidays & ordinary leisure to do Ambulance service on great & little occasions. They hardly ever get a pat on the back, & yet are absolutely essential to us, and I cannot begin to tell you what a <u>marvellous</u> effect it would have if you could possibly spare a day next summer. Oh dear – I do hate to ask you this, but the St John gets things like Investitures for the grand people, and I do feel that the thousands of working men who give up their hard earned leisure to cope with accidents & public occasions would feel so set up if you <u>could</u> have a look at them.

Please forgive me for asking you this, but you are so understanding about these things. <u>Please</u> don't give me away, as it really has nothing to do with me. I am being an interfering busybody, but the St John order is run by <u>old</u> <u>old</u> men, & they forget the rank & file! I felt I would so like to ask you this – it means so much to these excellent people. At all public functions the police notify the London District as to how many men & nurses they require, & the Brigade carry out these street duties absolutely free – a service gladly given by people like porters, postmen, shopmen etc. If you <u>possibly</u> can – it would be wonderful if you could inspect them.

Your loving sister in law Elizabeth

~

Tuesday undated [17 November 1936] to Queen Mary

145 Piccadilly

My Darling Mama,

Bertie has just told me of what has happened,* and I feel quite overcome with horror & emotion. My first thought was of you, & your note, just arrived as I was starting to write to you, was very helpful. One feels so helpless against such obstinacy. Would 10.30 be

---

* The King, who had been avoiding his family, had finally told his mother and brother that he planned to marry Mrs Simpson and that if his government could not accept this, he would abdicate. On 28 November, the Prime Minister, Stanley Baldwin, sent telegrams to the Dominions – Canada, South Africa, Australia, New Zealand and the Irish Free State – seeking their views on the possibility of the King marrying Mrs Simpson. Their answers varied in tone, but allowed the Prime Minister to conclude that no union, not even a morganatic one, would be acceptable.

too early for you tomorrow morning? Bertie has a meeting later on in the morning. If we don't hear to the contrary we will come at that hour. God help us all to be calm & wise.

Your devoted daughter in law, Elizabeth

~

Friday 20 November 1936 to Queen Mary

Wilton House
Salisbury*

My Darling Mama,

Thank you so very much for your letter, it was indeed kind of you to write so fully, and I am deeply grateful. What you say gives Bertie & I much courage and to know that we have your support at this turning point in not only <u>our</u> lives, but the lives of millions of people in the Empire is a wonderful encouragement & support.

Staying here, in a very normal English shooting party, it seems almost incredible that David contemplates such a step, & every day I pray to God that he will see reason, and not abandon his people.

I am sure that it would be a great shock to everybody and a horrible position for us naturally. However, it is no good going over the same ground again, but I must repeat that I do <u>not</u> know what we should do without you darling Mama. Please believe that Bertie & I will always do everything in our power to please you, and we do feel so thankful for your unfailing help & sympathy & wise advice.

It is a great strain having to talk & behave as if nothing was wrong during these difficult days – especially as I do not think that anybody here <u>dreams</u> of what is worrying all of us. [. . .] it is truly the sword of Damocles again.

Ever your loving daughter in law, Elizabeth

~

---

* Home of the Pembroke family.

23 November 1936 to King Edward VIII

145 Piccadilly
<u>Private</u>

Darling David,

Please read this. Please be kind to Bertie when you see him, because he loves you, and minds terribly all that happens to you. I wish that you could realize how loyal & true he is to you, and you have no idea how hard it has been for him lately. I <u>know</u> that he is fonder of you than anybody else, & as his wife, I must write & tell you this. I am terrified for him – so DO help him. And <u>for God's sake</u> don't tell him that I have written – we both uphold you always.

E.*

PS We want you to be happy, more than anything else, but it's awfully difficult for Bertie to say what he thinks, you know how shy he is – so do help him.

~

23 November 1936 to Helen Hardinge

145 Piccadilly

Dearest Helen,

It was very kind, and just like you to write me such a nice letter. I would love to see you, because there is nobody that I can talk to, and I know that you understand the horrible complications of the situation. It's bad whichever way one looks at it, both from our point of view, and the country's, and the <u>only</u> thing that matters is the support and sympathy of one's friends. I feel very depressed and miserable, and so am extra grateful for your support. You and Alec† are angels. E.

~

---

*   The Duke of York wrote a letter to his brother on the same day saying, 'I do so long for you to be happy with the one person you adore . . . I feel sure that whatever you decide to do will be in the best interest of this Country and Empire' (Philip Ziegler, *Edward VIII: The Official Biography*, Collins, 1990, p. 324).

†   The Hon. Alexander Hardinge, later second Baron Hardinge of Penshurst PC GCB GCVO MC (1894–1960), Assistant Private Secretary to George V, Private Secretary to Edward VIII and George VI. His wife Helen (née Cecil) was one of the Duchess's oldest friends.

3 December 1936 to the Hon. Sir Richard Molyneux

145 Piccadilly

My dear Dick

I have put off lunching with Oswald Birley,* because I do not feel able to cope today. I am sure that he will understand, & you too. It is a great help to us to feel that we have good friends like yourself, for indeed we both are unhappy & terribly worried. We have just arrived back from Scotland, to be greeted with the bombshell of the daily papers† – it is all so dreadful & <u>wasteful</u>. Please tell the Birleys how sorry I am.

Yours v. sincerely Elizabeth

~

6 December 1936 to May Elphinstone

The Royal Lodge

My Darling May

Thank you 1000 times for being so angelic to us at Carberry. I can't tell you what a joy it was to be with you all again, and I really don't think that we could have got through the Edinburgh functions, in the present state of unhappiness, unless we had been with you. It made all the difference, and I am <u>so</u> grateful. Bertie and I are feeling very despairing and the strain is terrific.

Every day lasts a week, & the only hope we have is in the affection & support of our family & friends.

I feel so sad, & yet there is only a very straightforward case – if

---

* Sir Oswald Hornby Joseph Birley (1880–1952), portrait painter 'producing high-quality faithful likenesses with insight and sympathy' (*Dictionary of National Biography*). In 1934 he painted a playful group portrait of the Windsor Wets which hung thereafter in Windsor Castle.

† On 3 December 1936 the British press broke the self-imposed silence it had observed all year – unlike its foreign counterparts – on the King's romantic affairs. When the Yorks stepped off the train from Scotland that morning they were greeted with newspaper placards: 'The King's Marriage'.

Mrs Simpson is not fit to be Queen, she is not fit to be the King's morganatic wife. The Crown <u>must</u> be above all controversy –

Thank you again for all your wonderful kindness.

Your very loving

Elizabeth

~

7 December 1936 to Osbert Sitwell

The Royal Lodge

Dear Mr Sitwell,

I am deeply grateful to you for your very kind letter, I wish that I could tell you how much encouragement & support we feel in what you say. In these last few days, when every minute has seemed an hour, we have been sustained & helped by the sympathy of our friends. Please believe that your letter has been read with real gratitude.

It is extraordinary how one's heart lightens at the kindness of friends, and I feel sure that you understand the great difficulties of the present situation – therefore your sympathy is <u>very</u> much appreciated. I thank you from my heart, & hope that we shall see you again soon.

Yours very sincerely,

Elizabeth

~

7 December 1936 to the Marchioness of Londonderry

The Royal Lodge

My dear Lady Londonderry*

I am so grateful to you for your very kind letter. Your sympathy is a great encouragement to us both during these terrible days that seem to last so long, and we are much encouraged by what you say.

---

* Edith Helen, Marchioness of Londonderry DBE (1879–1959), wife of seventh Marquess of Londonderry. She had written to the Duchess expressing her support and suggesting that Queen Mary's views on the King's wish to marry Mrs Simpson should be discreetly made known in order to give the country a lead. (RA QEQM/PRIV/PAL)

It is specially hard for my husband, involving as it does a much loved brother, and we are both feeling miserable, but sustained & helped by our friends indeed. Thank you from my heart for your kind thought in writing.

I do so agree with you about the calamity of Lord Beaverbrook & Lord Rothermere* bringing this very vital & constitutional matter down into an attack on Mr Baldwin. But I also think that it is <u>essential</u> for the Queen to remain outside any controversy – she <u>must</u> be above everything and her calm & dignity will prove to the people the futility of the cheap Press. I feel very sure of this – she must remain a serene and wise figure outside the ravings & ramblings of this agitated world. Do tell me that you agree with my view? Thank you again for your support, & kind thought in writing, & with messages from us both

I am, Yours affec.

Elizabeth

~

10 December 1936 to Queen Mary

145 Piccadilly

My Darling Mama,

I am so distressed that at this most vital and unhappy moment in the history of our country, I cannot leave the house to come & be with you.† Old Weir insists that I remain in my room, at least for today, and very unwillingly I have accepted his advice. My thoughts are continually with you, and we are sustained & encouraged more than I can say by your wonderful example of dignity and wisdom. Darling Mama, you are indeed a beacon of light to all the poor bewildered people who are now groping in the darkness of disillusionment, and with your leadership we must all combine to get the country back to what it was this time last year.

As I write, your message has come, & I shall look forward with great joy to your visit today at 3.

---

* Prime Minister Baldwin was convinced that the King had little backing in the country. However, both Beaverbrook and Rothermere, critics of Baldwin and proprietors of the *Daily Express* and *Daily Mail* respectively, backed King Edward VIII and used their newspapers to encourage support for his cause.

† The Duchess had another of her frequent bouts of flu throughout the abdication crisis.

I have great faith in Bertie – he sees very straight, & if this terrible responsibility comes to him he will face it bravely.

Much love, darling Mama,

your loving daughter in law

Elizabeth

~

Many years later, Queen Elizabeth reflected on the Abdication in her series of conversations with Eric Anderson:

'It was a terrible surprise to everybody when he [the King] decided that he had to leave. It was the whole Commonwealth who said no no, we don't want you to marry this lady. And it was just a terrible tragedy, it really was. We all loved the Prince of Wales and we all thought he was going to be a wonderful King. It was the most ghastly shock when he decided to go. It was a dreadful blow to his brother because, you see, they were great friends. It's a terrible, bitter blow when somebody you love behaves like that.

'Fortunately he was never crowned, and that was one of the good things he did. If he was going to make up his mind to go away, to do it before.

'I wonder. I don't think he ever wanted to be King. I don't think he thought of it as something he ought to do. Very odd. People do change in a strange way. He had this extraordinary charm, and then it all disappeared. I don't know what happened.

'Nobody knows, really. He was frightfully popular. Everybody adored him. I think he may have thought he was so popular that people would want him back, whatever. I imagine that might have been in his mind. Oh, he was immensely popular all over the Commonwealth. He was extremely attractive. That makes it all the more strange, the whole thing. He must have been bemused with love, I suppose.

'You couldn't reason with him, nobody could. The whole Government tried, everybody tried. The only good thing is, I think he was quite happy with her.'

~

King Edward VIII signed the Instrument of Abdication on the evening of 10 December 1936, and it was given legislative assent on 11 December. The Duke of York became King George VI and the Duchess of York his Queen Consort. The former King, now to be known as

Duke of Windsor, made a radio broadcast that night to explain his decision, and left by sea for France en route to Austria.

~

11 December 1936 to the Duke of Windsor

145 Piccadilly

Darling David

I am so miserable that I cannot come down to Royal Lodge owing to being ill in bed, as I wanted so much to see you before you go, and say 'God bless you' from my heart. We are all overcome with misery, and can only pray that you will find happiness in your new life.

I often think of the old days, & how you helped Bertie & I in the first years of our marriage. I shall always mention you in my prayers, & bless you, Elizabeth

~

12 December 1936 to the Most Rev. Cosmo Lang, Archbishop of Canterbury

145 Piccadilly

My dear Archbishop

I cannot tell you how touched I am at receiving your most kind and helpful letter today. I can hardly now believe that we have been called to this tremendous task, and, (I am writing to you quite intimately) the curious thing is that we are not afraid. I feel that God has enabled us to face the situation calmly, and although I at least feel most inadequate, we have been sustained during these last terrible days by many many good friends. I know that we may count you among them, and it means a great deal to us to know this. When we spoke together at Birkhall only three months ago, how little did I think that such drama & unhappiness was in store for our dear Country. Thank you from my heart for your unfailing sympathy & good advice.

I would love to see you soon, as there are so many things to talk over, and for many years now, you have been so kind and wise about our troubles & joys that I fear you cannot escape this time. We both feel our responsibilities very deeply, and though quite prepared for a difficult time, are determined to do our best.

Your dear kind letter has helped us more than I can say – we

were so very unhappy over the loss of a dear brother – because one
can only feel that exile from this country is death indeed. We were
miserable, as you know, over his change of heart and character during
the last few years, and it is alarming how little in touch he was,
with ordinary human feeling – Alas! he had lost the 'common touch'.
I thank you again from my heart for your wishes & prayers for our
future, we pray most sincerely that we shall not fail our country, & I
sign myself for the first time, & with great affection
    Elizabeth R

~

14 December 1936 to Queen Mary

145 Piccadilly

My Darling Mama

    I must write you one line to tell you that this evening Bertie gave
me the Garter.* He had discovered that Papa gave it to you on his
Papa's birthday June 3rd, and the coincidence was so charming that
he has now followed suit, & given it to me on his own birthday. I felt
that I must let you know this. [. . .]

    Ever darling Mama, your loving daughter in law
    Elizabeth

~

16 December 1936 to D'Arcy Osborne

145 Piccadilly

My dear D'Arcy

    Thank you so much for your dear, understanding letter. I do wish
that you had been here during these days of drama & tragedy and
disappointment. It is hard to believe that the one that we knew as
Prince of Wales could possibly have done what King Edward did.

---

* The Most Noble Order of the Garter, created in 1348, the United Kingdom's oldest and
highest order of chivalry. It is entirely in the gift of the monarch and is limited to twenty-six
members, including the monarch and the Prince of Wales.

    King George VI's official biographer, John Wheeler-Bennett, later wrote that the King's
gift of the Garter to the Queen was 'a public declaration of gratitude and affection to one who
had shared with him so bravely the burdens of the past, and was to bear with him so nobly
the trials of the future'. (John Wheeler-Bennett, *King George VI*, Macmillan, 1958, pp. 391–4)

I won't say anything about it, except that you can imagine what a misery it has been to the present King to lose a loved brother in such a way. He is tackling the business very calmly, and we can only do our best. Do let me know what the reaction has been in Rome. I hope that when you come home again you will come and see us in exactly the same way as before.

I am keeping an open mind about everything at the moment, so will wait until later to write more fully.

I have been feeling ill with influenza for the last ten days, so forgive an extremely unintelligent letter – everything seems like a bad dream. But the curious thing is that I am not afraid. Inadequate, but unfrightened.

I wish you a very happy Xmas, & do believe that the knowledge that we have your friendship and sympathy is a great support to us just now. I mean that from my heart.

Thank you again for your kind letter.

I am,

Yours very sincerely,

Elizabeth

~

17 December 1936 to Osbert Sitwell

145 Piccadilly

Dear Mr Sitwell,

I wish that I could tell you how much real pleasure your most enchanting Xmas present has given me. I have long wished to have a book about the Pavilion* & never dreamt that I could ever have such a lovely one. Not only are the illustrations & drawings exquisite, but the binding & coat of arms are also a dream of beauty.

Please believe that I am deeply grateful to you for your very kind thought of me, and I want to thank you from my heart for giving me such a very perfect present.

Also, I want to thank you for your sympathetic and understanding letter of last week. I cannot tell you what a help it has been to us in

---

* *The Royal Pavilion at Brighton* by John Nash, 1826, with a handsome tooled and gilt purple leather binding with a full coat of arms of George IV. (RCIN 1163283) The following year Sitwell gave her Humphry Repton's book of designs for the Pavilion (see p. 250).

the sad and tragic days that we have been through, to feel that we
have the support & wishes of friends like yourself.

One can hardly believe that we could have survived such drama
& tragedy, & yet, here we are, back at the old business – Buckling to,
doing our best, keeping the old Flag flying hoorah, and of course it is
the only thing that is worth doing now. I believe now, more than
ever before, that this country is worth sacrificing a good deal for. In
fact, if I was exiled, I should die, anyway in the spirit.

Again a thousand grateful thanks for the really beautiful book.

I am yours sincerely,

Elizabeth R

~

The new King and Queen, their children and Queen Mary spent
Christmas, New Year and most of January at Sandringham,
recuperating from the shock of the abdication and coming to terms
with the future.

The King was able to stop the sale, ordered by his brother, of
much of the Sandringham Estate. To the relief of the tenant farmers
and the Household, he also reversed many of the changes that
Edward VIII had made in the running of both Sandringham and
Balmoral.

Owen Morshead, the Royal Librarian at Windsor Castle, who was
at Sandringham over Christmas, found the King and Queen very frank.
The only topic of conversation was the new Duke of Windsor. The
King and Queen dwelt on his extraordinary personality – 'his amazing
power of charming people, his flair for making any party go'. The
Queen praised his 'unique talents' but was concerned that if he and
Mrs Simpson did not remain together, 'it would be dangerous to have
such a powerful personality, so magnetic, hanging about doing
nothing.'*

~

---

* Morshead, notes, 20 December 1936. (RA AEC/GG12) Sir Owen Morshead GCVO KCB
DSO MC (1893–1977), Librarian at Windsor Castle 1926–58.

14 January 1937 to the Most Rev. Cosmo Lang, Archbishop of Canterbury

Sandringham

My dear Archbishop.

I write to thank you most gratefully for the book on the Coronation that you have so kindly sent me. I have read it with great interest, and shall look at it very often I expect. I am afraid that I was very ignorant anent (as we say in Scotland!) the wonderful amount of History & tradition that goes to make the great ceremony, and after reading your book I realize even more, the significance of what we have undertaken. I feel now, rather as if I was coming to after a heavy blow on the head. I think that the shock of those terrible days in December was literally stunning, and a merciful numbness overcame one at the time. The return to life is rather unpleasant – we shall need all our courage in the days to come.

Thank you from my heart for your unfailing sympathy & understanding, it has been, & will be, the greatest help that we could wish.

I am,
Yours affec:
Elizabeth R

~

2 February 1937 to Queen Mary

145 Piccadilly

My Darling Mama

I do want to send you one line of grateful thanks for all your angelic kindness & help during our few weeks at Sandringham. I really do not know what we would have done without your unfailing sympathy & understanding through those first bewildering days when we were still stunned by the shock of David's going.

We shall never forget what you did for us, and shall always love you for it.

It was so wonderful having the old happy family atmosphere again. I feel sure that it is our great strength in these difficult days, and as for Bertie & myself, we shall do all in our power to keep it alive.

I am looking forward so much to coming at 11 tomorrow.

With all my love darling Mama, your always devoted daughter in law

Elizabeth

~

19 February 1937 to Osbert Sitwell

The Royal Lodge

Dear Mr Sitwell,

Thank you so much for your letter. I cannot tell you what a joy it is to receive an amusing and friendly one amongst the vast amount of begging letters, complaints, appeals, warnings, lunatic ramblings etc which go to make up one's daily postbag. Not forgetting bad poetry, bad drawings & paintings, bad music and other bad things sent by the mad and bad who seem to people the world. So you can imagine how one falls greedily on the few friendly letters that come, and yours was very welcome!

I must tell you first of all that we all thought your satire* absolutely brilliant. It really is perfect – it hits hard (and never too hard for me) and is wickedly amusing. I do congratulate you. [. . .]

You can imagine how deeply I feel about these people. I will not write about them though, & if, by the time I see you again I have any spirit left, I will tell you myself.

It's safer too!

---

* Sitwell had written a poem, 'Rat Week', for private circulation, in which he named and mocked many of those society figures who had first flattered King Edward VIII and Mrs Simpson and then jumped ship:

> Where are the friends of yesterday
> That fawned on Him,
> That flattered Her;
> Where are the friends of yesterday,
>
> Submitting to His every whim,
> Offering praise of Her as myrrh
> To Him?
>
> What do they say, that jolly crew,
> So new, and brave, and free and easy,
> What do they say, that jolly crew,
> Who must make even Judas queasy?

'Rat Week' was eventually published in book form in 1986.

May I ask whether you would be <u>very</u> kind and let me have a copy of your satire to put in the Windsor Castle Library? It would be quite private, but with other papers will be of great interest to future generations. Would you sign it? I would not trouble you, but I sent Lady Cholmondeley's copy back to her, & have none myself.

We have moved into temporary rooms at Buckingham Palace whilst our own are being done up, and escape here for weekends, which is very healing and peaceful. We are going through a fairly difficult time here in England. As you can guess, after an upheaval like that of last December's, gossip & ill natured stories are rife, and of course it is a heaven sent opportunity for Communist propaganda against Monarchies.

I feel rather 'Morning Post' saying that, but it's true, & their ways are so subtle. Gossip is a godsend when there is a wish to be cruel.

The whole situation is very interesting – I fully expect that we may be moderately unpopular for some time, but as long as our friends stick to us, one can shoulder any amount of trouble. Certainly what is called the <u>burden</u> of Kingship is truly said. The whole thing is a burden – when you are youngish and an Aunt Sally for verbal skittles, especially; & yet, the more difficult it all is, the more worth while. Anyway, I will tell you about it when we see you again, which I hope will be soon. You must come to Windsor in April, & see how Queen Victoria imposed her taste onto George IV's.

I shall look forward to your novel – if it seems long to you, it will of course seem much too short for your readers.

I am, always yours sincerely,

Elizabeth R

~

16 April 1937 to Kenneth Clark

Windsor Castle

Dear Mr Clark,*

I want to send you my very sincere thanks for telling me about

---

* Kenneth Clark, Lord Clark OM CH KCB FBA (1903–83), Director of the National Gallery, 1939–45; Surveyor of the King's Pictures, 1934–44. One of the great art historians of the mid-twentieth century, he was also an inspiring broadcaster, whose television series *Civilisation* was first broadcast by the BBC in 1969. He was an important adviser to the Queen as she built up her own private art collection.

the busts. I am delighted that I had the luck to get them, and Sir Eric Maclagan* has been most kind and forgiving about it.

I will never divulge the horrible truth, and I trust that your fair name will remain unsullied in Sir Eric's eyes!

I am communicating with Lord Gerald Wellesley,[†] and am looking forward so much to seeing them here.[‡] Sir Eric has just written to ask whether I will lend them to his Exhibition of Kings and Queens of England at the V & A this summer. After his honourable conduct I cannot refuse, so fear that they will not be seen here just yet.

I have changed the pictures round in my sitting room here in the way that you suggested, and am so pleased with their appearance. As I write, the Duchess of Cumberland[§] is looking down on me, and she looks heavenly on her new wall – I am already very fond of her.

I have lit the Gainsborough walky-talky[¶] (also D. of Cumberland) & it looks too lovely. Perhaps the next time that you come here, you will have a look at it, as it looks a little dry & crackly when lit.

It was a great pleasure to us to have been able to go round with you here, and we are so grateful to you for all your interest and good advice. The Rubens look wonderful now that they have come down from the sky, & Dick's hawk man[|] too – Goodness only knows what he is up to now!

I am, Yours very sincerely,

Elizabeth R

---

* Sir Eric Maclagan KCVO CBE (1879–1951), Director of the Victoria and Albert Museum, 1924–45. An inspiring and efficient administrator, he made the museum much more accessible and pioneered the sale of postcards and replicas. His obituary in *The Times* spoke of 'his fundamental honesty, sincerity and disinterestedness'.

† Lord Gerald Wellesley, later seventh Duke of Wellington KG (1885–1972), diplomat, soldier and architect, Surveyor of the King's Works of Art, 1936–43.

‡ The two marble busts, one of Charles I after Bernini, the other of William III, were placed in the Grand Vestibule of Windsor Castle.

§ Thomas Gainsborough's three-quarter-length portrait of Anne, Duchess of Cumberland.

¶ Gainsborough's *The Morning Walk* shows Henry Frederick, Duke of Cumberland, walking with his wife and sister-in-law.

| 'Dick', the Queen's friend Sir Richard Molyneux (see p. 187, footnote), who took an active interest in the Royal Collection, advising on matters such as picture hangs and the arrangement of rooms, especially at Windsor. The 'hawk man' was probably *Portrait of a Man with a Hawk*, attributed to the sixteenth-century Italian painter Girolamo Savoldo. (RCIN 405764)

~

King George VI and Queen Elizabeth were crowned at Westminster Abbey on 12 May 1937.

~

15 May 1937 to the Most Rev. Cosmo Lang, Archbishop of Canterbury

The Royal Lodge

My dear Archbishop

I write to you with a very full heart, to thank you for making our Coronation such a spiritual and wonderful service, & to congratulate you on the incredibly beautiful way that you did everything. I am sure that you have had many letters from people who were moved deeply by the immense significance of the day and I do want to add my affectionate and grateful appreciation of all that you did & meant to us that day.

I was more moved, & more helped than I could have believed possible. It is curious, on thinking it over now, that I was not conscious of there being anybody else there at the Communion – you told us last Sunday evening that we would be helped and we <u>were</u> sustained & carried above the ordinary fear of a great ceremony. Our great hope now, is that as so many millions of people were impressed by the feeling of service and goodness that came from Westminster Abbey, perhaps that day will result in strength and good feeling in individuals all over the world, and be a calming & strengthening influence on affairs in general.

I thank you with all my heart for what you have been to us during these last difficult and tragic months – a good counsellor and true friend – we are indeed grateful.

I am,

Your affec: friend

Elizabeth R

PART THREE

QUEEN

'Many an aching heart has found some solace in her gracious smile'

WINSTON CHURCHILL

ON 3 JUNE 1937, less than a month after the Coronation, the Duke of Windsor and Mrs Simpson married in France. To the dismay of Queen Mary, this was his father's birthday. Relations within the family had deteriorated since the abdication. The King and Queen, and Prime Minister Baldwin (who retired after the Coronation), were shocked to discover that the Duke had lied to them about his financial affairs. The Duke himself was angered because his family had not allowed his wife to assume the title Her Royal Highness (HRH). This was controversial because of the general rule that a wife takes on the status of her husband – as Elizabeth Bowes Lyon had on her marriage to the Duke of York. No member of the Royal Family attended the Windsor wedding – George V's Private Secretary, Lord Wigram, took the view that to do so 'would be a firm nail in the coffin of monarchy'.[1]

Queen Mary wrote to her daughter-in-law that the choice of date hurt her very deeply; 'of course she did it, but how can he be so weak, I suppose it is out of revenge that none of the family is going to the wedding.'[2]

At the beginning of October 1937, the Duke and Duchess visited Germany, where they met Adolf Hitler. This was ill judged. By this time, Hitler and Mussolini's aggressive policies were already forcing Europe towards the brink of war. The King and Queen were, like the vast majority of the British people, horrified by the prospect of another war only twenty years after the last, and they fully supported the new Prime Minister Neville Chamberlain's attempts to negotiate with Hitler. But by early 1939 they realized that Chamberlain's efforts had failed and they became as determined as anyone that fascism had to be confronted. Their visits to Canada, New York and Washington in 1939 were intended to rally democratic support against the dictators, as was their earlier visit to France in 1938. In September 1939, after Germany invaded Poland, Britain found itself at war for the second time in a quarter of a century.

The Queen wrote a note to herself the day after war was declared:

'My last cup of tea in peace! My last bath at leisure; and all the time one's mind working on many thoughts. Chiefly of the people of this country – their courage, their sense of humour; their sense of right and wrong – how will they come through the wicked things that war lets loose. One thing is, that they are at their best when things are bad, and the spirit is wonderful.'[3]

In the terrible world war that lay ahead for almost six long brutal years, all that had been instilled in the Queen by her family, all that she had learned from her contact with soldiers in the First World War, and all the public skills she had acquired since her marriage, she put to fine use for the country. She made it clear that evacuation was never an option for her, saying, famously, 'The children could not go without me, I could not possibly leave the King, and the King would never go.'

For much of the early part of the war, she and the King slept at Windsor, where their daughters lived, but were frequently in London (they could have been killed by a bomb which struck Buckingham Palace while they were there in September 1940). Morale on the Home Front was vital. The Queen constantly accompanied the King on visits to factories, schools, regimental headquarters and, above all, areas of London and other cities that had been badly bombed; she wrote to her mother-in-law Queen Mary, 'It does affect me seeing this terrible and senseless destruction. I think that really I mind it much more than being bombed myself.'[4]

In the first two years of the war, Britain suffered reverse after reverse. But the Queen refused to admit that defeat was even a possibility and the British people, remarkably, shared such confidence. The entry into the war of the United States after the Japanese attack on Pearl Harbor in December 1941 changed everything. Winston Churchill, who had become Prime Minister in May 1940, wrote in his war memoirs, 'Being saturated and satiated with emotion and sensation, I went to bed and slept the sleep of the saved and thankful.'[5]

When victory was finally won on 8 May 1945 hundreds of thousands of people gathered in front of Buckingham Palace. The King, the Queen and the Princesses appeared on the balcony – which had been surveyed to ensure that it was structurally sound – to salute the crowd and be saluted back. Joy abounded. Churchill, who joined the family on the balcony, later said, 'We could not have had a better King and Queen in Britain's most perilous hour.'[6]

The Queen, and even more the King, were exhausted by the effort of the war years. So was Britain itself. But there was more upheaval to come. The wartime coalition was dissolved and in July 1945 the people of Britain voted in a general election. They rejected Churchill in favour of a Labour government which promised the creation of a welfare state. From the Queen's point of view the story of the next six years was of tumultuous change in British society which she feared could damage the links between Crown and people, and of catastrophic decline in the King's health.

There were happy times, most particularly the engagement and marriage in November 1947 of Princess Elizabeth to Prince Philip of Greece. The Queen wrote to the Princess, 'That you & Philip should be blissfully happy & love each other through the good days and bad or depressing days is my one wish.'[7]

More happiness followed; in 1948 the King and Queen celebrated their Silver Wedding anniversary and then the births of their grandson Prince Charles in November 1948 and granddaughter Princess Anne in August 1950. But the Queen was preoccupied, above all, by her husband's condition.

In September 1951 a biopsy revealed a malignant growth in the lung. It was cancer, but that word was never mentioned. His physicians decided that the entire lung had to be removed. On the morning of the operation crowds gathered outside the Palace, where an operating theatre had been installed, and Churchill did something he had not done for many years – he went down on his knees and prayed.[8] So did millions of other people across the land. The operation was deemed a success and the Royal Family spent a happy Christmas 1951 at Sandringham. But in the early hours of the morning of 6 February 1952 the King died in his sleep.

The devastated Queen immediately wrote to her mother-in-law, Queen Mary, 'My darling Mama, What can I say to you – I know that you loved Bertie dearly, and he was my whole life . . . It is hard to grasp, he was such an angel to the children & me, and I cannot bear to think of Lilibet, so young to bear such a burden.'[9]

Princess Elizabeth, away in Africa, had overnight become Queen. She and Prince Philip flew back at once to London to assume a responsibility that each of them would carry out thereafter with an astonishing sense of duty.

The people showed their grief at the death of the unexpected King whom they had come to love. Over 300,000 of them waited in the bitter cold, in lines four miles long, to pass by his body as it lay in state in Westminster Hall. At the end of the day of his funeral, 15 February 1952, his widow Queen Elizabeth wrote, 'Today has been the most wonderful & the most agonizing day of my life. Wonderful because one felt the sincerity of the people's feelings, & agonizing because gradually one becomes less numb, & the awfulness of everything becomes real.'[10]

3 June 1937 to Queen Mary

Buckingham Palace

My Darling Mama,

We have been thinking so much about you today, with your memories of past days, and all the new anxieties added, and just send this little line of love to say how much we are with you in thought and sympathy and loving admiration.

Always your devoted daughter in law, Elizabeth

~

18 August 1937 to Queen Mary

Balmoral Castle

Darling Mama

I do hope that you are having a pleasant and peaceful time at Sandringham. I saw in the papers that you had made an expedition to Cambridge – I wonder whether you found anything nice.

I spent a very pleasant week at Glamis, & found my parents well. It was lovely & hot most of the time, & the garden a blaze of colour.

Here, everything seems much the same, & all the people well – Abercromby looks like a two year old, & Gordon* has grown a beard which suits him <u>very</u> well!

The garden has been very much cut down – the big border in front of the house has gone, & a great deal also in the lower garden. We shall have to try & put back the flowers as soon as possible. Also I do not know whether the gardener is any good yet – he <u>was</u> foreman I believe. [. . .]

---

* 'Abercromby', probably James Abercrombie Senr. (1865–1951), head stalker at Balmoral since 1924. His son James was also a stalker at Balmoral. Frank Gordon (1879–1954) had taken over as head stalker in January 1937.

We had such an amusing arrival here – I expect that Bertie told you – & were drawn by about 50 of the employees here up the drive to the Castle in a carriage with the pipers marching in front! The gentlemen & Lettice Bowlby* walked behind, looking like chief mourners, and altogether the cavalcade looked like a rather gay funeral! It was very delightful to be welcomed like that, but also very amusing.

Much love darling Mama.

I will write again soon,

Always your loving daughter in law

Elizabeth

~

21 September 1937 to Sir Walter Monckton

Balmoral Castle

Dear Sir Walter†

Thank you so much for your kind letter. I was most touched that you should think of writing so sympathetically and with such understanding and I appreciate your thought most deeply. I think that it would be an excellent thing if you were to write to the King at fairly regular intervals, for I feel that one of the main sources of anxiety of mind is the difficulty experienced of getting authentic news from abroad.

I do not think that the King is too badly worried, as he has great faith in your powers of persuasion & good advice, but I know that he would be immensely relieved if he could feel that there was no chance of the libel case coming off. The possibility even, is horrible to think of, and the whole thing so degrading. But we do feel so much

---

* Hon. Mrs Geoffrey Bowlby (1885–1988), née Annesley. Her husband, Captain Geoffrey Bowlby, was killed in the First World War. Lady in waiting to the Queen 1932–45.

† Walter Turner Monckton, first Viscount Monckton of Brenchley, GCVO KCMG MC PC (1891–1965), distinguished lawyer, later politician and banker, whom Edward VIII had asked to negotiate with the Prime Minister on his behalf in the weeks before the abdication. Monckton was a man of intellect and discretion; after the abdication, he performed an invaluable service liaising with the increasingly angry Duke of Windsor. The Duke had issued a libel suit against the author of a book, *Coronation Commentary*. This alleged that Mrs Simpson had been his mistress and that he had been drinking too much before the abdication. The King and Queen were appalled by the idea of the Duke being cross-examined in court. In the end the libel case was settled with Monckton's assistance in the Duke's favour.

encouraged by your help & kindness & wish to help, and I can imagine that the whole affair must be very difficult & troublesome to handle at times. One has seen with alarming clarity during the last two years how vitally necessary a stable Monarchy is for this Empire & the world, and as 'the Monarchy' really embraces the whole Royal family, we cannot afford any more scandals & insinuations.

I do hope that you have managed to have a real holiday – we have been very happy here. With again my grateful thanks for your kind thought,

I am,
Yours very sincerely
Elizabeth R

~

26 October 1937 to Queen Mary

Sandringham

Darling Mama

It is kind of you to suggest helping me with the presents for our people, and I cannot tell you how grateful I am to you for such an offer! You are so wonderfully clever at buying the right things, and if you would buy things for the people here, and/or the maids & valets of the Family, it would be a great help.

The children were thrilled at the idea of going to the Tower, & I am sure, adored their visit there with you.

Bertie's Speech went off quite well this morning. I must admit that I was very very nervous during the whole ceremonial!* The silence is most alarming, and the significance of the speech, as typifying the strong link between the Crown & Parliament most impressive.

The peace here seems so perfect after our busy days!
Ever, darling Mama, your devoted daughter in law
Elizabeth

~

---

*   This was the first time the King had opened Parliament; he and the Queen had both been nervous. Lionel Logue's help was still invaluable on such occasions.

7 December 1937 to the Hon. Sir Richard Molyneux

Buckingham Palace

My dear Dick

Will you come to Sandringham for Xmas, and help us with [three drawings of bottles, of increasing size, labelled Claret, Burgundy and Champagne respectively] etc – pull a few [drawing of a cracker]s & help us with that [drawing of a Christmas tree]? I hope that you are free – (not too free of course).

Yours sincerely

Elizabeth R

~

18 December 1937 to Osbert Sitwell

Buckingham Palace

Dear Mr Sitwell,

I wish that I could find words suitable to convey my delight in the lovely book on the Pavilion gardens,* that you so kindly sent me.

It is absolutely enchanting and exactly the sort of thing that gives me great pleasure. It is <u>fascinating</u> and I have spent hours looking at it & enjoying it. I do thank you with all my heart for such a delicious present. I feel very touched by your thought – and do so appreciate your unfailing and loyal friendship. In these days, one finds more & more that indeed the only things that count are friends, and the warmth & sense of security that they bring. All too rare alas!, but then, all the more precious. (Oh dear, I did not want to write the word prescious [sic] because I cannot spell it, what a bore!)

But please believe that I am <u>really</u> pleased with Repton's lovely book, and I thank you <u>very</u> <u>very</u> much.

With every good wish for Xmas & 1938.

I am, Yours very sincerely,

Elizabeth R

PS. What fun Hannah's† luncheon party was & how naughty you

---

* *Designs for the Pavilion at Brighton* by Humphry Repton assisted by his sons John Ades Repton and G. S. Repton [1806]. It is inscribed by Osbert Sitwell to Queen Elizabeth on the flyleaf. (RCIN 1160542)

† Hannah Gubbay (c. 1886–1968), née Rothschild, cousin of Sir Philip Sassoon and friend to both Queen Mary and Queen Elizabeth. She entertained them at her house in Hertford Street.

were going on about the Giorgiones! I enjoyed it enormously. My first luncheon party out since Dec: 1936.

And a thousand thanks for sending me 'Mrs Kimber',* I love it – do write some more poetry, yours is so good & so rare nowadays. Write us something hopeful & courageous for next year. After all, this is a grand little country, & as we can never be warlike, let us have some pride in it – we must be serious about <u>something</u>!

~

5 January 1938 to Princess Elizabeth

Sandringham
[Addressed to]
Her Royal Highness
The Princess Elizabeth
Gettingupforlunch
The Nursery
Sandringham

My Darling Lilibet

I am so glad to hear that you are better today, and hope that you will enjoy your lunch out of bed.

I am feeling much better too, but still a little achy and still living on tea! I hope by tomorrow that I shall be eating Irish stew, steak & kidney pudding, haricot mutton, roast beef, boiled beef, sausages & mutton pies, not to mention roast chicken, fried chicken, boiled chicken, scrambled chicken, scrunched up chicken, good chicken, nasty chicken, fat chicken, thin chicken, <u>any</u> sort of chicken.

Hope to see you soon – Goodbye darling from your very loving Mummy

~

5 January 1938 to D'Arcy Osborne

My dear D'Arcy,

I have so many things to thank you for, that I think I shall start at the latest & work back. First, that heavenly K*A*P*L*A*N.† He

---

* Osbert Sitwell's new novel.

† H*Y*M*A*N K*A*P*L*A*N, the humorous creation of an American writer, Leo Rosten,

arrived at the end of the first day of an attack of influenza, just when one felt that [one] could not look at a book, and after reading with tremendous enjoyment a few chapters, I slept well, & woke the next morning feeling vastly better. I put this miraculous cure down purely to Hermy [sic], and to your kindness in sending him to me. Thank you a thousand times. [. . .]

Thank you also, for sending me something so rare & so helpful.

And more thanks! For being such a wonderful friend. Your support and sympathetic understanding is appreciated more than I can ever say. During this last year the fact that you believed in us was a real encouragement, and I shall always be grateful for such a loyal friend.

As I told you before, you are one of the very few people in the world to whom I can talk intimately, and that is a great relief (to me). Especially nowadays, when I have already learnt that the people that one can trust implicitly are to be counted on the fingers of one hand.

I so much enjoyed our talks, & I was delighted to hear that you were impressed by a sense of vitality in this country. What people need is courage.

The only thing that worries me a little, is that now young people have rather given up religion in any form, they look more & more to individual leadership, or rather leadership by an individual, and that is going to be very difficult to find. It is almost impossible for the King to be that sort of leader.

For many years there was a Prince of Wales, who did all the wise & silly & new things that kept people amused & interested, & yet, because he did not, or would not realize that they did not want that sort of thing from their King – well he had to go.

It seems impossible to mix King and ordinary vulgar leadership – so what can we do? We don't want Mosleys,* perhaps something will turn up. In the old days Religion must have given the people a great sense of security & right, and now there seems to be a vague sense of fear. Or am I sensing something that isn't there at all. Perhaps it is me.

How beautiful your Cardinals must have looked in your green

whose stories of a Jewish immigrant to New York were collected into two books, *The Education of H*Y*M*A*N K*A*P*L*A*N* and *The Return of H*Y*M*A*N K*A*P*L*A*N*. The Jewish humour appealed to the Queen.

* Sir Oswald Ernald Mosley (1896–1980), English politician who founded the British Union of Fascists and, with his 'Blackshirts', tried to stir anti-semitic feeling in Britain. He and his wife, Diana Mitford, were interned as fascist sympathizers, 1940–3.

room – I am sure that your parties are exquisitely arranged, & great fun for everybody as well as yourself.

What a sadness that things aren't going any better in this troubled world. I listened to Mr Roosevelt's speech, & thought it rather boring. Rather the stuff we used to hear from old Ramsay, Snowden, Thomas* etc in the long ago. Higher-wages-let-people-buy-more+therefore-it-benefits-the-whole-community & so on.

However, he did say that democracies must stand together, tho' it's a bit vague.

We had rather an exhausting Xmas with the whole family here, however, they all got on with each other quite well, & nobody cried!

A very happy New Year to you D'Arcy & thank you with all my heart for your charming letters.

Elizabeth R

~

15 January 1938 to Duke of Windsor

Sandringham

Darling David,

When I received your little note this morning,† I rushed to my writing table, and after hunting about amongst the letters on it, I found the lost letter. I am furious and disappointed, because I left it addressed & ready to post, and have no idea what can have happened. I was getting worried as to the safe arrival of the knives, & you must have thought it very odd. I am glad you wrote about it, and I am delighted that you are pleased with the knives & forks. I enclose my little Xmas letter, but feel sad that it did not arrive at the right time – please read it now.

We have been here 3 weeks & the sun has not shone once – it is rather depressing. I hope that you had some warmth on the Riviera.

With love,

Yours

Elizabeth

---

* The Labour politicians Ramsay MacDonald, Philip Snowden and J. H. Thomas.

† The Duke of Windsor had written on 12 January saying he had received a box of cutlery with no accompanying note. He assumed it was a present intended for someone else and offered to return it. (RA EDW/MAIN/B/127)

<u>Enclosed</u>
Sandringham, 23 Dec 1937.

Darling David

I am sending you out by air-mail a small Xmas gift which I do
hope you will both be able to use sometimes. You may have got
hundreds of dessert knives & forks, but as these are old ones, perhaps
they <u>might</u> appeal to you, who like old things. I found them at our
old friend Rochelle Thomas.

Anyway, they take best wishes for Xmas & the New Year, of
health & happiness to both of you.

With love,
Yours
Elizabeth

~

19 March 1938 to Sir Kenneth Clark

The Royal Lodge

My dear Sir Kenneth,

Thank you so much for your letter telling me that you have
bought the two pictures* on my behalf. I am really glad to buy them,
for apart from the fact that I am anxious to start a small collection of
good modern pictures, I became extremely attached to the two in
question during the ten days that I spent in their company!

Please accept my very grateful thanks for the way in which you
'conducted the negotiations'.

I am pleased to learn that you think it may be of some small
encouragement to living artists, to know that I intend to buy <u>good</u>
modern pictures. It gives me pleasure to hear this from you, as I feel
it so important that the finer sides of life should be given a chance, in
these hurrying, ignorant, vulgar days that we live in.

I have no objection at all to a statement in the Press; may I see
what you propose to say before it goes in?

---

* *When Homer Nods*, portrait of George Bernard Shaw by Augustus John OM RA (1878–1961)
and *Chepstow Castle*, landscape by Philip Wilson Steer OM (1860–1942). Clark praised her
decision to buy the work of living painters. 'It is not too much to say that it will have an
important effect on British art in general' (quoted in Susan Owens, *Watercolours and Drawings
from the Collection of Queen Elizabeth The Queen Mother*, Royal Collection Publications, 2005,
p. 13).

Also would you kindly arrange for the bills to be sent to me direct?
With my thanks,
I am, Yours very sincerely,
Elizabeth R

~

23 June 1938 to the Most Rev. Cosmo Lang, Archbishop of Canterbury

Buckingham Palace

My dear Archbishop

I write to ask you a favour – on Monday next the 27th June there
will be a Memorial Service for my mother in London at the same
time as the funeral at Glamis, to which I am going and if it is <u>at all</u>
possible <u>would</u> you say a few of your lovely words about her?

If you are engaged (which I feel you may be) we shall not ask
anyone else, but I write to you at once, as there is nobody else whom
we would wish to ask, but yourself. I shall quite understand if it [is]
impossible for you to arrange it.

We are all feeling very unhappy – my mother was so much the
pivot of the family, so vital and so loving and so marvellously loyal to
those she loved, or the things she thought right – an Angel of
goodness & fun.

Please forgive me for trying to add yet another burden to the very
many that you shoulder, & believe that I shall so understand if you
cannot do Monday.

I am,
Yours affec:
Elizabeth R

~

Cecilia Strathmore died on 23 June 1938. The Strathmore family
gathered at Glamis and Lady Strathmore's funeral took place on 27
June. A simultaneous memorial service took place at the church of St
Martin-in-the-Fields, the parish church for Buckingham Palace; the
Archbishop of Canterbury said in his address: 'She raised a Queen in
her own home, simply, by trust and love, and as a return the Queen
has won widespread love.'

~

30 June 1938 to Arthur Penn

Birkhall

My dear Arthur,

I want to thank you, really and truly <u>from my heart</u>, for all your wonderful help and support during this last week. I don't know what we would have done without you, and I do not know whether you were amused or pleased by the way that the Lyon family turned as one to you, to solicit your help over such an intimate thing as the Memorial Service. That is what comes of being a loved old friend, and you did your part nobly.

I shall always be deeply grateful to you for your wonderful help and marvellously understanding sympathy. It is a curious thing, but I have always been terrified of my mother dying, ever since I was a little child, and now that it has come it seems almost impossible to believe.

But she has left so much behind her, and her influence will be strong with us, her children, all our lives. At Glamis this week we congregated in her sitting room & found comfort even in that.

Her <u>perspective</u> of life was so wonderful, each event was given its <u>true</u> importance, and that is a rare gift.

I was thinking today of how incredulous, slightly amused and <u>so</u> touched she would have been if she could have heard some of the appreciative things that her friends have said of her this last week.

She was modest to a fault, <u>very</u> proud & sensitive, and her judgement was never at fault. She had an uncanny instinct about human beings (whether they were nice or nasty) & has always proved right – Her taste too was so good and original, & if she had had more money to spend, would have left us many beautiful things in house and garden.

Now Arthur, I am writing too much about her, but I know you won't mind.

I have climbed one or two mountains, & spent my days amongst them, and feel very soothed – they are so nice & big & everlasting & <u>such</u> a lovely colour.

I am your grateful friend

Elizabeth R

~

2 July 1938 to Neville Chamberlain

Buckingham Palace

My dear Mr Chamberlain,

I write to send you my heartfelt thanks for your kind and sympathetic letter of condolence on the death of my mother. I was deeply touched by what you said, and thought it so wonderfully kind of you to write as you did, so understanding & so calm, when you were being harried in such a debate that evening. [. . .]

She had such a good perspective of life – everything was given its true importance. She had a young spirit, great courage & unending sympathy whenever or wherever it was needed, & such a heavenly sense of humour.

We all used to laugh together & have such fun. You must forgive me for writing to you like this, but you have been such a kind friend & counsellor to us during the last year, that I address you in the most friendly & grateful spirit. I was so sorry that we had to postpone the visit to Paris,* but as it was all Galas and Banquets and garden parties, it would have seemed rather a mockery to take part so soon, and the French have been very good about it, do you not think so?

With all my thanks,

I am, dear Mr Chamberlain,

Yours sincerely,

Elizabeth R

~

In September 1938 the Prime Minister, Neville Chamberlain, made several flights to Germany to try to make a settlement with Hitler. The Munich Agreement of September 1938 allowed Hitler to dismember Czechoslovakia and expressed the desire that Germany and Britain never go to war again. Chamberlain declared that this brought 'peace for our time'. Widespread euphoria greeted his announcement. The

---

* Lady Strathmore's death delayed by three weeks a planned official visit by the King and Queen to Paris which was intended to show the unity of two of Europe's most important democracies in face of the threat from the fascist dictators. In the interim, the Queen's dressmaker, Norman Hartnell, remade her entire wardrobe in white, the colour of deepest mourning for medieval queens. The effect in Paris was sensational.

King and Queen welcomed Chamberlain home from Munich by
appearing with him on the balcony of Buckingham Palace.*

~

Friday 30 September 1938 to Anne Chamberlain

Buckingham Palace

My dear Mrs Chamberlain

I have been thinking so much of you during these last agonising
weeks, knowing & understanding something of what you must be
going through. It is so hard to wait, & when it is on the shoulders of
your husband that such tremendous responsibilities rest, then it is
doubly hard. But you must feel so proud & glad that through sheer
courage & great wisdom he has been able to achieve so much for us
& for the World. Our gratitude is beyond words, & I can assure you
that our prayers that he might be sustained & helped through these
frightful days have been very real.

We have also felt most deeply for you, and do trust that the
Prime Minister & yourself will be allowed some real Peace, & soon.

I am, dear Mrs Chamberlain, yours very sincerely,

Elizabeth R

~

11 October 1938 to Osbert Sitwell

Balmoral Castle

My dear Mr Sitwell,

It was so kind of you to write me such a kind and sympathetic
letter during those terrible days that are passed. It was all such a
nightmare of horror & worry that I feel years older. But one good
thing is the fact that it was possible for sanity and Right to prevail at

---

* The Queen Mother later acknowledged to the historian D. R. Thorpe that this was an
error, though she thought it a 'venial' one. She acknowledged 'It was relief for ourselves, not
for Czechoslovakia.' (Author's interview with D. R. Thorpe.) It soon became clear that
appeasement had encouraged Hitler, rather than satisfying him. Queen Elizabeth later told
Eric Anderson that she thought Chamberlain was 'a good man. I think he really tried and,
whatever people say, it gave us that year. Because, as usual, they had practically got rid of the
army, stupid idiots. So that gave one year to re-arm and build a few aeroplanes.'

such a moment, and another, the marvellous way that the people of the country played up. They did not know very much of what was going on, and their courage & balance was (as usual) wonderful. Do you not think so? I shall hope to see you when you return to London – there is so much to talk about, and so few people with whom I can talk and keep my temper! Perhaps this will pass, I hope so with all my heart, for it is extremely boring both for myself and for my companions. [. . .]

I am, Yours very sincerely,
Elizabeth R
[. . .]

~

13 December 1938 to Sir Kenneth Clark

Buckingham Palace

My dear Sir Kenneth

Thank you so much for your charming letter. I was indeed touched by what you said in it, and can only repeat that we too, feel a deep regret that the heavy work of running the National Gallery, makes you feel that you must give up looking after our pictures.

It is so important that the monarchy should be kept in touch with the trend & life of modern, as well as ancient Art, and I hope that you will advise & help us along those lines?

Also, I do hope that you do not feel that you must give up immediately. Apart from the fact that we do not want to lose you, it would be a great help to find first of all a successor – and selfishly perhaps, I would like to have someone who is agreeable, & whom I can like, & talk to.*

Life is so worrying and troublesome nowadays, that it is a real distraction and encouragement to be able to lose oneself even for a few minutes among beautiful things, as apart from the ugliness and horror of so many of our problems.

I do understand what you feel about the difficulty you experience in running two large 'concerns', as it were. We are very sorry indeed, but do comprehend your feelings, which are most honourable.

---

* Sir Kenneth Clark remained *en poste* as Surveyor of the King's Pictures until 1944.

Yes, please, I would like to see the Sisley.*
I am, Yours Sincerely
Elizabeth R

~

9 February 1939 to Sir Kenneth Clark

Buckingham Palace

My dear Sir Kenneth,
    First of all I want to send you my very grateful, and I fear belated thanks for the most interesting and enchanting book of details.† It is fascinating and instructive & delightful, and I have so much enjoyed looking through it.
    It was indeed kind of you to send it to me, and I was so touched by your thought. [. . .]
    Thank you so much for sending the two pictures in for me to see. I like the Stanley Spencer‡ landscape very much. The Sickert§ is a little large & gloomy I find. But then, I am still very ignorant about the modern painters, and will ask you to come & look at them here when you return and to say what you think. Would Wednesday 15th at 12 o'clock suit you. If you have a meeting at that hour, the afternoon would suit me just as well.
    Please do not hesitate to let me know, I am, Yours very sincerely,
    Elizabeth R

~

---

* In 1939 the Queen bought a landscape by the Impressionist painter Alfred Sisley (1839–99).

† *One Hundred Details in the National Gallery*, published in 1938.

‡ Sir Stanley Spencer CBE (1891–1959), painter from Cookham-on-Thames, who studied at the Slade and served in the armed forces during the First World War; many of his strongest paintings adapted everyday scenes from Cookham to biblical stories.

§ Walter Sickert (1860–1942), leading British Impressionist painter who studied under J. A. M. Whistler and in Dieppe; moved from painting interiors with figures to robust landscapes.

5 May 1939 to the Most Rev. Cosmo Lang, Archbishop of Canterbury

Buckingham Palace

My dear Archbishop

I was so touched by your very kind and helpful letter, and feel that I must write you one line of affectionate thanks, which indeed comes from my heart.

You have always been such a wonderfully sympathetic and understanding friend to us both, and to know that we have your benediction and good wishes on our journey, is a great joy, and a great help. Sometimes, one's heart quails at the thought of the things that lie ahead, and then one counts one's blessings – and then things don't seem so bad!*

I am afraid that your holiday in the Mediterranean was very troubled and anxious – I am so sorry as you deserved a little real peace more than any man I know.

With my heartfelt thanks for your letter, I am,

Your affectionate friend

Elizabeth

~

6 May 1939 to Princess Elizabeth

RMS *Empress of Australia*

My Darling Lilibet

I do hope that you & Margaret got home safely & none the worse for all our goodbyes and journeys.

I am writing you this little letter, as a destroyer is coming off tomorrow to take mails, and tho' there is very little to tell you, I feel that if I don't write now, that you won't hear from me for weeks!

I hated saying goodbye to you & Margaret, but know that you

---

* In early May 1939 the King and Queen were to set off for a six-week visit to Canada and the United States to strengthen Britain's ties with both countries. War with Hitler was now seen as inevitable. Since Munich, anti-Jewish pogroms had grown ever more vicious in Germany and Austria and in March 1939 German troops occupied Prague. Chamberlain admitted that Hitler had misled him, and introduced compulsory military service for the first time ever in peacetime Britain.

will be happy with Miss C* & Alah, & that you will occasionally look at my 'notes'.

I can just see England in the distance now – the bit just beyond the New Forest where we enjoyed ourselves last summer! I do hope my darling, that if you want to know anything that you will send me a cable – I shall answer it at once.

We steamed through two lines of ships an hour ago (rather like the Coronation review) and they gave us a lovely send off. I thought of you both, & wished that you were here. I shall miss you horribly, but be good & kind & don't forget about fingers at Olympia, & smile politely!!

Goodbye my Angel, give Margaret a HUGE kiss, & an ENORMOUS one for yourself from

Your very loving

Mummy

PS My handwriting is very wobbly, because the ship is shivering like someone with influenza!

PPS Papa is writing to Margaret.

~

8 May 1939 to Queen Mary

RMS *Empress of Australia*

My Darling Mama

The Repulse† is leaving us tomorrow to return home, so I am taking the opportunity of writing you a letter in case she can take a bag. So far the journey has not been bad. It was rather rough (& big swell!) yesterday, and Catherine & a good many of the servants were laid low. However, it is pretty calm today, and they have all turned up smiling! It is rather foggy, and the foghorn moans hoarsely every minute or so – such a melancholy noise, & I much hope that we shall get better weather soon.

---

* Marion Crawford (1909–88), appointed governess to Princess Elizabeth and Princess Margaret in 1933 and known in the family as 'Crawfie'. She retired in 1949, having married Major George Buthlay in 1947, but her previously affectionate relationship with the Royal Family broke down after the publication in the USA in 1950 of her unauthorized book *The Little Princesses*.

† HMS *Repulse*, Renown-class battlecruiser launched in 1916, escorted the King and Queen thus far across the Atlantic. She was sunk in a Japanese air attack off Malaya in December 1941; 508 of her officers and men lost their lives.

The ship is quite comfortable, the food is good, but there are too many stewards & liftboys & messengers about – one falls over them at every turn. But they are so obliging & eager to do <u>anything</u> that we haven't the heart to send them away, poor things.

We felt very sad leaving you all on Saturday – it was nice that you all came to see us off, and I hope you had a good journey back in that horrible Pullman.

The Captain of the ship seems very nice & capable. We have not seen much of him as he is always on the Bridge owing to this annoying fog.

I found boxes & boxes of lovely flowers here, which kind people had sent, and some of them are on the ice, & will be fresh again in a few days.

There was one little thing that I quite forgot to tell you before I left, and that is, that Margaret gets very tired sometimes after those lovely visits that you take them [on] – she is so much smaller than Lilibet, & will never give up! So I wondered whether you would be very kind Mama, and if it is a picture gallery or large museum or something tiring, to tell Alah to take her home after an hour or so – I don't think that she will mind <u>very</u> much, and I do want her to grow, & not to get overtired with trying to keep up with her sister!

I do trust that things in Europe will settle down, & that there will be no major crises whilst Bertie is away.

I am starting to read the unexpurgated edition of 'Mein Kampf'* – it is very soap-box, but very interesting. Have you read it Mama?

I see on the news bulletin today, that David is going to broadcast to America this evening.† I do wonder whether this is true, and if it is, how troublesome of him to choose such a moment.

I will write again from Canada, & shall hope to write a more interesting letter than this! But life at sea is fairly monotonous as you know – better that it should be I suppose! There are lots of icebergs nearer Canada – so perhaps we shall see one – only <u>see</u> I trust!

With all my love darling Mama, ever your loving d-in-law
Elizabeth

---

* The two volumes of Adolf Hitler's *Mein Kampf* (My Struggle) were published in 1925 and 1926. The book expressed Hitler's hatred of Judaism and communism and his conviction that Germany should abandon democracy, rearm and expand.

† The Duke of Windsor broadcast an appeal for peace to the American people.

PS Forgive my bad hand-writing – there is a great deal of vibration.

~

13 May 1939 to Princess Elizabeth

RMS Empress of Australia

My Darling Lilibet

Here we are creeping along at about one mile per hour, & occasionally stopping altogether, for the 3rd day running! You can imagine how horrid it is – one cannot see more than a few yards, and the sea is full of icebergs as big as Glamis, & things called 'growlers' – which are icebergs mostly under water with only a very small amount of ice showing on the surface. We shall be late arriving in Canada, and it is going to be very difficult to fit everything in, and avoid disappointing people. It is <u>very</u> cold – rather like the coldest, dampest day at Sandringham – double it and add some icebergs, & then you can imagine a little of what it is like!

It is really a great anxiety being hung up here for so long, and the last thing that we expected. However, everybody is keeping cheerful, and the little band played Umbrellas, umbrellas,* etc today which helped to cheer <u>me</u> up.

I like to think of you and Margaret at Royal Lodge this weekend – I wonder if the garden is looking pretty, and if there are any Rhodies out in the wood.

Do ask Lord Wigram if he found a place for my Daphnes† – I sent him a message to ask him to very kindly select somewhere sheltered.

Do ask Alah if I ever mentioned to her that there is going to be an exhibition of personal furniture this summer at dear old 145 Piccadilly, and I promised to lend something from the nursery. Perhaps the little grandmother clock would do, and that little chair that you used to have. A very hard one covered in chintz!

We are all trying to behave like Guides & 'smile under difficulties' – and as whatever the conversation [it] usually comes back to ice & fog, it gets a little worn sometimes.

---

*   'The Umbrella Man', popular American song by Kay Keyser and his Orchestra in 1938–9.

†   *Daphne odora*, tender evergreen, bearing sweet-scented flowers in spring.

I do hope that you are enjoying your Saturday evenings with Mr Marten* – try & learn as much as you can from him, & mark how he brings the human element into all his history – of course history is made by ordinary humans, & one must not forget that.

Well, my darling, I am longing to see you both again, & I send you lots & lots of kisses and some pats for Dooks – Your very very loving Mummy

~

23 May 1939 to Princess Elizabeth

In the Train just after passing along the shore of Lake Superior

My Darling Lilibet

I am afraid that I never had one single minute in Ottawa to write to you, and this is the first opportunity on the train. All day we have been passing through lovely wild country. Rather like Scotland on a large scale. Great rivers & locks and pine woods, and for hours right along the Great Lake. It was bright blue, with many little wooded islands. This train is so rocky that I don't believe that you will be able to read a word.

We go round curves at full speed!

Papa & I have had a wonderful welcome everywhere we have been.

The French people in Quebec & Ottawa were wonderfully loyal; & [in] Montreal there must have been 2000000 people, all very enthusiastic & glad to have an excuse to show their feelings. Yesterday in Toronto it was the same, and we feel so glad that we were able to come here, & give the people an opportunity to show how British they are. (Oh this train!)

Today we have stopped to water the engine at various little places, usually consisting of a few wooden houses and a store. The people are so nice – they seem to be nearly all Scotch!

May 24th

We have stopped for the night at a little place called Kemnay in Manitoba half way across Canada. We spent the day in Winnipeg, a

---

* Sir Henry Marten KCVO (1872–1948) was Vice-Provost of Eton and gave Princess Elizabeth regular history lessons. In March 1945 he was knighted by King George VI on the steps of Eton College Chapel.

large town where all the business is done for the thousands of miles of farms round about. It rained in the morning, but cleared up in the afternoon, when we drove 28 miles, with cheering people & children all the way! Papa & I are bearing up very well. Tho' we are working very hard – from morning to night, we go in open cars & the good air keeps us well.

The train stops at little stations to get water or coal or ice, & there is always a crowd, & we go out & talk to the people. Yesterday there were some Indians with a baby in its wooden cradle, & <u>always</u> someone from Scotland! Usually Forfar or Glamis!

I am able to write much better now that the train is at a standstill – we have been travelling since Sunday and are getting quite used to the train.

I am absolutely <u>longing</u> to see you and Margaret again. What a hug you'll get when I get home. I wonder what Dookie will say!

I have had two delightful letters from you my darling. Thank you so very much. I am afraid that mine will be very slow in coming, as the distances are so great. What fun the Panda sounds.* I would love to see it.

Canada is a very beautiful country – I hope that you will see it some day. The people are very English – they think the same as we all do – luckily!

I am so sleepy & tired after our long day, that I think I must go to bed.

So good-night darling, from
Your very very loving
Mummy

~

27 May 1939 to Princess Elizabeth

Banff Springs Hotel

My Darling Lilibet
Here we are at Banff, in the middle of magnificent great mountains, & a river running just below the Hotel. We got here last night in time for dinner, a lovely evening, and like all Canadian

---

*   The Princesses had just visited London Zoo.

houses the Hotel was <u>boiling</u>! We opened every window, and I expect all the poor habitants will get pneumonia!

This morning we climbed a mountain nearby which took about 50 minutes. It was very like Balmoral only much bigger, & the pine trees smelt delicious in the hot sun. This afternoon Papa & I went for a buggy ride!! 'Thanks for the buggy ride' etc. Two nice grey horses & we rolled along on high old wheels – very wobbly but great fun.

After tea we went off in a car, & the first thing we saw was a great black shape in a little lake – a moose feeding on the water lily bulbs. Were we not lucky? Then we saw some beavers working at their dam – you remember Grey Wolf's* film? They do such wonderful things, & we watched them for some time. I did so wish that you & Margaret were with us then, as I know you would have loved them. Oh, & this morning we saw two baby black bears! They were so sweet, & not very shy.

It has been a great relief to get away from roaring crowds and incessant noise even tho' one is glad that the people are pleased to see us. Tomorrow morning we start off again. Church at 9.30 in the little church here, & then off to Lake Louise to catch the train.

At Calgary yesterday we saw a lot of Indians, and quite a lot of cowboys on 'bucking broncos' who came dashing along with us.

Papa & I are bearing up very well on the whole, tho' we have had a very hard ten days travelling, with <u>very</u> long drives in open cars through huge crowds. The next fortnight will be very hard work, but it is worth while, for one feels how important it is that the people here should see their King, & not have him only as a symbol. There is so little time to write, and I am afraid that my letters are badly expressed scribbles.

Please thank Alah and Miss Crawford for their nice letters. I was very glad to get them.

The mountains here are so high, that if you were looking out of the nursery window at B.P., you would have to raise your eyes to the sky to see the tops. It is very beautiful I must say.

Well my darling, I am sure that you are being wonderfully kind &

---

* The Queen meant 'Grey Owl', a 'Red Indian' naturalist, later revealed to be Archibald Belaney all the way from Hastings, who gave a 'cinema-lecture show' on Canadian animals to the Queens and the Princesses on Friday 10 December 1937. (Queen Elizabeth to her sister-in-law Fenella Bowes Lyon, 9 December 1937, RA QEQM/OUT/SHAKERLEY)

thoughtful for other people, and I am sure that Margaret is too. You mustn't forget that she is really very little, & sometimes you must control <u>yourself</u> when she is a little teasing. I know it is difficult, but you <u>can</u> do it, & I know you will.

I long to see you both again – days pass quickly please, and with many kisses & love to darling Margaret, Your very very loving Mummy

PS A nice pat for Dookie please. In one of the papers here there was a picture of you & M with Dookie, & it said 'an old Corgi of uncertain temper'!! Poor old Dookie.

~

1 June 1939 to Queen Mary

Jasper Park Lodge
Alberta

My Darling Mama

Bertie & I were deeply concerned when we heard the news of your horrible accident,* and we are so relieved to hear that you are going on well. I expect that you will feel the shock afterwards, and I do hope that you will be very very careful and take a <u>real</u> rest. It must have been absolutely <u>terrifying</u>, and thank God nobody was very badly hurt. You would have been touched to hear of all the anxious inquiries from all sorts & kinds of people here. At little wayside stations, Lord Mayors, politicians, <u>everybody</u> wanted to know how you were getting on. [. . .]

We have had a most touching reception everywhere – it has really been wonderful and most moving. All Canada is very pleased at the way the French Canadians received us, and are hopeful that the visit will bring lasting results in uniting the country. They are terribly divided in many ways – and the provincial Governments especially are jealous and suspicious of the Federal Government. But they are so young that I expect they will achieve unity in the end.

We spent a pleasant 2 nights in Victoria staying with the Lieutenant-Governor. They are charming people, and were such good hosts.

---

* On 23 May 1939 a lorry ran into Queen Mary's car in Wimbledon while she was returning from a visit to the Royal Horticultural Society's gardens at Wisley. Her car was overturned and she was badly bruised and shocked.

The trouble with these long days in the train, is that we stop very often for water, ice etc, and there are always crowds waiting, and one gets very little quiet.

In Ottawa we had a reception for all the journalists who are travelling with us in the pilot train – about 80 of them! They are really very nice, and were so shy and polite! The Americans are particularly easy and pleasant, and have been amazed I believe at the whole affair. Of course they have no idea of our Constitution or how the Monarchy works, and were surprised & delighted to find that we were ordinary & fairly polite people with a big job of work.

We have very long drives through the big towns, and I must say, we get very bored & tired, but both feel very well and so encouraged to feel the strength of feeling for the Empire here. More & more one feels that the hope of the world lies in the unity, sanity & strength for good in the British Empire – freedom is worth dying for.

We look forward so much to seeing you again before very long, and I do pray that you will feel no ill effects of your horrible accident.

With all my love darling Mama, ever your loving daughter in law Elizabeth

~

5 June 1939 to Princess Elizabeth

In the Train, Ontario

My Darling Lilibet

Here we are flying along round terrific corners through quite wild and untouched country – along the side of beautiful lakes & thousands of miles of woods & bush. We left the cultivated land the day before yesterday, & have been travelling hard & without stopping except for little places where we water & coal. There are usually a large bunch of children who have probably come over a hundred miles by canoe down the lakes, as there are no roads up here. Wouldn't it be nice to live in a place with no roads, only trails through the woods with the railway as the only link with civilization.

<u>June 6th</u>

We have been almost continually 'on show' all today, passing through a very thickly populated part of Canada after Toronto, and at every hour there are thousands & thousands of people waiting at the

various stops. They are so happy to have 'the King' with them, &
sometimes I have tears in my eyes when one sees the emotion in
their faces. It means so much to them to <u>see</u> the Sovereign who they
are so loyal to.

Tomorrow night we cross into the United States – I will try & write
a line from there, tho' I fear that every single moment will be occupied.

I was so glad to get your darling letter today. I do hope that the
colds are better, and am getting more & more excited at the thought
of seeing you both again! I should like you both to come down to
Southampton to meet us. Would you like to do this?

I think that you would like to see the 'Empress of Britain' coming
slowly in – will you tell Alec* to arrange this please? Get him to come
& see you – it will be all arranged already I expect.

Well, goodbye my darling Lilibet, I have so loved all your sweet
& <u>well written</u> letters, from your

   Very very loving
   Mummy

~

On 8 June, the King and Queen arrived by train in Washington DC in
an overpowering heatwave. They were the guests of President and Mrs
Roosevelt and their task, as they saw it, was to try to win American
backing for Britain's cause in the imminent war against Germany. It
was not easy; in 1935 Congress had passed the Neutrality Act,
specifically designed to keep the US out of any European war, and
isolationism was popular in the United States. From Washington the
King and Queen travelled to New York City and then to the
Roosevelts' country home, Hyde Park, in upstate New York.
Everywhere, they were well received. Later, the Queen recalled, *'It was
the first time an English King had ever been to the United States . . . We
didn't quite know what sort of attention we would have, but they were
tremendously welcoming. It was very valuable because the King was able to
talk to Roosevelt. Endless night talks they had, because Hitler was looming
then. In fact it was so close that we were going in a battleship, and had to
change to a liner in case it was wanted. It was as close as that.'*

~

---

*   Sir Alexander Hardinge; see footnote on p. 226.

11 June 1939 to Queen Mary

Hyde Park
On the Hudson, N.Y.

My Darling Mama,

I feel that I must write you one hurried line from this house before we leave tonight, to tell you of the great kindness & hospitality of the Roosevelt family towards ourselves. They are such a charming & united family, and living so like English people when they come to their country house.

We arrived in Washington in the most stupendous heat! I really don't know how we got through those 2 days of continuous functions mostly out of doors, as it really was ghastly. It is very damp heat, & one could hardly breathe. However everybody was very very kind & welcoming, & made us feel quite 'at home'. Yesterday we had a very long day in New York & the Fair, where of course we only saw our Pavilion (quite good & very interesting historically), Ireland, Africa, Canada, Australia etc. Some of the Pavilions looked very good – especially the Soviet! and Italy, but otherwise one big Fair looks much like another I believe. Everybody seemed genuinely pleased to see us, and at moments one really feels that one is at home in England! Especially here, where we arrived about 8 last night. One might be in an average English country house, with a wide hall, & big sitting rooms & rather small hot bedrooms.

Old Mrs R has the greatest affection & admiration for you Mama, & last night at dinner the President proposed your health in the most touching terms & quite impromptu addressing himself to his own Mother who was sitting opposite him. It was so nice & friendly, & of course I found tears coming into my eyes!

Today we went to Church in the little village Church. The service is exactly the same as ours down to every word, & they even had the prayers for the King & the Royal Family. I could not help thinking how curious it sounded, & yet how natural. It was just the sort of situation you would have appreciated – the drama of this happening in these days.

Then after church we had luncheon at little tables on the verandah of Mr R's little house near here. The tables were spread about under the trees, & he had all his own farm servants, gardeners etc at tables to right & left. It was a very friendly affair, and quite cool

& pleasant. Afterwards we went to <u>Mrs</u> R's own little house, where Bertie & the President & the sons bathed, whilst I sat in a chair in the shade watching them, & enjoying the first peaceful moment for many weeks. The President drove us <u>himself</u> in his car – he has some arrangement, as of course he is utterly paralysed about the legs. He is such a delightful man, and <u>very</u> good company. The sons are charming too, & the daughters-in-law pretty & <u>very</u> good mannered. I must say that they have all such lovely manners – easy & polished, & not shy.

I haven't got much time left before dressing for dinner, so will end hoping with all my heart that the effects of your horrible accident have left you.

So longing to see you again, ever your devoted daughter in law
Elizabeth
PS My complexion is ruined!

~

11 June 1939 to Princess Elizabeth

Hyde Park
On the Hudson, N.Y.

My Darling Lilibet
It was such fun talking to you both on the telephone today, and directly after we had spoken we went off for a picnic luncheon.

There were a lot of people there, and we all sat at little tables under the trees round the house, and had all our food on one plate – a little salmon, some turkey, some ham, lettuce, beans & HOT DOGS too! [. . .]

This evening, after dinner we are leaving, & tomorrow morning we start the last week of our trip. I must say that I don't think that I could bear very much more, as there comes a moment when one's resistance nearly goes. I am dripping at this moment so I hope that the paper won't get soaked!

We had two burning, boiling, sweltering, humid furnace-like days in Washington, and as we were busy from early morning till late, you can imagine what we felt like at the end of it! But everybody was <u>so</u> kind & welcoming, & one feels really at home here. Of course speaking the same language is a great link!

This morning we went to Church at the village Church, & the

service is <u>exactly</u> the same as ours. It seemed so nice somehow, &
homely.

I really haven't got very much time for writing, but wanted to
send you a word from the U.S.

Goodbye my darling, see you very soon,

Your very very loving Mummy

~

On 22 June the King and Queen arrived back in London to be greeted
by huge crowds of people singing 'Land of Hope and Glory' and 'God
Save the King' outside Buckingham Palace.

~

28 June 1939 to Lady Tweedsmuir

Buckingham Palace

My dear Lady Tweedsmuir*

After eight weeks I am at last able to make use of a stationary
writing-table!, and one of my first letters must be to you, who I have
so much to thank for. Your great kindness, and hospitality, & thought
for our comfort at Ottawa will never be forgotten by either the King
or by myself, and our gratitude indeed comes from our hearts.

It is really disgraceful how much the comforts of life allure one,
and I found myself sometimes thinking longingly of that lovely
bedroom & delicious bathroom, when we were travelling in the train,
& more particularly at The White House, where my bathroom was
about 90 degrees of heat!

It was so delightful staying with Lord Tweedsmuir and yourself,
you made us feel so much at home, and we felt truly sad when we
left you that Sunday at Ottawa.

Please accept our very deep gratitude for all you did for us, our
stay with you was perfect in every way, and I only hope that you
were not absolutely <u>dead</u> after that violent three days of functions <u>&</u>
being hostess.

---

* Wife of the Governor General of Canada, the first Baron Tweedsmuir (1875–1940), better
known as the author John Buchan. As she watched the King and Queen sail away from
Canada, she wrote, 'The line from Antony and Cleopatra came into my mind. I tried to push
the thought away, but it kept coming back: "The bright day is gone and we are for the dark." '
(Dorothy Laird, *Queen Elizabeth The Queen Mother*, Coronet, 1985, p. 241)

The books in the train were a great joy – I read a very good short Canadian history and <u>all</u> Mr James's Ghost Stories all over again!

I cannot begin to tell you what our feelings and memories are of the tour. Our chief emotion is one of deep thankfulness that it was such a success, for more & more one feels that a united Empire is the only hope for this troubled world of today. Sometimes I wonder whether we are not already fighting a war. A war of love & right thinking against the forces of evil. It was a curious sensation (and one that we had dreaded) of getting back over here to that horrible feeling of tension, rumour, and acute anxiety that had sapped our vitality for so many months before our departure for Canada. We find everybody very calm, very determined, and beginning to lose patience with the Nazi leaders, who seem determined to put a wrong construction on whatever any of our leading politicians say, and are still, I fear, certain that England will not fight. We must continue to pray that some means of preserving Peace will be found, and that Germany will realize that aggression & cruelty lead to destruction. We feel strengthened and encouraged by our trip, and filled with love and pride in Canada & her grand people.

With again my very sincere thanks for all your kindness, and with many kind messages to Lord Tweedsmuir,

I am,

Yours very sincerely

Elizabeth R

PS In Newfoundland I saw a most delightful photograph of Lord Tweedsmuir in an Indian headdress. Might I ask for a copy if you have one? It would give me great pleasure. ER

~

31 August 1939 to Queen Mary

Buckingham Palace

Darling Mama

I arrived here on Tuesday, and found Bertie very calm and cheerful despite the great anxiety that he is going through. It is indeed terrible that the world should be faced with a war, just because of the wickedness and sheer stupidity of the Nazis. One can only go on hoping & praying, that a solution will be found.

I am thinking of you so much at Sandringham, and so wish that I could come down and see you, but I do not like to leave at this critical moment. It is so wearing to be alone, and I do feel for you with all my heart.

This house is in a most extraordinary state! The garden entrance is being painted, also the Regency room & the Bow Room, and the walls outside our rooms are a network of planks and scaffolding preparatory to cleaning the stone, also the garden front is having various stones replaced – so you can imagine that the whole effect is one of complete upheaval.

The children we are leaving at Balmoral, & if war comes, they will go to Birkhall, anyway for the moment. It is awful to think of being parted, but one must see what happens before risking their coming south.

If David comes back here (I suppose he must if there is a war), what are we going to do about Mrs S? Personally I do not wish to receive her at all, tho' it must depend on circumstances, what do you feel about it Mama? I am afraid that if they do return, they will wriggle their way into things – tho' not come to court functions of course. It is a very difficult position, & a great nuisance, with many pitfalls. Lord Halifax* has just been to see Bertie, & remained to tea. What a wonderful man he is – such nobility of character & firmness of purpose – he is indeed a great man.

With all my love darling Mama, & we must have faith that good will prevail,

Your devoted Elizabeth

~

The Prime Minister, Neville Chamberlain, declared war on the morning of 3 September; his speech was broadcast by the BBC. The next day, the Queen wrote a four-page note describing her feelings.

~

---

* Edward Wood, third Viscount Halifax, KG OM GCSI GCMG GCIE TD PC (1881–1959), Conservative statesman, Foreign Secretary, 1938–40. A supporter of the policy of appeasement before the Second World War, he was British Ambassador in Washington, 1940–6.

Diary: 4 September 1939

I wish to try and set down on paper some of the impressions that remain from that ghastly day Sunday September 3rd 1939. And yet when one tries to find words, how impossible, & how inadequate they are to convey even an idea of the torture of mind that we went through.

Having tried by every means in our power to turn Hitler from his purpose of wantonly attacking the Poles, and having warned him of the consequences if he did so, and having been practically ignored by the Nazis, we knew on the night of Sept 2nd, that our request for a withdrawal of German troops from Poland would be refused, so that we went to bed with sad hearts.

I woke early the next morning – at about 5.30. I said to myself – we have only a few hours of Peace left, and from then until 11 o'clock, every moment was an agony.

My last cup of tea in peace! My last bath at leisure; and all the time one's mind working on many thoughts. Chiefly of the people of this country – their courage, their sense of humour, their sense of right and wrong – how will they come through the wicked things that war lets loose. One thing is, that they are at their best when things are bad, and the spirit is wonderful.

At 10.30 I went to the King's sitting room, and we sat quietly talking until at 11.15 the Prime Minister broadcast his message from Downing Street, that as the Germans had ignored our communications, we were at war. He spoke so quietly, so sincerely, & was evidently deeply moved & unhappy.

I could not help tears running down my face, but we both realised that it was inevitable, if there was to be any freedom left in our world, that we must face the cruel Nazi creed, & rid ourselves of the continual nightmare of force & material standards. Hitler knew quite surely that when he invaded Poland, he started a terrible war. What kind of mentality could he have?

As we were thinking these things, suddenly from outside the window came the ghastly, horrible wailing of the air raid siren. The King and I looked at each other, and said 'It can't be', but there it was, and with beating hearts we went down to our shelter in the basement. We felt stunned & horrified, and sat waiting for the bombs to fall.

After half an hour the All Clear went, & we returned to our rooms, & then had a prayer in the '44* room. We prayed with all our hearts that Peace would come soon – real peace, not a Nazi peace.

~

One of the Queen's principal concerns was for her children. She wrote to her sister Rose (Lady Granville) asking her to look after her two daughters should anything happen to her and the King. The letter has not been found, but in her reply of 6 September Rose wrote, 'I want to promise you straight away that in the event of anything happening to both you & the King, I would give up everything to try & make the two darlings happy, & try my very best to smooth their lives. I do realise that what I am promising is not an easy thing! – but I will keep your letter, as it would be a help if it ever came to an argument for their good. I have always loved them, & I think if they saw me a good deal, they would come to feel that there was someone to fall back on & rely on – & also someone to laugh at the old jokes with! [. . .] I do promise you that I will try my very best & will go straight to them should anything happen to you both – which God forbid!'[†]

~

8 September 1939 to the Most Rev. Cosmo Lang, Archbishop of Canterbury

Buckingham Palace

My dear Archbishop

I send you my affectionate and grateful thanks for your kind and very helpful letter received two days ago.[‡]

I must admit that I have had to call up all my reserves of strength

---

* The 1844 Room was so named because it was occupied by Tsar Nicholas I of Russia during his visit to England in 1844.

† RA QEQM/PRIV/BL

‡ In his letter the Archbishop had said he knew that the Queen would do everything to encourage the women of Britain, not least in 'spreading the spirit of your own sympathy and understanding and calm fortitude. Indeed I feel inclined to say to your Majesty what was said in the Bible story to Queen Esther, "Who knoweth whether thou art come to the Kingdom for such a time as this."' (5 September 1939, RA QEQM/PRIV/PAL/LANG)

and faith to cope with these last few days, and your inspiring words have given me fresh courage & hope. I <u>know</u>, as do all our people, that we are fighting evil things, and we must face the future bravely.

I shall try with all my heart to help the people. If only one could do more for them – they are so wonderful.

One thing I realize clearly, that if one did not love this country & this people with a deep love, then our job would be almost impossible.

The only hope for the world is love. I wish in a way that we had another word for it – in the ordinary human mind love has so many meanings, other than the sense in which I use it.

I hope that we shall soon meet again – if <u>only</u> it were in the clear bright air of dear Balmoral.

I trust that you have been provided with an adequate air raid shelter? How degrading it is, to have to rise from one's bed, & retire to the basement – I resent it hotly.

With again my grateful thanks for your letter, which I shall always cherish, & read when my courage fails a little.

I am,

Yours affec: & gratefully

Elizabeth R

~

26 September 1939 to Queen Mary

Buckingham Palace

Darling Mama

Thank you so much for your letter and enclosure. [. . .]

I returned this morning to London after a really lovely week at Birkhall. I went to see the refugees at Balmoral & Abergeldie, the children at the schools & in one or two cottages. A great many have gone back to 'the Gorbals' in Glasgow, a very bad slum, taking their children, but the ones who remain are happy, & trying their best to keep things clean & tidy & to help all they can. They are all Irish and of course Roman Catholic. Mrs Ross has done very well, and they are starting a work party for the mothers, to teach them how to sew for their children & themselves. They seem to be woefully ignorant of household matters, so that one hopes they will learn something useful at any rate.

The flowers were heavenly at Balmoral, masses of colour everywhere – it seemed <u>so sad</u> to see everything shut up & empty.

I motored to Glamis yesterday to see my father, who is very well thank God, stopping at Perth en route to visit the Black Watch Depot, where I met the chairman of the committee to provide comforts for the various Battalions. [. . .]

I do hope that life is becoming better for you gradually Mama darling. I do feel that it is terribly hard for you to be uprooted, & only your great courage will keep your spirits up.

I must say, that the first fortnight of September I really felt so miserable & disappointed & exhausted that life was almost horrible. I have tried hard to pull myself together, & summon all my faith, & hope & trust in the right, & do feel more able to stand up to things – for we <u>are right</u>.

I haven't heard a word about Mrs Simpson – I trust that she will soon return to France and STAY THERE. I am sure that she hates this dear country, & therefore she should not be here in war time.

I am so happy to hear from Bertie that you are coming here on Thursday – it will be so delicious to see you again.

With my love darling Mama, ever your loving daughter in law Elizabeth

~

2 October 1939 to Prince Paul of Yugoslavia

Buckingham Palace

My dear Paul,

Thank you a thousand times for your dear letter. It was such a joy to hear from you, and your words were most comforting at this terrible moment in our history. After the first ghastly shock that we all felt when war became inevitable, this country has settled down grimly, quietly, and with the utmost determination, to try and rid the world of this evil thing that has been let loose by those idiotic Germans.

It is truly a struggle of the spirit, evil thinking, arrogance and materialism, against truth, justice & liberty. Bertie & I, who went through the last War, feel deeply unhappy, but we both realize that the issue must be faced, and we are calmly trusting in the ultimate victory of good.

What breaks one's heart, is to see yet another generation going cheerfully off to face death. I went to see the Black Watch the other day, one of my regiments, and suddenly saw my nephew John Elphinstone* among the officers. I had not seen him before in uniform, and received a great shock, as I thought for an awful moment that it was my brother Fergus who was killed in France when serving with the same regiment. It was only for one second – a flash, a family likeness, but how tragic to think of all that ghastly waste.

And yet is it waste?

Humanity must fight against bad things if we are to survive, and the spiritual things are stronger than anything else, and cannot be destroyed, thank God.

I do feel so deeply for you & Olga parted from your dear boys, please do tell me if there is <u>anything</u> that we can do for them, we would be so glad to be of help at <u>any</u> time.

In a curious way the last 20 years seem to have been suddenly swept away and the last War has joined up on to this one. Perhaps we never finished it after all.

David's visit passed off very quietly. He and Mrs S stayed with Baba & Fruity Metcalfe,† & they have now returned to France, where let us hope they will remain.

I think that he <u>at last</u> realizes that there is no niche for him here – the mass of the people do not forgive quickly the sort of thing that he did to this country, and they <u>HATE</u> her! D came to see Bertie, and behaved just as if nothing had EVER happened – too extraordinary. I had taken the precaution to send her a message before they came, saying that I was sorry I could not receive her. I thought it more honest to make things quite clear. So she kept away, & nobody saw her. What a curse black sheep are in a family!

I am ordering a photograph for you, & one for Olga, and Mr Beaton‡ who is mincing away at some light war work, will execute

---

* John Alexander Elphinstone, seventeenth Lord Elphinstone (1914–75), son of the Queen's sister May and Sidney Elphinstone.

† Edward ('Fruity') Metcalfe MVO MC (1887–1957), Indian Army officer, joined the Prince of Wales's staff in 1922 and remained loyal thereafter; best man at his wedding to Mrs Simpson. Married 1925 Alexandra 'Baba' Curzon (1904–95), daughter of Lord Curzon.

‡ Cecil Beaton (1904–80), fashion and society photographer. His first series of portraits of the

my order as soon as possible. I believe he is a telephone operator. Can you not imagine him saying, 'Number darling'? 2305? 'Oh <u>divine</u>, my dear,' etc etc.

Sometimes I feel that we are all living in a terrible nightmare, don't you?

When so many people in the world <u>long</u> for peace, it seems very hard not to be able to obtain it. The people here are beginning to make jokes about Hitler. That is rather a good sign, for they usually joke about things when they are too serious to be taken seriously – if you know what I mean. He is usually known as Old Nasty. Very childish!

Everything in this country is completely upside down. All the big houses are either maternity homes or hospitals or schools, London is completely black at night, everybody working hard & united as never before, and the balloon barrage swimming over our heads like pretty fishes when high, & very like elephants & sheep when low!

I do hope that you are quite well again. Bertie & I think so often of you & Olga & all you have to bear. How lucky Yugoslavia is to have you.

With our best love to you both, ever your devoted friend, Elizabeth.

PS

Oct 11 1939

I kept my letter back in case the photographs arrived, but as they have not come, I send 2 or 3 baby snapshots taken at the same time – just to amuse you & Olga!

~

6 November 1939 to the Most Rev. Cosmo Lang, Archbishop of Canterbury

Buckingham Palace

My dear Archbishop

You very kindly said today, that you would look through my broadcast,* and I now send you the skeleton. I have purposely made

---

Queen was made in 1939. Thereafter he became one of the Royal Family's most constant and successful portraitists.

* The Queen had been urged to broadcast to the women of Britain and the Empire. She made the broadcast on Armistice Day, 11 November 1939.

it very simple, as I wish to speak to the simple women who are a little perplexed about this War.

One thing I notice is – that I have not brought God into my few words. If you think that I should say anything about our faith in divine guidance – <u>please</u> do suggest a sentence or two. I think that it would be right & helpful myself – if you agree, I should be most grateful for any suggestions. It was so delightful seeing you today. We always feel refreshed & strengthened when we have talked with you. I wonder if you will think my idea of a broadcast too homely? It is <u>so</u> difficult.

Ever yours affec:

Elizabeth R

~

The Queen's Broadcast, 11 November 1939

The last time that I broadcast a message was at Halifax, Nova Scotia, when I said a few words of farewell, to all the women and children who had welcomed The King and myself so kindly, during our visits to Canada and the United States of America.

The world was then at peace; and for seven happy weeks we had moved in an atmosphere of such goodwill and human kindliness, that the very idea of strife and bloodshed seemed impossible. The recollection of it still warms my heart and gives me courage.

I speak today in circumstances sadly different. For twenty years, we have kept this Day of Remembrance, as one consecrated to the memory of past and never to be forgotten sacrifice, and now the Peace which that sacrifice made possible has been broken, and once again we have been forced into war.

I know that you would wish me to voice, in the name of the women of the British Empire, our deep and abiding sympathy with those on whom the first cruel and shattering blows have fallen, the women of Poland. Nor do we forget the gallant womanhood of France, who are called on to share with us again the hardships and sorrows of war.

War has at all times called for the fortitude of women. Even in other days, when it was an affair of the fighting forces only, wives and mothers at home suffered constant anxiety for their dear ones, and too often the misery of bereavement. Their lot was all the harder because they felt that they could do so little beyond heartening, through their own courage and devotion, the men at the front.

Now this is all changed, for we, no less than men, have real and vital work to do. To us, also, is given the proud privilege of serving our Country in her hour of need.

The call has come, and from my heart I thank you, the Women of our great Empire, for the way that you have answered it. The tasks that you have undertaken, whether at home or in distant lands, cover every field of National Service, and I would like to pay my tribute to all of you who are giving such splendid and unselfish help in this time of trouble.

At the same time, I do not forget the humbler part which so many of you have to play in these trying times. I know that it is not so difficult to do the big things. The novelty, the excitement of new and interesting duties have an exhilaration of their own. But these tasks are not for every woman. It is the thousand and one worries and irritations in carrying on war-time life in ordinary homes which are often so hard to bear.

Many of you have had to see your family life broken up – your husband going off to his allotted task – your children evacuated to places of greater safety. The King and I know what it means to be parted from our children, and we can sympathise with those of you who have bravely consented to this separation for the sake of your little ones. Equally do we appreciate the hospitality shown by those of you who have opened your homes to strangers and to children sent from places of special danger. All this, I know, has meant sacrifice, and I would say to those who are feeling the strain: Be assured that in carrying on your home duties and meeting all these worries cheerfully, you are giving real service to the Country. You are taking your part in keeping the home front, which will have dangers of its own, stable and strong.

It is, after all, for our homes and for their security that we are fighting, and we must see to it that, despite all the difficulty of these days, our homes do not lose those very qualities which make them the background as well as the joy of our lives.

Women of all lands yearn for the day when it will be possible to set about building a new and better world, where peace and goodwill shall abide.

That day must come. Meantime, to all of you, in every corner of the Empire, who are doing such fine work in all our Services, or who are carrying on at home amidst the trials of these days, I would give a message of hope and encouragement.

We have all a part to play, and I know you will not fail in yours, remembering always that the greater your courage and devotion, the sooner we shall see again in our midst the happy ordered life for which we long. Only when we have won through to an enduring peace shall we be free to work unhindered for the greater happiness and well-being of all mankind.

We put our trust in God, who is our Refuge and Strength in all times of trouble. I pray with all my heart that He may bless and guide and keep you always.

~

12 November 1939 to Lady Helen Graham

Buckingham Palace

Dearest Nellie,

I cannot begin to tell you how glad I am that you are coming back in the spring for a 'wait'. I really do not think I could bear to lose you altogether. [. . .] I do want you to know how deeply grateful I am. In fact words can never tell you what I feel in my heart. All through these years, and particularly the last three years, when life became so complicated and difficult, your wonderful understanding and never failing sympathy, your courage and your sense of proportion, and your delicious & perfect sense of humour have made the whole difference to my days. I wish that I had your gift of words, so that I could put on paper how much I feel. [. . .]

Yours affec:

Elizabeth R

PS This is not a farewell letter – it is just what I am thinking at the moment. ER

~

15 November 1939 to Viscount Halifax

Buckingham Palace

My dear Lord Halifax

I send you 'Mein Kampf', but do not advise you to read it through, or you might go mad, and that would be a great pity.

Even a skip through, gives one a good idea of his mentality, ignorance, and obvious sincerity. I forgot to ask you today whether you were comfortable at the Dorchester?

It's so exciting, & sounds so rackety & gay!

I must ask Dorothy whether I may come one day to see you, & view your new home.

I trust with all my heart that you will achieve a day or two in the country soon.

Ever yours sincerely
ER

~

6 December 1939 to Prince Paul of Yugoslavia

Buckingham Palace

My dear Paul

[. . .] Everybody here has settled down to war conditions, and tho' every single individual loathes this war, it has made them all the more determined to try & end aggression. It is really rather horrible, the way this all crops up every few generations – this time we must try & produce a more lasting Peace.

Bertie is in France,* & thank God seems well, & standing up to the strain & anxiety in excellent fashion. I am busy going round seeing things and talking to people – I feel that it is so important that the people can feel free and able to tell me anything they like. Their cheerfulness & courage sustains me to a great degree. It's such a pity

---

* The King had made a vist to the British Expeditionary Force in France where morale was not high among soldiers waiting for action in the cold. The trip was a great success in encouraging the troops. One member of the Force put it strongly, 'We feel ready for any number of Hitlers now.' (Extract from a letter to Molly Cazalet from a cousin in the BEF enclosed with a letter from Molly Cazalet to Queen Elizabeth, 16 December 1939, RA QEQM/ PRIV/PAL)

that Ribbentrop* only made friends with people like Lady Cunard†
when he was here as Ambassador – do you suppose that he made his
calculations of the British character & reactions to events from a
study of her & her friends?

I do hope that you are keeping well, tho' you must be going
through an intolerable strain – the world is indeed in a miserable
state.

Kenneth Clark is doing such excellent work organizing work for
artists, giving concerts in the empty National Gallery, & such useful
things.

Oh, and Paul, I am being painted by Augustus John! He has made
the charcoal drawings, one lovely one, & starts the real thing next
week. I shall be so interested to see what he produces.

I have bought a very attractive Duncan Grant‡ (St Paul's from
over the river) & have got a little Sickert, at last. [. . .]

Please give dearest Olga my best love, & with much to yourself as
well,

ever your affect:

Elizabeth

PS Poor old Aunt Louise§ was ninety one – it was a mercy really
that she died.

PPS I am living here alone, & am the <u>only</u> member of the family
in London!! Keep the old flag flying. Hooray!

~

---

* Joachim von Ribbentrop (1893–1946), leading Nazi and intimate of Hitler. German
Ambassador to London, 1936–8; Foreign Minister, 1938–45. In London he was much disliked
for his pomposity and bad manners. In 1945 he was put on trial at the Nuremberg Military
Tribunal and found guilty of war crimes, crimes against humanity and other crimes; along
with other defendants, he was hanged on 16 October 1946.

† Maud 'Emerald' Cunard (1872–1948), famously lavish hostess. During the abdication crisis,
she was a supporter of Mrs Simpson.

‡ Duncan Grant (1885–1978), landscape, still-life and portrait painter, forever associated with
the Bloomsbury Set – Virginia Woolf, Vanessa Bell, Lytton Strachey. Lived in East Sussex
where their vividly painted house, Charleston, became a popular attraction after Grant's death.

§ Princess Louise, Duchess of Argyll (1848–1939), sixth child of Queen Victoria and Prince
Albert.

1 February 1940 to Viscount Halifax

Buckingham Palace

My dear Lord Halifax

I am deeply touched and most grateful, that in the midst of your very busy life you have found time to send me 'Ghosts' (I love 'em), and also to let me know about D'Arcy Osborne. I am glad that he is staying on at the Holy See – he loves Rome, <u>and</u> the Pope, <u>&</u> the Cardinals, and I hope that the good relations already established will continue to prosper. With my heartfelt thanks for your kind note, and for the book,

I am, Yours very Sincerely
Elizabeth R

~

1 February 1940 to Osbert Sitwell

Buckingham Palace

My dear Mr Sitwell,

I thank you with all my heart for your kindness in sending me your sister's most lovely anthology.* It is indeed full of most wonderful things, and I enjoy her introduction so much. I am very ignorant about poetry, and her descriptions and explanations of different poems make it intensely interesting & illuminating. Do tell her what a joy it is giving me.

I am sending you the photograph of myself. I hope that it is the one you wanted.

Ever yours sincerely,
Elizabeth R

~

---

* Edith Sitwell (1887–1964), poet and critic, sister of Osbert and Sacheverell. She appeared deeply unconventional, often wearing a turban, brocade gowns and masses of jewellery. Both her poetry and her exotic sense of dress excited controversy and she made public enemies. But she enjoyed enduring friendships and was much admired by Queen Elizabeth. In 1940 she published two collections, *Edith Sitwell's Anthology* and *Poems New and Old*.

26 February 1940 to May Elphinstone

The Royal Train

My Darling May

I cannot tell you how refreshed, revitalised and better in every way I feel, after my 3 days in your and your family's company. The last few months have been such a ghastly climax to two anxious years, and sometimes one feels very depressed, tho' not able to show it! My visit to Carberry was a marvellous relief – it is very healing to be with people one loves, and you are all so angelic to me always. Thank you a million times for all your kindness – I always love coming to Carberry. I love sitting lazily in bed in the morning, drinking good tea, & listening to the Elphinstones yelling at each other from their bedrooms, WCs or down the passages! And I love having a good laugh or a good discussion about interesting things.

It is marvellous the amount you have done, & are doing, darling. You have the pioneering spirit, and that is why you are a good leader. [. . .] Everybody is most grateful for all you are doing. Did you talk to any of those old Captains & fishermen today? I hope so, for they were a wonderful lot. What courage. Curse those beastly Germans for machine gunning innocent fishermen.*

I felt so deeply for you when John remarked calmly that he was going to France. [. . .]

Thank you a million times for my heavenly moments of relaxation at Carberry. Life in London is so intensely worrying & anxious that I was really <u>longing</u> for a change of thought & scene.

Goodbye darling, from your
very loving
Elizabeth

B and I got out of the train this evening, just before dark, & walked up a stubble field, & along a little road between beech trees. So quiet & refreshing.

~

---

* Yorkshire fishermen were the first British civilians to be attacked. In January and February 1940 their trawlers were dive-bombed and and machine-gunned off the coast of Scarborough.

1 April 1940 to Sir Alexander Hardinge

Buckingham Palace

My dear Alec

First of all, may I wish you many happy returns of today? One can hardly believe that 20 years* have passed since you entered these portals! At the same time I want to thank you from my heart for all you have done for us. We have had three very difficult and sometimes very sad years together – hardly any real peace, & certainly no peace of mind. One can only trust that better days lie ahead, tho' I sometimes wonder whether <u>we</u> shall ever see them. But as long as our children do, then one can put up with anything.

Many thanks for your notes about the Y.W.C.A.† I don't agree with all your points, but directly after I had written you a note last night, the King told me of certain projects in view at this moment. If anything comes of it, the neutrals won't like it at all. We've got to beat the Germans, and I expect it will annoy all those countries who stay out, & a message in that case might do more harm than good.

It is obviously not meant for propaganda, and the reason why I think the Y.W.C.A. is the only organization possible to speak to at this moment, is that it is international in character, & is closely linked with us here. There is no other audience whom I would choose, and it <u>is</u> a very important one, with a great many working class members all over U.S. and Canada.

Of course the best way to do it, would be to have a reception at the Central Club in London, and I could say a few words, including a message of goodwill to our American co-workers. That would be most innocent, wouldn't it. I shall probably have to go to something for them very soon, they are doing grand war work, & it would be an opportunity to link up with the U.S.

---

* Hardinge had started work in the Royal Household as Assistant Private Secretary to King George V in 1920.

† The Queen had been asked by the American YWCA to make a broadcast to the National Convention of the YWCA at Atlantic City, New Jersey, on the eighty-fifth anniversary of the founding of the YWCA in London. The Americans had been disappointed that, as Patron of the YWCA in Great Britain, she had not visited their headquarters in New York in 1939. The Queen did make the broadcast, on 13 April 1940.

What a pity we didn't have a birthday cake today! We will on the 25th anniversary. ER

~

1 April 1940 to Viscount Halifax

The Royal Lodge

My dear Lord Halifax

I am deeply grateful to you for the trouble you have taken over the message to the Y.W.C.A. in U.S. It seems such a very trivial thing to give even a moment's thought to, especially at this moment. I would like to assure myself, before deciding to do it, that anything we intend to do in a warlike manner in the near future, is absolutely honourable and right.

Because I do not feel that I can talk of high ideals and the right ways of life, if at the same time the neutrals are accusing us of not keeping our word. We <u>must</u> beat the Germans, but the neutrals won't like it whilst it's going on!

If they mind very much, a broadcast from me might do more harm than good.

With my heartfelt thanks for your never failing sympathy & understanding towards us both,

I am, Yours very sincerely
Elizabeth R

~

17 May 1940 to Neville Chamberlain

Buckingham Palace

Dear Mr Chamberlain,

I must write you one line to say how deeply I regretted your ceasing to be our Prime Minister.* I can never tell you in words how much we owe you. During these last desperate and unhappy years, you have been a great support and comfort to us both, and we felt so safe with the knowledge that your wisdom and high

---

* After the failure of the Norwegian campaign, there had been a vote of no confidence in Prime Minister Chamberlain. He resigned and Winston Churchill became Prime Minister on 10 May 1940, the day the German army invaded France.

purpose were there at our hand. I do want you to know how grateful we are, and I know that these feelings are shared by a great part of our people.

Your broadcast was superb. My eldest daughter told me that she and Margaret Rose had listened to it with real emotion. In fact she said: 'I <u>cried</u>, mummy.'

These last few days have been so terrible in every way. Although one knew that carnage had to come, it is hard to sit here and think of those young men being sacrificed to Hitler.

You did all in your power to stave off such agony, and you were right.

We can now only do all in our power to defeat this wickedness and cruelty. It is going to be very hard.

With again my heartfelt thanks for all you have done for this dear country of ours,

I am,

Yours very sincerely,

Elizabeth R

~

11 June 1940 to Eleanor Roosevelt

Buckingham Palace

My dear Mrs Roosevelt

I was deeply touched by your kind thought in writing me such a charming and sympathetic letter. I do appreciate what you said, and send my heartfelt thanks.

Sometimes one's heart seems near breaking under the stress of so much sorrow and anxiety. When we think of our gallant young men being sacrificed to the terrible machine that Germany has created, I think that anger perhaps predominates, but when we think of their valour, their determination and their <u>grand</u> spirit, then pride and joy are uppermost.

We are all prepared to sacrifice <u>everything</u> in the fight to save freedom, and the curious thing is, that already many false values are going, & life is becoming simpler and greater every day.

It is very encouraging to know that the United States is gradually beginning to realize the terrible menace of the Nazi way of living. We who have lived near it for some years, to some degree understood the danger, but it is all far worse than our simple peace loving people could ever take in, until faced with the awful reality.

I must tell you how moved I have been by the many charming, sympathetic and understanding letters which I have received from kind people in the United States.

Quite poor people have enclosed little sums of money to be used for our wounded, or sailors, or mine sweepers. It really has helped us, to feel such warmth of human kindness & goodness, for we still believe truly that humanity is over all.

Sometimes, during the last terrible months, we have felt rather lonely in our fight against evil things, but I can honestly say that our hearts have been lightened by the knowledge that friends in America understand what we are fighting for.

We look back with such great pleasure to those lovely days we spent with you last June. We often talk of them, and of your & the President's welcome & hospitality. The picnic was great fun, and our children were so thrilled with the descriptions of the Indian singing & marvellous clothes – not to mention the Hot Dogs!

The most wonderful relays of hospital comforts and clothes have been arriving here from the United States – we are so deeply grateful for such invaluable help.

Now that the Germans have started their bombing and destruction here, the clothes will be doubly welcome in the many little homes where all personal belongings are lost – blown skyhigh.

It is so terrible to think that all the things we have worked for, these last twenty years are being lost or destroyed in the madness of such a cruel war. Better housing, education, nursery schools, low cost of living & many others. But perhaps we have all gone too hard for material benefits, & ignored the spiritual side of life. I do believe that there is a gradual awakening to the needs of the spirit, and that, combined with adversity and sorrow overcome, will lay the seeds of a far better world.*

In one of the nice letters I have had recently from America, a lady

---

* Three days after the Queen wrote this letter, German troops entered Paris and the Queen broadcast a message of encouragement to the women of France, praising the ardour with which the French army was fighting and the sacrifices which Frenchwomen were now prepared to make to save their country. On 22 June the French government surrendered and Hitler made a triumphal entry into Paris (see p. 608 footnote).

wrote of the sorrows of 'your world'. It seems such a curious distinction, her world and our world are apparently different! I did not feel that at all when I was with you all last year.

Please give my kind messages to the President. We do so admire his great work & wise statements, and I hope with all my heart that we may meet again someday.

With all good wishes to you both,

I am,

Yours very sincerely,

Elizabeth R

~

24 July 1940 to Queen Mary

Buckingham Palace

Darling Mama

I have been thinking over your very kind suggestion about a birthday present, and the other day at Spink I found some very pretty enamel ash trays at £4 each – if you would like to give me a couple of those I would be <u>delighted</u>, or <u>one</u>. I have four here, and they are very charming.

I do hope that you have not been disturbed <u>too</u> much lately by air raids. It must be so exhausting. Mary [the Princess Royal] has arrived for a few days, & she will be our last guest for a few weeks, as I have arranged with George & Marina* to be away, & some of the housemaids are having their hard earned holidays. This house has been full ever since the War started, and as we have a depleted staff it is rather hard on the servants. Uncle Charles and Olav† seem to have

---

*   George, Duke of Kent, and his wife, Princess Marina.

†   As the German armies swept across Europe, the royal families almost all tried to flee. Queen Wilhelmina of the Netherlands was the first to arrive in London; the King met her at Liverpool Street station and brought her to stay at Buckingham Palace. Next were King Haakon VII of Norway ('Uncle Charles') and his son, Crown Prince Olav – they too came to stay in the Palace. The Queen later recalled, 'I remember when all these poor Kings, who were harried by the Germans, arrived one by one, as did Queen Wilhelmina. In one air raid, I remember stepping over a recumbent King of Norway and his son, both snoring away on the floor. An extraordinary life. It really was. Too peculiar. And they made one go down to the shelter, but it was horrible. I hated going down there. In fact I didn't in the end because you felt claustrophobic – very nasty.' (*Conversations with Eric Anderson 1994–5*, RA QEQM/ADD/ MISC)

completely settled down here! I am really a little worried, and have tried to get them to take a house in the country for a bit, as tho' we love having them, it is rather a bore never to be alone. So far all efforts have failed but as Mary wants to give up Green Street, we thought we might rent it from her, and lend it to Uncle Charles. This is only an idea, & it may come to nothing of course. Both my footmen go quite soon, and as our pages take turns in looking after Uncle C & Olav, this makes another little complication. However, they are all being splendid, & working very well.

I do hope that we shall meet again soon, and with all my love dearest Mama,

Ever your loving daughter in law
Elizabeth

~

20 August 1940 to Queen Mary

Windsor Castle

My Darling Mama

I am so sorry not to see you this week, and hope so much that you will be coming to London soon again.

I am staying here all this week (I hope), as I want to be with the children, and of course spend Margaret's birthday with her. It is lovely here – delicious weather, tho' too many air raid alarms! We refused utterly to descend into the bowels of the earth on Sunday when the sirens went at 1.15 [p.m.]! Having visited Uncle Arthur* after Church, we arrived home hungry & sore of throat with shouting at him & to be deprived of luncheon was too much, we felt! So we ate happily, whilst tin hatted Wardens peered reproachfully at us now & then. [. . .]

What magnificent deeds our airmen are doing. They are certainly fired by the crusading spirit – do you not think so?

Everything very dry here, and the Park is quite yellow.

Poor Olav – he must be very anxious about Märtha & the children – it will be a great relief when they reach America safely. I suppose that the Germans are furious at them leaving Sweden, and

---

* Prince Arthur, Duke of Connaught (1850–1942), third son of Queen Victoria, Colonel of the Grenadier Guards. He was succeeded as Colonel by Princess Elizabeth.

are making themselves as unpleasant as possible in consequence. It is
tragic that the Americans are not more united as a people – I suppose
a country has to suffer to find its soul. Poor things.

With all my love darling Mama, I do trust with all my heart that
you are feeling well under the strain of all these air battles. I do think
you are brave.

Ever your loving daughter in law
Elizabeth

~

13 September 1940 to Queen Mary

Windsor Castle

My Darling Mama,

I hardly know how to begin to tell you of the horrible attack on
Buckingham Palace this morning. Bertie and I arrived there at about
¼ to 11, and he and I went up to our poor windowless rooms to
collect a few odds & ends. I must tell you that there was a 'Red'
warning on and I went into the little room opposite Bertie's room to
see if he was coming down to the shelter. He asked me to take an
eyelash out of his eye, and while I was battling with this task, Alec
came into the room with a batch of papers in his hand. At this
moment we heard the unmistakable whirr-whirr of a German plane.
We said, 'Ah a German' and before anything else could be said, there
was the noise of aircraft diving at great speed, and then the scream of
a bomb. It all happened so quickly, that we had only time to look
foolishly at each other, when the scream hurtled past us, and
exploded with a tremendous crash in the quadrangle.

I saw a great column of smoke & earth thrown up into the air,
and then we all dashed like lightning into the corridor. There was
another tremendous explosion, and we & our two pages who were
outside the door, remained for a moment or two in the corridor
away from the staircase, in case of flying glass. It is curious how
one's instinct works at these moments of great danger, as quite
without thinking, the urge was to get away from the windows.
Everybody remained wonderfully calm, and we went down to the
shelter. I went along to see if the housemaids were all right, and
found them busy in their various shelters. Then came a cry for
'bandages', and the first aid party, who had been training for over a

year, rose magnificently to the occasion and treated the 3 poor casualties calmly and correctly.

They, poor men, were working below the Chapel, and how they survived I don't know. Their whole workshop was a shambles, for the bomb had gone bang through the floor above them. My knees trembled a little bit for a minute or two after the explosions! But we both feel quite well today, tho' just a bit tired. I <u>was</u> so pleased with the behaviour of our servants. They were really magnificent. I went along to the kitchen which, as you will remember, has a glass roof. I found the chef bustling about, and when I asked him if he was all right, he replied cheerfully that there had been un petit quelque chose dans le coin, un petit bruit, with a broad smile. The petit quelque chose was the bomb on the Chapel just next door! He was perfectly unmoved, and took the opportunity to tell me of his unshakeable conviction that France will rise again!

We lunched down in our shelter, and luckily at about 1.30 the all-clear sounded, so we were able to set out on our tour of East and West Ham. The damage there is ghastly. I really felt as if I was walking in a dead city, when we walked down a little empty street. All the houses evacuated and yet through the broken windows one saw all the poor little possessions, photographs, beds, just as they were left. At the end of the street was a school which was hit, and collapsed on the top of 500 people waiting to be evacuated – about 200 are still under the ruins. It does affect me seeing this terrible and senseless destruction. I think that really I mind it much more than being bombed myself. The people are marvellous and full of fight. One could not imagine that life <u>could</u> become so terrible. We <u>must</u> win in the end. Darling Mama, I do hope that you will let me come & stay a day or two later. It is so sad being parted, as this War has parted families.

With my love and prayers for your safety, ever darling Mama, your loving daughter in law,

Elizabeth

PS Dear old B.P. is still standing, and that is the main thing.

~

5 October 1940 to Owen Morshead

Memorandum:

1. Have you the Plays and Sonnets of Shakespeare in a not too small print? I am in my room with a mild attack of influenza, & would like to browse in Shakespeare.

2. I see that there is a new book out about the King, by Keith V. Gordon.* It is very badly reviewed in the Times Literary Supplement – what a pity that any ignorant person may write trash about the Throne.

~

19 October 1940 to Queen Mary

Windsor Castle

My Darling Mama

Thank you so much for your two dear letters. We are now all recovered from our influenza, and have returned to normal life. So much happens each day, that one does not know where to begin, when writing letters. It was dreadful about poor Kensington Palace. I have not yet been able to go & see the damage.

A land mine exploded in St James's Park on Tuesday morning early, & when Bertie & I reached Buckingham Palace that morning, there was not one pane of glass left in the front or in the quadrangle. Most of the window frames have gone, and it will be terribly difficult to keep the house clean. However, everybody, including Williams† & dear Mrs Ferguson‡ were perfectly calm (perhaps the calmness of despair!) and when we were there yesterday, the glass was still being swept up. It really makes one wild with rage to see all the insane destruction of beautiful & so often dearly loved buildings. To think that so much beauty should be sacrificed to Nazi brutality is horrifying. Yesterday we waited anxiously for some hours, as there was an unexploded land mine in St James's Park, quite near the

---

* *North America Sees our King and Queen*, Keith Gordon, Hutchinson, London, 1939.

† Major Thomas Williams held the post of Superintendent at Buckingham Palace, in the department of the Master of the Household, and was responsible for furnishings.

‡ Janet Ferguson, housekeeper at Buckingham Palace, 1936–54.

Palace. We trembled for our few remaining panes of glass! Luckily it
was made safe, & we breathed again.

Bertie & I are now using the Belgian suite, and he the '44 room as
a sitting room, with the furniture from his own room upstairs. It
makes a charming room & the windows have so far survived. I talked
to Williams last week about the silk on the walls of the little Chinese
room, and tho' a little torn, I feel sure that on a new back it will be
quite sound again. It was a miracle that no more was destroyed, and
indeed, darling Mama, we must plan to reconstruct everything after
this war is over. It is <u>very</u> kind of you to suggest replacing the
Chinese lantern – I do hope you & I will be able to restore much that
has gone.

We felt <u>so</u> sorry about the windows at Marlborough House. I do
hope & trust that all your <u>lovely</u> things are safe.

Yesterday Bertie & I went to see poor Great Cumberland Place
where a land mine has wrecked all the surrounding houses. It is a sad
& terrible sight, but thank God, <u>very few</u> casualties. We went on to
Stoke Newington, where they were still digging people out from a
block of flats which collapsed on top of them. They fear two hundred
dead, owing to the fact that the water main burst, & drowned many.
There were many amazing rescues – one man diving into the water
through a tiny opening, & saving some lives. I do <u>hate</u> these visits so
desperately Mama. I feel quite exhausted after seeing & hearing so
much sadness, sorrow, heroism and magnificent spirit. The
destruction is so awful, & the people too <u>wonderful</u> – they <u>deserve</u> a
better world.

With my love darling Mama, ever your loving daughter in law
Elizabeth

~

25 October 1940 to May Elphinstone

Windsor Castle

My Darling May

I was so delighted to get your letter, and to know that you have
heard from John.* I wonder whether one could get any food or

---

* John Elphinstone had been serving in the 1st Battalion, the Black Watch. He was captured
near Dunkirk in 1940 and spent the rest of the war in German prisoner-of-war camps, including

clothing to him through Paul of Yugoslavia? Shall I try? It must be done very anonymously of course, but it might be worth while to try. It seems ten years since I last saw you – it is so sad being cut off from the family, tho' I occasionally see David who is <u>very</u> busy, and doing very good work I believe.

We are sleeping here at the moment, & spending the middle of the week in London, as we have practically not one pane of glass at poor old Buckingham Palace. However, they are getting on fairly well with the boarding up, but the house is very draughty!

The last 'incident' (that is the name for devastation) was a land mine in St James's Park, which not only blew out all our windows, but the window frames as well! We have been attacked here 2 nights running, but don't say a word will you, as we don't want the Germans to know anything that might help them aim!, and it was the first time that the children had actually heard the whistle and scream of bombs. They were wonderful, & when I went to say good-night to Margaret in her bed, I said that I hoped she wasn't frightened etc, & she said, 'Mummy, it was just like when you take a photograph that doesn't come out – all grey & blurred, & you see several hands and arms instead of one', & it is so true, really very much what one feels like.

It makes me <u>furious</u> seeing the wanton destruction of so much. Sometimes it really makes me feel almost <u>ill</u>. I can't tell you how I <u>loathe</u> going round these bombed places, I am a beastly coward, & it breaks one's heart to see such misery & sadness. On the other hand, the spirit of the people is so wonderful, that one feels ashamed to mind so much for them.

I do hope that Andrew will go to India – it would be a wonderful change for him, & so interesting.

Please give Sidney my love & a kiss. I mean a X and not a sssss of course.

Also to Elizabeth & Margaret – please tell E to write to me & tell me what she is doing.

A great deal of love to yourself
from your very very loving
Elizabeth

Colditz. He was particularly close to his aunt, the Queen, and on his release in 1945 she was the first person he called. He settled in Scotland, and in 1951 he bought the Drumkilbo estate on the borders of Angus and Perthshire.

PS [. . .] Have you got a PIG? We have organised a very successful collection of waste food for our pigs. It is amazing the amount of waste in the country.

~

31 October 1940 to Queen Mary

Windsor Castle

My Darling Mama

I do so agree with you in what you say in your letter received today, as to the eventual planning and rebuilding of London. So far, Bertie has insisted on seeing every big plan or scheme, the last being poor Wellington Barracks. Of course, by the time rebuilding comes, Lord Reith* may not be in command, but it is just as well to make the position clear to him, <u>and</u> to his successors.

Taste (especially in private building such as hotels) has been deplorable these last twenty years, and it is very important that it should improve after this War. I imagine that whole great areas of the East End will have to be rebuilt eventually, but I expect that the LCC [London County Council] will have something to say to that. Carlton House Terrace makes such a fine facade, that any rebuilding there, should certainly be in harmony. The poor Devonshires' house is a sad sight, but of course it is detached, & therefore not such a problem. Oh why did they not drop a bomb on the German Embassy. I believe the interior had been made very vulgar by that horrible Ribbentrop, & it would have been no loss.

All those lovely Crown houses in Regent's Park <u>must</u> be rebuilt in the Regency manner. Perhaps they will be able to combine beauty <u>and</u> utility for once! Houses like 145 Piccadilly are much more of a problem. We realised two or three years ago that the day was fast approaching when no private person would be able to live in them, and I daresay that the whole block will be rebuilt, in, let us hope, good taste. What great problems await us all! But first we must win the War, & tho' it may be long, I cannot & <u>will</u> <u>not</u> accept any idea of defeat. I am sure that you feel the same darling Mama.

---

* John Reith, first Baron Reith, PC KT GCVO GBE Kt CB TD (1889–1971), Minister of Works (1940–42), creator and first Director General of the BBC.

I wake rather early these days and spend an hour or so thinking in that early morning clarity, of all the blows & possible blows that have come to us, and tho' we may have a few more in the Middle East, I do feel great hope in our ever growing Air Force and national unity. We have had to take such great reverses, as only a truly great people can take disasters, and possibly so much disappointment & horror will steel our people, & take them to great heights of sacrifice and courage. I do feel that material things like comfort, money and self were getting too much hold before the War, and it only shows how much stronger the human spirit is than anything else. In fact, the people are living a truly Christian life – being good neighbours & living for each other as never before; which, with the things of the spirit, seem to me to be real Christianity.

I went to see poor Xenia* last week, as they had had bombs all round them, & had lost their windows. She was so good, but rather shaken. We are thinking of offering her Wig's [Clive Wigram] house at Balmoral as a temporary escape from all the noise & horror.

The poor wife of Andrew of Russia† was dying there, & I went in to see her poor thing. By ill luck, a piece of bomb had penetrated the roof, and hit her in the middle of the forehead. She was rather proud of this in a way, but one could see that she had not much longer to live. It is a mercy. I sent my car for Xenia this morning, to take her to the funeral, as really my conscience pricks rather. That someone who has been through so much should, at her age, be blasted by guns & bombs, seems very hard.

Bertie is away visiting troops, and I have been in London two days. It is most unpleasant, but everyone is wonderful.

With my love darling Mama, & so many thanks for your dear and interesting letter.

Ever your loving daughter in law
Elizabeth

~

* Grand Duchess Xenia Alexandrovna of Russia (1875–1960), eldest daughter of Emperor Alexander III of Russia and sister of Emperor Nicholas II. She had lived in England since escaping the Russian Revolution. The King and Queen lent her Craigowan, the house on the Balmoral estate used by the monarch's private secretaries, including Lord Wigram, and she lived there for the remainder of the war.

† Prince Andrei Alexandrovich (1897–1981), son of Grand Duchess Xenia and her husband Grand Duke Alexander Mikhailovich. His wife Elisabetta died of cancer on 29 October 1940.

7 January 1941 to Queen Mary

Sandringham

My Darling Mama

I am <u>thrilled</u> with the photograph of the lovely clock which you &
the family are so kindly giving me. I can hardly wait until I return to
Windsor to see it, and send you most loving & grateful thanks for
such a perfect present. I am certain that it will suit my room in poor
Buckingham Palace, when we can start living there once again, and
I shall look forward to 'placing' it <u>so</u> much. We are all feeling much
better for our quiet stay at dear little Appleton.* Mabel Butcher &
Marrington† worked absolute <u>miracles</u> over carpets & lights, and
every room has a carpet which fits perfectly, and even the furniture
fits!

The drawing room here has new armchairs & sofas from the Hall
at Sandringham, the radio, & the piano from the drawing room at
Sandringham. It makes a very comfortable living room, and as I have
my writing table in Bertie's room, the lady can use the drawing room
all the morning for writing.

The children are looking quite different already – I am afraid that
Windsor is not really a good place for them, the noise of guns is
heavy, and then of course there have been so many bombs dropped
all around, & some so close. It is very difficult to know what is the
best thing to do with them.

The weather has been very bad here, and snow lies everywhere.
Bertie has shot every day possible, and looks much refreshed. All the
people seem very well, and on Saturday the Women's Institute's tea
party takes place! How I wish that you and Mary were to be there to
sing & laugh – I believe there are to be patriotic 'tableaux' this year –
I wonder who will be Britannia!

We went to see the Newfoundland soldiers who are living in the

---

*   Sandringham House was closed for the duration of the war. Instead, the Royal Family used
the much smaller Appleton House, on the estate. This had been the English home of Queen
Maud of Norway, Edward VII's youngest daughter, until her death in 1938. It was inconspicu-
ous and easily managed. A large air-raid shelter was built on to one side of the house and this
proved impossible to remove afterwards without causing damage. By the 1960s dry rot had
spread through Appleton and it was demolished.

†   Mabel Butcher, housekeeper at Sandringham, 1928–51; Robert Marrington, tapissier
(responsible for furnishings) at Sandringham, 1925–68.

beautiful new Church School. They seem quite happy, but it is sad to see them there instead of the children.

It seems almost unbelievable that one can spend days here so like the good old pre-war ones. It is a real refreshment, and our own visit to Sheffield seemed less of a burden in consequence.

Our Xmas at Windsor was rather tragic, because Lilibet & I both felt terribly ill for 2 days. It was a sort of internal flu, which Bertie had too, and made everything a great effort. It was disappointing too, because George & Marina came for 3 nights, & we retired to bed once before dinner, & also poor Alexandra* developed German measles, so that we were rather parted!

I am anxiously watching the children for signs of the first spots!

I am very sad at losing Dorothy Halifax† who is a real pillar of strength to me, but feel sure that the Americans will like and admire them both, as we do.

I am still enraged beyond <u>words</u> over the futile and wicked destruction of the City of London. The Guildhall one can never forgive, and I am beginning to really <u>hate</u> the German mentality – the cruelty and arrogance of it.

With all my love, darling Mama, and directly the days get a little longer, we shall hope to pay you another visit, which will be something to look forward to, indeed, for us,

Ever your very loving daughter in law
Elizabeth

~

14 January 1941 to the Duke of Kent

Buckingham Palace

Darling George

Mama has sent me a photograph of a lovely clock to be given to me for Xmas by the family. Darling, thank you so <u>very</u> much for your share, also Marina, and really I feel that it is too much after all your divine presents to us at Xmas. [. . .]

---

* Princess Alexandra of Kent LG GCVO (1936–), daughter of the Duke and Duchess of Kent.

† Lord Halifax had taken up his appointment as British Ambassador to the United States.

We had a marvellous fortnight at A[ppleton]. Horribly cold, but somehow cleansing and upholding. [. . .]

The drawing room (where you used to urge Aunt Maud [the Queen of Norway] round the room, whilst I bucketed round clasped to [Crown Prince] Olav's tummy) was made comfortable & gay. The new chairs and sofas from the hall at S, a piano & a radio almost over-furnished it, & it was marvellously hot.

Poor Sandringham looked so forlorn, surrounded completely by waves of barbed wire, & (hush please) but Bertie has done away with all those very large & ugly clumps of shrubs & trees, so that it looks a little naked & uncherished.

Everything goes on much the same, & 'Annie' was in grand form. I went to the Women's Institute party, and this year we had very patriotic tableaux! If only you could see them. Dear Mrs Way, as Neptune, glaring furiously through a tangle of grey hair & seaweed, & Miss Burroughs (the Verger's daughter) as Britannia were HEAVEN. The words were spoken by Mrs Fuller's cook, who was draped in the Union Jack, and it was all perfect.

Please thank darling Marina for her sweet letter, and with much love & many heartfelt thanks for the present,

Ever your loving sister in law
Elizabeth

~

7 February 1941 to Elizabeth Elphinstone

Buckingham Palace

My Darling Elizabeth

Thank you so much for your letter. I can imagine so well what you are feeling about your jobs, but I am sure that unless you hear of something definite which you know you can do – it is much better to stick to your present ones.

Personally I think the kind of work that you are doing now is extremely important.* The life of the country must go on, & the

---

* Elizabeth Elphinstone worked as a Voluntary Aid Detachment (VAD) nurse, an organization founded in 1909 to provide nursing services which was widely deployed throughout the First and Second World Wars. She was also involved with the 'Girls' Diocesan Association', which may account for the Queen's comments in this letter.

human side is just as vital to the future as making munitions or planes. Especially the children; helping to mould their characters & make them good citizens – make them feel 'What can I <u>do</u> for my country', & never 'What can I get out of my country' – that is good work. [. . .]

I do feel so <u>deeply</u> for you & your mother being brotherless & sonless for the moment. I can't bear it either, as I always look upon John and Andrew as part of <u>my</u> family! A mixture of nephews & brothers – very nice & vulgar & delicious. I have longed to write to John [in a German POW camp] & have hesitated <u>in case</u> it did any harm. Will you send me his address, & I will get some plain paper & sign Peter, & perhaps that would be alright. [. . .]

We had a very interesting tour round air stations a week or two ago. The weather was ghastly, and we had great difficulty in getting about. Ice & snow & blizzards, and everywhere we arrived there was a 'Jerry' overhead! It became quite a joke in the end. But it <u>is</u> refreshing to see the actual fighting men, & their modest & completely calm attitude isn't it? It gives one courage.

I am still just as frightened of bombs, & guns going off, as I was at the beginning. I turn bright red and my heart hammers, in fact I'm a beastly coward but I do believe that a lot of people are, so I don't mind! Well darling I must stop, and I do feel sure that all your present work is useful, and if you can put in a little refresher in nursing – well all the better.

Tinkety tonk old fruit, & down with the Nazis
always your loving
Peter

~

5 March 1941 to Princess Margaret

The Royal Train, near Peebles

My Darling Margaret,

I do hope that you are feeling <u>much</u> better, and beginning to sit up and eat once again. It seems a long time since I said goodbye yesterday morning. After a busy day in dear old London at darling old Buckingham Palace with all its ducky little cardboard windows, we left last night in the train for Scotland. Today we spent from 9.55 to 5.15 in Glasgow, and visited a lot of factories shipyards & docks etc.

This morning we came to Peebles (PEEBLES FOR PLEESURE as the old lady said) and the country is <u>lovely</u>. There is a wide river rather like the Dee – I can hear it rippling & surging outside the train; and rather low hills, very green & empty – very few houses, and clumps of beeches. It really is most attractive. [. . .]

Please tell Lilibet that I will write to her next – I write to you first because you are an INVALID, and I promised to write you a letter.

Well, my darling, don't eat too much roast beef, boiled mutton, Irish stew, haricot mutton, beefsteak pudding or lamb chops whilst you are in bed. Just have a few eggs beaten up with onions, sprinkled with lemon juice, & served in a banana skin and you will soon be well.

Goodbye my angel from your <u>very</u> loving Mummy

~

8 March 1941 to Princess Elizabeth

Glamis Castle

My Darling Lilibet

There is really very little to tell you, but I thought you might like a letter from Glamis. The season is late up here, and the grass is very <u>yellow</u> looking & dry, & the trees look very grey & lifeless, but there are a lot of snowdrops, and it's refreshing to smell good Scotch air.

I went to see Fanny this afternoon, & McInnes* who was looking <u>blooming</u>! He told me what he had to eat when a child in the Western highlands. They lived on a smallholding, with one cow. They had porridge for breakfast with milk. Then for mid-day meal they practically always had fish & potatoes. Either dried herrings, or fresh herrings, & various sorts of potato dishes. Then milk in the evening. A <u>very</u> wholesome diet, & they all grew strong & happy on it. They never had 'butcher's meat'. I was interested, as I am sure it is what all modern doctors urge people to eat.

Yesterday we spent with the Poles.† They were very nice, & we walked along a mile of coast which they are guarding. We were asked occasionally to go down what looked like a large rabbit hole, & how

---

*   Donald McInnes, head gardener at Glamis, 1918–53. Fanny was his wife.

†   The Polish government in exile, together with many Polish troops, had moved to Britain. Polish soldiers and airmen played a major role throughout the rest of the war.

we did it, I don't know! But we did, & came out again very nearly doubled up!

I saw Margaret E who looked very well, & asked a lot after you. Grandfather seems better, but he is still rather weak & in his room.

Well, my darling, I am looking forward very much to seeing you & Margaret next week.

Lots of kisses from your v. loving Mummy

~

21 March 1941 to Queen Mary

Windsor Castle

My Darling Mama

Thank you so very much for your dear letter. I am so distressed to hear of your horrid cold, and the very tiring and depressing cough. What a nuisance for you. I do trust that you will throw it off soon. If only you could go away for a little change. Is there no house in Devonshire where you could go for a week or two of sun & quiet? It would be such a help to the cough, tho' I know how difficult travelling is in these days.

I am so longing to see you again, & shall hope to motor down very soon if you feel up to a visit. It seems years since Bertie & I last talked with you.

We had a very interesting time in Scotland, and visited Edinburgh, Glasgow, Aberdeen and Dundee. All the people were in good heart, and working very hard.

All the voluntary services splendid, and a good spirit of co-operation everywhere. Glasgow had not been bombed when we were there but were prepared & ready for the worst. I am afraid that they had a very bad time in Clydebank, where those horrible slummy tenements are real death traps.

Aberdeen has had a good many bombs, & a certain number of casualties, but seemed quite cheerful.

We spent one day with the Polish Army, which was really rather delightful. We inspected the coast defences, and various regiments, lunched with General Sikorski* & his staff, & then watched a 'Parade

---

* General Wladyslaw Sikorski (1881–1943), Polish military and political leader. After the German occupation of Poland, he became Prime Minister of the Polish government in exile

march' in Forfar. They marched past Bertie, doing a sort of minor goose step, only more of a <u>stamp</u> and it was most impressive! The Scottish people love the Poles, and they are extremely popular. There are many billeted in Glamis village, and every one of the village people are delighted with their guests.

One does feel so sorry for the poor men, so cut off from their families, & hearing nothing but dreadful tales from poor Poland. They seemed very pleased to see us, and received us with shouts of 'God preserve the King' or some such Polish noise, and their manners are really exquisite. And what with extremely good-looking young Counts and Princes loose in the countryside, I tremble for the love stricken young ladies of North East Scotland! [. . .]

Bertie is in London as usual, & is seeing the Prime Minister – I will keep this letter until he returns, in case there is anything to tell you.

Bertie has returned, and seems quite satisfied with existing affairs. Of course he is very anxious about Yugoslavia, & very anxious about our shipping & all the many dreadful anxieties that are on his mind. But, as he says, we are doing our very best in whatever field one can mention, & Anthony Eden* is still out there, which is very helpful. When I say 'satisfied', that is not a good word, for of course he cannot be <u>satisfied</u>, but he is <u>hopeful</u>, which is everything. One trembles rather for Greece, doesn't one. Poor George,† he has been splendid, & so are his people.

With all my love darling Mama, and so hoping to see you soon, from your loving daughter in law

Elizabeth

~

---

and Commander-in-Chief of the Polish armed forces in exile. He died when his plane crashed just after take-off from Gibraltar in July 1943.

* Robert Anthony Eden, first Earl of Avon, KG MC PC (1897–1977), Conservative politician. As Foreign Secretary, 1935–8, he vigorously opposed the appeasement of Germany and eventually resigned in protest. In 1940 Churchill appointed him Secretary of State for War, and then Foreign Secretary when Lord Halifax was appointed Ambassador to the United States. He remained Foreign Secretary throughout the war.

† King George II of the Hellenes (1890–1947), second cousin of King George VI and first cousin of the Duke of Edinburgh. Greece had fought off an attack by Italy in 1940, but was now facing invasion by the German forces as they swept through the Balkans. Despite brave resistance, Greece was overwhelmed by the end of May and King George, who had moved with his government to Crete, was forced to flee to Cairo and then to England.

On 20 March 1941, the King and Queen visited Plymouth which, as a naval port, had been heavily bombed. That night, after they left, the port was subjected to another massive bombardment.

~

23 [22] March 1941 to Viscountess Astor

Windsor Castle

Dearest Lady Astor,*

Since early yesterday morning when I first heard of the savage attack on dear Plymouth, I have been thinking of you all without ceasing. I have been praying that the people may be helped to find courage, and ability to face such a terrible ordeal, and I am certain that they have all this spirit already.

Words are not invented to say even mildly what one feels, but having just left you after such a happy and inspiring day, one feels it all so bitterly, and so personally. My heart does truly ache for those good mothers and children and all the splendid workers.

This is one of the hard things about being King and Queen of a country that one loves so much. Every time this sort of murderous attack is made, we feel it, as if our own children were being hurt. All we can all do, is to do our very best, and leave the rest in God's hands.

I know how much you love the people, and how much you have striven to better their lives in Plymouth, and my sympathy is <u>very</u> deep and sincere.

I long to hear how Virginia House fared, also the Club and Toc H† as I fear they were in the shopping centre.

Oh, curse the Germans,

---

* Nancy Witcher Astor, Viscountess Astor, CH (1879–1964), American society beauty and the first woman to sit as a Member of Parliament in the House of Commons. She was MP for Plymouth Sutton, 1919–45. A witty and outspoken woman, she made enemies, and in the second half of the 1930s she was so closely identified with appeasement that some called her 'The Member for Berlin'.

† A Toc H hostel was opened in Plymouth in February 1941 to give shelter to those made homeless by the endless German bombing of the naval city. Virginia House was originally the old Batter Street Congregational Chapel, built in 1704. After the First World War, Lord and Lady Astor had bought the site and amalgamated it with the Victory Club next door to create the Virginia House Settlement, a well-equipped and very popular social club. The building was indeed bombed in the Second World War.

With love and thanks for your devoted service to humanity,
Yours affect.
Elizabeth R

~

23 April 1941 to Viscount Halifax

Buckingham Palace

My dear Lord Halifax

Here, at last, is the photograph that I promised to send you, and I do hope it is the one you wanted.

Cecil Beaton is so busy photographing fighter pilots just off or just back, that it was some weeks before I could procure the copies of this print! It seems rather pre-war, but rather refreshing to see tulle instead of tweed. Everything seems to be going on much the same since you and Dorothy left us.

We have had a few black moments lately, but adversity seems to suit our people better than success, and the two recent inhumane attacks on London have stiffened people amazingly.

This morning, we went down to East & West Ham, where the whole place is <u>flat</u>, and everywhere we stopped the people were magnificent. Words fail me – <u>you</u> know this spirit – it is unbeatable. It is self-sacrificing and noble – they are indeed true Christians. How I wish that people would not mix up Christianity & religion with a capital R.

It is all there for anyone to see – <u>living</u> and true.

I am sure that you are sad, as I am, about Paul & Yugoslavia.* I am sure that he was afraid & perhaps weak, but with all his faults I would trust him before any of these politicians. He was always terrified of a coup d'etat, as of course it would mean the

---

* Hitler had demanded that Yugoslavia join the Tripartite Pact which had been signed on 27 September 1940 by Germany, Italy and Japan. King George VI made personal appeals to Prince Paul, now Regent of Yugoslavia, but the Prince was unable to resist Nazi pressure. He did, however, insist on a clause stating that neither German troops nor war materials were to transit his country. As events turned out, he was powerless to see these terms were met. News of his government's signature to the Pact provoked fury in Yugoslavia and between 26 and 27 March 1941 Prince Paul was ousted in a coup d'état. By the end of May 1941 the whole of the Balkans was in fascist hands. Prince Paul and Princess Olga were forced into exile. The Queen did not condone Prince Paul's decisions but was understanding of his predicament and remained friends with him and Princess Olga.

disintegration of such an uncomfortably sham country. I cannot imagine why they did not return Croatia to Hungary years ago. What a lot of trouble it would have saved them.

The Prime Minister lunched with us today. He seems well, and every time he goes to visit Dover or a blitzed town, he takes a couple of Americans with him. They have to look at devastation, and face facts! Rather successful. We had some close shaves since you lunched here before leaving for the U.S. – I mean that Buckingham Palace has had some close shaves, as we were in Scotland when about 9 bombs fell in the forecourt and demolished the garden entrance. The house is still standing, tho' one or two ceilings have come down.

Please tell Dorothy to write to me, & tell me her news. I miss her very much, and we both miss you as well. But how important that you should be in Washington. I do hope that the feeling that you are both doing a vital work for our country helps you in your exile. I know that your hearts are here, & that your prayers are with us, as ours are with you. Ever yours sincerely

Elizabeth R

~

The relationship between Churchill and the King and Queen had become ever closer. It is an established practice of Britain's constitutional monarchy that the Prime Minister holds a confidential conversation with the monarch every week. During the war, these became weekly lunches and the Queen was almost always present. This was unique – never before or since has the consort of the monarch attended such private meetings. The Queen later recalled, 'The King told me everything. Well one had to, you see, because you couldn't not, in a way. There was only us there. So obviously he had to tell one things. But one was so dreadfully discreet, that even now I feel nervous sometimes, about talking about things. You know, you knew something and you couldn't say a word about it, when you heard people talking absolute nonsense.'

Churchill wrote to the King, 'I have been greatly cheered by our weekly luncheons in poor old bombed out Buckingham Palace, & feel that in Your Majesty and the Queen there flames the spirit that will never be daunted by peril, nor wearied by unrelenting toil.'*

---

* 5 January 1941, RA PS/PSO/GVI/C/069/07.

On 6 May 1941 Churchill discussed with the King and Queen Operation Tiger, a plan to get more tanks and aircraft to Egypt. It succeeded overall, though one transport ship with fifty tanks on board hit a mine and sank in the Narrows off Malta, en route to Alexandria. Churchill wrote to the Queen on 9 May, 'Madam, Tiger started with 306 [tanks]. One claw was torn away & another damaged last night. The anxiety will last another day at least. More than half is over.'* In the end 250 tanks and 50 aircraft reached Alexandria.

On the evening of 10 May, London suffered a huge air raid – almost 1,500 people were killed and 1,800 injured, 2,000 fires were started and 11,000 houses destroyed. Parliament and Westminster Abbey were both hit.

~

12 May 1941 to Winston Churchill

Windsor Castle
The Day of Our Coronation

The Queen thanks Mr Churchill <u>most gratefully</u> for his kindness in sending news of the progress and safe arrival of Tiger. Even though he lacks a claw or two, it is to be hoped that he will still be able to chew up a few enemies. Any risk was well worth taking.

The Queen is dreadfully sorry about the House of Commons, & the damage to Westminster Abbey.

~

29 July 1941 to Osbert Sitwell

Buckingham Palace

My dear Mr Sitwell,

I am so disappointed that you have chosen to come to London the very week we leave to look at troops, and I shall not be back here until Friday. It would have been so delightful to see you, and to pass a few observations on current events. Please do let me know when you are here again, for it is several weeks since I have met anyone <u>not</u> for the first time!

I have just bought two absolutely charming pastels of Queen Victoria

---

* RA QEQM/PRIV/PAL.

and Prince Consort by Winterhalter. They are so young looking, &
the Prince Consort has a most appealing & melting look in his eye – I
can almost understand how delectable he must have been at that age.
I would like to show them to you, they are so human & soft. [. . .]

   I am, Yours very sincerely,

   Elizabeth R

~

10 August 1941 The Queen's radio broadcast to the women of America

It is just over two years since I spoke to the American people, and my
purpose then was to thank countless friends for much kindness.

It is to those same friends, and of even greater kindness that I want
to speak to-day. We, like yourselves, love peace, and have not devoted
the years behind us to the planning of death and destruction. As yet,
save in the valour of our people, we have not matched our enemies,
and it is only now that we are beginning to marshal around us in their
full strength, the devotion and resources of our great British family of
Nations, which will in the end, please God, assuredly prevail.

Through these waiting months, a heavy burden is being borne by
our people. As I go amongst them, I marvel at their unshakeable
constancy. In many Cities, their homes lie in ruins, as do many of
those ancient buildings which you know and love hardly less than we
do ourselves. Women and children have been killed, and even the
sufferers in hospital have not been spared; yet hardship has only
steeled our hearts and strengthened our resolution. Wherever I go,
I see bright eyes and smiling faces, for though our road is stony and
hard, it is straight, and we know that we fight in a great Cause.

It is not our way in dark days to turn for support to others, but
even had we been minded so to do, your instant help would have
forestalled us. The warmth and sympathy of American generosity has
touched beyond measure the hearts of all of us living and fighting in
these Islands. We can, and shall, never forget that in the hour of our
greatest need you came forward with clothes for the homeless, food
for the hungry, comfort for those who were sorely afflicted. Canteens,
ambulances and medical supplies have come in an unceasing flow
from the United States. I find it hard to tell you of our gratitude in
adequate terms, though I ask you to believe that it is deep and sincere
beyond expression.

Unless you have seen, as I have seen, just how your gifts have been put to use, you cannot know, perhaps, the solace which you have brought to the men and women of Britain, who are suffering and toiling in the cause of freedom.

Here in Britain, our women are working in factory and field, turning the lathe and gathering the harvest, for we must have food as well as munitions. Their courage is magnificent, their endurance amazing. I have seen them in many different activities. They are serving in their thousands with the Navy, Army and Air Force; driving heavy lorries, cooking, cyphering, typing, and every one of them working cheerfully and bravely under all conditions. Many are on the land, our precious soil, driving the plough and making a grand job of it. Others are air raid wardens or ambulance-drivers, thousands of undaunted women who quietly and calmly face the terrors of the night bombings, bringing strength and courage to the people they protect and help. I must give a special word to the nurses, those wonderful women, whose devotion, whose heroism, will never be forgotten. In the black horror of a bombed hospital they never falter, and though often wounded, think always of their patients and never of themselves.

And I need not remind you, who set as much store by your home life as we do, how great are the difficulties which our housewives have to face nowadays, & how gallantly they are tackling them.

I could continue the list almost indefinitely, so manifold is the service which our women in Britain are giving. But I want to tell you that whatever the nature of their daily, or nightly, tasks, they are cheered by the evidence of your thought for them. We like to picture you knitting on your porches, serving in your committee rooms, and helping in a hundred ways to bring relief to our civilian garrison here.

Though I speak for us all in Britain, in thanking all of you in America, I feel I would like to send a special message of thanks to American women.

It gives us strength to know that you have not been content to pass us by on the other side; to us, in the time of our tribulation, you have surely shown that compassion which has been for two thousand years the mark of the Good Neighbour. Believe me – and I am speaking for millions of us, who know the bitter, but also proud, sorrow of war – we are grateful. We shall not forget your sacrifice.

The sympathy which inspires it springs not only from our common speech and the traditions which we share with you, but

18. The Duchess of York trying her hand at the coconut shy
at the Fresh Air Fund Fair in Epping Forest, July 1923.

19. The Duke and Duchess of York at the closing ceremony
of the Empire Exhibition, October 1925.

20. The Duke and Duchess of York, April 1925.

21. The Duke and Duchess on tour in Australia, May 1927.

22. The Duchess and Lady Strathmore with the Princesses.

23. The Duchess, King George V and Queen Mary with Princess Elizabeth and Princess Margaret at Y Bwthyn Bach, in the grounds of The Royal Lodge, 1934. The play house was given to Princess Elizabeth on her sixth birthday by the people of Wales.

24. The Duke of York with the Princesses.

25. The Prince of Wales, the Duke of York and the Princesses.

26. The Coronation of King George VI. Left to right: the Princess Royal, the Duchess of Gloucester, the Duke of Gloucester, Queen Mary, King George VI, Queen Elizabeth, the Duke of Kent, the Duchess of Kent, Queen Maud of Norway.

27. A Christmas invitation to Sir Richard Molyneux, founder of the Windsor Wets, the secret club of which the Queen had been patroness since 1931.

28. The King and Queen on board the *Empress of Australia*, bound for Canada, May 1939.

29. The King and Queen in Washington DC with President and Mrs Roosevelt, and the President's aide, Major-General Edwin Watson, June 1939.

30. The King and Queen surveying the damage caused by the bombing of Buckingham Palace, September 1940.

31. The King and Queen in the gardens of Buckingham Palace, May 1945, photographed by Cecil Beaton.

32. The King, Queen and the Princesses with General Smuts at Drakensberg, March 1947.

33. The Royal Family on the balcony of Buckingham Palace following the marriage of Princess Elizabeth to Prince Philip.

even more from our common ideals. To you, tyranny is as hateful as it is to us; to you, the things for which we will fight to the death are no less sacred; and – to my mind, at any rate – your generosity is born of your conviction that we fight to save a Cause that is yours no less than ours: of your high resolve that, however great the cost and however long the struggle, justice and freedom, human dignity and kindness, shall not perish from the earth.

I look to the day when we shall go forward hand in hand to build a better, a kinder, and a happier world for our children.*

May God bless you all.

~

28 August 1941 to Queen Mary

Balmoral Castle

My Darling Mama

We have been having a very happy time here for the last week, and Bertie is looking so rested and well. It is a great relief that it has been possible to arrange this little visit, as it is doing everyone good, especially the children, who look ten times better, with pink cheeks and good appetites! The past year has been so hard, and I feel so grateful for this break.† [. . .]

With all my love darling Mama, ever your loving daughter in law Elizabeth

~

On 7 December 1941 the Queen heard on the wireless news of the Japanese assault on Pearl Harbor. She said afterwards that she realized at once what it meant – America would at last enter the war against fascism alongside Britain. As the US declared war on Japan, so did Britain. Hitler then declared war on the United States.

---

* The Queen was determined to do everything possible to encourage American support for the British war effort. Churchill helped draft her speech which President Roosevelt said 'was really perfect in every way and . . . will do a great amount of good'. (Wheeler-Bennett, *King George VI*, p. 530)

† Queen Elizabeth later recalled such wartime visits to Balmoral: 'It is such a very happy house, and I remember thinking when we came up in those awful days of 1941 and 42 how clean it felt, in a way pure, & I still feel that now.' (Queen Elizabeth to Queen Elizabeth II, 3 September 1982, RA QEII/PRIV/RF)

America's entry into the war was an extraordinary boost for British morale. But victory was still a distant prospect. While the King and Queen were in South Wales they learned that the battleship *Prince of Wales* and the battlecruiser *Repulse* had been sunk by Japanese bombers off the coast of Thailand. The loss of these great ships and over 800 men cast a gloom across the nation.

~

9 December 1941 to Queen Mary

In the Train

My Darling Mama

Thank you so very much for your charming letter. I do feel ashamed at not having written for so long – the days go by so quickly, & weeks pass before one has noticed. And so much has happened lately. Let us hope that the battle in Libya will turn in our favour, for tho' our men always fight magnificently, we seem to have no <u>luck</u>. So far Hitler has had a lot, <u>and</u> the supreme advantage of years of secret arming. But we seem to be gradually pulling up, and if only the poor Americans keep calm & start working in earnest, we may get sufficient weapons to cope with the Germans.

The Russians have done well, haven't they? They must have got an <u>enormous</u> army. It looks as if the Japanese caught the Americans out rather badly with their sudden attack. I expect they will have a bad time, for the US is not well armed, & their pilots have no experience, and it does take a long time to learn total war methods, which those horrid Japanese have much used. I do feel rather sorry for them (the US), tho' they have persistently closed their eyes to such evident danger, for they are a very young and untried nation.

We are down in South Wales this evening, for a two days' visit to the mining valleys & some industries, and I am writing in the train. I suppose that we are not so very far from Badminton.* How I wish that we could meet. Perhaps a little later on you will allow us to come down to you for a night, and some talk, for we have not seen you since July! [. . .]

---

* Queen Mary lived with the Duke and Duchess of Beaufort (her niece) at Badminton House in Gloucestershire throughout the war.

My very nice footman Mervyn Weavers is missing – I am very sorry, for he was a particularly nice and well educated young man, and was already a sergeant pilot. He went off in a Wellington and never came back. I fear that there is little hope. Oh this cruel war, & the sorrows the German spirit has brought to so many young wives, for he was happily married. [. . .]

Forgive rather a dull letter, but I feel rather bemused after the shocks and anxieties of the last weeks,* and a little tired this evening.

Hoping with all my heart that we shall meet soon, ever, darling Mama, your loving daughter in law

Elizabeth

~

28 December 1941 to Queen Mary

Windsor Castle

My Darling Mama

I write to thank you with all my heart for the lovely rug which you kindly gave me with the family. It will be most useful, and I am delighted to have something so useful and so colourful. [. . .]

I expect that we shall have a very difficult time in this New Year, for the Americans have been caught out, and things must work up to a climax, but I do feel confident, don't you Mama? Confident in the valour and good sense of the British people, & confident that good sense will prevail in the end.

We send you every good wish for a happier New Year, and may it help to bring victory to our cause.

With much love darling Mama, ever your very loving daughter in law

Elizabeth

~

---

* On 19 September 1941 John Bowes Lyon, Master of Glamis, grandson of the Earl of Strathmore, was killed in action in Egypt. Before his death was confirmed, the Queen wrote to Queen Mary on 5 October: 'It is very sad news that my nephew John is missing in Egypt . . . He is a dear affectionate boy and I do trust that he may be spared. I am afraid that my father will be grieved, for he is the eldest of his eldest son, and one feels for the family succession.' (RA QM/PRIV/CC12/177)

19 January 1942 to J. P. Morgan [incomplete draft]

Buckingham Palace

My dear Mr Morgan

I cannot tell you how deeply touched the King & I were, at your kind thought in sending such exciting & lovely parcels. They were opened with great interest, and actually they were the first personal parcels that we have received at all! What really created a stir was the <u>cheese</u>! If you ever send any more, the cheese is most gladly received as we do not have any ourselves, feeling that every crumb should go to the heavy workers in industry who need all they can get. But apart from the excellent contents, what really pleased us was the evidence of your thought for us in these terrible but glorious days.

I wonder when we shall all meet again on the hills in Scotland? It will be some long time I think, but tho' things are still very hard & difficult, & reverses abound, somehow the world seems to have balanced itself better with the United States <u>in</u> the fight against evil thinking & evil doing.

We went through an unpleasant time last year being bombed very violently, and fighting back all we knew, and all through those long months, I don't think that it ever entered anybody's head that we might be beaten by that kind of low savagery. It was terribly moving when we went to visit & try to help all these poor people, who in one night lost <u>everything</u>, home, possessions & sometimes their children. But always one heard, 'well I've lost all I had, but thank God they missed the factory', or '<u>I'm</u> all right, but poor Mrs Jones next door is far worse off' etc. I never heard a grumble, and indeed the good neighbour was uppermost all the time. Truly, one felt grateful for such a good & real Christian spirit. If they don't go to Church, so many of them are <u>living</u> a Christian life, & it was wonderful. It is very terrible too, and we both felt years older after last winter.

I do pray that America will not have to go through such horrors, tho' I feel quite sure that if it does come, she will take it all in her stride and rise above it.

It is a great sadness to us that the dear Archbishop* is resigning,

---

* Cosmo Lang retired as Archbishop of Canterbury in spring 1942. The Royal Family had relied on him for spiritual and moral support, particularly at the time of the abdication and

for he has been, not only a great friend but a trusted adviser for many years. It is just like him to insist on going before he gets too old. [The letter ends here.]

~

27 February 1942 to Elizabeth Elphinstone

Buckingham Palace

My Darling Elizabeth

I received your last letter in the train yesterday. Somewhere between——and——[sic]. Directly we arrived back in London last night, I rang up old Hitler, & quite politely asked him to make up his mind for once & all about his beastly old invasion. If he wasn't going to risk it, well & good, but if he <u>was</u> going to come, well, for goodness sake he must decide – <u>now</u>. I told him that, apart from the trouble of having to mine the beaches, and the perpetual sharpening of the Home Guard's pikes, my niece Miss E was having her plans held up, and she must really be considered a little.

After a good deal of havering & evasions, I pinned him down to saying that the end of March was O.K., so that you will be able to come south with a clear conscience & no risk of being cut off from your hospital & kith and kin.

Why does kin & kith sound wrong? And what, may I ask are kith? Are you my kith, or only my kin. Answer me that. [. . .]

I do hope that you will come down next month, and I shall look forward to seeing you so <u>VERY</u> much. I am afraid that London is rather gloomy, with nobody to ring up or to go & see. Sometimes one feels quite lonely, it is so rare to see a friend, but how very exciting when one dear old face turns up! [. . .]

Your <u>very</u> loving
Peter

~

---

since the beginning of the war. Queen Mary described him as 'our friend in weal and woe'. (Queen Mary to Queen Elizabeth, 13 January 1942, RA QEQM/PRIV/RF)

5 March 1942 to Arthur Penn

Buckingham Palace

My dear Arthur,

I wish that I could tell you how deeply I feel for you at this moment.* It seems like yesterday that I went through what you must be going through, and I know how useless words really are, for it is the separation which matters. But other things come, such as talking of a much loved mother with others who loved her too, lovely memories come crowding, and one must say thank you for a beautiful life like your own mother's. But the hardest to bear, tho' in my case the most selfish, is the lost feeling. To be loved by your mother is wonderful and so safe, a unique love different to any other. That 'going home' feeling, knowing that a loved person is waiting for you full of eager interest in the smallest of your joys or troubles, that is very hard to lose.

Your family life has always been so perfect, and this loss must be almost more than you can bear. I do wish that I could help you, tho' only time can do that, but I do send my most heartfelt sympathy, and my prayers that you may be given strength and courage during these days of sorrow.

Yours ER

~

10 April 1942 to Queen Mary

The Royal Lodge

Darling Mama

Enclosed are the 100 coupons, and I do hope that if you want any more you will let me know.

We were so very happy that you were able to come to Lilibet's confirmation, and I am so glad that you liked the very simple little service.† I thought the Archbishop was wonderful, so straightforward and so inspiring, and it was sad to feel that it was his last appearance at a family 'festival'. He has been such a good & wise friend to us

---

* This letter was written on the death of Arthur's mother, Constance.

† Princess Elizabeth was confirmed on 28 March 1942 in the Private Chapel at Windsor Castle by Cosmo Lang, the Archbishop of Canterbury.

both, and we shall miss his intensely human and sincere advice, given so simply and kindly at various moments of stress.

I like the new Archbishop* too, but a great intellect sometimes dims the eager kindness & understanding which a truly wise simplicity is so ready to pour out, tho' I am <u>sure</u> that he will be a support & friend in the future.

We were so glad that Harry & Alice were able to come to us for a night when Mary was staying as well. George also came, and we were so happy to be together again.

Bertie & I, & the children came here for Good Friday, & Lilibet went to her first Communion on Easter Sunday. It was very peaceful and lovely, just Bertie & she & I. The little Chapel was beautifully decorated, & we walked there on a deliciously clear early morning, & came back here to breakfast & Easter eggs for the children. It was so nice to be together & quiet after these years of war & turmoil & perpetual anxiety, for even a few moments of true peace.

I have learnt that peace is only of the mind really. If only we can bring a true peace to this poor suffering world after this War is over, well, all the anguish & sorrow will have been worth while.

We feel so much better for the week spent here – the first visit in two years! Everything has been very worrying abroad; but the rest has given us both more courage & ability to cope with the unending anxieties that arise every day.

We return to London next week, and will be back at Windsor for weekends about the 21st April.

Lilibet was so thrilled by the <u>lovely</u> jewel you gave her, it was angelic of you darling Mama, & I was enchanted too!

Very much love, & so hoping to see you soon again, ever your loving daughter in law

Elizabeth

~

---

* Most Rev. William Temple (1881–1944), formerly Archbishop of York, appointed Archbishop of Canterbury in 1942. Author of philosophical and theological works of which probably the most influential was *Christianity and Social Order* (1942). Joint founder, with Chief Rabbi Joseph Hertz, of the Council of Christians and Jews, 1942.

5 June 1942 to Doris Vyner

In the Train

My Darling Doris,

I have just received your wonderfully brave and beautiful letter, and can only say how I am thinking of you <u>all</u> the time, and praying with all my heart that your great courage will take you through these terrible days, as it has the last fortnight.

As you say, it is wonderful that Elizabeth* had her heart's desire, and happiness and laughter, and that she will not know sorrow or despair – I know what you must feel about that, and also Doris, I know a little of what you & Clare must be going through. I feel somehow as if all this is part of myself, and if I can share your sorrow, I pray God that I may be allowed to share in the inspiration of your tremendous courage and hope and faith. Your letter was like a shining light in a dark world, and I feel absolutely confident that your great spirit will take you through <u>all this</u>.

Darling Doris, if only loving thoughts could help. I am thinking of you & Clare & the boys all the time. Later on, let me know when you feel like seeing me, & I will come so gladly.

With <u>all</u> my love & everything I have, Elizabeth

~

9 July 1942 to the Hon. Sir Richard Molyneux

Buckingham Palace

My dear Dick

<u>Of course</u> – Do prowl a little at Windsor, whenever you feel like it.

It seems a long time since you came to see us. What about the weekend of July 18th. You can give a little much needed advice to Kelly† about my portrait. It is a great difficulty finding the time for sittings in these busy days, but he is painting hard (& well), I think.

---

* Doris and Clare Vyner's daughter, Elizabeth, born 15 January 1924, was named after her godmother, the Duchess of York; she died of meningitis while on active service as a Wren, on 3 June 1942.

† Sir Gerald Kelly RA (1879–1972), British artist, who was engaged for much of the war at Windsor on full-length portraits of the King and Queen.

I bought 2 pretty gilt mirrors from Partridge the other day. Do let me know if you see any worthy Windsor or Buckingham Palace things to buy, for you know the right sort.

I have given orders to the Grenadiers at Windsor to let off rifles, tommy guns, machine guns, Lewis guns & mortars at you, also the Bofors guns are keen to get a hit. I hope you'll enjoy your little strolls. Yours ER

~

31 August 1942 to David Bowes Lyon*

Buckingham Palace

My Darling David

I was so glad to get your letter, and do hope that by now Rachel[†] has been able to find a house, and that your work is being congenial as far as possible. Do let me know how it all goes, and who you like etc. Don't bother about who you dislike!

If we could only have a real victory, even a small one, it would all help. It will come alright, but the waiting is hard. I don't believe that anybody realises the ghastly difficulties & dangers of the last 3 years, or how magnificently our people have faced it all. They have sacrificed so much & so willingly – I do admire them.

We came back here last week after ten days at Balmoral, for the funeral of poor George. It does seem such a dreadful waste, and he was doing such very good work, and becoming so helpful to Bertie. We shall miss him very much, for he was always gay, and in touch with such a wide circle – which to us is so important, and so affectionate. It really is terrible, and so few to do those sorts of jobs now.[‡] [. . .]

---

* David Bowes Lyon went to Washington as head of the Political Warfare Executive in 1942, remaining there until 1944. There are many references to him in this role in the diaries of Sir Robert Bruce Lockhart (*The Diaries of Sir Robert Bruce Lockhart*, vol. II: *1939–1965*, ed. Kenneth Young, Macmillan, 1980).

† Rachel Bowes Lyon, née Spender-Clay (1907–96), wife of David.

‡ The war had brought out the best in Prince George, Duke of Kent. He had insisted on being given wartime military duties and was created Air Commodore in the Royal Air Force. His task was to inspect RAF facilities at home and abroad. On 25 August 1942 he took off in a Sunderland flying-boat from Invergordon in Scotland bound for an RAF base in Iceland. There was thick fog and the plane hit the top of a mountain near Wick. The news came to Balmoral

Please give Rachel my best love, and do remember that just to be your own natural, polite, darling selves is the best way to help your work.

Your very loving
Elizabeth

~

13 September 1942 to Osbert Sitwell

Buckingham Palace

My dear Mr Sitwell,

It was most kind of you to send me a copy of Gentle Caesar,* and I have read it with great interest. [. . .]

It was also very kind of you to write about the tragic death of my brother in law. It is really a terrible loss, both to ourselves and to the country. He was much more like a brother to me, & I could talk to him about many family affairs for he had a quick & sensitive mind & a very good & useful social sense, & we had a great many jokes too. Some ancient ones which are <u>always</u> funny – you know the kind! It is terrible for his dear wife, for she was so utterly devoted to him, & leant on him for <u>everything</u>. She is very brave & the little baby is a consolation too.

I saw Mrs Ronnie about 3 weeks ago. She was at Braemar & quite miserable there. She came over to Balmoral, & it was too pathetic to see this little bundle of unquenchable courage & determination, quite helpless except for one very bright eye. I had not seen her for a couple of months, & was very shocked and sad at the change. But with all her weakness there was just the same tenacity of purpose, & I felt full of admiration for such a wonderful exhibition of 'never give in'.

I hope that you will come to luncheon with us when you are in London. I am not there just now, but am returning next week.

I am, Yours very sincerely,
Elizabeth R

~

in the middle of dinner and the King passed the Queen a note stating that his brother was dead. All members of the family, especially his mother, Queen Mary, were devastated. The King and Queen did their best to comfort his widow, Princess Marina, and their three children, Prince Edward (who succeeded to the title), Princess Alexandra and Prince Michael.

* *Gentle Caesar: A Play in Three Acts*, about Tsar Nicholas II, by Osbert Sitwell and Rubeigh James Minney.

27 September 1942 to Osbert Sitwell

Balmoral Castle

My dear Mr Sitwell,

I am most grateful to you for your great kindness in writing to me about Mrs Ronnie's last illness and her funeral.* I was very anxious to hear what had happened, and am so thankful that her spirit departed so peacefully. She had such a tremendous love of life and people, and was so obviously living by strength of mind alone, that I was afraid she might have fought to stay in this poor suffering (but I do not believe <u>thinking</u>) world.

I shall miss her very much indeed (as I know you will, for she was truly devoted to you), she was so shrewd, so kind, so amusingly <u>un</u>kind, so sharp, such fun, so naughty ('amn't I naughty'), that must be very Scotch to say 'amn't I', and altogether a real person, a character, utterly Mrs Ronald Greville and no tinge of anything alien.

It is terribly sad to think that she has gone, and such a strong personality had she, that I know when I pass a great blind hideous mass of masonry like the Dorchester Hotel, that I shall think of her sitting unbowed by war or illness in that ugly sitting room surrounded by ambassadors & statesmen.

Do you remember those wonderful weekends at Polesden? I shall look forward to talking them over someday when we meet again, they seem so far off and delectable & idle and rich and careless, & yet I remember one was deeply worried at the same time.

I cannot tell you how deeply touched I am at your kindness in writing – there was nobody else who would have thought of it, & I have been ill and am still in bed, but beginning to feel extremely depressed, which shows convalescence, I believe – so hope to be getting up in a few days.

It must have been dreadfully sad at the funeral at Polesden – she was really so lonely in her living, so utterly without family, I felt too sad for her sometimes.

With again my thanks, I am, Yours very sincerely,
Elizabeth R

~

---

* Mrs Ronald Greville died on 15 September 1942.

30 September 1942 to Arthur Penn

Balmoral Castle

My dear Arthur,

Many thanks for sending me the information about Mrs Ronnie's will* – Poor old lady, I felt there was nothing much but will power left when she came here in August, and she had plenty of courage.

Will you write to Mr Russell saying how touched I am to be remembered by Mrs Greville etc and tell him that when he has any more information for me, to write to me <u>direct</u>. It is much simpler and better, and to have things on paper is also an advantage. [. . .] I won't say a word to anybody about the legacy and hope to keep it quiet.

I have stopped the box just in time, so hurriedly enclose this letter.

I am beginning to feel better, but have narrowly escaped death from the <u>antidote</u> for pneumonia. The cure is <u>not</u> the berries, nor is it OK, in fact I must ask Peter Cheney† to invent a word to describe it, because I don't know one bad enough! ER

~

30 September 1942 to King George VI

Balmoral Castle

My Darling Bertie

[. . .]

I <u>do</u> wish that you were here darling, or that I was with you; tho'

---

* The details of Mrs Greville's will were published in *The Times* on 8 January 1943. She left £1,564,038 gross and she bequeathed 'with my loving thoughts' much of her jewellery to the Queen, including drop diamond earrings, a tiara, and a diamond necklace that was said to have belonged to Marie Antoinette. Mrs Greville left Princess Margaret £20,000. To Queen Victoria Eugenie of Spain, who had lived in exile since 1931, she left £12,500 'with deep affection and in memory of the great kindness and affection which her Majesty has shown me'. Mrs Greville also left £10,000 to Osbert Sitwell, which made him feel 'very rich'. A few months after her death he visited her old French maid Aline, who still lived at Polesden Lacey. He reported to the Queen that the rest of the staff, whom he and she called 'the Crazy Gang', had been disbanded – but they had 'brought off a big coup with the sale of Mrs Ronnie's cellar – an appropriate <u>finale</u>'. (Osbert Sitwell to Queen Elizabeth, [18] April 1943, RA QEQM/OUT/SITWELL)

† Perhaps a reference to Peter Cheyney (1896–1951), a writer of crime fiction, whose books sold widely at the time.

of the two alternatives I would prefer you to be here with me! I feel that I am getting on so slowly. Three whole days since you went, and I really feel just the same. In fact today I have felt very tired, a heavy yet empty head and limbs, & very conscious of them. But I daresay tomorrow I shall feel quite different again.

Did you read Edward Halifax's speech in America about ten days ago? One of his good 'Christian' speeches, I thought bits of it were excellent.

Do read 'St George or the Dragon'* if you have time. It is really worth reading, & it is well divided up so you can take your time over it.

The children's colds are better, & Margaret is looking less pale – Lilibet had a coughing fit out stalking today, half because she wanted to be very quiet! Just the end of her cold.

Well darling angel, I must stop, and shall be speaking to you on the telephone tomorrow morning, long before this letter is posted even!

Goodbye Bertie darling, I do hope you'll have lovely weather next week, how I wish I was to be there,

from your very very loving
Elizabeth

~

7 October 1942 to Arthur Penn

Buckingham Palace

My dear Arthur

[. . .]

There are two things I would be grateful if you would do for me.

1. Find out what Battalions of my regiments† are in this country

---

* *St George or the Dragon: Towards a Christian Democracy* (1941) by Godfrey Elton, first Baron Elton (1892–1973), historian, Labour politician and author.

† Among the many regiments of which the Queen was Colonel-in-Chief or Honorary Colonel over the years were the King's Own Yorkshire Light Infantry, the Black Watch, the Queen's Bays, the 7th Queen's Own Hussars, the Manchester Regiment, the 9th Queen's Royal Lancers, the Bedfordshire & Hertfordshire Regiment; other regiments or units of the armed services with which she was associated included the Irish Guards, the Women's Royal Naval Service and the Royal Army Medical Corps.

who can have plum puddings at Xmas. I am sure it would be easier to find out from the Colonels – Black Watch, London Scottish (by the way, why didn't the old silly tell me that One Bn was going abroad), Yorkshire Light Infantry, and of course the Bays are away.

The Toronto Scottish and Saskatoon Light Infantry and Black Watch are still mouldering out their lives in the South of England I suppose. Can I have the information pronto, as the puddings must be ordered at once.

2. Would you write a nice note to the RAMC man to thank for the Brooch? Please tell him that I was hoping to thank them personally at a gathering in London, but circumstances intervened, and so I write instead.

Wildish weather here. [. . .]

ER

~

10 October 1942 to King George VI

Balmoral Castle

My Darling Angel

[. . .]

It is really terrible what the Germans are doing now in Europe, they seem to have lost every vestige of decent behaviour, or I suppose it's really that they know that all their sham & pretence of taking a little country purely for its own good is wearing thin, & their true nature is coming out. Beasts.

As for the way they are treating the Dieppe prisoners,* it is pure barbarism, straight back to the savage age from which they have never emerged.

I do think that it was a great mistake for us to threaten to treat their prisoners the same here. It is very lowering and schoolboy & tit for tat, which is never the slightest use. Because they murder & rob,

---

* In August 1942 an Allied raid carried out on the German-controlled French port of Dieppe, by a largely Canadian force, ended in disaster with more than 3,000 troops killed, wounded or captured. The Germans discovered an Allied battle plan that involved the shackling of German prisoners of war. In response, Hitler ordered that the same be done to Canadian prisoners – which caused Churchill to order that German POWs in Canada be shackled too. Both orders were soon rescinded.

is no reason why we should follow this bad example. I was very
distressed when I read it in the paper.

It will be a great relief when 'something' happens at last, for I am
sure it is very hard & bitter and nerve-racking for all the people in
this country who know nothing of plans, to see month after month
going by, & nothing great happening, & only hearing how the brave,
the magnificent, the practically <u>holy</u> Russians are fighting the whole
German army. We want the headlines ourselves – <u>and</u> a few decent
press correspondents who can write about decent men in decent
English – the stuff they send is awful, don't you think? Darling,
couldn't you send a special message, short & to the point, to the
millions of loyal Indians whom nobody ever hears of? It would
remind the Americans too, that all Indians are not traitors, & that the
King still means something in India. I don't suppose your 'advisers'
would like this idea – much too straightforward and not nearly
cringing and roundabout enough.

I am so thankful that you had a good week at dear little Appleton,
I was miserable to miss it, as I love Sandringham in October, <u>&</u> the
partridge days.

I shall send this by bag today, but am not sure if you will get it
tomorrow or Monday when you return.

Why <u>won't</u> those people in W. [Whitehall] answer? It's those
cowardly secretaries of yours darling, they are all getting very Foreign
Office & dithering, and are really not firm enough.

Letting down the Monarchy and all that! Well, well! Goodbye
darling from your very loving Elizabeth

PS Rather a silly letter, but I <u>feel</u> a little silly.

~

12 October 1942 to Arthur Penn

Buckingham Palace – internal

My dear Arthur,

1. And much the most important. Thank you very much for the
book. The author definitely knows his potatoes, and I think the whole
story is absolutely the berries. The way that dame Pearl gets a ripple
on, there was a baby for you – oh boy.*

---

* The short stories of the American writer Damon Runyon (1880–1946) were filled with

2. Will you contact that old geezer Hartigan and ask him the form about foreign bodies who wish to affiliate. If it's OK by the R.A.M.C. I am all in favour of bringing in any link with the Colonies etc. But don't you have anything to do with a phoney set up like the War Office. They would only pull a fast one on me, and I'm just not taking any. Get that?

3. OK to Lord Hampden's request.

4. Tell that mug in the Scottish office that he may have a photograph for the Land Galy's [Girls'] carnival in Glasgow. [. . .] put it on the train to Bonnie Scotland and I'll OK it, if it's OK.

And may I ask what the hell the Ministry of Information means by hiking photos of me around. Tell 'em where they get off. Tell 'em to scram, and goddam quick. [. . .]

Be your age Arthur. I'm through now – nothing like a good business letter to clear the brain. ER

~

13 October 1942 to Queen Mary

Balmoral Castle

My Darling Mama

It seems rather a long time since I last wrote to you, and this stupid illness having kept me in bed so long made letter writing rather difficult. I am feeling much better, and am coming south next week, tho' I have promised the doctors not to do very much for a few weeks.

I want to ask you something <u>very</u> private. We have invited Mrs Roosevelt to come over here and see something of the work our women are doing all over the country.* She will stay with us a couple of days, and then go all round the place. I wondered whether by any chance you would care to have her for one night at Badminton when she is down in the West Country?

I do not know if this would be at all possible, or if you felt able to invite her, tho' I am sure she would <u>love</u> to come & see you. The whole affair is such a deadly secret owing to the flying risk, that

---

gamblers and hustlers who spoke Runyonese – a colourful mixture of slang and formality. This style appealed to the Queen's sense of humour, rather as the P. G. Wodehouse and the Hyman Kaplan stories did.

* At the President's suggestion, the Queen had invited Eleanor Roosevelt to come to London.

nobody knows of this visit at all, except us and the American Ambassador & Lady Reading (inevitably!).* If you smiled upon this idea, would you send me one line darling Mama, and I will get hold of her programme & suggest a date to you. She may possibly arrive towards the end of next week, and spend the first few days in London. I am glad that she is coming over, because she is a practical, intelligent woman, and will probably take hints back with her that will help the American women to organise themselves for war.

I have told nobody of this proposed guest, & only hope that people will be discreet, tho' I do think that official people in London are terribly talkative. [. . .]

I must tell you that Mrs Greville has left me her jewels, tho' I am keeping that quiet as well for the moment! She left them to me 'with her loving thoughts', dear old thing, and I feel very touched, I don't suppose I shall see what they consist of for a long time, owing to the slowness of lawyers & death duties etc, but I know she had a few good things. Apart from everything else, it is rather exciting to be left something, and I do admire beautiful stones with all my heart. I can't help thinking that most women do!†

The country is looking divinely beautiful up here. Golden birches and scarlet rowans flaming against the russet of the bracken & the brown and blue hills. One or two lovely days lately, after a truly bad August & September.

Is it not terrible the way the Germans are behaving all over Europe. The mask is off at last, and the true savagery is emerging now that there is no need to pretend that all these small countries were taken over for their own good. Murders & deportations, children sent away from their families, & now the unspeakable treatment of prisoners.

---

* Stella, Dowager Marchioness of Reading, GBE CStJ (1894–1971). The daughter of Charles Charnaud, in 1931 she married the first Marquess of Reading (d. 1935). A dedicated public servant throughout her life, she founded the Women's Voluntary Service (later the WRVS) in 1938 and served on many public bodies such as the Factory and Welfare Board, the Central Housing Advisory Committee and the Personal Service League; later she became Governor and then Vice-Chairman of the BBC.

† Queen Mary replied, '[. . .] I can understand your pleasure about the jewels. [. . .] I never had any such luck – but I am not really jealous, I just mention this as it came into my mind!' (Queen Mary to Queen Elizabeth, 16 October 1942 (misdated November, RA/QEQM/PRIV/RF)

I must admit, that I think our retaliating was a very great mistake
– if the Germans murder & steal, there is no reason why we should;
& I am sure that it puts us in a bad position to treat the German
prisoners here badly. I do pray that some solution will be found, for it
is so awful to return to the bestiality of the Middle Ages.*

I do hope that we shall meet again soon. I still cannot quite
believe that George's dear, vital spirit is not still with us. As time goes
on, one misses him more and more, and I do grieve to think of the
great blank it must mean to you. He is indeed a terrible loss to us all.

With my best love darling Mama
ever your loving daughter in law
Elizabeth

~

16 October 1942 to Osbert Sitwell

Buckingham Palace

My dear Mr Sitwell,

I am so deeply grateful to you for your great kindness in sending
me your Autobiography to read. I have just finished the first volume
& cannot begin to tell you how fascinating I have found it. [. . .]

I was very touched that you wished me to read it in typescript,
very pleased too. I immediately felt better after the first chapter, &
called for a steak half way through the second, and have never looked
back since. So I am doubly grateful to you – first for the sparkle and
glitter of your autobiography, all a'shimmer with sumptuous and
lovely words, & secondly for such an aid to convalescence. I read it at
Balmoral, where very fortunately, I was ill, I really rather enjoyed my
three weeks in bed – the first time that I have been laid aside in peace

---

*   Throughout 1942, there had been more and more reports of the Nazi plan to liquidate the
European Jews, which had been formulated at a secret conference on Lake Wannsee in January
1942. Thus on 20 June 1942 the *Daily Telegraph* carried a story headlined 'GERMANS MURDER
700,000 JEWS IN POLAND'. In early December, Jewish groups in Britain appealed to the
Queen to intercede with the government on behalf of Polish Jews; there is no record of the
Queen's response (Council of Jewish Women's Organisations to Queen Elizabeth, 3 December
1942, RA QEQM/PRIV/MISCOFF). On 17 December, the Foreign Secretary Anthony Eden
told the House of Commons that Jews in Europe were being subjected to 'barbarous and
inhumane treatment'. The House then stood in a two-minute silent tribute.

    The Queen's reference to the mistake of Allied retaliation against the Germans was a
repetition of her earlier concern about shackling prisoners after the Dieppe raid.

& quiet since the war. I needed it very badly, & it was heaven seeing nobody at all except a nice tactful nurse & a Scottish doctor or two.

I read a lot of [Robert Louis] Stevenson again, and a 'Genji' or two, & Beckford's Travels (which you gave me some years ago) & I found some heavenly stories by F. Marion Crawford,* in which the hero and heroine always went through terrible trials, but always won through to an intricate but happy ending. And after a few horrid modern books by horrid journalists, I was pining for something good when, hooray! Your letter arrived offering to let me read the autobiography.

The country was looking so beautiful. The grass & the bracken yellow & brown & rusty, & the birches and rowans golden & blazing against the dark hills – most satisfying & soothing. [. . .]

I am Yours very sincerely

Elizabeth R

~

19 October 1942 to Queen Mary

Balmoral Castle

My Darling Mama

Thank you so much for your telegram & letter. I have told the American Ambassador of your invitation, and asked them to write direct to you at Badminton the moment the programme of visits has been settled. Mrs Roosevelt is now leaving on the 20th, & by way of arriving evening of 21st, but of course everything depends on the weather. She will spend some days in London, & is going to Chequers† for the weekend. I am sure that she will be so pleased at being asked to visit you.‡

---

* Francis Marion Crawford (1854–1909), American author of romantic adventure novels and horror stories.

† The country residence of the British Prime Minister, in Buckinghamshire.

‡ Mrs Roosevelt in fact arrived on 23 October. She was shocked by the damage done by German bombing and by the conditions at Buckingham Palace. She noted the draughtiness, the lack of windows, the black line painted around the bath to show the maximum water allowed and the fact that no fires could be lit until December. Her first night at Buckingham Palace was memorable – while they were at dinner news came through to Churchill of impending victory at El Alamein – the first British victory in three years of war. Touring the country and visiting American troops, Mrs Roosevelt was impressed by the unity and

We are leaving for London this evening, and I must admit that I do not look forward to London life again. It is <u>so</u> dreary at Buckingham Palace, so dirty and dark and draughty, & I long to see the old house tidy and clean once again, with carpets & curtains & no beastly air raids. I feel so sorry for poor Mrs Ferguson & the housemaids, for it is most depressing having to look after a house that is half ruined!

I am putting Mrs R in my own bedroom upstairs. I have had some small windows put in, and she can use Bertie's own sitting room as mine is dismantled and windowless. It is quite a problem to put up <u>one</u> guest nowadays! She is only bringing a secretary with her, & travels very simply and quietly.

Much love darling Mama, ever your very loving
Elizabeth

PS I was deeply interested to read David's letter to you & Bertie. It is a good thing to communicate, but what a typical 'attitude'! <u>We</u> are always in the wrong!

~

2 November 1942 to Queen Mary

Buckingham Palace

My Darling Mama

[. . .] I wonder how the visit [of Mrs Roosevelt] went off, and if you found her agreeable and clever. I thought her a charming guest when she stayed here for her short visit, so interested in all our war efforts, & so understanding and sympathetic of our ideals and difficulties. I only hope that she is not seeing almost <u>too</u> much in such a short time! [. . .]

I have seen Marina and Paul several times – poor Olga I am sure has a very difficult time with Paul. He mopes & sulks I imagine, partly because he is hurt at his position, & partly because he was in the wrong (through pure sense of duty), & that is always bitter. I am sorry for him tho', & do hate to think that our old friend is in such a position. Marina seems much better, and still very brave, & trying to take up the threads of her life again. Poor darling, one's heart aches

---

determination of the British people and their gratitude for American help. (Wheeler-Bennett, *King George VI*, pp. 550–1)

for her in that little house, with such <u>very</u> lively children! The new
governess looked very nice, & Marina likes her enormously which is
most fortunate.

We are here, now, and it is rather unpleasant; cold and dreary
(but of course not too bad). I feel complaining when one thinks of the
discomfort of most people's lives, and we are really very lucky.

Much love darling Mama,

ever your loving

Elizabeth

~

2 December 1942 to Sidney Elphinstone

Buckingham Palace

My dear darling Sid

I was just taking up my pen to write to your wife, my sister,
Lilibet's aunt, John's mother, Fox's mistress (that reads bad) etc, when
your letter & the charming book* arrived, so I am writing to you
instead. Thank you a thousand times for your very kind thought in
sending it, the illustrations really are marvellously good, and John's
talent is remarkable. How clever of him to have done it, I am sure
that the book will have a great success.

The woodcock is specially good, and altogether the drawings are a
triumph.

I should love to write and tell him so – will you be very kind &
send me his address?

Also, can I send him a photograph of myself? I have got one
which he likes, & which he wanted kept for him.

I was starting a letter to May for two reasons, one to thank her
for a delightful letter, I will write to her in a few days, & the other to
say that yesterday I saw a little man who had escaped, & who had
been a long time with John in Germany. He said such very nice
things about him, & how much he had done to keep up morale by
being cheerful himself, & he would be very glad to write to you &
tell you anything he could. This man, Major Challoner, is a funny

---

* *The Rough Shoot*, Esmond Lynn-Allen and John Elphinstone, Hutchinson, 1942. This book
was published while John was in a POW camp.

nervy little man, intensely energetic & capable & talkative, and
perhaps you would be able even to see him later on.

I enclose his address, in case you or May would like to 'contact'
him. I am sure that John would be a help to other less courageous
ones, & the fact of the book being achieved shows great
determination & grit. We had the pleasure of the company of your
youngest daughter* for a Sunday at Windsor. She was her usual
depressing unattractive self, and that unfortunate lack of any kind of
sense of humour is really very trying. It must be sad for you when
she comes home for the hols, dreary & downhearted, & frowning at
those dirty stories of yours.

London is HORRIBLE. Cold and dark. Can you get coal from
your own pit,† or is it all whisked off?

Ever your affect.

E

~

21 December 1942 to Sir Kenneth Clark

Buckingham Palace

My dear Sir Kenneth,

Thank you very much for your letter, the information it contained
interested me enormously. I am hoping very much to see the
exhibition of French pictures, possibly next Thursday if I can manage
it.

I was asked to open the R.I.B.A Exhibition, but had to decline, as I
do not want to start 'formal' openings until the Germans are really
beaten, I shall absolutely come & visit it, I am sure it will be
fascinating.

The new ballet sounds thrilling and I imagine that Mr Piper's‡ art

---

* Margaret Elphinstone (1925–), later Mrs Denys Rhodes. One of the Queen's favourite
nieces, she spent much of the war living with the Royal Family. In 1990 she became a lady in
waiting to Queen Elizabeth and was with her when she died. Her memoir *The Final Curtsey*
was published in 2011.

† The Carberry mine was owned by the Deans & Moore Edinburgh Collieries Company. It
was opened in 1866 and closed in 1960.

‡ John Piper (1903–92), British artist renowned for his landscapes and architectural paintings,
as well as for his abstract work. During the Second World War he was commissioned to
record bomb damage in London and elsewhere, and in 1941 the Queen asked him to paint a

would be supremely suited to the ballet – I hope that Mr Walton's music will be 'dancey' – he is such a good composer.*

Yes, I will be delighted to lend a Piper for Sweden. I would like to know which one you consider suitable, as there are one or two almost too 'Macbeth' for perfection. I am very anxious to see the new series – on a lovely spring day Windsor can look <u>almost</u> smiling! I do hope that I shall see them soon.

It was most kind of you to let me know all this good news of the arts. It is nice to know that during this most terrible of wars the arts have risen above incredible difficulties; & have brought hope, & relaxation & beauty to many millions of people. We have to thank you for magnificent leadership in this connection – we are very grateful.

With my best wishes to you & Lady Clark for a happy Xmas, & a happier New Year,

I am, Yours sincerely,

Elizabeth R

~

3 January 1943 to Osbert Sitwell

Appleton

My dear Mr Sitwell,

Thank you very much for your two nice and interesting letters. First of all, don't you think that '1943' is much easier and more pleasant to write than '1942'? Anyway, I trust that it will be as happy a year as possible for you. The only thing is that the United Nations†

---

series of watercolours of Windsor Castle and buildings in Windsor Home Park and Great Park. Over the next three years he produced two extensive sets of drawings, amounting to the most important commission the Queen ever made. Although she had doubts about the prevalence of dark colours and stormy skies in the pictures (the King famously joked that Piper had had bad luck with the weather), the Queen appreciated their quality and gave them a prominent place in her collection.

* Sir William Walton OM (1902–83), British composer, notable for *Belshazzar's Feast*, for *Façade* (his collaboration with Edith Sitwell) and for the patriotic film scores he wrote during the Second World War, among them the music for Laurence Olivier's *Henry V*.

† When the war began in September 1939 the allies against Germany were Britain, France and Poland. The British dominions – Australia, Canada, New Zealand and South Africa – soon also declared war on Germany. After Pearl Harbor, President Roosevelt devised the phrase 'The United Nations' for the Allies, and in January 1942 the Declaration of the United Nations

are beginning to give me that <u>groaning</u> feeling if you know what I mean. After Dunkirk and during & after the battle of Britain one had an arm-stretching sensation of freedom and independence, and tho' much that happened was horrible & terrifying beyond words, yet there was magnificence as well. Now I am conscious of a closing in of too many countries with all their jealousies, bitternesses & unintelligent criticisms, and yet this must be a wrong feeling, for it is so very important to keep together & work together to win the peace.

But what I am really writing to you about is the poetry reading.* It sounds very exciting and delightful, and I do hope that I shall be able to come to it, and bring my eldest daughter. I might also bring Margaret, for I believe that she would enjoy it madly, but I will leave that until later to decide.

What a wonderful list of English poets you have collected – and even if a few fall out, it will still be a marvellous gathering. What about the Poet Laureate?† Don't you think he ought to come & read a verse or two of welcome to me, written of course especially for the occasion! [. . .]

I am sure that this year is going to be a difficult one because everyone is expecting so much. I am always a little alarmed when a sense of optimism sweeps the country tho' I have infinite trust in the level heads of the Britons who live in these Islands. [. . .]

I have just started reading another book, 'The Fall of Paris' by a Russian.‡ The blood of workmen is running in the streets, but it may become less biased and [more] enjoyable soon. Have you read it?

I do hope that your autobiography is going ahead well, and

---

was signed by 26 countries. This became the basis for the international body which replaced the League of Nations in 1945.

* Sitwell had proposed a poetry reading for the Queen to help 'keep the arts alive'. The details of time, place and participants were not easy for him to arrange. With great talents often came great egos. Eventually the reading took place before the Queen and both Princesses at the Aeolian Hall in New Bond Street on 14 April 1943. The Princesses found it hard not to giggle when T. S. Eliot incanted from *The Waste Land*, and loved it when another poet was booed by his friends for exceeding the time limit. The Queen thought Osbert Sitwell's sister Edith was among the best – she read 'beautifully'. (Anderson, *Conversations*, RA QEQM/ADD/MISC)

† John Masefield OM (1878–1967), Poet Laureate from 1930 until his death.

‡ Ilya Ehrenburg (1891–1967), Soviet writer and propagandist who was allowed by Stalin to travel widely in Europe in the early years of the war.

that you are not too cold to work. I did so greatly enjoy the first part.

With my best wishes for this New Year,
I am, yours very sincerely,
Elizabeth R

~

25 January 1943 to the Right Rev. Edward Woods, Bishop of Lichfield*

My dear Bishop,

I am so delighted with the book about Elizabeth Fry,† and send you my most grateful thanks for such a charming and interesting account of a great woman. She was such a sympathetic character, and I am enjoying the book quite enormously.

I am enchanted always by your choice of books, and do deeply appreciate your kindness in sending me such good reading matter. Please, please continue to do so, and I look forward with delight to any future recommendations on your part. The children simply loved the little booklet about Elizabeth Fry: she appeals very much to the young.

With all my thanks,
Ever yours sincerely
Elizabeth R

~

14 February 1943 to David Bowes Lyon

Buckingham Palace

My Darling David,

[. . .] I have [. . .] been thinking of Glamis & how lovely it is on

---

* Edward Woods, Bishop of Lichfield (1877–1953), became, in the words of a member of her family, the Queen's 'personal bishop'. He helped both her and the King with speeches and corresponded frequently with the Queen. He argued in one letter that the suffering of war would be unbearable unless one could be sure 'that God is in the midst of it all, & that out of this raw material of evil He is creating something good'. The Queen agreed – she believed that the horror of fascism showed what could happen when a great nation abandoned the teachings of Christ. The war made her, if anything, more devout. Most of her letters to Bishop Woods were lost in a fire in the 1980s.

† Elizabeth Fry (1780–1845), prison reformer, Quaker minister and gifted preacher.

a June day, & how delicious in early October with the rather yellow
light on the stubble. And I can even see Mother coming over Earl
John's bridge in those short sharp rushes which looked so odd
until one realised that she was being butted lovingly along by
an enormous sheep! The longer the war goes on, & the more
horrible everything gets, the more often do I think of the old days
& how happy we were. We really were lucky, because we laughed
a great deal, and lived in such lovely places & liked the country
best. I do think that it is high time that you came home for a
freshener. I am sure your work must be very hard & difficult, and
everyone says that you are doing it so well. I am sure sometimes
you must need all your self-control & tact too, which is very
exhausting. A few weeks of hard headed, sensible, experienced old
London would be a rest. Do try & nip over darling, I am longing to
see you again.

The more Americans I see, the more I like them, & the more I
realise how extremely ignorant they are of the ways of the world.
[. . .] I mean by 'the world' the bigger things of being able to judge
others correctly, & not be too politically innocent, & more balance
when things are either good nor bad. [. . .] They seem to have got the
essential things like love of family & freedom of religion & thought,
and all they need is a little political experience. I take a motherly
interest in them, because I like them. I hope it is all right writing like
this, but I know you won't quote me.

People seem to be working hard as ever here – some of the by-
elections are a bit odd. I suppose they usually are. [. . .] it is easy for
an independent candidate to promise the electors the earth, abuse the
Government about pensions & soldiers' wives' pay, laud poor
Winston to the skies, and stab him in the back by getting elected! I do
wonder what sort of a House of Commons we shall have after the
war. [. . .]

Well darling I must stop. We are having more air raids again –
they are dropping bombs just anywhere. They hit a big school last
week & killed a lot of children in Lewisham. I went to see the worst
hurt ones in hospital this week, & gave them some bananas that
Dicky brought the children from Casablanca. It made me all the more
determined to beat those unspeakable Huns, to see those little faces,
so good and so hurt for the sake of Nazi propaganda. I grind my teeth
with rage. But it happens every day – pure murder.

My best love to Rachel, I am hoping to write to her very soon.
Your very loving
Elizabeth
PS I do hope the children are well – it must be blissful to be
together again.

~

19 February 1943 to Queen Mary

Windsor Castle

My Darling Mama

At last the photographs of Lilibet & Margaret have arrived, and
I am at once sending a copy of the one you wanted. I do hope that it
is the right one. They are not very well printed, but that is wartime
paper restrictions I believe. I am also enclosing one of Bertie which
I rather like, in case you would like to have it, and one of Lilibet
wearing the Grenadier badge and pretty brooch given to her by the
officers of the regiment.

It seems such ages since Lilibet & I came down to pay you that
little visit. I do hope that you're well, and have had no more painful
accidents when tree-felling. [. . .]

The Americans don't seem to have handled the North African
political situation very well, do they? [. . .] I do wish that they would
let us do more there, for at least we have great experience (as a
country) in political matters, and it is no use letting the ex-Vichy
French get the upper hand. I don't see how poor Eisenhower can deal
with a very difficult military situation, <u>and</u> an impossible political one
as well – it didn't work in Egypt did it, we had to send Oliver
Lyttelton* out as adviser. I do hope that the Americans will send a
good man to N. Africa. The only drawback is: have they got one!
They are so very nice, & do make such awful mistakes! [. . .]

I wonder what will happen if Gandhi† dies? What an old

---

*   Oliver Lyttelton, first Viscount Chandos (1893–1972), soldier, businessman and politician,
Conservative MP for Aldershot, 1940–54, Minister of State and member of War Cabinet
(1941–2).

†   Mohandas 'Mahatma' Gandhi (1869–1948), the leader of Indian nationalist opposition to
British rule. Inspired by the doctrine of non-violent civil disobedience, with Nehru he led India
to independence in 1947.

blackmailer he is, practically committing murder to gain his own ends, it is all very dreadful [. . .]

I am so glad the Government were firm about the Beveridge report* last week. For however much one wants to help people to a more secure feeling in the future, how can one contemplate social security unless we have world security first. And even when the war is won, which please God we shall do in time, I wonder whether we shall be able to pay for such luxuries for our people. It is much better not to promise things that may be impossible to bring to pass. Do forgive me for inflicting such a long letter on you, so full of my own dull opinions.

Very best love darling Mama, ever your loving daughter in law
Elizabeth

~

5 March 1943 to Osbert Sitwell

Buckingham Palace

My dear Mr Sitwell,

Thank you so much for letting me know the date and place of the Poetry Reading. I shall look forward to it immensely. [. . .]

I want to thank you very gratefully for telling me of 'The Gobi Desert'.† I was enthralled and soothed and given hope in an extraordinary way by the book.

I think that the quality which shines through it is love. The kind of love of humanity that Christ had. If only there was more of it in this poor suffering bewildered world. I was deeply impressed by the book and some parts of it can be read over & over again.

There is an absorbing little book called 'Education for a World Adrift' by Sir Richard Livingstone‡ of Oxford. I wonder whether it would interest you at all? It does seem so important that we should

---

* *Social Insurance and Allied Services* (1942), written by William Beveridge (1879–1963), British social reformer and economist. His seminal work, always known as the Beveridge Report, was the foundation for the post-war welfare state constructed by the Labour government elected in 1945.

† By Mildred Cable (1878–1952) and Francesca French (1871–1960), intrepid Protestant missionaries who, with Francesca's sister Eva (1869–1960), travelled and proselytized throughout China, 1901–36. Together they wrote over thirty books about China and their Christian purpose.

‡ Sir Richard Winn Livingstone (1880–1960), British scholar and educationalist, Vice-Chancellor of Oxford University, 1944–7. Other publications include *A Defence of Classical Education*.

improve the education of our people before <u>other</u> grand plans come into being.

I am, Yours very sincerely

Elizabeth R

~

19 March 1943 to Sir Alexander Hardinge

Buckingham Palace

My dear Alec,

I think that Sunday April 11th would be the best date to choose for my talk to the women of the Empire.* I cannot be sure that I can do it on that date, but will try very hard to be ready by then.

It is a very difficult proposition, as one would like to congratulate women on the way they are tackling men's jobs, & yet they must be ready to stand down (& by) after the war.

I <u>do</u> hope that the King's visit to the Fleet will be properly handled by the press.† I do not hope for much, but must admit that I am not very happy about it; & not counting Canadians & Americans even a few English people are beginning to feel a little uneasy at the way any news of the King's activities are usually either ignored altogether or placed in the 'snippets' columns of the so-called 'national' press. Please don't say anything about this matter to me <u>on paper</u> as I am worried about it, and would prefer to <u>talk</u> to you some time on this extremely difficult and extremely important and irritating subject. ER

~

21 March 1943 to King George VI

Buckingham Palace

My Darling Angel

I do hope that you are not too tired after your long journey, and that all went well. I am longing to see you, & hope you will ring me on arrival at B.P. I do hope you won't be too bored, but I am afraid

---

* The Queen had been urged by people of all political persuasions to make a broadcast to the women of the Empire, praising them for all they were doing for the war effort.

† The King had gone to Scapa Flow, Orkney, to visit the Home Fleet.

that your ceiling has fallen down in the Regency Room, and
therefore, when you get back today, you will find your writing table
in the '44 Room.

I am only so thankful that it happened today, & not tomorrow, &
I am sure that all that side of the house must be very 'disgruntled' by
that heavy first bomb.

Best love darling

E

~

1 April 1943 to Lady Helen Graham

Buckingham Palace

My dearest Nellie,

I am deeply grateful to you for saying that you will look over
these drafts, & give your advice.*

I have tried many alternatives myself, & am rather flummoxed!
I would so like to bring in something about the great responsibility of
being free. People seem to take freedom for granted, and yet it rests
on the individual completely.

Also the importance of giving. It's no use planning for better
things if it's all 'take' – we must all give too.

So many of the ideas people (especially women) send to papers
etc are all things they think they want – never a word of how to live
together as a brotherhood!

Much love and so many thanks again.

Yours ER

~

6 April 1943 to Winston Churchill

Buckingham Palace

My dear Mr Churchill

I am deeply grateful to you for saying that you will look over the
enclosed very rough draft of my broadcast. I send it to you in the

---

* The Queen trusted Lady Helen's judgement and sought her advice on many speeches.

knowledge that it is not very good, but I am sure that you will be ruthless with the extra bad bits, & cut them out firmly!

We are just off to the North East of England.

I am, Yours very sincerely,

Elizabeth R

~

11 April 1943 to Sir Alan Lascelles*

Buckingham Palace

My dear Tommy

Thank you so very much for your kind note. If the broadcast I made this evening had any message, it was thanks to your co-operation & help.† I am quite sure that I could not make one without you, for you understand what I feel about things, and I am truly grateful to you. What agony these things are! It's funny, but when I talk into those dumb-looking little microphones, I think of the grey & narrow streets of places like South Shields or Sunderland. If one can help those gallant people, everything is worth while.

Yours in gratitude

ER

~

11 April 1943 The Queen's radio broadcast to the women of the Empire

I would like, first of all, to tell you just why I am speaking to you tonight – to you, my fellow-countrywomen all over the world. It is not because any special occasion calls for it; it is not because I have any special message to give you. It is because there is something that,

---

* Sir Alan 'Tommy' Lascelles PC GCB GCVO CMG MC MA (1887–1981). Appointed Assistant Private Secretary to the Prince of Wales in 1920, he found the Prince's irresponsibility intolerable and resigned in 1929. In 1935 he became Assistant Private Secretary to King George V and then to King Edward VIII and King George VI. In 1943 he succeeded Sir Alexander Hardinge as the King's Private Secretary.

† The speech benefited from advice from Tommy Lascelles, Winston Churchill and the Bishop of Lichfield. Lascelles commented in his diary that this was 'a curious trio of collaborationists, who are unlikely ever to be in literary partnership again'. (Alan Lascelles, *King's Counsellor: The Wartime Diaries of Sir Alan Lascelles*, ed. Duff Hart-Davis, Weidenfeld & Nicolson, 2006, p. 122)

deep in my heart, I know ought to be told you; and probably I, in the position to which I have been called, am the best person to do it.

Most of us, at one time or another in our lives, have read some fine book that has given us courage and strength, and fresh hope; and, when we lay it down, we have wished that, though we are strangers to him, we could meet the author and tell him how much we admire his work, and how grateful we are for it.

Something of the same kind I should like to say to you. For you – though you may not realise it – have done work as great as any book that ever was written; you too, in these years of tragedy and glory, of crushing sorrow and splendid achievement, have earned the gratitude and admiration of all mankind; and I am sure that every man, who is doing his man's share in the grim task of winning this war, would agree that it is high time that someone told you so.

Some of you may feel that I am exaggerating your own share in that task. 'What have I done?', you may ask, 'compared to what my boy has to put up with, dodging submarines in the Atlantic or chasing Rommel across Africa.' In your different spheres, believe me, you have done all that he has done, and in different degrees endured all that he has endured. For you, like him, have given all that is good in you, regardless of yourself, to the same cause for which he is fighting – our cause, the cause of Right against Wrong; and nobody, man or woman, can give more.

There is no need, surely, for me to say in detail how you have done this. Perhaps, constantly travelling, as the King and I do, through the length and breadth of these Islands, I am fortunate in being able to see a clear picture of the astonishing work that women are doing everywhere, and of the quiet heroism with which, day in day out, they are doing it. This picture, I know, is being reproduced in many similar aspects all over the Empire, from the largest self-governing Dominion to the smallest Island owing allegiance to the Crown. We are indeed very proud of you.

How often, when I have talked with women engaged on every kind of job, sometimes a physically hard or dangerous one – how often, when I admired their pluck, have I heard them say 'Oh, well, it's not much. I'm just doing my best to help us win the war.' Their courage is reinforced, too, by one of the strongest weapons in our national armoury – a sense of humour that nothing can daunt.

With this weapon of amazing temper, that turns every way, our people keep guard over their sanity and their souls. I have seen that weapon in action many, many times in the last few years – and how much it can help in the really bad times.

'Work' is a word that covers a very wide field. It is hard to define in a single phrase, but if you take it as meaning doing something useful that helps others, then you will see that your work, whatever it may be, is just as valuable, just as much 'war-work' as that which is done by the bravest soldier, sailor or airman who actually meets the enemy in battle.

And have you not met that enemy too? You have endured his bombs; you have helped to put out the fires that he has kindled in our homes; you have tended those he has maimed; brought strength to those he has bereaved; you have tilled our land; you have, in uniform or out of it, given help to our fighting forces, and made for them those munitions without which they would be powerless; in a hundred ways you have filled the places of the men who have gone away to fight; and, coping uncomplainingly with all the tedious difficulties of war-time – you, the housewives, many doing whole-time, and many part-time, jobs – you have kept their homes for them against the blessed day when they come back.

Many there are whose homes have been shattered by the fire of the enemy. The dwellings can be rebuilt, but nothing can restore the family circle if a dear one has gone forever from it. A firm faith in reunion beyond this world of space and time, and a fortitude born of the resolve to do one's duty and carry on to the end, are true consolations. I pray they may not be denied to all who have suffered and mourn.

All of us women love family life, our homes and our children, and you may be sure that our men overseas are thinking just as wistfully of these homes as we are – some of the dear and familiar homes they left behind, others of the new homes they mean to make for the young wives of the future. These men – both at home and abroad – are counting on us at all times to be steadfast and faithful. I know that we shall not fail them, but, fortified by the great experience in this war of our strength in unity, go forward with them, undismayed, into the future.

I feel that in all the thinking and planning which we are doing for the welfare of our Country and Empire – yes, and concern for other Countries too – we women as home-makers have a great part to play in re-building family life as soon as the war ends.

I would like to add, with my fullest conviction, that it is on the strength of our spiritual life that the right re-building of our national life depends.

In these last tragic years many have found in Religion the source and mainspring of the courage and selflessness that they needed. On the other hand we cannot close our eyes to the fact that our precious Christian heritage is threatened by adverse influences. It does indeed seem to me that if the years to come are to see some real spiritual recovery, the women of our Nation must be deeply concerned with Religion, and our homes the very place where it should start; it is the creative and dynamic power of Christianity which can help us to carry the moral responsibilities which history is placing upon our shoulders. If our homes can be truly Christian, then the influence of that spirit will assuredly spread like leaven through all the aspects of our common life, social, industrial, and political.

The King and I are grateful to think that we and our family are remembered in your prayers. We need them and try to live up to them. And we also pray that God will bless and guide our people in this Country and in our great family throughout the Empire, and will lead us forward, united and strong, into the paths of victory and peace.

~

13 April 1943 to Winston Churchill

Buckingham Palace

My dear Mr Churchill

Please accept my most grateful thanks for your contribution to my broadcast to our women. I put it in, just as you wrote it, and am certain that those words will comfort many an aching heart.

I am so sorry not to be at the 'Picnic'* today, & hope that conversation will flow unchecked by that incessant prowl round the table by attentive varlets!

With all my thanks for so kindly helping me with my message,

I am, Yours very sincerely,

Elizabeth R

~

---

* Churchill's private weekly lunch with the King and Queen at Buckingham Palace.

15 April 1943 to May Elphinstone

Buckingham Palace

My Darling May

Thank you so very much for your angelic letter about my broadcast message. It was so very difficult to know <u>what</u> to say – the field is so enormous, & what to put in, & what to put out was a <u>nightmare</u>! If you really thought it helpful I feel very happy. One does so long to tell women how truly brave & self sacrificing they are, & perhaps by praise making the <u>very</u> few butterflies feel a little ashamed!

You have done such wonderful work, & your example has I know meant a great deal to the women who work with & for you – very hard too I know.

Goodbye darling,

Your v. loving

E

~

18 April 1943 to Sir Alan Lascelles

Windsor Castle

My dear Tommy

I expect that you have seen in today's papers that the Prime Minister has sent a message to the Viceroy of India congratulating the Indian troops on their great work in Africa during the last year or so. I do feel that this is so <u>very</u> wrong, for it is certainly for the King to send such a message, the first one, and <u>not</u> for the P.M.* It is so troublesome, as I know that the King was waiting for an opportunity to send a personal word of congratulation on the work of <u>his</u> troops, for I believe they are very loyal to the K. Emperor. I do wish that you would raise this matter with the King tonight or tomorrow, as I am sure it is a suitable thing to bring up with the P.M.'s private secretary, saying, that the King was wishing to send <u>his</u> message etc. Of course, the King will send a special word some time I imagine, but it looks so very bad for the Prime Minister to butt in with words addressed to

---

* Throughout the war, the Queen was determined to see that the King received credit for all he did. She felt that too often politicians tried to steal his limelight.

the Princes & peoples of India. It makes people angry, & does
undermine the King's position. What a bore in the future, if we have
Stafford Cripps* sending such messages on his own, without waiting
for the head of the State to do it. We must not let all these things go
by; up Private Secretary and at 'em.

Please try & do something – it can be very friendly & polite. ER

~

Undated [11 June 1943] 11.15 a.m. to Queen Mary

Windsor Castle

My Darling Mama,

I have just heard that Bertie has landed <u>somewhere</u> in Africa[†] &
taken off again for his destination, so I hope that the major part of his
journey is safely over. I have had an anxious few hours because at
8.15 I heard that the plane had been heard near Gibraltar, and that it
would soon be landing. Then after an hour and a half I heard that
there was a thick fog at Gib, and that they were going on to Africa.
Then complete silence until a few minutes ago, when a message came
that they had landed in Africa and taken off again. Of course I
imagined every sort of horror, and walked up and down my room,
staring at the telephone! It was unlucky not being able to land at
Gibraltar, and one gets so anxious over the oil running low & other

---

* Sir Stafford Cripps (1889–1952), Labour politician, British Ambassador to the Soviet Union,
1940–2. President of the Board of Trade, 1945–7, and then Chancellor of the Exchequer,
1947–50. Later, Queen Elizabeth would recall to Eric Anderson: 'I remember when Stafford
Cripps came to stay. He was a vegetarian and he had an omelette for lunch. And I remember
my children's faces – horror. This man gulping up their weekly ration, you know. I've never
forgotten it.' (*Conversations with Eric Anderson 1994–5*, RA QEQM/ADD/MIS)

† In summer 1943, Allied victories in North Africa enabled the King to visit his armies in the
field. On 11 June 1943 he set off from Northolt aerodrome, travelling incognito as 'General
Lyon'. The visit was an outstanding success and gave the King the headlines that the Queen
thought his work always deserved. He met General Dwight Eisenhower, the Commander of
Allied Forces in North Africa, knighted General Bernard Montgomery in recognition of his
triumph at El Alamein, and mingled with troops.

He also made an overnight voyage on the cruiser HMS *Aurora* to Malta. The island
fortress had held out against two years of endless bombing and blockade by the Axis powers.
The King had awarded the islanders his personal decoration, the George Cross, and was
determined to go there in recognition of their courage. It was dangerous – Sicily, only sixty
miles away, was still in fascist hands. His arrival caused spontaneous joy and he was mobbed
by weeping, cheering people. He was greatly moved.

things, but I believe that he ought to be at Algiers (I suppose) by lunch time, & getting into a hot bath and having a good meal.

He took Alex [General Alexander] with him last night, & Mouse Fielden* too, who I have great faith in. I will let you know any news I get, but fear it will be very sparse, & Bertie will be on the move for the next ten days.

What a relief it will be to have him back again. I already feel that he has been away for days, & it is barely 12 hours!

Thank you a thousand times for the notes on the trains. I have put the paper with the lace ones.

Much love, darling Mama, ever your loving
Elizabeth

~

14 June 1943 to King George VI

Windsor Castle
12 o'clock

My Darling Angel

I have just received your telegram, and Eric[†] tells me that if I send a note up to London by 2.30, it will probably get to you. I am so <u>thankful</u> that you had a comfortable journey, and I do hope that you weren't too tired. I was very relieved to hear that you had arrived safely, as it seemed an endless time waiting here! It seems <u>weeks</u> since you went off, and I am counting the days until you return. I do hope that the warm sun will do you good, and that the change of <u>everything</u> will be a real tonic – I am sure you badly need it after these 4 years of grinding work and anxiety. I don't like to write very freely, as one never knows what might happen to letters in these days! So I am very discreet.

At the moment it is <u>raining</u>! Eric is being so very kind and helpful,

---

* Air Vice Marshal Sir Edward Hedley 'Mouse' Fielden GCVO CB DFC AFC (1903–76), Captain of the King's Flight for King Edward VIII and King George VI and the Queen's Flight for Queen Elizabeth II until 1962. During the Second World War, he flew risky missions to drop off and pick up agents in occupied France. He remained a friend of Queen Elizabeth and frequent visitor to the Castle of Mey until his death.

† Sir Eric Charles Mieville GCIE KCVO CSI CMG (1896–1971), Assistant Private Secretary to George VI, 1937–45; he had previously served as Private Secretary to the Governor Generals of India and Canada.

& so far I have signed 4 little ERs, and so I trust have not let you down yet! Noël Coward is doing a film, in which one scene is the lying in state of Papa, and they want to borrow 4 Yeoman of the Guard and a standard so as to get details right. I felt sure that you would wish these 'objets' lent, as otherwise they are bound to make a mess of it. The lying in state scene is very short, & nobody says a word, so I imagine it will be quite moving & <u>not</u> annoying.

Lilibet is in bed with a cold, & Margaret has gone down to Frogmore to help the Sea Rangers cook their lunch! I shall be back in London Wed: morning, & if a chance comes will send you another little note.

I think of you all the time, and do pray that you will have a really interesting & not too exhausting time. All my love darling, from your very loving E

Have you seen Clare Vyner? I wonder if you'll get a chance. If you see any of my regiments, do give them a special word of greeting & congratulation from me.

I miss you <u>terribly</u>.

~

17 June 1943 to King George VI

Buckingham Palace

My Darling Angel

Here is another letter which I hope you will get soon.

The news of your arrival in Africa has given everyone a great thrill here, and thank goodness the papers have big headlines and news of your doings (4 days old naturally) today. Everybody is very interested, and I am sure it would have been a great mistake to keep it all dark until your return. As it is, there is great excitement and admiration combined. I <u>do</u> hope that you are keeping well. From the account of your first two days you seem to be leading a very strenuous life – please don't get overtired, & do save up all the tit bits & amusing or interesting things to tell me when you get home.

I took the children to the ballet yesterday which they loved. We all miss you terribly, and Buckingham Palace feels very lonely and more lugubrious than ever! Eric has been quite excellent, & so helpful and kind. Tommy takes over today, and I have only signed about half a dozen papers each day, so not much happening.

I don't like to write too freely as I said before, not knowing what might happen to this letter, but I think of you all the time, & am so happy to know what pleasure you are giving to everybody in Africa, as well as everybody here. I look forward enormously to your return, but don't hurry back now that you are out there, & take in every bit of sunshine <u>possible</u>.

I wonder how your lunch with the Americans went off? It sounded a lovely meal.

Goodbye darling, all my love
& everything from your very
very loving
Elizabeth

~

24 June 1943 to Queen Mary

Buckingham Palace

My Darling Mama,

I have just heard that Bertie is likely to arrive in England early tomorrow morning, so I hasten to send you this line to let you know the pleasing news.

I have had no direct news at all from Africa, beyond two wireless messages from Bertie to say he was well, and that he was having a very strenuous and interesting time. The accounts in the various newspapers are really the best news until he gets home.

I enclose a message received late Tuesday evening from Joey* which you might care to see. I would have loved to see Malta & Tripoli. It must have been a very emotional moment & full of feeling & drama. Of course we will send a message the moment he arrives, and unless the weather gets bad I trust with all my heart that he will be home by breakfast time. I feel that the trip has been very exhausting for him – those thousands of miles & endless inspections & heat. He looks very thin in photographs, but [I] hope he will have a quiet day in Algiers yesterday, and not feel the strain too much.

---

* Lieutenant Colonel Sir Piers 'Joey' Walter Legh GCVO KCB CMG CIE OBE (1890–1955), equerry to the Prince of Wales, 1919–36, then to King George VI until 1946. In 1941 he was appointed Master of the Household.

Much love darling Mama, I know how relieved you will be when he is safely home again, ever your loving daughter in law

Elizabeth

~

17 October 1943 to David Bowes Lyon

Buckingham Palace

My Darling David

Thank you so much for your letter safely received. I shall be very glad to see Miss McGeachy, and will talk to her about the Churchy Women, tho' honestly darling I don't think that I feel very holy at the moment, & just couldn't think of a word to say to them. Just because I said last spring that I believed in Christianity & home life, I am considered practically a mother superior, & clergymen raise their hats to me with sort of special gusto! But I really will try & broadcast some time, if only I could find the right reason & the right moment.

[. . .]

The children are very well, and what a beastly time it is for people growing up. Lilibet meets young Grenadiers at Windsor, & then they get killed, & it is horrid for someone so young. So many good ones have gone recently, including poor Wigram's son, Francis. He was a nice clever boy, just the sort we shall need so badly after the war. Well darling, I must stop.

Lots of love to Rachel & yourself,

from your very loving

Buffy

~

23 October 1943 to Queen Mary

Buckingham Palace

Darling Mama

I was so glad to receive your kind letter at Balmoral, and I have told Bertie of your suggestion about the underground factories. They sound most interesting, and I know that he wants to see them some time. He has been very busy lately, and it has been so difficult to make any plans. Somehow the war seems to have got to such a tremendous moment – so anxious and with such possibilities, and yet such dangers. One feels quite exhausted by the immensity of the huge battlefields, stretching right across the world, and by the great amount of misery caused by the Germans. What people – words fail one. [. . .]

We saw the Archbishop of York* the other day. He was quite interesting about his trip to Russia, but I think one of his most vivid memories was of the vast quantities of food & drink he had to assimilate! Apparently the Russians still entertain their important guests with endless eating & vodka – very difficult to cope with, fresh from this rationed & austere country! [. . .]

With so much love darling Mama, ever your very loving daughter in law

Elizabeth

~

20 November 1943 to Queen Mary

Windsor Castle

My Darling Mama

I cannot tell you what a joy it was to be with you at Badminton, or how much I loved our talks & the opportunity of discussing so many things & events. It was all so delightful, and you were so angelically kind as usual, and we were so happy during our short visit.

It was a particular pleasure to us that we were able to bring Lilibet, as owing to the war we so seldom go away together, and she did so enjoy herself.

Our Arabian luncheon went off very well, & the two brothers were most beautiful, true Arabs with marvellous dignity and lovely manners. It was rather a strain having to talk through an interpreter, but it all seemed to go smoothly. They brought Bertie a diamond studded sword from King Ibn Saud,† & they were very pleased when Bertie drew out its curved blade and said that it would do to cut Hitler's head off!

---

* Most Rev. Cyril Forster Garbett GCVO PC (1875–1955). In September 1943 Garbett was invited to Moscow by the newly installed Patriarch Sergius I. Stalin used the visit to claim that there was full freedom of worship in the Soviet Union. In an interview in the *New York Times* Garbett supported this line, but during the Cold War he denounced communism as anti-Christian.

† Ibn Saud (1876–1953), the first king of the unified state of Saudia Arabia.

Field Marshal Smuts* has arrived here, & we have had a most interesting talk. He seems pleased with Lilibet, which is nice, as I think he is a good judge. This morning he gave us a talk in Chapel instead of the Dean's sermon. It was very kind of the old man, & is something which the soldiers who heard him will never forget. He put into such fine & plain words the great things for which we are all fighting, truly the Freedom of Man, and it was most inspiring.

I am very busy here turning out boxes & drawers to find old bits of stuff for the dresses in the Pantomime. Luckily Chinese clothes are easy to make from odds & ends, & I hope they will be successful.

With all my love darling Mama, & with my loving thanks for our delightful visit, we do so love being with you, ever your loving daughter in law

Elizabeth

~

30 November 1943 to Sir Osbert Sitwell†

Buckingham Palace

My dear Sir Osbert,

I write to thank you for the most charming book of poems‡ which you have so kindly sent me. I am enjoying them immensely. [. . .]

Thank you also for your last letter. Yes, I have read the Gentleman from San Francisco§ and thought it a wonderful story – it remains in the memory.

---

* Field Marshal Jan Christiaan Smuts OM CH ED KC FRS PC (1870–1950), Prime Minister of the Union of South Africa, 1919–24 and 1939–48, statesman, soldier and philosopher. He led the armies of South Africa in the First World War and was a British field marshal during the Second. He was instrumental in founding the League of Nations and, later, the United Nations; he wrote the preamble to the UN Charter. He was a friend of the King and Queen, who greatly admired him; the Queen later recalled that he 'was wonderful with the children, which was so nice. He was a great Greek scholar and they sat and listened to what he said.' (Conversations with Eric Anderson, 1994–5, RA QEQM/ADD/MISC)

† Sitwell had succeeded to the baronetcy on the death of his father, Sir George Reresby Sitwell, the fourth baronet, on 9 July 1943.

‡ *Selected Poems Old and New*, Duckworth, 1943.

§ 'The Gentleman from San Francisco' (1915), short story by the Russian author Ivan Bunin (1870–1953), the first Russian to win the Nobel Prize for Literature. It was translated into English by D. H. Lawrence.

Have you read Arthur Koestler's last book?* I did not like it quite so much as Darkness at Noon, and during a slight attack of influenza I read a most horrid thing called Between the Thunder and the Sun,† which left an unpleasant taste in that it gave importance to all the things & people which & whom I look upon with contempt & distrust. Most unimportant anyway. I am now reading Mrs Gaskell's Wives & Daughters‡ to help me back!

The children are busy with their pantomime§ and all the oldest jokes are being resurrected & used boldly once more. We are making the clothes from old curtains & black-out stuff, and tho' the panto is 'Alladin', or is it 'Aladin', some dreadfully Japanese touches are creeping in, including such atrocities as Nip off to Nippon & such things! If you are in London on the 17th or 18th Dec:, it might amuse you to go to see it one of those afternoons, & perhaps stay the night at Windsor? Do let me know if this were possible, as I hope to be there and it would give us the greatest pleasure to see you again.

I am so glad you wrote 'England Reclaimed', those delightful characters should be preserved – I do <u>hope</u> that radio & press & films won't destroy all individualism in England. At Sandringham there exist still a few very original country people, quite untouched by modern vulgarities, but I suppose that Norfolk is still far away enough to preserve such delights.

I am, Yours very sincerely
Elizabeth R

~

---

* *Arrival and Departure* (1943), final novel in the trilogy by Arthur Koestler (1905–83) which began with *The Gladiators* (about Spartacus) and then *Darkness at Noon* (about the Soviet show trials). *Arrival and Departure* dealt with Koestler's life as a Hungarian refugee.

† *Between the Thunder and the Sun*, by James Vincent Sheean (1899–1975), American war correspondent and writer.

‡ Elizabeth Gaskell (1810–65), Victorian novelist, author of *North and South* and *Cranford*. Her books were filled with detailed observation of life at every level of society and are prized by social historians as well as by general readers.

§ The Windsor wartime pantomimes were an important event in the year for the Princesses and their friends.

11 February 1944 to Sir Kenneth Clark

Buckingham Palace

Dear Sir Kenneth,

Thank you so much for your letter which I received before Xmas – and I delayed writing to you until I knew a little more about all the postwar projects for exhibiting our pictures. It is very sad to think that you cannot do the arrangements, but as I do not think the Exhibition at the Royal Academy will take place for some time yet, there will be plenty of time to discuss it all, and I hope you will come & see me one day soon, when we can at least get a rough idea mapped out, and speak also, of finding your successor. It is too sad but I quite see that you must get the National Gallery going again, & therefore that you cannot give enough time to our pictures. I suppose they really need cataloguing too.

I am so pleased with the new set of Piper drawings, some of them are really exquisite, and on the whole I think I like them better than the first set. The King likes them enormously too, and altogether I am <u>delighted</u>.

A few months ago I bought a strange & rather fascinating picture by Paul Nash,* which he calls the 'Landscape of the Vernal Equinox'. It is slightly 'magic', & changes towards evening in a most mysterious manner. In fact, I sometimes expect to see a new tree, or a mysterious elemental coming out of the wood! I wonder what you would think of it. If you are free, could you come & see me on Friday 18th afternoon next at about 2.45. If you are engaged, please do not hesitate to say so, and I can suggest an hour next week instead.

With again my thanks for your kind letter of Dec 21st.

I am, Yours very sincerely,

Elizabeth R

~

---

* Paul Nash (1889–1946), British landscape and surrealist painter. He was an official war artist in both world wars. *Landscape of the Vernal Equinox* was one of the Queen's most important purchases. A visionary painting, in which Wittenham Clumps, an ancient British camp in the Thames Valley, is portrayed as in a dream, with the sun and moon together in the sky. The Queen told Eric Anderson, 'It's a wonderful picture, imaginative and fascinating.' However, Princess Margaret told Anderson that 'We said, poor Mummy's gone mad. Look what she's brought back. At the age of twelve we weren't, I suppose, into that sort of thing.' (*Conversations with Eric Anderson 1944–5*, RA QEQM/ADD/MISC)

27 February 1944 to Sir Osbert Sitwell

Buckingham Palace

My dear Sir Osbert,

I am so delighted to have that charming book which belonged to the Prince Consort, and I send you my grateful thanks for your very kind thought in giving it to me. We do not seem to have progressed very much since the days of the Hero of Alexandria,* and paper & printing and trouble-taking in 1851 were much superior to 1944! Down with utility, & up with expensive creamy paper & lovely bindings & all that. (After the War.) (Patriotic afterthought.) It is an entrancing book, and will be much prized by your sincere friend,

Elizabeth R

PS Please keep the bookplates.† I meant that you should keep them. I wonder when you will next be in London as I would much like to see you.

~

7 March 1944 to Lady Violet Bonham Carter

Buckingham Palace

Dear Lady Violet‡

I was so touched to receive your charming letter, and so delighted to hear that your son§ has regained that gaiety of mind & spirit, which

---

* Hero (Heron) of Alexandria (AD 20–62), Greek mathematician, scientist and inventor who created many mechanical devices, including a water organ, a fire engine and what is thought to be the earliest steam-powered engine.

† The Queen had enclosed two 'Elizabeth R' bookplates.

‡ Lady Helen Violet Bonham Carter DBE (1887–1969), daughter of Herbert Asquith, Britain's last Liberal Prime Minister; married Maurice Bonham Carter, 1915. Lady Violet was also a leading Liberal politician and diarist and in 1964 was created Baroness Asquith of Yarnbury, a life peerage.

§ Mark Bonham Carter (1922–94), commissioned in the Grenadier Guards in 1941, captured in Tunisia and then escaped from a prisoner-of-war camp in Italy; he walked 400 miles to rejoin British forces and was mentioned in dispatches. In November 1943 he met Princess Elizabeth as Colonel of his regiment and, Arthur Penn told the Queen, was very impressed. 'It was a new experience for him to find friendliness so allied to dignity and kindness to a perfect naturalness. He left treading on air' (20 November 1943, RA QEQM/PRIV/PAL/PENN). Bonham Carter became a Liberal politician, publisher and human-rights activist and was created a life peer in 1986.

the strain & agony of all he went through must have greatly tested. He is so absolutely <u>charming</u> in every way, everyone is so fond of him, and I am so glad to know that the respectable routine at Windsor has rested and restored him. There is a 'governess & schoolroom' atmosphere there at the moment which, in these days of war, is very healing! [. . .]

I am so sorry that he is leaving, for though we only get to Windsor for weekends, it is a delight to see him occasionally, & he will be greatly missed, not least by his Colonel!

I am, Yours very sincerely,

Elizabeth R

~

11 April 1944 to Queen Mary

Sandringham

Darling Mama

I was so glad to receive your letter last week, and many thanks for writing. It is very sad to think that two such real old friends have gone, tho' I think that Mrs Rawlings'* death was a great relief, as she had been so unhappy & suffering, and there was so little that could be done to relieve the poor old thing. I think too, that it was a mistake her living so near to her beloved Castle. She hated leaving it, and couldn't bear to think of another housekeeper there, and all these feelings combined with such ill health made her very miserable. I hope that the dear old thing is now at peace, and I trust that she won't return to haunt Windsor Castle – I can almost imagine seeing that spare black silk figure whisking down a dark passage, jangling her keys! How devoted she was to you and <u>how</u> she loved Windsor.

I must admit that I do too, & I am glad to say that Lilibet has also a great affection and admiration for the whole place, one gets a very great sense of <u>history</u> there too.

We are in the throes of trying to find a new Dean – not an easy matter in these days, and so important to get the right man. There seems to be a sad lack of the vintage of Cosmo Lang.

---

* Amelia Rawlings, housekeeper at Windsor Castle, 1912–39. A formidable figure, she was devoted to Queen Mary, who thought highly of her. In her retirement she lived in Windsor Home Park.

Bertie did the Maundy at Westminster,* & the dear old Archbishop [Lang] looked very well & wise & completely & utterly bald. I do feel how immensely lucky we were to have him for the Coronation, for we both felt the depth and meaning of that great service of dedication with all our hearts and souls, and he raised the whole thing above pageantry & history, & made it so <u>personal</u>. I am sure that the present Archbishop [William Temple], clever & nice as he is, could never have raised it all to such spiritual heights, or felt so deeply about it, as the old one.

I have had a bit of bad luck, & through these lovely spring days here I am in bed with a sort of flu. [. . .] Luckily Bertie is well, & he and the children are out all day on their bicycles, & seem most happy. They are rat hunting this afternoon – what a sport!

We have a very nice temporary equerry from the R.A.F. called Townsend.† He is a Battle of Britain fighter pilot, & charming and fits in beautifully. [. . .]

We are so looking forward to seeing you on the 21st, and then we can discuss dates etc for visits. How one <u>prays</u> that the War may end soon, and then <u>what</u> a Europe to re-make – devastated, starving & unlawful to a degree. [. . .]

With so much love darling Mama, ever your loving daughter in law

Elizabeth

PS I am giving Lilibet a small diamond tiara of my own for her 18th birthday, & Bertie is giving her a little bracelet to wear now. It is almost impossible to buy anything good, but he may find something secondhand.

~

4 May 1944 to Elizabeth Elphinstone

Buckingham Palace

My Darling Elizabeth

Thank you so very much for your charming letter.

I do so understand what you feel about nursing – it is a very great pity that intelligent & well trained V.A.D.s are not given more of a

---

* On Maundy Thursday, the monarch traditionally distributes silver coins to the elderly.

† Group Captain Peter Townsend CVO DSO DFC and Bar (1914–95), equerry to King George VI, 1944–52, and to Queen Elizabeth, 1952–3.

chance to take responsibility and prove their worth, but, as you say, it's no good discussing that now, and I know that the pigs and sheep & cows are mooing and baaaing & grunting & that you long to answer their call. I really think that it is high time that you came down for a week or so, and then we could discuss the whole question, for it is a big subject to write about, and there is much to think over.

I expect that with an income of your own, even a small one, farming would be an ideal life. And you do like country things best, don't you? I think that if I couldn't occasionally rest the eye & the spirit by a glimpse of green fields or purple mountains, I would go stark staring mad. Life is so very complicated sometimes, the problems are so vast, the whole picture of the world so black and unhappy, that one feels a very strong urge to be able to look at nature & remember how small & petty human beings are, & gather a little fresh strength from the everlasting hills.

One thinks so much of these big problems nowadays, that I feel I don't give enough time or thought to one's own home things. Anyway, it would be heavenly to see you – do you know that it's over six months, nearly seven, since Balmoral? Do come and stay for a week. You can have a room (with no view) and I would ADORE it.

Come on – Your very loving Peter.

It is delicious having Andrew [Elphinstone]. He is such fun, & so intelligent & so good-looking. He has just bought me a piano, or rather he found it & I paid for it and he plays on it, & I listen!

~

Thursday 4 May 1944 to Sir Osbert Sitwell

Buckingham Palace

My dear Sir Osbert,

Thank you so much for your letter. [. . .]

I spent last week in Norfolk and the beauty of the countryside was amazing. It was so lovely that one could hardly bear it. It was such luck hitting the week in the year, because the week before nothing much was out, and this week it's all there, & last week one could watch the leaves unfolding and the lilac coming out, & the double cherry trees blazing. How lovely it was. I noticed that some of the young soldiers minded the beauty very much – it is true that the war does make anything as glorious as England in April very agonising. It makes me think of

'Years of gladness,
Days of joy,
Like the torrents of spring,
They hurried away'*

It's all very sad. [. . .]
I am, Yours sincerely
Elizabeth R

~

18 June 1944 to Arthur Penn

Windsor Castle

My dear Arthur

I simply cannot <u>tell</u> you how much I feel for you over this ghastly tragedy of this morning.[†] It seems so cruel that you, so good, so kind, and such a true and appreciated friend should have to suffer like this, and in such a terrible way. I know that your great courage and great heart will take you through this agony, & into the better days, and I am sure that you know that all my thoughts and <u>most</u> sincere prayers are yours.

I feel quite stunned by it all and <u>what</u> you must feel – I do pray that you may be helped and sustained. Oh Arthur, it all seems so terrible – we must be brave – I know you are and I shall try all I know in <u>case</u> one can help. Yours ER

~

---

* From *The Torrents of Spring* by Ivan Turgenev (1818–83), translated by Constance Garnett, London, Heinemann, 1897.

† After the D Day landings on 6 June 1944, Hitler unleashed new weapons against Britain, first the pilotless V-1 flying bomb, and then the V-2 rocket. Known as doodlebugs, the V-1s flew in straight lines from their launch sites across the Channel and when their noisy engines stopped they fell, causing panic and great damage. Almost 3,000 civilians were killed and 10,000 homes were destroyed in just one month.

On Sunday 18 June the engine of a V-1 bomber cut out just after it had crossed the Thames and it fell between Parliament and Buckingham Palace on the Guards Chapel in Birdcage Walk as Sunday morning service was being conducted, killing sixty-three servicemen and women and fifty-eight civilians. Among them was Olive, sister of Arthur Penn. He was working at the Palace when the disaster happened; he went straight to the Chapel to help, and there he found his sister's body.

Wednesday 21 June 1944 to Sir Osbert Sitwell

Buckingham Palace

My dear Sir Osbert,

I do wish that I could find words to tell you how very <u>very</u> much I have enjoyed your enchanting book of essays.* [. . .]

It has been an exhausting few months with the anxiety over our invasion of France lying heavy on the heart & mind, and now these great battles raging, & so many precious people killed, makes the days long & worrying. But truly, your essays were a great help, & <u>most</u> cheering and sustaining. Now we have to fight the new attack on London, and once again it is the people who will 'take it' and let us hope, give it back after the war, by remembering that the Germans are dangerous, & insisting on our remaining strong. What a lot of war we have seen in our generation. On Sunday in Church I weakly let a tear leave my eye, thinking of the sorrows of so many good & brave people, & feeling unhappy for them, & as I did so, I felt a small hand in mine, & the anxious blue eye of Margaret Rose wondering what was the matter. As she touched me, I remembered with a dreadful pang that I did exactly the same thing to my mother, when I was just about Margaret's age. I remembered so vividly looking up at my mother in church, & seeing tears on her cheeks, & wondering how to comfort her. She then had 4 sons in the army, & was so brave. I could not bear to think that <u>my</u> daughter should have to go through all this in another 25 years. It must <u>not</u> be.

We were bounced about by a bomb last night, but always hope for the best!

With again my true thanks for the book.

I am, Yours very sincerely,

Elizabeth R

~

26 June 1944 to Sir Kenneth Clark

Buckingham Palace

My dear Sir Kenneth,

Thank you very much for your two letters. I am most relieved to

---

* *Sing High! Sing Low!* (1944).

hear that you think the pictures in Buckingham Palace should be left where they are for the moment, as I feel that the accommodation at Windsor is rather strained, and anyway there are far too many valuable objects there already!

I am also very pleased to hear about the cellar at Hampton Court, & do pray that the lovely old place may be preserved from the fury of the Germans. This [the V-1 bomb] is such a different type of attack, and one must not make the mistake of being 1940-minded in fighting it.

I do hope that both you and Lady Clark are well? Last week we had to use our shelter a certain amount & I much enjoyed the pictures – some of them are really lovely, & one would never get tired of them. I was thinking that if I had put a couple of Matthew Smiths down there, they would not have soothed one, after being slightly bounced about by a bomb, in quite the same way as did Mr P. Potter or Mr Hobbema or Mr Van de Something. I must try and learn a little about them, I am so grateful to them!*

With so many thanks for your letters, I am, Yours very sincerely, Elizabeth R

~

27 June 1944 to Princess Elizabeth

Buckingham Palace

My Darling Lilibet

This is just a note about one or two things in case I get 'done in'†
by the Germans! I <u>think</u> that I have left all my own things to be divided between you & Margaret, but I am sure you will give her anything suitable later on – such as Mrs Greville's pearls, as you will have the Crown ones. It seems silly to be writing these sort of things, but perhaps it would be easier for you darling if I explained about the jewels.

---

* Many of the small Dutch landscapes in the Royal Collection had been hung on the walls of the shelter, including works by Paulus Potter (1625–54) and Meyndert Hobbema (1638–1709), all of gentle landscapes with cows, horses and figures. Matthew Smith (1879–1959) was a British painter, greatly influenced by Matisse and the Fauves. The Queen owned one of his typically brightly coloured oil paintings.

† The Queen's concern at being 'done in' was probably caused by the V-1 flying bomb. Westminster and the Palace appeared to be on one of the direct lines of flight on which these 'doodlebugs' were launched. After the Guards Chapel was destroyed, another doodlebug fell on Constitution Hill, blowing out seventy-five yards of the Palace wall. The King, Queen and Prime Minister took to holding their Tuesday 'picnics' in the Palace air-raid shelter.

I am sure that you would find Cynthia Spencer & Dorothy Halifax very helpful over any difficult little problems, & of <u>course</u> Granny!!

Let's hope this won't be needed, but I <u>know</u> that you will always do the right thing, & remember to keep your temper & your word & be loving – sweet – Mummy

~

8 July 1944 to Queen Mary

Windsor Castle

Darling Mama

It would be too delightful if you would come to luncheon on my birthday, there could be no nicer 'treat'! But I do think that, if by then the flying bombs are still being a bore, you should put it off, as the whole thing is so very unpleasant and your journey might be rather difficult.

One exploded this side of the Copper Horse* yesterday evening, & I thought my windows were coming in! We lost a few at Royal Lodge, but I am most thankful to say that nobody was hurt, even at the Workshops which was quite close. But let us hope that by August 4th the situation will have improved.

It is too kind of you to say that I may find a present. The other day I found a pretty Fabergé cornflower in a crystal pot, so charming in these grim & grey days that I thought it would look cheerful in my shelter room at B. Palace! If you would care to give a little towards it, I would <u>love</u> that.

We spent two very interesting and lengthy days this week going round our own bomber stations, and the American VIIIth Air Force as well. It was also very agreeable to feel out of reach of the disgusting robot bombs for a little time!

The Americans were so very nice, and charming hosts. We saw a formation of Forts† coming home after a mission in France – it was really very dramatic seeing these great ships cruising round waiting their turn to land, firing two green lights for successful results, & a red if any wounded on board. They [the American servicemen] seem to be

---

*   Equestrian statue of George III at the end of the Long Walk in Windsor Great Park.

†   Boeing B17 Flying Fortress bombers, one of the principal aircraft deployed by the United States Air Force in the strategic bombing of Germany.

most efficient, and ready for anything, and making friends all the time, which is so important.

We are returning to London on Tuesday, & I admit quite frankly that it is much worse than the Blitz of 1940 – I don't quite know why. Perhaps because after 5 years of war people have been through so much that this extra burden lies heavier. Also there is something very inhuman and beastly about death dealing missiles being launched in such an indiscriminate manner.

Edward and Dorothy Halifax came to dine this week – they are so delightful, & such a pleasure to have people to whom one can talk quite freely. It seems so rare nowadays, alas!

I am so glad that Marina's children are with you. They really are very sweet now, & I am sure that it will do Alexandra a lot of good to be with you. I know that Lilibet & Margaret learnt a great deal on their visits to you in the old days.

Much love darling Mama, ever your very loving daughter in law Elizabeth

~

17 July 1944 to Queen Mary

Buckingham Palace

Darling Mama,

I must quickly write and say how sorry I am that in the stress of bombs etc, I quite forgot to tell you about Mary Palmer.* I was on the point of writing when your kind letter came, & in answering I stupidly omitted to include this item of news. She seems a most charming girl, well educated, poised, intelligent and delightfully natural & unshy, and I do hope that she will be a success. I am so vexed that I did not tell you before the announcement came out, as I meant to do. She has been working in a day nursery in London, amongst the Gibraltar refugees, and as (thank goodness) they are now being sent home, that particular work is coming to an end. Bertie likes her very much and she has come from good stock which has served its country well.

We have a very busy week behind us, and we saw two aspects of the battle of the robot. Wednesday we toured gunsites in the South,

---

* Lady Mary Palmer (1920–2000), daughter of third Earl of Selborne. The first lady in waiting appointed to Princess Elizabeth, she served in the Royal Household until 1950. Married 1944 Anthony Strachey (d. 1955); 2nd 1981 St John Gore.

and spent the afternoon with a battery of heavy guns. The bombs came over fairly frequently, and the guns let go everything at them, tho' without much success. An occasional fighter came hurtling past on the tail of one of the robots, and one flew straight into the bursting shells, & my heart nearly stopped, as he started to wobble about, & we thought he had been hit. However, the bomb crashed a little further on, & the fighter seemed to recover. But really war is <u>very</u> exhausting! This particular site was a mixed battery, & the girls are doing very well indeed. They all looked so well, and though they are constantly on the alert night & day, they do get their sleep which is the main thing. The food was good, & well arranged tents & good beds.

The worst part was getting back to London through Croydon & Streatham which get a great many hits.

On Friday we went to fighter stations, and heard a lot about their work in shooting down these things. Some squadrons were operating in Normandy in support of our troops, and it was very inspiring to talk to these shy modest & very brave men. At one place there was a squadron of Norwegian fighters, such splendid young men, & mixing so well with ours. We saw two French squadrons, quite good too. Air Marshal Coningham* told me that a little while ago, some of the French in one squadron were Fighting French, some were Vichy & some were pro Giraud,† & feeling ran so high, & became so bitter that they took to sending each other little black coffins, & daggers & rude letters, until he had the brilliant idea of removing the squadron leader and sending in two good New Zealanders who in no time had the whole thing running smoothly and happily! It just shows how well they react to the right leadership, someone they can really trust. [. . .]

Much love darling Mama, your loving daughter in law
Elizabeth

~

---

* Air Marshal Sir Arthur Coningham KCB KBE DSO MC DFC AFC RAF (1895–1948), First World War flying ace; in the Second World War he commanded the Desert Air Force supporting the Eighth Army in North Africa, including at El Alamein, and was commander of tactical air forces in the 1944 Normandy campaign. On 30 January 1948, he presumably died with all the passengers and crew of an airliner which vanished without trace on a flight from the Azores to Bermuda.

† Henri Giraud (1879–1949), French general who took part in the Allied invasion of North Africa in November 1942. His relations with General de Gaulle were poor and he retired in 1944.

On 23 July 1944 the King set off for a ten-day trip to visit his troops in Italy under the command of General Alexander.*

~

26 July 1944 to King George VI

Buckingham Palace

My Darling Angel

I have a chance to send you a line by Walshie who thought he could deliver it to you, so here it is!

I do hope that you had a good journey, and that the tum tum tummy is behaving nicely, & not revolting at the climate, or the chianti, or the macaroni or spaghetti! It seems at least a month since you left, & the children and I are longing for your return. Everybody is well – the guide and Ranger camp was a great success, & 'Captain' & 'Skipper' parted without actually coming to blows which shows what a great success it was! I do hope that you are being able to see the troops, and not being <u>too</u> exhausted. Please give Alex [General Alexander] my greetings, and tell him I think he's a magician to weld British & Canadian & Polish & French and Goums† into one great Army – And such a splendid one too.

There is very little to tell you from here – Lilibet and I have signed a few papers dismissing people from the Services for various 'orrible offences! Also a bill which they want approved in a great hurry called the Validation of Wartime Leases Bill, & I hope that this is alright, tho' I do think it is wrong to ask for approval for the next day as it comes up for a second reading. It really doesn't give time to look at it! Well darling, I shall look forward tremendously to your return – Don't use any water that is not boiled – most important. From your loving and rather lonely Elizabeth

PS. Weather better and sky full of great big bombers!

~

---

*   Field Marshal Harold Alexander, first Earl Alexander of Tunis KG OM (1891–1969). During the Second World War he served as a commander in Burma, North Africa and Italy, eventually rising to become Supreme Allied Commander, Mediterranean Theatre. After serving as Governor General of Canada, in 1952 he became Minister of Defence in Winston Churchill's Cabinet.

†   Moroccan soldiers who served with the French army.

26 July 1944 to Queen Mary

Buckingham Palace

Darling Mama

Thank you so very much for your angelic note. I know that you understand my secret intense anxiety when Bertie goes off on these visits,* for one cannot feel happy about the long journeys by air, and all the hazards are great. But he feels so much not being more in the fighting line, and I know that it heartens the troops, & one swallows one's anxieties!

Lilibet & I went to see him off. It was nearly dark when we drove onto the airfield, and we at once got into the aircraft, & looked at all the arrangements. It really is quite comfortably arranged, with a nice little kitchen to prepare the food. When I went into the cockpit to see where the pilots sat, the first thing I saw through the glass was a flying bomb caught in the searchlights, & coming straight for the plane! I really felt, well this is too much, and averted my eye in anger! Luckily it buzzed over, and was going strong when I looked again! What emotions one goes through these days. I haven't heard a word from Bertie, but only reports that he had arrived at Naples, & then at Alex's HQ. I will let you know directly I hear any more news.

I think that he thought he would not see Beppo or any of the Italian Government as things are still a little 'mixed up'.†

Today I went to see a large American hospital at Oxford. It was very well run, & very full of wounded, some fresh from Normandy. One feels so sorry for the poor boys, they feel things so much, & are so homesick!

Much love darling Mama, ever your loving daughter in law

Elizabeth

~

* On the eve of his departure the King wrote to the Queen saying that although he did not expect anything to happen to him 'there are some matters which might want clearing up.' He said that she would 'naturally go on living at Buck. Pal, in this Castle [Windsor], Sandringham & Balmoral for the present until such time as Lilibet is on her own. I hope Royal Lodge, Appleton & Birkhall will always be your house on the private estates. The former is our home; the house we built and made for ourselves in Windsor Park.' RA QEQM/PRIV/RF)

† 'Beppo' was Crown Prince Umberto of Italy (1904–83), to whom his father King Victor Emmanuel III had handed over most of his powers since his country's September 1943 armistice with the Allies. King George wished to avoid an official visit to Rome, and the government agreed that for political reasons it was inadvisable for him to see any Italian political leaders or members of the Italian Royal Family.

10 August 1944 to Sir Osbert Sitwell

Buckingham Palace

My dear Sir Osbert,

Your birthday present has just this moment arrived, and as I am on the point of leaving for the station to go to Yorkshire, I will quickly send you this word of thanks, and shall look forward immensely to reading 'A Letter to My Son' in the train. It was most kind of you to think of sending it.

What a <u>tragedy</u> that Rex Whistler should have been killed.* I know how much you must feel it, and I too, feel great sadness.

In this vulgar age we live in, with so much ugliness around us, his exquisite taste and essentially good & noble outlook on life are a terrible loss to England.

In great haste, & with all my thanks,

I am Yours very sincerely

Elizabeth R

~

19 August 1944 to Queen Mary

Balmoral Castle

My Darling Mama

[. . .]

We came here via Yorkshire where we spent a day with the Canadian bomber squadrons, and the peace & beauty are even more heavenly after the violent two months just passed. We have had a lovely week with fine weather, for which we feel most grateful! Marina seems very happy at Birkhall, & is out all day with the children. We have met for picnics, & she brought Eddy to lunch after Church – he is a dear little boy, & much improved in manners.

The children are well, and it is so nice to see very bright eyes and pink cheeks again – the life at Windsor is really rather trying now, but they are really very good about it all.

One hears a lot now of the hopes that Paris will soon be freed,

---

* Rex Whistler (1905–44), British artist, designer and illustrator. He wrote letters embellished with beautiful drawings to the Queen, amongst others. He was killed by a mortar bomb near Caen on 18 July 1944, while serving with the Welsh Guards during the Normandy invasion.

but it leaves me quite cold compared to the longing I have that London may be freed from incessant bombardment. I don't think that anybody has any conception of the strain and horribleness of the whole thing, and people are so wonderful about it all. Up here, away from it all, I find that I think all the time of those little rows of houses, & everyone carrying on so splendidly amongst all the ruin and death – one feels almost conscience stricken to be so peaceful and quiet. It is marvellous too! [. . .]

Much love darling Mama, ever your loving
Elizabeth

~

4 October 1944 to Sir Alan Lascelles

Balmoral Castle

Dear Tommy

I am so very glad to hear that the Home Guard are to keep their battledress, boots & cape, and I am so grateful to you for letting me know so promptly. I am sure that this little douceur will be very well received, for I feel that many of those good brave self sacrificing people were rather depressed by their sudden & rather curt dismissal by radio.* I felt rather depressed too.

Perhaps the King will be able to give them a medal or flash or something, soon. It would be nice if he could announce it himself, say at the farewell parade. It gives so much more pleasure that way, & much more personal as well which is what matters. The George Cross & medal gained so much from being announced by the King himself.

We have had the most awful weather here, driving rain & cold & strong winds, but everyone is most friendly one toward another, & a little energy seems to be creeping back into the poor tottering human frame, which is a mercy.

We had a most exciting lesson & sermon on Sunday from

---

* The Queen was dismayed by the government's decision to disband the Home Guard. She recalled 'this splendid spirit of loyalty and determination which brought the Home Guard into being during those critical days of 1940'. (Queen Elizabeth, message to Commanding Officer (Lieutenant Colonel Hon. Michael Bowes Lyon) 31 July 1944, RA QEQM/PS/ENGT/1944/43)

Zachariah, about a flying roll & an ephah, & when Mr Lamb* was
describing to us what an ephah was (mooor than a boooshle of
wheat) & that when the lid was removed from the ephah, sitting on
the corn was a WOMAN, & this woman was a WICKED woman, his
tones became so denouncing that the kirk was stilled like magic, & all
the Manchesters† leant forward eagerly to hear <u>how</u> wicked was this
WICKED woman. But their coughing was smothered for nothing,
for the lid was quickly replaced on the ephah, and it was picked up,
wicked woman & all, & whisked off to Babylon by two women, 'and
the wind was in their wings, for they had wings like the wings of a
stork', & that was the end of the ephah & the wicked woman. The
flying roll was passed over.

 ER

       ~

9 October 1944 to Arthur Penn

Balmoral Castle

My dear Arthur,

 I return the letters from Eric Coates. I <u>trow sir</u>, we mustn't <u>waste
Coates</u> or <u>my hat</u>, he might get the <u>boot</u>.‡ Then the Master of the
King's Musick will have to pull up his <u>socks</u>, or Coates will get hot
under the <u>collar</u>, and his <u>pants</u> will be deafening. But I'll put my <u>shirt</u>
on the M of the KM, and he will probably be in<u>vested</u> with the <u>garter</u>.
To be continued.

 I shall be returning next week to the house I hate most in the
world [wartime Buckingham Palace], and shall hope to find you well.

---

* Dr John Lamb, Minister at Crathie 1937–63. He died in 1974, and Queen Elizabeth wrote
to his son Jock saying, 'My mind often goes back to those happy Balmoral days, & the laughter
& the jokes, & delicious tea at the Manse, & Dr Lamb glowing with vigour after his dip in the
icy Dee!' (RA QEQM/OUT/MISC)

† Soldiers of the 7th Battalion, the Manchester Regiment, stationed at Balmoral at this time.
The Queen became their Colonel-in-Chief in 1947.

‡ Sir Eric Coates (1886–1957), composer of many well-known pieces of light music, including
the film score for *The Dam Busters* and the theme tune of *Desert Island Discs*. He had written
asking permission to dedicate to the Queen his orchestral suite *The Three Elizabeths*. The three
were Elizabeth I, Elizabeth of Glamis and Princess Elizabeth. They were celebrated respectively
by a musical salute to the pageantry of Tudor England, a pastorale with a Scottish atmosphere,
and a stirring march evoking Princess Elizabeth as the leader of the Youth of Britain. His
dedication was accepted.

I think this last six months has been the most miserable of the whole war. So many wonderful people being killed gives one a permanent ache in one's heart for their relatives.

[. . .]

Yours ER

~

6 November 1944 to Queen Mary

Buckingham Palace

Darling Mama

One line to say that my Father is very ill, and I am going up to Glamis tomorrow night. He had influenza about a month ago, & he has never really recovered, and he is now extremely weak & there is not much hope of his regaining strength.

One feels great sadness at this moment, but he has always been so active & virile, that one could not wish him to live as an invalid.

You are always such an angel of understanding & sympathy, & you will know how one feels at this breaking of many links.

Your v. loving

Elizabeth

~

7 November 1944 to David Bowes Lyon

[Telegram]

FATHER DIED VERY PEACEFULLY IN HIS SLEEP THIS MORNING. SO GLAD YOU ARE COMING OVER.* ELIZABETH

~

13 November 1944 to Queen Mary

Buckingham Palace

Darling Mama

It was such a joy to be with you yesterday, so comforting &

---

* David Bowes Lyon replied that, as his father had already died, he would not fly home from Washington because 'I did not feel justified in taking this trip in war-time when all is over.' (Bowes Lyon Papers (SPW))

helpful too, and I felt much better after our talk, ranging as it did over many subjects.

There was one matter which I had intended to ask you about. It really has nothing to do with me, except that I became extremely interested over a scheme put up by Miss Amy Buller and the dear old Bishop of Lichfield among others, to use part of the Royal College of St Katharine's in Regent's Park as a centre for the study of the Christian philosophy of life.* It would be so wonderful if one could attract, particularly, the teachers of psychology, science, medicine, etc from the great universities all over the country, for they many of them seem to be almost pagans, and there seems to be absolutely nowhere where clever people can go to study and discuss the Christian way of life from an intellectual angle. It might lead to such great things if only one could get it started, and I believe that the scheme comes up to you as Patron of the College, and I do so wonder what you feel about it. The College seems an ideal place with its old associations with the Queens of England, and though of course it would have to be an experiment, there would be room for that, as well as its more ordinary & excellent work in the East End. There is nothing like it in the country and I did so want to ask you whether you liked the idea or not. Miss Buller is such an interesting little woman, I wonder whether you have seen her since she wrote 'Darkness over Germany', and she has seen so much of university life & its lack of intelligent Christian guidance. I am sure that people are badly taught about religion, if at all!

So sorry to write at such length darling Mama, ever your loving daughter in law

Elizabeth

~

---

* The war had convinced the Queen that Christianity was vital to the recovery of Britain. In 1944 she met Amy Buller (1891–1974), who had been horrified by the ease with which the Nazis came to power in Germany, a country she knew well. Miss Buller told the Queen of her ambition to create a college to inculcate Christian principles. The Queen, who had been impressed by Miss Buller's book, *Darkness over Germany*, promised to help find a site. In 1947 Cumberland Lodge, a residence in Windsor Great Park, fell vacant and the King and Queen offered it to Miss Buller's Foundation. She became warden and Elizabeth Elphinstone her deputy. St Katharine's College changed with the times (its name becoming St Catharine's, and then Cumberland Lodge), but it continued to flourish into the twenty-first century.

14 November 1944 to David Bowes Lyon

Buckingham Palace

My Darling David,

It was terribly sad that you were not able to come over for the funeral, though I quite agree that you did the right thing. [. . .] Father weakened so quickly that only May got there in time, and one must be very thankful that he had such a quick and peaceful death. The night nurse told me that he was breathing very lightly on Tuesday morning, & just gave a little sigh & stopped breathing. It couldn't have been better, but it is extraordinary how one misses him isn't it?

I can't tell you what nice letters I've had from all sorts and conditions of people, & so many stress Father's 'kindness to one and all' & him being an 'aristocrat', meaning I suppose that class meant nothing to him, Charles May or Crabbe or Bertie or Nurse Barrie or a Bishop, or Rory or me, or Olive Drummond, all the same.*

Of course there is that awful feeling of one's old home not really being a home any longer, which is a horrid thought, and I felt very sad during the 3 days at Glamis last week. But one must face up to it, and the main thing is that Glamis should go on as a centre of good will, & let us hope, good example and real leadership. Pat was awfully nice and is determined to live at Glamis.† If only Dorothy could move, I think that they would settle there at once. He seems to really love the place, and perhaps he will become more ordinary & easy when he is 'himself' at Glamis.

The funeral was much the same as Mother's, and it was very simple & just right.

Pat, May, Rosie and I went in the car, & in front, just behind the coffin walked Bertie, Mike and Sidney. [. . .] It was all just right.

One feels very sad, and I am afraid that you will feel it all so much darling, being so far away.

---

* Charles May, agent at St Paul's Walden. George Crabbe, head forester on the Glamis estate; Nurse Barrie probably worked with one of the doctors from nearby Forfar; Harry Gilbert Grey Rorison (1879–1963), Rector at Kirriemuir, 1928–48, also serving the Chapel at Glamis; Chaplain at Glamis Castle, 1948–60; Olive Drummond, a local friend of the family.

† Patrick Bowes Lyon (1884–1949), Queen Elizabeth's eldest brother, was known as the Master of Glamis until the death of his grandfather in 1904, when he became Lord Glamis. On his father's death he became the fifteenth Earl of Strathmore.

I have given Tommy your message and he will do what he can. I enclose a letter from Alah, so nice, dear old Alah.

Goodbye darling,

your very loving

Buffy

The new fun is rockets. Less trouble than flying bombs because you can't take shelter, & it's just luck or perhaps the Almighty keeping an eye.

~

14 November 1944 to Winston Churchill

Buckingham Palace

Dear Mr Churchill

I was very much touched by your kind letter of sympathy, and I send you my heartfelt thanks for such understanding & helpful words. It is a very sad moment for us all, my Father loved us, and we loved him, and it was so comforting for me to go home, and feel even now, with old age coming on, that I was a loved child. That has gone, but I am very grateful to have had him so long, & it is good to know that Glamis was a centre of good will & unity for the people around.

I am glad that you had a successful visit to France,* & only hope that the cold was not too trying. Do you think that there is any chance of London being 'liberated' in the coming months? My heart aches for our wonderful brave people, they have been tried so high, & of course can go on, but it really is rather a bore to feel that one might be blown to pieces at any moment. There is no limit to their courage & cheerfulness, and I long for them to have a lightening of their burden.

With again my thanks for your kind letter,

I am, Yours very sincerely,

Elizabeth R

~

---

* Paris was liberated on 25 August 1944, and Churchill received a rapturous welcome when he visited the city on 11 November.

1 January 1945 to Mrs Way

Buckingham Palace

Dear Mrs Way*

The thoughts of the King and myself have been so much with you & your sons these past few days, and I do want to send you this personal note to say how deeply we feel for you in your great sorrow. Our sympathy is most heartfelt, & we share your grief, for we looked upon Way & yourself as old & true friends, and are deeply distressed by his death.

He gave such good and faithful service to his King, and when we came to Sandringham, the first place that our steps turned to, was always to visit you & your dear husband. I know how bravely you are facing this sad time, & am so thankful to hear that two of your sons are with you.

With our deepest sympathy,

I am, Yours very sincerely,

Elizabeth R

~

26 January 1945 to Queen Mary

Appleton

My Darling Mama

It was most kind of you to write so sympathetically about Michael's illness, and I am so grateful to you for your dear thought. I am thankful to say that he is now well on the road to recovery, thanks to our old friend M & B!†

We have had a very agreeable and <u>icy</u> cold visit here, punctuated with bad colds & flu, & now Margaret has got mumps (luckily very mild), and so Lilibet & I may be catching after next week. It is a great bore, the whole place is full of it, Ruth Fermoy‡ has it, the Birkbecks and all the schoolchildren and so it has been difficult to avoid.

---

* Mrs Way's husband George had just died. He was a gamekeeper at Sandringham, 1911–43, and kennelman, 1943–4.

† Produced by May & Baker in 1936, the first effective antibiotic.

‡ Ruth Roche, Lady Fermoy, DCVO OBE (1908–1993), lady in waiting and close friend of Queen Elizabeth and maternal grandmother of Lady Diana Spencer.

I think that your idea of Lilibet visiting some hospitals is a very good one, and it had occurred to me too. She is going to do a course in mechanics with the ATS* when we return to London, tho' this is to be kept quiet for the moment, and I think it will be a good thing for her to have a little experience from the inside into how a women's Service is run. She will learn something about the inside of a car as well, which is always useful. The course takes about six weeks I believe, & she can do it by day, & I do hope it will be a success.

She has been working fairly hard with Henry Marten and has learnt quite a lot of European and constitutional history. He is such a good teacher. I long to join in myself, only am always in London during the week.

The Russians seem to be getting on very well, oh how one prays that with us pressing all along the West, & the Russians all along the East, that the Germans may be compressed & harried & beaten at last. They have brought such untold agony on the world – I do <u>hope</u> that we shall stay well armed after this war, for it is the only way to stop another one.

The Greek affair† was very depressing, wasn't it? One could hardly believe that the Press and the intellectuals of the socialist party could be so blind as to back up a gang of bandits who wanted to seize power by force. We have suffered so much in the fight for what is called Freedom, it was very sad that at this moment people could be so misled as to what freedom means. It certainly doesn't mean government by tommy gun, and one can only hope that it has done good in the end by making people see the dangers of armed rebellion.

Much love darling Mama,
ever your loving daughter in law
Elizabeth

~

* The Auxiliary Territorial Service was formed in September 1938 as a women's voluntary service and the Queen became its Commandant in Chief in 1939. It was given full military status in 1941. The women served in a variety of roles ranging from cooks and clerks to drivers, radar operators and 'ack-ack' anti-aircraft gun crews. At its peak the ATS numbered over 200,000 women. In 1949 it was disbanded and the WRAC (Women's Royal Army Corps) took its place.

† After the Germans had fled Greece, violence between Royalists and Communists grew. The Queen was dismayed by the way in which the press and the BBC appeared to support the Communists.

14 February 1945 to Sir D'Arcy Osborne

Buckingham Palace

My dear D'Arcy,*

I was so pleased to get your letter today, and I want to thank you also for a very charming and interesting letter which I have been meaning to answer ever since it arrived in August. Like you, I find it extremely difficult to write to one's friends nowadays. I suppose that it is partly because one is exhausted by the agonies of war, & partly because there is so little to write about except war, and the effects of war. It will be delightful [to] see you again when you next come on leave, and there are thousands of things that I want to discuss with you.

Your account of Italy is very sad. I do wish that we could take them over, & govern them, & give them a start, & some hope for better things. Are they cultivating the fields again, because food is such an important start to sane thinking.

How one longs for the war to end. Life is very hard here in London for most people, tho' they are wonderfully patient and self sacrificing, and even when they are being blown up by day & night, are still passionately interested in the poor French, or those poor Chinese, or those poor refugees, or those poor starved Indians in Bengal. I do believe that we are the most warm hearted people in Europe, or outside, with a great sense of obligation towards the more unfortunate people who don't happen to belong to the British Empire!

I am so glad to hear that you have a house at last.

[Not signed off]

~

---

* D'Arcy Osborne was heroic as Envoy Extraordinary and Minister Plenipotentiary to the Holy See during the war. He was part of a small group of diplomats and churchmen who helped conceal some 4,000 escapees – Allied soldiers and Jews – from the Nazis.

Major Sam Derry, an escaping soldier, described Osborne in the Vatican in 1943: 'Seldom have I met any man in whom I had such immediate confidence. He welcomed us warmly, yet I found it impossible to behave with anything but strict formality ... I was almost overwhelmed by an atmosphere of old-world English courtliness and grace which I had thought belonged only to the country-house parties of long ago ... I felt as though I had returned home after long travels, to find that royalty had come to dinner, and I had to be on my best behaviour.' (Owen Chadwick, *Britain and the Vatican during the Second World War*, Cambridge University Press, 1986, *passim*)

20 March 1945 to the Hon. Sir Richard Molyneux

Buckingham Palace

My dear Dick

It is curious that your letter arrived today, because last night the King & I were saying that we had not seen you for <u>AGES</u>, and I said that I would write & ask you to come and spend a weekend at our little weekend cottage. And, lo and behold! on my table this morning what do I see? That well-known writing – is it? Can it be? Yes! No – Yes; it <u>is</u>! I suppose that my thoughts whizzed out of the window here, turned sharp right, cut across the Green Park, past the Ritz, down Berkeley Street, and entering your flat, elbowed their way through the guests thronging your hall, & crashed into your mind. Anyway, I was very pleased to hear from you, and we do hope that you will be able to come and see us very soon. Can you come to Windsor next Saturday 24th? Or perhaps Saturday 7th April would suit you better.

Mr Kelly has very nearly finished the portraits, & I shall be so interested to hear what you think of them.

Down with Hitler!

Your friend ER

~

10 April 1945 to Queen Mary

Buckingham Palace

Darling Mama

Thank you so much for your letter. It was so really delightful having you for that little visit on Sunday, and we all enjoyed it very much.

Margaret has not been very well lately. [. . .] I am longing to take her and Lilibet to Appleton for a little change of air, for Lilibet really was bad with mumps, and she is tired (like young people do get tired) with her really hard work at the Motor Company – I don't mean tired <u>of</u> it, for she likes it so much, but tired by the day's hard work! But it has been such a success I am thankful to say, and the experience will be of use to her in the future. [. . .]

Mama, if by the mercy of God we are spared further murderous onslaughts by the Germans, and no more flying bombs & rockets come over, could you not come to Windsor for a week or a fortnight, from there you could easily come up to London for any business or shopping & it would be so nice for us. I only suggest this as a possibility, as there is plenty of room there, & conveniently close to London, and there are so many <u>preliminary</u> plans to make for the Great Move [back to Marlborough House] when it comes, and it is sometimes easier if one can just cast an eye on things oneself.

Please don't trouble to answer, but if, later on, this idea appeals to you, just let us know.

Much love darling Mama,

Ever your loving daughter in law

Elizabeth

PS You would not mind if we were not at Windsor during the mid week.

~

Victory in Europe was finally declared on 8 May 1945. All of Britain celebrated. Hundreds of thousands of people gathered in front of Buckingham Palace to cheer the Royal Family – and the King and Queen allowed the Princesses to mingle with the ecstatic crowds.

In a speech in the House of Commons, Winston Churchill praised the work of the King and 'his gracious consort, the Queen' throughout the war. She had, he said, 'been everywhere with him to scenes of suffering and disaster, to hospitals, to places shattered the day before by some devastating explosion, to see the bereaved, the sufferers and the wounded, and I am sure that many an aching heart has found some solace in her gracious smile.'*

~

12 May 1945 to Doris Vyner

Windsor Castle

My Darling Doris,

Your note has just arrived, and it is impossible for me to say what is in my heart for you. Words are just useless, and I can only send you <u>all</u> my love and constant thoughts and prayers. This cruel blow†

---

* Hansard, 15 May 1945.

† Charles Vyner (b. 1926), the son of the Queen's oldest friends, Clare and Doris Vyner, was killed over Burma on 2 May 1945. Flying in support of Allied landings to capture Rangoon, his

is one which I have <u>prayed</u> that you and Clare might be spared, and both the King and I are absolutely heartbroken for you. Such grief is so utterly personal, and one feels so helpless to say or do anything – Oh Doris, I cannot <u>bear</u> to think of your sorrow – only your great courage can sustain you, that, and the sharing of this great & added burden with Clare. You will be able to help him so much, and he you. I have never in my life read a letter so ringing with courage and unbeaten spirit, as yours today. How proud Charles must be of you, he had such a gay and gallant spirit himself, and your reaction to this crushing blow is so wonderful. Darling Doris, all my most loving thoughts are with you all the time; if ever you want me I shall come <u>at once</u>, even just to be with you a moment. I feel so deeply for Clare too – you are our dearest & best friends, & your sorrows are our sorrows – if <u>only</u> we could lighten them for you.

<u>All</u> my love my darling brave Doris, Your always loving E

~

14 May 1945 to Sir Osbert Sitwell

Buckingham Palace

My dear Sir Osbert,

I have to thank you for two delightful & kind letters and also for sending me your enchanting and fascinating book, Left Hand Right Hand.*

I have been trying to write for weeks, but somehow have found it very difficult to put two words together and even now I fear that this letter won't make much sense! I feel rather numbed by the emotions of the last weeks, and on top of all the great anxieties of the last years, this has made me feel stunned as well, so you will understand a rather stupid letter, I hope!

I have read your lovely book with such enjoyment and admiration. It was thrilling to read it again, and everybody is full of praise for such a superb work.

I would so like someday to see your Pipers – have you seen mine of Windsor? I thought that some of your drawings looked lovely.

---

plane crashed into the sea. The news reached his parents only on 12 May 1945, four days after VE Day.

* The first volume of Osbert Sitwell's autobiography.

It is almost impossible to believe that the dreadful war is over, and Germany truly beaten; – the sense of relief from bombs and rockets is very agreeable at the moment, and I hope that people won't forget too soon. They have shown such a noble and unselfish spirit all through the country during these long years of war, and I long for them to keep at the same high level in the days to come.

Our people respond so magnificently when they are asked to do hard things, to die, to smile amongst the wreckage of their homes, to work until they crack, to think of their neighbour before themselves; and the more difficult the things you ask of them, the more response you get. It's been so wonderful; and all that spirit will be needed now, more than ever, for the whole world looks (even if some unwillingly) to these Islands for leadership in decent living and thinking. We must do it somehow. [. . .]

With again my heartfelt thanks for sending me your book,

I am your very sincerely,

Elizabeth R.

~

11 June 1945 to Queen Mary

Buckingham Palace

My Darling Mama

It is wonderful to think that you are back at Marlborough House after all those years of war, and this is just to send my fondest love, & to say what joy we feel on your return.

It has really been very lonely not having any member of the family in London and it is so splendid that you are the first to return.

This bunch of roses comes with so much love.

Ever your devoted

Elizabeth

~

26 July 1945 to Queen Mary

Buckingham Palace

My Darling Mama

It would be so delightful if you would come to tea on my

birthday. I think that we may be going to the races at Ascot in the afternoon, & should be back by 4.30.

The election has been rather a shock,* and I think that Bertie felt it very much, as Winston has been such a great support and comfort all through these terrible years of war. He is a great man, of great vision, and his leadership has meant so much to so many. People's memories are short, alas!, and one must try now to build up another good, sound government. But the material is not too inspiring.

With a great war raging, & a Potsdam Conference sitting, really is not the time to have a change of government! We both feel very tired & today has been very depressing, but Bertie is wonderful, and tho' he looks rather pinched in the face, he is so calm and good, tho' I know he is worried to death. You have been through all these things Mama, & understand it all so well. It is hell, isn't it.

Your very loving daughter in law
Elizabeth

~

On 15 August 1945, after the US dropped atomic bombs on Hiroshima and Nagasaki, Japan surrendered and thus the Second World War came to an end. August 15 1945 has ever since been known as V-J Day. The Japanese government's formal surrender took place on board the battleship USS *Missouri* in Tokyo Bay on 2 September 1945.

~

15 August 1945 to Lady Helen Graham

Buckingham Palace

My dearest Nellie,

I am so very distressed to hear that your recovery has had this setback, and these few lines bring you all my love and most understanding sympathy. [. . .] This day has brought the end of the war – one can hardly take it in. I do pray that all the sacrifices &

---

* The result of the post-war general election was announced on 26 July. The Conservatives, still led by Winston Churchill, were defeated, and Labour, pledged to create a welfare state, won by a majority of 146. The King wrote to Churchill, 'how very sad I am that you are no longer my Prime Minister . . . I shall miss your counsel to me more than I can say.' (Wheeler-Bennett, *King George VI*, p. 637)

comradeship & love which people have felt for each other will not
fade.

All my love dearest Nellie,

Your <u>very</u> affec:

Elizabeth R

~

22 August 1945 to Sir Osbert Sitwell

Buckingham Palace

My dear Sir Osbert,

[. . .]

There has been so much happening that I feel rather dazed, don't
you? One fears that this winter is going to be difficult, little fuel, no
more clothes, monotonous and sparse food, & no bombing to liven
us up. But people are not being killed & that's the main thing.

Yours very sincerely,

Elizabeth R

~

18 September 1945 to Queen Mary

Balmoral Castle

Darling Mama

[. . .]

I do trust that David's visit will go off well, and that he won't
have any press conferences.* He ought to say that his visit is private
and refuse to see the press, for it is most indiscreet to start something
which the family have avoided so successfully here. I pray that his
visit will give you pleasure, for whatever the sad events of the past, it
is very hard for a mother to be parted from her son.

Lilibet is getting on quite well. One leg had some bad gashes on
it, and is healing slowly, and the doctor has ordered complete rest.
It is most unfortunate, but might have been so much worse. There is

---

* The Duke of Windsor had been appointed Governor of the Bahamas in 1940. He made his
first post-war visit back to Britain in October 1945. He stayed with Queen Mary, who was
delighted to see her 'dear eldest son'. She was relieved that he had not brought his wife with
him. He saw the King, but not Queen Elizabeth. (Owen Morshead, Notes on conversation
with Queen Mary, 18 February 1946, RA AEC/GG/12/OS/2)

nothing so dangerous as a horse bolting among trees, and we are thankful that her eye escaped, for she had a scratch across the eyelid.

[. . .]

I am afraid that Aunt Alice* will think that Bertie and I have aged a lot, and look rather haggard and ravaged! and one's clothes are so awful! But those years of anxiety and the horrible effects of bombing and destruction must leave a mark I suppose, so I hope she won't be too surprised.

Everything goes well here, and to my joy Bertie has taken to stalking again, which means he has more energy, and it is doing him good. He was very tired when we got up here at the end of August, for the summer had been very exhausting. [. . .]

Your very loving daughter-in-law
Elizabeth

~

8 October 1945 to Arthur Penn

Balmoral Castle

My dear Arthur,

I return the letter written in Paris. It whisked me back all those years in a twinkling, and I suddenly remembered what fun it was and how carefree we all were, and how much we laughed, and how late we sat up! Thank you <u>so</u> much for letting me see your very amusing account of the journey. [. . .]

Au-revoir, Ta Ta you can hear him say to the Marchioness Clerkenwell† as he wishes her good day (one of my father's songs).

ER

~

---

* Princess Alice, Countess of Athlone (1883–1981), the last surviving grandchild of Queen Victoria, was married to her second cousin once removed, Prince Alexander of Teck (created Earl of Athlone, 1917), the brother of Queen Mary. He was Governor General of South Africa, 1924–31, and in 1940 he succeeded Lord Tweedsmuir (John Buchan) as Governor General of Canada.

† Perhaps 'Molly the Marchioness', by Lionel Monckton (1861–1924), popular composer of musical comedies.

Oh, Molly was tall and fair to see,
Her manners were frank, her language free;
She met with a noble Lord when he
Was fishing a neighbour's water . . .

19 December 1945 to the Hon. Sir Richard Molyneux

Buckingham Palace

My dear Dick

Bowling through Berkeley Square today, it suddenly struck me to ask whether you were planning to spend Xmas anywhere particular, or whether you would care to come & spend it with us at hideous ugly germ ridden old Sandringham? I only write this note in case, because of course you may be off to a party, and old S may be a bit dull!

In any case, I hope you will come for a few days later, as it is 6 years since we have had a room or two 'spare'! If you are already too engaged, a merry Xmas! if not, you just wait. ER

~

31 December 1945 to Mrs Beevers

Sandringham

Dearest Nannie B

A number of your babies' Mothers have banded together to collect & give you a small gift in token of our love & gratitude for all you have done for us.

We find it almost impossible to buy anything nice in these days of empty shops, so we are wondering whether you would care for the money to be used to buy an annuity, which might be the most useful in the end. I have asked for the form to be sent to you, and if you will just fill it in where it is marked X, the whole thing will be quite private.

I do hope you will agree to this, and the gift comes with all our love. I shall send you the list of mothers, and every one of them was so pleased & delighted to join. The writing was all done by Mrs Carnegy of Lour,* and I thought it might be very nice to have a little tea party in the Spring, & I will collect some mothers & we can all talk over old days!

    With my love,
    always your affect.
    Elizabeth R

~

---

*   Violet Carnegy of Lour (1897–1965), wife of Lieutenant Colonel Ughtred Elliott Carnegy of Lour. They had three daughters.

1 January 1946 to Sir D'Arcy Osborne

Sandringham

My dear D'Arcy,

[. . .]

It is rather a sad thought but both my daughters have never set foot outside these Islands! For some years before the war they were not only too small, but dictators strutted in Europe, & for six years they lived under fairly warlike conditions here, so that when people are kind to each other again, I can see that they will be off & away to travel & see for themselves. Indeed, they have hardly even met a foreigner! It is too extraordinary & wrong.

I feel that people are gradually becoming more sensible here, but manners are not too good – they were so exquisite during the war – perhaps it was too great a strain!

I am enclosing a small photograph [of the Royal Family on the balcony on VE Day] with our very best wishes for the New Year. Those days of victory passed in a sort of daze – one could hardly believe that the killing & anguish was over. I do pray that we shall get <u>real</u> Peace soon. [. . .]

Your very old friend

Elizabeth R

~

6 January 1946 to Eleanor Roosevelt

Sandringham

My dear Mrs Roosevelt

I do want to send you a word of cordial greeting on your arrival in England, and say how much we are looking forward to meeting you again.

So much has happened to this poor battered world since those days when you visited us at Buckingham Palace, & now so many hopes are centred on this great 'getting together'* which starts next week.

---

* The United Nations was created, following an international conference in San Franscisco, on 24 October 1945. Its first General Assembly, with fifty-one nations represented, opened at Central Hall, Westminster, on 10 January 1946. On 17 January the Security Council met for

I do hope that your stay here will be a pleasant one, & if you can manage it, I would be so glad if you could come to us for a weekend. It would be so delightful to renew our friendship, & I will suggest a date a little later, when you will perhaps know your plans ahead more clearly.

With all good wishes,
I am,
Your sincere friend,
Elizabeth R

~

15 May 1946 to Queen Mary

Buckingham Palace

Darling Mama

Thank you so much for your note. We are looking forward very much to your visit to Royal Lodge on your birthday, and are so delighted that you are coming to us. [. . .]

There is one thing which I am so anxious to ask you darling Mama, and I feel that I was such a bore about it during the War that I hesitate to bore you again. But I feel that you understand my strong feelings on the subject, and therefore ask whether you would contemplate putting our dear old friend the Bishop of Lichfield (Woods) onto the Council of St Katharine's (Regent's Park). He is such a rock, & so sensible, and owing to the impossibility of building for the next few years, I do believe that my fond hope of a place where students can study the Christian philosophy may come to pass – if St Katharine's will back it for a year or two. Lord Salisbury has offered Hatfield – he is very keen about the plan, and I am sure that the Bishop of Lichfield could explain the whole great idea if you would place him on the Council. I do hope you don't mind me suggesting this, but I do feel that this country depends so largely on our democracy being <u>Christian</u>, that one ought to fight tooth and nail the rather 'Nazi' spirit of paganism that is so rife.

Please forgive me if I have suggested something which is in any

---

the first time and on the 24th the General Assembly adopted its first resolution, on the peaceful uses of atomic energy and the elimination of atomic and other weapons of mass destruction. The cornerstone of its permanent headquarters in New York was laid in October 1949.

way difficult, but the whole trend of education nowadays is so utterly
material, & so dangerous for the future. I am sure that the Bishop
would only be a help, & never try to force any new ideas on to St
Katharine's.

Much love, darling Mama, Your loving daughter in law, Elizabeth

PS We thought of having a luncheon party here on Victory March
Day, & do hope you will come.

~

25 September 1946 to Viscountess Cranborne

Balmoral Castle

Dearest Betty,

[. . .]

We have just returned here after two very crowded days in
London, trailing round 'Britain can make it' (but no one can get it)*
with Mr & Mrs Attlee† & Sir Stafford Cripps, saying goodbye to
[King] George of Greece‡ who goes to a difficult job I fear, goodbye
to Mr Harriman;§ being given orders & honours by Nepalese generals,
trying to choose chintzes for the trip to South Africa, and to return to
this haven of air & light is almost to good to be true. I know that I
would die if I had to live in London all my life – one only exists
there. But do you remember what fun it used to be? So gay & so
friendly & so elegant – I am so glad to have known it – I even
remember carriages & horses, & geraniums in window boxes & ices

---

* Bread had not been rationed during the war – but now it was. All other foods, clothing
and fuel were in short supply or rationed. 'Britain Can Make It' was a massive 1946 exhibition
put on at the Victoria and Albert Museum by the Council of Industrial Design (later the
Design Council) to promote post-war British industry.

† Clement Attlee, first Earl Attlee, KG OM CH PC FRS (1883–1967), leader of the Labour
Party; Deputy Prime Minister, 1940–5; Prime Minister, 1945–51. Violet (Vi) Attlee, his wife,
worked closely with him and drove him everywhere throughout the country. The Queen told
Eric Anderson, 'I think the King faintly dreaded such a complete change, but actually Mr
Attlee turned out very good. He and the King got on very well. And he was a very good
Prime Minister, I think.' (*Conversations with Eric Anderson 1994–5*, RA QEQM/ADD/MISC)

‡ Following the plebiscite calling for his return, the king was going back to Greece after over
five years in exile. He faced the thorny task of managing the political factions of the country.
He died childless in April 1947 and was succeeded by his brother Prince Paul.

§ W. Averell Harriman (1891–1986), American Democrat politician, businessman and diplomat. In 1941 he became US Special Envoy to Europe.

at Gunter, & polo at Hurlingham, & tennis in the squares, & all those old fashioned things! Ah me!

Thank you again dearest Betty for the photographs, & <u>how</u> we loved having you & Bobbety here – it was a real joy to us both.

With much love from your affec:

Elizabeth R

~

8 October 1946 to King George VI

*RMS Queen Elizabeth**

My Darling Bertie

I sent you a little message at lunch time today, and as there is five minutes before tea, I thought you might like a letter from your wife whilst at sea! We have been all over the ship, & I must say she is quite beautiful and very comfortable. It is so good for people to see that we have got taste & good workmanship in this country – oh how I hate utility and austerity, don't you?

It's all wrong.

Well, darling I must fly, the children have just returned from the engine room, and tea is calling.

I <u>do</u> hope that Sandringham is nice and warm.

Your very very loving

E

~

9 October 1946 to John Elphinstone

Balmoral Castle

My Darling John

Since leaving lovely Glenmazeran[†] last Thursday, this is really the

---

* RMS *Queen Elizabeth*, then the largest ocean liner ever built, was launched by the Queen on the Clyde in September 1938. War delayed her commercial service – she first served as a troopship. She was fitted out for the first time as a liner only in 1946. During the 1950s she and her sister ship *Queen Mary* dominated the transatlantic passenger market until air crossings took over. She had an ignominious end: in 1972 she caught fire and was wrecked in Hong Kong harbour.

† John Elphinstone had returned from his German prisoner-of-war camp after VE Day.

first moment I have had in which to write you a line to say how TREMENDOUSLY I enjoyed my visit there. I was so looking forward to seeing the house and the country, and I thought both enchanting.

You were so angelic to Lilibet & me, & we adored our visit, and would so love to come again please, if you can bear it!

It was so kind of you to have arranged such a wonderful day for Lilibet. She was absolutely thrilled!

And the whizzbang! My! My!

A million thanks,

Your very loving

Peter

~

12 November 1946 to Sir Osbert Sitwell

Buckingham Palace

Dear Sir Osbert,

I am wondering whether you are going to be in London on Wednesday Nov 20th, for on that evening we are going to the Academy to gaze at our pictures in comparative peace, & it would be delightful if you would care to come at 9.30 pm or after.

We shall ask a very few friends who might like to wander round quietly. I am enjoying seeing our pictures well lit & well shown, & it has revived my wish to build a pretty gallery at Buckingham Palace. But with the present rate of house building I fear it will be many years before such a thing is possible.* I shall leave a legacy I expect! If you and your sister would like to come on the 20th, we would be enchanted.

Glenmazeran was the sporting estate at Tomatin in Inverness-shire bought by John's father, Sidney.

* An exhibition of paintings from the Royal Collection had long been mooted. After the war, the collection was gradually reassembled from its various wartime hiding places. The pictures were cleaned and restored as necessary and the 'The King's Pictures' opened at the Royal Academy in November 1946. It was the first large art show to be held in London since the war and over 366,000 people came to see it. The Queen arranged a private view and supper for friends at the Academy on 20 November 1946. Queen Elizabeth's wish for a gallery at Buckingham Palace came true many years later, when the Duke of Edinburgh suggested that the bomb-damaged Chapel be converted into a small public gallery to display changing exhibitions from the Royal Collection. The Queen's Gallery was opened in 1962. In 2002 it was incorporated into a new, larger gallery built to commemorate Queen Elizabeth II's Golden Jubilee.

I do hope that you are well and not feeling cast down by the bleakness of life. I find London very gloomy, & everybody behaves as if they were deaf. They don't listen to anything anybody says – but perhaps they are right.

Hoping to see you before long.

I am, Yours v sincerely

Elizabeth R

~

After the war, Royal Tours of Australia, New Zealand, Canada and other Dominions were planned as a way of thanking their peoples for the sacrifices they had made. South Africa was the first such destination and the Royal Family set sail in HMS *Vanguard* on 1 February 1947. It was one of the coldest winters in memory; the workings of Big Ben froze solid and so did the Thames, and there were constant power cuts. The King and the Queen were both reluctant to leave the country in such circumstances, but their welcome in South Africa was as warm as the weather, even in the traditionally anti-British Boer territories. The abundance of the country was astonishing, but the journey, much of it by train, was exhausting, particularly for the King. Towards the end of the tour Princess Elizabeth celebrated her twenty-first birthday and made a moving radio broadcast to her people in which she pledged that 'my whole life, whether it be long or short, shall be dedicated to your service.'

~

Saturday 1 February 1947 to Queen Mary

HMS *Vanguard*

My Darling Mama

I believe that a helicopter is going to land on this ship today, so I shall take the opportunity of a mail to send you one line of love. It is horrid to think that we shall not see you for so long, but May will soon be here, and a happy reunion.

Our cabins seem very comfortable, & we are settling in busily. We got up early this morning, & left a very grey & snowy England as dawn lightened the sky – I wish that one could feel happier about the state of the country, so many homeless is a terrible thing, and so bad for home life in general.

With so much love darling Mama,
Ever your loving daughter in law
Elizabeth
PS Arthur has got the School of Needlework in hand, & Jack
Spencer will, I hope, prove a good choice as Chairman.

~

21 February 1947 to Queen Mary

Government House
Cape Town

My Darling Mama,

This is the first opportunity that I have had to write to you, as the
last four days have been so busy we had hardly time to breathe!

This morning Bertie opens Parliament so we have an hour or two
of quiet until 11.30.

Everybody has been very kind here in Cape Town, and I think
that the visit is going well. There are so many serious racial problems,
but so far all sections of the community have been most welcoming.

Yesterday we went out to Paarl and Stellenbosch, two very
Nationalist and Afrikaans speaking towns, and had the most delightful
reception – very nice country people, and they had prepared a picnic
on the top of a mountain with a staggering amount of home made
food! Lovely old Dutch recipes and French Huguenot dishes – Bertie
and I were stunned by so much, & then we descended the mountain
and had luncheon under the trees, again a mass of food, & we nearly
burst! The tables looked so lovely piled high with grapes & peaches &
pears, & beautiful flowers – and all good simple home grown food –
the people here are very lucky to be able to grow so much for
themselves. We find that we simply cannot eat all they offer us! I will
write more fully from the train – we start today on this immense tour
– I do hope it won't be too tiring for Bertie. We are thinking of you
all shivering at home, and wish we could help. I see that the Indian
thing is out today, poor Dickie* will need our prayers. Your very
loving E

~

---

* The British colonial administration of India, headed by Lord Mountbatten, the last Viceroy,

9 March 1947 to Queen Mary

The White Train

My Darling Mama

We are just back in this comfortable but very wobbly train, after 3 days in Bloemfontein. We stayed at Government House which has just been built, and is very pretty & well arranged tho' small for a large party such as ours. I enclose a photo in case you would care to see it. I think that Lady Duncan* had a good deal to do with the building of it, and the laying out of the garden.

Bloemfontein is a great centre of Nationalism, and practically all the Town Council & the Administration are Nationalist, & were rather suspicious to start with. The members of the provincial council are mostly old Boer farmers, men of iron, but fine old men, & we all got on very well together. Six of them had fought against us in the Boer War, & proud of it!

There was of course, a garden party, & a Ball, & children's gatherings, and yesterday we went by air to their little game reserve, where we had lunch with the members of the provincial Council and their wives, & over meat broiled over an open fire, we became quite friendly, & I think that they softened towards us. It was hardly worth flying out to see a few buck, but it <u>was</u> worth the friendly picnic atmosphere & chance of making friends.

Today we went to Church in the Cathedral, then to the Zoo which is in a very lovely garden, & this afternoon we visited some farmers & called on old Mrs Steyn, widow of the old President of the Free State, & she sent you many messages, & said that she always remembered a luncheon in London when you were Princess of Wales, & how much she admired you. A wonderful old lady, & very interesting about the old days. [. . .]

---

had hoped to give independence to a united India. But the demands of Hindu and Muslim leaders proved impossible to reconcile and Mountbatten presided over the partition of India into two countries – the mostly Muslim Pakistan and the mostly Hindu India. New borders had to be drawn and independence to both countries was granted at midnight on 14/15 August 1947. Mountbatten was criticized for the speed with which he had insisted Partition be carried out. Terrible bloodshed occurred as millions of people crossed from one new country into the other.

* Lady Duncan (Alice), widow of Sir Patrick Duncan (1899–1943), Governor General of South Africa, 1937–43. She shaped the gardens at Government House and, a South African herself, stayed there after her husband's death.

We think of home all the time, and Bertie has offered to return, but Mr Attlee thought that it would only make people feel that things were getting worse, and was not anxious for him to come back. This is a very difficult and anxious time, and the British people seem to be taking it very magnificently.

I wore your lovely tiara for the Opening of Parliament, & I told the Press that you had lent it to me for the purpose, & they were all delighted. Do please forgive this abominable writing, but the train shakes & sways, & it is difficult to write.

We find that the stops every two hours are rather exhausting, but we try to get out & talk to people because they <u>are</u> so nice, & some come a very long way, carrying babies, & standing patiently for hours, & one meets the ordinary citizens in this way.

Delia [Peel] & Mima* are great helps, & the two equerries are learning quickly, for being War appointments, they have never seen this sort of thing. I rather miss Joey Legh – he is so good on these trips & can speak with authority on occasions, which is very useful.

I have ordered you some crystallised fruits – they are just making this year's, so I hope they will arrive fresh.

Much love darling Mama,

Ever your loving daughter in law

Elizabeth

~

16 April 1947 to Queen Mary

The White Train
Bechuanaland

Darling Mama

Today we left Bulawayo after a very strenuous but interesting visit to Southern Rhodesia, which included a trip across the Zambesi to N. Rhodesia.

Government House at Salisbury is charming, and I would have

---

* Lady Harlech DCVO (1891–1980), née Lady Beatrice ('Mima') Gascoyne-Cecil, daughter of the fourth Marquess of Salisbury; wife of fourth Baron Harlech. Lady of the Bedchamber to Queen Elizabeth (1947–67). Lady Harlech and Lady Delia Peel were the Queen's two ladies in waiting on the South African tour; Lady Margaret Egerton (later Colville) was lady in waiting to the two Princesses.

liked a few more days there, to see a little more of the country, & to collect one's thoughts & impressions. But everything has been a great rush, which was inevitable I suppose, as it would have meant at least another three weeks added on to the tour if we had gone a little more slowly.

Rhodesia is most attractive, a very agreeable mixture of British & good Colonial, and a nice feeling of freedom everywhere. I think that they need British capital, because one sees signs of American infiltration through commerce, and they are so loyal, & all try & 'buy British', even if it is a little more expensive. Anyway, our goods are excellent, which is most pleasing.

This Country is terribly dry. They are going through a bad drought poor things.

The Kennedys* were very nice & charming hosts – it was delightful to stay <u>with</u> someone! One misses that so much in South Africa. [. . .]

Bertie is rather tired – the pace has been very hot, and the weather at the Victoria Falls boiling – I do hope that the trip home will rest him a little, tho' the journey out was not really peaceful.

He has worried so much about affairs at home, & this tour has been really exhausting on top of all that. I think that it was high time that a visit was paid in South Africa, & if it proves successful, then it is all worth while.

We are <u>so</u> looking forward to seeing you darling Mama,
Ever your loving
Elizabeth

~

---

* Major General Sir John Kennedy GCMG KCVO KBE CB MC (1893–1970), and his wife Catherine. He was Assistant Chief of the Imperial General Staff during the Second World War; Governor of Southern Rhodesia, 1947–53. Sir John told Queen Elizabeth later that he took the King around the grounds of Government House and they looked at a tree planted by King Edward VIII when he was Prince of Wales. The King reflected, 'My brother never had the good fortune I had when I married my wife.' (Sir John Kennedy to Queen Elizabeth, 14 January 1959, RA QEQM/PRIV/PAL)

26 April 1947 to May Elphinstone

HMS *Vanguard*
At sea

My Darling May

Thank you a thousand times for your angelic letters, it really was dear of you to write, and I can't tell you how glad I was to get them & hear some news from home. Our tour was so concentrated and such a rush, that there literally wasn't a moment for letter writing, so I thought I would send you a line from this ship, & hope that you will get it before we meet!

I long for you to come out to South Africa & see the wonderful, glorious flowers and shrubs – though we were not there at the right time, the profusion & terrific colours just took my breath away! There were a few heaths still in flower in Cape Colony, just enough to give one an idea of the wonderful sight it must be when they are all out, and hibiscus & frangipani, & morning glory (which at once made me think of Mother) not to mention roses & lilies and delphiniums and chrysanthemums & dahlias all mixed up together! There were beautiful flowering shrubs in Rhodesia, and when we stopped at St Helena, I managed to pick a wild Arum lily growing by the road!! It was much bigger and thicker than those round the altar at Easter!

It was an extremely interesting tour, as it is such a complex country, with the white races quarrelling & hating each other, and the black races growing enormously in numbers . . .

They were marvellously kind & welcoming to us – even the old Nationalist Boers, reared to hate England, gave us a very hearty welcome, and I do hope that our visit has done good.

It would be a thousand pities if S. Africa became a Republic, because the Crown is really the only link now left, & I do trust this will not happen, tho' there have been quite strong feelings for one in recent years.

One feels the lack of an English Governor General – it is really very unsuccessful to have a local, however nice, because he can never feel free to do things or take a lead, which is badly needed.

I am thankful to say that I got through the tour alright, tho' very, very tired – one feels quite sucked dry sometimes – I am sure that crowds of people take something out of one. I can almost feel it going sometimes, and it takes a little time to put it back.

Well, darling, it will be <u>wonderful</u> to see you all again – we have been 10,000 feet up in the air, and a mile & a quarter below the earth, but a little bit of England & Scotland will be heaven.

I do hope that the garden survived the ghastly winter – & that you have kept well, likewise my darling Sid.

Please give him a kiss on his nice pink cheeks, or two kisses – one on one pink cheek, & one on the other, & to end up with, one on the tip of his dear little nosey posey, & many to yourself

from your very loving
Elizabeth

~

7 July 1947 to May Elphinstone

Buckingham Palace

My Darling May

This is one line to tell you <u>very secretly</u> that Lilibet has made up her mind to get engaged to Philip Mountbatten. As you know, she has known him ever since she was 12, & I think that she is <u>really</u> fond of him, & I do pray that she will be very happy. Your Elizabeth had a long talk with him on Sunday & liked his interest in many things & ideas, which was nice. But I did want you to know before it was announced darling.

We are keeping it a deadly secret, purely because of the Press, if they know beforehand that something is up, they are liable to ruin everything!

Your very loving
E

~

Philip Mountbatten, the son of Prince Andrew of Greece and Princess Alice of Battenberg, great-granddaughter of Queen Victoria, was born in 1921 and went to school at Gordonstoun in Scotland. He had a distinguished war in the Royal Navy and was mentioned in dispatches. He was a good-looking and strong-willed young man, and Princess Elizabeth had been attracted to him for many years. At Balmoral in September 1946 the young couple decided to marry; the King and Queen persuaded them to wait until after the South African trip to announce their engagement. They did so on 10 July 1947.

~

9 July 1947 to Prince Philip

Buckingham Palace

My dear Philip,

I am <u>so</u> disappointed to be laid aside with this laryngitis, because I particularly wanted to see [you] & tell you how happy we feel about the engagement, and to say how glad we are to have you as a son-in-law. It is so <u>lovely</u> to know you so well and I know that we can trust our darling Lilibet to your love and care.

There is so much that can be done in this muddled & rather worried world by example & leadership, & I am sure that Lilibet & you have a great part to play. It's not always an easy part, for it often means remaining silent when one is <u>bursting</u> to reply, & sometimes a word of advice to restrain instead of to act! But I have great confidence in your good judgement, & am certain that you will be a great help & comfort to our very beloved little daughter.

I am determined to get up tomorrow, but I have to speak to you on my fingers! But anyway, this little note brings you my fond love, and the assurance of my true affection – and <u>please</u> do feel that you can come & talk to me about anything you feel like talking about, & I shall always be ready to help in any way possible.

Ever your affect aunt*
Elizabeth

~

10 July 1947 to Sir Osbert Sitwell

Buckingham Palace

My dear Sir Osbert,

It was so kind of you to send your good wishes on the engagement of our daughter, and I was much touched to receive them. We feel very happy about it, as he is a very nice person, & they have known each other for some years which is a great comfort. Everyone has been so kind about the announcement, & having minded so much about Mr Molotov's 'No's',† I think that people feel like a moment of rejoicing over a young lady's 'Yes'!

---

* The Queen was not, in fact, Prince Philip's aunt. His father was King George V's first cousin, and his mother was King George VI's second cousin. No doubt both the Prince and the Queen considered 'Aunt' more suitable to their difference in age.

† Vyacheslav Molotov (1890–1986), senior Soviet politician and diplomat. As Minister for

I want to thank you also for the very delightful book, 'A Free House'.* I have only had time to glance at it, but it looks <u>enchanting</u> – What an extraordinary man Sickert must have been, and what a lot he had to say. That's one thing I enjoy very much in painters – they have so much to say, & so much to criticise.

I loved sitting to A. John – he was such fun and never drew breath except when the Griller Quartet† came & played next door and put him off completely. He quite rightly said that he couldn't possibly listen <u>and</u> paint. Myra Hess‡ came & played one day, & that was so delicious that it put him off even more!

The day that the Griller Quartet was coming to play, I was sitting to A. John, & he was painting hard, when my page came into the room and said in a rather trembling voice, 'The gorillas have arrived,' which terrified us both, and I expect poor A. John had a vision of several shambling baboons coming in to say how much too long my nose was, & wasn't one eyebrow higher than the other.

I have really suddenly remembered this, & it all comes from Sickert, so I hope you will forgive such a rambling & boring letter of thanks.

I would so love you to come & see the picture gallery here. Anthony Blunt§ has re-hung the pictures, & we have brought the two enormous Van Dycks from Windsor. Will you be here when we return from Holyrood on the 25th? Would you be so kind as to let me know some time, & then perhaps you could find a day.

Foreign Affairs, in 1947 he condemned America's Marshall Plan, which offered aid to Europe, as 'imperialism', and refused to allow European countries already under Soviet influence access to its funds.

* A collection of the writings of the painter Walter Sickert edited by Osbert Sitwell.

† A fine string ensemble which played from 1931 until the early 1960s.

‡ Dame Myra Hess (1890–1965), celebrated British concert pianist who organized popular lunchtime concerts at the National Gallery during the war.

§ Anthony Blunt (1907–83), appointed Surveyor of the King's Pictures in 1945, succeeding Sir Kenneth Clark; Surveyor of the Queen's Pictures, 1952–72. Knighted in 1956, but stripped of his knighthood in 1979 after he was exposed as a Soviet spy. Queen Elizabeth later recalled: 'Blunt was a tremendous expert on Poussin, whom he particularly adored. He was another person one learned a bit from. And he could lecture in French, which I thought was so clever. Poor man. It was a long time after his wickedness, he had probably forgotten all about it. Wasn't it extraordinary that people got like that at Cambridge? I couldn't do that. I really couldn't. To be a traitor to your country to me would be the worst thing.' (*Conversations with Eric Anderson 1994–5*, RA QEQM/ADD/MISC)

I am so very sorry to hear that you are still in pain. It is such a horrible infliction, and I hope that you will soon feel better. The treatment sounds quite awful, & most agonising – only bearable if it is really doing good.

With again all my thanks for your kind letter,

I am, Yours very sincerely,

Elizabeth R

~

Prince Philip and Princess Elizabeth were married in Westminster Abbey on 20 November 1947. On their honeymoon, first at the Mountbatten home, Broadlands, in Hampshire and then at Birkhall, the Princess and her new husband wrote loving letters to her parents. The Prince, who had been created Duke of Edinburgh on his marriage, wrote to the Queen, 'Lilibet is the only "thing" in the world which is absolutely real to me and my ambition is to weld the two of us into a new combined existence that will not only be able to withstand the shocks directed at us but will also have a positive existence for the good . . .'*

~

24 November 1947 to Princess Elizabeth

Buckingham Palace

My Darling Lilibet

Your most angelic letter has given me the greatest joy, I have read it, and re-read it, and each time I feel more thankful for our darling little daughter! You have written so sweetly & wisely, and thank you with all my heart.

Papa & I are so happy in your happiness, for it has always been our dearest wish that your marriage should be one of the heart, as well as the head, and we both love Philip already as a son. I do pray that he will feel truly at home with us, & I know that he will be a great help to us both.

I must admit that I have been thinking about you for nearly every minute since you drove away on Thursday! This is only natural, because one's child is part of one's life, and marriage is such a great step, and

---

* 3 December [1947], RA QEQM/PRIV/RF.

we do love you so very much. So your letter was very welcome, for it told me of your happiness & of Philip's love and care for you.

Darling Lilibet, no parents ever had a better daughter, you are always such an unselfish & thoughtful angel to Papa & me, & we are so thankful for all your goodness and sweetness.

It is lovely to think that your happiness has made millions happy too in these hard times, & it is a wonderful strength to the country that we can feel like one big family on occasions. As you say, 'we four' have had wonderful fun & much laughter even through the darkest times, and I look forward to more fun & laughter with 'us five'. Thank you again my darling for your wonderful letter which I shall always keep.

That you & Philip should be blissfully happy & love each other through good days and bad or depressing days is my one wish – a thousand blessings to you both from your very very loving Mummy

~

30 November 1947 to Princess Elizabeth

Sandringham

My Darling Lilibet

It was lovely having a few words on the telephone, and Birkhall sounds rather heavenly. If the snow is on the ground, you & Philip ought to borrow a couple of Gordon's night shirts, & go hind shooting – I am sure he wears enormous night shirts!

We have had four very typical days here – 3 shooting all round the pit holes & fields which was great fun.

Today we walked to church, very cold, & as the church was nice & warm & Hector the Rector's* sermon rather long, everybody went fast asleep! [. . .]

This afternoon we went across the Park which looked like the prairie. Covered with ponies & horses & herds of cattle & droves of sheep, with Billy & Jane† contemplating a new young horse. Then we went past York Cottage to the Kennels & played with the dogs for

---

*   The Rev. Hector Anderson, Rector of Sandringham, 1942–55.

†   Sir William Fellowes KCVO (1899–1986), agent at Sandringham. He started work there for Edward VIII in 1936 and retired under Queen Elizabeth II in 1964. He and his wife, Jane, remained friends of the Queen Mother all their lives.

some time. We were then frozen with cold, & ran all the way home & here I am.

I do miss you terribly, but must get used to it. It is so important to have one's own home when one is married, & after all, we shall see you often, & I long to see you both installed in your house with your own things round you. I do hope they will hurry up with Clarence House, because with all the work nowadays it is so useful to have a H.Q., & then you can get away to Windlesham* with a feeling of relief & relaxation.

I forgot to say, do tell Jock [Colville]† some time, to keep in touch with 'the family' over engagements made or refused, likewise patronage or Presidents, as otherwise one is liable to get overlapping which is wasteful. I shall tell Tom‡ to do likewise. So many people write round the family asking the same thing.

Darling angel, everybody enjoyed the wedding <u>enormously</u> – I have had really touching & wonderful letters from people saying how deeply moved they were, and even people who one might have thought would not have been touched by beauty or religious feeling – one never knows – the older I get, the more surprises I get!

Goodbye darling, I do hope you have a delicious time, ever your very very loving

Mummy

~

1 December 1947 to the Duke of Edinburgh

Buckingham Palace

Dearest Philip,

This is the first time I have written to you as my son in law, and it is only to send you my love, and to say how much I am thinking of you & Lilibet, and how deeply I wish you every lovely happiness

---

* Windlesham Manor, Surrey, close to Windsor Great Park, briefly home to Princess Elizabeth and Prince Philip before they moved to Clarence House.

† Sir John Rupert 'Jock' Colville Kt CB CVO (1915–87), civil servant who worked with Winston Churchill during the war. He was Private Secretary to Princess Elizabeth, 1947–9, and then returned to work for Churchill. His diaries, *The Fringes of Power: Downing Street Diaries 1939–1955* (1985), provide an intimate description of Churchill at war and peace.

‡ Major Thomas Harvey DSO CVO (1918–2001), former Scots Guards officer who was Queen Elizabeth's Private Secretary, 1946–51.

possible. It is such a joy to know that you will cherish & look after her, because however independent minded women are nowadays, they still need a man to lean on!

I do hope that you won't find public life too trying; for the people are demanding when they like you, but you will have the comfort of knowing that you are giving so much towards the happiness and stability of the country. Also, I remember at Balmoral last year, you told me that you had always played a lone hand, and had had to fight your own battles, & you will now have a great chance for individual leadership, as well as 'married couple' leadership which is so important as well. As a family we do try to work as a team, but each going their own way, and I am sure that you will make very valuable contributions towards the common pool. I am certain too, that as times goes on, you will be able to help Papa very much. He will talk to you on subjects that you will be able to support him on, and I do look forward to that, for he has many & great burdens to bear. Oh dear, how my pen runs on, I really just meant to send you a line of love, and here I am on the third page!

Do write me a line & tell me how Lilibet is – she sounds blissful, and I feel so happy about the future. I do hope that Windlesham will be a success, and in the meantime please do use this house as a hotel, & lodge here whenever you want. It has often been used by newly married people whilst they are getting settled in, & tho' it's a bore not to be able to go straight into your own house, we love all the family to feel that they can come to Hotel Buckingham whenever they want. Now I won't go on for another page, but with much love, dearest Philip, ever your devoted Mama

Elizabeth

PS I fear this has missed 2 bags

~

26 April 1948 to Arthur Penn

Buckingham Palace
12 o'clock midnight

My dear Arthur

This is the first moment that I have had today to write you a line of thanks for your enchanting present for our silver wedding.*

---

* The present was a glass salver engraved by Laurence Whistler inscribed with the words

It is quite <u>perfect</u>, and it is quite the most delicious, amusing, lovely and delightful object that one could imagine. Thank you a thousand times.

Also I thank you with all my heart for your letter. You are such a dear friend and one who has sustained and helped me through many a hard year and anxious moment. For all this I am deeply grateful. [. . .] ever your affectionate friend

Elizabeth R

~

27 July 1948 to Sir Alan Lascelles

Buckingham Palace

Dear Tommy

Prince Bernhard* was very vague today, but I think that Pss Margaret will probably go over about the 3rd September & stay over the Abdication (!) & the Coronation, returning about 8th or 9th. I told him that she will take a lady & a gentleman, & he said, O.K., O.K., so apparently all that is quite easy. Of course she is staying with Princess Juliana for the visit, and goes purely as a 'gesture' from us to our good friends.

Nothing to do with Holland, but I feel unhappy about this idea of making us all 'citizens'† instead of subjects of the King. It didn't do France any good, & such a bother to bring up the subject instead of leaving it quiet. One must be careful of thin ends of wedges, & this I feel to be most sharp edged. I don't believe that Mr Attlee thinks about these things, but why should it affect the United Kingdom at all. Let Canada be citizens & then subjects – the subjects will fade

'The Queen on her Silver Wedding Day, the twenty-sixth of April 1948, from her devoted Servant and Treasurer, Arthur Penn'.

* Prince Bernhard of the Netherlands (1911–2004), Prince Consort of Queen Juliana (1909–2004) who became Queen of the Netherlands on the abdication of her mother, Queen Wilhelmina, in 1948. She in turn abdicated in favour of her daughter Princess Beatrix in 1980. Abdication in the Dutch Royal Family was the norm; in Britain it was the unhappy exception.

† Until 1948, nationals in the United Kingdom, the Dominions and some colonies had been entitled to call themselves 'British subjects'. The British Nationality Act of 1948 created the new status of 'Citizen of the United Kingdom and Colonies' for all Commonwealth subjects, and allowed them to settle in the UK. Subsequent legislation limited the automatic right of abode, and the British Nationality Act of 1981 abolished the 1948 definition of citizenship.

away, but the people of these Islands must be <u>first</u> subjects of the
King as long as we have a King. Do you agree?

ER

~

6 August 1948 to Sir Osbert Sitwell

Balmoral Castle

My dear Sir Osbert,

I am enchanted with the book which you have sent me for my
birthday, and send you so many thanks. It is quite unique, with those
charming gilded portraits of King George III and his family, and I like
the 'affectionate advice' of Goldney 'to the King on his happy choice
of a GOOD QUEEN' very much.* [. . .]

We have been here a week, & so far it has rained quite steadily
for six days. In a way it is rather peaceful, quiet & misty & green, and
gives one a moment to gather oneself together after the last six
months of unending functions & visits & political worries. It is
curiously difficult to achieve any real peace of mind nowadays – it is
rather like the war, one lives from day to day, don't you find it so?
One sees people doing & thinking such foolish things, it is really
<u>infuriating</u> sometimes. [. . .]

Before leaving London, we went to the Victoria Palace to see the
'Crazy Gang',† and that quite restored me, & an evening of a real
English music hall audience gave one back a lot of faith in one's own
people. They laughed so heartily, & so kindly.

I do hope that your visit to America will be interesting and not
too exhausting. I am sure they will be so pleased to have you there.
I wonder whether you will be back before we start on our long tour
of Australia and New Zealand in January. I do hope so.

---

* Edward Goldney, *A Friendly Epistle to the Deists and a Rational Prayer recommended to Them,
in order for their conversion to the Christian Religion* (1759).

† The Crazy Gang, a much loved group of English entertainers – comedians, singers, actors
– who had enduring stage and film successes from the early 1930s to the late 1950s. Their
principals included Bud Flanagan, Chesney Allen, Jimmy Nervo, Teddy Knox, Charlie
Naughton, Jimmy Gold and 'Monsewer' Eddie Gray. Among their most famous and popular
songs was 'Underneath the Arches', a tender evocation of the homeless who slept rough. Their
kind Cockney humour was particularly popular, indeed poignant, during the war.

With again my thanks for the delightful book & for your great kindness in remembering my birthday, your thoughtfulness truly touches me very deeply.

Yours very sincerely,
Elizabeth R

~

The King's health had been giving him and the Queen concern all year. The South African tour had exhausted him and led to considerable weight loss, and he now suffered from constant cramps and numbness in the feet and legs. In November 1948 he was diagnosed with the onset of arteriosclerosis and his doctors insisted that he should cancel the tour of Australia and New Zealand. There was a danger of amputation and he was confined to bed with his legs in clamps. This treatment avoided amputation but concerns about his condition continued to grow.

~

Sunday 14 November 1948 to Queen Mary

Buckingham Palace

Darling Mama

Just a line to let you know that Lilibet is well and the baby not quite making up its mind when to arrive. [. . .] I hope it will come soon because it is certainly showing signs of coming, but like all babies won't be hurried. But it's always trying waiting about, & I hope for Lilibet's sake that it won't be too long now.

Since writing this, I have received your letter for which many thanks. I was going to suggest coming to see you to talk about Bertie & our change of plans, but perhaps you would prefer to come here? Would tea tomorrow or Tuesday suit you, it would be so delightful to have a talk, & I am sure that Bertie would love you to come.

I have been terribly worried over his legs, and am sure that the only thing is to put everything off, and try & get better.

I am afraid that Australia & NZ will be desperately disappointed – but what else could one do – I do hope they will understand that it is serious.

Much love darling Mama,
Your very loving daughter in law
Elizabeth

~

Prince Charles Philip Arthur George was born that day, 14 November 1948.

~

20 November 1948 to Queen Mary

Buckingham Palace

Darling Mama

Next Thursday would suit me very well for our shopping expedition. I shall look forward so much to another 'sortie' with you. Your letter touched me so deeply when you mentioned the uplift received from a visit to Lilibet & the baby – One has lived through such a series of crises & shocks & blows these last years, that something as happy & simple & hopeful for the future as a little son is indeed a joy.

Lilibet was so delighted with her presents –
Your loving daughter in law
Elizabeth

~

8 December 1948 to Queen Mary

Buckingham Palace

Darling Mama

Thank you so much for your letter about the picture of King George III.* I do so agree that we must buy it for the Collection, & I have told Arthur Penn to go to £1500 just to be on the safe side. It is wonderfully kind of you to say that you will give four hundred towards its purchase, and of course darling Mama, you shall have it for Marlborough House, and it is so nice to think that it will be an 'opposite' to one you have there already.

I am so terribly sorry that your cough is so tiresome, but I am sure that the only way to combat such an infliction is to keep it very quiet. But <u>what</u> a bore for you – I am so sorry.

It was very sad for me to see so much of the old silver from

---

* The full-length portrait of King George III, described as 'Studio of Allan Ramsay', came from the collection of Lord Home. It was later hung in the hall of Clarence House.

Glamis at Christie's.* I have bought a certain amount of it today, which I hope will someday belong to a new Lord Strathmore. But one is sad to see such a break up of well loved things – tho' luckily my brother has kept a few very 'family' pieces. Sir Stafford Cripps† does not make it easy these days!

Much love darling Mama, & please be <u>very</u> careful even tho' it bores & tries you because you are <u>very</u> precious to us, your loving children

Elizabeth

~

12 December 1948 to Queen Mary

Buckingham Palace

Darling Mama

The doctors have just been, and are very anxious that Bertie should stay here for another three weeks to do this treatment in the same atmosphere, so that very reluctantly we have had to give up the idea of Xmas at Sandringham. Bertie wishes me to say how terribly sorry he is, & you can imagine how sad I am, and we do hope that you will come for a little visit later on. If all goes well we should go down the first week in January, and it will be wonderful to be together again.

The doctors are very pleased with Bertie's progress, and I think that is one reason that they are so keen to <u>continue</u> the treatment here, & not risk any setback due to change of atmosphere.

It is a great disappointment that we cannot go to Sandringham until after Xmas, and I know that you will feel it very much. You <u>will</u> come here on Xmas Day won't you, and we shall try and make it as cheerful as possible.

With all these tremendous personal blows lately, one sometimes feels quite dazed, & occasionally I feel it a strain to be gay & cheerful, but that will pass, & I can only be deeply thankful that darling Bertie

---

* This sale took place at Christie's, Spencer House, on 8 December; the catalogue lists for sale 'Important Old English Silver, Objects of Vertu and a Charles II Gold Porringer and Cover, sold by order of the Earl of Strathmore', the Queen's eldest brother, Patrick, the fifteenth Earl.

† Stafford Cripps was now Chancellor of the Exchequer and taxes had been increased.

is really on the mend. I think that 2 or 3 weeks ago, the doctors were desperately worried, and it is his own courage & perseverance which has brought him through.

Darling Mama – we <u>are</u> so sorry about Xmas –

Your loving daughter in law

Elizabeth

~

27 December 1948 to Winston Churchill

Buckingham Palace

My dear Mr Churchill

I was deeply touched by your kindness in sending me a copy of your book 'Painting as a Pastime',* & I send you my warmest thanks for such a delightful Xmas present.

I think that it is one of the most enchanting books which has been written for many years, and I am so glad to have it inscribed by yourself, and bound, as an extra treat, in lovely blue. It has given me really great pleasure, & I am most grateful indeed for your thought of me.

We have been through many deep experiences & emotions during the last months, & tho' sometimes one feels that they have been almost <u>too</u> vampire & have drained away something of the joy of living, yet one also feels closer than before to the good beating heart of the British people. God bless the people – they <u>are</u> good people, and when one feels depressed or frustrated (this often) a little talk with a painter, or a plumber or a steel worker or a nice angry English gentleman soon puts one right!

With again my thanks, & with every good wish for 1949,

I am,

Yours sincerely

Elizabeth R

~

---

* Churchill had enjoyed painting since the 1920s; he found it an excellent way of relaxing and he became remarkably accomplished. Most of his works were landscapes, many of them done in the South of France and Morocco after his electoral defeat in 1945.

February 1949 to Queen Mary

Sandringham

Darling Mama

I was so delighted to hear from you, and am glad to be able to say that Bertie continues to make good progress. He <u>looks</u> so much better too, and I think that if it can be arranged that he doesn't plunge into engagements that tire, he should go on improving slowly. He very much enjoys a morning rabbit shooting, which tires him less than 'going for a walk', and tho' he still does about 4 hours a day treatment, he gets out for longer too.

The weather has really been lovely, and mostly sunny, and I feel a different person! What with the gnawing anxiety about Bertie, & the baby's arrival & a general tiredness I began to feel most useless, & everything a very great effort. But I am beginning to feel more alert and energetic, & am so thankful!

Lilibet went off on Saturday, & we miss them and the darling baby dreadfully. He did so well here, and was really too angelic by the time he left.

It was cruel luck getting measles, & she had it very severely poor darling, but was looking very well by the time she left here.

We are boiling with rage and disgust over the Sunday Express's horrible & vulgar article about poor Margaret.* It is so hard on her kind nice host and hostess, & is particularly mean as one cannot do anything about it. If this sort of thing happens, nobody will want to ask her, and it is so unfair on a young girl. And no mention of her lady in waiting or the fact that it was a house party for the Lingfield races. Oh dear, it is all very annoying. [. . .]

Much love darling Mama,
Ever your loving daughter in law
Elizabeth

~

---

* After Princess Elizabeth married Prince Philip, Princess Margaret's romantic life became a subject of enduring obsession to the popular press. Newspapers in those days were mild by comparison with later, but their attentions were often intrusive and unwelcome.

5 January 1949 to Prince Paul of Yugoslavia

Buckingham Palace

My dear Paul

I was so touched by your very kind letter of sympath
Bertie's illness, and I write to thank you, & to say that he
really making progress, & I think that in a few months he
to take up his life again. He is doing all his work now, but
in bed nearly all day, which is very boring, as rest is essenti
the circulation back to his legs.

It is curious what a lot of people have had this particula
since the war – the doctors say that it is a direct result from
& strain & mental worry – can one be surprised, when one l
the poor torn world & its problems.

I do so hope that you are really better for your treatment
Switzerland. I expect that the mental anguish of the last years
affected you, and I do trust that you will really get better.*

The baby is so sweet, & Lilibet & Philip are enchanted, and
are so happy for them.

How nice it would be to talk about things again!

Here, you would find great stability & a sense of unity, even
ideas & bubbles of semi-thought are irritating people –, but after
great misery of the war, I think that people are now beginning to
their thoughts & sense of balance, & they do try to 'love their
neighbour as themselves'.

With our love, and so many thanks for your very kind letter,
Ever yours affect:
Elizabeth

~

---

* Prince Paul and Princess Olga had endured exile in Nairobi and then in Cape Town after
the coup that toppled him from the regency of Yugoslavia in 1941. Their lives improved
considerably after the King and Queen overrode official advice and met them on their 1947
tour of South Africa. They moved to Paris in 1949 and restored many of their British
friendships. Prince Paul had been declared an enemy of the state by the post-war Communist
regime in Yugoslavia but was officially rehabilitated by the Serbian courts in 2011. He died in
1976, Princess Olga in 1997.

5 March 1949 to Sir D'Arcy Osborne

The Royal Lodge

My dear D'Arcy,

Thank you so very much for your last letter. I feel that I haven't written to you for ages, but the last year has been rather like the war in a minor degree! Daughters getting engaged, and daughters marrying, and daughters having babies, & the King getting ill, & preparing for a tour of Australia & New Zealand, & then having to put it off – all these things are very filling to one's life, and I feel ashamed at the few letters I have written.

I do hope that all goes well with your life, and that you are as happy in Rome as you used to be. I do wish that I could see it before I die, but it doesn't look very hopeful at the moment. The King is really getting on very well, though it will be fairly slow progress, and one good thing is that he is having the first rest since 1936.

I am sending this letter by the King's P. Secretary Edward Ford,[*] who is going to Rome for a few days in the King's aeroplane. Also with him is Peter Townsend, who is a very nice, ultra sensitive ex-flying man, who was in the Battle of Britain, & nearly flew himself into a nervous decline. He is our equerry.

If you come across him, do be very kind & give him a big hello (that's how we talk in England now that spring is nearly here).

Margaret (daughter) is grown up now, and a great delight to us both. She is funny, & makes us laugh (en famille!), and also loves people & seeing & doing things. I do hope that she will be useful.

The baby is very delicious, and makes a very nice soft innocent topic of conversation in a rather horrid, unkind world!

I do hope that you are coming over this year, as there are millions of things to talk about, and we haven't seen you for far too long.

I am sure that 66 Via Giulia is lovely – do paint some pictures of the rooms & bring them with you when you come,

---

[*] Sir Edward William Spencer Ford GCVO KCB ERD DL (1910–2006), Assistant Private Secretary to King George VI and then to Queen Elizabeth II, 1946–67. On the morning of 6 February 1952 it fell to Ford to report the death of the King to Winston Churchill. He found the Prime Minister working in bed and told him that he brought him bad news. 'Bad news?' said Churchill. 'The worst.' (Bradford, *George VI*, pp. 607–8)

Your sincere but totteringly aged friend
Elizabeth R
Edward or Peter will give you news of us.

~

Sunday 8 May 1949 to Princess Margaret

The Royal Lodge

My darling Margaret,

[. . .] We read with great interest what you are doing & seeing, but after the first few days in Capri when the papers were at their most vulgar and irritating, everyone was so annoyed with them, that they are now being super discreet. [. . .] So we adore your letters, & pass them hungrily from hand to hand. I do hope that all is being delicious & that you are soaking in beauty and sunshine. Do you like Italian food? You might bring back some good recipes for macaroni a la Milanese or whatever it is, because our food is becoming more & more monotonous.

Yesterday evening we went over to see Charles who was too heavenly, and concentrated madly on his sponge when in the bath.

Monday

Just got a message to say that you are ringing up tomorrow. Hurray!

I am just off to London & will finish this there.

Tuesday BP

It was heavenly hearing your darling little voice so clear.

[. . .]

Papa is down at Royal Lodge this week, & I think that he is really better. He is taking an interest in his rhododendrons, & making plans for more planting, & altogether beginning to perk up. I am sure that if he can go on as he is doing, & not get exhausted in London, he will soon be back to his old form. [. . .]

I remember Florence so well, & I wonder whether you will love it. I do wish that you could have stayed in a villa, but a hotel is always an experience. Do you have coffee & rolls & honey for breakfast? And lunch at 12? Darling, we do miss you, but are so happy to think that you are seeing so much. It does broaden one's outlook on life, & gives one a vague idea how other countries live.

I shall write again very soon, and with a hundred kisses and a &

a,* ever your very very very very very very very very very very very
loving Mummy

~

15 July 1949 to the Duke of Edinburgh

Buckingham Palace

Darling Philip,

Would you be very kind & glance through the enclosed little
article, which has been written by old Miss Poignand to go opposite a
reproduction of Halliday's portrait† of yourself.

She occasionally writes little pen portraits for magazines, which
helps her to earn small amounts of money She was asked to write this
by Woman's Journal which has a large circulation.

I thought it quite innocuous, and if you don't mind it, would you
please just put it in an envelope & send it back to me, with O.K. or
not on your life or whatever you feel.

How did you enjoy your dance with the glamorous new wife of
the Regent of Irak‡ – She is BEAUTIFUL, isn't she?

Much love, Mummy or Mama

~

21 July 1949 to Eleanor Roosevelt

Buckingham Palace

My dear Mrs Roosevelt

It was so kind of you to write to me about the King, and I am
glad to be able to tell you that he is really better, and with care
should be quite well in a year or so. It is always a slow business with
a leg, and the great thing is not to get overtired during convalescence.

---

* Probably a reference to a Scottish marching song, with the refrain 'Wi' a hundred pipers
an' a', an' a' [and all, and all]' commemorating Bonnie Prince Charlie's entry into Carlisle
during the 1745 Jacobite rising against the Hanoverian monarchy in Britain.

† Edward Irvine Halliday (1902–84), British portrait painter, trained at the Royal College of
Art and the British School of Rome. In 1948 he drew both Princess Elizabeth and Prince Philip.

‡ Crown Prince Abdulla of Hejaz GCB GCVO, Regent of Iraq, 1939–53. His 'glamorous new
wife' was his second of three, Faisa el Tarabulsi. In 1958, both he and his nephew, King Feisal
II, were murdered in a coup d'état which overthrew the monarchy.

You can imagine how difficult this is to achieve with the world in its present state, & worries & troubles piling up! However, he is making such good progress, & for that I am profoundly grateful.

I was much interested to hear your account of the visit of some of the English people at the United Nations to Hyde Park. I am sure that they enjoyed it enormously, and we often think of the happy time we had there with you and President Roosevelt.

I fear that the story that Margaret is going to the United States this Autumn is not true, alas! I do hope that someday she will be able to visit America, as I am sure that she will love it as much as we did in those far off days of 1939. We all hope that you will come over here for another visit before too long, because you know, we are always so very happy to welcome you here.

I am sure that you find that people are recovering very quickly from the effects of that long and agonizing war. One feels that the anguish & worry reveals itself long after, & last year was bad, & now one feels a definite revival of spirit & serenity.

With all our good wishes,

I am, yours very sincerely,

Elizabeth R

~

Prince Philip had resumed his naval career after his marriage. He worked first at the Admiralty and then in 1948 took a staff course at the Naval Staff College, Greenwich. In 1949, he was posted to Malta as the First Lieutenant of the destroyer HMS *Chequers*, the lead ship of the 1st Destroyer Flotilla in the Mediterranean Fleet. Princess Elizabeth joined him in Malta and there they lived as a naval officer and his wife. It was a happy time.

~

29 November 1949 to Princess Elizabeth

Windsor Castle

My Darling Lilibet

I have been thinking so much of you, and hoping that you are having a lovely & interesting time, & united once more with Philip – It must be such a joy to be together again after so many weeks apart.

I was very glad to hear that you had arrived safely – that Sunday seemed endless!

[. . .] I am sitting at my writing table in my sitting room at Windsor. Everything is grey & blue outside, & looking most beautiful and romantic. I really believe that Windsor looks its very best in November – such lovely lights, & mysterious towers looming out of the haze, and the sentries in their grey greatcoats & black bearskins look exactly right. The band has just marched away down the hill, & the music is getting fainter, & now they have just changed to bom bom bom – & those high little penny whistles. I do love this place!

Papa & I looked in to see Charles after Toby's* wedding. He was very busy in the nursery, and greeted us so kindly. He really is too delectable, & Papa was enchanted by him. He cheers one up more than one can describe – there is something so sweet & innocent & good about a baby, all the unkind or worrying things just don't exist when one is with him.

Hooray hooray, your letter has just arrived. Thank you a million times darling. It is such a pleasure to hear how much you are enjoying life in Malta. I see a little piece in the papers most days saying that you had called on the Governor, or visited a ship, or danced somewhere, & that keeps one in touch. How are they getting on with the rebuilding? [. . .]

Clip Clop Clop – what do you think that was? Margaret & Peter riding past the window! I had a little theatre party the other evening, & we went to Hammersmith to see 'Let's make an opera' by B. Britten.†
Mark & Julian & Laura & Peter & Pam Ruthven & Jamie & M & me.‡

---

* Lieutenant Commander George 'Toby' Marten DSC, equerry to the King, married Mary Anna Sturt at Holy Trinity, Brompton, on 26 November 1949.

† Edward Benjamin Britten, Baron Britten, OM CH (1913–76), one of the greatest twentieth-century British composers, perhaps best known for his operas such as *Peter Grimes*, *Billy Budd* and *Midsummer Night's Dream* and for his *War Requiem*. In 1948 he and his partner, the tenor Peter Pears, founded the Aldeburgh Festival, in their home town on the Suffolk coast. It began with classical music but was expanded to include poetry, drama, literature and art. It continued to flourish past Britten's death. The Queen Mother and the Queen both admired Britten and Pears, and what they had done for music in Britain and for cultural life on the east coast. The Queen Mother later nominated Britten for an honorary degree at London University. He and Pears became friends of both Queens; they often stayed at Sandringham and Queen Elizabeth attended many concerts at Aldeburgh.

‡ Probably Mark Bonham Carter, Julian Amery, Laura Smith, Peter Townsend, Jamie Granville and Princess Margaret.

We had to learn songs & sing them with the little opera – one was about birds, & we had to do owls, whilst the gallery sang Chaffinches saying 'Pink Pink' on a <u>very</u> <u>very</u> high note – Julian & I did not like our owls, so we had a resistance movement & sang very high pink pinks which shocked the surrounding owls!

It must be rather heavenly at Malta, is it warm? Can you lie in the sun, & how is Bobo – I do hope that a warm climate will help to get her quite well. Now I must take the dogs out – Susan on a lead because she strains every nerve to get at the sentries. Back to London next week & don't forget darling that the French President pays a visit in March.

Please give Philip my very best love, and a great deal to your darling self whom we all miss so much,

from your very loving
Mummy

~

21 December 1949 to Princess Elizabeth

Buckingham Palace

My Darling Angel

This is a little letter to wish you a <u>very</u> happy Xmas. I am so glad that you are to spend it with Philip, tho' we shall miss you horribly. The first Xmas without our very darling daughter – but never mind, it is quite right to be with the hub of your universe!

I went to see Charles yesterday, & he seemed in very good form. I think that his teeth are worrying him a bit, but otherwise he is very well. Of course a rather violent attack such as he had, takes a little time to get over, and he may be a few days yet before he is absolutely back to form.

Miss Turner is <u>mad</u> about him, and I think it was a good thing to have her there, as it was rather a terrifying responsibility for Nannie alone. She really has been very good & quietly coping.

I <u>love</u> the picture of Clarence House – it is very attractive, & thank you so very much. Darling, I've had trouble over what to send you out for a Xmas present. I shall send you a small present, & keep my other more useful ones here.

Papa seems well, but gets a bit tired with all the worries – Uncle

David* came & had one of his violent yelling conversations, stamping up & down the room, & very unfairly saying that because Papa wouldn't (and couldn't) do a certain thing, that Papa must hate him. So unfair, because Papa is so scrupulously fair & thoughtful & honest about all that has happened. It's so much easier to yell & pull down & criticize, than to restrain, & build, & think right – isn't it.

I am feeling quite gaga with Xmas preparations! On Sunday we did all the Royal Lodge servants & gardeners & policemen etc, & then went to Windsor, & did Mrs Bruce & Lucking & the housemaids & Simpson etc.† On the Friday we had the servants ball at Windsor. – We had '20 questions' & 'Ignorance is Bliss' – great fun. Then the presents for everybody here on Monday! Then the servants ball here last night, with a show including Jimmy Edwards &, yes!! Frankie Howerd!‡ He is exactly the same off stage, as on, oh yes, come now, ladies & gentle<u>men</u> – etc! I danced with Evitts – we had an impassioned talk about the footmen – with Hailey, bending over me kindly in a waltz, and an endless dance with Lance, & my dress was too long, & he stepped on it every other twirl.

Then we had a Paul Jones,§ & I danced with a tool-maker from the outskirts of London, nephew of one of our charladies, he cheered me by saying that he loved his work, & had a grand 'guvnor', & then I was claimed by a smart but seedy looking individual, who said in a fruity voice that he had just had a letter from Philip saying that the weather was lovely in Malta – you know the frenzied conversations one has with utter strangers! But, after keen questioning, I found that he really belonged to Dickie [Mountbatten], & had lived at Chester Street!

Then I had a <u>samba</u> with Jack Crisp, everyone else stood round & watched, except for some swoopers & twirlers who executed the most magnificent bonga-bongas all round us. But it went quite well – & I think that everyone seemed happy.

---

* The Duke of Windsor.

† Alice Bruce, Stanley Lucking, George Simpson, Reginald Evitts, Cyril Hailey, Thomas Lance and Jack Crisp were members of staff at Windsor, respectively housekeeper, foreman, head gardener, yeoman of the plate pantry, page and footmen.

‡ Jimmy Edwards (1920–88) and Frankie Howerd (1917–92), popular comedians who each enjoyed great success in radio, television and film.

§ Popular dance, sometimes known as a mixer, in which everyone frequently changes partners.

Darling Lilibet, I do miss you so much – but I love to think that you are having sun & fun, & above all a change, & a look in to another form of life.

Papa & I were so lucky, because we have tried so many different ways of life – We did night club life madly for a few years, but also mixed with dinners & country house visits, & big game shooting in Africa, & visits to Paris & Oslo & Belgrade & Rome and Brussels & Australia and MALTA, and out of the welter, one gradually found one's feet & head. You are so young, & you are also 'finding out' – & I am sure that your life in Malta must be one of the 'finds'.

Lots of love darling, & so many good wishes for a very happy Xmas, from your very very loving

Mummy

~

21 December 1949 to the Duke of Edinburgh

Buckingham Palace

Darling Philip,

This is to bring you all the best wishes for a happy Xmas – I am so very glad that Lilibet is going to spend it with you, and I hope that you will have a blissful time together.

I am sending you a tiny token present for your sitting room. It is made of teensieweensiekite, or some such stuff, found I believe in Norway, & will do for your guests to flick their ash into. Anyway, it brings all my love and blessings. We do miss you! It seems literally years since you went back to sea, & I do hope that you are finding the life really worth while & creative.

I did think it was wonderful how you plunged into the life of the country here during your two years ashore, and I wonder if you realize how tremendously it was appreciated.

Life is so complex nowadays, what with radio, & press & general depression, and what you gave, & can give, in leadership & courage & example is a great inspiration to all the people. I sometimes wonder if you think Papa & I are rather olde worlde about some things – I expect you do, & quite right too, because that is how the world goes. I remember thinking my father a bit old world, & so he was!

But I do hope that you will come back to work ashore some day

– there is so much to be done, and so much to be learnt – so many
people to meet, & so many ideas to be discussed & accepted or
discarded, and you have a good mind & brain, fit for wide horizons –
Someday?

Dearest Philip – we are so fond of you, and <u>so so</u> glad that you &
darling Lilibet are so happy.

With all my love, & so many good wishes for Xmas & very
successful and happy New Year, ever your loving Mum

Elizabeth*

~

25 January 1950 to Sir Osbert Sitwell

Sandringham

My dear Sir Osbert

[. . .]

I do hope that you are really better now. It was such fun having
a talk at a supper table when you came to our party at Buckingham
Palace – it reminds me of the old days (only 10 years ago!) to sit at
a small round table eating rather dusty food, with sleepy footmen
standing round, & distant music occasionally coming through. But it
is sad to be practically the only people who can give a party in one's
own house (even one a year), and I don't believe that we have dined
out more than four or five times since 1939. It is strange; but perhaps
if we can eventually rid ourselves of food rationing, <u>tiny</u> dinners will
be given & minute entertainments be arranged. What fun Hannah's

---

* Prince Philip replied:

'I'm sure I don't deserve half the kind things you say. These last two years have been a
wonderful experience and a most valuable one. I have learnt a great deal about what "goes
on" and in years to come the knowledge gained will come in very useful.

'I have the most unbounded admiration for the way in which you and Uncle Bertie
manage to do the enormous number of things you do without letting it become automatic.
Your example and help have been a constant source of strength during a rather hectic period.

'You say in your letter that I think you are Olde Worlde. I don't really think that my
own ideas are sufficiently clear to be able to stigmatize anybody least of all yourself. Perhaps
my education and life so far have caused me to think differently and therefore hold different
views but I hope that they are sufficiently open-minded not to be "modern" for modernity's
sake. If and when we disagree I assure you that I listen to and digest your views as those of an
exceptionally intelligent and enlightened person and try to reconcile them with my own. It
seems to me that the best way to form an opinion is to rub views with other people!

'Your loyal and devoted son in law, Philip' (RA QEQM/PRIV/RF)

luncheons were in her very small drawing room in Hertford Street. We must bully her until she has a house, or a flat, where she can entertain us all once again.

Some day you must come to Sandringham, for it is pure undiluted Edwardian, and utterly hideous, & every table is completely covered with valueless objects.

All the woodwork is shiny brown, the carpets red with blue splodges, and the central heating consists of great gusts of hot air blown at one out of sinister holes in the wall. If anyone has a cold in the head, the germs congregate in these holes & multiply exceedingly, and are then puffed out again in thousands & millions, stronger & more determined than any microbes I have ever known. Nobody escapes.

But I am very fond of it all & love being here.

[. . .]

Yours very sincerely

Elizabeth R

~

3 March 1950 to the Duke of Edinburgh

Buckingham Palace

Darling Philip,

The two exquisite plates which you & Lilibet so kindly gave me for Xmas, have now gone to Royal Lodge, and greatly enhance the collection there. [. . .]

I feel that I haven't seen you for years. I was so interested in that admirable letter you wrote to Papa, so clear & most illuminating about the Navy, & the difficulties of turning over from war to semi peace. And the descriptions of your visits, most fascinating. You certainly can write a letter! Which alas, is a rare thing nowadays, & so delightful & important.

We are just beginning to recover from the election, the excitement on Friday was terrific, and though unfortunately the result is a stalemate, it was very well fought, polite and reasonable & people took it seriously thank God. For the problems are so tremendous, & one really needs all men of good will to combine their brains & talents to bring us through these difficult days.*

---

* The first general election since the Labour victory of 1945 was held on 23 February 1950. Labour won a narrow majority of just five seats over all other parties.

March 17th

I thought I would hang on to this letter & tell you a little about the visit of M. Auriol.* It all went off very well indeed, and it was greatly enjoyed by Londoners, who packed the streets & gave the President & Madame a very good & cordial welcome. We were blessed by three lovely spring days, & the processions & functions were pretty & successful. Papa & I were quite as tired by trying to talk French (because of course we were glued to each other at every meal) as by the banquets etc. We were given a delicious dinner at the French Embassy, & our food seemed extremely dry & sparse & uninviting after their wonderful dishes!

The Ballet was really good, & Covent Garden looked a dream with décor by Oliver Messel. We did so miss you Philip, and I do hope you will be here for the next State visit (when & who I don't know) because one gets a real good laugh in between.

I am sure you must be longing to hear of Lilibet. She seems very well, and is looking extremely pretty as you may have seen from press photographs. She misses you terribly I think, and is looking forward with all the force of her ardent & controlled nature to meeting again. When one is parted from one's husband one misses the little tendernesses & thoughts & kindnesses most of all, & especially just now for a reason which is just too wonderful. I am so glad for you both. [. . .]

Best love, darling Philip, & I pray for your happiness & guidance every night – from your loving Mama, Elizabeth

~

27 March 1950 to Peter Cazalet

Buckingham Palace

Dear Peter,†

Now that we have recovered a little from the excitement and

---

*   Vincent Auriol (1884–1966), President of the French Fourth Republic, 1947–54.

†   Peter Cazalet (1907–73), racehorse trainer. After the war he and his friend Anthony Mildmay, a brilliant amateur jockey, set up a racing stable of jumpers at his home, Fairlawne in Kent. In 1949 they persuaded the Queen and Princess Elizabeth that they should buy Monaveen, who raced in the Queen's colours in the 1950 Grand National.

Over the years Peter Cazalet trained over 250 winners for Queen Elizabeth. His second

emotion of Saturday, I feel that I must tell you how pleased we were
with the way that Monaveen ran. It really was a creditable
performance, because a mistake like that must take a lot of stuffing
out of a horse, and to come on to 5th was very good. Of course I had
steeled myself for anything! – falling at the first fence, being knocked
down, almost any disaster, but I must say that the race was far more
thrilling than I could have imagined.

The next thing is to try and win the National again, if not next
year, the year after that! [. . .] I have great confidence in Monaveen –
he must be a great hearted horse, and we must hope for next year.

Yours very sincerely
Elizabeth R

~

24 April 1950 to Princess Elizabeth

Buckingham Palace

My Darling Lilibet

I was so delighted to get your very interesting and amusing letter,
and thank you so very much for writing. I have started several letters
to you, and each time I have either rushed off to sit to Simon Elwes,*
or dashed off to meet Anthony Blunt, or 'are you coming' from Papa,
or 'will you look at this letter' from Margaret, or 'Mrs Bruce is
outside the door' etc., & I have never managed to finish a letter!
However, this time I <u>WILL</u>, I <u>WILL</u>. First of all, Charles is too
heavenly & very well, and trying hard to say new things. [. . .]

Papa and Mummy get smacking kisses every night – I am sure
that you will think he has grown quite a good deal. Nanny has been
very nice, and so easy & friendly, and seems very happy at Royal
Lodge which is I suppose an ideal place for small children.

The pram can be in the little sunk garden & an eagle eye can be
kept from the nursery window!

It's been snowing <u>hard</u>. The wind icy & Charles was fascinated by

wife Zara was an exuberant hostess and, in the 1960s, Queen Elizabeth enjoyed their house
parties at Fairlawne.

* Simon Elwes RP RA KM (1902–75), British war artist and portrait painter. In 1945 he nearly
died from a stroke; his right hand and side were paralysed so he taught himself to paint with
his left hand. He painted many members of the Royal Family.

the snowflakes. He pressed his little face against the window, &
watched them falling for ages.

We have come up for a couple of days of 'things', & tomorrow M
& I are going to see Dior's clothes at the French Embassy – I always
feel very solid & tweedy & wrongly dressed under the eye of those
exquisite creatures!

I hear that you are coming home on the 3rd – how lovely, & how
horrid for you & Philip. But it is wonderful to hear that he may be
home in July. I really long to see the boy again, & one does miss his
cheerful outlook on life, amongst other things.

There is to be a division on the budget this week, & if the
Government doesn't get a majority I suppose it means a difficult
decision for Papa. However, perhaps nothing will happen once again.

Darling, I think of you so much, and am so looking forward to
next week – I do hope that you will have a good trip. I shall not be
back until late, as I am launching the Ark Royal* on that day, but will
ring you when I get back.

Very much love my darling, & lots to Philip from your
Very loving
Mummy

~

14 May 1950 to Earl and Countess Spencer

Balmoral Castle

Dearest Cynthia and Jack†

I have become used to violent contrasts in our life, but I don't
think that I have ever known such a heavenly one, as our evening at
Althorp yesterday. To leave the absolute inferno of noise & rush &
oil fumes at Silverstone, with those thousands & thousands of caviar
like people, & to find oneself in such an atmosphere of sheer beauty
& love & peace was a pleasure that I simply cannot describe to you.
I shall never forget the wonderful impression of that beautiful park in

---

* Queen Elizabeth was fond of the aircraft carrier HMS *Ark Royal* and visited it often, as she
did its successor, also *Ark Royal*, which she launched in 1981. In November 2001, some four
months before her death, she visited her second *Ark Royal* for the ceremony to mark its
recommissioning after extensive refitting.

† 'Jack', seventh Earl Spencer (1892–1975). Countess Spencer DCVO OBE (1897–1972) née
Lady Cynthia Hamilton. Lady of the Bedchamber to the Queen 1937–72; paternal grandmother
of Diana, Princess of Wales.

the evening sunlight, and the sight of the Pytchley hounds on the green grass. And seeing the most lovely and cherished of English houses once again – & even more lovely than I had remembered – it was all the greatest joy, and I do want to thank you both for such kindness, and for giving us two hours of sheer delight.

I do think that it is so wonderful the way you have both kept it all looking so perfect. I know what a tremendous struggle it must be, and also what a great deal it means to people who love good & beautiful things in this horrid moment of uncertainty & bad taste.

Thank you a thousand times

from your affec.

Elizabeth R

~

24 May 1950 to Peter Cazalet

Buckingham Palace

Dear Peter,

I do want to send you a few words of my sincere sympathy over Anthony's tragic death.* I can imagine what a terrible blow it must have been to you, and if we who knew & loved & admired him, felt a shock and great sadness, what it must have meant to you I do not like to think. The only comfort is, that I am sure that nothing good is ever wasted in this world, and Anthony's wonderful example of courage & integrity and good sportsmanship has helped & encouraged many less valiant spirits during these last few difficult years, and that is something which goes on. We do badly need people like Anthony, and I am sure that millions of people felt a real sense of loss when they read of the sad accident.

I know how close you were to each other, & the sympathy I feel for you is very heartfelt.

Yours v sincerely,

Elizabeth R

~

---

* Anthony Bingham Mildmay, second Baron Mildmay of Flete (1909–50), amateur steeple-chaser, who had introduced the Queen and Princess Elizabeth to National Hunt racing. Lord Mildmay had disappeared while swimming off the coast of Devon in May 1950. His loss was a blow to racing as well as to all those who knew him.

21 June 1950 to Sir Osbert Sitwell

Buckingham Palace

My dear Sir Osbert,
    Thank you so much for letting me know about the exhibition
of Henry Walton* pictures. I hope very much to be able to see it,
and I feel sure that it will be <u>enchanting</u>. I love a small collection of
pictures, one does not get exhausted or bemused, and one has time to
linger before a favourite instead of that terrible feeling of 'I haven't
seen the last 4 rooms'. I do want to thank you too for letting me see
the proofs of your latest volume† – as usually it is <u>perfect</u>, and
fascinating, and I am full of admiration & gratitude.
    Yours very sincerely,
    Elizabeth R

~

21 July 1950 to the Duke of Edinburgh

Buckingham Palace

Darling Philip,
    We are all so thrilled at your promotion,‡ and I do want to send
you a thousand congratulations. It is too exciting and I cannot
imagine how on earth you got through all those frightful exams. It
must have been tremendously hard work, and I think quite splendid
to have done it.
    It will be wonderful to have your <u>own</u> ship – may I come & visit
you if you bring her back here?
    We are all looking forward so <u>very</u> much to your return. It will
be delicious to see you again, and I expect that Lilibet will be
overjoyed. She seems wonderfully well, tho' I haven't seen much of
her lately as I have been travelling about a good deal. Charles is too
angelic for words – such a strong manly little boy, & extremely brave
too!
    He cracks his head against things & only looks surprised & rubs

---

*   Henry Walton (1746–1813), British painter.

†   *Noble Essences: A Book of Characters*, Macmillan, 1950.

‡   Prince Philip was promoted to Lieutenant Commander and given command of the frigate
HMS *Magpie*.

the place! He is such a darling, & a very good joker too – <u>how</u> he will love having you home.

Much love, & a bientot, Your loving Mama

~

15 October 1950 to Queen Mary

Balmoral Castle

Darling Mama,

My time in Scotland is coming to a close, and I shall very soon be in London, and hoping so much to see you. It seems an age since we last met, and I do hope that you are keeping well, and able to get about & enjoy life without any horrid pain.

The weather here has been deplorable, very cold and incessant gales, but Bertie managed to go out most days, and is really better I think. He walked much better, and was not nearly as tired in the evening. It is a great and blessed relief to see him stronger and more able to cope with the many worries & difficulties of life nowadays.

It was the greatest joy to have Lilibet and the darling children* here. They left last night and the house seems very empty and forlorn today.

Charles is really too angelic, and is such a clever child. His memory is prodigious, and he takes a deep interest in everything. He is such a friendly little boy and everyone here loves him.

This place is looking lovely now, the birches are all gold, and the flowers still gay in the garden.

Much love darling Mama, and so hoping to meet soon,
From your loving daughter in law
Elizabeth

~

7 December 1950 to Peter Cazalet

Buckingham Palace

My dear Peter,

Ever since the race on Saturday I have been thinking about writing to you, and somehow find it very difficult to know what to

---

* Princess Anne Elizabeth Alice Louise, second child of Princess Elizabeth and the Duke of Edinburgh, was born on 15 August 1950.

say. It was such a real tragedy, and such a terribly sad thing that such a good game horse as Monaveen* had to be put to rest. I am so very glad that Crocker Bulteel† is having him buried at Hurst Park – it is a comfort in a curious way and such a kind thing to do.

I have thought of very little else these last few days, and with a real sense of loss, I do feel very grateful for the fun & excitement that we have had with that lionhearted horse.

I suppose he really was killed by his courage and eagerness, & such qualities are splendid ones in a horse.

I have received so many touching & genuinely sad letters from people all over the country, starting with one from our Irish parson at Sandringham who had followed Monaveen 'because he belonged to us all in a rather special way'. Quite a lot of people have said the same.

Would you tell your head stable man how terribly sorry I am; & how grateful I am for all the care he gave Monaveen. I shall always remember how he never left him at the time of the Grand National.

Will you thank Zara for her angelic kindness & tact at Hurst Park? I was so touched, & I felt very stupid because I longed to shed a tear, & didn't dare, & I knew she understood.

When I was in the aeroplane I was able to let a few tears fall for Monaveen.

It must have been so ghastly for you, because not only the cruel loss of a grand horse, but the fact that memories of Anthony came flooding back, all combined to make it a bitter blow. I don't think that any other horse will ever have quite the same sentimental feeling for me.

I have just received your letter, for which many thanks. I am so relieved that Grantham is progressing & hope that he will mend quickly,

Yours very sincerely
Elizabeth R

~

---

* Monaveen won many races in the course of 1950 but at the end of the year, ridden by Tony Grantham, he fell and broke his leg at Hurst Park. He had to be put down at once. Grantham broke his ribs in the accident.

† Sir John Crocker Bulteel (1890–1956), racing administrator, who developed the racing programme at Ascot.

12 December 1950 to Princess Elizabeth

Buckingham Palace

My Darling Lilibet

I have put off writing before this, because I knew that you were in Greece, & now I am using Margaret as messenger. I do hope that you had a delightful visit. I do envy you seeing all those wonderful & beautiful places and I am longing to hear about it all.

Wasn't it a terrible thing about Monaveen. I really think that it was one of the saddest days of my life. One moment seeing the horse in the paddock, looking, honestly, a hundred per cent better than last time, & going tremendously well in the race, & then, ten minutes later, he was dead. It was such a shock, & the worst of it was, that everyone was so upset, & so unhappy & so kind, & I <u>longed</u> to weep, & one's voice became high & cracked, & it was almost unbearable. Somehow, Monaveen was all mixed up with a 'first venture', & Anthony, & all the fun & excitement of last year, & sharing with you, and it seemed so sad that such a gallant & great hearted horse should have to be put to rest. It cast a real gloom over England – everyone was sad for the loss of a good & popular horse. [. . .]

I have been over several times to see Charles & Anne. They are angelic & seem very well. I hope that they will enjoy Sandringham, for I think it's pretty dull for Charles at Clarence House, not that <u>he</u> would ever know that, as he is always busy!

Papa has had a painful attack of lumbago, or something like it, but is better now.

We had a very enjoyable visit to Broadlands, & a charming & cosy party. Dickie was very executive in a delicious way, & rushed into the dining room at least 4 times before each meal, to see if it was ready! But they were so kind, & we loved our visit. [. . .]

Darling, I do hope that you will have a <u>very</u> happy Xmas, & please give Philip lots of love, & I miss you terribly, & tho' I long to see you, am <u>very</u> glad to think that you are together.

From your very very loving

Mummy

PS Mikie [her brother Michael] had a flare up, & had his kidney removed. He is going on well, but it is a bad few days for him.

PPS May old Miss Poignand see the children? She longs to.

~

29 December 1950 to Princess Elizabeth

Sandringham

My Darling Lilibet

First of all I want to thank you a thousand times for the lovely stockings. They are a perfect present, and I am so delighted to have them. [. . .]

Charles has been <u>so</u> good, & I assure you that I don't spoil him – he is very easily managed & Mabel* <u>is</u> good with him isn't she? He comes to visit me in the morning about 9.45, & likes to sit on the bed playing with my little box of rather old lipsticks! They are all colours, & they rattle & he loves taking the tops off. Then we look at a book in which there is a picture of a man in a kilt playing the pipes. This is the Pipe Major of course, & he gets the book shut on him, & endlessly 'where <u>can</u> the Pipe Major be?' Is he under the eiderdown, in Charles's pocket etc. etc.! Sometimes Margaret plays 'Blaydon Races' to him after tea. He likes that because it has a line 'all with smiling faces', so it's called 'Miling faces.

I can't tell you how sweet he was driving to the station before Xmas. He sat on my knee, occasionally turning to Papa & giving himself an ecstatic hug, as if to say, isn't this fun. He sits bolt upright doesn't he, just like you used to. He is a brave little boy, but I think he's sensitive, & you will have to see that he doesn't get frightened by silly people.

And as for Anne!

Well, she is too delectable for words. She comes down after tea, & is laid on the sofa whilst Nannie stays outside, & she is surrounded immediately by a ring of adorers. She hasn't cried once, & coos & gives short vulgar laughs, & is altogether delicious. I know that you will be enchanted with her when you see how she has developed. She is so pretty & neat & very feminine! Philip will see such a huge difference, I am sure she'll give him a tremendous glad eye! I can't tell you what a difference it makes having your darlings here – the whole place cheers up, & especially old Grannie.

---

* Mabel Anderson (1927–), nanny to royal children through six decades. She started work as assistant nanny to Prince Charles in 1949. He once described her as 'a haven of security, the great haven'. She retired in 1981 but remained close to the family; in 2010 the Queen invited her on a cruise of the Western Isles.

Darling, I had a terrific day on Tuesday. I didn't think that I would be able to get away on Boxing Day but early that morning I simply couldn't bear it, & ordered the car & rushed off to Kempton! The roads were very icy all round here, but alright from Newmarket, & I got there at 1.30, rather cold & stiff.

After a hurried lunch, we went to see Manicou,* who was walking round, looking right & left in that charmingly intelligent way. [. . .] The race was very good, & tho' Silver Flame was always very close, Manicou seemed to have that little bit of speed again at the end. Peter was almost speechless, and very pleased with him I think. [. . .]

I left again soon after 3, & ran into thick fog London side of Newmarket, stopped for tea with Cecil,† & then crawled on in horrible fog & icy roads. The fog cleared later, but the road was terrible, & we crept along with the back wheels swinging all over the place. Got home about 8. But it was the greatest fun – & I loved every moment of it.

Jan 5th. [1951]

We have just returned from London & the lunch for the Prime Ministers. All seemed very happy & friendly with each other, & I do hope that the meeting will give a little more sense of security, which is what is needed. The only one absent was Liaquat‡ but I hear that he is coming in a day or two. Nehru§ was quite friendly in his abstracted way, but I think is worried about India & the turmoil in Asia – but all the P.M.s were determined to try & help him all they could, which was very nice & really so <u>like</u> a family party! Mustn't let him feel out of it, & cheer up old man sort of feeling.

---

* Manicou was the second racehorse the Queen acquired. A dark bay with a white star on his forehead and two white socks, the Queen loved him. He became incurably lame and at stud sired many horses, including The Rip and Isle of Man, two of her later favourites.

† Sir Cecil Charles Boyd-Rochfort KCVO (1887–1983), successful racehorse trainer who trained for King George VI, Queen Elizabeth and Queen Elizabeth II until his retirement in 1968.

‡ Liaquat Ali Khan (1895–1951), lawyer and political theorist who was one of the creators of Pakistan after the partition of India in 1947. He served as first Prime Minister of Pakistan from 1947 until his assassination four years later.

§ Jawaharlal Nehru (1889–1964), Indian politician and lawyer, one of the principal leaders of the movement for independence from Britain in the 1920s and 1930s. After that ambition was achieved in 1947, he became the first Prime Minister of India, a position he retained until his death. He was one of the leaders of the international non-aligned movement.

Nannie told me that the other evening Sugar & Johnnie [dogs] were sort of playing outside the nursery, & somehow Charles thought that you were coming. His face lit up & he said 'Mummie!' in a voice of bliss – Wasn't it delicious. I am sure that he misses you, & Philip, who is so wonderful with children.

The weather has been GHASTLY. Snow & ice, & now it's thawing & <u>pouring</u>. I do hope that it has stopped raining in Malta. Grannie seems <u>much</u> better, & we only just prevented her going with Margaret & 4 gentlemen to a small dance of the Birkbecks – 'Oh if <u>only</u> I was ten years younger' moaned Grannie, watching them going off with real envy! She is wonderful. [. . .]

Margaret simply <u>adored</u> her visit to you. She was thrilled & amused, & liked the people she met very much. The only thing was, she said, that just as she was beginning to get to know people, it was time to go away, which was very sad. But she said that you & Philip were too angelic to her, & I know that she would have loved to stay longer. You asked me to let you know, & I quite agree that sometimes the Sphinx isn't in it with darling Margaret!

Goodbye darling angel, lots of love to Philip

from your very loving Mummy

~

31 January 1951 to Princess Elizabeth

Sandringham.

My Darling Lilibet

I was so delighted to get your delicious letter. Papa & I said '<u>what</u> a good letter Lilibet writes, full of news & thought & amusing too.' I wish that I could tell you what a joy Charles and Anne are to me.

Every day he has new words and new ideas, and I shall miss them quite terribly when you return.

Nearly every day we discuss your return – 'Mummy will come in an aeroplane & then get into a car etc, & then she will drive up to the front door, & she will get out, & there will be Charles waiting, & Mummy will say "<u>Hullo</u> Charles" & then arms are opened wide, & "Papa too".' Oh dear, how sweet they are.

Did you hear that the other day when Charles was getting down from his high chair, he bumped his leg, & patting that sturdy limb he said 'Mind my nylons' which was, of course exactly what he heard daily! I don't suppose that he had the vaguest idea what it meant!

Darling, I <u>am</u> so looking forward to seeing you again, & I do hope that the weather will improve by next week for your flight.

I keep on hearing what pleasure your being in Malta gives to everybody, and I am sure that you will be terribly missed when you leave.

Shall you go back in the Spring? [. . .]

The world situation is chaotic to say the least of it. But if one can tide over this dangerous period, & if the Americans can be persuaded to <u>think</u> before they act, then perhaps we shall get away from the immediate danger of war. But how everything has deteriorated these last 3 years.

Here, prices are <u>roaring</u> up, which is very bad. State ownership does not work. I can't think why the Government doesn't do what worked well in the war – a high authority over individual industries – you could have state interference at a high level, & yet keep competition, without which all industry seems to wilt and almost die.

Oh silly imitators of Marx – how foolish they are. [. . .] Goodbye darling, so looking forward to your return, from your very very loving

    Mummy

~

7 April 1951 to Princess Elizabeth

The Royal Lodge

My Darling Lilibet

The children went off yesterday morning, and we felt very sad & terribly quiet after they had gone. I can't tell you what a difference it makes having those heavenly little creatures in the house – everybody loves them so, and they cheer us up more than I can say. Thank you very very much for letting them come. [. . .]

Charles was angelic at the Coldstream Colour giving. He sat in his pram on the right of the steps going down from the East Terrace, & when it was over, he walked round with Papa & me to the saluting base just outside the tunnel door, & stood with us on the dais. When I said 'You must salute the Colours Charles', he raised a small white gloved starfish of a hand to his hat in the gravest & most entrancing way!

We spent most of the time after tea in the Chapel! Every day! That little door on the right of the altar leading to the Dean's dressing room, & the steep little stair up to the pulpit had a tremendous allure, and after playing trains in those pews, which are ideal for the purpose, we toiled up another steep stair to the organ loft (passing a very exciting tiny window on the way), where Charles enjoyed himself madly playing the organ – silently of course!

But it was a wonderful place to play in, and even the upstairs 'boxes' where we used to sit are perfect to explore, aged 2½. One morning when he was paying me a visit in my room, he had a large stick & was marching up & down, being the sentry. He did not know that I was watching him, & really he was so funny that I had great difficulty in not laughing aloud. He stamped, exactly right, & after presenting arms, saluted in a perfect & nonchalant way, all this done very quickly & with a stern & serious face!

Anne is growing hard, & sits bolt upright. I think that she is going to be tall, she is long in the body, & very pretty too. She has lovely eyes, hasn't she?

Mrs Bruce adored having the babies, & Madame Corpsleger [Lightbody]* & Mabel & Agggeness† were such nice guests – always cheerful & happy. Altogether it was too delicious having them. [. . .]

Darling, I've just received your letter, & do hope that the Colour ceremony went off well. [. . .]

I do hope too, that Rome will be delicious. Don't overdo things and get too tired – it can be very exhausting in the spring, & people are inclined to get relaxed throats – so please be careful.

Lots of love to Philip, from your very very loving

Mummy

PS Papa is much better – that flu got him very down, & he took a long time to shake it off.

Did Philip hurt himself when his pony fell? I wonder if you have any good manipulators – so important.

~

* Helen Lightbody (1908–87), nanny to Prince Charles and Princess Anne from 1948 to her retirement in the 1950s.

† Agnes Macdonald Couper, nursery maid, 1950–6.

17 September 1951 to Queen Mary

Balmoral Castle

Darling Mama

Thank you so very much for your dear and understanding letter. It is very worrying about Bertie, and I feel miserable being up here, and feel most cut off. He was very insistent that I should stay here, & not accompany him to London. Partly, I think, he had a faint hope of returning here, and partly he did not want to agitate people too much, but I hope to come down for a day or two anyway this week. It is too unfortunate that the Palace is in such a bad state, our rooms being painted, scaffolding everywhere, but thank goodness we kept the Belgian suite open in case of emergency. I have been dreadfully worried all the time up here, as Bertie was really very unwell with a bad cough & so unfortunately caught a bad cold, & tho' he really was feeling much better last week, he was far from well.

I do pray that the doctors will be able to find something to help the lung recover.

Your dear letter was a great comfort, and I do thank you with all my heart for writing to your very loving daughter in law

Elizabeth

~

The King's health gave great concern throughout the year. He was in need of constant rest, and X-rays showed a shadow on his left lung, which his doctors declared was pneumonitis and could be cured by penicillin. At the end of August, at Balmoral, he caught a chill and the Queen insisted his doctors come to Scotland to see him. They, in turn, prevailed upon him to return to London for one day, to have further tests and X-rays. A specialist in malignant diseases of the chest joined the team and a biopsy from the left lung revealed a tumour, but the word 'cancer' was never used. Instead the doctors published bulletins which talked of 'structural changes' to the lung. It was indeed lung cancer, however, almost certainly caused by his heavy smoking, though the link was not then widely understood.

On 23 September, the King's left lung was removed; thousands of anxious people waited outside the Palace for news to be attached to the railing. Winston Churchill said, 'I did a thing this morning that I

haven't done for many years – I went down on my knees by my
bedside and prayed.'* Millions prayed with him.

~

23 September 1951 to Queen Mary

Buckingham Palace
2.30 p.m.

My Darling Mama

I have just seen the surgeon, and he is very satisfied with the
operation, which is a marvellous relief. Bertie stood it very well –
about 3 hours of it, and if he goes on as he is now, the doctors will be
pleased. He said that we must be anxious for 2 or 3 days, because of
reaction & shock etc., but his blood pressure is steady, & his heart
good. It does seem hard that he should have to go through so much,
someone as good as darling Bertie who always thinks of others – but
if this operation is successful, he may be much stronger in the future.

What a long hell the morning has been! Endless waiting, & I
thought of you so much darling Mama – such moments are true
torture. One must have real faith & trust in the goodness of God.

Your loving Elizabeth

~

23 September 1951 to Sir Alan Lascelles

Buckingham Palace

My dear Tommy

Thank you so much for your letter. I am sure that today the King
was utterly surrounded by a great circle of prayer, and that he has
been sustained by the faith of millions. There must be great strength
in such an uprising of spiritual forces.

If only he has a good 2 days, one will feel much more confident.

This last few weeks has been pure hell, hasn't it. I quite agree
with you that there should be a Council of State. Anything to save
the King the little things that must be done. You can imagine that
I do not want to see the Duke of Windsor – the part author of the
King's troubles. [. . .]

---

* Sir Alan Lascelles to Queen Elizabeth, 23 September 1951 (RA/QEQM/PRIV/ MISCOFF).

Thank you again for your unfailing support given so unsparingly through your own days of anguish. I shall always be <u>very grateful</u> for that.

ER

~

15 October 1951 to Princess Elizabeth

Buckingham Palace

My Darling Lilibet

We have been following your journey step by step,* and the B.B.C. has given quite a good account every evening.

I remember nearly all the places so far, so can imagine you & Philip at all stages of your journey. I am sure that you have had a wonderful welcome, & don't you think Canada a wonderful country? I think of you a very great deal, and I do pray that you won't get absolutely exhausted, not only by endless stops, but by the agonizing worry of trying vainly to keep up to time & not disappoint people who have waited hours. On looking at your 'schedule', I imagine that they have run the times terribly close. They nearly always do!

I really think that Papa is getting stronger (I nearly put gaining strength!), and he is today sitting in the audience room for lunch & tea. His voice is still very hoarse, but he is beginning to take an interest in things again, and once he makes a start, he will, I am sure, get on quicker. It must be slow I suppose, but the doctors are pleased, & he is a little more cheerful.

I would have written before, but got stricken down on Thursday night with a sort of violent flu, which knocked me out for a day or two, & I am just up today in my dressing gown, so fear I have very little news of the children. I saw them on Wednesday when they came over to see one of the night sisters, and they seemed very well.

---

* Princess Elizabeth and Prince Philip set off on a tour of Canada on 7 October 1951, delayed slightly by the King's illness. The Princess's Private Secretary, Martin Charteris, carried sealed envelopes containing the draft Accession Declaration and Messages to Parliament, to be opened should the King die. In the event, nothing detracted from the triumphant 10,000-mile journey undertaken by the young couple. Prince Philip was a special attraction – young women screamed when he waved. The Princess was pleased by her husband's 'succès fou' and the growth of his 'legend'. (Princess Elizabeth to Queen Elizabeth, 4 November 1951, RA QEQM/ PRIV/RF)

I can't believe that it is very good for them to live in a completely empty house, & if later on Nanny seems happy, shall I ask them to stay for a week or two? I think that Charles gets a bit bored with nursery 'patter' don't you? But I will only do this if you think it a good thing.

Everything seems to have gone to pot in Egypt, and I don't wonder with the deplorable Government we have had for so long. They will defer to, & take the advice of the Americans, & much as we like our Canadian neighbours [that is, the United States], do we think much of their judgment on foreign affairs.

Any government that comes in here next week is in for a mess.* Oh dear, it is really terribly worrying & dangerous to realize how little we are listened to at the moment.

And I wonder sometimes whether the bulk of the people realize it, they have had their thoughts glued on to rations & shortages, & housing problems & making sure that nobody rises higher than the lowest, and it is difficult for them to raise their eyes to look wider & higher, & see what is happening to them. But I do think that they have a marvellous sense of balance, & am quite sure that their good sense will save them (some day!).

I am longing to hear your impressions of everything – the French, the Mounties, the delicious people at the little unexpected stops, poison pen Perrick,† your staff, & particularly about Blair House‡ when you get there. Don't forget to give warm personal messages to Mr & Mrs Truman from Papa & me – & anybody else that you think right.

Have you managed clothes all right? It sounds a nightmare for Bobo [MacDonald] of dividing and planning, but I am sure that she has been splendid, & a great support. One really could not do these tremendous tours without a clever & kind maid.

Don't forget to put a bit of inflection into your speeches, especially for coming over the radio darling. They have been excellent so far, so clear too, & good pauses – Philip came over splendidly – it sounded very well indeed.

---

* On 25 October 1951, the Conservatives, led once more by Winston Churchill, won the general election with a majority of seventeen seats. The King was happy to invite his wartime companion to form a government once again.

† Eve Perrick (1916–95), well-known journalist on the *Daily Express*.

‡ Presidential guest house close to the White House.

Margaret is busy cleaning anything & everything in this house! We shall soon be shining like the morning sun!

Papa & I are so proud of you & Philip, & so glad that it is all going so well. We think of you all the time, & with all the rush & tiredness, one stores up wonderful experiences, & perhaps a little more understanding & wisdom – doesn't one? Goodbye darling, from your very loving Mummy

~

26 December 1951 to Arthur Penn

Sandringham

My dear Arthur

You know that there are various unusual objects which one is mad about, and toasting forks are my real weakness. I simply love your most charming present and send you <u>many</u> <u>many</u> grateful thanks.

I shall use it a great deal because we nearly always hot up the toast in London by pronging it on a silver fork and burning one's fingers at the fire, so my lovely new old toasting fork will be HEAVEN to use. It is so kind of you, Arthur, and I am so very grateful.

With all wishes for a better 1952 and with a thousand thanks, not only for my delicious present, but also for all your wonderful help and support through bad days and good days.

Yours with dreams of fresh crunchy toast
Elizabeth R

~

After a family Christmas at Sandringham, where the King had been weak but happy, Princess Elizabeth and Prince Philip set off for Kenya on the first leg of the long Australasian tour which the King and Queen had had to forego because of the King's illness. At London airport on 31 January, the King stood gaunt and hatless as he and the Queen waved their daughter goodbye. The King and Queen were themselves planning a private trip to South Africa for the King to recuperate in the sunshine.

~

2 February 1952 to Princess Elizabeth

Sandringham

My Darling Lilibet

I send you one line to tell you that the children are very well, and we had a successful journey down yesterday. Charles spent at least an hour going up & down the train 'to see if Anne is all right', and made a wonderfully unwholesome tea of half a crumpet, 2 chicken sandwiches, one ham sandwich and the ice cream!

This afternoon Margaret & I took Charles & Anne to Brancaster. Whilst Nanna & Mabel pottered about with Anne, Charles rushed straight down to the sea, & managed to get his feet nice & wet! It was a lovely day, cold & sunny.

We think about you & Philip <u>so</u> much, and it seemed so extraordinary to talk to you yesterday, and to think of you in Nairobi so soon after that horrid good-bye at Heathrow. I could <u>not</u> help one huge tear forcing its way out of my eye, & as we waited to wave goodbye, as you taxied off, it trembled on my eyelashes & I saw both d'Albiac* and Whitney Straight† eyeing it in a sidelong & agitated manner! I did hate saying goodbye to both you darlings, & we felt terribly sad & bereft when you had gone.

I do pray that all goes well, & I am quite sure that you will give immense pleasure wherever you go. People react to goodness & kindness in a wonderful way.

Papa seems pretty well, & I do hope that a good soaking from the sun will do him good. But he does hate being away from all his responsibilities and interests – & I don't expect we shall stay long!

Lots of love darling from your very loving Mummy

~

On 5 February the King went rabbit shooting, while the Queen and Princess Margaret visited the painter Edward Seago at his home near by. That evening the King and Queen looked at some of Seago's pictures which the Queen had brought home, and had an enjoyable dinner with Princess Margaret. The King then retired to bed in his

---

* Air Marshal Sir John D'Albiac KCVO KBE CB DSO (1894–1963), Commandant London Airport 1947–57.

† Air Commodore Whitney Straight CBE MC DFC (1912–79), Deputy Chairman (later Chairman) of the British Overseas Airways Corporation (later British Airways).

ground-floor room. In the morning his servant, James Macdonald, brought the King his tea and found that he had died in his sleep. The Queen was told and rushed to his room.

The report of the King's death was met with grief throughout Britain, the Commonwealth and many other parts of the world.

The new Queen, Elizabeth II, and Prince Philip were given the shocking news in Kenya; they flew back at once and were met at the airport by Winston Churchill and other political leaders on 7 February. They then journeyed to Sandringham to join the rest of the family. The King's coffin was brought by special train to London and lay in state in Westminster Hall; over 300,000 mourners passed by to pay their respects.

On Friday 15 February the King's funeral took place in St George's Chapel, Windsor, and there he was buried. Winston Churchill's wreath read simply 'For Valour'.

~

Wednesday 6 February 1952 to Queen Mary

Sandringham

My Darling Mama,

What can I say to you – I know that you loved Bertie dearly, and he was my whole life, and one can only be deeply thankful for the utterly happy years we had together. He was so wonderfully thoughtful and loving, & I don't believe he ever thought of himself at all. He was so <u>devoted</u> to you, & admired and loved you. It is impossible for me to grasp what has happened, last night he was in wonderful form and looking so well, and this morning, only a few hours ago, I was sent a message that his servant couldn't waken him. I flew to his room, & thought that he was in a deep sleep, he looked so peaceful – and then I realised what had happened.

It is hard to grasp, he was such an angel to the children & me, and I cannot bear to think of Lilibet, so young to bear such a burden. I do feel for you so darling Mama – to lose two dear sons, and Bertie so young still, & so precious – It is almost more than one can bear –

Your very loving

Elizabeth

~

Saturday undated [9 February 1952] to the Duke of Edinburgh

Sandringham

Darling Philip,

You could not have written me a more comforting & wonderful letter, and I do thank you with all my heart for your understanding & sweetness. Papa was so devoted to you, as I am, and that is one of the sad things about his death, because I am sure that as the years went on you would have grown closer even than you have been, and he, I know, was so happy to discuss things with you, & found you such a staunch support.

We both felt so happy that darling Lilibet had such a good & true man as her husband, and that you have that mutual understanding & love which makes the hard things possible to overcome, the sorrows more bearable, & the joys the greater.

I have the greatest confidence in both of you & do thank God for such dear children.

You know that you can count on me to uphold you with all the strength & love that I have – if ever you need it.

Your loving
Mama

~

11 February 1952 to Arthur Penn

Buckingham Palace

My dear Arthur,

How can I ever thank you enough for all your wonderful support & sympathetic understanding during these last dark days. You helped me more than I can say, and I am deeply <u>deeply</u> grateful.

To be upheld by one's friends gives one that little bit of extra courage so badly needed, and your kind thoughtfulness & delicacy will never be forgotten by your grateful
Elizabeth R

~

11 February 1952 to Lady Delia Peel

Buckingham Palace

Darling Delia

It was so wonderful to see you today, and Lilibet & Margaret & I felt so comforted by even the sight of your dear face. You have the gift of making one feel braver, and we truly felt better even after a glimpse. The children have been wonderful all through these awful days.

[. . .] I did so hope that he might have had even a few years of better health to use his energy & creativeness for nice things & good things. I expect that God knows best, & I am tremendously grateful for having had him, tho' it seems <u>such</u> a short time.

Thank you for your letter which I loved. I do so like being reminded of nice things we did together.

Your loving

ER

~

12 February 1952 to Sir Alan Lascelles

Buckingham Palace

My dear Tommy,

I do want to try & tell you something of the deep gratitude I feel for all your loving and wonderful service to the King through perhaps the most difficult years any sovereign has passed through. Your advice & support were greatly cherished by the King – he respected your judgement completely, & how often I have heard him say, 'I must discuss this with Tommy' & know that he would get such a wise & balanced view of the question.

I am sure that at the Coronation he dedicated himself utterly to his country & people and he never deviated from the path he chose. And you helped him to walk that path, and I, who loved him most dearly, want to thank you with all my heart for all you have done to help him.

I am glad beyond words that you will be at the side of our daughter.

I am, Yours sincerely

Elizabeth R

PS The King was very <u>fond</u> of you.

~

Friday 15 February 1952 to Sir Alan Lascelles

Buckingham Palace

My dear Tommy

I am so very grateful to you for re-drafting my message. You have put in just what I wanted & I thank you so much. Today has been the most wonderful & the most agonizing day of my life. Wonderful because one felt the sincerity of the people's feelings, & agonizing because gradually one becomes less numb, & the awfulness of everything becomes real.

I am sure that the King would have been pleased, today. ER

PS I did not tell Arthur that I had showed you my poor words, but tomorrow I shall tell him that you saw, & suggested alterations.

~

18 February 1952 Queen Elizabeth's message to the nation

I want to send this message of thanks to a great multitude of people – to you who, from all parts of the world, have been giving me your sympathy and affection throughout these dark days. I want you to know how your concern for me has upheld me in my sorrow, and how proud you have made me by your wonderful tributes to my dear husband, a great and noble King.

No man had a deeper sense than he of duty and of service, and no man was more full of compassion for his fellow men. He loved you all, every one of you, most truly. That, you know, was what he always tried to tell you in his yearly message at Christmas; that was the pledge that he took at the sacred moment of his Coronation fifteen years ago.

Now I am left alone, to do what I can to honour that pledge without him. Throughout our married life we have tried, the King and I, to fulfil with all our hearts and all our strength the great task of service that was laid upon us. My only wish now is that I may be allowed to continue the work we sought to do together.

I commend to you our dear Daughter: give her your loyalty and devotion: though blessed in her husband and children she will need your protection and your love in the great and lonely station to which she has been called. God bless you all: and may He in his wisdom guide us safely to our true destiny of Peace and Good Will.

~

18 February 1952 to Winston Churchill

Buckingham Palace

My dear Mr Churchill

I was deeply touched by your very kind letter, and want to thank you from my heart for the comforting and sympathetic things you wrote to me.

It is very difficult to believe that the King has left us. He was so well, the day before he died, so gay, & full of plans & ideas for the future. I am sure that he was looking forward to some slightly less anguished years, with perhaps a little time to give to fairer things, such as making gardens which he loved, planning vistas and re-hanging pictures at Windsor, and other very English things which he never had time for.

One thing I am very thankful for, and that is that you returned as his Prime Minister before he died. I am sure that you must have realized his pleasure & delight in having you at the head of his government, and how much he looked forward to seeing you, & discussing affairs of state.

It is very kind of you to say that you will come and see me at some later date. I shall look forward to your visit very much, & I adore talking about the King with someone who knew him well.

With again my thanks for your unfailing sympathy & support, I am, Yours very sincerely,

Elizabeth R

PART FOUR

QUEEN MOTHER

'There's something about her that's kept very young'

TED HUGHES

DESPITE HER GRIEF, Queen Elizabeth showed fortitude. Less than a fortnight after the death of the King, she announced that in future she wished to be known as 'Queen Elizabeth The Queen Mother', though it was not a title she liked. She knew she was now the *ancien régime*. She would no longer be at centre stage in the life of the nation but would be playing a supporting role to her daughter. But she was only fifty-one and she could not contemplate being relegated to 'the no earthly use class'.[1]

Gradually, the tide of sorrow which had almost submerged her withdrew. She began to rebuild her life around several core elements. The most important was family – her daughters and her grandchildren. Prince Charles was, from infancy, a great favourite; throughout her life she lavished love upon him – and he returned it. In November 1952 she wrote to D'Arcy Osborne, 'Charles is a great love of mine. He is such a darling & so like his mother when she was a small child.'[2]

Widowhood could not mean retirement. 'The very important thing is to be busy,'[3] Queen Elizabeth believed, and she followed such advice herself after the death of the King. As she grew older she worked unceasingly for the charities, regiments and other organizations with which she was associated. Her list of patronages grew to over three hundred and she could rarely say no to a new one.

The Queen Mother also became, in her second half-century, one of the best-travelled members of the Royal Family, undertaking many tours of North America, Africa and Australasia, as well as taking holidays in France and Italy. The enthusiasm she generated on her official travels showed her that she could still help foster Britain's links with its former imperial possessions, which were now part of the Commonwealth, and improve relations with other countries. Even her official tours were laced with the fun which she tried to impart to everything she did. She had always loved flying and in Africa or Australia would take to the smallest local planes without any anxiety.

In the summer of 1952, a few months after the King's death,

Queen Elizabeth went to stay in Caithness in the north of Scotland
with one of her closest friends, Doris Vyner, and her husband Clare.
Their remote house overlooked the sea and the Orkney Islands
beyond. Together they chanced upon a little ruined castle on the coast
and its delighted owner sold it to Queen Elizabeth for a token £100.
It was a whimsical purchase but, over the decades ahead, the Castle of
Mey gave enormous pleasure to her and her friends.

She developed her passion for racehorses. The Queen, like other
monarchs before her, concentrated on flat racing, and so the Queen
Mother took up steeplechasing, the poor relation of the flat, which
attracted a rather louche and amusing crowd of people. Mother and
daughter each became immersed in the joys and sorrows of the turf,
knowing well the lines of individual horses, the records of jockeys,
trainers and owners, the going under different conditions of every
racetrack in the kingdom. For five decades their letters to each other
were filled with racing gossip and the performances of their respective
horses. Racing was all the more fun because it was such a contrast
to royal life – far from being predictable, it was always thrillingly
uncertain.

In the decade following the death of the King, Britain began to
experience an extensive social revolution. In the 1960s and 1970s, as
the state took over more and more areas of life and as Britain became
a more open, less judgemental society, deference was sometimes
replaced by indifference, scepticism and satire. The monarchy seemed
remote and out of date to London-led cultural revolutionaries. But
others saw the institution and particularly the Queen Mother as the
embodiment of the traditional values on which they depended.

Throughout, she was informed by a conviction that individuals
were more important than the state and that the extension of the
government's reach into every area of life did 'not absolve us from the
practice of charity or from the exercise of vigilance. The English way
of progress has always been to preserve good qualities and apply them
to new systems.' She, like other members of the Royal Family, felt this
especially in the matter of health care. The National Health Service,
created by the Labour government in 1948, should continue to use
charitable volunteers to 'show that sympathy and compassion were
still freely given'.[4]

In 1993, in her annual speech to the Sandringham Women's
Institute (a group she much enjoyed), she looked back fifty years to

the time 'when the skies above us were filled with aircraft of the American 8th Air Force, stationed all around us in East Anglia'. There had been many changes since then, she said, 'some good, and some not so good, but through all those changing scenes of life we can feel the strong beat of the English heart'.[5]

She kept her own heart young not only by being busy but also by always winning new young friends. Many of them stayed with her at the Castle of Mey, probably the most relaxed of her households. At the end of her eighties she became close friends with the poet Ted Hughes, with whom she exchanged affectionate letters for a decade.

Her friendship with Hughes gave joy to her nineties, but it was in many ways a wretched decade for the Royal Family. Princess Anne's marriage ended in divorce in 1992 and so, later, did the marriage between Prince Andrew and Sarah Ferguson. But the most damaging rupture of all was between the Prince and Princess of Wales. Their separation was announced at the end of 1992, shortly after the fire which devastated large parts of Windsor Castle.

In all these sadnesses, Queen Elizabeth spoke to many of her relations, but she was careful not to commit her views to paper, not even in private letters. She had always been discreet about the Royal Family. By the 1990s, when leaks were constant, she was even more careful.

When her hundredth birthday arrived in August 2000, Queen Elizabeth had lost most of her eyesight, but she still wrote to and saw many friends, she still carried out public engagements and she still, in every way, celebrated life. The event was marked by a spectacular pageant on Horse Guards Parade in which representatives of all the organizations with which she had been associated during her life marched past her and Prince Charles. She loved it, and so did all those taking part.

For the next twenty months she continued, growing weaker, but still visiting her homes in Scotland, still entertaining friends, still writing letters.

28 February 1952 to Lionel Logue

Buckingham Palace

Dear Mr Logue

I am so grateful for your very kind letter, and very much touched by what you write.

I am indeed sorry to hear you have been so ill, & it was most kind of you to make the effort to write to me.

I think that I know perhaps better than anyone just how much you helped the King, not only with his speech, but through that his whole life, & outlook on life.

I shall always be deeply grateful to you for all you did for him.

He was such a splendid person, & I don't believe that he ever thought of himself at all. I did so hope that he might have been allowed a few years of comparative peace after the many anguished years he has had to battle through so bravely.

But it was not to be.

I do hope that you will soon be better, & with again my heartfelt thanks,

I am, Yours very Sincerely,
Elizabeth R

~

13 March 1952 to Peter Cazalet

Buckingham Palace

My dear Peter,

[. . .] I think that your letter, like many others, got sent to the Queen by mistake and it was sent back to me here, so to make quite sure, would you put your initials in the corner of the envelope, & "personal" on top, when you write again? Owing to the fact that we are both ELIZABETH there is a slight muddle at the moment.

Yours sincerely,
Elizabeth R

~

Sunday undated [?late February–March 1952] to Queen Elizabeth II

The Royal Lodge

My Darling Lilibet

I am so sorry that I collapsed this evening, just when I didn't want to, but I have been feeling very unhappy all today, and I suppose that talking about leaving Buckingham Palace just finished me off. I was longing to talk to you about plans anyway, as naturally you must move back to B.P. in the Spring, & I have been trying to think of these things all this week – and somehow when I wanted to discuss it with you, it all went wrong! I am quite sure that next time will be absolutely alright.

I expect that the best plan would be for you & Philip to move into the Belgian rooms, because you are quite independent there, & Papa & I lived there all through the war as you know.

That would give me time to move my things without any ghastly hurry, and I could be quite self contained upstairs, meals etc, and you would hardly know I was there. I do implore of you to put the children upstairs for the moment – it will only be for a short time, & my little rooms would be desperately uncomfortable for children, nurses & you. It is so important to keep a few rooms for yourselves – it is like having a house within a house where you can have all your own things, & when you move up to Papa's & my rooms, I am sure that you will see what I mean.

It is so angelic of you both to tell me I can stay on for a bit at B.P., and I am most grateful for your thoughtfulness. I know that it took Granny some months to pack up everything, & I fear that I shall need some time too.

But what is a few months in a lifetime anyway! Thank you darling for being such an angelic daughter, & I do love you so,

Your very loving
Mummy

~

31 March 1952 to Viscount Davidson

Buckingham Palace

My dear Lord Davidson*

I was so deeply touched by your kindness in sending me the account of your talk with the King, and I want to send you my heartfelt thanks for your thought in writing so charmingly of such a personal and poignant episode.

Your little story brings those days back to me so clearly, tho' they always seemed very close to the King & I. In fact only a few days before he died, we were saying how incredibly quickly the years had sped by since we married, & how it seemed only yesterday that we started our life together. Perhaps having lived through such turbulent & troublesome years, made the time go so quickly, there were so many things that we wanted to do, & so many plans we made, but during the War we said, 'after the War', & after the War it was 'when things improve', so alas, they did not materialise very often.

As you told me your story so well, & so delicately, I must tell you that we were ideally happy, due to the King's wonderful kindness & goodness and thought for others. I never wanted to be with anyone but him, & during the last ten terrible years, he was a rock of strength and wisdom & courage. So that in thanking you for your letter, I thank you also for the advice you gave the King in 1922.

I am
Yours very sincerely
Elizabeth R.

~

* John Campbell Davidson (1889–1970) had been MP for Hemel Hempstead and was created Viscount Davidson in 1937. In 1922, he had been introduced to Prince Albert by the Prince's equerry Louis Greig, as a member of a Parliamentary delegation. According to his own account, he realized that the Prince was deeply unhappy, and the Prince then told him that he had lost the only woman he would ever marry. Davidson told him that he must never give up hope but must persevere – and that his own wife had refused him many times before she accepted him. Davidson's advice seems to have encouraged the Prince to continue his suit and 'play the long game'.

Davidson kept an account of the conversation and, soon after the death of the King, sent it to the Queen Mother. He wrote that he had kept this encounter 'in the secret recesses of my memory ever since, and I am only releasing it now, because in Your Majesty's terrible loneliness I believe it may bring one tiny grain of comfort.' The Queen Mother's reply suggests that he was correct. (Lord Davidson to Queen Elizabeth, 26 February 1952, RA GVI/ADD/MISC/COPY)

28 April 1952 to the Marchioness of Salisbury*

Windsor Castle

My dearest Betty,

Thank you so very much for your angelic letter. I cannot tell you how touched I am that you should invite me to stay, and you can imagine how much I would love to be with you. If you are to be at Cranborne later on in the summer, could I come then?

I know that it is a healing place, with its great beauty & serenity & peace, & I know that I would love to be with you & Bobbety, who are so wonderfully understanding about that strange and devastating thing called sorrow.

There is no doubt that it changes one's whole life, & one's outlook on life, & I find everything a perpetual battle & struggle. But, as you know, the King never gave in, and I am determined to try & do what he would have wished.

Thank you so much too for sending me that charmingly expressed letter from Bob Thayer. It is so wonderful to know that Americans appreciated those qualities that the King had, which are not the glittering obvious ones, but things like truth & valour & strength.

Dearest Betty, you are such a good & angelic friend, and I long to see you again. Perhaps you will come & see me at Buckingham Palace where I return next week.

The blossom here is too lovely for words, & everything a glorious & tender green – almost unbearable.

With my love, ever your devoted friend
Elizabeth R

~

3 May 1952 to Sir Osbert Sitwell

Windsor Castle

My dear Sir Osbert,

It was delightful to see you again the other evening, and I wished that I could have made more sense because there is so much that I want to talk about, but the noise was so terrific, and the plunge for

---

* Lord and Lady Cranborne had become fifth Marquess and Marchioness of Salisbury on the death of his father in 1947.

me so sudden that I felt slightly bewildered. But it was a great pleasure to sit next to you at that wonderful dinner served so exquisitely by all those beautiful Frasers, and I was so glad to see you looking well, & in such good heart.*

I did tell you, I think, that I tried to write to you, for I was deeply touched by your two kind letters and somehow I could not say what I wanted just then.

You write in such a very understanding way, & I knew that your sympathy was so real, & I was very grateful for what you said.

It is very difficult to realise that the King has left us, he was so much better, & so full of plans & ideas for the future, and I really thought he was going to have some years perhaps less anguished than the last fifteen. I think that those years after the war were terribly anxious & frustrating and it was all very hard & grinding work, and I longed for him to have some peace of mind. He was so young to die, and was becoming so wise in his Kingship. He was so kind too, and had a sort of natural nobility of thought & life, which sometimes made me ashamed of my narrow & more feminine point of view.

Such sorrow is a very strange experience – it really changes one's whole life for better or worse, I don't know yet.

I hope you will come and see me in London, & perhaps we might get Hannah [Gubbay] too, which would be very stimulating.

Yours very sincerely,

Elizabeth R

~

* This was Queen Elizabeth's first foray into social life since the death of the King. The 'beautiful Frasers' were members of the family of Brigadier Simon ('Shimi') Christopher Joseph Fraser, seventeenth Lord Lovat DSO MC TD (1911–95), a courageous commando officer during the Second World War. He and his men helped to take Sword Beach on D Day.

The hostess of this dinner may have been Lord Lovat's sister Magdalen Fraser, the Countess of Eldon, Queen Elizabeth's friend and a member of the Windsor Wets. She was renowned for her beauty, as was her sister Veronica Fraser, wife of Sir Fitzroy Maclean. A third 'beauty' may well have been Rosie Lovat, the wife of Lord Lovat.

21 July 1952 to Queen Elizabeth II

Sandringham

My Darling Lilibet

I feel that I must tell you the most extraordinary & wonderful thing that has happened to me, which is, that when I arrived here on Saturday evening, I felt an amazing feeling of relief & peace, which I have not felt since Papa died.

It was just as if Sandringham opened its arms to me, & I sank into them thankfully. I can't explain it, but I feel quite different here, and in a way it's a great surprise. I suppose that when one is in great anguish, everything that happens each day opens a wound, & tho' this place is utterly bound up with Papa, I love the people & all that happens here, & to be amongst them is a relief & a healing.

Isn't it amazing – I <u>can't</u> get over it.

When Papa succeeded, I remember we said to Granny, 'you must always come to Sandringham when<u>ever</u> you want to, and please treat it as your home', and I would so love it if you would say that to me too. I wouldn't come often, but it is all so bound up with our life together, & it would be wonderful to be able to come once in a while.

I wonder whether this feeling will last! I don't suppose it will, but I felt I must tell you – it is almost as if Papa said 'come in darling, & rest'.

Perhaps one is closer to him than one knows.

Good bye darling, from your very loving Mummy

~

6 August 1952 to Arthur Penn

Buckingham Palace

My dear Arthur

When I was staying up in Caithness I passed a dear little Castle down by the sea,* and when I visited it, I discovered that it was going to be sold for nothing, just the value of the lead on the roof.

---

* Barrogill Castle, which Queen Elizabeth first visited when staying with Clare and Doris Vyner at their nearby home, The House of the Northern Gate. The Castle was cheap to buy but not to restore to habitable condition nor to maintain thereafter. Queen Elizabeth changed

This seemed so sad, that I thought I would buy it & escape there occasionally when life became hideous! The old man who has lived there a long time was very anxious to give it to me, but I resisted the kind gesture and he has now offered it to me for £100!

It might be rather fun to have a small house so far away – the air is lovely, and one looks at Orkney from the drawing room! The only sad thing is that part of the roof was blown off in the great gale last January, and I shall have to put in electric light of course. The grid runs past the door luckily.

Do you think me mad?

ER

~

Tuesday undated [?early August 1952] to Queen Elizabeth II

Buckingham Palace

Darling, I do hope that you don't think me too temperamental for words, I don't often give way, but somehow it all comes welling up when I talk to you & Margaret, & I long for the day when I shall feel alright again. You must bear with me for a bit – I am sure that I shall regain iron control again very soon. The thought of going to dear Birkhall is very extraordinary. If you can imagine yourself going there without Philip, without Charles, without Anne, or Nanny (!) or Bobo you can imagine my feelings! Your very loving Mummy

~

6 August 1952 to the Marchioness of Salisbury

Buckingham Palace

My dearest Betty,

Owing to various unforeseen complications, I have had to put off my visit to Holyrood in September, which is very sad. But, please will you come next year instead, & we will have all the things we want to see & hear. I am terribly disappointed as I long to see you & Bobbety.

If you feel very strong for the simple life, do come & stay austerely with me at Birkhall after you leave Balmoral. You know

---

its name to the more romantic original name, The Castle of Mey, and it gave her, and many of her friends, immense pleasure for the rest of her life.

how small & uncomfortable the house is, but the welcome would be
ENORMOUS, and it would give me such real pleasure to feel that
you were coming dearest Betty. Bobbety could have his Australian to
lunch.

What fun your party was on Friday. Winston was so angelic
about the King – he has such tender understanding, & I was so
touched & helped.

With my fond love,
ever your loving friend
Elizabeth R

~

31 August 1952 to Queen Mary

Birkhall

Darling Mama

It was so very kind of you to reply so quickly, and I am indeed
delighted to hear about the silver dishes and sauce boats. They will be
very useful and I am deeply grateful to you for lending me these
things.

It is so difficult nowadays to collect enough for running a house,
and your kindness will ease the situation greatly.

I wonder if you saw in the paper about the old Castle in
Caithness? When I was staying with the Vyners I saw this small castle,
& heard that it was going to be allowed to crumble away. It belongs
to a nice old man called Imbert-Terry, and I felt that it was such a
wrong thing to happen to an interesting old place, that I said I would
try & keep it going, anyway for the moment.

It is near the sea, with lovely views, & might be nice for a change
sometimes, and perhaps one could lend it to tired people, for a rest.
It will only need a housekeeper, and will be rather fun to do up
gradually.

I am sure that dear Sandringham is looking attractive now, and I
do hope that the 'open garden' days do not disturb you too much.

With again my loving thanks for your kindness about the silver,
I am your devoted daughter in law
Elizabeth

~

15 September 1952 to Edith Sitwell

Birkhall

My dear Miss Sitwell

It was so very kind of you to send me a copy of your <u>lovely</u> book.* It is giving me the greatest pleasure, and I took it out with me, and I started to read it, sitting by the river, & it was a day when one felt engulfed by great black clouds of unhappiness & misery, and I found a sort of peace stealing round my heart as I read such lovely poems & heavenly words.

I found a hope in George Herbert's† poem, 'Who could have thought my shrivel'd heart, could have recovered greennesse? It was gone quite underground.' And I thought how small and selfish is sorrow. But it bangs one about until one is senseless and I can never thank you enough for giving me such a delicious book wherein I found so much beauty & hope – quite suddenly one day by the river.

It is such an entrancing collection of beautiful & unusual things, & must have taken a lot of digging & delving to find so much variety. I am deeply touched by your thought of me, I love being given books, and I send you my <u>warmest</u> thanks.

I am, yours very sincerely,
Elizabeth R

~

3 October 1952 to the Marquess of Salisbury

Birkhall

My dear Bobbety

Thank you so much for your kind letter.

I must admit that I had to screw myself up a good deal to finally say that I would go to S. Rhodesia, but I do admire [Cecil] Rhodes, &

---

*   Edith Sitwell had sent her a copy of her new literary anthology, *A Book of Flowers*.

†   George Herbert (1593–1633), English poet, Parliamentarian and priest. Among his poems which became popular hymns are 'King of Glory, King of Peace', 'Let all the world in every corner sing' and 'Teach me my God and King'. He described his poems as 'a picture of spiritual conflicts between God and my soul'.

I hope very much that Federation will ultimately prove a success, and if a visit would help in any way of course I am glad to go. [. . .]*

It has been rather cold & windy here, but I have not been very conscious of the weather, & I can't quite remember what has happened, except that Lochnagar has twice been glittering with snow. I went to Beaufort for two days, where the Lovats live a beautifully feudal existence, surrounded by a mass of glorious children. It is obviously a happy life, lots of cream & butter and faded tartan and local leadership. A useful life, as well as an enjoyable one.

I had a very nice visit from Winston yesterday.† He was absolutely charming & very interesting, and I realised suddenly how very much I am now cut off from 'inside' information. He is truly a remarkable man, & with great delicacy of feeling too.

Please give Betty much love, & I hope so much to meet later on.

Yours very sincerely,

Elizabeth R

~

29 November 1952 to Sir Alan Lascelles

Sandringham

My dear Tommy

Thank you so much for your letter about Mr Wheeler-Bennett,‡ and for sending me his book about Hindenburg.

From what you say, I do feel that he sounds a suitable person to undertake a life of the King, especially if he really wants to do it.

---

* The British government was attempting to forestall the growing demands of African nationalists for full independence from their colonial masters by creating a federation of Northern and Southern Rhodesia and Nyasaland.

† Winston Churchill visited the Queen Mother at Birkhall while he was making the Prime Minister's annual autumn visit to the sovereign at Balmoral. According to his daughter, Lady Soames, Churchill took it upon himself to tell the Queen Mother that she still had a vital role to play in public life. Her lady in waiting, Lady Jean Rankin, said, 'I think he must have said things which made her realise how important it was for her to carry on, how much people wanted her to do things as she had before.' (*The Queen Mother Remembered*, ed. James Hogg and Michael Mortimer, BBC Worldwide, 2002, p. 161)

‡ The Queen Mother was concerned to choose an appropriate official biographer for the King. Tommy Lascelles suggested John Wheeler-Bennett, a distinguished military historian, who had also been helped by Lionel Logue to overcome a stammer. After the Queen Mother and the Queen had invited Wheeler-Bennett to stay in Scotland, they agreed with the choice. His lucid biography, *King George VI, His Life and Reign*, was published in 1958.

I have the greatest confidence in your choice, as I know that you, more than anybody understands what is needed, and if you like him personally, I expect that we shall too. I would very much like to meet him, and perhaps this could be arranged when I come back to London.

It will not be an easy book to write – so many years taken up with war, and such a short political life after the War.

If only the King had been allowed a few years of comparative peace – he would have had a chance to ease down a bit, & do all the things he had planned, or some of them anyway.

There can be very few Kings of England whose reigns were so harried & harassed by troubles & worries & anxieties on such an immense scale. First the abdication, & all the agony of mind – I doubt if people realize how horrible it all was to the King & me – to feel unwanted, & to undertake such a job for such a dreadful reason, it was a terrible experience.

Then the War with all its agony, & then 'after the War', which was a dreadful strain on the King. I suppose that we have been through a revolution and, as usual, people hardly realized what was happening to them.

All this crammed into 15 short years – it is a dizzy thought.

But you are the important person as regards the book. You will probably have to write a good deal of it yourself, in notes etc, as nobody else can do it. I will do all I can to help, tho' it is difficult.

I suppose that one will never feel the same again. I talk & laugh & listen, but one lives in a dream & I expect that one's real self dies when one's husband dies, and only a ghost remains. The only things that rouse me to anger are when people look at me in a penetrating way, & say 'are you feeling BETTER' and the other people who say 'but what a wonderful death for the King – how that must comfort you'. If only they knew!

I shall hope to see you next week in London, here we have had cold pure days, with blue skies, & such kind welcomes from all the old friends.

Yours
Elizabeth R

~

29 November 1952 to Sir D'Arcy Osborne

Buckingham Palace

My dear D'Arcy,

I was so glad to hear from you, tho' <u>very</u> sad to think that with all our confabulations & discussions your friends cannot save you from liquidation – I am sure that a ring, or just one jewel might help, but you were adamant. I can't tell you how much I enjoyed having you at Birkhall – perhaps you realised how agonizing life was to me, & how one could not bear seeing people, and how you were one of the <u>very</u> few friends I wanted to see – you were so kind & understanding, and I was so very grateful to you. Next year I hope to be more brave.

I was so very touched by the letter written by your Swiss friend – he must be charming & kind. I enclose a little note, & wonder whether you would send it on to him when you next write. I hope that I have addressed it right?

Charles & Anne are very well, & Charles is a great love of mine. He is such a darling & so like his mother when she was a small child.

With all wishes for a happy Xmas from your friend,

Elizabeth R

~

5 January 1953 [misdated 1952] to Prince Paul of Yugoslavia

Sandringham

My dear Paul,

The chocolates that you kindly sent me are too excellent for words, and I send you my warmest thanks for your charming thought. The extraordinary thing is, that they are <u>all</u> so good. I have never had a box of chocolates before which didn't have pink flavoured with bath salts, or nougat made of iron filings & sand, and it is so exciting to <u>know</u> that yours are all delicious.

Thank you a thousand times.

I rather love being here, because every stick & stone & every corner reminds me of Bertie. He was always so happy here, and adored the estate & the people, and in his short time did so much to improve and beautify the place. I feel that he is so close to me here.

As the time goes on I miss him more & more – he was always so good & loving & thoughtful, & so much <u>fun</u> to be with – you knew him well, & of course he had developed and strengthened his already strong character through those long years of war, and life is immensely dreary without him.

We were hardly ever apart during our married life – except when he was abroad visiting troops etc, so Paul, you can imagine how horrid life is. This sounds rather complaining, but I don't mean it like that, & only write freely because I know that you were fond of Bertie.

It was so delightful seeing you again, & I do hope that we shall meet again before too long. It is delicious seeing Olga occasionally and hearing your news.

David is staying here for the shooting, & is very well.

With again all my thanks for the chocolates, & with my fond love to Olga,

Ever yours affect.

Elizabeth

~

3 February 1953 to Queen Elizabeth II

Buckingham Palace

My Darling Lilibet,

It was so lovely being at Sandringham with you & Philip & Margaret, and I felt very set up by the end of January. I can't quite believe that it has come to an end and that delicious time of skies & keepers & clear (or foggy) cold air is over. You were so angelic, & kind, & thoughtful, and I did so adore being with you.

It is so difficult to try & carry on, having lost all one's interests – the gardens, farming, pictures etc, and I am so thankful to still have the horses. It is so much more amusing to have them at Sandringham, & I should hate to have them anywhere else, as I always connect them with you!

I do hope that I shall be able to keep them going – perhaps someday I shall win a race, & that would help!

I went down to Canvey Island* yesterday – it was terribly like the war all over again, the same defiance, the same 'I don't care' & I felt

---

* The east coast had been hit by the worst storms and flooding in decades. The Queen Mother visited some of those rendered homeless.

quite shattered & exhausted by memories, & the sad reality of the present tragedy. Poor little homes – poor dogs & cats, kind policemen & St Johns – oh it is so horrible.

Your loving Mummy

~

2 March 1953 to Queen Mary

Buckingham Palace

My Darling Mama,

I cannot <u>begin</u> even to tell you how touched & grateful I am by your very kind suggestion that I might wear your robe at the Coronation. This has greatly eased my mind, because I know that it would have been very difficult to shorten my own Coronation robe, & I was beginning to wonder what would happen.

I do think it so dear and kind of you, and I shall see that your beautiful robe is taken great care of, and I send you my very warmest thanks.

I am so terribly sad that you have had such a horrid time, & felt so unwell for the last week,* and I do so hope that you will soon feel better.

It is so miserable for you, & all our thoughts are with you all the time.

With my love, and more thanks – ever your devoted daughter in law

Elizabeth

~

---

* Queen Mary died peacefully at Marlborough House on the evening of 24 March 1953. Her official biographer commented that 'by undeviating service to her own highest ideals, she had ended by becoming, for millions, an ideal in herself'. (James Pope-Hennessy, *Queen Mary*, Allen & Unwin, 1959, p. 622) Following the death of Queen Mary, Queen Elizabeth hoped to be able to move into Marlborough House. However, it was deemed too expensive and she and Princess Margaret moved into Clarence House nearby in May 1953, a few weeks before the Coronation. The Queen eventually gave Marlborough House to the Commonwealth Secretariat.

13 April 1953 to Lady Doris Vyner

Birkhall

My Darling Doris,

So often we have shared moments of great sorrow & suffering, & I was so afraid that last week might have been one of intolerable anguish to you & Clare. But you were both so <u>wonderful</u> & so composed & brave, that one would never have known how deeply you must have felt, both before, during and after that <u>lovely</u> dedication of the Memorial.* It was so wonderful that you both wished me to be there, and I can never tell you how touched I was at being asked.

The whole conception of the memorial is so perfect, these two young, brave hopeful figures, so deeply moving – how <u>terribly</u> proud you must be through all the suffering and torture of mind.

It was so heavenly being with you & Clare, & once again I subsided into a delicious feeling of 'being with friends'. There is nothing like it to heal wounds – so often one's own silly mind which doesn't rest makes them worse, and I am so very grateful for all your loving Kindness.

The DINNER PARTY was so splendid. So smooth & sophisticated, those just right cocktails, the wonderful food & drink, the ROLLS in their NAPKINS, the sparkling conversation – it was so right, & such a good idea to have it then.

Thank you again & again, darling Doris, from your ever loving, Elizabeth R

~

27 May 1953 to Queen Elizabeth II

Clarence House

Darling Angel, I don't want to bother you when you are so busy, but I must somehow borrow a row of diamonds for the Coronation, & if I <u>don't</u> hear from you I will get hold of one of Granny's† – O.K.? Your loving Mummy

~

---

* Clare and Doris Vyner had erected a monument to their children, Elizabeth and Charles, at Fountains Abbey, one of the greatest medieval monasteries in Britain, of which they were the last private owners. The Queen Mother dedicated the memorial on 9 April 1953.

† From photographs of the Coronation, it seems that the Queen Mother wore three separate

12 June 1953 to Sir Alan Lascelles

Clarence House

My dear Tommy,

Thank you so much for your kind letter.

I have really felt quite shattered by the whole thing,* and cannot help feeling that it would never have happened if the King had been here.

I have not mentioned it to anyone except the Queen, but I would like to talk to you, soon, please. I have nobody I can talk to about such dreadful things. Have you mentioned it to anybody belonging to me? I wondered today if Arthur knew.

It is a great comfort that you understand the human side of such tragedies – for so they are to the young.

Yours very sincerely

Elizabeth R

~

---

necklaces – probably her own Coronation necklace given her by the King in 1937, the Teck collet necklace, which first belonged to George III's daughter Princess Mary, Duchess of Gloucester, and the necklace that Queen Alexandra was given as a wedding present by the City of London in 1863.

* Queen Elizabeth was referring to the romance between Princess Margaret and Group Captain Peter Townsend, of which she had been unaware until recently. Since the death of the King, which had devastated her, Princess Margaret had become ever closer to Townsend, wartime flying hero, equerry and now divorcé. At the end of 1952, Townsend told Tommy Lascelles that he and the Princess were in love and wished to marry. Lascelles was horrified, in particular because divorce was still widely frowned upon as contrary to the teaching of the Church. The two young people told the Queen Mother in February 1953 and she was distraught. The romance became public after the Coronation. Lascelles was concerned for the position of the Queen as head of Church and state. Under the Royal Marriages Act of 1772, no lineal descendant of King George II who was under twenty-five could marry without the Sovereign's consent. After reaching twenty-five, such a marriage could take place unless Parliament objected. In this case, the Queen would have to act on the advice of her ministers – and Lascelles felt certain that they would not advise her to allow her sister to marry a divorced man in a registry office. The Prime Minister, Winston Churchill, was at first seized with the romance but, on reflection, decided he would not recommend consent being given to the marriage unless Princess Margaret renounced all her royal rights.

7 July 1953 to Queen Elizabeth II

In the Train [visiting Southern Rhodesia]

My Darling Lilibet

We have just finished a day in the train stopping at places like Gwelo, Que Que, Gatooma, Hartley etc, & it seems a very short time since we were all alighting at the same places, & being urged back into the train by Papa!

They have all <u>doubled</u> in population since we were there, new factories springing up, & lots of young people, especially men, looking very tough & happy & prosperous. I am sure that this country has a great future, tho' it will have to go through the teething troubles of Federation. [. . .]

The stewards on the train are all South Africans – one was with us in 1947 – very nice, & for our first dinner on board we had eight courses! I sent for the menus & <u>pruned</u>!

It is rather difficult not having anyone who has ever been on a tour, and I do miss Peter [Townsend] very much.* He had experience, & I find that alas! this only comes through silly mistakes. One was terribly spoilt having Tommy [Lascelles] & Michael [Adeane]† I suppose.

The Comet flight was very successful, and we were lucky enough to have good weather. Khartoum is the bugbear. But my goodness, we all felt ghastly for at least 5 days – but now the heart has stopped bumping, & the knees are stiffening and apart from Margaret complaining dreadfully of the cold in her sleeping cabin, & coughing rather ostentaciously (can't spell it) on the platforms, we are feeling restored. [. . .]

Your very loving Mummy

~

---

* On 30 June 1953, the Queen Mother and Princess Margaret set off on a tour of Southern Rhodesia, now merged with Northern Rhodesia and Nyasaland into a federation. Queen Elizabeth had been asked by the British government to make the tour in the hope that it would help give credence to the new federal entity.

Peter Townsend had been due to accompany them, but that was deemed inappropriate following publicity about his romance with Princess Margaret.

† Michael Adeane, Baron Adeane PC GCB GCVO (1910–84), soldier and courtier, Assistant Private Secretary to King George VI 1945–52, Assistant Private Secretary and then Private Secretary to Queen Elizabeth II 1952–72. He guided the Queen on a path of constitutional rectitude.

9 July 1953 to Sir Osbert Sitwell

Royal Tour
Southern Rhodesia

My dear Sir Osbert,

I have been meaning to write to you for many weeks, and this is the first opportunity I have had to thank you for 2 letters & the delightful book of short stories. I read one story between Beirut & Khartoum as the Comet magic-carpeted us through the sky, one in Salisbury, & now I am spending 2 nights at a hotel called Leopard Rock and I have been reading more stories in between gazing at the most glorious mountains. It really is such very beautiful country, range after range of blue mysterious hills, fading away into far far away, and a great plain stretching away for ever between the mountains. The light is exquisite, the sun bright & hot & the air cool. I love the immensity of Africa, one feels a great rhythm all the time, but how much more beautiful England is.

I do hope to see you when I return.

This country is very cheerful, hardworking & loyal & English, full of young, eager people who are going to make a great country of it and NO DEATH DUTIES!

Yours very sincerely,
Elizabeth R

~

23 August 1953 to Queen Elizabeth II and the Duke of Edinburgh

Birkhall

Darling Lilibet & Philip,

Being at Balmoral with you was HEAVEN. Thank you both, darlings, for being so angelic, it all means so much to me, and it was such fun being with my children & grandchildren and laughing & talking & being a family, which is the only thing worth living for.

Your very loving Mummy

~

7 November 1953 to Queen Elizabeth II

Clarence House
11 p.m.

My Darling Lilibet,

I have just got back here, and I must write one line to tell you why I had to rush away when you produced a statue of Papa.* It was because I knew that I was going to burst into floods of tears, and I am sure that you realized this & understood.

I could <u>not</u> look at a statue of my beloved husband in front of all those people.

I did not know that a model had been done, or that a site had been chosen, & it was such a shock, & I felt terribly upset.

I must send this line to explain, tho' I am sure you know how I felt darling,

Your very loving Mummy

~

11 November 1953 to Sir Alan Lascelles

Clarence House

My dear Tommy

Here are volumes four and five of the King's note books.

When reading them, memories become almost too vivid to bear, and one feels at once transported back to those days when everything went against us, & yet one was convinced that in the end we would win.

You will remember that the King kept these notes groaningly for <u>reference</u> & not as a Diary.

Yours very sincerely
Elizabeth R

~

---

* The statue of King George VI by William McMillan was erected just off the Mall in 1955. On 24 February 2009 a statue of Queen Elizabeth by the sculptor Philip Jackson was unveiled as a permanent memorial to her. In preparation for this, the statue of King George VI was moved slightly forward from its original position. The Prince of Wales said in his speech, 'At long last my grandparents are reunited in this joint symbol, which in particular reminds us of all they stood for and meant to so many during the darkest days this country has ever faced . . .'

23 November 1953 to Queen Elizabeth II

Clarence House

My Darling Lilibet,

I have tried to telephone you several times today, but you have always been engaged which I <u>quite</u> understand. It must be a ghastly day for you,* poor darling.

I wanted to know 2 things. One, if the children come here in Feb:, would it be possible for my lady in waiting to sleep at BP?

Also, what have you done with Papa's letter.

Also, would you tell Nanna that they are to come here later? I am thinking of good nights etc.

Your v. loving
Mummy

~

14 December 1953 to Queen Elizabeth II

Clarence House

My Darling Lilibet,

This brings you all my most loving wishes for a happy Xmas. It won't seem at all the same here with you & Philip away, but we shall all be thinking of you very much.

I am sending you a little Fabergé clock which I do hope will be useful. I thought it such a pretty <u>clean</u> colour, like strawberry ice, & as Fabergé things are now becoming scarce, I thought you might like it for your table. Anyway, it brings you a <u>great</u> deal of love.

The children are very well. They were at R. Lodge for the weekend, & we took a <u>great</u> <u>deal</u> of exercise! They adore the pony at

---

* The Queen Mother thought the day 'ghastly' for the Queen because she was leaving, without her children, for a five-month tour of the Commonwealth. As Duchess of York, she had had to embark on a similar tour in January 1927.

The Queen Mother enclosed a letter from Mrs Fisher, the wife of the Archbishop of Canterbury, in which the Prelate's wife offered suggestions as to how to deal with the stress presented by the forthcoming tour. She thought one should begin every day with stillness, to stop one's mind running. ' "Think of God", "Know that I am God" and recall and realize some simple facts. "In whom we live and move and have our being", "I cannot draw another breath except thou givest me power", "The day is thine". The whole process being simply one of letting go of oneself and all the duties into his Hands.' On the envelope the Queen Mother wrote, 'Read in aeroplane or ship. I think it is helpful.'

Windsor, & rush down there in the mornings, & ride, & it seems a
great success. Charles appears to enjoy himself hugely, & so does
Anne. On Sunday afternoon I took them to the Farm. Thank God
for the Pellys!* There are so many wet & dangerous things to avoid.
Having unpacked some of the eggs which had just been carefully
packed, we went into the chicken runs, where Anne found a large
& heavy tin food container hung by a small bit of iron, & swung it
about until it nearly fell on her head. After picking up some eggs the
children rushed ahead into the cow shed, & turned on every tap with
great abandon!

Having scooped Charles down from some tottery straw bales,
which threatened to fall & engulf him at any moment, we then had a
dear little cat hunt by some dogs who I always thought of as quite
nice Corgis and Sealyhams. But not when a cat appears! Ravening
wolves & blood-thirsty tigers aren't in it!

Having extricated the children from among the calves, they
unfortunately saw some farm machines & had to climb up on each
one. Gleaming knives & rusty sharp prongs abounded, and of course
their joy was great when a cart full of manure was found!

They then saw a pram with a baby in it, and it was with the
greatest difficulty that I could persuade them to leave it. They cooed
and patted its hands and leant lovingly & heavily over it!

'Mummy has promised us a baby' I heard Charles saying proudly
to Mr Pelly, as they walked away. Being a sailor, he took the
information quite calmly. Having leant over the pigs, & fed the cows
etc etc etc, we came home – the children fresh as paint, & me? – well,
perhaps well exercised is the word!

But they have been so good, and talk about you & Philip a lot.
'My papa says' etc. The weather has remained very warm & still &
grey, almost too hot for tweeds!

M'as tu vu† is well, & runs again on Saturday at Hurst Park. Peter
[Cazalet] doesn't think he will win, as he has to give Miss Paget's
Shock Tactics a lot of weight. But it will be interesting to see how he
does.

He ran very well at Lingfield, and pulled out a nice little bit of

----

*   Shaw Farm, in Windsor Home Park. Adrian Pelly was the farm manager and his sister
Andrea kept house for him.

†   M'As Tu Vu, a bay gelding foaled in 1946, won six races between 1953 and 1956.

speed after the last fence. It was very exciting, & absolutely extraordinary to see a horse <u>win</u> again!

I have been terribly busy since you left, and seem to have done a great many very boring things!

Fergie* & Betty came for the night last weekend. What a nice person he is, so good & kind to his mother. I am thankful that he is going to stay on in the Scots Guards, and he is blissfully happy too.

[. . .]

I do so hope & pray that you won't get <u>too</u> overtired in N.Z. & Australia. I know the deadly strain all too well – it's the length of it all that kills. If only you can get to bed in good time.

I can't tell you how much I miss you darling, it's awful having nobody to talk to about things – I can talk to Margaret up to a degree, but I see very little of her.

This I am very glad of for her sake, as she has been lunching & dining out a great deal. Even a lunch with Billy Wallace!† I felt quite cheered up.

I will write again very soon, & in the meantime <u>all</u> my love. I think of you so many times a day.

Your very loving Mummy

~

28 December 1953 to Queen Elizabeth II

Sandringham

My Darling Lilibet,

First of all, I want to thank you and Philip for the <u>lovely</u> plates, which will join the others and which have given me <u>great</u> pleasure. They are beautiful & such a wonderful surprise when I found them on my table. It was too angelic of you both darling.

The children all enjoyed Xmas, it passed off without any major colds or rows! There was the usual tense excitement after tea, with Charles & Anne galloping down the passage to the Ballroom, being brought up short at the door by Marrington with his hand on the

---

*   Fergus Bowes Lyon (1928–87), Queen Elizabeth's nephew. He became the seventeenth Earl of Strathmore in 1972; in 1956 he married Mary McCorquodale (1932–).

†   William Euan Wallace (1927–77), a debonair man about town and friend of Princess Margaret.

switch, & then the 'oh's' & 'ah's' & 'isn't it <u>BEAUTIFUL</u>' when the Tree was revealed. They then all rushed at their tables, & settled down very happily to undoing parcels etc. [. . .]

On Xmas we all went to Holy Communion at 8.45, & then all the children came to the 11 Service. Anne behaved like an angel, & the only time her voice rang out was ordering Nanna to 'kneel down properly'. They adored putting a coin in the bag, & then at the end when we all filed out, Charles took up a position at the altar rails & <u>stared</u> at Mr Anderson. He would have stayed there for hours I believe!

In the afternoon we listened to your broadcast which came through remarkably well, and everyone was delighted with it. Then I gave the presents for you [to the staff], there was one excellent moment when Ainslie announced 'Mr Smith, estate blicklayer', which was the signal for hearty laughter & jolly good jokes about blicks!

On Sunday Marina & Eddy & Alexandra & Michael & Olga & Paul & Elizabeth arrived!* So I have had to move into Granny's room, which is very nice & light, but very cold. There is no heating or power points in her rooms. Would you agree to me telling Marrington to fix a radiator & put in power plugs when I move out? One really must have them nowadays, & also a fixed basin in the bathroom. If all these things are done, I think that you will like the rooms, & it will give Philip a sitting room too. I believe that Papa had pipes laid in Granny's rooms all ready for the radiators to go in – she had a thing about heating, as we know to our costs.

It seems very odd to look out of the window and <u>not one</u> pheasant on the lawn! Such a thing can't have happened for many generations.

The horses seem very well – Birdcage Walk, Contango & Rodney are down at Appleton, & the 3 two year olds & Devon Loch are at Wolferton.

By the way darling, I got a large hotel bill for their stay at Wolferton last year, which was a bit of a surprise on the top of pretty big bills for food etc, which naturally is an understood thing. But I wondered whether you knew about the weekly rent down at

---

* Princess Marina of Kent, her children Prince Edward, Princess Alexandra and Prince Michael; Prince Paul of Yugoslavia, his wife Princess Olga and their daughter Princess Elizabeth.

Wolferton, & if it is the usual thing – I had never thought of it I must say! Anyway it's all paid up to now, & of course I want to do the right thing – I just hadn't heard of that one I suppose.

Manicou is looking too glorious for words – he really is a model horse, & has quite recovered his bloom. But no foals I fear! What do you think one ought to do. Isn't it all sad & difficult. Bradly thinks that Devon Loch might get sound.

I thought that I would go over to Newmarket one day, Cecil [Boyd-Rochfort] kindly asked me to go to lunch. I hear that Rohays [his wife] is much better.

The servants' Balls went very well, but of course you & Philip were greatly missed. The one at Windsor was, as usual, the nicest (for me) & I had a waltz with Lord Freyberg* [. . .] which was very exciting as it was the dance when balloons descend from the roof. [. . .]

The children are so well & being very good. This is such a good place for them, and I hope to stay here till the very beginning of February.

Dermot wouldn't send the little Windsor pony, in case it was ruined here, but the Scotts have lent the tiny pony again, so I hope it will be a success.

I did feel so deeply for you over that awful train accident. It complicates everything so much, & in a small country like NZ must make a great impact.†

I follow your journey with such deep interest, & being able to visualise so much is a great help. I remember Fiji & Jamaica so vividly, also Auckland & Rotorua etc.

Lots of love darling, from your very loving Mummy

~

---

* General Bernard Cyril Freyberg, VC, GCMG, KCB, KBE, DSO and three bars (1889–1963), first Baron Freyberg, Governor General and Commander-in-Chief of New Zealand 1946–52, Deputy Constable and Lieutenant Governor of Windsor Castle 1952–63.

† On Christmas Eve 1953, shortly after the Queen and Prince Philip arrived for their official tour of New Zealand, the overnight express from Wellington to Auckland fell off a bridge, killing 151 of the 285 people on board. This was the worst rail accident in New Zealand history.

10 January 1954 to Queen Elizabeth II

Sandringham

My Darling Lilibet

The children are very well. I took them to church this morning, and they went out during the hymn before the sermon. As they got to the end of the pew, & Mabel was opening the door, Anne spotted Mr Anderson advancing up the aisle to lead the Bishop to the pulpit. She bounded up to him, & very politely shook hands & said goodbye! It really was rather delicious, & Mr Anderson, tho' surprised, behaved very well, & bowed politely. The Bishop unfortunately was bowed in prayer, so missed the charming interruption to the service!

Charles has started his lessons with Miss Peebles [governess], & seems to be happy with her. She comes to breakfast & lunch, & seems very nice 'about the house'.

The great game in the evening is dumb crambo. It is a great success, & they adore acting, tho' the rhyming is slightly vague. Something to rhyme with 'stop' – 'pheasant' said Charles triumphantly – that's the way it was played at first, but now they are getting much better at rhyming.

Hugh & Fortune [Grafton]* have been here this week which was very nice, I do so like them both.

I have cut everything down so as to have as few servants as possible, so I hope the expense for you will be quite small. It is quite easy really, & as there is no shooting, no parties. Charles Moore† was here this week, & he & Hugh & Arthur went out several times after woodcock & got some old cocks which Dodd wanted, & enjoyed it tremendously. Do you remember what fun we used to have, beating out the garden & ponds ourselves? There is nothing there this year, tho' I see quite a lot of water hens out of my window!

---

* Hugh Grafton, eleventh Duke of Grafton, KG DL (1919–2011), Chairman and later President of the Society for the Protection of Ancient Buildings and member of other bodies devoted to Britain's heritage. Married 1946 Anne Fortune Smith, Mistress of the Robes to Queen Elizabeth II since 1967. Close friends of Queen Elizabeth, who later accompanied her on happy private trips to France and Italy.

† Captain Charles Moore, CVO, MC, Croix de Guerre (1880–1965), Irish Guards Officer and horse trainer to King George VI and Queen Elizabeth II, 1937–63. The Queen's early successes as a racehorse owner – between 1954 and 1960 she twice headed the list of winning owners – were attributed to his skilful management.

The weather has been very good on the whole, a few days of cold & frost which was a very good thing.

Margaret & I went over to lunch with Cecil on Tuesday, & saw the horses out. Aureole* looked wonderfully well, & seems to have thickened out tremendously. [. . .]

Dear Manicou looks such a picture. I wonder if he would do for someone kind to ride out with horses at Newmarket. Hobbs has Finure of course, & Murless has Red April, but they must be getting on, & perhaps in a year or two they would like a beautiful ride like Manicou. He has got something special, hasn't he darling? I don't know what it is, but even Charles feels it! [. . .]

We miss you so much, and do wish that May wasn't so far away.

We follow your journeys very well by the papers, and some good news reels. How well one knows the procedure, & how monotonous it becomes. But one simply can't think of any other way of letting people see the sovereign, than getting up on a dais & driving round a town. It's really all they want, & with fine weather I am sure that everyone has a good chance of a look. I do hope that you are keeping well, & getting enough sleep. How is Philip – men are sometimes even more exhausted than women – I do trust that he isn't tired. It makes just the whole difference in the world doing things together – one gets such moral support, doesn't one. I find that doing things without Papa nearly kills one – he was so wonderful. And if one had to go off on one's own, there was always the nice feeling of arriving home, & rushing to his room to say 'I'm back', & he was always interested in everything.

I believe that was why he was such a good King, because no detail was too small for him, & he minded what happened to people – Queen Victoria had it very strongly, & I think that you have that gift too. [. . .]

It's rather sad to think of Tommy & Joey & Ulick all gone in a year. [. . .] I am sure that Michael [Adeane] will be a very good successor to Tommy, tho' I suspect that the latter was probably the best private secretary for a hundred years. Don't you think so?

---

* The best colt that ever carried the Queen's colours, he came second in the Derby in 1953, and in 1954 won the Coronation Cup at Epsom and the Hardwicke Stakes and the King George VI & Queen Elizabeth Stakes at Ascot.

With lots of love darling, I don't know if you will ever wade through this letter, from your very loving

Mummy

~

10 March 1954 to Queen Elizabeth II

Clarence House

My Darling Lilibet

Your 'family' letters have been a great success, and I have kept them together so that you can enjoy them in a year or so!

I went to Cheltenham last week – staying with the Spicers, and we had some very good racing. M'as tu vu started off jumping very well, but about half way round he suddenly stopped, and Francis pulled him up.

It was rather disappointing, but I wasn't surprised, as he did not do very well in his last races. Francis* said that he hit a fence rather hard, & then he felt him going lame – so very sensibly pulled up. Peter, I know, likes the horse, but if he doesn't run well at Lingfield I would like to take him out of the National. How disappointing racing can be, but also what fun! There is always hope. And I do like horses!!

Darling, I do hope that you aren't too tired. I remember so well how tired we got in 1927 – one just gets through and yet, thank goodness, one is uplifted & carried on by the wonderful loyalty & affection.

And one feels again, how moving & humble-making, that one can be the vehicle through which this love for country can be expressed. Don't you feel that? When one is exhausted, & maddened by the idiocy of everybody, one is sustained by the feeling that people need a sovereign – it can be a help to know that. [. . .]

Lots of love darling – I will write again soon. I have been desperately busy – from morning to night, and am feeling really fairly well. Considering that life without Papa is a perpetual strain & anguish, I am really quite O.K.

Your very loving

Mummy

~

---

* Richard ('Dick') Francis CBE FRSL (1920–2010), successful jockey and crime writer.

28 March 1954 to Queen Elizabeth II

The Royal Lodge

My Darling Lilibet

It was so lovely talking to you today, and I always wish that I could tell you more interesting things when we talk! But I am so anxious to hear how you & Philip are, & the children so eager to talk, too, & Margaret poised to snatch the receiver, so that I become bemused and forget all the exciting & boring news I have to tell you!

I can hardly <u>believe</u> that you will be home in just over six weeks. I do hope that you will have good weather on the homeward trip, so that you can relax & rest a bit. I believe that you are going to Balmoral shortly after you arrive, that ought to be very agreeable & comforting.

The children seem very well, and I feel sure that Miss Peebles is a success. Do you remember what you felt like at 5 or 6 years old? I think that one doesn't remember enough, and one really felt very deeply about things, and you may find Charles much older in a very endearing way. He is intensely affectionate & loves you & Philip most tenderly – I am sure that he will always be a very loving & enjoyable child to you both.

I have heard of a very good music teacher (tell you when you get home). [. . .]

To change the subject – The Pactolus 2 year old went very lame – Did I tell you? Anyway I got hold of Strong, & he goes down at weekends to treat him. He has a badly wasted muscle behind his shoulder, isn't it sickening – but I do hope that he will become sound again. He is easily my favourite, the most charming and beautiful horse, with a lovely disposition – he really is too nice for words. [. . .]

Wasn't he nice, & wasn't he a B—E.

I feel very anxious about the polio in Western Australia, & shall be very glad when you are all safely out of [reach of] any possible infection. [. . .]

I took Anne to Chapel this morning. She was too angelic, and sang the psalm & hymns in a very penetrating voice, quite tuneless & extremely loud, & reduced everyone to happy laughter. She was absolutely natural, & luckily never looked at Mr Gillingham who was enjoying it all immensely, and she really was too heavenly for words. She is very intelligent, & very sensitive & <u>very</u> funny!

I have been without a Comptroller again! Adam Gordon* came into my room a month ago, & had to suddenly sit down, & said he felt very giddy. I opened the window, & rushed him home to bed, & the doctor found that he had 'vertigo' – that balance in your ear that can go wrong, so that you can't stand up properly. Isn't it sad for him, poor little man. He has gone to the South of France to recover.

Well, darling, I need not say how wonderful I think you & Philip have been, & are – it is a great source of pride & joy to your very very loving
Mummy

~

26 August 1954 to Queen Elizabeth II

Birkhall

My Darling Lilibet

It was so delicious being at dear Balmoral once again, and it worked its usual magic on me, and I felt much calmer and better by the time I had to leave.

You know how much I adore being with you & the children, and without exaggeration, these moments are my only happiness in this curious grey unreal world that I live in without Papa. That sounds rather groaning, but it's true, and therefore those days with you all were so wonderful, and do help to give me courage. It's very funny, that sometimes one feels so <u>frightened</u> – isn't it silly.

So thank you with all my heart darling, for your unfailing sweetness & thoughtfulness; and the darling children are a perpetual joy, so I am very grateful.

With much love to Philip, I was so sad to see him only for a minute, but he looked so well, & I long to hear more of his trip.

Your very loving
Mummy

~

---

* Lord Adam Granville Gordon KCVO MBE (1909–84), a major in the Royal Artillery and mentioned in dispatches during the Second World War. He succeeded Group Captain Peter Townsend as Comptroller and Assistant Private Secretary to the Queen Mother and stayed in the post until 1974.

13 September 1954 to Arthur Penn

Birkhall

My dear Arthur

[. . .] Thank you so <u>very</u> much for your last survey of the financial front. I am so grateful for all the trouble you are taking, & for the thought you have given to the many problems. [. . .]

I don't think that Mey will be very heavy – one must spread it out, and anyway I am praying for that.

So let's hope for the best.

Perhaps an old person will leave me a million, <u>what</u> fun we'd have!

I am so looking forward to seeing you here,

Yours ever,

Elizabeth R

~

26 September 1954 to the Marchioness of Salisbury

The House of the Northern Gate
Dunnet
Caithness

Darling Betty,

I was wafted away on Friday morning, fresh from the delightful sophistication of a Rattigan* evening, straight into the sea & sky atmosphere of far away Caithness. I am writing in a little white room with the sea on three sides of the house, the wind, I am sorry to say, banging & whistling at the windows, the sea & sky blue & wild, and every moment of my delicious evening with you very clear in my mind. I enjoyed it all so <u>very</u> much, and am more touched than I can say by your sweet kindness in taking me to the theatre, and that heavenly dinner, & such nice people, & oh, what a pleasure it all was.

---

* Sir Terence Rattigan (1911–77), successful British playwright. Eclipsed at the end of the 1950s by the rise of younger and less conventional playwrights such as John Osborne and Harold Pinter, he came back into fashion. He was knighted by the Queen Mother in 1971 and wrote to congratulate her on the way she conducted such ceremonies, remarking that for almost everyone receiving honours 'those few proud but nerve-wracking seconds of confrontation represent the high pinnacle of their lives.' He realized she was well aware of this. (5 December 1971, RA QEQM/PRIV/PAL)

Thank you a thousand times, I enjoyed <u>every</u> moment; from seeing
Bobbety's face when he saw the foie gras, the wonderful eternal thrill
of seeing the curtains go up, the excellent brilliant play, Mr Rattigan's
round face, arriving at your lovely house, Mr Foster's enthralling
stories of murder, eating far too much very good food, sitting in your
drawing room after dinner surrounded by those glorious gay flowers,
and the joy of being with you both. Oh, it was fun.

Your loving friend
Elizabeth R

~

In October 1954 the Queen Mother embarked, in the *Queen Elizabeth*,
on a tour of the US and Canada. The main purpose of the trip was the
presentation of funds raised in memory of the King for the training of
young people from the Commonwealth in the USA. In New York she
stayed with the British Permanent Representative to the United
Nations, Sir Pierson Dixon, and his wife, in their official home in
Riverdale. In Washington she stayed at the residence of the British
Ambassador, Sir Roger Makins, and his wife. On her return Winston
Churchill wrote to her saying, 'The maintenance, and continuous
improvement, of friendship between the English-speaking peoples, and
more especially the friendship between these islands and the great
North American democracies, is the safeguard of the future. Your
Majesty has made a notable contribution to this end.'[*]

~

5 November 1954 to Queen Elizabeth II

The White House
Washington

My Darling Lilibet
This is really the first opportunity I have had of putting pen to
paper, as we have been dashing and rushing without stopping, & I
have often sat down & picked up a pen, & then, knock on the door,
can I speak to you for a minute! You know how it is.

I think that New York went off all right. The Dixons were very
kind, & it made all the difference staying with them, tho' it was about

---

[*]   25 November 1954, RA QEQMH/PS/VIS/1954/USA

25 minutes from the city. A very nice house, & how <u>wonderful</u> the American bathroom things are – millions of towels, large, medium, small, tiny, face flannels, in great profusion, and of course taken away at once if you even pick one up!

I find the whole thing a most tremendous effort, & it really is ghastly not having any family to laugh with. I have never been on a trip before alone, & it is hell.

Everybody is <u>so</u> kind, but very foreign – tho' I do like the Americans very much. The main thing I have found that is wrong, is, that I have no equerry. It really is absolutely vital, and I can't tell you how often I have longed for dear Patrick [Plunket].* Will you tell him how much I miss him, not only his work, but himself! Oliver [Harvey, her Private Secretary] is desperately busy coping with programmes & idiotic speeches & things like that, & I never realized how much one depended on someone to arrange & do liaison with all these protocol minded people.

The Pajama Game[†] was <u>wonderful</u> – very good tunes & I wish Margaret had come too.

I went shopping one day which was rather funny. The press came to the first shop, & I kept on meeting Eve Perrick round every counter! At the next one, a surging crowd of excited ladies filled the whole place, & about fifty policemen not only kept them away, but successfully made it impossible to see the goods! We got into a lift, & stopped it half way up & held a conference for about five minutes, Jean & me, 2 secret service people, four N.Y. policemen & the manager! We decided to make a run for it, & as we got out on a top floor, the doors of the <u>other</u> lift opened, & a mad rush of ladies roared out. It was exactly like a Marx brothers film, & I must say terribly funny. We eventually found a haven in a 'Boutique', & the hungry hordes were barred out.

I have <u>never</u> hated anything so much as the two big dinners, Columbia University, & the English Speaking Union. One sits on a

---

* Patrick Plunket, seventh Baron Plunket KCVO (1923–75), equerry to King George VI 1948–52 and to Queen Elizabeth II 1952–75. Deputy Master of the Household 1954–75. His early death from cancer deprived the Queen of one of her most trusted and responsive aides.

† Popular Broadway musical which had opened on 13 May 1954 and ran for over 1,000 performances. It has since become popular among local and amateur groups around the world.

dais, having dinner under a terrible glare of television & film lights, & you know how much I hate eating in public. It really is a nightmare, & they give one gigantic bits of meat, bigger than this sheet of paper, practically raw, & then instead of gravy, they pour a little blood over it. Oh boy (I always think of Margaret).

I had a very nice evening with the Douglases,* & then flew here yesterday. It's all very different to the Roosevelts – terribly protocol, and faintly stiff. The security is fantastic, I have some very nice secret service people – they are just like nannies, & look after one, & look also faintly disapproving or rather loving. I'd like to have one or two to bring home.

Today at lunch, a huge cake arrived, & Mrs Eisenhower said that it had been sent to me, & specially baked, & added, quite naturally, 'of course the secret service men were there to check all the ingredients, & watch every bit of the baking'. Isn't it extraordinary. There are some bad characters about I guess.

Oh, what about Landau? I want to get Charles [Moore] on the telephone & hear about the race – I imagine it was very <u>very</u> heavy.

Darling, how are you – I am looking forward madly to returning home – is Honey all right? I do hope he is quite well. And the darlings.

Your <u>very</u> loving
Mummy
PS Very best love to Philip

~

13 November 1954 to Princess Margaret

Government House
Ottawa

My Darling Margaret,
I thought of you a lot in Virginia. They are so nice. [. . .] I longed for you to be there & hear their Southern drawls. Miiiighty kind, mam, they say, taking longer than you can believe to say 'mighty'. [. . .]

---

* Lewis Douglas (1894–1974), distinguished Democrat politician from Arizona, and his wife Margaret 'Peggy' Zinsser. US Ambassador to Britain 1947–50; he played an important part in the Marshall Plan for the rebuilding of Europe and in the management of the 1948 Berlin airlift. Queen Elizabeth dined with the Douglases in New York.

The Americans were very nice & welcoming, they are very warm hearted, & know our family so well. It's really rather ghastly how much they look to us to lead in family life etc, & they know Charles and Anne better than I do! [. . .] Lots of enquiries after you – the Press were terribly nice about you – the only one of us who hasn't been to US they say rather sadly! [. . .]

Your very loving
Mummy

~

17 January 1955 to Sir Alan Lascelles

Sandringham

My dear Tommy,

Thank you so much for your nice and very amusing letter. I would love to hear Shane Leslie's son lecture on Flying Saucers,* as I adore hearing about the glorious god-like beings that step out and converse so sweetly with strangers. It's such an amusing madness, and has grown to such beautiful proportions, and what is extraordinary too, is the fact that these people from Venus or wherever they come from are so NICE. They are kind & benign and loving, & presumably, good. It's all most encouraging!

Many thanks also for your comments on my possible visit to the Loire. I have always wanted to visit the Chateaux, & it would be so delicious to go to France without any real time-table or set programme. I shall come to you for advice & information if I may. [. . .]

Yours v. sincerely,
Elizabeth R

~

---

*   Sir John Randolph Leslie, third Baronet (1885–1972), Anglo-Irish diplomat and writer, first cousin of Winston Churchill. His son, Desmond, was a Spitfire pilot during the Second World War and co-authored one of the first books on UFOs, *Flying Saucers Have Landed* (1953).

9 September 1955 to Princess Margaret

Birkhall

My Darling Margaret,

I sometimes wonder whether you quite realise how much I hate having to point out the more difficult and occasionally horrid problems which arise when discussing your future.*

It would be so much easier to gloss them over, but I feel such a deep sense of responsibility as your only living parent, and I seem to be the only person who <u>can</u> point them out, and you can imagine what anguish it causes me.

I suppose that every mother wants her child to be happy, and I know what a miserable & worrying time you are having, torn by so many difficult constitutional & moral problems.

I think about it and you all the time, and because I have to talk over the horrid things does not mean that I don't suffer <u>with</u> you, or that one's love is any less.

I have wanted to write this for a long time, as it is a thing which might sound embarrassing if said. Your very loving Mummy

~

11 October 1955 to Princess Margaret

The Castle of Mey

My Darling Margaret

It is so difficult talking of anything personal on the telephone, because one feels that so many people are listening most eagerly.

But I did want to say darling, that I know what a great decision you have to make fairly soon, & to beg you to look at it from every angle, and to be <u>quite</u> sure that you don't marry somebody because

---

* In August 1955 Princess Margaret had her twenty-fifth birthday, the age at which, in theory, she could marry without the consent of the sovereign. The press once again became frantic, if not aggressive, speculating over her intentions, demanding that she make up her mind. She replied to this letter saying: 'Darling Mummie, Your letter did help so much. Thank you for writing it – as you said it's easier to write than say – but please don't think that because I have blown up at intervals when we've discussed the situation, that I didn't <u>know</u> how you felt.' She said that Peter Townsend was coming over from Brussels (where he was Air Attaché at the Embassy) soon so that they could discuss everything. (RA QEQM/PRIV/RF)

you are sorry for them. Marriage is such a momentous step and so intimate, and it is far, far better to be a little cruel & say 'no' to marriage unless you are quite quite sure.

Some people make wonderful friends & confidants, & not such successful husbands and there is so much giving in a happy marriage, & sometimes real sacrifice, & it must be on both sides.

When I said 'sorry' for somebody earlier in the letter, I meant sorry for their devotion & patience, not for them themselves. You know what I mean.

Poor Peter has had a ghastly time, but I am sure that he would agree that a marriage could not be truly happy unless both were prepared to face the extraordinary difficulties of a very difficult situation with clear consciences.

Oh, I do feel for you darling – it is so hard that you should have to go through so much agony of mind.*

Your very loving Mummy

~

29 October 1955 to Rachel Bowes Lyon

Clarence House

Darling Rachel

I can't tell you how much I enjoyed my delicious little visit to you & David.

It came at a moment when I had been dreadfully worried and harassed, and it was wonderful to be able to relax & talk normally for even 24 hours. Thank you, more than I can say, for your kindness, & gentle understanding.

I know that you realise the anguish of all we have been through

---

* For the Princess, the crisis deepened week by week. Anthony Eden, Winston Churchill's successor as Prime Minister, although himself divorced, refused to support her marriage to Townsend. It became clear that if she went ahead, she would have to renounce her royal status. *The Times* denounced the very idea of the marriage. For Princess Margaret, the choice was hard – between her love for Townsend and her devotion to her God, to her sister and to the institution to which her whole family had dedicated itself. She said later that when she met Townsend at Clarence House they had both decided at exactly the same moment that 'It's not possible. It won't do.' (Princess Margaret to Toni Untermeyer, 23 November 1955, Bellaigue Papers) On 31 October 1955 she and Peter Townsend issued a joint statement saying that they had decided against the marriage.

with Margaret, & it was very comforting to be with you & David, and I can never thank you enough.

Your very loving & grateful sister in law
Elizabeth

~

23 January 1956 to Queen Elizabeth II

Clarence House

My Darling Lilibet

I wish that I could tell you how much I loved being with you all at Sandringham, or how touched and enchanted I am by your angelic kindness & thoughtfulness.

The time I spend there at Christmas is a <u>real</u> joy, and gives me so much courage for the rest of the year.

The feeling of being together with you & Philip & the darling children is a wonderful help, and I felt a different person when I left last week. One of the things I love best is when you pop in to my room to say good morning! It is the nicest thing I know, & those sort of moments which I miss so terribly, and one feels soothed & uplifted by such sweetness on the part of one's child! The familiar outings such as getting into the Ford to go shooting, feeding the bantams, walking home from Church, staring at horses, the films, the meals, the servants all make one feel 'belonging' again, and I can never thank you & Philip enough for your heavenly kindness and understanding towards your very very loving

Mummy

PS The race was rather disappointing on Saturday, as at one moment it all looked so hopeful. But it was a wonderful race, & I wish you could have been there.

~

7 February 1956 to Queen Elizabeth II

Clarence House

My Darling Lilibet

I was just sitting down to write to you, when your heavenly letter arrived, for which I thank you a <u>thousand</u> times. It was wonderful hearing your news, and I do feel so deeply for you over the ghastly climate. It must make you feel so exhausted, and I do hope that the heat won't get you down too much.

You are approaching the half way mark which is encouraging – and the visit is being such a marvellous success, tho' I fear at a cost to yourself and Philip. [. . .]

I am 'doing a Granny', and taking them [the children] to see a small Exhibition at the Imperial Institute today. It is about Nigeria,* & I expect that they will be as bored as you & Margaret were when Granny dragged you round museums! I promise they won't be long tho', and it might be well arranged.

Last week was very very cold, & the colder it got, the cooler the central heating here became, & by the time the coldest day for 100 years arrived the heating went off altogether.

When you were gasping in Nigeria, we were trembling with cold here! I heard that Elizabeth Arden was over for a few days, so I saw her, & of course we talked purely horses! I was amused to see in the paper the next day, that when some journalist asked her why she trained with Cecil, she answered, 'Because the Captain is tops – doesn't he train for the Queen' – which seemed an adequate reason!

Margaret & I went to Holy Communion yesterday morning, & we had special prayers for you & a very nice one about Papa.

Well, darling, I fear this is a scrappy and dull letter, especially compared [with] yours which was glowing in colours & interesting items, but it brings you both a very great deal of love, & prayers that you won't get too done in by the heat. I will write again,

from your very very loving

Mummy

Mummy is so easy to write that I sometimes put in too much Mummmmy.

~

---

* The Queen made an official tour of Nigeria, 28 January to 16 February 1956.

28 March 1956 to Peter Cazalet

Clarence House

My dear Peter,

I am sending you this little box as a memento of that terrible &
yet glorious day last Saturday.*

Glorious because of Devon Loch's magnificent performance, &
terrible because of that unprecedented disaster when victory seemed
so sure. I know that you & I will always feel an ache about it all, as
will poor Francis, and the only slight consolation is that Devon Loch
is now the hero of the day!

I feel rather agonized, don't you, but it was a great comfort to be
able to talk it all over with you afterwards, & we must now pray that
such a gallant horse will go on to another great race, perhaps next year.

I looked at the television this evening, & there was a nice picture of
Devon Loch, looking extremely distinguished & splendid! I have had
several letters asking for photographs of 'a great horse', which is quite
touching, and I only hope that he won't be given too much weight.

I am sure that you know how very deeply I feel for you. I am
beginning to learn more of the immense amount of thought & work
that goes into the preparation of a horse for racing, and I can
understand a little of the anguish you must have felt at such a cruel
blow.

Once again, I send my heartfelt sympathy to you & all in the
stable, & we won't be done in by this, & will just keep on trying – for
another day.

Ever yours sincerely,
Elizabeth R

~

* In the 1956 Grand National, Queen Elizabeth's horse Devon Loch, ridden by Dick Francis,
was leading and seemed certain to win until he 'pancaked' in the approach to the finishing
line. It was a terrible moment for owner, trainer and jockey – and for the crowds who had
been cheering the horse on. Queen Elizabeth did not show her disappointment as she
comforted Francis and Cazalet in the enclosure. 'That's racing,' she said. (*The Queen Mother
Remembered*, ed. Hogg and Mortimer, p. 194; Elizabeth Longford, *The Queen Mother*, Weidenfeld
& Nicolson, 1981, p. 149) With this letter she enclosed a silver-gilt box with her crest, inscribed:
'PETER CAZALET IN MEMORY OF DEVON LOCH'S GRAND NATIONAL from Elizabeth
R 1956'.

12 April 1956 to Queen Elizabeth II

The Royal Lodge

My Darling Lilibet

I did so love my week at Windsor, and send millions of thanks for so much sweetness & thought and care for your venerable parent. It is always a wonderful joy to be at Windsor which I love very deeply, and where every corner & object has a memory for me. One knows the pictures so well, and to see & enjoy them again, gives a nice feeling of continuity, and I never tire of admiring the Castle from every angle. But specially it was a treat to be with you & the children, and I loved the outings to Frogmore & the polo, & felt so happy to have the companionship of <u>family</u>, again.

You can't imagine how deadly everything is when one is alone – When one is young one feels that life goes on for ever, & I was utterly happy with Papa & you & Margaret. That is why I feel that it would be so marvellous if you thought of having more children – Charles & Anne will so soon be much older, & it would be so good for them too.

I longed for more children, but somehow everything seemed against us – do give it much thought darling, & forgive me for mentioning it.

With again all my most loving thanks for my heavenly week, always your very loving
Mummy

~

14 October 1956 to Sir D'Arcy Osborne

Invercauld*

My dear D'Arcy,

It was <u>so</u> kind of you to remember to send me that enchanting French book, & I have enjoyed it immensely. Thank you <u>very</u> much. I am so grateful. I <u>do</u> wish you could have been here this week. After the horrid weather, which you sampled, & which went on without interruption for day after day, suddenly unbelievable glory came to

---

* Invercauld Castle, near Balmoral, lent to Queen Elizabeth by the Farquharson family for six weeks while building works were going on at Birkhall.

Deeside. On Monday, the sun came out – the hills turned blue, & the birches became so gold that one can only stare & wonder & be grateful. I have looked & looked & stared all this week, and longed for a friend who would also stare & enjoy. The birches really do look like the fireworks called 'Golden rain', and I don't think that one could see a lovelier sight.

I leave here on Tuesday, for rather horrid London, & shall look forward very much to your arrival at Birkhall next year. Keep a whole week, or ten days – do.

Your affect: friend. ER

~

14 January 1957 to Sir Osbert Sitwell

Sandringham

My dear Sir Osbert,

The delightful book of the lakes of Scotland arrived safely, and I write to thank you most warmly for sending me such a charming present.

It is wonderful to hear that you are writing poetry, and I hope that means you are well & busy as ever.

Do you remember the glorious Poetry readings of past years?

I wish that we could have another some day – it might be very instructive too, as so much has happened since those far off days of ten years ago.

It is being very enjoyable here, & fairly peaceful except for political upsets. I feel so sorry for Anthony Eden,* who has given so much of his life to serving his country, and then when things go a little wrong, he is allowed to go with scarcely one word of thanks from Press & public. He has great courage, & could not be mean or spiteful, and I personally can remember particularly what able & generous support he gave Winston all through the war. So one feels sad for him just now.

---

* Anthony Eden succeeded Churchill as Prime Minister in 1955 and was engulfed in the Suez crisis the following year. President Nasser of Egypt nationalized the Suez Canal; the British and French governments deemed this to be an illegal seizure of a crucial asset and they secretly conspired with Israel to occupy the Canal Zone. President Eisenhower condemned this action and Eden was compelled to withdraw British forces; he resigned in early January 1957. Harold Macmillan succeeded him as Conservative Prime Minister.

I have not seen Hannah lately, but am hoping to attend one of her all male luncheon parties in the Spring! [. . .]

I do hope that we can have a meeting when you return to beautiful England. I suppose it will not be until summer time, but it seems a very long time since we had a talk.

With again my very grateful thanks for the enchanting book,

I am, yours very sincerely,

Elizabeth R

~

28 January 1957 to Queen Elizabeth II

Sandringham

My Darling Lilibet

I wish that I could tell you how much I loved being here with you for such a heavenly long visit. I look forward to it madly as being a time when I can really see you and the darling children in comparative peace, and I am deeply grateful for all your angelic kindness & thoughtfulness towards me. It is so curious that this is the only place where I can find a sort of peace of mind – I suppose it is because every bit is associated with happy memories, and I am quite blissful to [go] out by myself, & visit the horses or look at the marshes. I do wish that you could have had one really quiet week at the end of January [. . .] with nothing to do! But it was difficult, and thank you so very much for letting me stay on for a bit. I am sure I shall build up a good resistance to flu, because it does make one feel so ill for so long, & such a waste of time!

I do hope that you are really feeling better, & it was wretched luck having that attack just before the horrible tooth, and I felt miserable for you. John Griffin [Queen Elizabeth's Press Secretary] survived 2 days, & then retired to bed, & his temp: is 102!!

It has been a wonderful month of happiness darling & I do feel fortunate to have such a kind & loving daughter, and I thank you again a thousand times for such a heavenly time.

Your very loving

Mummy

~

1 July 1957 to Lady Clark

Government House
Salisbury
Rhodesia

My dear Lady Clark,

I have journeyed many thousands of miles since I left lovely Saltwood on Saturday morning, but very vivid in my mind is the picture of your incomparable home, and I shall never forget the beauty and extraordinary atmosphere of the Castle on that glorious June evening.

I do not know how to thank you and Sir Kenneth for all your great kindness and hospitality – it was a most delightful experience staying with you, and I loved every moment of that enchanted night at Saltwood.

From the first thrill of suddenly coming upon the Castle set so splendidly amongst the deep green of the trees, to the wonderful and romantic walls, the perfect cocktail party (everyone nice and no noise!!) the delicious dinner, and the pleasure of seeing such lovely pictures and objects in such a setting – all was exquisite and enjoyable, and I am deeply grateful to you both for such a pleasure.

I really was carried away by the beauty, and set out for Dunkirk* which as an emotional experience I dreaded, greatly heartened and strengthened by my visit. I do like to think of you both living in that heavenly place, making it even more beautiful and to be loved every year – I always 'feel' a place, and Saltwood affected me enormously – It did something to my spirit, a sort of calming and yet elevating effect which was extraordinary, and <u>most</u> comforting!

But above all the great beauty was the kindness and

---

* Queen Elizabeth had made a day trip to Dunkirk to unveil a memorial to the British troops who had been evacuated or killed there in 1940. In order to make an early start across the Channel, she had stayed with Sir Kenneth and Lady Clark at Saltwood Castle, their home near the Kent coast. The stay had been arranged by Arthur Penn, who had written with his customary courtesy to Sir Kenneth on 28 March 1957: 'Her Majesty, as I have said, readily recognizes the domestic difficulties which beset us all nowadays, and that is why she is anxious to make this proposal with diffidence . . . If it would be of the slightest assistance to you it would be quite easy to supplement your staff by sending down a manservant to help with the luggage and meals, and, I have no doubt, a kitchen maid if this would be welcome to Lady Clark, though from what I have heard of your hospitalities I think this may well prove unnecessary . . . Yours sincerely, Arthur Penn'. (Clark Papers)

thoughtfulness of my host and hostess – I was so very touched by such goodness, and I shall always carry with me the happiest memories of such a perfect visit.

With heartfelt thanks, I am,

Yours very sincerely,

Elizabeth R

~

In January 1958, Queen Elizabeth set off on a round-the-world journey – the first member of her family to do so by air. After flying across Canada, she arrived in New Zealand at the start of a five-week tour of that country and Australia.

~

9 February 1958 to Queen Elizabeth II

Government House
Wellington
New Zealand

My Darling Lilibet,

This is really the first opportunity I have had of writing to you, and you will receive a letter written with rather a trembling hand, under a bleary eye! It has been hard going since I arrived here, but the welcome has been very heartfelt I think, & everyone speaks of yours & Philip's visit with great love & feeling. I went to the races yesterday, & when I gave the Cup to old Sir Ernest Davies who had won the race, he roared up to the microphone & said that he wished to present me with Bali H'ai* the winner as a present from all the sports people of New Zealand!! You can imagine my feelings! And at once I thought of you & Margaret saying 'what has Mummy done now', & Charles Moore's face of half 'boo' & half 'ha ha'! Actually he won the St Leger here, & this race was a mile & a half, & he's a gelding, so don't let's worry too soon.

It was terribly hot in the North, & I was still feeling the effects of that horrible flu, but gradually felt better, until today, when I spent an

---

* Bali H'ai, a black gelding, turned out to be an excellent horse, winning several races before becoming lame. He was Queen Elizabeth's first flat runner.

anguished hour in the Cathedral here trying not to fall down! My
head started to go round just like it did in London before I left, & my
knees trembled so much that the service paper rattled & rustled! It
was really an agony, & the first time in my life that such a thing has
happened to me – I know that it is only the result of that horrid
disease we got at Sandringham, & I pray that it will die down again.
[. . .]

Darling, I hope that all goes well, & I hope that I shall be able to
revive & do my bit in Australia.

Your v. loving
Mummy

~

18 February 1958 to Queen Elizabeth II

Government House
Canberra

My Darling Lilibet

I feel that I have written you such scrappy & flu-ridden letters so
far, & today I hope to send you a better one! At the moment I am
free of that foul disease, so life is looking up, and my three days here
have been a positive rest after the mad rush of N.Z.

It is lovely to be in such a nice house, & looking out on such a
lovely view. Did you not find it restful?

The welcome in N.Z. was deeply touching. I do think it
wonderful to find such burning loyalty nowadays, and what a mental
rest to find serious, well written newspapers. One had forgotten how
vulgar ours have become, & it was quite a shock to return here to the
headliny, gossipy, untruthful kind of writing. They are rather more on
the American pattern here, aren't they. So far they are quite polite, &
go on the old old stories of how tired I am, & how much my feet
hurt, & how tired the staff is, & how I <u>must</u> dye my hair otherwise
how could it still be dark etc. etc.!! Quite harmless, & quite funny
sometimes. Dennis Mitchell* really is [a] splendid person. He has had
a very great deal of work with all this incessant flying, & keeps

---

* Group Captain (later Air Commodore Sir) Dennis Mitchell (1918–2001). During this tour
he took the place of Mouse Fielden, Captain of the Queen's Flight. He succeeded Fielden in
that post in 1962.

everyone happy. I thought I would tell you this in <u>case</u> you see
Mouse [Fielden].

Mr Macmillan had a tremendous success here. They all loved him,
& Dorothy, and I am sure that his tour & his speeches & his
friendliness have done immense good. The first time a P.M. has done
this sort of thing I imagine. [. . .]

Dr Evatt* came to see me yesterday, & gave me a picture – You
know how he & Mr Menzies† loathe each other, & Mr Menzies gave
me a very good traditional Australian painting, so Dr Evatt cunningly
outdid with an excitingly modern one!

They are so political here, aren't they? I must fly darling
(literally!), & will write again soon.

A very great deal of love from
your loving
Mummy

~

18 February 1958 to Cecil Boyd-Rochfort

Government House
Canberra

My dear Cecil,

The other day in New Zealand, I presented a Gold Cup to the
owner of the horse that won it, & in return he presented me with the
horse! I was rather taken aback, but as it was done in public, there
was nothing to do about it!

I wondered whether you would be very kind, & take the horse
for anyway a little time, & see what you think of him? I feel that the
owner, a rich old man of 86 [Sir Ernest Davies], will be very
disappointed if he doesn't go to a stable, and of course the eyes of all
the racing people in NZ are on him.

He won their St Leger, & this Gold Cup of a mile and a half, I

---

* Herbert Vere Evatt QC KStJ (1894–1965), Australian politician and lawyer, President of the
United Nations General Assembly, 1948–9.

† Sir Robert Gordon Menzies, KT, AK, CH, QC (1894–1978) Australian politician, Prime
Minister, passionate Anglophile and monarchist. He first became Prime Minister in 1939, and
ensured that Australia was a close wartime ally of Britain. By the time he retired in 1966 he
had served 18 years in the post, longer than anyone else.

think. I do hope that you will have room for him, & if he is not good enough, off to Peter Cazalet, I suppose!

I am, yours very sincerely

Elizabeth R

~

22 February 1958 to Princess Margaret

Government House
Sydney

My Darling Margaret,

I was so delighted to get your delicious letter, so full of news, and of interesting things. I am thrilled to hear about the Epstein.* I do admire his work, & was wondering for a long time whether he would be a good person to do Papa's tomb in St George's [Chapel]. If he could do something grand & yet loving, I am sure it would fit into that lovely place. What do you think, having sat to him?

I have been hurtling about as usual & was very glad to be in my dear Queensland. [. . .]

[I have been] staying on a station called Coochin Coochin with three glorious maiden ladies called the Miss Bells. They were heaven, rather over excited, & never drew breath and they had some very beautiful nephews, all called Bill. The real country Australian is really a knock out. Very tall, with long legs encased in tight trousers, blue eyes, a drawl, & a Stetson – they are too charming for words, & the American cowboy is a mere nothing compared. [. . .] I am thinking of you at Fairlawne, & hope that you found the dear beautiful unsuccessful horses well. The trouble is that they look so well in the stable, & perform so poorly on the racecourse.

So looking forward to seeing you again my darling. Only about 2½ weeks, & you will clasp a mottled, beady eyed mother in your arms once again. Tiny red eyes, & hideous sunburn!

Your very loving Mummy

~

---

* Princess Margaret was sitting to the sculptor Sir Jacob Epstein for a portrait bust and wrote enthusiastically to her mother: 'he is *so* nice [. . .] and has old, strong workman hands with very thick fingers with which he delicately places tiny worms of clay on the head. It was fascinating seeing him build it up from nothing. I don't care if it's awful, it's such fun going.' (12 February 1958, RA QEQM/PRIV/RF) Although Epstein was approached about the King's tomb, in the end Queen Elizabeth chose to have a chantry chapel built at St George's Chapel instead of a traditional tomb with an effigy.

1 March 1958 to Queen Elizabeth II

Government House
Melbourne

My Darling Lilibet

I was so enchanted to get your letter today, giving me the news I have been pining for, and it was so interesting, & so full of really pithy steeplechasing gossip that I felt quite close to it all again!

I also got a telegram saying that Opalescent had hurt his fetlock. I do hope that it isn't serious, & I hear that you quite rightly sent him to Miss Wilmot. It would be a bitter blow if he didn't come back, because I have always had nice dreams about him, & tho' those things are silly, they <u>are</u> fun.

I have just had a very enjoyable day's racing at Flemington, with an objection to the Queen Elizabeth Cup. It was rather sad, as the winner Sailor's Guide was a very popular Victorian horse, & there was a roar when he won. Then a huge groan for an objection, and an agonized wait of 10 minutes. The second (who objected) was owned by a Sydney bookmaker, so you can imagine the tension! Then the objection was overruled & another roar went up! I think that you saw this race, & didn't Mr Underwood win it?

I got up early this morning, & went to see Landau. He looks very well, & has got some very nice foals I believe.

I am just hanging on, but this tour is just a little bit too much, as they literally haven't left a minute for breathing. Luckily the weather here is lovely, and one feels revived.

I went to Tasmania for lunch yesterday. That's the form! It was a gloriously crazy day, & I haven't laughed so much for years! First of all, we arrived in a howling gale, which is always faintly funny.

Sir Ronald Cross had an A.D.C. from the Grenadiers who was having ghastly trouble with a huge bearskin, & I thought he had gone mad when he conducted me firmly to the <u>back</u> of the Guard of Honour. I had visions of inspecting their backs, when on a word of command, they revolved, & we faced each other bravely. Then on arrival at their house, there was drawn up a lot of Army nurses to inspect. As I started down the line, a particularly vicious blast took <u>all</u> their hats off, & being round & flat, they rolled away like little bicycles!

Then the public address system broke down when I was making

my very boring speech, & then we had a mad chauffeur who obediently slowed down on approaching a group of people, and then accelerated violently when passing them, so all the poor things saw was a pair of white shoes, as I was thrown back against the seat & my feet shot into the air. Let us hope that they thought they saw little white hands waving.

Darling, when I wrote about the English papers, I was only remembering that they never put in anything that the family does, & I only mind for the Australians. Because they give one such a tremendous and loyal welcome here, and don't understand when our papers are not interested. I don't care a damn about <u>myself</u>, as I'm sure you know, but I do think that from prestige & all that, it is very sad the 'looking in' of our very bad Press. They don't look out at all.

[. . .]

Will you arrange about the train on the Wed. for Cheltenham? I shall be so cold, & so mottled in the face I expect, that I shall lean on you for plans. Tiny red eyes, sunk into a sunburnt, wrinkled face, a reddish nose & quite deaf. That will be your dear little mother. 'Good on yer, Mum' – 'Come back soon' – How nice they are & how wonderfully loyal. I have been deeply touched by their very true feelings of love, & <u>amazed</u> at their enthusiastic reception.

Longing to see you darling Lilibet, from your very loving Mummy

Shall we meet Monday evening? I don't want to be alone for dinner.*

~

3 June 1958 to Sir D'Arcy Osborne

Clarence House

My dear D'Arcy,

This is to ask you a VERY IMPORTANT question. WHEN ARE YOU COMING HOME?

---

* Queen Elizabeth's flight back to London was eventful. The Qantas Super Constellation developed engine trouble in Mauritius and again in both Uganda and Malta. She arrived home sixty-eight hours late. When the Qantas manager in London apologized, she reassured him, 'It could have happened to anyone. I feel very sorry for the crew; they all worked so hard.' (Laird, *Queen Elizabeth The Queen Mother*, p. 337)

Is it to be in July, or are you going to do the same as last year and come later on?

I do hope that you will be able to face the rigours of Birkhall once again. Your stick is awaiting you in the hall, & when I left it yesterday, it was hanging out of the stand with such a beseeching look on its handle-face, obviously longing for the firm but tender clasp of the Osborne fingers.

If you come in July, I shall be at Sandringham from the 26th for about ten days, do come too.

I have just been to Birkhall for ten days' fishing. The first weekend it rained solidly for 2 days & the river roared & was unfishable. Then I caught a flu germ, & had to stay in for three days when the weather was lovely & the river perfect. Then when I was well again, it started to rain & the river roared & became unfishable, & then I had to come back to London! Wasn't it sad?

Do you think that poor honourable General de Gaulle will be able to galvanise the French into combining a little for the sake of France?* I do hope so.

I am so glad that the new apartment is such a success. I am sure that you have made it lovely, & I long to see it.

Ever your affectionate friend,
Elizabeth R

~

5 June 1958 to Cecil Boyd-Rochfort

Clarence House

My dear Cecil,

Thank you so much for giving me details of poor Bali H'ai's setback.

It was kind of you to write so fully, and it is indeed sad that we shall not see this summer how he measures up to our English horses.

---

* Queen Elizabeth had loved France since childhood and had admired de Gaulle ever since meeting him when he led the Free French Forces in England during the German occupation of France. In April 1960 de Gaulle made a state visit to London and the Queen Mother stood on the balcony of Clarence House to watch his carriage drive up the Mall to Buckingham Palace. As the carriage drew opposite the house, it paused and the General rose to salute her.

When, in January 1963, de Gaulle magisterially said 'Non!' to Britain's application to join the European Economic Community (as it then was), Queen Elizabeth was not outraged. Her sympathies were with the Commonwealth and with individual European countries, not with a bureaucratic institution.

I have felt so much for you over all your anxieties & dramas connected to the Derby. It really was <u>cruel</u> Alcide going wrong like that, and certainly Miner's Lamp had very little luck in the race.

Those weeks before must have been most trying, and I did feel for you very deeply. Horses are the nicest thing in the world, but they do manage to give one headaches occasionally!

I hope that your evening with Mr Guggenheim* went off all right – I thought he was so nice & modest, & sporting to take these long trips to see his horse run.

I am, Yours very sincerely,
Elizabeth R

~

24 July 1958 to Princess Margaret [in Canada]

Clarence House

My darling Margaret,

I have a feeling that Canada gives one a boost – even with very hard work – do you agree? They are so nice, & so loving, and the Mounties are so beautiful & so romantic. It all helps. [. . .]

I gave a cocktail party for 200 Bishops from overseas – by the time that 8 o'clock came, they were in cracking form! They tucked into all the canapés & tossed down martini after martini, especially the Americans who I am sure had been entertained on warm sherry for weeks before!

Lilibet seems really better at last – it has been a horribly obstinate germ, I do hope that it is now dead. [. . .]

Your very loving
Mummy

~

30 January 1959 to Sir D'Arcy Osborne

Clarence House

My dear D'Arcy,

I can't believe that at last I am coming to Rome! It really is too exciting, and I am looking forward to it all so much. It is the first time

---

* Harry Guggenheim (1890–1971), American businessman, philanthropist and fellow racing enthusiast.

in my life that I am to visit a place just for pleasure, and I hope it all works out. I think that Margaret will probably come with me, but that is not settled, so nothing to be said at the moment. I shall love to come to luncheon with you, and place myself in your hands as to plans – and of course I will visit the school for orphans – that is one thing I am determined to do.

As to your luncheon party. All your suggestions sound delectable, but I rather favour your American friends the Laurence Roberts. What fun it will be (at last) to see you in Rome, & in your own house – oh I do hope it all comes off.

Already I am inundated with anxious letters from low Protestants in this country over my projected visit to the Pope.* I wish that one could convey to these people (who are simple & good) that if one goes to Rome, the Pope, being a Sovereign, must be visited out of politeness if nothing else. There is great ignorance & fear still about the R. Catholic religion – possibly because they are so well organised.

D'Arcy, I was so grieved to hear about your brother [who had just died]. The links with one's childhood are so precious, & so comforting, & one hates them to be broken. I <u>am</u> so sorry.

Please do discuss with the Ambassador about my visit. I am sure that you know the sort of things I would like to see, & the sort of things I ought to see!

Oh to be in Rome when April's <u>here</u>!

Your affec friend,

Elizabeth R

~

In early 1959 Queen Elizabeth made an official tour of Kenya and Uganda – the first time she had visited East Africa since her safari with the Duke of York in 1924–5. Much of colonial Africa was experiencing what Harold Macmillan later called 'the winds of change'. Ghana was the first British colony to win its independence, in 1957, and it was followed by Nigeria, Sierra Leone, Tanganyika (Tanzania), Uganda,

---

* Queen Elizabeth received 112 letters from members of the public concerned that she was to visit the Pope during her trip to Rome. This unofficial visit took place, with Princess Margaret, in April 1959; she did have an audience with Pope John XXIII and she unveiled a monument to Lord Byron in the Borghese Gardens.

Kenya, Nyasaland (Malawi) and Northern Rhodesia (Zambia) through the 1960s. All became members of the British Commonwealth, an organization which, throughout her reign, Queen Elizabeth II has tended assiduously. She later said that its growth marked 'the transformation of the Crown from an emblem of dominion into a symbol of free and voluntary association. In all history this has no precedent.'

The British government considered cancelling the Queen Mother's 1959 trip because of the unrest; in the event she was received with courtesy and enthusiasm.

~

21 February 1959 to Princess Margaret

Government House
Entebbe
Uganda

My Darling Margaret

I have been so rushing about that I haven't had time to write any letters except a scribble to Lilibet, but I have thought of you every day, and now at last I have a <u>whole</u> morning! So I will quickly start before someone comes in to ask questions!

Kenya was very crowded as to programme, but goodness, what a <u>beautiful</u> country it is! The cool air in the evenings revives one after grilling in the sun in the wrong sort of clothes, and the people were so welcoming & loyal.

It was so annoying at Mombasa – <u>terrific</u> heat, and when I went to the Arab quarter for welcomes & speeches, each Sheik who came to be presented, looked gravely at my flushed & streaming face, & red eyes (v. small too) and said 'We <u>DID</u> so love having <u>Princess Margaret</u> here – I <u>do</u> hope she comes again soon, soon'. And then on to the Women's thing, where the Indian ladies looked at my crumpled dress, & said 'Oh we <u>did</u> love having <u>Princess Margaret</u> here, she was wonderful', & the English ladies said 'It was marvellous having Princess Margaret', & the Goan ladies said etc etc!

And as for the Commissioner there, he spoke of nothing but you & the visit, & the visit & you & you, and as he was saying it, I thought of how you would be amused.

But they <u>did</u> love having you darling as you can guess.

I had a lizard in my room all night, & it hung over my bed looking at me with bulging eyes. I felt quite embarrassed.

I came here on Wednesday, & had a busy day in Kampala yesterday, with 3 speeches, & a degree giving in my Chancellor's robes in <u>great</u> heat, & ending up with a Tattoo at night, which was so gloriously English that it was almost funny.

The K.A.R. [King's African Rifles] doing marvellous drill, & re-enacting a battle in Burma, splendid massed bands, all African, except for a very white conductor, wonderful African dancing, & then quite suddenly a skirl of the pipes, & out came 8 Scottish dancers looking <u>exactly</u> like they do in the forecourt at Holyrood, the ladies in white dresses & plaids, and the men in beautiful kilts, & they danced an intricate & pretty reel. [. . .]

On Thursday I lunched with the Kabaka, & before lunch we went into a room filled with people, & he introduced me round them all. My brother Andrew, my brother Frederick, my brother Henry, my brother Frank, my brother John, my brother Michael, my brother George, my brother Mark, my brother Peter, my brother – oh breathless it was. I think that there were 19 of them. [. . .]

Betty & Bobbety [Salisbury] have suddenly turned up here, as their aeroplane has something wrong with it, & they are here for a few hours. I must rush & see them. Goodbye my darling, from your
 Very loving
 Mummy
 PS I do hope that the French play is a good one!

~

14 April 1959 to Cecil Boyd-Rochfort

Clarence House

My dear Cecil,

Thank you so much for your letter about Bali H'ai. I am glad to hear that he is doing well and hope very much to be able to see him run – I shall be in Rome on April 25th, but might be able to get to Chester on May 7th. Anyway I will have a good try! It is, unfortunately, the week of the Shah of Persia's visit, so a bit complicated.

It was splendid Parthia winning his race – what an exciting & rather agonising time of year this is!

All the hopes & some of the fears loom up, & the future is so
unknown, but most thrilling,

I am, Yours v sincerely

Elizabeth R

~

12 October 1959 to Peter Cazalet

The Castle of Mey

My dear Peter,

Thank you so much for your letter about the horses. [. . .] I am
only here for a weekend to make some arrangements in the house
before the winter sets in. It is still warm, and the sea in front of the
house is full of seals. They lie about on the rocks, looking very
benevolent, and rather like people one knows. They really are
charming.

I do hope that you will have a successful Cheltenham and I
greatly look forward to this winter's racing.

I am, Yours very sincerely,

Elizabeth R

~

23 March 1960 to the Marquess of Salisbury

Clarence House

My dear Bobbety

How kind of you to ask me to dine on June 28th. I would love to
come, and shall look forward greatly to seeing you & Betty again.

So much has happened since I saw you last, & apart from political
& world affairs, the nicest has been my daughter Margaret's
engagement!* She is so serenely happy, & he is very nice.

---

* Princess Margaret had fallen in love with Antony Armstrong-Jones, a young, attractive and
rather Bohemian society photographer. In August 1959 the Princess wrote to him from Balmoral,
'You've made me happy. Are you pleased? I am . . . I left London tremendously NOT in
turmoil' (14 August 1959, Snowdon Papers). On her birthday, 21 August 1959, she waited in
her room at Balmoral to take his call and wrote to tell him how happy she now was. 'Dare
one say that word . . . I'm afraid of stating it' (22 August 1959, Snowdon Papers). Their
engagement was announced, to widespread astonishment, in February 1960 and their marriage
took place in Westminster Abbey on 6 May that year. They became the Earl and Countess of

Oh, & the Baby!* He is also <u>very</u> nice!
Ever yours,
Elizabeth R

~

7 May 1960 to the Duke of Edinburgh

Clarence House

Darling Philip,

I do want to send you one line of warm & grateful thanks for your kindness and understanding to Margaret on her wedding day.

It was such a comfort to me, to see you bringing her up the aisle, for it does matter so much on that great day in one's life, to lean on the arm of a strong & loving person.

I do thank you with all my heart, & also for being so sweet to her during the last years. It must have helped her a lot, for I think she felt terribly lost when her father died.

Bless you – your loving m-in-l, E

~

22 May 1960 to Princess Margaret

Government House
Lusaka
Northern Rhodesia

My Darling Margaret

After the tremendous bustle and noise and hoorays & beauty of your wedding day, you suddenly disappeared, and I feel that I haven't seen you since you were about 9 years old! I long to hear a little news of your life in the yacht, & I do hope that it has been a wonderful time for you both. I do think that the wedding was perfect, and I

Snowdon. From honeymoon in the Royal Yacht *Britannia*, Princess Margaret wrote to her mother to thank her 'for being so absolutely heavenly all the time we were engaged, you were so encouraging and angelic and it is something that is difficult to express on paper because it is really thanking you for being you' (16 May 1960, RA QEQM/PRIV/RF).

The Snowdons had two children, David and Sarah. Sadly, the marriage, which began in great happiness, ended in divorce in 1978.

* Prince Andrew Albert Christian Edward, the Queen's third child, was born on 19 February 1960.

have had such charming and touching letters from so many people, saying how glorious it all was.

I felt that it was a <u>real</u> wedding service, holy & beautiful, and you looked heavenly darling.

I am so longing to see you again, and what I want you to know is, that until you have a country house of your own, I hope that you will always come to Royal Lodge when you want to.

Don't ask me, just say you are coming, and I hope it will be <u>often</u>.

How uncomfortable Government Houses are! Tiny bath towels, no lights to dress by, & board-like sheets! But great kindness, & one mustn't be beastly.

I have had the usual gruelling tour, and so far it has gone happily. It is a wonderful country, & the people love it so much.

I went to Barotseland, which is quite delightful. Everyone falls on their knees when they see one – not grovelling but enormously natural & polite.

No roads, and a vast plain, which every year is inundated by the mighty Zambesi, too beautiful for words, because the water is just going down now, & the tall grass is growing through the water, & this endless vista of shimmer & light is really fascinating.

The old Paramount Chief is a good ruler, & nobody can approach him except on their knees! I think we might introduce this at Clarence House, it might be an excellent idea!

The only bother about Africa is that one can get malaria and typhoid and smallpox and cholera and bilharzia (nasty) and yellow fever and black fever & I expect pink fever & blue fever & GREY fever (bad) and beige fever (the worst), & huge animals knock on one's door, & great beasts fly in at the window, and all the time at Royal Lodge the garden is quiet & lovely, & the azaleas are out.

Ah well, Livingstone & Rhodes made it alright.

Darling, lots of love to you both, & please write me a small letter saying that you are happy & that all is blissful.

Your very loving
Mummy

~

25 August 1960 to Queen Elizabeth II

Birkhall

My Darling Lilibet

I simply loved my short but perfect visit to Balmoral, and sank happily into the dearly loved atmosphere of well remembered smells of stone & stocks, & children's feet running by, & that delectable baby [Prince Andrew], & the door opening & you staggering into my room with that heavenly creature in your arms, & the Moderator [of the General Assembly of the Church of Scotland], & the picnics & the card games & the cinema, & <u>especially</u> being with my children.

That is always the real treat, & the time went far too quickly. Thank you so very much darling, & Philip also, for all your sweetness & kindness to me. Do tell Philip that if he finds that too much grouse driving to get through becomes burdensome, I would gladly take Slioch off your hands. It works very well with Corndavon, & wouldn't affect any of the other shooting on Gairnshiel, & would save anyway one day, or two. It is rather trying having a very great deal of shooting, & leaves too little time for stalking & fishing & climbing about looking for birds! Anyway, you & he can remember this, <u>in case</u> you wish to be relieved of some ground. Of course I would pay a rent too!

Thank you again darlings for my lovely visit,

from your very loving

Mummy

~

17 February 1961 to Queen Elizabeth II*

Clarence House

My Darling Lilibet

I am just going off to Royal Lodge, & taking Charles back for his last 2 days of convalescence. [. . .]

He seems to have recovered from the measles – he had it pretty badly, and if he gets mumps (which he might), it might be better to snatch him back to have it with Anne!

---

* The Queen was on an official tour in India.

She, poor darling, has had a temp: of 99 for over a week, & I did ring up Dr Sheldon to try & make him <u>do</u> something about it, and he is, at last, going to give her some medicine. She seems quite well in herself, except for a cough, & I rather think that she is very 'thick' in her throat, & that there is the trouble.

Feb 19th. It was wonderful having a talk yesterday, & very reassuring to hear your voice & hear that you were surviving. Today, I took Charles up to London, & we attended the BIRTHDAY PARTY of Andrew! We left here, on a glorious English Feb: day – hot sun, blue sky, no wind, & joined the agonizing queue of cars for London. [. . .]

When we got up to the nursery, there was Andrew looking absolutely angelic, Anne Tennant's son looking slightly red & angry, & Christa's* baby looking very brown & exhausted. We sat down to a glorious nursery tea, except for a sweet little girl, who I <u>think</u> is Christa's, except that she doesn't speak much English, who refused to sit at the table, & crouched by Andrew's pen, & spurned any effort to give her food or drink. This <u>devastated</u> the Nannies (3), but they took it very well, & bright conversation at the table, took minds off such a dreadful affair!

The conversation consisted of,

Wah! Eeeeeeee! Ungh! (from Andrew) – accompanied by a beaming smile, & banging on his chair –

Boolah, boolah boolah, belooo belooo thump (Tennant)

Grrrrrrrrrr, & again grrrrrr (young Christa)

The noise was terrific, & everyone enjoyed themselves very much. The cake was cut, with great difficulty, by Andrew, & the proceedings ended by me escaping at about 5.30, & arriving back here just as darkness was falling, & having to take the dogs for a tiny walk in the dark!

I am not sure, but I think that the darling English are going mad. That they can sit about, led by Lord Russell, & hope to achieve anything except making England a laughing stock, is very sad, and I can only hope that if <u>too</u> many people are <u>too</u> silly, that the dear

---

* Christina, Princess of Hesse (1933–2011), daughter of Prince Christoph of Hesse and Sophie, Princess of Greece and Denmark (the youngest of the Duke of Edinburgh's four sisters). She married Prince Andrej of Yugoslavia in 1956 and they had two children, Maria Tatiana (b.1957) and Christopher (b.1960), the little girl and the baby mentioned in this letter.

English will once again pull themselves together, and realize what is happening.*

I have not given you much news of the steeplechasing, because it has all been so depressing. I didn't want Peter [Cazalet] to run Double Star the other day, because he ran badly the time before, & I am sure he gets bored with racing. [. . .]

I also sometimes wonder whether I ought to give up my racing – yet it is the only thing that I enjoy (not quite true!). On the other hand it is not nearly so much fun now that you & Margaret never race† – perhaps someday things will look up, so one mustn't despair.

I think that it is wonderful what you & Philip have done in India – I have always felt, that the glorious influence of Queen Victoria and the British Army, & the supreme I.C.S. [Indian Civil Service] have laid such a foundation of trust & good government, that even politicians cannot break something as good.

Everyone has been ill here – I have survived so far, but have not been feeling very gay – I rather think that I have missed my usual dose of flu, it certainly gives one a rest, & a respite!

With all my love, & I think of you so many times during the day, & my goodness, such prayers at night!

Your very loving

Mummy

PS I am terribly sorry that there are so many blots – the nib is a bit uncertain.

~

7 April 1961 to Miss Penn

The Royal Lodge

My dear Miss Penn,

When I went to my sitting room at Clarence House yesterday and saw the lovely clock‡ on the table, I instantly thought, that is just

---

* The Campaign for Nuclear Disarmament (CND) was formed in 1958 with Bertrand Russell, third Earl Russell (1872–1970), philosopher, historian and activist, as its President. In 1960 he created a splinter group, the Committee of 100, which favoured more direct action. In 1961 he was arrested while leading a sit-down demonstration.

† In fact, the Queen did continue to race, but only on the flat. Queen Elizabeth always concentrated on steeplechasing.

‡ A Sheraton bracket clock, c. 1780, from the collection of H. H. Mulliner.

what Arthur* would like, and when I read your letter, and realized that he wanted <u>me</u> to have it, I found a tear was falling.

I am so deeply touched by his thought of me & I shall always treasure the clock. I have tried, once or twice, to write to you, to try & tell you how eternally grateful I shall always be to Arthur for his wonderful support & unselfish & devoted service to me & my family.

He was such a great and wise person, and that he is no longer there, with his balance & right advice on all the many problems that assail one, is a terrible loss. Clarence House is certainly not the same place without him, & he is continually missed by all my Household & all the servants.

He was so marvellous in always making himself available to listen to their troubles & perplexities, & the wonderful mixture of fun & understanding of human nature with which he solved their problems, always sent them away happy.

For myself, to be able to have Arthur for wise counsel in so many difficult situations, & to be able to share the pleasure of beautiful things, & to laugh was something which has meant more to me than I can ever say, both in happy days and sad days.

If we all miss him so much, I cannot bear to think what the loss must mean to you.

I do feel for you so much and for Eric and Prue† who love him too.

How wonderful to have lived a life such as Arthur lived, spreading gaiety & kindness around you, & goodness & courage as well. He was a great example in how to live on this earth.

I am <u>so</u> glad to have the clock, & when I look at it I shall think of his exquisite taste & knowledge, & be so thankful for his long friendship.

I am, Yours very sincerely,
Elizabeth R

~

---

* Arthur Penn, Queen Elizabeth's friend since her early years, adviser since her marriage, and Treasurer until he died on 31 December 1960. This letter was to his sister Marjorie Penn.

† Lieutenant Colonel Sir Eric Penn (1916–93), Comptroller Lord Chamberlain's Office, 1960–82, and his wife Prue, née Stewart-Wilson (1926–), later an extra lady in waiting to Queen Elizabeth.

23 May 1961 to Queen Elizabeth II

Birkhall

My Darling Lilibet

You remember that I told you yesterday that Bali H'ai had run so badly in the Yorkshire Cup, well, I heard from Cecil this morning saying that he had a very small knot just above the near hind joint (the same leg as before, only higher) and he sounded doubtful if he would be sound again. It's very sad, as he ran so well at Kempton. I shall have to try & get another N.Z. horse!

My goodness, racing can be disappointing – you've had your fill too.

It is so lovely up here – so green & so brilliant in light, and I do think that it is a real holiday. I like it, because I can get away from ladies in waiting (however nice!) for the whole day, & with luck, only have an evening meal together!

I have been thinking such a lot about Charles – I suppose that he will be taking his entrance exam for Eton soon – I do hope that he passes, because it might be the ideal school for one of his character & temperament. Also, however good Gordonstoun* is, it is miles & miles away, & he might as well be at school abroad. Also, all your friends' sons are at Eton, & it is so important to be able to grow up with people you will be with later in life. And so nice, & so important when boys are growing up, that you & Philip can see him during school days, & keep him in touch with what is happening – he would be terribly cut off & lonely up in the far North.

I am sure that it must be a worry to Philip & you, because one loves one's old school, but if he can get into Eton it would solve many difficulties, one being religion. It's always a tricky one with the heir to the Throne, & one would not be involved in any controversies in a staunchly protestant place like Eton Chapel!

I do hope you don't mind my writing my thoughts on this subject, but I have been thinking & worrying about it all (possibly without cause).

---

* Prince Philip believed that Eton was too close to Windsor and to London and that Prince Charles would be harassed by the media there. (The age of the paparazzi had just begun.) Knowing also how much Prince Charles loved Scotland, Prince Philip argued that he should attend his old school, Gordonstoun in Morayshire. Prince Philip's view won the day.

With a great deal of love,
from your very loving
Mummy

~

20 June 1961 to Sir D'Arcy Osborne

Clarence House

My dear D'Arcy,

How kind of you to write about my broken bone.* It is a great bore because one cannot get a shoe on, & therefore I cannot hop round hospital wards, shipyards, universities, garden parties, picture galleries, boys' schools, girls' schools, race meetings, agricultural shows, civic centres, slum clearances, horse shows, regimental reviews, and all my usual treats!

I am <u>so</u> looking forward to seeing you in July. If you are arriving on the 28th, I shall be at Sandringham then, and would love it if you could come down for the weekend. It is a very easy journey, & you could have a peaceful 2 days, sitting in the garden (if fine) or in the house (if wet). Do think about it.

I was so pleased to get your letter about the Queen's visit to Rome, and so glad it all passed off so happily. I was delighted to know that she paid you a visit and I read about it in one of the papers here, who said that 'on leaving the house of her old friend she called out "Goodbye darling".' I suppose that some ever eager journalistic ears heard her say 'Goodbye D'Arcy'!!

I have had a very busy six months – there seems to be more to do than ever, & I look forward to the clear cold beauty & peace of Scotland. Will you be coming to Birkhall? Oh do.

With so many thanks for your letter,
Ever yours,
Elizabeth R

~

---

* In the diary kept by the lady in waiting on duty, Lady Jean Rankin recorded that after dinner at Windsor, following the Garter celebrations, Queen Elizabeth fell and hurt her foot on the way to bed. An X-ray the next day showed that the big toe on the left foot was broken. (RA QEQMH/DIARY/1961:12,13 June)

20 August 1961 to Cecil Boyd-Rochfort

Balmoral Castle

My dear Cecil,

Thank you so much for your letter.

I greatly enjoyed my short visit to Freemason Lodge & thought that both the horses looked so well. If dear old Bali H'ai doesn't stand training, I am sure that the best thing is to send him back to Sir Ernest, don't you? He would arrange a de luxe journey for him, & he would sink into a petted old age in New Zealand. I suppose that leg would never stand hurdling now? He would be too strong for any lady that I know, unless it was an amateur Miss Pat Smythe!* [. . .]

The grouse are very bad up here – & the river rather empty of fish!

I am, yours v sincerely
Elizabeth R

~

19 September 1961 to Queen Elizabeth II

Birkhall

My Darling Lilibet

I do want to thank you for all your thoughtful kindness over the funeral, & the journey down & back, & your understanding during those sad days.†

Darling David was so truly devoted to you, he really loved you, & would have done anything for you. He was one of the few people in the world who would tell one the truth about people or things, & if it was unpalatable, he said it so nicely that one didn't mind. It is like a light going out in one's life, we have always been so close, I knew what he was thinking even.

I have had such wonderful letters from all kinds of people –

---

* Pat Smythe (1928–96), one of Britain's top female show jumpers and a popular figure.

† David Bowes Lyon, the Queen Mother's youngest and closest brother, the other of their mother's 'Two Benjamins', died of a heart attack while staying with his sister at Birkhall, on 13 September 1961. The Queen knew how much her mother would miss him and did everything she could to cherish her in the days that followed. His widow Rachel continued to live at St Paul's Walden and it was then taken on by their son Simon and his wife Caroline. The Queen Mother stayed with the family there at least once a year.

nobody could have had more real friends, & one feels that his life must have been greatly shortened by the unending help he gave so freely to others.

Anyway darling, it made <u>all</u> the difference that you came, not only to me, but to poor Rachel as well – thank you for <u>everything</u> from your v. loving

Mummy

~

20 September 1961 to Graham Sutherland

Birkhall

My dear Mr Sutherland,*

I have just been reading your letter to Ralph Anstruther, & feel that I must write you one line to say that I absolutely understand about the portrait.

When I was sitting to you in my ancient white hat (I did so enjoy the sittings), I wondered whether you would find the sort of portrait that the University wanted rather difficult to achieve, and if you do find time to finish the small work, I would be very thrilled to see it. [. . .]

~

10 November 1961 to Queen Elizabeth II

Clarence House

My Darling Lilibet

I have been thinking so much of you all yesterday & today, & hope that you are not already exhausted by parades & gatherings

---

* Graham Sutherland OM (1903–80), British artist of many talents, was commissioned by London University to paint a portrait of its Chancellor, the Queen Mother. He suggested she wear a feathered hat and they had seven sittings in early 1961. He produced a lively, sympathetic sketch which she liked and hung in Clarence House. But he then decided that he would not be able to produce a portrait that the University approved and so withdrew from the project. In 1961 he was completing a massive tapestry, *Christ in Glory*, for the new Coventry Cathedral, which replaced the original church bombed in the war. In place of Sutherland, London University commissioned a portrait of Queen Elizabeth by Pietro Annigoni. Her letter to Sutherland is an unfinished draft found among her papers and may not have been sent.

& Mr N[krumah]! I am sure that you were right to go, & really if one listened to all the faint hearts, one would never go anywhere.*

Perhaps you would like to hear a little local news. When I got into my carriage at Paddington yesterday morning, Peter Cazalet was already there, & as we settled into our seats (including Charles) he told me that a strange thing had happened at Fairlawne, the day before. (He being safely at Newbury.)

A large chauffeur driven car arrived, in it a very pretty girl, very well dressed, who said that she had come from M. Boussac who was sending some horses over to Peter, & that Peter had said that she could look round the stables. Poor Jim (the head lad) naturally believed this & took her round the horses, and the fascinating thing is, that apparently she is the important member of a dope gang. Isn't it extraordinary? Poor Peter was in a great stew, & all the horses have had to be changed from box to box. [. . .]

Isn't it extraordinary that it could be so important nowadays to nobble a steeplechaser? I thought that you would be amused & interested by this little tale of what goes on nowadays.

Peter was in a stew about Laffy, who runs at Cheltenham tomorrow, & on his running at Newbury will probably be a hot favourite. He has been changed round!

Rather a dull day's racing yesterday – Young Rajah ran with credit behind Saffron Tartan, & some real cracks, but I did not really enjoy it. I think that I was so tired from all the worries of last week!

Charles is coming up on Sunday for lunch, & then I will take him down to R. Lodge & break the journey with tea (& eggs!). Darling, I do hope that all goes well, & I think & pray for you both all the time.

Your very loving
Mummy

~

---

* In November 1961, the Queen visited Ghana. The British government and the United States were concerned lest its first President, Kwame Nkrumah (1909–72), tilt too far towards the Soviet Union; the Queen's visit was to be a gesture of British and thus Western goodwill. There had been unrest in the country before her departure and consideration was given to cancelling her trip. She insisted on going and the visit was a great success.

13 February 1962 to Sir D'Arcy Osborne

Clarence House

My dear D'Arcy,

I <u>am</u> so sorry to learn from your letter which has just arrived, how poorly you have been feeling. I send you very much sympathy, for there is nothing so dispiriting as to climb back to health after 'a turn'.

Everyone expects to get well at once, but it takes quite a time, & I do hope that you will soon feel really better.

If you eventually reach Lausanne, perhaps the wonderful doctors there will re-organize you completely, & I shall hope to see you here in July completely restored!

I am so delighted that your picture show was such a marvellous success. Thank you very much for sending me the catalogue, & I do congratulate you with all my heart.

The world staggers on, from one crisis to another, but I have a feeling that human beings are beginning to become accustomed to these rather bogus upheavals, & take them more philosophically than the slightly hysterical reporters & newscasters!

I do hope that you will soon be better,

Ever your affect: friend

Elizabeth R

~

1 August 1962 to Rachel Bowes Lyon

Clarence House

My Darling Rachel

I have started several times to <u>try</u> and tell you how deeply I felt for you when I spent that lovely weekend at St Paul's Walden, & have torn up all my attempts to say what I feel – they were <u>inadequate</u>.

Your courage & faith are so wonderful, & how proud David would be of you. To carry on, as you do, to perpetuate his love of Pauly, & his understanding of people, & the important things of life, is a splendid effort, & the whole dear place is <u>alive</u> with David's spirit.

I can never tell you how deeply grateful I am for your understanding of my close feeling for David. Life is very bleak without him, but I cannot bear to think of what <u>you</u> must be going through. He has left something so <u>strong</u>, hasn't he – perhaps that is really the point of human life & living, to give, & to create new goodness all the time.

I love to think of beloved Paul's Walden still being a centre of all these good things, & that is purely your doing.

Bless you darling Rachel for your giving & loving spirit – ever your devoted Elizabeth

~

7 February 1963 to Sir D'Arcy Osborne

Clarence House

My dear D'Arcy,

Your perfectly heavenly picture of Birkhall is giving me the <u>greatest</u> pleasure, and I do want to thank you with all my heart for giving me something so <u>very</u> nice.

Dear Birkhall, with the little river running by, & the great metropolis of Ballater looking glamorous in the distance – I hope that you will come again this year. [. . .]

D'Arcy, one or two of your old & loving friends have sent a small sum to your banking account in Rome, in case it might come in handy some time. They hope you won't mind, it is just to show their true affection. [. . .]

Ever yours,
Elizabeth R

~

27 October 1963 to Cecil Beaton

Clarence House

My dear Mr Beaton

It was so kind of you to send me a copy of your wonderful book of portraits of my family, and I do want to thank you for giving me such a charming present, I find it very nostalgic looking through the pages. The years telescope, & I suddenly remembered what I felt like when I wore those pre-war garden party clothes – all those years ago.

It is absolutely fascinating to look back, and I feel that, as a family,

34. The Queen, the Duke of Edinburgh, Queen Elizabeth and Princess Margaret, Coronation Day, 2 June 1953.

35. Queen Elizabeth with the jockey Dick Francis in 1956, the year he rode her horse Devon Loch in the National.

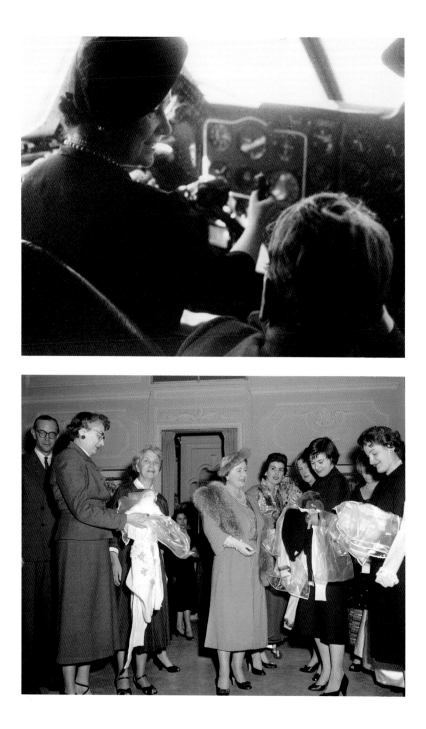

36. At the controls of a Comet, 1952.

37. Queen Elizabeth at Saks 5th Avenue, November 1954.

38. On tour in Bulawayo, July 1957.

39. On tour in Canada, June 1962.

40. With veterans of the Boer War at
the Royal Hospital, Chelsea, 1966.

41. Attending a reception for the London
Scottish Regiment, of which Queen Elizabeth
was Honorary Colonel, April 1967.

42. As Chancellor of
the University of London,
at the Students Union
Commemoration Ball,
February 1970.

43. With Prince Charles and John Elphinstone on Cordavon in the early 1970s.

44. At Birkhall with the Queen and Princess Margaret at Gairnshiel picnic lodge.

November 2nd 1977

My dear Sir Frederick

I do want to send you a line of very warmest Congratulations and hoorays on your receiving the O.M.

Everyone is delighted, & when one thinks of your glorious Ballets, and when you have put our English ballet — on a pinnacle,

one is full of gratitude — and so thrilled that your genius has been acknowledged in this way.

I am, ever yours Elizabeth R

45. A letter of congratulation to the choreographer Sir Frederick Ashton, who had been a close friend for many years.

46. Queen Elizabeth with her horse, Special Cargo, which had just won the Whitbread Gold Cup at Sandown Park, April 1984.

47. Queen Elizabeth enjoying a pint of bitter that she had pulled herself during a visit to The Queen's Head in Stepney, July 1987.

48. Queen Elizabeth with her friend Dick Wilkins, a leading City figure of the 1960s and '70s.

49. Queen Elizabeth with her nephew Simon Bowes Lyon and his wife Caroline watching the village parade at St Paul's Walden in honour of her ninetieth birthday.

50. One of Queen Elizabeth's last public engagements, in November 2001, at a reception marking the reformation of 600 Squadron, Royal Auxiliary Airforce, of which she was Honorary Air Commodore.

we must be deeply grateful to you for producing us, as really quite nice & _real_ people!

The photographs are so lovely, and the whole book marvellously produced. I am sure that it will give pleasure to a great many people, & to no-one more than,

Yours gratefully,
Elizabeth R

~

27 December 1963 to the Duke of Leeds

Sandringham

My dear D'Arcy,

How _very_ kind of you to give me such a lovely book for Christmas. I am thrilled with the beautiful [Augustus] John drawings & pictures, they are so exquisitely reproduced, & the book is giving me immense pleasure. I do want to thank you with all my heart for remembering me in this delectable way.

I do hope that all is going well with your extremely complicated Duchess life – I am sure that you are being wildly generous to them all, & I only hope that there will be something left for you, when you have finished with lawyers etc.

Will you be able to come over a little earlier than usual next year?

I wonder too, if you are going to take your seat in the House of Lords – what a lot of interesting extras are attached to a Dukedom!* We are a big family party here, some dear children & everyone getting on with each other!

With again my heartfelt thanks for the splendid book,
Ever your affec: friend
Elizabeth R

~

---

* D'Arcy Osborne unexpectedly became Duke of Leeds in 1963. A bachelor, he had no heir and the title died with him on 20 March 1964. Queen Elizabeth's letters to him were returned to her after his death by his cousin Robin Campbell, who told her that Osborne had had a stroke on 16 November 1963 and never fully recovered consciousness. In his final months, he was cherished by devoted friends, including his housekeeper Giuseppina, who had been with him some twenty years. (QEQMH/GEN/1964/LEEDS)

31 December 1963 to Sir Osbert Sitwell

Sandringham

My dear Sir Osbert,

I am so delighted to have the programme of Rossini's La Gazza Ladra, and am so touched by your giving me such a charming Christmas present. The occasion must have been a very gala performance, with such a well bound book of the words, and the golden watered silk inside is so gay and lovely . . .

I do hope that you are really better?

It would be so nice to meet again, & when I return to London I shall try & find out whether you would care for a little visit.

I am going to Australia and New Zealand at the beginning of February, & return the end of March.

It is curious that fate takes me continually to Canada, Australia and N. Zealand, & tho' I love the people, there are so many other places that I long to see.

I have never been to Spain, & only a few places in Italy, & so hardly anywhere in France, & time is getting short!

I spent a few days in Touraine in the spring, & saw some lovely places. Most of the owners suffering as we are, from lack of money, too much taxation & few servants, & most of the houses are open to the public.

At one divine house where I lunched, do you know who my host's true English hero was?

The Duke of Bedford! How he packs 'em in.*

With again all my thanks, ever yours very sincerely

Elizabeth R

~

---

* Woburn Abbey, the ancestral home of the Russell family and the Dukes of Bedford. Heavy death duties were imposed after the death of the twelfth Duke in 1953, and his son decided that in order to restore and keep the house he would have to open it to the public. Woburn was one of the first great houses to become a popular tourist attraction.

11 February 1964 to the Prince of Wales*

Sister Agnes

My Darling Charles,

I can't tell you how touched & delighted I was to receive your beautiful flowers, and I thought it was wonderful for you to arrange it so far away at Gordonstoun.

This is the first letter that I have written since the operation,† & that is why there is a funny little O by the date, which was me trying to get my pen to work!!

Anyway, thank you darling, simply a thousand times for the flowers, & also for your dear letter. [. . .]

I believe that the stitches are coming out today, & I am feeling much better, so hope to be home before too long. I remember the agony you went through when laughing too much at Hattie Jacques,‡ it really <u>does</u> hurt!

Mummy brought Andrew to see me yesterday. He brought me a sweet little bunch of snowdrops that he had picked himself, & in return I gave him a bunch of freesias in a nice basket, which he went away clutching happily.

David§ came on Saturday. He sat on my bed & ate the grapes that he'd brought me! Quite right!

This is a very nice place, with charming nurses, but it's very noisy. Last night the boiler got on fire at 2 am, & half the fire engines in London arrived to put it out. Greatly enjoyed by all!

I was terribly distressed at having to put off my tour, as so many people had worked so hard & so long to arrange it, but these things happen & so suddenly, & I must try & go some other time.

I <u>do</u> wish that the door would open, & that <u>you</u> would be there!

---

* Prince Charles had been created Prince of Wales, the title traditionally conferred on the monarch's eldest son, in July 1958.

† The Queen Mother had been admitted to King Edward VII's Hospital for Officers, commonly called 'Sister Agnes' after its founder and first matron Agnes Keyser, for an emergency appendectomy. This meant that, to her disappointment, she had to cancel a long-arranged trip to Australia and New Zealand.

‡ Hattie Jacques (1922–80), popular English comedy actress who starred in *ITMA*, *Hancock's Half Hour* and fourteen *Carry On* films.

§ David Armstrong-Jones, Viscount Linley (1961–), son of Princess Margaret and Lord Snowdon.

But with any luck, you will be coming when Mummy has the baby,*
& I shall look forward <u>so</u> much to seeing you then.

With lots of love & <u>most</u> loving thanks for the flowers & letter,
from your devoted

Granny

~

19 February 1964 to the Duke of Edinburgh

Clarence House

Darling Philip,

I was so touched to get your charming letter, and thank you most
gratefully for your sympathy & good wishes. It was really quite an
enjoyable experience (after the first 2 or 3 days) to be in Sister Agnes.

I felt just as if I was in a ship, my room was exactly like a rather
small cabin, and one felt agreeably isolated from the madding world.
Except that one night the boilers got on fire, & every fire engine and
every fireman in London converged on the hospital. I narrowly
escaped being pushed out of the window, but fortunately the fire was
put out before I had to be 'saved'.

It was rather an agony having to put off my tour in NZ and
Australia. You know the amount of work & planning that goes on for
so many months beforehand, and I really felt miserable to have to let
so many people down – including the yacht.

However, there was nothing to be done about it, & perhaps lucky
not to have got ill in the aeroplane!

Much love, your devoted Mama,

Elizabeth

~

20 February 1964 to Cecil Beaton

Clarence House

My dear Mr Beaton

It was so kind of you to send me such lovely flowers & such a

---

* The baby that the Queen was expecting was her fourth and last child, Prince Edward
Antony Richard Louis, born on 10 March 1964.

charming letter, and I really am most deeply touched to be
remembered in this way.

The freesias are here in my room, looking so cool & so beautiful,
and are giving me very real pleasure. It is very nice to be home again,
but after the first day or two in Sister Agnes', I began to enjoy being
tucked away in a small cabin. One felt gloriously isolated, with
endless time to think, & only the <u>very</u> nicest people to peer in for a
<u>few</u> minutes. It was a truly enjoyable experience, apart from the fact
that kind people sent me modern novels to read, and they were so
loathsome, & so perfectly horrible, that I felt quite sick with distaste.

I think that we must be living through a moment of bad taste in
many forms of art, & I hope that the English will revolt soon.

With again many thanks for your most kind thought.

I am,

Yours very sincerely,

Elizabeth R

~

28 March 1964 to Princess Margaret

HMY *Britannia*, Trinidad*

My darling Margaret

[. . .] I always have very bad luck with the drinks! Perhaps because
I am considered a frail invalid, I am always given delicious fruit drinks
with so little alcohol that one feels quite sick! Then I ask timidly if
I might have just a <u>very</u> little gin in it, & then too much is put in,
& I have to ask for a little more ice to stop my throat being burnt, &
so it goes on! This usually at Government Houses, I may say! [. . .]

Your very loving

Mummy

~

---

* After her operation, the Queen Mother took a two-week cruise in *Britannia* in the Caribbean
to convalesce.

16 August 1964 to Princess Margaret

The Castle of Mey

My Darling Margaret

Thank you so <u>very</u> much for sending me that delightful &
amusing group [photograph] of the christening.* Everyone looks very
happy, & tho' I look a little pale & definitely exotic in my Kenyatta
hat, I think I give a touch of oriental splendour to the otherwise
impeccably dressed ladies. Groups are such fun, and I study this one
with enormous pleasure.

I <u>long</u> to hear how you are getting on, where you are staying &
what you do all day. I do hope it's being fun, and real relaxation, &
very warm. Here, the weather has been grey & misty & still, until
today when there is an easterly gale raging, & horizontal rain. It's
really quite agreeable sitting in a warm little room & hearing the
weather crashing at the Castle, until one has to take the dogs out!

The days go by very quietly here, so there is very little to tell you.
If one goes out exploring in the car, one usually finds some lovely
view, or some tremendous clifflike rocks by the sea, or a dear little
house which I long to buy & do up!

I want to put a 'cap' on a turret on top of the tower, and do ask
Tony if fibre glass is strong enough to withstand gales of wind & rain?
[A drawing of a tower follows, with four floors marked 'my sitting
room, my bedroom, Olivia's† room, Suckling's‡ room'.] And with the
exquisite architectural drawing I will bring this interesting &
informative letter to a close, & remain

Your very very loving Mother, Mummy

~

---

* The christening in Buckingham Palace of Lady Sarah Armstrong-Jones, later Chatto
(1964–), daughter of Princess Margaret and the Earl of Snowdon.

† The Hon. Mrs John Mulholland DCVO (1902–84), daughter of first Viscount Harcourt.
Lady in waiting to Queen Elizabeth 1950–84.

‡ Gwendoline Suckling (1905–90), Queen Elizabeth's dresser 1952–72.

11 January 1965 to Mrs Leone Poignand Hall

Clarence House

Dear Mrs Poignand Hall

Thank you so much for your kind letter giving me details of dear Miss Poignand's last days.* I am so thankful that her last hours were so peaceful, and that she was able to talk to you that last Saturday. I shall always be deeply grateful for the wonderful & affectionate loyalty she showed to me & to my family. She shared our joys & sorrows to the full, & I have nothing but happy & loving thoughts in my mind when I think of her through the years that have gone. And how we used to laugh too! That was a delightful side of her character.

It is very sad to feel that such an old friend has gone, but I am thankful that she is now at peace.

I am, Yours very sincerely,

Elizabeth R

~

29 June 1965 to Noël Coward

Clarence House

Dear Mr Coward,

Thank you so much for the charming photographs – they bring back vividly many delightful memories of that heavenly luncheon party in Jamaica, and I am so pleased to have them.

I enjoyed it so much – seeing your delicious house with that spectacular view, the splendid food, and those enchanting guests made it all utterly enjoyable, and a delicious moment of relaxation.

It was the nicest bit of my visit to Jamaica and I can quite see what a wonderful and inspiring place it must be to work in – I hope so much to see you when you come to England. [. . .] Could you not come down to Sandringham for the night of Tuesday July 20th – when a famous Russian cellist (I can't spell him) is playing in one of

---

* Beryl Poignand, Elizabeth Bowes Lyon's governess, confidante and friend during the First World War and after, died in January 1965. Queen Elizabeth had kept in touch with her always and had helped arrange her nursing-home care. She last visited her in December 1964. After her death, her family returned all Queen Elizabeth's letters to Clarence House – they were later sent to the archive at Glamis.

our lovely old Churches? It would be such fun to see you and to show you dear Edwardian Sandringham.*

I am, Yours very sincerely,
Elizabeth R

~

26 February 1966 to the Prince of Wales

The Royal Lodge

My Darling Charles,

I was so delighted to get your lovely long letter [written from Timbertop, part of Geelong Grammar, Australia] – It was so descriptive, and gave me such a vivid impression of your very varied journey. Some of it sounded great fun!

I do hope that life at Timbertop is agreeable, & not <u>too</u> much like school. I hope that you will be able to nip over and see me at Canberra – is this arranged yet? It will be such a joy to see you, and I shall be able, I hope, to give you all the latest news of home.†

At the moment I am rather isolated from the family. Because Mummy and Papa are in the Caribbean, Uncle Harry and Aunt Alice are in Jamaica, William is in Nigeria,‡ Margot and Tony leave on Monday for Hong Kong – <u>you</u> are in Australia, & only a few children and poor dear old Granny are left to carry on!! We shall do our best!

---

* Queen Elizabeth had admired Coward since first seeing *Cavalcade* in 1931. More recently she had enjoyed spending weekends with him at Fairlawne, the home of Peter and Zara Cazalet, where Coward would always entertain the guests, with his songs and his wit. On a visit to Jamaica in early 1965 to receive the first honorary degree awarded by the University of the West Indies, she went to an enjoyable lunch at his home, Firefly Hill. When she invited him to Sandringham to hear the Russian cellist Mstislav Rostropovich, Coward asked her if he should brush up his Russian. 'It is limited at the moment to "How do you do?", "Shut Up you Pig", and "She has a White Blouse". But I am eager to improve' (RA QEQM/PRIV/PAL). She mourned his death in 1973, and in March 1984 she unveiled a memorial to him in Westminster Abbey.

† In March 1966 the Queen Mother made the trip to Australia and New Zealand which her appendectomy had delayed in 1964. She had an enthusiastic reception throughout both countries. The trip was enhanced for her by the fact that Prince Charles, on leave from Gordonstoun, was studying for two terms at Timbertop, the rural outpost of Geelong Grammar School in Victoria. They met in Canberra and together they visited the Snowy Mountains hydro-electric project in New South Wales.

‡ The Duke and Duchess of Gloucester and Prince William of Gloucester.

Life goes on here in the same old way, and I have been doing the Investitures for Mummy, & occasionally going racing, & signing documents, & having quite a time with darling little Busy Bee – the puppy Mummy gave me. She is angelic, and very clever and <u>very</u> naughty!

Today Andrew and Edward and Mabel [Anderson] came down from London to have tea. We spent some crippling time in the little Welsh house, & I am still slightly bent. Andrew dug up quite a lot of the garden, and Edward was just angelic.

It looks as if we are to have another election. Rather an agony, but I suppose Mr Wilson feels he has a very small majority.*

On the other hand the socialist government have already done quite a lot of legislation, so one hopes they won't plunge into too much more. There are already so many rules, regulations & taxes that one feels the people are rather over burdened.

It has apparently been <u>very</u> cold at Balmoral, so let us hope that those wily old grouse won't start making their nests too early this year. Wouldn't it be wonderful to have a really good year once again?

Pearl† is in the seventh heaven because he got a 20 pounder on the first day of this season. A wonderful start.

This month has really been terribly wet – nothing but endless driving rain, & the whole country is waterlogged.

Darling Charles, I do hope that you can get a good look at Australia. They are such splendid people – all the best of the qualities of the English are theirs, & there is nothing better in the world.

I can't tell you how much I look forward to seeing you next month, & with much love, ever your devoted, idiotic, supine, sentimental, vacillating, keenonfishingandshootingandallthosedelight-fulthings and very loving

Granny

~

---

* Harold Wilson, Baron Wilson of Rievaulx KG OBE FRS FSS PC (1916–95), Labour politician and Prime Minister, won the 1964 general election with a majority of four seats. In May 1966 he called another election and won a ninety-six-seat majority.

† James Pearl, keeper at Birkhall, 1949–76.

10 April 1966 to Peter Cazalet

HMY *Britannia*

My dear Peter,

What a disastrous season for horse tragedies! I am so sorry to hear of the latest victims, and one begins to wonder whether horses are becoming more brittle, for they seem to break down with great regularity. I do feel for you, because it is so depressing for the stable. I only hope that they are mendable tendons – it is too sad about Bel Ambre. He looked such a strong young horse & I hope that he will become sound for next year.

I got the Australian broadcasting people to put on the Grand National for me, and nearly went mad when I heard that Kapeno was going easily up with the leaders & also nearly died when that foul Beechers did him in – I wonder if he remembered it, I believe they do sometimes. You really have had bad luck this year, isn't it strange how when things begin to go wrong, it almost seems catching. [. . .]

I had a very hectic & hard working time in South Australia where I went racing & saw the big race (2 miles) won by a splendid gelding from New Zealand! [. . .]

Then on to West Australia where I stopped at a place called Esperance where it was 110 of heat! It's a fine country, & bursting with optimism & plans for the future. Very nice people too.

Then on to Canberra, where Charles, my grandson, joined me, and we spent two days in the Snowy Mountains, looking at the vast network of dams & power houses, until we nearly went mad!

Then I flew on here, & joined the yacht, which is a wonderful relief, & tonight we sail for New Zealand. About the only letters I have had so far is one from you saying that Bel Ambre had broken down, & one from Cecil [Boyd-Rochfort] saying that Charlot had sprained his near force suspensory, & that the vet had put on antiphlogistine & the whole leg blew up! Much too hot, I suppose, & burnt the poor fellow!

So I haven't got any very happy thoughts for the moment!! But NEXT YEAR!

I do hope your flu is better.

Love to Zara, ever yours,

Elizabeth R

~

21 April 1966 to the Earl of Snowdon

Wannaka Hotel
New Zealand

Dearest Tony,

I have just seen your Indian pictures in the magazine* and do want to send you one line to say how beautiful they are. It is a tremendous feat to condense such a vast tapestry into one article and I found the whole thing entrancing. How you survived those three weeks, I don't know! The colours must be divine in India. I thought the picture of the man spinning silks with a bicycle wheel had such lovely pinks and reds and apricots, and the Gauguin-like backs of the holy men of Benares fascinating.

This is a very beautiful place of great mountains and lakes and rivers but by now I am rather longing to get home and hear those yelling dogs, and play with the grandchildren and burn with rage at politics!

Much love from your exhausted mother in law,

Elizabeth

PS I was photographed in a river, wearing supremely unbecoming clothes, by 35 photographers. Pure hell.

~

9 May 1966 to Brigadier Sir Bernard Fergusson

Clarence House

My dear Bernard†

I really can't believe that after all the discussions & plans and postponements & flying journeys that I have actually BEEN to New Zealand! That this wonderful visit eventually came off, is a source of great joy to me, and I can never thank you & Laura sufficiently for all your kindness & thoughtfulness and immense help in every way.

It was all such fun too, and tho' naturally one got a bit tired

---

* After his marriage to Princess Margaret, Lord Snowdon had resumed his photographic career with great success. He had just published a pictorial essay on India in the *Sunday Times Magazine*.

† Bernard Edward Fergusson, Baron Ballantrae of Auchairne and the Bay of Islands KT GCMG DSO OBE (1911–80), soldier, military historian and the last British-born Governor General of New Zealand. Married to Laura Grenfell (1920–79).

sometimes there was always something interesting & invigorating to
restore one to normality.

I have so many delightful memories. Nearly being swept away by
that rapidly rising river, the agony of Anzac Day, the glorious beauty
of Wanaka, that dear old lady toppling on to me clutching her glass
of gin & tonic, that old man who was just going to tell me why he
thought that the Duke of Windsor would never ascend the throne
(you <u>must</u> find out some day!), that unforgettable scene of Laura &
Frances* in their tiaras, & swathed in the chef's cooking apron,
preparing eggs in the galley, the touching farewell from the Britannia,
& dozens more amusing & moving memories.

The love & loyalty of the N.Z. people is something I shall always
treasure – long may it be part of their philosophy of life. [. . .]

This is a lovely moment to return to England. The cherries are
bowed down with blossom, & the birches & chestnuts a most tender
green. The azaleas are coming out, and one falls in love with Spring
all over again.

With again my warmest thanks for helping to make my visit such
a supremely happy & memorable one, & with my love to Laura,

I am, Yours very sincerely,

Elizabeth R

~

10 July 1966 to the Prince of Wales

The Royal Lodge

My Darling Charles,

I am writing to you just before going to Chapel. I shall walk over
in a few minutes, & will meet Mummy & I hope Andrew driving up
a little fast (a little late!) & go into that familiar smell, & listen to the
canticles sung rather badly with Ernest Pearce's soaring tenor
dominating the singing, & it will all be much the same.† (I hope!)

---

* Dame Frances Campbell-Preston DCVO (1918–), Laura Fergusson's sister. Lady in waiting
to Queen Elizabeth 1965–2002. Kind, witty and outspoken, she later wrote an autobiography
in which she described Queen Elizabeth's household with affection as a pre-1939 'world of
butlers, chefs, housekeepers, housemaids, pages and footmen in smart uniforms, kitchen maids,
chauffeurs and gardeners.' (*The Rich Spoils of Time*, Dame Frances Campbell-Preston (with
Hugo Vickers), Dovecote Press, 2006, pp. 268–311)

† Ernest Pearce, the wounded soldier whom she had met at Glamis in 1915, was still working
as a gardener at Royal Lodge.

I do wish that you could be there too. It seems <u>such</u> a long time since you have been away, and I miss you so much.

Thank you a thousand times for your fascinating letter about New Guinea and Queensland – it all sounded deeply interesting & great fun too. What a chance to see places & people under such agreeable circumstances.

I am just back from Chapel. It <u>was</u> just the same! Only Papa was there too, as he hadn't got to go to Cowdray until later. Mr Ward gave everyone absolute stick for not going often enough to Holy Communion – everyone looked, & felt, rather sheepish!

When I got back from N Z in May I went up to Birkhall for a week's fishing. Alas, there were no fish in the river – The water was high & cold, & the fish simply wouldn't leave the lower water. They were catching quite a lot below. Fishing about 6 hours a day I managed to get <u>2</u>!! Poor Pearl was very sad, and as for Brown,* he hadn't even <u>one</u>! It really was slightly depressing but there were one to two nice days, & I love being by the Dee anyway so was quite happy. [. . .]

The hills were still covered with snow, so I couldn't extract much grouse news from Macintosh, but the rumour is 'fair to middling'.

I have had a very busy summer, & been to Northern Ireland & Yorkshire & Wales & Scotland, & endless things around London, so am looking forward to bonnie Scotland in August.

I shall hope to go to Balmoral for a couple of days on the 18th – I <u>do</u> hope that you will be there by then.

I had a pretty strenuous tour in New Zealand, and the fishing was a failure! One nice little river was rising so rapidly that I nearly got marooned in the middle of it. There were huge trout swimming about literally under my feet, & I was reduced to taking the line in my fingers and dangling the fly over their noses! They took not the slightest notice, but I did hook a fine big fish later but the fly had been so badly tied that it broke at once – very disappointing.

Mummy is looking very well and very pretty – I am sure she is longing to see you again.

Goodbye, darling, from your very loving, Granny

~

---

* Robert Urquhart Brown, ghillie at Balmoral since 1932.

15 August 1966 to Benjamin Britten

The Castle of Mey

Dear Mr Britten,

I am so delighted to have the record of Curlew River, and Ruth [Fermoy] and I have listened to it with such real pleasure.

It sounds so lovely in this silent place, where only the sea & the gulls & the wind are to be heard, and I am deeply grateful to you for sending me such a charming gift.

I did so enjoy the Burning Fiery Furnace, and it was an added pleasure to hear it in your company. It is so beautiful and so moving. I long to hear it (and see it) again.

With my warm thanks for giving me such a lovely record,

I am, Yours very sincerely

Elizabeth R

~

15 December 1966 to the Prince of Wales

Sister Agnes*

My Darling Charles,

I cannot tell you how touched I was to get your marvellous pink roses, and then your sweet letter.

Thank you a thousand times – the roses are too lovely and scenting my room, and I am so very grateful for your thought of me.

It would be wonderful if you had five minutes to nip in here, but I know how much you have to do, and anyway I shall be ringing Mummy in the morning.

I am <u>delighted</u> that you are going to Trinity – I am sure that you will enjoy it to the full, & be able to make the most of the opportunity of getting to know that splendid character Lord Butler† –

---

*   Queen Elizabeth had been diagnosed with cancer of the colon. A successful operation to remove the tumour was carried out on 10 December at Sister Agnes, King Edward VII's Hospital for Officers.

†   Richard Austin Butler, Lord Butler KG CH DL PC (1902–82), distinguished Conservative politician better known as Rab Butler, who had been Chancellor of the Exchequer, Home Secretary and Foreign Secretary but was twice passed over for Prime Minister. Among his greatest achievements was shepherding the reforming 1944 Education Act through Parliament. In 1965 he was appointed Master of Trinity College, Cambridge.

I feel sure too, that he is one of the few <u>wise</u> men just now, & full of humour as well as being a statesman.

So longing to see you darling Charles – from your very loving Granny

~

7 August 1967 to the Prince of Wales

The Castle of Mey

My Darling Charles,

This is just a little line to tell you how greatly touched I was that not only did you remember my birthday but that you gave me such an entrancing & interesting present. I really am enchanted with it, and it will be a <u>great</u> treasure.

I do hope that you are enjoying your trip in Britannia, & that it will rest & relax your darling mother – I thought she looked tired, & no wonder with so many horrid anxieties & political worries to deal with.

See if you can look after her well darling Charles, & even persuade her to sit in a comfortable chair & REST (occasionally!). She is very precious to us all.

Such lovely weather here. I do wish that you were looking in later this week, but I hope that the polo will be great fun.

Again, a thousand thanks for your lovely present.

Ever your loving
Granny

~

3 April 1968 to Cecil Boyd-Rochfort

Clarence House

My dear Cecil,

Thank you so much for your letter about Capstan. I do hope that he goes on well, of course he was a late foal, & must be still a baby, & will I suppose mature late. I expect that you had this very cold weather at Newmarket, I do hope that it warms up soon. I am quite glad that the National Hunt season is nearing its end, because I have had such a series of disasters! Blood vessels, hearts, bad backs, over reaches, tendons, have taken their toll, & it's usually the hopeful ones!

What awful things horses can do to themselves – and yet, after perhaps a long bleak time, <u>one</u> win can change everything! Hope springs eternal they say, and, I suspect, especially in racing.

I do hope that you will have a good season, you certainly deserve one.

I am,

Yours very sincerely

Elizabeth R

~

6 June 1968 to Rose Kennedy

[Telegram]

SO DEEPLY SHOCKED & GRIEVED TO LEARN OF THIS GREAT TRAGEDY.* I SEND YOU MY TRULY HEARTFELT SYMPATHY, & THE ASSURANCE OF MY THOUGHTS & PRAYERS IN THIS MOMENT OF SORROW. ELIZABETH R QUEEN MOTHER

~

26 December 1968 to Osbert Sitwell

Windsor Castle

My dear Sir Osbert,

How very kind of you to think of me at Christmas time, and to give me such a delightful present.

The book is charming, & such fun, as I hadn't read 'The Lays'† for years, & it still seemed familiar. I do want to send you my <u>warmest</u> thanks.

My daughter Margaret so much enjoyed her visit to you last summer, & was thrilled with the beauty of everything around Florence. I do hope that I shall be able to come out one day, & that I may have the pleasure of paying you a visit. It seems so long since I saw you, & so many sad things have happened. That Hannah [Gubbay] should have died was terribly sad, and there will never be anyone like her again. The last time I lunched with her, she seemed desperately frail & crippled, but just as funny & crisp as ever. We all

---

* Senator Robert Kennedy was assassinated in Los Angeles on 5 June 1968.

† *The Lays of Ancient Rome* by Thomas Macaulay.

spoke of you, & wished that you could have been there. As it is, it has turned into the last 'Bowler Lunch' – those enjoyable feasts which started in Hertford Street, so many years ago. You & Malcolm and James & Bobbety and Alex – what a rattle of conversation – only interrupted by urgent orders from Hannah 'to have just one bit more chicken'! [. . .] Oh how sad it is when familiar people disappear. But, on a happier note – there are very nice young ones coming on.

With again my warmest thanks for your charming present,

I am,

Yours very sincerely

Elizabeth R

~

11 May 1969 to the Prince of Wales

HMY *Britannia*

My Darling Charles,

I was so <u>delighted</u> to get your dear letter, and thank you most warmly for writing. I was longing to know how your time was going at Aber, and am so relieved to know that all is going well.

I can imagine how difficult it must be, to be catapulted from an agreeable & sophisticated base like Cambridge where one has friends, into an utterly strange environment.* Hullo – I've picked up a different pen, & it's much blacker. I think I'll go on with it!

I do hope, with all my heart, that you will find it all worth while. As life is really one long experience, I am sure that these long weeks will add a lot to yours.

The press are perfectly foul, but I am sure that they don't achieve their object (if they even <u>have</u> one) by being beastly. The English don't really like it, & darling, I can't tell you what charming and heartwarming things I am always hearing about you. Everyone loves you, & is proud of you, and I absolutely <u>know</u> that you will be able to do wonderful things for this country, not only in leadership, but by being your own kind hearted, loving and intelligent & <u>funny</u> self! It

---

* After Trinity, Cambridge, Prince Charles studied at Aberystwyth University. On 1 July 1969 the Queen formally invested her eldest son as Prince of Wales at Caenarfon Castle, Wales. Much of the ceremony was designed and directed by Lord Snowdon, the Constable of the Castle.

would be intolerable if one couldn't laugh, even when things are dismal, and I love your jokes! Ever since you were a little boy, you have made your desiccated old grandmother laugh immoderately, & long may you continue to do so.

I am longing to see you again, & hear more of your life in Wales – the Welsh people are so nice, & I am sure that they will take you to their hearts.

The darling yacht is being, as always, a haven to return to after very busy days.

I am off to Birkhall next week but gather that the Dee is EMPTY of fish. Isn't it ghastly – poor Pearl, poor Brown. I will let you know how empty the Long Pool, Red Brae, Polveir, Little Polveir, Fir Tree etc are.

Lots of love darling Charles from your very devoted Granny

~

8 July 1969 to the Earl of Snowdon

Clarence House

Dearest Tony,

I thought that the whole setting of the Investiture at Carnarvon was so perfect and arranged with such marvellous taste that I feel I must send you one line of heartfelt congratulation on a really <u>super</u> result. I know how much thought and hard work you must have put into this immensely important piece of our island history and <u>everyone</u> was thrilled by the beauty of the scene. Tony, I thought the scarlet chairs were marvellous and the delicate structure of the covering to the dais most beautiful. It is so lovely to know that this day, so important, to you, is also a sort of turning point for the people of our country. You've done so much to achieve this, well done.

Your loving mother in law,
ER

~

4 December 1969 to the Duke of Edinburgh

Clarence House

Dearest Philip,

I was so grieved to hear the sad news this morning,* & this is just a little note to give you my loving sympathy & to assure you of my affectionate thoughts & prayers.

However much one longs for someone to be at peace, the break with the past & with one's childhood is very painful to bear.

I do feel for you with all my heart.

Your loving Mama in law,

Elizabeth

~

12 February 1970 to Lady Diana Cooper

The Royal Lodge

My dear Lady Diana,†

Your delightful luncheon party was such a treat last week, and I could not have enjoyed it more. To meet dear friends in such an enchanting setting is ideal, and it was specially nice to see Noël [Coward], who is rather elusive nowadays. I thought that Little Venice is too charming for words, so white & watery & elegant, and I loved seeing you again, in your own heavenly house.

Thank you a thousand times for asking me & for being so kind to me.

I am, ever,

Yours affec:

Elizabeth R

~

---

* Prince Philip's mother, Princess Andrew of Greece, died at Buckingham Palace on 5 December 1969.

† Lady Diana Cooper, widow of Duff Cooper and mother of John Julius Norwich, lived in Little Venice, with the Regent's Canal on her doorstep.

10 August 1970 to Benjamin Britten

The Castle of Mey

Dear Mr Britten,

I was so very touched that you and Mr Pears should have arranged that heavenly afternoon at Sandringham, and I don't think that anybody could ever have had a more perfect birthday present.

It was the kindest idea on your part, and gave me the greatest possible pleasure, not to mention the rest of the audience who were blissfully happy with the lovely programme and glorious singing.

There are some things in one's life that are memorable and I shall never forget the concert at Sandringham or the wonderfully kind and generous thought that made it possible.*

With again my warmest thanks to you both,

I am yours very sincerely

Elizabeth R

PS I open this letter, to add further grateful thanks! The record of 'Les Illuminations' has arrived and Ruth and I have played it several times and listened with the greatest joy. There is no sound here except the shushing of the sea and the crying of the seabirds, & this music is exactly right for the atmosphere here of sea & sky and & silence.

Thank you very very much, I find it extraordinarily moving. ER

~

14 August 1970 to the Prince of Wales

The Castle of Mey

My Darling Charles,

I was so very touched that you should give me such a beautiful birthday present, and I am absolutely thrilled with the glass bowl. The inscription is so marvellous and I assure you it will be one of my real treasures. I have not brought it up here, as it is so heavy, this is one of its beauties, for glass should either be very weighty or light as air, and I am already looking forward to seeing it again.

---

* The concert of music by Mozart and Britten was given by Britten and Peter Pears on 1 August 1970.

Darling Charles, you are an angel to give me something so personal & so imaginative, and I do thank you with all my heart for your loving thought of your hoary headed aged old crone of a grandmother.

I am looking forward SO much to seeing you all here on the 16th – it is one of my greatest treats to be with the family even for a few hours.*

With my fond love & gratitude, ever darling C, your hoary headed and aged old crone of a Granny

~

7 February 1971 to the Rev. Anthony Harbottle

Royal Lodge

Dear Mr Harbottle,[†]

I was so touched by your very kind note yesterday & I do want to thank you for what you said, & also to say how comforting it is to have the assurance of your thoughts & prayers.

As the years go by, though the pain is still there, more & more comes the feeling of <u>thankfulness</u>.

Thankful for the King's life here, & thankful beyond words to have shared it.

With my gratitude, I am yours sincerely,
Elizabeth R

~

---

* The Queen and her family enjoyed an annual summer cruise of the Western Isles of Scotland in *Britannia*. It was one of the few times they could relax together without much press intrusion. They developed the tradition of stopping off at the little port of Scrabster to go to lunch with Queen Elizabeth at the Castle of Mey. These were convivial occasions much enjoyed by all the family.

† The Rev. Anthony Harbottle LVO (1925–2009), Chaplain of the Royal Chapel in Windsor Great Park, 1968–81. A distinguished lepidopterist and the first person in Britain to breed the New Pale Clouded Butterfly, he had served in the Royal Marines during the war. After he left Windsor, he would write every year to the Queen Mother on the anniversary of the King's death, to express his kind sympathy. Every year she replied, equally kindly.

18 June 1971 to Lady Penn

Windsor Castle

Dearest Prue,

It was so very kind of you & Eric to ask me to lunch <u>and</u> tea AND martinis on Sunday.*

I loved coming, and adored the lovely concert – and meeting so many delightful people.

Benjamin Britten always creates such a marvellous <u>atmosphere</u> when he conducts or plays. It is happy, kind, friendly, & becomes relaxed <u>and</u> excited if that is possible!

He is so charming and natural & kind that somehow the people listening get infected as well. I shall never forget the scene as the helicopter soared into the air. All the dear seeing off party behaving like leaves in the wind, and then the wonderful surprise of that exquisitely arranged portable bar!

It absolutely saved our lives, & there was enough for the Air Marshal as well.

I do thank you with all my heart for giving me such a delicious day. I am so so grateful.

With my love,

Ever yours affectionately

Elizabeth R

~

3 October 1971 to the Prince of Wales

Birkhall

My Darling Charles,

I was so delighted to get your letter, and to hear a little of your life at Dartmouth.† It all sounds immensely busy, and terribly concentrated.

---

*   Queen Elizabeth flew from Royal Lodge by helicopter for lunch with the Penns to attend a concert at the Maltings at Snape and returned in the evening. Lady Penn sent a copy of this letter to Benjamin Britten and he replied, 'How kind of you to let me see that letter from Queen Elizabeth, & what a nice one it is. She is a lovable and remarkable woman, & it was a great pleasure to have her with us. I hope she will come back! I only wish someone could persuade her to call me Ben like the rest of them!' (21 June 1971, Penn Papers)

†   The Prince of Wales began his naval career in September 1971, with a six-week training course at the Royal Naval College, Dartmouth.

You have certainly had to put a great deal into very short periods – learning Welsh in a jiffy, learning to fly in an extraordinarily short time, and now learning to be a Naval Officer in a twinkling.

I look forward to the day when you can come to Scotland, stay right on into October! Let it be soon!

We had our last day's grouse driving yesterday. [. . .] The hills looked too lovely for words, blue & slightly misty, like the bloom on a grape. The last day of the fishing we all fished MADLY, but I had to leave the Streams of Gairn* empty handed, with dozens and dozens of fish jumping and head and tailing and laughing at Pearl and me!

I am so looking forward to having a glimpse of you in Japan. I have ordered a new kimono – and I MUSTN'T forget my fan.†

Lots of love from your TREMBLY OLD GRANDMOTHER

~

3 December 1971 to the Prince of Wales

Clarence House

My Darling Charles,

It was so lovely getting your dear letter, and I was so interested to hear how your life was turning out on board [the Prince was serving on HMS *Norfolk*, a guided-missile destroyer], & what sort of people were round you.

Life has been going on much the same here – it is always a very busy time of year made more so by Mummy's chicken pox, as I had to do the investitures etc. But in a way it was really a boon, as she actually has a REST for a week or so.

There was a delightful day's shooting here on Monday (of course I mean at Windsor). [. . .] it was a glorious still autumn day in the Park, with the sun shining and the oaks looking blue and misty, & a splendid lot of pheasants. Everyone kept on saying, as one does in England, isn't it a BEAUTIFUL day. I had to go up to London after lunch, & when I got to the Copper Horse & looked down the Long

---

* One of the best pools on the River Dee at Birkhall. Ashe Windham, one of Queen Elizabeth's devoted younger courtiers, once caught twelve salmon there before breakfast.

† The Prince of Wales had received the Order of the Chrysanthemum, Japan's highest honour, that year.

Walk, there was nothing to be seen at all – everything completely wiped out by the thickest fog that I have ever seen. Isn't it extraordinary that you can be basking in blazing sunshine at one moment and then 50 yards away everything blotted out.

There are many worrying things at home at the moment – unemployment is very bad, & so many boys leaving school can't get jobs. One wishes that one could have a year or even six months of national service of some sort. It does help to prepare people for life, as you know so well. But I suppose that there are practical difficulties in the way. I suppose that after the war there was such an acute shortage of everything that factories sprang up everywhere & labour was short too, & we have now caught up & we were producing too much, & some of it too expensive to sell abroad. One always hopes that things find their own level in the end, but I fear this brings sorrow & worry to many people. [. . .]

But I must not write to you about gloomy news, tho' all your life I have talked to you freely about EVERYTHING. That is because I love you dearest Charles, & I thought of you SO much on your birthday. I wrote out a telegram, & then thought how the system on board would break down if too many signals came, so I tore it up, & now wished I hadn't.

A great deal of love from your CRUMBLING OLD GRANNY

~

Thursday 16 December 1971 to the Earl of Snowdon

Clarence House

Dearest Tony,

Just a line to say how deeply, deeply touched I was by your call this morning and for your most comforting letter. It was very dear of you to write for of course one can't help minding such venomous observations, especially coming from our revered House of Commons!* I am so grateful not only for your letter but for the kind

---

* The Royal Family, and the Queen Mother in particular, were under attack over financial matters. In 1970 the new Prime Minister, Edward Heath, set up a House of Commons select committee on the Civil List, by which the monarchy was financed. The committee included such implacable critics of the monarchy as William Hamilton, Labour MP for Fife (1917–2000). Hearings began in May 1971 and in December that year the matter was debated in the House of Commons. Labour Members of Parliament, led by Willie Hamilton, made fierce criticisms

and loving thought behind it, and I send you my love and heartfelt thanks. Ever your very affect and very old woman, Elizabeth

~

undated [29 April 1972] to the Lord Mayor of Norwich

[Telegram]

I AM DELIGHTED THAT NORWICH HAVE TODAY BECOME CHAMPIONS OF THE SECOND DIVISION. PLEASE CONVEY MY WARMEST CONGRATULATIONS TO THEIR MANAGER AND TO ALL MEMBERS OF THE TEAM AND MY BEST WISHES FOR NEXT SEASON IN THE FIRST DIVISION. ELIZABETH R QUEEN MOTHER

~

20 May 1972 to the Prince of Wales

Birkhall

My Darling Charles,

It is rather curious that I was just thinking 'I must write to Charles about Brown'* when your letter arrived. It is indeed a terribly sad thing to happen. I never thought of Balmoral or the river without Brown, he is so much part of all one's happiest memories – that little light compact figure, so courteous & so full of fun & such a pleasure to spend a day with. I really felt very mournful when I went up to fish Suspension and Garlum the other day.

He taught me to fish and my mind went back to the old days & all the fish I had hooked or lost in those lovely pools, & Brown's sharing one's thrill at landing a fish, or tactful sympathy when that ghastly empty feeling told one that the hook had come out! [. . .]

When I arrived here a week ago it was absolutely FREEZING. Icy winds, snow pouring down on Lochnagar, the river in flood, & I wondered whether one would ever see the river fishable. However,

---

of the Queen Mother and Princess Margaret, with Hamilton demanding to know of the Queen Mother's staff, 'What the blazes do they do?' Princess Margaret he dismissed as 'an expensive kept woman' who did 'even less than her old Mum'. In the end, the House of Commons, controlled for now by the Conservatives, fixed the Civil List for ten years so that there need not be a disagreeable debate every year.

*   Robert Brown had recently died.

after two or three days it started to go down, & we have been fishing hard for the last few days. [. . .]

The ground here is covered with primroses & violets & cowslips & anemones, the birches are just coming into leaf, & the cherries are in full flower. It is such a lovely time of year, & such a relaxing one. No changing for dinner – we eat rather early & fish later, and tho' this week is supposed to be a rest, all muscles ache like fun, backs practically broken in two, shoulders in agony, usually a slight cold in the head & a small chill in the tummy, bruised feet & legs & probably a twisted knee, but it's all worth it!

I <u>DO</u> wish you were here. [. . .]

A great deal of love darling Charles, from your very devoted Granny

~

5 July 1972 to Sir Bernard Fergusson

Clarence House

My dear Bernard

I am absolutely delighted that you are to become a LORD, and I send you warmest congratulations on this honour, so truly well deserved. I think that <u>everyone</u> was pleased to hear the news, & no one more pleased than your guest in New Zealand, your hostess in Britannia & your Colonel in Chief! What nice links they make!

Ever, yours

Elizabeth R

~

17 July 1972 to Rachel Bowes Lyon

Clarence House

My darling Rachel,

I have spent many happy weekends at St Paul's Walden, but I really think that this last one was the most heavenly of all!

Everyone was <u>so</u> nice, and the feeling of unhurried relaxation was perfect. One moved from one pleasure to another so smoothly; from Church (always so nostalgic) to that lovely walk round the garden (all the new paths), on to that peaceful visit to Simon and Caroline, & a joy to see those darling children, marvellous lunch, no hurry, just lie in the long chair & read, wander down to the pond, happy tea, & calmly off to the Canadian log cabin. Lovely day, darling Rachel, ending with the greatest treat in the world, to hear Joyce* doing her inimitable and wonderfully funny and touching selections.

Thank you a million times, it was all blissful, with much love ever your devoted

Elizabeth

~

17 August 1972 to the Duke of Edinburgh

The Castle of Mey

Darling Philip,

I have hung your lovely picture† over the fireplace in the dining room, where it looks absolutely perfect.

It really has made all the difference to the room, and the colour is exactly right, as it reflects the light and sky outside which I can see from where I sit. I am enormously grateful to you for giving me such pleasure, thank you a thousand times.

With my love, ever your affec Mama,

Elizabeth

~

6 March 1973 to the Earl of Snowdon

Clarence House

Dearest Tony,

I cannot tell you how greatly I enjoyed the lovely lunch party on Sunday. To eat marvellous food in the company of dear friends in a

---

* Joyce Grenfell OBE (1910–79) witty actress, comedienne, song writer, who entranced generations and who had a family connection with Rachel Bowes Lyon through Waldorf Astor, Rachel's uncle. In the Second World War she toured the world entertaining Allied troops. Afterwards she performed constantly on the BBC and played in many film comedies such as *The Happiest Days of Your Life* and the original *St Trinian* films. Her comic monologues delighted everyone – including Queen Elizabeth.

† Prince Philip had enjoyed painting for many years. He gave the Queen Mother two paintings which she hung in the dining room at the Castle of Mey – one was of the east face of the Castle's tower, the other a view of St Kilda painted from the Royal Yacht.

very pretty house is my idea of bliss! It was all such fun and having dropped David back at school I went to Royal Lodge in a daze of martinis, red wine, that excellent yellow stuff <u>and</u> CHAMPAGNE. It took me a few hours to surface!

Your affec.

ER

~

27 June 1973 to Edward Cazalet

Clarence House

My dear Edward,*

I cannot tell you how grateful I am to you for making my visit to Fairlawne on Monday so much happier than I could have dared to hope. I did dread the saying goodbye to Jim & the lads & the jockeys, <u>and</u> the horses, and you were so kind and understanding about it all, that I managed the goodbyes without <u>actually</u> crying. I really cannot thank you enough, for I am sure you must have felt very sad yourself. I am sure that the happiest moments of my life, since the King died have been at Fairlawne, or in disasters or triumphs on the racecourse with Peter. He was a strong and splendid person, and I do feel so deeply for his family at this moment.[†]

---

* Sir Edward Cazalet DL (1936–), barrister, High Court judge and authority on P. G. Wodehouse; son of Peter Cazalet and his first wife Leonora, step-daughter of Wodehouse.

† The last of the 250 winners Peter Cazalet trained for Queen Elizabeth was Inch Arran, which won the Topham Trophy at Liverpool in March 1973. Cazalet was by this time terminally ill with cancer; he and Queen Elizabeth watched the race on television together at Clarence House. Nothing could have moved the pair of them more than their horse's victory. Cazalet died on 29 May 1973.

Queen Elizabeth said goodbye to Fairlawne after twenty-four years on 25 June 1973. She saw each of the stable lads and jockeys separately and gave them each a present – a mix of cufflinks, travelling alarm clocks, small silver objects, all inscribed with her crest and initials. Edward Cazalet recalled, 'They all knew how much she loved her horses and how much interest she had taken in everyone who worked at Fairlawne. There was not a dry eye in the place as she was driven out of the yard for the last time.' (Edward Cazalet to the author, 21 May 2012)

Queen Elizabeth moved her horses from Fairlawne to the stable of Fulke Walwyn (1910–91) at Lambourn, sometimes known as 'The Valley of the Racehorse', in Berkshire. He also trained successfully for her and she became fond of him and his wife Cath. When Fulke Walwyn died, aged eighty, in February 1991, Cath took out a training licence and continued to train for Queen Elizabeth until 1993.

With all my thanks, & my heartfelt hopes that glorious Fairlawne will go on to be a happy family home. I am, Yours affec
Elizabeth R

~

29 June 1973 to the Prince of Wales

The Royal Lodge

My Darling Charles,

I have just been down to the little greenhouse to see how the melons are getting on, and of course I instantly thought of YOU! I had a happy memory of you coming after polo, and sitting in the saloon with a huge slice of melon. It made me wish so much that this could happen again. Of course it will, and not before too long, I hope.

I have just seen two big great squirrels on the terrace outside my window as I write. The dogs are after them, but they are up the big oak tree. There are far too many healthy young ones just now. I must get the keeper to have another blitz on the horrid things.

Mummy and Papa went off to Canada on Monday – I never feel quite happy until they are back again.

We seem to be very short of Counsellors of State, at the moment there is only Anne & me to do the papers & receive the Diplomats [. . .] as Margaret is away, so I look forward madly to the time when you are home again, not only for your physical presence darling, but for your signature as well!

I do hope that you are having an interesting time, to help to combat the 'being away'* feeling. We do all miss you terribly and long for your return. I still think of that lovely family weekend at Balmoral, as a sort of glorious oasis. Wasn't it lovely being together & walking up Glen Beg, & laughing & chatting. A time to remember.

Otherwise life plods on, with Ascot over, garden parties coming, hospitals to open, galas to attend, & it all makes one so deeply grateful for the marvellous peace of this little house. I have come down for a night, & am now off to Devonshire, & back to London on Monday.

I lunched at Blenheim on Tuesday (things in Oxford) and at

---

* The Prince of Wales was serving in the 845 Naval Air Squadron, based at Yeovilton.

Hatfield on Wednesday, & it was fascinating thinking of the difference in the two houses, the magnificence of 1720 and the also magnificent but much more domestic architecture of Tudor days. It is lovely that they survive and are lived in.* However, nothing beats Windsor!

Lots of love, darling Charles, from your very loving GRANNY

~

14 December 1973 to Benjamin Britten and Peter Pears

[Telegram]

MAY AN IGNORAMUS OF A MUS DOC HONORIS CAUSA SEND HER GRATEFUL THANKS TO TWO BELOVED MUSICIANS FOR THEIR CHARMING MESSAGE OF WELCOME. SHE ALSO WOULD ADD A HOPE THAT THEY WILL SPEND A HAPPY AND JOYOUS CHRISTMAS†

ELIZABETH R QUEEN MOTHER

~

20 February 1974 to Benjamin Britten

Clarence House

Dear Ben,

I cannot tell you how greatly touched I feel that you would like me to be Patron of your glorious Festival. Of course I would be delighted to be associated with one of the best things that has happened to England's music, and I do hope that I can have another chance to come to a concert during the summer.

I hope also that you are really beginning to feel better & stronger after such a bad time – the hours pass so slowly when one is not well, and you must be longing to get back to what in 'horse parlance' is called strong work.‡ I don't really feel that I am half musical enough to have the honour & pleasure of being your Patron, but I accept

---

* Blenheim Palace in Oxfordshire and Hatfield House in Hertfordshire, homes of the Spencer Churchill and Cecil families respectively.

† On 6 December 1973, on her receipt of an Honorary Doctorate of the Royal College of Music, Britten and Pears had sent Queen Elizabeth a telegram welcoming her 'to the ranks of honourable musicians'.

‡ Britten had been suffering from ill health, particularly heart problems, for some years.

with joy, and am deeply grateful that you should wish me to be
linked to Aldeburgh in this happy way.

I am,

Ever yours,

Elizabeth R

~

4 June 1974 to Sir John Betjeman

Clarence House

Dear Sir John*

I was so pleased when you gave me a copy of your lovely words
at Stratford, & I would like to send you a word of very warm thanks.
Your poem was so perfect for the occasion. It was such a happy day,
wasn't it? The English are so splendid when they are doing something
for somebody else, and all those volunteers, having achieved so much,
made one feel 'hooray'. It was wonderful that you could be there, and
did you not think that all those good people lining the river gave one
an excellent feeling that England is absolutely all right. It was all such
a splendidly un-BBC occasion. Too many nice ordinary people
enjoying a nice ordinary occasion is strictly against the rules!

With again my thanks for the encouragement you gave to all
those dedicated people on Saturday,

I am,

Yours sincerely

Elizabeth R

~

14 July 1974 to Lord Clark

Clarence House

My dear Lord Clark,

I was talking to Jock Colville the other day about the fascinating
Churchill Centenary Exhibition which is being held in the Fine Rooms
in Somerset House, and which is, alas!, languishing for lack of visitors.

---

* Sir John Betjeman CBE (1906–84), Poet Laureate from 1972, broadcaster, gentle but passionate
defender of English traditions, countryside and especially Victorian architecture. Queen Elizabeth
loved his poetry and his other enthusiasms. He was a frequent guest at Royal Lodge. At Stratford
on 1 June Queen Elizabeth reopened the Upper Avon River, which had been unnavigable since
the nineteenth century, and Betjeman recited his poem composed for the occasion.

This seems a very sad state of affairs, and we both felt that if it were at all possible for you to be wonderfully kind and do a few minutes' film for the BBC, walking around the Exhibition, talking partly about Somerset House & the magnificent ceilings and chimney pieces etc, & partly about two or three of the most interesting things in the Exhibition itself that it would be the most marvellous help.

A great many people do not seem to know that Somerset House even exists, and if you felt able to contemplate doing this thing, I am sure that people would <u>flock</u>.

I do hope that I am not asking too much, but you are really the only person who can do something like this, and you would make it all sound so exciting, and so worth while.

Apparently the BBC would be thrilled to have a few minutes from you on 'Nationwide', and Jock would be only too happy to take you on a preliminary 'run-around', if the idea appeals to you at all.

Winston was such an extraordinary man, & the Exhibition does give a splendid picture of his gloriously varied life – and it seems a waste that more people do not see it.

Please forgive me for bothering you with this plea, and if you feel at all disinclined, of course I shall understand.

Jock's (he is now Sir Jock!) address is 19 St James's Square.

I adored your last book, and I long for Civilisation* to be shown again – it should really appear every year.

I am, Yours very sincerely,

Elizabeth R

~

18 August 1974 to Sir Ralph Anstruther

The Castle of Mey

My dear Ralph†

It was too sad that you could not come to the COCKTAIL

---

*   BBC television series created by Lord Clark which traced and celebrated the triumph of Western civilization through its art. It was a model of public service broadcasting which was hard to equal.

†   Sir Ralph Anstruther (1921–2002), Coldstream Guards officer, courtier, Treasurer to Queen Elizabeth after the death of Sir Arthur Penn. His attempts to bring order to Queen Elizabeth's finances were never-ending.

PARTY, as I am sure you would have adored it! Everyone (like the Hildreths) brought utterly unknown ladies, and Mrs M. became quite intoxicated. There was an awful moment when I was talking to the Baronetess and the Provost of Wick, & he said 'to whom have I the honour of speaking', & then of course I could only mutter feebly, as I could <u>not</u> remember her name, & then, fortunately I remembered Ackergill, so all was well, & he instantly invited her to visit the Town House & 'write her name'!

About the Drum Horse. It really is nothing to do with either Alastair [Aird] or Martin [Gilliat], only me!* Some years ago my daughter Margaret presented a Drum Horse to her Regiment & then they amalgamated with one of mine, & when this old boy retired, I thought that it would be nice to present one in my turn.†

John Miller kindly ransacked Edinburgh for a suitable horse, & <u>four</u> arrived at the Mews in London, & the Queen & I chose this huge fellow, who has been drawing a dray, poor thing. He is now at Knightsbridge Barracks, where the Blues are trying to tidy him up, & make him look smart. So, he can safely be paid for.

So beautiful here – we have been so fortunate, & I wish that you could have had a little longer of Caithness.

Yours

ER

~

---

* Lt-Col. Sir Martin Gilliat GCVO MBE (1913–93), soldier and courtier, Private Secretary to the Queen Mother, 1959–93. He shared his employer's love of people (and steeplechasers) and contributed mightily to the spirit of bonhomie that pervaded Clarence House. His friend Martin Charteris, formerly Private Secretary to the Queen, chose P. G. Wodehouse's phrase 'like a prawn in aspic' to describe how well he fitted into Queen Elizabeth's Household.

Captain Sir Alastair Aird GCVO (1931–2009) joined Queen Elizabeth's staff as an equerry in 1960, became Comptroller of her Household in 1974, and Private Secretary after the death of Martin Gilliat in 1993. He carried on the welcoming traditions of Clarence House and was courteous, unflappable and meticulous in his attention to detail.

† The Queen Mother had learned that the drum horse of her regiment the Queen's Own Hussars was being retired. She asked the Crown Equerry, Sir John Miller, who was in charge of the Royal Mews, to find a suitable horse. He did so, through the St Cuthbert's Co-operative Society in Edinburgh; the price was £300. The regiment accepted the horse with pleasure and named him Dettingen.

4 March 1975 to Sir Cecil Boyd-Rochfort

Clarence House

My dear Cecil,

It was most kind of you to write to me about Tammuz's victory in the Schweppes Hurdle.* It was a great thrill & after about 25 years as an owner of horses running under National Hunt rules, my very first big race! As you say, it was an extra pleasure that the horse was bred by the Queen, & perhaps Highlight will breed another good one. Of course, Porchy† was very pleased, as Tammuz was a Tamerlaine child!

I was very interested to hear that High Veldt has done so well in South Africa. I remember that Charles [Moore] had a great opinion of him. It was very sad that Aureole had to be put down this year. I was so fond of the dear old horse, & he was always the first person that I went to visit at Sandringham. He was a real character, wasn't he? and remained so into his old age. And what an influence he (& Feola‡) have had on breeding all over the world.

It is very hard nowadays to find a good 3 mile steeplechaser, so, don't forget, if you see a hopeful young horse in Ireland, do let me know!

Next week, Cheltenham, I have 2 runners – One Sunyboy (by Mourne) which I bought from Lady Beaverbrook this last year; Isle of Man by Manicou (my old horse) & if the going is good Game Spirit§ in the Gold Cup. Cheltenham is not my lucky course, but, thank goodness, in racing, hope springs eternal!

With my thanks again for your kind letter.

Elizabeth R

~

* The Schweppes Hurdle, run at Newbury. Tammuz was ridden by Bill Smith. The race carried a purse of £9,000, Queen Elizabeth's most valuable win to date.

† Lord Porchester, later Lord Carnarvon (1924–2001), close friend of the Queen and her racing manager from 1969.

‡ Feola was an outstandingly good brood mare at the Royal Stud at Sandringham from 1938 to 1953; Aureole in his turn had sired many winners there.

§ One of Queen Elizabeth's favourite horses, trained by Peter Cazalet and Fulke Walwyn, Game Spirit never succeeded in winning the Cheltenham Gold Cup but won 21 other races for her. Sunyboy and Isle of Man were also successful horses, the latter winning 14 races.

23 May 1975 to the Prince of Wales

Clarence House

My Darling Charles,

It seems such a LONG time since I have seen you, and the only glimpse I have had of your dear phig in recent weeks is a picture of you rising from below the ice, wearing, in a traditional Goon manner,* a BOWLER.

We missed you TERRIBLY at Easter, a time I always love at Windsor, only a small family party, & as a treat, tea by the lake at Frogmore.

This year, for some reason, I had tea with Mabel & an occasional Edward, on our ONLY tea picnic, and we had a most enjoyable gossip about the whole family!

[. . .] I went to Persia for a week really because I have always longed to see Persepolis. That was a real pleasure, & more moving than I had ever imagined, but apart from the 2 Poets' tombs at Sheraz and Persepolis, I found the whole country agitating and uncertain. I don't really like being driven at 60 miles an hour through crowded streets, with so many police, & so many soldiers surrounding one – and I do feel for the Shah trying to be a 'do-Gooder' AND a practical Dictator.†

They loved your short stay there, and I think that more visits from people like us (non political) might give them a lift.

I went up to Birkhall for a week (I have just got back) and the river was too high for most of the pools, & only dear old Polveir produced a fish! I fished every day for 6 days and only managed to catch one at, literally, the 12th hour before flying South, in Polveir. Pearl, who was by then becoming almost suicidal at the horrid behaviour of the salmon, was over the moon with pleasure and relief!

---

* *The Goon Show*, broadcast by the BBC Home Service from 1951 to 1960, starred Spike Milligan, Harry Secombe and Peter Sellers in various ludicrous if not surreal conversations and situations. Prince Charles was a great enthusiast for the show's madcap humour.

† Queen Elizabeth's official visit to Iran was undertaken on the advice of the British government, anxious to improve relations with the Shah. Her analysis of the country as 'agitating and uncertain' was correct – the Shah's attempts to modernize Iran while retaining his autocracy failed. Four years later he was overthrown and the country was engulfed in a brutal Islamist revolution which did incomparable harm at home and abroad for decades to come.

I still feel a lovely glow on skin and spirit from those few days in the most heavenly part of Scotland. To hear the birds singing, & the river flowing by gives one fresh hope & courage. How fortunate we are to be able to be quiet and free in that glorious place. Do come back soon, and in the meantime (as they say at Balmoral), I send you a great deal of love, from your utterly decrepit

Granny.

~

1 July 1975 to Benjamin Britten

[No address]

Dear Ben,

The day that I spent at Aldeburgh will always remain in my memory as a truly happy one. It was a real pleasure to come to the Red House and talk with you and Peter and Peg* – and that delicious cold champagne was just right after a journey by helicopter!

The concert was pure bliss, and I was deeply moved by your glorious new piece.

It was so very kind to have a Patron's Choice, and I felt very humble & most honoured to be allowed such a treat![†]

It was, altogether, a lovely day, and, I wasn't late for lunch!

It is so marvellous that you are feeling stronger and I hope that you will continue to feel better & better, & that more wonderful music will come pouring out, to delight & enchant us all – with my warmest thanks to you and to Peter for so much kindness.

I am, ever yours

Elizabeth R

PS Ruth and I came home all aglow!

~

---

* Princess Ludwig of Hesse and by Rhine (1913–97), née Margaret Geddes. Her husband, who died in 1968, was a great-grandson of Queen Victoria. They were close friends of Benjamin Britten and Peter Pears, and 'Princess Peg' became President of the Aldeburgh Foundation.

† The Patron's Choice concert, with pieces chosen by Queen Elizabeth, began with Britten's *Prelude and Fugue for Strings* and ended with Berlioz's *Nuits d'été* sung by Janet Baker.

14 August 1975 to Queen Elizabeth II

The Castle of Mey

My Darling Lilibet

I have so many things to thank you for! The beautiful candlesticks, the wonderful surprise of Ben Britten's music,* & the glorious dinner party. It was angelic of you to think of so many delightful and spoiling things, and, darling, I am so very grateful and send you a <u>million</u> thanks.

The candlesticks are so original & pretty, and I shall enjoy using them enormously. As for the music, it is <u>so</u> exciting, and when one thinks how ill Ben has been, the fact that he had the will & the ability to write something special, is really marvellous. I never dreamt that I could ever be the recipient of such a 'Birthday Offering', and I am <u>so</u> thrilled, and <u>so</u> touched.

It was such a wonderful thought on your part.

The birthday dinner was simply heavenly, and I can never thank you enough for such a lovely celebration. So many dear friends, all enjoying themselves like anything, made it all <u>so</u> happy. Also, I thought that it was wonderful of Philip to come all the way up for it, as I know how hard it is to tear oneself away from the dear yacht.

It made a perfect end to an extraordinary day, and Fergie & Mary [Strathmore] & me ended up by having a cup of tea in the garden at Clarence House!

Is it really all right if I come for a couple of days on Wed. 27th? If you are <u>quite</u> sure that it won't wreck your party?

With all my love,
your very loving
Mummy

~

---

* The Queen had secretly asked Benjamin Britten to compose a piece of music for her mother's seventy-fifth birthday on 4 August 1975. He proposed writing a cycle of seven songs for the harp, using poems by Robert Burns. The Queen was enthusiastic. Britten called the composition *A Birthday Hansel*, which is a Scottish word for gift. The composition was presented to Queen Elizabeth at a birthday party given by the Queen in August 1975 and the work was first performed at Uphall, Ruth Fermoy's home near Sandringham, on 16 January 1976. The audience included the Queen, the Queen Mother and Princess Margaret, Lady Fermoy, Britten himself and his nurse, Rita Thomson. Peter Pears was the tenor and Osian Ellis played the harp. (Queen Elizabeth II to Sir Benjamin Britten, 12, 22 January, 25 March and 26 April 1975, Red House Archives, Aldeburgh)

18 August 1975 to Benjamin Britten

The Castle of Mey

Dear Ben,

    I don't think that I have ever had a more wonderful surprise in my life, than the moment when I set eyes on your Birthday Hansel. I am absolutely thrilled and delighted by this glorious birthday gift, and I do want to thank you with all my heart for your kindness in composing this very special and exciting music. The poems are so touching and so beautiful, and Ruth has just been playing the harp music on our old upright here!

    I love the Early Walk, the Sweet Rosebud, & his – Burns' – touching love of little birds like linnets. I have never heard 'My Hoggie' – poor Hoggie, what a charming little poem. And I love 'Flow gently, sweet Afton', what lovely things you have chosen for your lovely music.

    I honestly do not think that anything in my life has given me greater pleasure than your birthday gift.

    It is very precious to me, and will, I am sure, give joy to your countless grateful admirers.

    I am, ever yours

    Elizabeth R

    PS I often think of the happy day I spent at Aldeburgh.

~

1 September 1975 to Queen Elizabeth II

Birkhall

My Darling Lilibet

    Another heavenly three days at Balmoral has flown by, and I am writing to thank you a thousand times for my lovely visit. It is such a tremendous treat to be with you & the children, and every moment was very precious. There is something so uplifting & courage making about being with young people – Charles is <u>so</u> funny, & makes one laugh & also so serious about serious things, such a good mixture, and Andrew is so marvellously uninhibited, & so gay and good natured, one can only feel cheerful with him! Also the darling little ones, so good to see them growing the right way. It was all so happy, & so glorious to have a chance of a talk with you and I really felt set up by Sunday!

There is something rather like hard work when one is in one's own house, the food, the dramas, the grumbles, the guests (getting them out of the house!), landrovers always breaking down etc etc, so I did feel wonderfully rested at Balmoral.

With a million thanks from your very loving

Mummy

~

19 September 1975 to the Duke of Edinburgh

Birkhall

Darling Philip,

Thank you so much for sending me 'Trousered Apes'. From what I have already read, I feel that I shall agree most heartily with what Professor Williams says! It is so terribly easy for people to get so used to reading & seeing violence & vulgarity that they come to accept it as normal.*

There is one thing that I wanted to talk to you about the other evening, then forgot! There is a great machine cutting the grass & weeds on each side of the road past this house from Ballater.

The verge is only a couple of feet wide, & has never been cut before, & I feel is immensely valuable to the little birds & small animals – & insects.

Possibly you could get C. McHardy on to it & think of what a dead waste of ratepayers' money!†

Much love, ever your devoted Mama,

Elizabeth

~

---

* *Trousered Apes: Sick Literature in a Sick Society*, by Duncan Williams (1971). Williams's argument was that 'Great literature is that which over the centuries sustained and elevated mankind ... Such art involves a prodigious effort and concentration on the part of its creator and demands a cultivated response from its audience ... It therefore constitutes a minority culture ... detested and feared by the majority of contemporary artists and writers with their egalitarian aims and allegiance.' The book created a stir when published but then fell out of print.

† Colonel ('Charlie') William George McHardy MC CVO, resident factor on the Balmoral Estates, 1965–79.

24 November 1975 to Prince Paul of Yugoslavia

Clarence House

My dear Paul

[. . .]

A very sad thing has happened. My beloved nephew John Elphinstone died very suddenly some days ago. It was a heart attack. He has always been to me like a semi son, and I now feel my heart very heavy.

He suffered rather badly in the War, & had a horrid time in Colditz, but he was a dear, kind & very brave person – and never grumbled about all he went through. It is terrible, as one gets older, to lose the younger generation, isn't it? You have always been so affectionate towards my family, that I wanted you to know this latest very real loss.

Please don't forget that your room is waiting for you, whenever you feel like a few days in London.

With much love to Olga & yourself,

ever your affect:

Elizabeth

~

25 November 1975 to the Prince of Wales

Clarence House

My Darling Charles,

The Gala at Covent Garden in aid of the Royal Opera Benevolent Fund is on Dec 18. I do hope you will be able to come that evening?

Also I would love you to meet Prince and Princess Clary* if you ever have a moment. They had huge properties in Czechoslovakia (Bohemia), and have lost EVERYTHING (even his own private diaries which are in a museum in Prague) and never a murmur of regret or boo-hoo. Splendid old people, & the last of that Great Generation.

Is lunch any good [. . .] perhaps you could give me a ring one evening?

---

* Alfons, Prince Clary and Aldringen (1887–1978), and his wife Princess Ludwine (1894–1984). The family were the lords of Teplitz (Teplice) in north-west Bohemia, next to Saxony, from 1634 until 1945. The Prince was a man of great courtesy, a historian, an art lover and a fine raconteur who had many friends in London.

I do hope that all is going well with you. I have a heavy heart at the moment, as John E was so much part of my life, past & present, & such a dear, good person.

With all my love, ever your loving GRANNY

~

19 February 1976 to Fulke Walwyn

Clarence House

My dear Fulke,

Just a line to say how thrilled I was that Sunyboy brought off the 300th winner at Ascot. You had got him on such good form, and he won so well, and it was lovely that it all happened on 'home ground'.

What a relief! Now we can run the horses without this awful 299 hanging over us.

With my thanks to you, I am, yours ever,

Elizabeth R

~

25 April 1976 to Queen Elizabeth II

The Royal Lodge

My Darling Lilibet

It was so wonderful being with the family for Easter at Windsor, and I don't think that I ever remember a more beautiful or peaceful week-end. I had been looking forward intensely to coming, and I can't tell you how revived I felt after those few days!

Somehow the three months after Christmas had been very difficult, what with one thing & another, and nowadays the only places I can relax in, are when I come to you, three times at Windsor, & the weekend at Balmoral.

It is really a joy, and such an enormous help to be surrounded by the darling children, & so many old jokes crop up, which also helps. You & Philip are always so angelic to me, and I always hope that I am not like Granny & stay too long!

I galvanized myself just enough to go to Sandown & present the Whitbread Gold Cup* to a dear little dairy farmer from Devonshire,

---

* The 1976 Gold Cup at Sandown was won by Otter Way, ridden by Jeff King and trained by Oliver Carter.

who had bred & trained the horse himself, bought the mare on Dartmoor with a lot of black cattle, & sent her eventually to a £10 stallion, & one felt that this is the lovely side of National Hunt racing, & what it's all about.

The flat horses all looked wonderfully well, & Riboboy seemed to win very well. John Howard de Walden's horse was 3rd, & looked a splendid type.[*]

Darling, how can I ever thank you enough for my heavenly visit – & don't forget about getting the pages to kneel & do the Garter up, they <u>should</u> be lissom boys, and will save us the agony of watching an aged Knight, purple in the face, trying to do the nearly impossible.[†] It's the difficulty of getting <u>up</u> which is so agonizing. John Abergavenny was very nearly brought down last year!!

Your very loving
Mummy

~

23 September 1976 to Dame Freya Stark[‡]

Birkhall

Dear Dame Freya,

It was a great joy to find the third volume of your 'Letters' waiting for me here, and it has come at exactly the right moment for I have just got to the end of volume II. I cannot tell you how much I am looking forward to reading it, or how deeply grateful I am to you for giving me such a perfect present.

I have enjoyed volume II quite enormously, and I am still feeling stunned at the thought of you riding 8 hours a day whilst having

[*] Lord Howard de Walden (1912–99), racehorse owner and breeder of great skill, three times elected as a senior steward of the Jockey Club.

[†] The Order of the Garter is the senior British order of chivalry, founded by King Edward III in 1348 and limited to the sovereign and twenty-four knights, conferred for service to the nation or to the sovereign personally. Its emblem is a blue garter with the famous motto 'Honi Soit Qui Mal Y Pense', worn by knights below the left knee. The sovereign invests new knights with the insignia of the Order – including, as well as the garter itself, the blue velvet mantle, the collar and badge, and star – during a Chapter of the Order in the Throne Room at Windsor Castle.

[‡] Dame Freya Stark DBE (1893–1993), British travel writer; her letters were published in eight volumes from 1974 to 1982, followed by a one-volume selection, edited by Caroline Moorehead, in 1988.

MEASLES! I remember how ill I felt when I had it years ago, and I cannot imagine how you survived. Sheer courage and determination I expect.

I am thrilled to start on volume III, and I think that I told you that I read one or two letters each day, so I make the reading of the book last a lovely long time.

With my warmest thanks, I am, ever yours sincerely,
Elizabeth R

~

2 November 1976 to the Prince of Wales

Clarence House

My Darling Charles,

Thank you so much for your dear letter. I know exactly how you feel about beloved Balmoral.

Somehow the whole place, the river, the mountains & the people are in one's BONES, and to leave it is really agony. I usually go to the Eagle's Nest (where the hut is) and walk up the hill behind, for my last look at the hills & trees before leaving for London, and it is always a moment of emotion. I think that we are lucky to have a place to love and to get our roots down, but oh! It is hard to leave.

What a lovely idea to come to you after the Cenotaph.* I would love to do this and I do hope that you will all come back here to lunch afterwards. Crackly potatoes?

I was SO sad not to see you in Scotland, but you were busy, and I know how precious every minute becomes [the Prince was now commanding the minehunter HMS *Bronington*].

I do hope that Andrew enjoyed his day with you – he was so looking forward to it.

Goodbyeeee, don't sigheeee, wipe the tear Baby dear from your eyeeee.†

---

* The 11 November Armistice Day celebration commemorating the dead in two world wars and other conflicts, at which the sovereign and other members of the Royal Family as well as politicians, high commissioners and ambassadors lay wreaths.

† The chorus of Weston & Lee's song had been famous since it was first heard in 1917:

Goodbye-ee, goodbye-ee, / Wipe the tear, baby dear, from your eye-ee! / Though it's hard to part I know, / I'll be tickled to death to go. / Don't cry-ee, don't sigh-ee, / There's a silver lining in the sky-ee, / Bonsoir, old thing, cheer-i-o, chin, chin, / Nap-poo, too-dle-oo, / Goodbye-ee.

I can't wait to come aboard at glamorous Tower Pier – why not cruise up the river and anchor off glorious Datchet? Or go aground off glorious Datchet?

A great deal of love from your loving GRANNIE

~

11 June 1977 to the Duke of Edinburgh

Clarence House

Dearest Philip,

At the end of this most memorable & happy week I just long to write a few lines to say how much you have meant during these 25 years,* not only to darling Lilibet, but to the family and the whole country.

Your strength and wisdom & courage have been such a wonderful help & comfort to us all, and as it is not easy to <u>say</u> these things, I send you a few loving thoughts on paper from a grateful & extremely affectionate Mama, E

<u>Please</u> no answer, just a wink at the Installation on Monday!

~

29 August 1977 to Queen Elizabeth II

Birkhall

My Darling Lilibet

I simply cannot believe that a whole year has passed since I sat down to try & thank you for another heavenly 2 days (or to be precise 2½) at Balmoral. As usual, it was wonderful being there with you & the family, and I hated leaving you all yesterday.

I was thinking in Church, looking at the row of brawny knees†

---

*   The Queen was celebrating her Silver Jubilee.

†   The row of brawny knees (in kilts) belonged to Prince Charles, Prince Andrew and Prince Edward. Of the Queen's children, only Princess Anne had already married; in 1973 she wed Mark Phillips, who shared her love of horses and Three Day Eventing. An accomplished horsewoman, Princess Anne was a member of the British Eventing Team at the 1976 Montreal Olympics. She and Mark Phillips had two children, Peter and Zara; the latter inherited her mother's equestrian skills and was a member of the British Eventing Team at the London 2012 Olympics, gaining a silver medal. The Phillips marriage ended in divorce in 1992. Later that year the Princess married Timothy Laurence, a commander in the Royal Navy who had served as an equerry to the Queen.

on your left, how proud you must be of those darling creatures – so good looking & gay & clever. And such good company! How I hope that they will all find dear, charming, pretty, intelligent, kind & GOOD girls to marry! I always feel sad having to say goodbye, & this house seems rather lonely at first. I was so lucky to have had David [Bowes Lyon], & then John [Elphinstone] to be 'family' – how sad that they all died so young.

The week hasn't started very well, as one of the Basset boys has just shut his finger in the car door, & been whisked off to Aberdeen for an x-ray! I was dreading a fly in the eye in this wind, so perhaps a finger is safer, poor little boy.

Thank you a thousand times darling for such a blissful visit, & I hope that you will have a <u>real</u> rest & much enjoyment.

Your very loving
Mummy

~

2 November 1977 to Sir Frederick Ashton

Clarence House

My dear Sir Frederick

I do want to send you a line of very warmest congratulations and hoorays on your receiving the O.M.*

<u>Everyone</u> is delighted, & when one thinks of your glorious Ballets, and where you have put our English ballet – on a pinnacle, one is full of gratitude – and so thrilled that your genius has been acknowledged in this way.

I am, ever yours,
Elizabeth R

~

---

* The choreographer Frederick Ashton was appointed to the Order of Merit in October 1977. Queen Elizabeth had admired his work since the 1930s. In 1985 she celebrated her eighty-fifth birthday at Sandringham by dancing with him to a wild mazurka played by Mstislav Rostropovich, the exiled Russian cellist.

26 August 1978 to the Prince of Wales

Balmoral Castle

My Darling Charles,

I am so thrilled with the beautiful trays, and very touched that you should have given me such a perfect birthday present. It is such a lovely picture of Balmoral that I feel it should be hung up, & not insulted by drops of tea or milk. Thank you a thousand times. I really do love it.

Darling, I can't tell you how moved I was to read your foreword to the Country Life book.* I don't deserve such wonderful words, and FAR the best moments of my life in these latter years have been watching you with admiration and deep love, and laughing with you, and discussing with you, and just enjoying being in your company! Hooray for jokes, even moderate ones!

With all my loving thanks from your devoted GRANNY

~

23 September 1978 to Lady Katharine Farrell†

Birkhall

Dearest Kitty

It was angelic of you to write me such a charming letter about my new appointment,‡ and I am so grateful. I have never seen

---

* The Prince had written: '. . . ever since I can remember, my grandmother has been the most wonderful example of fun, laughter, warmth, infinite security and, above all else, exquisite taste in so many things. For me, she has always been one of those extraordinarily rare people whose touch can turn everything to gold – whether it be putting people at their ease, turning something dull into something amusing, bringing happiness and comfort to people by her presence or making any house she lives in a unique haven of cosiness and character. She belongs to that priceless brand of human beings whose greatest gift is to enhance life for others through her own effervescent enthusiasm for life . . .' (Foreword by HRH The Prince of Wales to *The Country Life Book of Queen Elizabeth the Queen Mother* by Godfrey Talbot, Country Life Books, 1978)

† Lady Katharine Farrell (niece of Lady Diana Cooper) and her husband Charles were old friends and Queen Elizabeth enjoyed bucolic summer lunches at their home in Oxfordshire. Other guests often included the philanthropist Paul Getty and his wife Victoria. Getty's love of almost all things English was similar to that of Queen Elizabeth herself.

‡ Queen Elizabeth was installed in the historic post of Warden of the Cinque Ports in 1979. She enjoyed her annual visits to these once strategically vital harbours on the Kent coast and

Walmer Castle and I believe that the outside is romantic and the inside a little austere but I am longing to pay it a first visit. Some day you must come to stay there and we will sing a rousing chorus of 'I do like to be beside the seaside'.

    With my love, ever yours affec:

    Elizabeth R

~

30 December 1978 to Sir Charles and Lady Johnston

Sandringham

Dearest Natasha & Sir Charles*

    How could one ever have too many Pushkins!

    I am so delighted to have a copy of the American edition, and when one starts reading, it all seems new again, and I am full of delight, and also deep admiration of the tremendous knowledge and skill that has gone into such a marvellous translation.

    You are angels to give me such a perfect Christmas present, and I send you a thousand grateful thanks.

    With my love, and every good wish for the New Year,

    ever yours affect.

    Elizabeth R

~

4 February 1979 to Queen Elizabeth II

The Royal Lodge

My Darling Lilibet

    It is almost impossible to believe that those lovely weeks at Sandringham have gone by so terribly quickly! You know how much I look forward to January, plugging through those endless engagements in October & November, I felt encouraged by thinking of the bliss to come, and I can never thank you enough for letting me

---

would stay at Walmer Castle, which her staff from Clarence House furnished and fitted entirely for her short sojourns.

* Sir Charles Johnston GCMG KStJ (1912–86), senior British diplomat who translated Russian poetry, including Pushkin's *Eugene Onegin*, and whose wife Natasha was a member of the Georgian Royal Family. They were friends of Queen Elizabeth and regular, enthusiastic guests at Royal Lodge.

stay such a long time – I do love being there with you, and soaking in the dear family atmosphere. I feel totally relaxed, & oh! the pleasure of not having to order the food, or 'can I see you for a few minutes', and all the bothers of one's own house. I really feel a new person, and it lasts quite a long time! [. . .]

I have come to the conclusion, that at my age one begins to love a pattern of life. No hurry to get up in the morning, short walk with the dogs past the Church (hopeful), 12.45 off to Anmer or Wolferton, delicious gay lunch, lots of nice people. A little shooting, a look at the mares on the way home, feed the dogs, take them for a walk in semi-darkness, write a letter or two, go down for a drink & a talk – Dinner – BED – lovely calming life, & a real rest.

I am very fond of all your people, & I do hope that R. Fellowes will turn out wise, & a help.*

I went to Sandown on Friday, Fulke [Walwyn] very gloomy about Special Cargo† who had coughed & faded a bit, and I have never seen anyone as surprised as him when the horse won! But the great pleasure for me, was watching dear old Isle of Man sailing over the Railway fences, just like old days, and he only got beaten half a length or so by a good horse that was giving weight to. He looked like his old self, and was biting his loving lad with great zest after the race!

Back at Royal Lodge with the ground still hard, & not a sign of a snowdrop or an aconite. Margaret is here, well except for a cough, & E. Elphinstone for the weekend.

Darling Lilibet, how can I thank you enough for my happy time at Sandringham, also Philip who was most kind & affectionate to his long-staying M. in L.!

Lots of love from your
very loving
Mummy

~

---

* Robert Fellowes, Baron Fellowes GCB GCVO QSO PC (1941–), son of Sir William Fellowes, the Queen's Land Agent at Sandringham, and his wife Jane. Joined the Royal Household in 1977 and was Private Secretary to the Queen 1990–99, a difficult decade. Married to Jane, elder sister of Lady Diana Spencer, later Princess of Wales.

† One of Queen Elizabeth's favourite horses, Special Cargo went on to win the biggest race she had ever won, the Whitbread Gold Cup at Sandown in 1984, as well as several other major races. A statue of him was erected at Sandown.

24 February 1979 to Queen Elizabeth II

The Royal Lodge

My Darling Lilibet

Your journeys have been very fully reported in the papers, and I have been reading with great interest all the rather unusual things that you have been doing!* I don't know how hot hot [sic] it is, but you always look cool.

Here, everything rumbles along in the same old way, strikes everywhere, and yesterday the Civil Service joined in, and even annoyed Dr Owen.† In the old days the C.S. could not strike, but I suppose nowadays they include every sort of nationalised things, and yesterday people arriving by air had a marvellous time smuggling at the airports, because the customs men were on strike!

The Investiture this week went well, & there was a young sailor who had done extremely brave things when there was an explosion in an atomic submarine, & crept through scalding steam in darkness to see what was wrong. I said to him, 'that must have been a terrible experience' and he replied 'Not half as terrible as this', which was rather nice. He was white with apprehension & fear!

No racing news except that Upton Grey ran on Thursday, jumped badly, & ran abominably. I expect he's sickening for some disease – I do hope that there is a reason. I must say that it is rather depressing having mediocre horses, and one can't even run them to see if they are any good.

Charles has got into trouble by saying in his innocent way that management is not good in this country!! It is always fraught with danger if you criticize one side, and everyone is having a lovely time giving their ideas on the subject!

The Tongas came to tea – he has lost 90 pounds, & ate a hearty tea.‡

Darling, your letter has arrived. Thank you a thousand times, it is

---

*   The Queen had embarked on a tour of the Middle East (to Kuwait, Bahrain, Saudi Arabia, Qatar, the United Arab Emirates and Oman).

†   Dr David Owen, Foreign Secretary in the Labour government, 1977–9; afterwards co-founder of the Social Democrat Party, peer and negotiator for peace in Bosnia.

‡   Tāufaʻāhau Tupou IV (1918–2006) became King of Tonga on the death of his mother Queen Salote, who gave great pleasure to the London crowds when she drove to the Coronation in an open carrage despite the rain. His Queen was Halaevalu Mataʻaho ʻAhomeʻe.

so full of information & amusing happenings, & I am so grateful – I will keep it carefully for you. How exciting being given pearls, there is nothing nicer, & such a relief not being given huge echoing caskets.

The snow has gone for the moment, & a few snowdrops have come up, but the plants look shrivelled & cold. I can't wait for you to return, it is horrid when you are away, & what with Margaret in Mustique, the Gloucesters in Australia, Aunt Alice [Duchess of Gloucester] leaving this week – there seems to be nobody of the family except old Aunt Alice [Countess of Athlone] & me, with an occasional Charles.

With a great deal of love,
from your very loving
Mummy

PS I haven't yet been to see the dogs, because I thought that it might upset them & perhaps they would expect YOU.

~

25 February 1979 to Princess Margaret

The Royal Lodge

My Darling Margaret

It is so particularly cold this morning that my thoughts winged toward you, hoping that you are nice and warm in Mustique! It must be heavenly, & I trust that all is going well, & that you are really enjoying it all.

Here, things go on much the same, strikes, frost etc! [. . .]

The children came over for lunch yesterday, & seemed very well.* Unfortunately, David can't come to the Film Performance, because he is leaving school a few days early to go on a geographical expedition. I expect that it will be much more fun than our evening!

I am afraid that there is really no interesting news.

Last weekend Charles came to stay, also quite unexpectedly

---

* Princess Margaret and Lord Snowdon had divorced in 1978. Queen Elizabeth remained on close terms with Lord Snowdon for the rest of her life. She was a loving and dependable grandmother to their children, David and Sarah.

Nicholas Soames,* & then Hugh van Cutsem† turned up, as his
aeroplane couldn't leave from Heathrow.

I thought, how sickening Margaret not being here, as I know you
have some very dull weekends here, and suddenly 3 nice young
gentlemen turn up! So annoying. Anyway, they were very nice, & we
had a good laugh, & Hugh came to your detested Mattins, & enjoyed
it madly! Isn't it curious, the R.C.s who only have Mass, find the well
remembered Mattins very enjoyable.

A lovely 'diary' letter‡ has just arrived from Lilibet – I will keep it
until your return, to which I am looking forward <u>very</u> much, it is
horrid being totally alone in London, except for an occasional look-in
from Charles.

Much love darling from your loving
Mummy

~

15 August 1979 to Lady Katharine Farrell

The Castle of Mey

Dearest Kitty,

I was very touched that you should remember my birthday and I
write to thank you and Charles most warmly for such glorious
flowers [. . .]

Here one lives at the very furthest tip of these islands, and when
the sun shines, the sea is amazingly blue and the quality of the light
so lovely. I wish that some day you could come here. One feels so
beautifully far away and the newspapers come too late to be readable.

With my love and a thousand thanks,
I am ever yours,
Elizabeth R

~

---

* Nicholas Soames, MP for Mid Sussex, grandson of Winston Churchill. A convivial and loyal
friend of the Prince of Wales.

† Hugh van Cutsem, a Norfolk neighbour. He and his wife Emilie were close friends of the
Royal Family, particularly of the Prince of Wales.

‡ Queen Elizabeth II usually sent long letters to her mother while on official tours abroad.

26 April 1980 to Queen Elizabeth II

Clarence House

My Darling Lilibet

It seems too shaming that I started to write to you last Tuesday week, on leaving Windsor, and have started several times since, only to be done in by various ailments, really to thank you for another lovely Easter week. It was such luck having that glorious weather, and what with the bliss of picnics at Frogmore, and heavenly 'family' evenings, the week went by far too quickly. I do love being at Windsor, tho' I equally love being at Sandringham, and I am sure that it is quite possible to love different places in different ways, each as much as the other. And then, what about Balmoral! I adore that place. Possibly, as one gets older one's memories become more precious, and such odd things come to mind. When walking down to Frogmore, I always think of how TIRED I felt, pottering down the hill with Granny & Grandpapa! Curiously enough, I don't feel half as tired at 79 as I did at 28!! Count your blessings! Ha Ha.

With very much love, and a million thanks for yet another most happy Easter week,

ever your loving

Mummy

~

22 May 1980 to the Prince of Wales

Craigowan Lodge

My Darling Charles,

I cannot tell you how thrilled and amazed I was to find that huge LOG CABIN sitting so happily amongst the trees by the side of Polveir! It looked as if it had always been there, and I can never thank you & the other kind donors sufficiently for thinking of such a marvellous present.*

And the nicest thing is that I can visualize all the next generations

---

* For Queen Elizabeth's eightieth birthday, family and friends clubbed together to buy her a Scandinavian log cabin which was erected by her favourite pool, Polveir, close to Birkhall on the River Dee. The cabin was an inspired gift – it was much used for picnic lunches over the years to come. It was often called 'The Old Bull and Bush'.

having lovely picnics there, you, & perhaps your grandchildren and great-grandchildren! With the water either roaring or trickling by & the occasional flop! of a fish which refuses to be caught.

The amount of times that I have, muffled up and shivering with cold, sat eating lunch with frozen fingers which are too atrophied to hold a stuffed roll – these days are now past, and I shall bask in the luxury of a wood fire, lolling back in a comfortable chair, and BLESSING you & the family and friends for this total change in my fishing and picnic life. Thank you a million times from your grateful & loving GRANNY

~

5 August 1980 to Queen Elizabeth II

Clarence House

My Darling Lilibet

How can I ever thank you sufficiently for all the wonderful arrangements that you made for my birthday. St Paul's, the Garden Party, the Holyrood evening, were all such happy affairs, & enjoyed by everyone who was there.

And now the FUR COAT! Never in my wildest dreams did I think that I would actually own one! You are such a kind and loving angel, & I am deeply deeply grateful.

Thank you my darling a million times –
Your very loving
Mummy

~

5 August 1980 to Princess Margaret

Clarence House

My Darling Margaret

How can I ever thank you sufficiently for arranging two such marvellous evenings at Holyrood and Covent Garden?

Everything was perfection, & what was so splendid, was that not only me, but everyone simply adored them. I know what a lot of trouble you took over the many details, and I am everlastingly grateful.

And then the FUR COAT! The biggest & most exciting surprise of my life. It really was angelic of you & Lilibet to even think of such a wonderful present, and thank you, my darling a thousand times.

Your very loving & grateful

Mummy

~

22 October 1980 to Queen Elizabeth II

Birkhall

My Darling Lilibet

As you are away for so long,* I thought that perhaps you might like to have a word from soaking wet, thick misty, soggy Aberdeenshire! This has gone on for at least four or five days, succeeding the coldest few days that I can remember here! Thick snow on the hills, <u>icy</u> north wind, & frequent showers of snow & sleet! Last Saturday I went over the hill to Brechin & on the top of Cairn o' Mount looked down on a lovely landscape, golden sunshine & clear blue skies! What a funny climate we live in.

I do hope that all is going well – I follow your journeys in the papers, & now you are with my old pal Bourguiba.† I do hope that you didn't have to eat soft poached eggs in your fingers, as I had to do at a dinner party with Bourguiba.

I go south on Thursday, pausing to plant a rose tree in Aberdeen en route for the airport. How I do hate planting the first of 80 roses – I had to do it here the other day, & all over the place, & if I ever get to 81 there won't be any room anywhere in England & Scotland for any more <u>roses</u>, thank goodness.

It seems ages since you left here, & I am <u>so</u> looking forward to your return. I do hope that you have kept well – Italy and N. Africa are bad tummy places, so hope you have a good store of Arsenicum.‡

A great deal of love darling, & to Philip

from your very loving

Mummy

~

---

* The Queen was on tour in Tunisia.

† Habib Bourguiba (1903–2000), President of Tunisia. Queen Elizabeth had made an official visit in 1961, four years after Tunisia gained independence from France.

‡ *Arsenicum album*, a homeopathic remedy.

28 March 1981 to Lady Diana Cooper

Clarence House

Dearest Lady Diana,

Once again I am writing to thank you for a perfect lunch party, and a <u>most</u> enjoyable Noon cocktail party. Your neighbours are so delightful and amusing and varied, and it is great fun to watch the famous HOUSE POISON doing its work, voices rising, conversation becoming more & more sparkling, & even the dear faces of the clergy becoming a tiny bit roseate. Oh, it is such fun, and I adore coming to see you, & I enjoy myself madly in the lovely & relaxed atmosphere that you create round you, & I am deeply grateful to you for giving me such a heavenly treat.

With so many heartfelt thanks, I am,

ever yours affec:

Elizabeth R

~

17 May 1981 to Sir Ralph Anstruther

Clarence House

Dear Ralph,

I thought that [France]* this year was better than ever. Such charming hosts, and lovely chateaux [. . .]

PS I have a strong feeling that BRITTANY is on the *tapis* for next year. What do you think?

With so much gratitude, I am, ever yours,

Elizabeth R

~

---

* Queen Elizabeth had hankered since the mid 1950s to revisit France, which she had loved as a young woman. In 1963 this dream came true and over the next thirty years she made twenty-two private tours – progresses, perhaps – through different regions of France and then Italy, staying in some of the loveliest chateaux, visiting churches, galleries and other sites of historical interest. The visits were complicated for her Treasurer, Sir Ralph Anstruther, and her hosts to arrange, but they were greatly enjoyed. The maid at one chateau where she stayed commented, 'La Reine Mère est bien plus commode que Madame.' (Anstruther account, 5 April 1965, RA QEQMH/PS/VIS)

21 May 1981 to Lady Katharine Farrell

Birkhall

Dearest Kitty,

I am still glowing with pleasure at the memory of that delightful 'conducted tour' that you so kindly arranged last Sunday. [. . .] I shall never forget driving up that secret green lane and coming suddenly upon that hidden and mysterious house untouched through the centuries and inhabited by the right sort of rather mysterious people! I liked them so much and they were so kind and welcoming. The house was thrilling, those great beams made granite by age and the garden absolutely crowded with green cones all jostling each other. One felt transported into another age, and what was very nice was the feeling that house and garden were greatly loved. Then back down the green lane into our own age and a delectable tea party with the Carringtons.* I hadn't been 'out to tea' for absolutely ages and I adored it.

And I adore the Carringtons! It's so comforting to know two people who one can truly admire. [. . .]

With my fond love, ever yours affec:

Elizabeth R

~

20 October 1981 to the Earl of Snowdon

Clarence House

Dearest Tony,

I was thrilled to receive an invitation to open (or perform the opening ceremony) at the recently completed great bridge† at Old House and I would like to congratulate you most heartily on bringing this great project to a happy conclusion. I have read many articles in the press about the extreme difficulties of the terrain, the

---

* Peter Carington, sixth Baron Carrington KG GCMG CH MC PC DL (1919–); married to Iona (1920–2009). A politician of distinction, Carrington was Foreign Secretary in Mrs Thatcher's government. He resigned in April 1982, accepting responsibility for the Foreign Office's failure to anticipate Argentina's invasion of the Falkland Islands. Such principled resignations were by this time rare in British politics.

† Lord Snowdon had designed a bridge to cross a stream on his property, Old House in Sussex.

depth of water, the strong current, and of course the great length of the many spans. It will be a great pleasure for me to take part in this momentous occasion and I suggest that we have a meeting with your agent at some future date to discuss ways and means and dates. But, bar chaff, it looks so pretty, much at home with the various shrubs and weeping trees. With my love, ever your affectionate ER

~

23 July 1982 to Andrew Parker Bowles

Clarence House

My dear Andrew

I have been thinking of you so much this week, since the senseless and cruel happenings, and I do want to send you a line of truly heartfelt sympathy.*

That precious men and beloved horses should have to suffer like this, is beyond comprehension, & I think that it has all aroused anger & revulsion everywhere. One feels so proud, that the next day they were riding past here, en route for the Horse Guards, looking magnificent.

I can imagine how agonizing it must have been for you.

I am, ever yours,

Elizabeth R

~

5 August 1982 to the Prince of Wales

Clarence House

My Darling Charles,

Ten thousand loving thanks to you & Diana for the most useful and badly needed birthday present that one could imagine. All

---

* Colonel Andrew Parker Bowles, Lieutenant Colonel in the Blues and Royals. Son of Queen Elizabeth's friend Derek, and a frequent visitor to the Castle of Mey, sometimes with his wife Camilla. On 20 July 1982, the IRA committed twin atrocities in London – they blew up the bandstand in Regent's Park when a band from the Royal Green Jackets was giving a concert; this attack killed seven bandsmen and wounded many in the audience. On the same day an IRA car bomb in Hyde Park killed three soldiers and seven horses from the Queen's Life Guard (found from the Blues and Royals). One horse, Sefton, suffered a severed jugular and Parker Bowles ordered a groom to staunch the wound with his shirt. The horse survived and became something of an icon. Parker Bowles and his wife divorced in 1995, and in 2005 she married the Prince of Wales, becoming HRH The Duchess of Cornwall.

Bishops seem to be ten feet high and six broad, so the splendid chair will receive the Episcopal bottom with comfort & elegance, whilst the Episcopal throat gulps down the post sermon gin and tonic. Perhaps I shall get the chance to relax in it on a week day.

I am so glad you like the little gold mug – a difficult one for even a strong baby to break.*

With so much love & thanks, ever your loving Granny

~

18 October 1982 to Queen Elizabeth II

Birkhall

My Darling Lilibet

Thinking of you in great heat & chiffon, I write, as usual, in a downpour of rain and thick wool!

It has really never stopped since you left,† and everyone is amazed, & we all ask 'Where is our lovely frosty Golden October', to which there seems no answer. But all the same, I would rather be here in the grey days than in London in sunshine.

I follow your travels on the television & papers, and it all sounds fascinating & now, very far away. I do hope not too tiring, tho' I expect that the yacht is salvation. [. . .]

It is a fortnight since you left, and I always count the days until you return, which means another fortnight, and to think of the immense amount you are doing, & how little I am doing! Pottering down to the Log Cabin, walking back through the wood, which, by the way, I couldn't do yesterday, because the river had come over the bank & inundated the little path.

I saw Special Leave win at Ascot – he looked splendid & did it so well – I do hope & pray that he goes on well. Michael‡ kindly sent me copies of the photographs of the foals. I like to think of you poring over them & dreaming dreams! [. . .]

---

* Prince William Arthur Philip Louis, first child of the Prince and Princess of Wales, was born on 21 June 1982.

† The Queen was on an official tour of Australia and the Pacific islands.

‡ Sir Michael Oswald, KCVO (1934–), the Manager of the Royal Studs at this time, and Queen Elizabeth's Racing Manager from 1970 to 2002. He and his wife Lady Angela, a lady in waiting to Queen Elizabeth from 1981 to 2002, accompanied her on her racing engagements.

Geordie is <u>much</u> better & full of life. Only one back leg is weak, & he manages quite well now that he has learnt which one works at certain important moments!

A great deal of love darling
from your very loving
Mummy

~

3 December 1982 to Catherine Walwyn

Royal Lodge

My dear Cath,

It was so kind of you to write me such a sweet letter of sympathy last week, and I was very touched by what you said. Everything is now back to normal, except for a slight feeling of jetlag!*

We haven't had much luck with the horses the last season or two, I feel that poor Fulke has been saddled with a rather unlucky owner! But things will change I am sure, & one always thinks 'next time', which is a comfort.

Anyway, I love having horses with Fulke, he is a wonderful trainer, and I always enjoy my times with you & him.

With my warmest thanks,
I am, ever yours affectionately,
Elizabeth R.

~

8 January 1983 to Edward Cazalet

Sandringham

My dear Edward,

It was so kind of you to send me the book with the fascinating dedication to my naughty cousins!†

---

* A fishbone had lodged in Queen Elizabeth's throat and she had needed an operation under anaesthetic to remove it.

† P. G. Wodehouse's first book, *The Pothunters*, was published in 1902, and sold well enough to encourage him to leave the Hong Kong and Shanghai Bank to start his career as a writer. It was dedicated to Joan (1888–1954), Effie (1889–1981) and Ernestine 'Teenie' (1891–1981) Bowes Lyon, the young daughters of Hon. Ernest Bowes Lyon, Queen Elizabeth's uncle. Wodehouse had an avuncular relationship with them and told their mother, 'I occupy in your house a

The eldest (& naughtiest) was extremely pretty so that might have been a reason!

Anyway, I am delighted to have the book, and send you my warmest thanks, and every possible good wish for 1983,

& I am, ever yours,

Elizabeth R.

~

17 February 1983 to Sir Charles Johnston

Clarence House

Dear Sir Charles

What a delightful lunch that was yesterday, & I write to thank you and Natasha most warmly for your kindness in asking me to such a truly enjoyable occasion.

It is such a wonderful feeling, eating delicious food amongst the treetops of London, and I felt so happy and relaxed in the warm and friendly atmosphere that you both created.

I greatly enjoyed meeting Mr James* (the first Socialist Democrat†that I have actually met!), and I do hope that I was not too outspoken at lunch about that particular party!

One can't help feeling a bit uncertain about people who leave the good old Labour party to invent a 'Social' (What's that) 'Democratic' (equally mysterious) party – perhaps rather up a Don's street!!

With again my thanks for a splendid lunch,

& with my love to Natasha

I am, ever yours,

Elizabeth R

~

---

position equivalent to that of cold beef . . . If there is nobody new to talk to, the Lyon cubs talk to me' (Robert McCrum, *Wodehouse: A Life*, Viking, 2004, pp. 53–4).

* Clive James CBE AM (1939–), Australian writer, broadcaster, poet and wit.

† The Social Democratic Party, formed in 1981 by four senior Labour politicians, Roy Jenkins, David Owen, Bill Rodgers and Shirley Williams, who believed the Labour Party had become too left-wing. In 1988 the party merged with the Liberal Party to form the Liberal Democrats.

28 February 1983 to Queen Elizabeth II

The Royal Lodge

My Darling Lilibet

When I begin a letter to you, I always think, how dreadfully dull it is going to be! and this time it is just the same!

The only really hot news is that Blackie has had his remaining teeth out, (being poisoned says Mr Grimes) and is now sleeping off the effects of the anaesthetic.

Your news is always interesting & thrilling, and thank you very much for your first letter.* I sent it on to Charles & Anne. Now, you are approaching America, & I am hoping that the BBC has turned loyal and will give us some good pictures. They are such <u>nice</u> people (Americans, not BBC), so kind & overwhelming, I really believe that they mean it.

Since you left these shores life goes on much the same. Anne & I have done some Ambassadors, & she has been really splendid. [. . .]

You will not be surprised to hear that the reluctant Master Andrew blotted his already tarnished copy book again today at Kempton. He dropped himself out in a <u>very</u> hot race, & then fell! I have an awful feeling that he hates jumping. [. . .]

It is such a comfort to write this to you, because I know you understand one's feelings, so do forgive me. In fact, I have no one to boo hoo to about the horses – I won't do it again! Not <u>just</u> yet!

I think about you all the time, we all do, and I am sure that the present tour will do a <u>tremendous</u> lot of good. So much love darling Lilibet, & lots to Philip,

ever your very loving
Mummy

~

On 20 March 1983 the Prince of Wales, with the Princess of Wales and their son, Prince William, landed in Alice Springs for an official visit to Australia. They were away for over a month. Queen Elizabeth wrote to the Princess of Wales congratulating her on the success of the tour,

---

* The Queen was on her way to the USA and Canada after visiting Jamaica and the Cayman Islands.

during which the Princess had been the centre of obsessive media attention. The Princess replied, saying she was 'enormously touched by your letter – the thought gave me a lot of happiness. Charles is the one who deserves all the credit by showing me what to do, and how to do it, always patient and ready to explain. The whole Tour seems to have helped me a great deal on how to cope with my public duties, so all in all, a good experience!'*

~

19 April 1983 to the Prince of Wales

Clarence House

My Darling Charles,

The enormous tour seems to be going <u>so</u> well, and I do hope that you are both surviving the strain. It is so nice to be <u>wanted</u>, and this shows through all the pictures & news reels and I do think that you and Diana are being <u>MARVELLOUS</u>.

I remember so well our visit over fifty years ago, all by ship and train – dinner at 6 o'clock etc, and how dreadfully tired one sometimes felt, but, at the same time, uplifted by the love & loyalty shown to us. I don't think that things have changed too much?

Here everything goes on much the same. Heavy going for the horses, buckets of rain, and everything beginning to come out. At Royal Lodge the magnolias are flowering marvellously, & the camellias [are] very good, and even the tulips are nearly out! You will be coming home to see your garden full of colour.

I do hope that some day you will take on Royal Lodge. So convenient to London and you will carry on the garden, & make it more beautiful!

Darling Charles, thank you so much for your lovely, long, & illuminating letter. It was most interesting to know your views on Australia. I gave it to Mummy to read, & she was also deeply interested.

We all felt rather sad at Easter, with you & Diana in Australia, Andrew in America & Edward in N.Z. and even Sarah [Princess Margaret's daughter] in Eleuthera. <u>How</u> I look forward to your

---

* Princess of Wales to Queen Elizabeth, 19 May 1983, RA QEQM/PRIV/RF.

return, & it is wonderful how much pleasure you have both given,
and with so much love, ever your very loving Granny.

~

18 September 1983 to Fulke Walwyn

Birkhall

My dear Fulke,

Just a line to say how deeply distressed I was to hear the sad news
of gallant little Gay George.*

You must feel his loss terribly, because there was something very
special about him, wasn't there?

There is something very touching when courage and beauty go
together, and I always loved seeing him in his box when I was
looking at my horses.

It so often seems to be the good ones, but they are never
forgotten – I am sure.

Please don't answer this letter, I just wanted to send my
sympathy, & I am ever yours,

Elizabeth R.

~

19 November 1983 to Queen Elizabeth II

Clarence House

My Darling Lilibet,

Your visit to Kenya seems to have gone very well, and I do hope
that parts of it were enjoyable and sometimes amusing. There have
been many photographs and television pictures, which is splendid.
Tho' you haven't been away all that long, it seems ages and I look
forward so much to your return.

Things go along much the same here, tho' it seemed very odd not
to have you at the Cenotaph and the Albert Hall.

The family came to dinner here after the latter, and they all
seemed in good form, and you've never seen such complicated eaters
and drinkers (or non-drinkers)! Can't eat meat (it was only little pieces
of veal), wouldn't touch the mirabelles (smelled of brandy) etc etc!

---

* Gay George, a handsome dark-brown horse owned by the Duke of Devonshire and trained
by Walwyn, fell at a fence at Warwick and died.

It really was funny, as they are all comparatively young – & very choosy. But they were all very nice. [. . .]

The ground continues iron hard, & I don't think that I shall have any runners in the near future. The poor trainers are going mad, because they simply can't get the horses fit. It is very frustrating, & one sees walk-overs for lovely prizes!

Dear old Olav* was very well, and slept happily through the Remembrance at the Albert Hall, only waking up tactfully when there was clapping!

Darling old Blackie is slowing down rather quickly. He occasionally has a good day, but his left eye has gone, and he can only see me about 12 yards away.

I must try and find another couple of dogs, for life would be intolerable without their company. Geordie is very well, and would, I think, accept young ones coming in.

It is always difficult starting again, for these two know one's every movement – when one gets up or goes to bed, what clothes are hopeful, which car means the country etc etc! [. . .]

All your hats & dresses look lovely on the tele – <u>&</u> you darling.

Much love to Philip, from your very loving Mummy

~

1 March 1984 to Prince Philip

Clarence House

Darling Philip,

Thank you a thousand times for giving me a copy of your latest book.† I am so looking forward to reading it – I hope that you saw some of the excellent reviews in the papers?

I simply can't imagine where & how you find the time to write on such very varied subjects, & what research it must involve.

Much love and many thanks from Mama E

~

---

*   King Olav V of Norway.

†   *Men, Machines and Sacred Cows*, a collection of Prince Philip's views and speeches, published by Hamish Hamilton. Later in 1984, *A Windsor Correspondence* was published – this was a collection of Prince Philip's letters to and from the Right Rev. Michael Mann, the Dean of Windsor. Their letters dealt with evolution, fundamentalism and morality.

6 August 1984 to the Prince of Wales

Clarence House

My Darling Charles,

I simply cannot tell you how touched I was that you made that dash from plane to plane, to come to lunch on my birthday. It made all the difference in the world, and thank you a thousand times.

And I must thank you for the charming table for the terrace at Royal Lodge – just what I needed and wanted, a perfect birthday present. You really are an angel.

It will be wonderful if you can manage those few days at Birkhall in October. I think now of the beauty of the hills, and the peace of mind that comes when one walks on them, no screaming police sirens & no hurry hurry – oh bliss.

Once again, a million thanks darling Charles for your dash here – and your lovely gift. I do hope that your visit went well.

So much love, from your devoted Granny

~

3 October 1984 to Queen Elizabeth II

The Castle of Mey

My Darling Lilibet

I hope that all is going well in Canada, and that you are not totally exhausted. It sounds terribly strenuous. [. . .]

Last week I went over to the Isle of Man, & opened the Commonwealth Conference for you. They all seemed happy together, & were going for endless bus rides round the Island, which sounded very dull! I stayed with a nice Admiral called Cecil, last C-in-C Malta I think, & they were most kind.* It is rather curious that I have been both to the Isle of Man & Northern Ireland within a year, & in both places so many memories of darling Rosie, and the gardens she had made & left behind her.†

---

*   Rear Admiral Sir Oswald Cecil KBE CB (1925–), became Lieutenant Governor of the Isle of Man in 1980, a post he held for five years.

†   Earl Granville, husband of Queen Elizabeth's sister Rose, was Lieutenant Governor of the Isle of Man 1937–45, Governor of Northern Ireland 1945–52. One of Queen Elizabeth's older sisters, Rosie died in 1967.

On Monday I went down to Rosyth to the re-commissioning of Resolution, & lunch with the Admiral, another nice one! I went all round the submarine full of mysteries, and full of cheerful and delightful sailors! Naval people are always so easy & nice to talk to, don't you find? [. . .]

With <u>so</u> much love darling Lilibet, from your very loving
Mummy

~

6 February 1985 to Queen Elizabeth II

Clarence House

My Darling Lilibet,

How can I even <u>begin</u> to thank you for that wonderful visit to Sandringham? It was pure bliss from beginning to end, and I came away feeling a totally new person. It is like a galvanizing rest cure, I suppose some of it comes from being with you & the family, and the rest being able to go out in the good air, & being able to spend a lot of time with the horses, and being able, once again, to live a happy family life.

You are such a kind angel to me, and I suppose that you are one of the few people that I can talk to freely, & it is all wonderful.

I do mind so much what happens to you all, & long for you to have peace & happiness in your own home.

Darling, a million grateful thanks for your endless thoughtful kindness, from your very very loving
Mummy

~

22 March 1986 to Henrietta Knight

The Royal Lodge

Dearest Henrietta*

It was so dear of you to give me that lovely photograph of Dangerous Game, and I do hope that he gets a run before the end of the season. Fulke did not think that he was quite ready for Friday,

---

* Henrietta Knight B.Ed (1946–), successful racehorse trainer, whose husband, the former champion jockey Terry Biddlecombe, rode many times for the Queen Mother.

perhaps coming over from Ireland is a bit of a shock, new food, new water, new lad, but he seems to have settled down very happily.

I still miss Doctor McCluskie very much! He was such a lovely young horse, & I had watched him growing & maturing, & perhaps one had one's dreams too soon!

Congratulations on all your winners – it is <u>marvellous</u>.

With my love and thanks,

I am, ever yours affect.

Elizabeth R

~

10 April 1986 to Queen Elizabeth II

Clarence House

My Darling Lilibet

I did so love my Easter week at Windsor, and send a million thanks for all the fun and kindness. It is always a joy to be with <u>you</u> and to have such a glorious family party as well, made it all very special. I miss it all dreadfully when I leave, and the first day or two here were very depressing and <u>DULL</u>!

I thought that Sarah* fitted in very happily, didn't you? She is such a cheerful person, and seems to be so thankful & pleased to be part of a united family, & is truly devoted to darling Andrew. It seems most hopeful which is a comfort. [. . .]

But, darling, I was touched beyond words by your concern for my hopeless racing account. Just like you, & I have managed to pay in a certain amount, and hope to find homes for several horses which will help. Oh, for the good old days when hay was twelve pounds a ton, & no huge vets' bills for poisoning poor horses!

With so many loving thanks for my heavenly visit, all so familiar & so full of memories,

from your very loving and slightly nostalgic

Mummy

~

---

* Sarah Ferguson married Prince Andrew, Duke of York, and became Duchess of York on 23 July 1986. They had two children, Princess Beatrice and Princess Eugenie; they were divorced in 1996.

28 June 1986 to the Right Rev. Robin Woods, former Dean of Windsor

The Royal Lodge

My dear Bishop,*

It was a great joy to see you at the Windsor reception, and thinking of old days, it seemed exactly right that we should meet in St George's Hall! It is most kind of you to give me a copy of your autobiography, and I shall read it, I know, with great interest and pleasure.

I have, this minute, returned from a few days in Tuscany, so I have only had time to read the first few chapters, and learned for the first time how long your dear father had to be in Switzerland and how marvellous was his recovery from tuberculosis.

He meant a great deal to the King & myself, and was our 'Librarian' for many years, and I think that it was he who gave my husband a book called 'The Upper Room', which gave him a great deal of thought & evoked much discussion!†

It is curious, how in a fairly long life some moments remain so vivid in one's memory. And one is, prayers in the Chapel before going to bed, when we were staying with your parents at Lichfield. A moment of tranquillity and peace never to be forgotten.

With again my warmest thanks for the delightful book,

I am, ever yours

Elizabeth R

~

2 May 1988 to Queen Elizabeth II

Clarence House

My Darling Lilibet

Every day I read about endless things that you are doing, and

---

* Bishop Robin Woods KCMG KCVO (1914–97), son of Right Rev. Edward Woods, Bishop of Lichfield, whom the Queen had valued as a spiritual counsellor. Edward Woods was 'Librarian' to the King and Queen in the sense that he often sent the Queen books dealing with religious matters, particularly during the Second World War. Robin Woods was a distinguished Dean of Windsor, 1962–70; he reorganized the Chapter and was the founder of the inter-faith consultation centre, St George's House, in which Prince Philip played a major role.

† *The Upper Room* described the work of Toc H.

hope so much that you are bearing up? You look very happy & pretty in the pictures so perhaps you are!

Here everything seems to go on much the same, IRA murders, horses running badly, rain pouring down, and an occasional uplift when Dick Hern* has some lovely horses winning races!

I believe that your lovely filly has got over her horrid accident, & it will be very interesting when she runs.

I went over to see Charles's new offices [in York House, St James's Palace], which seem a great success. Anyway, it means that he does see his office people, & also visiting foreigners etc in a more handy place! It was so funny, I couldn't help remembering when Uncle David† lived there, and going to dances after the theatre etc, & the thrill of being partnered by Fred Astaire! It's rather a pity that one couldn't have plaques put up to remind one of the unlikely residents who lived there, Uncle David with his rather smart entourage, & Uncle Harry‡ to succeed in quite a different way of life.

I went to see the Australians 'on guard' next door, & they were so nice. They adored their visit and they were all absolutely exhausted! They were so touched by their visit to Windsor, and were all going back there, to have a photograph taken in the Long Walk with the Castle in the background. What a lot of good it has done.

I count the days when you are away, and the time of your return is now not too far. I am going up to Birkhall for just about ten days on May 11th, the day after you return, so perhaps you will give me a ring when you feel able?

Dash has gone to join your corgis at Windsor, and Ranger is dreadfully lonely, he keeps very close to me, & moons about in a most depressed way! She is very much the moving spirit.

So much love darling, from
your very loving
Mummy

~

---

*   Dick Hern CVO (1921–2002), racehorse trainer to the Queen.

†   The Prince of Wales, the future King Edward VIII.

‡   Prince Henry, Duke of Gloucester.

On 3 June 1988 Queen Elizabeth spoke at the unveiling of an
English Heritage blue plaque to mark the residence of P. G.
Wodehouse at 17 Dunraven Street, London W1

I am particularly pleased to have been invited to unveil this plaque as
for many years I have been an ardent reader of P. G. Wodehouse.
Indeed, I am proud to say that his very first book 'The Pothunters'
was dedicated by him to members of my family.

Sir Pelham Wodehouse succeeded in the great ambition of so
many novelists: not only has he brought new words and expressions
into the English language but he has also created characters whose
names have become household words – Jeeves and Bertie, Lord
Emsworth and his prize pig, the Empress of Blandings, and even Aunt
Agatha, to name but a few, live on as immortal characters.

Nevertheless I think that Wodehouse's greatest gift is that fifty or
sixty years after many of his books were written they still make us all
laugh, and I am sure that generations to come will continue to laugh
at them just as much as we have done. What an encouraging thought
for the future!

P. G. Wodehouse lived in this house from 1927 until 1934, and I
am delighted to unveil the plaque which now records this.

~

19 July 1988 to Rachel Bowes Lyon

Clarence House

Darling Rachel

Another heavenly weekend at St Paul's Walden is over, and now I
have many happy memories to enjoy. It was thrilling to see your new
garden, and I was amazed at how much you have achieved in such a
short time. You really are a Garden Wizard!

I loved wandering round the old Barns and Flea House, &
remembering some of the old characters who seemed to live there.
Will Wren's parlour, and Charles May's shed, were always full of
fascinating & exciting objects when we were children, and the Brew
House with its dangerous deep well, and chaff cutting machine, were
very special and rather frightening!

And once again, the garden and wood, so beloved and so full of
memories, were looking wonderful.

Thank you a thousand times for a truly happy visit, and I am, as always,

your loving
Elizabeth

~

10 September 1988 to Camilla Cazalet

Birkhall

My dear Camilla,*
You wrote me such a charming letter about our beloved Freddy [Ashton], and it is hard to believe that such a dear friend has left us.†

I think of the word <u>integrity</u> when I think of him, he was so wonderfully honest in his opinions, and I think thank goodness his great genius will live on in his works.

And what fun he was to be with! Such laughs, and we were always so amused by what I called his 'marble profile' when he was displeased with a play or some unpleasing music, real rigid displeasure!

Oh, how we shall miss him, I don't think that he had the faintest idea, how dear he was to his friends, so modest was he.

With so many thanks for your letter, I know what a great blank this will be to you, who was always so wonderful to him,

& I am ever your affec
Elizabeth R

~

24 September 1988 to the Prince of Wales

Birkhall

My Darling Charles,
Monday, Tuesday and Wednesday of this week seem now like a lovely dream, & no one but you could have thought of such a marvellous, imaginative and brilliant birthday present. When sitting in a butt, and gazing at those glorious mountains, I was whisked back in time & those fifteen years just rolled away, and I felt so happy and

---

* Camilla, The Hon. Lady Cazalet (1937–), daughter of sixth Viscount Gage, wife of Edward Cazalet.

† Sir Frederick Ashton died on 19 August 1988.

carefree. [. . .] Everything was perfect, including the weather! I shall
never forget the beauty of the Monday at Corndavon, sitting outside
the Old Lodge, surrounded by dear friends. It was all too wonderful
for words. I was so pleased that I am still able to walk up that steep
hill to the second drive after lunch!! One is <u>so</u> grateful to be mobile!
I do love those undulating hills. Their grandeur and peace seem to
make one's own troubles & anxieties seem so small.

It was, I am sure, one of the happiest 3 days in my life, all due to
your dear self, and my thanks do come straight from my heart.

With so much love from your very loving Granny

~

26 December 1988 to the Prince and Princess of Wales

Clarence House

Darling Charles and Diana,
You have given me the most <u>marvellous</u> Christmas present, and I
can now look forward to <u>hours</u> of glorious Hancock.*

Thank you a MILLION times from your extremely grateful
Granny

~

11 February 1989 to Ashe Windham†

Clarence House

My dear Ashe,
What a delightful reunion that was the other evening!

It was such fun having it down in that cosy old kitchen at Pratt's
Club, with that very old trout hanging on the wall, and the card
tables set out all ready for endless games of dominoes or six pack
bezique or whatever true Pratt-ites play.

I know that the lovely idea of an 'old comrades' dinner party was

---

* Tony Hancock (1924–68), English comedian and actor, famous for the BBC series *Hancock's
Half Hour*.

† Ashe Windham CVO (1957–), Irish Guards officer, equerry to Queen Elizabeth and extra
equerry to HRH the Prince of Wales; from 1996 Chairman of the Queen Elizabeth Castle of
Mey Trust. By way of thanking Queen Elizabeth for her hospitality at the Castle the previous
summer, Windham organized annual midwinter dinners for her guests and equerries.

all yours and Mikie [Strathmore's] idea, and I do want to thank you very warmly for arranging such a happy treat for us all.*

Everyone seemed in excellent form and 'doing alright' which is always a relief nowadays.

I do hope that you will be able to come up to Birkhall in May, between 10th and 20th and see if buying off the nets on the Dee is having any effect. Perhaps it is to too soon to say.

With again <u>so</u> many thanks for a wonderful evening, I am ever yours,

Elizabeth R

~

11 February 1989 to Dame Freya Stark

Clarence House

Dear Dame Freya,

I was so thrilled and very touched that you should wish me to have a copy of the latest volume of your Letters, and I do want to send you my warmest thanks for giving me such a delightful present.

I particularly love the letters from the desert, so vivid and so beautifully descriptive, I almost feel that I am standing with you, gazing into the distance & feeling content.

I often think of the day when I came to visit you in Asolo.† You were standing at the top of the stairs, holding a glorious bunch of roses, and wearing an extremely becoming hat, and you gave me such a lovely welcome, & showed me the layout of the garden, and that day remains with me as a very happy memory.

Once again, may I thank you for the precious book.

I do hope that we shall meet again in heavenly Asolo

& I am, ever yours,

Elizabeth R

~

---

* A member who visited the Club before this dinner recalled a sign on the wall with words to the effect 'Gentlemen, the Club will be closed for dinner on 9 February 1989. I will tell you why afterwards. Devonshire.' (Pratt's was owned by the Duke of Devonshire.)

† Asolo, a Renaissance hill-town in the Veneto where Dame Freya lived for most of her life and where Queen Elizabeth visited her while touring the Palladian villas of the region in 1987.

24 June 1989 to Sir Antony Acland

Clarence House

Dear Sir Antony*

It was so kind of you to send me such a full account of your visit to Hyde Park,† and I thought that your speech to open the Exhibition was perfect. Reading it brought back so many memories of our tour in Canada & the U.S. The shadow of Hitler was looming over us at home in England, and it was wonderful to find such support and understanding in both those great countries, & one felt less alone.

Our visit to Hyde Park was full of incident, and the most delightful & funny things happened.

The house, I believe, belonged to old Mrs Roosevelt [. . .]. There were two steps down into the dining room, & one by one the various courses crashed to the floor as the butler & co fell down the steps. To be treated with roars of laughter by the President, and black looks from his mother! Then at Church on the Sunday morning, as we arrived, we saw a large notice outside the Church saying 'Church of the President', and under it some wag had written 'Formerly God's'.

I think that the King and President Roosevelt had some very good talks (closely attended by Mackenzie King) about bases etc, and all the Roosevelts were kindness itself, and it was all very happy & relaxed. Isn't it strange about history, what people <u>really</u> remember of our visit was Hot Dogs!

I hope that you will let me know if you are coming to London, as I would be so glad to see you both, & hear some news of the dear old U.S.

With again my warmest thanks for your letter, I am, ever yours sincerely,

Elizabeth R

~

---

*   Sir Antony Acland KG GCVO GCMG (1930–), Permanent Under-Secretary of State at the FCO, 1982–6; British Ambassador in Washington, 1986–91. He then became Provost of Eton College until his retirement in 2001.

†   Hyde Park, New York State, the home of President and Mrs Roosevelt, to which the King and Queen had made their memorable visit in 1939, weeks before the outbreak of the Second World War.

5 September 1989 to Queen Elizabeth II

Birkhall

My Darling Lilibet

I adored my precious two days at Balmoral, in fact 2½ with that lovely picnic in your new tent, and it was, as usual, a great joy to be with you all. There is something so <u>special</u> about Balmoral, always the same happy atmosphere, the family, the outings, the piper, it was all <u>such</u> fun.

It was so nice to hit off Peg [Hesse] & Tiny,* I so enjoyed seeing Peg getting a tiny bit tiddly in the evening (can I top you up) and on thinking it over, I can understand why she said 'I feel so lonely', because, I think that as you get older you feel rather isolated in a curious way, with only very few people or family left on your wavelength.

I believe that next weekend is Prime Minister weekend, so if convenient & helpful do bring her [Margaret Thatcher] to tea.†

With so much love and a million thanks from your very loving Mummy

~

30 December 1989 to the Hon. Lady Johnston‡

Sandringham

Dearest Libby

How very kind of you to give me a copy of Sarah Legh's§ letters & diaries. It is really fascinating, and takes one right back to those far-

---

* Sophie, Princess George of Hanover (1914–2001), sister of Prince Philip.

† Margaret Thatcher, Prime Minister 1979–90. Queen Elizabeth admired Thatcher for her patriotism and her robust approach to the problems of Britain. At private meals, Queen Elizabeth amused her friends by lowering her glass out of sight to 'toast' those of whom she disapproved, such as some Socialist or Liberal politicians, and raising it to those whom she favoured, like General de Gaulle or Mrs Thatcher.

‡ Queen Elizabeth's goddaughter Elizabeth Johnston (1927–95), younger daughter of second Baron Hardinge of Penshurst (see p. 226 footnote) and his wife Helen (née Cecil), Queen Elizabeth's friend from girlhood. Wife of Lieut-Col. Sir John Johnston, Assistant Comptroller then Comptroller of the Lord Chamberlain's Office 1964–87.

§ Sarah Legh was the wife of Sir Piers 'Joey' Legh. Her son, Alfred Shaughnessy, the scriptwriter of the London Weekend Television series *Upstairs Downstairs*, edited *Sarah: The Letters and Diaries of a Courtier's Wife 1906–1936* (1989).

off days & people who one had forgotten – Some of the entries
'lunched with so-and-so at the Ritz he came to tea later' reminded me
of my debutante days, when one was thrilled by that sort of thing!

I remember dancing with a nice young American* at Lady Powis'
ball in Berkeley Square (aged 17) and the amazement and thrill when
the next day a huge bunch of red roses arrived!

In those days flowers were very rare!

Sarah was talked of as little Mrs Shaughnessy, & was extremely
attractive, &, I suppose, quite young.

A thousand thanks for such an entertaining Christmas present, &
with my love,

I am, ever your affect.

Elizabeth R

~

Good Friday 13 April 1990 to the Duke of Edinburgh

Windsor Castle

Dearest Philip,

I am so sorry to have kept this book† so long! I found it
fascinating, especially the letters from prison; she must have had an
extraordinary memory for detail, which does help to give the book
extra 'family' interest.

So many thanks & love from

Mama E

~

4 August 1990 to the Prince of Wales

Clarence House

My Darling Charles,

It was a heaven-sent idea of yours to give your most loving
Grandmother such a delectable musical birthday present! The Concert
was superb and was greatly enjoyed not only by the loving

---

*   Sam Dickson – see letter to Beryl Poignand, 13 June 1918 (p. 59).

†   *A Romanov Diary: The Autobiography of Her Imperial and Royal Highness Grand Duchess George
of Russia* (1988); the Grand Duchess was Prince Philip's aunt. The book includes letters written
by her husband from prison during the Bolshevik Revolution; he was shot in 1919.

grandmother, but by <u>all</u> the guests, from the Poet Laureate* to William.† Dear Rostropovich was in great form and I loved the Thistle and the Rose‡ – so beautifully sung by Maria McLoughlin in her splendid scarlet dress. The whole conception of the evening was so touching, so delicate, and I can <u>never</u> thank you enough darling Charles for thinking of something so rare and so memorable.

The orchestra also was perfection, and having Raymond§ to conduct, a real inspiration, and so I can only say from my heart, a thousand thanks for an evening of bliss for us, and encouragement to the young composers, and with endless love from your devoted GRANNY

~

---

* Ted Hughes OM (1930–98), British poet, named Poet Laureate in 1984. He became a friend of Queen Elizabeth after she had invited him to dinner at Sandringham in summer 1987. They shared a love of Britain, the countryside and fishing. She found his craggy good looks 'very striking' and he found her 'interested in everything, amused by everything. Her secret is – one of her secrets – to be positive about everything.' (Ted Hughes to Gerald Hughes, 18 May 1991, Ted Hughes papers, Manuscript Archives and Rare Book Library, Emory University.) In the 1990s the friendship meant a great deal to each of them.

† William Tallon RVM (1935–2007), Steward to Queen Elizabeth, who joined the Royal Household in 1951 and remained with Queen Elizabeth until her death. He was a flamboyant, engaging character with good taste and good cheer; the mutual affection in which he and Queen Elizabeth held one another, his cheekiness and his generosity with martinis and other libations helped make her Household one of the most relaxed and amusing in the Royal Family.

‡ *The Thistle and the Rose*, a song cycle for soprano and choir, commissioned by Prince Charles from the British composer Patrick Doyle (1953–) to celebrate the Queen Mother's ninetieth birthday.

§ Raymond Leppard (1927–), conductor and harpsichordist. He grew up in Bath and he first encountered the King and Queen when they visited the city after it was heavily bombed in the so-called Baedeker raids, which targeted Britain's heritage, in April 1942. Leppard was a schoolboy serving meals at an improvised soup kitchen for the homeless and saw the 'magical and powerful effect' the King and Queen had as they went 'climbing over rubble, talking to everyone, unguarded and caringly sympathetic'. He saw them as 'the symbol of the spirit of England'. (Raymond Leppard, *On Music*, Pro/Am Music Resources, New York, 1993, pp. 442–3.) Later he became a good friend of Queen Elizabeth and often played the piano for her.

18 August 1990 to Ted Hughes

The Castle of Mey

My dear Poet Laureate

I have been reading and re-reading your wonderful poem* with admiration and amazement, admiration for its beauty and nobility, and amazement that you managed to put into glorious words, the whole history of the last ninety years.

And slipping from horror words like Stalin and Hitler suddenly into lovely things like a salmon lying under a white stone.

There is a white stone in my favourite pool on the Dee, Polveir, and there is nearly always a fish under it, just moving in a languid way against the stream.

And you even remembered when Mickey Mouse came upon the scene!

I wish that I knew enough words to tell you what immense joy your poem has given me, it is so beautiful and so moving, there are several passages that make me cry, and this happens every time I read it.

And your kindness in writing it out in your own hand has touched me very deeply, it will be my greatest treasure.

I think that this must be rather a good place to read a poem. There is only the sea and the immense sky, and the images that you create in your great poem seem to float in one's mind, in fact every time I read it a new one appears.

My thanks do indeed come from the grateful heart of
Elizabeth R

~

* Hughes had written, for her ninetieth birthday, an epic poem called 'A Masque for Three Voices', which was an exploration of the great, awful and lovely moments of the century. He began with lines on the significance of monarchy:

> A royalty mints the sovereign soul
> Of wise man and of clown
> What substitute's debased those souls
> Whose country lacks a crown
> Because it lies in some Swiss bank
> Or has been melted down . . .

'A Masque for Three Voices', first published in the *Weekend Telegraph*, 4 August 1990.

27 April 1991 to the Earl of Snowdon

The Royal Lodge

Dearest Tony,

What an enchanting luncheon party that was on Friday! I can never thank you enough for arranging such a wonderful visit to Oliver's 'suite'.* I had always wanted to see it and I found it entrancing. It could not possibly have been conceived by anyone else, so brilliant, and so original and so glowing. I loved the dining room, so clever to cover the glass with huge motifs so that you never saw yourself but just felt that you were in an exotic garden. It's wonderful that you managed to save it and to find such talented and sympathetic people to carry out the work of restoration. They were so charming and I loved meeting them. It was such a happy visit and one that I shall always remember with much gratitude and it was also great fun.

With a thousand thanks, I am ever yours affectionately

Elizabeth

~

12 July 1991 to Lord Wyatt of Weeford

The Royal Lodge

Dear Lord Wyatt,†

It is always a great pleasure to visit Cavendish Avenue, and last Tuesday was an extra treat, because I had never seen your charming house in daylight!

It all looked so lovely, with that beautiful garden giving such a feeling of peace and tranquillity.

And then one turned inward to find a starry company, full of sparkling conversation both witty and wise, and as usual, I soon found myself being vastly entertained, & best of all, greatly cheered up!

---

*   Oliver Messel (1904–78), designer and uncle of Lord Snowdon. In 1953 he created a suite at the Dorchester Hotel, which included a lavish mix of rococo and baroque styles and a 'considerable dose of fantasy'. It was said to have been adored by such stars as Noël Coward, Marlene Dietrich and Elizabeth Taylor. In the late 1980s Lord Snowdon restored the suite and he gave occasional lunch parties there with eclectic groups of people.

†   Woodrow Wyatt, Baron Wyatt of Weeford (1918–97), British politician, journalist and writer. A committed follower of Margaret Thatcher, he was also close to Rupert Murdoch and wrote a political column for the *News of the World*.

Your guests were all so nice and so interesting. I was very pleased to meet Lord Weidenfeld* for the first time, & I can see how he gets his reputation for charm, for he was most kind & delightful company at lunch.

It was most kind of you to ask me to such a splendid lunch party, and I enjoyed it no end – you have such a wide range of fascinating friends, & I do love meeting some of them.

With a thousand thanks to you & to Lady Wyatt, I am, ever yours

Elizabeth R

~

25 January 1992 to Ted Hughes

Sandringham

Dear Mr Hughes

I am so delighted with the enchanting little book† that you have so kindly given me.

The paper is so rich & rustling, and the printing so fine and clear, just right for the beautiful poems that are contained in this really fine edition. I do want to thank you most warmly for giving me something so precious, and it is giving me <u>such</u> pleasure.

It is lovely to have the poems that I know so well all handy in this book, what a treat! Thank you also for your letter, with its thrilling description of landing a fish in such wild & stormy conditions. It must have been too exciting for words, & I felt an envious thrill myself when reading of the battle with the fish and the wind and the rocks.

Thinking about fish, I shall be up at Birkhall from May 9th for a fortnight, and if you would care to come up to the Dee for a few days, it would be very nice for us, but, alas! I must tell you that our river is getting less and less fish each year.

But there is always the odd one, and with luck, a sea trout!

With again my thanks for the book, and my deep gratitude to our Poet Laureate, I am ever yours sincerely

Elizabeth R

---

*   George Weidenfeld, Baron Weidenfeld GBE (1919–), one of Britain's most distinguished publishers and philanthropists who fled from Nazi Austria to Britain in 1938.

†   *Rain-Charm for the Duchy*, a collection of Hughes's Laureate poems, published in 1992.

PS I think that the notes at the end of the book are splendid, and most helpful to the young minds.

~

5 February 1992 to Queen Elizabeth II

Clarence House

My Darling Lilibet

I can hardly believe that 36 hours ago we were walking past John Chinaman* to pick some hamamelis! It is here in my room, smelling delicious and reminding me of incredibly happy days at Sandringham. I do think that it is really wonderful of you & Philip to have me for such a long visit. It is such bliss to settle down and really do nothing except visit the horses and the neighbours and play a soothing game of patience in the evening.

I don't think that I could battle with life, unless I had this glorious January. It is better than ten bottles of tonic or twenty bottles of Arnica.†

I do hope that you too feel rested and relaxed after those weeks of open air & much exercice – how <u>do</u> you spell it?

London is looking particularly damp and dismal, and at this moment there is a maniac lady screaming outside my window.

<u>Later</u>

I never had time to finish this letter in London, so I am now writing at Royal Lodge. Absolutely nothing out in the garden, it is strange how very late everything is this year.

Darling Lilibet, I do wish that I could find adequate words to tell you how much I loved my visit and how sad I was to leave. But I am <u>very</u> <u>very</u> grateful, for your loving kindness and care (I have brought the stick!)‡ and for everything else, honestly I have never been so well looked after and with very much love

I am your very loving

Mummy

~

---

* The affectionate nickname for a golden statue of Buddha in the grounds of Sandringham.

† One of Queen Elizabeth's favourite homeopathic cures.

‡ The Queen and Princess Margaret were constantly urging their mother, usually without success, to take more care of herself. The stick was a recent gift.

22 February 1992 to Nigel Jaques

The Royal Lodge

Dear Mr Jaques,*

I was so deeply touched to receive your charming letter of remembrance on Feb 6th, and I do want to thank you with all my heart for writing as you did.

I was so interested to see that you used the words 'affectionate respect' in describing the boys' feelings on that day, especially as nowadays one feels that the press, radio and television are sadly lacking in any respect for our institutions and traditions. Perhaps the schools can make up for this lack.

Your letter gave me much comfort <u>and</u> pleasure, and I am ever, yours sincerely,

　　Elizabeth R

~

5 June 1992 to Ted Hughes

The Royal Lodge

Dear Mr Hughes

I wish that I could find some elegant and suitable words to convey to you the immense pleasure that your beautiful Picnic poem† has given me. When I read it, here in Windsor Park, I find myself transported at once to my beloved hills, and to the 'steep frowning glories of dark Lochnagar' (Lord Byron!!), and to the birds and the deer and the elusive salmon and the dear creaking pines. It is such a wonderful and <u>loving</u> poem, and I send you my most hearty thanks for giving us something so special.

---

* Nigel Jaques, master at Eton and frequent guest at Royal Lodge, wrote to her on the anniversary of King George VI's death recalling how, at Eton, the boys had responded to the news in February 1952.

† Hughes appealed to Queen Elizabeth's lifelong enjoyment of mystical matters. In 1919 she had given D'Arcy Osborne her 'Magic Stone' – and then requested it back. On his recent visit to Birkhall, on a picnic below Lochnagar, she asked Hughes if he thought trees could communicate with each other. This led him to write his picnic poem: 'And what were the great pines whispering? / We would have liked to know. / With rooty thoughts and needle tongues / They murmured: "There they go / Looking for mountain sunshine just / In time to meet the snow! / Toasting Queen Victoria / For blazing the trail to Lochnagar."'

Much to my annoyance, the moment you left Birkhall, the water warmed, the snow in the Cairngorms melted, and the fish were encouraged to attempt the long haul to the higher stretches of the river. If you will come again next spring, I think that you should stay a little longer, and catch the river in all its moods.

In the village next door to Sandringham there is a much revered Pub called The FEATHERS – So, perhaps when we have our Mushroom Beano, we might discover there, in darkest Norfolk

<u>THE GREAT WHITE LIGHT</u>

There are always ancient goings-on in Norfolk, so we must Beware.

Once again, my heartfelt thanks to our splendid Poet Laureate, for the pleasure his lovely verses give us, and with many messages to Mrs Hughes I am, ever yours

Elizabeth R

~

3 February 1993 to Queen Elizabeth II

Clarence House

My Darling Lilibet

How can I ever thank you enough for my heavenly weeks at Sandringham. It is something that I look forward to the whole year, and this year it was all just as perfect as ever. Somehow one always feels <u>safe</u> in that dear old house, surrounded by family and loved familiar objects. It is so happy, and I wallow in it! In fact, I wallow too much, and having done nothing but enjoy myself, for the whole of January, I find it extremely difficult to get back into London routine.

I do hope that you feel rested and relaxed after all the ghastly happenings of last (& this) year.* I do think that you have been marvellous, & so does everybody.

---

* In 1992 the monarchy was beset with troubles. The Palace announced that the Duke and Duchess of York were to separate and then in June the *Sunday Times* began to serialize a book called *Diana: Her True Story*, which created a sensation, especially when it became clear that the Princess had covertly given her version of events to the author, Andrew Morton. The Queen Mother was appalled – loyalty came close to duty in her canon. She was greatly saddened at the end of the year when the Prince and Princess of Wales announced their separation.

Oh how I miss the lovely air, and <u>especially</u> the chats round the card table, & a chance to talk.

With a million thanks darling Lilibet, & very much love from your grateful and hopping lame

Mummy

~

21 April 1993 to the Duke of Edinburgh

Clarence House

Dearest Philip,

I am returning the 'Edinburgh Relations Table'* with many thanks for letting me have it to peruse. What amazing research.

I found it most interesting and it will of course be very useful for reference.

With so many thanks & my love from your affec Elizabeth M

~

21 June 1993 to Queen Elizabeth II

Clarence House

My Darling Lilibet

I think that this must be a slightly unusual letter to thank you for an Ascot week at Windsor!

Considering that I spent it hunched over the television instead of leaping in and out of carriages & rushing off to the paddock did make

---

On 20 November 1992, fire damaged large parts of Windsor Castle. The Queen was distraught and stayed the weekend with her mother at Royal Lodge. Then a fierce newspaper campaign was launched, demanding that the Queen, not the government, should pay for the restoration. Four days after the fire, the Queen made a remarkable speech in which she said '1992 is not a year on which I shall look back with undiluted pleasure. In the words of one of my more sympathetic correspondents, it has turned out to be an "annus horribilis".'

*   The Edinburgh Tables: an updated version of the original Mountbatten relationship tables. These were prepared by Earl Mountbatten of Burma, based initially on the memory of his mother, Victoria, Marchioness of Milford Haven, in 1939. They were first published by him on the Viceregal Press in New Delhi in 1947, when he was the last Viceroy of India. The Edinburgh Tables, started by Prince Philip in 1991, traced the descendants of the grandfathers of both the Queen and himself – namely King George V and the fourteenth Earl of Strathmore & Kinghorne, and King George I of Greece and Prince Louis of Battenberg (later the Marquess of Milford Haven).

it a little different, but, all the same it was <u>wonderful</u> to be at Windsor, and thank you simply a thousand times for all your loving care and thought for your still slightly dizzy*

Mummy

~

18 July 1993 to Ted Hughes

Clarence House

Dear Mr Hughes

Please forgive me for being so long in thanking you for your charming letter and for the enchanting Verses. We have lately been battered by tragic happenings† and I found it hard to put pen to paper.

But the saga of Miss Dimsdale has given me such great pleasure that I feel greatly restored. I only wish that I could find suitable words to show my gratitude for such lovely and amusing verses. Thanks to you Miss Dimsdale has surfaced and I enclose a short note of thanks [from her]. She is obviously <u>thrilled</u>.

I hope that all goes well with you and that we shall see you when spring comes.

I am ever yours
Elizabeth R

[Enclosure in Queen Elizabeth's hand]

Dear Poet Laureate
Thank you with all my heart for finding me.
I never knew who I was.

---

* Queen Elizabeth had been feeling unwell and did not go to the Ascot races or attend the Garter ceremony at the beginning of the week.

† In addition to the recent misery in her family, Queen Elizabeth's Private Secretary, Martin Gilliat, died on 28 May 1993. He had been a happy presence in her life for almost forty years. Then, on 6 July, Ruth Fermoy, one of her greatest friends, also died of cancer. The Queen Mother and the Princess of Wales, Lady Fermoy's granddaughter, went to the funeral together.

Hughes's whimsical poem recalled happier moments. On his last visit to Birkhall they had seen a young woman collecting moss near their picnic place. They decided she must be a 'Nymph of the Glen' and Hughes invented a fantasy life for this woman he called 'Miss Dimsdale'. In her reply the Queen Mother extended the joke.

Was I the deep pool in Polveir or the snow on Lochnagar, or the sad call of the curlew, or the dark encircling Pines or just a Dream –
But now I know who I am – & thank you,
I am your grateful
Emily Dimsdale

~

14 August 1994 to Lord Wyatt of Weeford

The Castle of Mey

Dear Lord Wyatt,

I am so delighted and thrilled with the two delightful books that you have so kindly given me, and I send you my warmest thanks for the most enjoyable of birthday presents. [. . .]

I was especially pleased to see 'Colonel Bramble'* again, for I struggled through it, many years ago, and having totally forgotten the story I shall now have the immense pleasure of reading it in English!

I have just been watching an old film of our visit to Southern Africa very soon after the War, and the Queen's speech from Cape Town in which she dedicated her life to the service of her Country.

This was when she came of age, & even Mr Murdoch† couldn't deny that this is just what she has done.

With again much gratitude, and I shall hope to see you when I return to London, and I am ever yours,
Elizabeth R

~

---

* *The Silence of Colonel Bramble* by André Maurois (1885–1967), a fictionalized account of Maurois' time as Churchill's interpreter on the Western Front. Maurois was a writer of distinction as well as a great Anglophile. He served with the Free French forces and in June 1940 he helped the Queen write a broadcast to France on the day the Germans entered Paris. The words she spoke were eloquent – 'Pour moi qui ai toujours tant aimé la France, je souffre aujourd'hui comme vous' – and 'Une nation qui a, pour la défendre, de tels hommes, et pour l'aimer, de telles femmes, doit, tôt ou tard, forcer la victoire.' Maurois praised her, saying that her words would give his countrymen and women hope for the future. (André Maurois to Queen Elizabeth, 26 June 1940, RA QEQM/PRIV/PAL)

† Rupert Murdoch AC ASG (1931–), Australian-born media mogul and proprietor of British newspapers *The Times*, the *Sunday Times*, the *Sun* and the *News of the World*. He saw himself as anti-establishment and was often critical of the monarchy.

10 October 1994 to Ted Hughes

The Castle of Mey

My dear Ted,

I was so thrilled to receive your letter telling me of the fascinating history of the Poet Laureates' BUTT of SACK* and I am not only very grateful but extremely touched that you should wish me to share in this lovely gift. A crate of Oloroso sounds like a dream, and a crate of Fino a glorious treat. That you should think of me in this way has given me enormous pleasure and my thanks are truly from my heart. Perhaps we should have a feast to celebrate such a delightful happening – I could invite Miss Dimsdale, and you could invite your tin man, as long as he is altogether again. I am sure that they would be enchanted to have a sip of such beautifully named nectar. I have read your letter again and again. It takes one straight out of this rather gloomy world into a world of sun and warmth and kindness, not to forget the wine that maketh glad the heart of man! It is all very exciting and makes me feel so happy. I am writing this in the dark with a very bad pen, so not very legible I fear.

With again my most hearty thanks,

I am,

ever yours

Elizabeth R

~

19 October 1994 to Susan Crawford

Birkhall

Dearest Sue†

I was so delighted to get your lovely letter, and the deeply touching [poem] 'can one love a dog too much' which of course brought a huge lump into my throat and several tears.

I don't think that one can love a dog <u>too</u> much – they give one such love and loyalty themselves and deserve all that we can give back.

---

* The sherry growers of Jerez annually presented Hughes, as Poet Laureate, with a 'Butt of Sack', about six hundred bottles' worth.

† Susan Crawford (1941–), leading equine artist and portrait painter, married to Major-General Jeremy Phipps. Her Jack Russell terrier had just died of poisoning in Oman.

But here comes the heartbreak – and I do feel for you <u>so</u> much – some dogs are so <u>special</u> & leave one so utterly forlorn.

Oh we do miss you here, the stags are roaring round the house, Charlie's* laugh ringing out & no Sue. Promise to try & come next year.

Jeremy is just leaving so I must send this with him.

Much love from

Elizabeth R

~

10 June 1995 to Ted Hughes

Clarence House

My dear Ted,

I was absolutely thrilled to receive the glorious saga of Miss Dimsdale's pursuit of the elusive Potter all written in your own beautiful clear hand. I love every line of every verse, and wonderful pictures came into my mind of Andrew Haig[†] and Elizabeth Basset[‡] leaping over the hills hot on the Potter trail. The end is marvellous & now, when I see the big flat head of a dog otter on the Dee, I will be reminded of the Rev Potter, and of his mysterious disappearance.[§]

I am wondering now, whether the Rev. had a secret passion for Miss Dimsdale – hence the footsteps on the frosty lawn, and as they are both dream people could a dream wedding be a possibility? I can see the announcement in the Daily Telegraph – A wedding has been

---

* Charlie Palmer-Tomkinson, (1940–), Hampshire farmer known for his sporting prowess and good-natured laughter. He and his witty wife Patty were close friends and skiing and stalking companions of the Prince of Wales.

† Major Andrew Haig, CVO (1910–2003), Deputy Ranger of Windsor Great Park and Surveyor of Windsor Estate, from 1960 to 1974. He was close to the Queen Mother, who invited him to stay with her at Birkhall to fish on the Dee almost every year between 1974 and 2000. James Pearl, the long-serving ghillie at Balmoral, was his former batman.

‡ Lady Elizabeth Basset, DCVO (1908–2000), daughter of seventh Earl of Dartmouth. In 1931 she married Ronald Lambart Basset, who died in 1972. She loved racehorses, opera, parties, gossip, poetry and God. She joined the Queen Mother's Household in 1959 and, true to the spirit, the example (and the desire) of her employer, she retired only when she was 85. The Queen Mother shared her faith and in her Introduction to Lady Elizabeth's first book, *Love Is My Meaning – An Anthology of Assurance* (1973), she wrote that people would 'find in the pages what in our hearts we believe but find hard to say'.

§ The Reverend Cedric Potter was another of Hughes's whimsical creations.

arranged and will shortly take place between Julia eldest daughter
of Doctor Dimsdale and Rev. Cedric Potter Rector of Knoware.
I wonder where the happy union will take place. Possibly on the steep
frowning glories of dark Lochnagar.

Forgive all this nonsense, and with a thousand thanks
I am,
ever yours
Elizabeth R

~

18 August 1995 to Ted Hughes

The Castle of Mey

My dear Ted,
Your beautiful poem is giving me infinite pleasure, and I am so
thrilled to have a copy written in your own hand. Your theme is so
wonderful the root, the branch, the leaf the story of nearly one
hundred years, it's all so lovely and I keep on reading it, & always
finding something so glorious and poetic. How fortunate I am to have
a friend who is a great poet! Lucky lucky me!

And lucky me sends you her heartfelt thanks for the best birthday
present ever. I am truly deeply touched by your tender thought, and I
am with gratitude and affection, ever yours
Elizabeth R

~

29 January 1996 to Simon Bowes Lyon

Sandringham

Dearest Simon,
I was so deeply distressed that I was unable to get to darling
Rachel's* funeral, and I was thinking about it all the morning &
almost felt that I was taking part.

The roads were closed here & I couldn't get through which on
that particular day was cruel.

What a blank that brave spirit will leave.

---

* Rachel Bowes Lyon, widow of Queen Elizabeth's brother, David, and mother of Simon,
died on 21 January 1996.

And yet there is a great deal that will always be with us, her courage and her humour, and her <u>great</u> loving kindness.

I know that when my heart fails me that I shall hear Rachel saying come on now, don't give up. I feel for you so much as a family & send you all my sympathy & love

& I am ever your affect,

Elizabeth

~

9 February 1996 to the Rev. Canon Dendle French

Clarence House

Dear Mr French*

Thank you very much indeed for sending me a copy of your beautiful address at Rachel's funeral. I was absolutely heart-broken that I could not get to the service, but most of the roads were closed and there was no way of getting to Hertfordshire. I could visualise it all, but I was terribly sad not to be with the family.

So, I am particularly glad to have a copy of your Address.

I know that if, in the future my heart fails me at the prospect of doing something difficult, I shall hear the beloved Rachel saying 'oh go on, I know you can do it'.

<u>She</u> had endless courage.

With again my thanks

I am, yours very sincerely,

Elizabeth R

~

10 June 1996 to Prince Philip

Clarence House

Dearest Philip,

Many congratulations and loving good wishes on your birthday, and many thanks for lending me your strong right arm at Epsom!

Have a happy day!

Mama E

~

---

* The Rev. Canon Dendle French, Vicar of St Paul's Walden, 1978–94. On his retirement, he became Chaplain of the Chapel of St Michael and All Angels, Glamis Castle, 1994–2010.

2 September 1996 to Queen Elizabeth II

Balmoral Castle

My Darling Lilibet

What a treat it is staying at Balmoral! So I thought that I would write to you from this address to thank you a thousand times for a really heavenly weekend. Saturday was such fun – I did so enjoy going out shooting, sitting in the sun & eating a mutton pie whilst gazing at the hills. My idea of bliss. It is a rare treat for me nowadays, and took me straight back to those happy days of long ago.

I thought that the garden was looking particularly good, <u>and</u> the vegetables, & I walked back toward the cricket ground, & the path had all those same bits of horse manure that seemed to belong there!

It was <u>so</u> nice to catch a glimpse of some family. Today is very grey, I hope that it is better at the beautiful pile in Teesdale!*

With so much love from
your very loving
Mummy

~

7 January 1997 to Admiral Sir John Slater

Sandringham

My dear Jock†

Thank you very much for giving me a copy of Broadsheet, it is fascinating to read, and the illustrations are brilliant and I am not surprised that this edition received an award.

I notice that the Royal Navy is falling victim to the modern fashion of immensely long titles!

'Chief Strategic Systems Executive Business Unit' is not bad!

---

* Queen Elizabeth's ironic remark refers to Holwick Hall, a house not renowned for its beauty but nevertheless much loved, where the Queen and the Duke of Edinburgh were on a private visit to the Earl of Strathmore, Queen Elizabeth's great-nephew.

† Admiral Sir John Cunningham Kirkwood 'Jock' Slater GCB LVO DL FRSE (1938–), equerry to the Queen 1968–71. He became First Sea Lord in 1995, a post he held until his retirement in 1998. *Broadsheet* was the First Sea Lord's newsletter for the Royal Navy and Royal Marines, of which he always sent a copy to Queen Elizabeth. He was often a guest at the Castle of Mey.

May I send you and Annie my best wishes for a happy New Year,
& with again my thanks,

I am, ever yours,

Elizabeth R

~

15 February 1997 to Ted Hughes

My dear Ted,

I wish that I could find the right words to be able to tell you how
thrilled and delighted I was with the enchanting 'The Prince and his
Granny'.*

First of all, the Prince read the verses to his Granny (very nicely)
and since that happy occasion, the Granny has read them again and
again. You must have the most observant eye in the world!

To remember the Police Brass Band, the lemon curd, the grim
guns, the beach, the picnic Lodge in the trees, the wheels on the
gravel, they all make lovely memories.

I specially love the last verse about Houghton, the 'timeless place'
and the moonlight deer.

They sometimes escape from the Park at Houghton, and when
I see them flashing through our woods, I shall think of our revered
Poet Laureate, and of the many delights he has brought to us all.

With an IMMENSE amount of gratitude from the Prince's
Granny.

Elizabeth R

~

3 May 1997 to Queen Elizabeth II

Clarence House

My Darling Lilibet

I have an extraordinary feeling that lovely Easter weekend at
Windsor was all a dream! Beautiful hot days at Frogmore enjoying
heavenly picnics, all so green and yellow, and that delightful baby
having his lunch with us, it all seemed too good to be true, but

---

* An affectionate comic remembrance by Hughes of the Queen Mother's visit to the
Sandringham Flower Show with Prince Charles in July 1996.

it was, and I send you a thousand thanks for those blissful four days.

I came away feeling a different person, all that fresh air and walking and laughing was a real tonic and great fun. [. . .]

With again a thousand thanks from

your very loving

Mummy

~

26 June 1997 to Sir Antony Acland

Clarence House

Dear Sir Antony

It was such a joy to come to Chapel at Eton on Sunday, and once again I found the whole Service beautiful and so moving.

It is so refreshing and encouraging to see all those excellent boys, & one couldn't help wondering is there a future Prime Minister amongst this throng, a Bishop, an explorer or even a Tam Dalyell!*

The reception after Chapel was so well arranged, and one felt that one was meeting and talking to some of the really important people who made up all Eton, the river, the groundsmen, the history tutors, the classics & language enthusiasts, and you not only knew them all, but you also knew their names!

It was a most happy visit, and with thanks to you both,

I am, ever yours

Elizabeth R

~

7 February 1999 to the Rev. Anthony Harbottle

Royal Lodge

Dear Mr Harbottle,

I was deeply touched to receive your very kind letter of remembrance on Feb. 6th.

---

* Sir Thomas ('Tam') Dalyell Loch, eleventh Baronet (1932–), an exuberant man of strong opinions, Labour MP for West Lothian from 1962 to 1983 and for Linlithgow from 1983 to 2005.

You wrote such charming & beautiful words about the King, & they gave me such comfort.

I do hope that all goes well with the Harbottle family.

I am, ever yours sincerely & gratefully.

Elizabeth R

~

29 August 2000 to Lady Elizabeth Shakerley*

Birkhall

Dearest Liza

What a wonderful birthday present!

I have never seen such perfect garden furniture, lovely, handy and comfortable chairs, and tables that are exactly the right size and shape.

Thank you a thousand times for arranging such a delightful 'family' gift – I am truly very deeply touched by your tender thought.

The picnic baskets have already proved splendidly useful and a great addition to our outings.

With my love and endless thanks from your affect

GA Elizabeth

~

21 October 2000 to Susan Crawford

Birkhall

Dearest Sue

I wish that I could find the right words to tell you how <u>much</u> I love the wonderful triptych of my beloved grandson.[†] It is so brilliant, I can't decide which I like best, the full-face or the profiles they are all so like him, and to have it to look at is one of the nicest things that have happened to me for a very long time.

Thank you a million times for such a heavenly present.

---

* Lady Elizabeth Shakerley (1941–), granddaugher of Jock Bowes Lyon, Queen Elizabeth's brother.

† Triptych portrait of the Prince of Wales painted by Susan Crawford for Queen Elizabeth's hundredth birthday.

You have painted it with such love and understanding which makes it even more precious.

It was such a delight to have you and Jeremy here, much too short. With my love, I am ever your affectionate

Elizabeth R

~

December 2000 to Sir Michael Peat*

Birkhall

Dear Sir Michael

I was so delighted and thrilled to receive such a wonderful birthday present from the members of the Queen's Household.[†]

The pictures of the saloon at the Royal Lodge are very beautiful and are giving me the most enormous pleasure.

The painter is one of my favourites, and he has got the 'feel' of the room so perfectly, with the light pouring through the windows. I send you my deep gratitude, and I would be very grateful if you would convey my warmest thanks to all those who took part in this splendid gift, and

I am, ever yours sincerely,

Elizabeth R

~

4 June 2001 to Lady Katharine Farrell

Clarence House

Dearest Kitty,

I do love coming to lunch with you and Charles. It is always such fun, such charming people, such glorious grub, and the wonderful feeling of relaxation and laughter which makes one feel so happy.

It was sad that Mr Getty could not be there, but perhaps it was better that he was in his own bed, and not in yours![‡]

---

[*] Sir Michael Peat, GCVO (1949–), Keeper of the Privy Purse and Treasurer to the Queen 1996–2002, Private Secretary to the Prince of Wales 2002–5, Principal Private Secretary to the Prince of Wales and the Duchess of Cornwall 2005–11.

[†] Two watercolours of the Saloon at Royal Lodge by the Scottish artist Hugh Buchanan.

[‡] At a previous Farrell lunch, Paul Getty, who suffered from ill health, had been taken unwell and had to retire upstairs. He died in 2003.

The hedge is <u>enormous</u> and the arch much prettier than Marble Arch. I can't believe that I saw its very beginning.

Dearest Kitty, it was a heavenly lunch party and I wish it was not over. Will you tell those dear ladies that their lovely bouquet is flourishing and a joy.

With my love and endless thanks, from your affec
Elizabeth R

~

5 July 2001 to Princess Alexandra

Clarence House

Darling Alexandra,

What a heavenly luncheon party that was!

I love coming to lunch with you and Angus* – you always have such charming people and it is all such fun and so cosy. It is the highlight of July and what a treat to have Andrew and Debo† who hardly ever appear in London.

They are very special.

With a thousand thanks for a lovely happy visit and much love from your devoted aunt
Elizabeth

~

August 2001 to the Prince of Wales

The Castle of Mey

My Darling Charles, Thanks to your marvellous birthday present I shall now be able to wrap myself from nose to toes in a huge and heavenly Bath Towel. Thank you a <u>thousand</u> times, they are just what I needed. [. . .]

Here the sun is shining, the sea is shining, and lovely white clouds are floating about. Of course in five minutes the whole scene can

---

* Sir Angus Ogilvy KCVO PC (1928–2004), British businessman, married to Princess Alexandra.

† Andrew Cavendish, eleventh Duke of Devonshire KG MC PC (1920–2004), and his wife Deborah, Duchess of Devonshire DCVO (1920–). Both were long-standing friends of Queen Elizabeth.

change, angry waves, leaden sky and a howling wind, not to mention the crying of the sea birds and growling of seals.

I do hope that Birkhall is being its own dear self, and with endless gratitude for your wonderful present,

from your always loving Granny

~

Queen Elizabeth's one hundredth birthday in 2000 had been celebrated with enthusiasm throughout Britain. Together with Prince Charles, she watched and waved (standing much of the time) in Horse Guards Parade as hundreds of the organizations, regiments and charities with which she was associated marched gaily past her. Her sight was so poor by then that she could see very little, but that did not spoil her obvious enjoyment.

In her one-hundred-and-first and one-hundred-and-second years, Queen Elizabeth became ever more frail – and ever more indomitable. She was determined to carry on counting her blessings and living every day as fully as possible, for according to one of her favourite maxims 'tomorrow you might be run over by a big red bus!'

In November 2000 she tripped and broke her collar bone, but after six weeks in bed she was up again and in spring 2001 she fulfilled all her usual commitments. She went to lunch in June 2001 at All Souls, Oxford, with some of the cleverest people in the land, a regular occasion which she and they always enjoyed.

She attended Royal Ascot but then needed a stay in King Edward VII hospital to have a transfusion to make good a serious iron deficiency. She insisted that the necessary treatment be carried out overnight so that she could be back to greet the customary crowd of well-wishers at Clarence House for her one-hundred-and-first birthday. Prince Charles congratulated her on having her 'iron constitution so comprehensively re-ironed'.*

There was an elegiac quality to her visits to the Castle of Mey and Birkhall in summer 2001. She gathered old friends around her, danced an eightsome reel and insisted on going to see her old ghillie, Charlie Wright, at his home on the Dee. To get to him she had to walk on her sticks across a hump-backed bridge – and back again.

She continued to show extraordinary courage. In November 2001

---

* Prince of Wales to Queen Elizabeth, 8 August 2001, RA QEQM/PRIV/RF.

she flew by helicopter to Portsmouth, to take part in the rededication of one of her ships, the aircraft carrier *Ark Royal*, and she made a short speech to the 1,200 people on board to greet her. As usual, she went to dinner at the Middle Temple, took lunch with the Trustees of the Injured Jockeys Fund, attended a last race meeting at Sandown Park, where her horse First Love won, and then, despite another painful fall, joined her staff Christmas party at Clarence House, before spending Christmas 2001 with her family at Sandringham.

January 2002 brought the year of the Queen's Golden Jubilee and growing public appreciation of all that Elizabeth II had achieved since the death of her father the King. But the family was pre-occupied by the worsening health of Princess Margaret. The Princess died on 9 February 2002. Queen Elizabeth was still at Sandringham and she flew by helicopter to her daughter's funeral in St George's Chapel, Windsor Castle. She managed to stand as the Princess's coffin was borne out of the Chapel at the end of a tranquil service.

She then went home to Royal Lodge and, though weaker than ever, held her annual lawn meet for the Eton beagles and her house party for the Grand Military Race Meeting at Sandown Park. Her horse First Love, her last ever runner, won again.

Easter fell early that year, on 31 March; in the week beforehand, Queen Elizabeth made many calls to friends who thought she was saying thank you and farewell. She was eating very little now, but would take a small glass of champagne with scrambled eggs in the evening – she said this reminded her of late night suppers with the Duke in the early years of her marriage.

On Good Friday, she declined further and on Easter Saturday, 30 March 2002, a contemplative day for Christians anticipating the resurrection, she died, with the Queen and her grandchildren Sarah and David at her bedside.

In the week before her funeral at Westminster Abbey, hundreds of thousands of people lined the cold March streets to pass by her coffin as it lay in state in Westminster Hall, as they had for the King half a century before. In that time the nation had changed almost beyond recognition, but at the beginning of the Golden Jubilee Year the British people showed their continuing support for the monarchy by honouring the Queen Mother and her daughter, the Queen. (Ten years later, in 2012, the Queen celebrated her Diamond Jubilee to even more gratitude, affection and applause.)

The Prince of Wales gave a heartfelt tribute to his grandmother in which he described her as 'the original life enhancer [. . .] wise, loving, with an utterly irresistible mischievousness of spirit.' Above all, he said, 'her heart belonged to this ancient old land and its equally indomitable and humorous inhabitants.' In a television address on the night before the funeral the Queen also spoke from the heart. Thanking people for their 'overwhelming' tributes to her mother, she hoped that 'sadness will blend with a wider sense of thanksgiving, not just for her life but for the times in which she lived – a century for this country and the Commonwealth not without its trials and sorrows, but also one of extraordinary progress, full of examples of courage and service as well as fun and laughter. This is what my mother would have understood, because it was the warmth and affection of people everywhere which inspired her resolve, dedication and enthusiasm for life.'

In his eulogy, the Archbishop of Canterbury, Dr George Carey, said that the Queen Mother had about her, in George Eliot's lovely phrase, 'the sweet presence of a good diffused.' He spoke of her sense of Christian duty and of her optimism, and he ended with words from the Book of Proverbs – '. . . many have done excellently, but you exceed them all.'

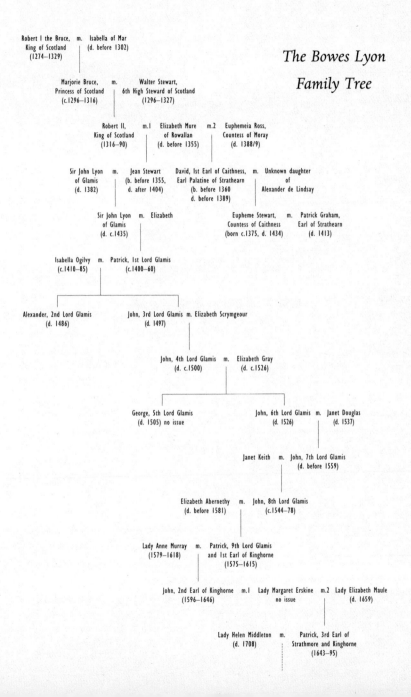

The Bowes Lyon
Family Tree

Robert I the Bruce,   m.   Isabella of Mar
King of Scotland   (d. before 1302)
(1274–1329)

Marjorie Bruce,   m.   Walter Stewart,
Princess of Scotland   6th High Steward of Scotland
(c.1296–1316)   (1296–1327)

Robert II,   m.1   Elizabeth Mure   m.2   Euphemeia Ross,
King of Scotland   of Rowallan   Countess of Moray
(1316–90)   (d. before 1355)   (d. 1388/9)

Sir John Lyon   m.   Jean Stewart   David, 1st Earl of Caithness,   m.   Unknown daughter
of Glamis   (b. before 1355,   Earl Palatine of Strathearn   of
(d. 1382)   d. after 1404)   (b. before 1360   Alexander de Lindsay
                                            d. before 1389)

Sir John Lyon   m.   Elizabeth   Eupheme Stewart,   m.   Patrick Graham,
of Glamis   Countess of Caithness   Earl of Strathearn
(d. c.1435)   (born c.1375, d. 1434)   (d. 1413)

Isabella Ogilvy   m.   Patrick, 1st Lord Glamis
(c.1410–85)   (c.1400–60)

Alexander, 2nd Lord Glamis   John, 3rd Lord Glamis m. Elizabeth Scrymgeour
(d. 1486)   (d. 1497)

John, 4th Lord Glamis   m.   Elizabeth Gray
(d. c.1500)   (d. c.1526)

George, 5th Lord Glamis   John, 6th Lord Glamis   m.   Janet Douglas
(d. 1505) no issue   (d. 1526)   (d. 1537)

Janet Keith   m.   John, 7th Lord Glamis
                     (d. before 1559)

Elizabeth Abernethy   m.   John, 8th Lord Glamis
(d. before 1581)   (c.1544–78)

Lady Anne Murray   m.   Patrick, 9th Lord Glamis
(1579–1618)   and 1st Earl of Kinghorne
                        (1575–1615)

John, 2nd Earl of Kinghorne   m.1   Lady Margaret Erskine   m.2   Lady Elizabeth Maule
(1596–1646)   no issue   (d. 1659)

Lady Helen Middleton   m.   Patrick, 3rd Earl of
(d. 1708)   Strathmore and Kinghorne
                              (1643–95)

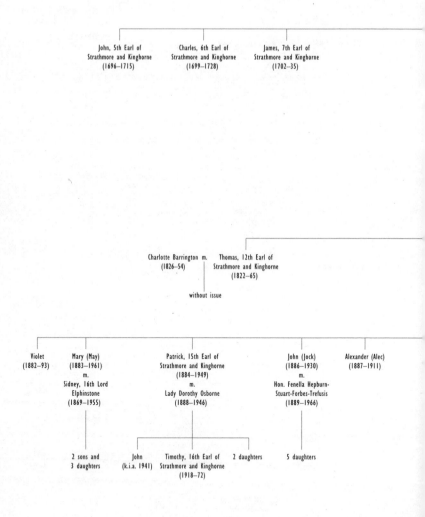

John, 5th Earl of
Strathmore and Kinghorne
(1696–1715)

Charles, 6th Earl of
Strathmore and Kinghorne
(1699–1728)

James, 7th Earl of
Strathmore and Kinghorne
(1702–35)

Charlotte Barrington m.
(1826–54)

Thomas, 12th Earl of
Strathmore and Kinghorne
(1822–65)

without issue

Violet
(1882–93)

Mary (May)
(1883–1961)
m.
Sidney, 16th Lord
Elphinstone
(1869–1955)

Patrick, 15th Earl of
Strathmore and Kinghorne
(1884–1949)
m.
Lady Dorothy Osborne
(1888–1946)

John (Jock)
(1886–1930)
m.
Hon. Fenella Hepburn-
Stuart-Forbes-Trefusis
(1889–1966)

Alexander (Alec)
(1887–1911)

2 sons and
3 daughters

John
(k.i.a. 1941)

Timothy, 16th Earl of
Strathmore and Kinghorne
(1918–72)

2 daughters

5 daughters

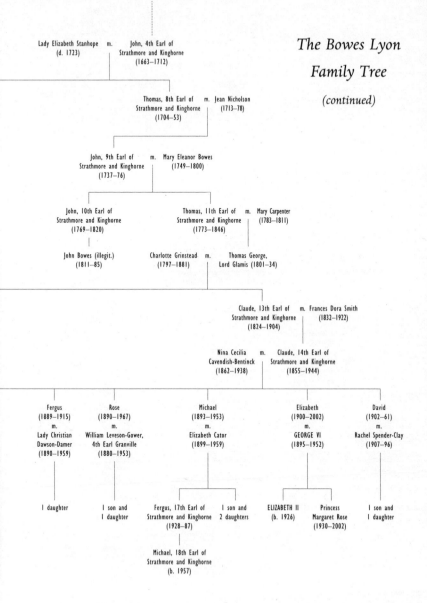

The Bowes Lyon
Family Tree

(continued)

Lady Elizabeth Stanhope   m.   John, 4th Earl of
(d. 1723)   Strathmore and Kinghorne
                                                (1663–1712)

Thomas, 8th Earl of   m.   Jean Nicholson
Strathmore and Kinghorne   (1713–78)
(1704–53)

John, 9th Earl of   m.   Mary Eleanor Bowes
Strathmore and Kinghorne   (1749–1800)
(1737–76)

John, 10th Earl of   Thomas, 11th Earl of   m.   Mary Carpenter
Strathmore and Kinghorne   Strathmore and Kinghorne   (1783–1811)
(1769–1820)   (1773–1846)

John Bowes (illegit.)   Charlotte Grinstead   m.   Thomas George,
(1811–85)   (1797–1881)   Lord Glamis (1801–34)

Claude, 13th Earl of   m.   Frances Dora Smith
Strathmore and Kinghorne   (1832–1922)
(1824–1904)

Nina Cecilia   m.   Claude, 14th Earl of
Cavendish-Bentinck   Strathmore and Kinghorne
(1862–1938)   (1855–1944)

Fergus   Rose   Michael   Elizabeth   David
(1889–1915)   (1890–1967)   (1893–1953)   (1900–2002)   (1902–61)
m.   m.   m.   m.   m.
Lady Christian   William Leveson-Gower,   Elizabeth Cator   GEORGE VI   Rachel Spender-Clay
Dawson-Damer   4th Earl Granville   (1899–1959)   (1895–1952)   (1907–96)
(1890–1959)   (1880–1953)

1 daughter   1 son and   Fergus, 17th Earl of   1 son and   ELIZABETH II   Princess   1 son and
                      1 daughter   Strathmore and Kinghorne 2 daughters (b. 1926)   Margaret Rose   1 daughter
                                            (1928–87)   (1930–2002)

                                            Michael, 18th Earl of
                                            Strathmore and Kinghorne
                                            (b. 1957)

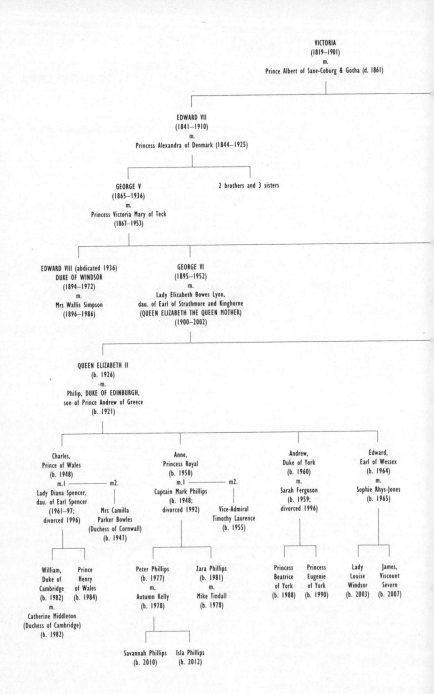

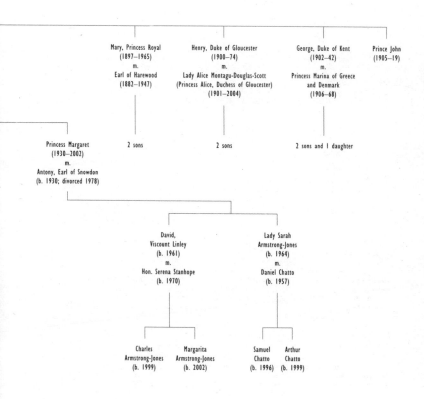

The Saxe-Coburg & Gotha

(1837–1917)

and Windsor

Family Tree

3 brothers and 5 sisters

Mary, Princess Royal
(1897–1965)
m.
Earl of Harewood
(1882–1947)

Henry, Duke of Gloucester
(1900–74)
m.
Lady Alice Montagu-Douglas-Scott
(Princess Alice, Duchess of Gloucester)
(1901–2004)

George, Duke of Kent
(1902–42)
m.
Princess Marina of Greece
and Denmark
(1906–68)

Prince John
(1905–19)

Princess Margaret
(1930–2002)
m.
Antony, Earl of Snowdon
(b. 1930; divorced 1978)

2 sons

2 sons

2 sons and 1 daughter

David,
Viscount Linley
(b. 1961)
m.
Hon. Serena Stanhope
(b. 1970)

Lady Sarah
Armstrong-Jones
(b. 1964)
m.
Daniel Chatto
(b. 1957)

Charles
Armstrong-Jones
(b. 1999)

Margarita
Armstrong-Jones
(b. 2002)

Samuel
Chatto
(b. 1996)

Arthur
Chatto
(b. 1999)

NOTES

Abbreviations

BUA   Birmingham University Archives
BIUY Borthwick Institute, University of York
CAC   Churchill Archives Centre, Cambridge
NLS   National Library of Scotland
RA   Royal Archives
SPW St Paul's Walden Bury

All quotations from Queen Elizabeth's conversations with Eric Anderson in 1994–5 are taken from transcripts in the Royal Archives (RA QEQM/ADD/MISC)

Preface

1 Roger Fulford, *Dearest Child*, Evans Brothers, 1964, pp. 1–2
2 Duchess of York to Lady Strathmore, n.d. [27 April 1923], Glamis Archives (RA)
3 Lady Strathmore to Duchess of York, 27 April 1923, RA QEQM/PRIV/BL

PART ONE: ELIZABETH

Introduction

1 Lady Cynthia Asquith, *The Queen*, Hutchinson, 1937, pp. 22–3
2 Conversations with Eric Anderson, 1994–5, RA QEQM/ADD/MISC
3 Käthe Kübler, *Meine Schülerin – die Königin von England*, Hermann Eichblatt Verlag, Leipzig, 1937, pp. 7–8, 10
4 Asquith, *The Queen*, p. 41
5 Käthe Kübler, *Meine Schülerin* p. 12
6 Asquith, *The Queen*, p. 44
7 Exercise book, 1911, Bowes Lyon Papers (SPW)
8 RA QEQM/PRIV/DIARY/1
9 Conversations with Eric Anderson, 1994–5, RA QEQM/ADD/MISC
10 Kübler, *Meine Schülerin*, p. 10
11 Asquith, *The Queen*, p. 67
12 Lady Elizabeth Bowes Lyon to Beryl Poignand, 22 May 1917, Glamis Archives (CH)

Letters/Diaries

10 February 1909: Glamis Archives (CH)
1 January 1910: RA QEQM/PRIV/DIARY/1
16 July 1910: RA QEQM/OUT/ELPHINSTONE

20 November 1910: Glamis Archives (CH)

13 December 1910: Glamis Archives (CH)

16 December 1910: RA QEQM/OUT/SHAKERLEY

17 February 1911: Bowes Lyon Papers (SPW)

11 October 1911: Bowes Lyon Papers (SPW)

26 December 1911: RA QEQM/OUT/MISC

17 February 1912: RA QEQM/PRIV/DIARY/1

[undated diary entry] March 1912: RA QEQM/PRIV/DIARY/1

10 May 1912: Glamis Archives (RA)

19 September 1912: Glamis Archives (CH)

17 October 1912: Glamis Archives (270/11)

3–7 January 1913: RA QEQM/PRIV/DIARY/2

15–18 April 1913: RA QEQM/PRIV/DIARY/2

18 July 1913: Glamis Archives (RA)

30 November 1913: Bowes Lyon Papers (SPW)

26 June 1914: Glamis Archives (CH)

27 June 1914: Glamis Archives (CH)

20 October 1914: Glamis Archives (CH)

9 August 1915: Glamis Archives (CH)

26 August 1915: Glamis Archives (CH)

31 August 1915: Glamis Archives (CH)

14 September 1915: Glamis Archives (270/11)

16 September 1915: Glamis Archives (CH)

26 December 1915: Glamis Archives (CH)

6 February 1916: Glamis Archives (CH)

17 March 1916: Glamis Archives (CH)

25 March 1916: Glamis Archives (RA)

28 March 1916: Glamis Archives (CH)

4 April 1916: Glamis Archives (CH)

19 April 1916: Glamis Archives (CH)

26 April 1916: Glamis Archives (CH)

1 May 1916: Glamis Archives (CH)

23 August 1916: Glamis Archives (CH)

17 September 1916: Glamis Archives (CH)

20 October 1916: Glamis Archives (CH)

25 October 1916: Glamis Archives (CH)

26 October 1916: Glamis Archives (CH)

27 January 1917 [misdated 1916]: Glamis Archives (CH)

3 May 1917: Glamis Archives (CH)

6 May 1917: Glamis Archives (CH)

22 May 1917: Glamis Archives (CH)

9 October 1917: Glamis Archives (CH)

21 October 1917: Glamis Archives (CH)

26 November 1917: Glamis Archives (CH)

5 January 1918: Glamis Archives (CH)

9 January 1918: Glamis Archives (CH)

7 February 1918: Glamis Archives (CH)

13 March 1918: Glamis Archives (CH)

22 March 1918: Glamis Archives (CH)

23 March 1918: Glamis Archives (CH)

20 April 1918: Glamis Archives (CH)
26 May 1918: Glamis Archives (CH)
13 June 1918: Glamis Archives (CH)
21 September 1918: Glamis Archives (CH)
1 October 1918: Glamis Archives (CH)
22 October 1918: Glamis Archives (CH)
27 November 1918: Glamis Archives (CH)
5 January 1919: Glamis Archives (CH)
undated [22 March 1919]: Glamis Archives (CH)
undated [6 April 1919]: Glamis Archives (CH)
17 April 1919: Glamis Archives (CH)
undated [31 August 1919]: Glamis Archives (CH)

PART TWO: DUCHESS OF YORK

INTRODUCTION

1 Lady Elizabeth Bowes Lyon to Beryl Poignand, n.d. [1 July 1919], Glamis Archives (CH)
2 Lady Elizabeth Bowes Lyon to Beryl Poignand, n.d. [23 September 1920], Glamis Archives (CH)
3 Queen Mary to Duke of York, 24 January 1923, RA GVI/PRIV/RF/11
4 Duke of York to Lady Elizabeth Bowes Lyon, n.d. [25] and 26 January 1923, RA QEQM/PRIV/RF
5 Lady Elizabeth Bowes Lyon to D'Arcy Osborne, n.d. [28 June 1923], RA QEQM/OUT/OSBORNE
6 Lady Elizabeth Bowes Lyon, diary, 25 April 1923, RA QEQM/PRIV/DIARY/3
7 Dorothy Laird, Queen Elizabeth The Queen Mother, Coronet, 1985, pp. 63–4
8 Duchess of York to Lady Strathmore, 26 April 1923, Glamis Archives (CH)
9 John Wheeler-Bennett, King George VI, Macmillan, 1958, p. 151.
10 Duke of York to King George V, 22 July 1924, RA GV/PRIV/AA61/213
11 Conversations with Eric Anderson, 1994–5, RA QEQM/ADD/MISC
12 King George V to Duke of York, 28 November 1924, RA GV/PRIV/AA61/228
13 Queen Mary to Duke of York, 2 December 1924, RA QM/PRIV/CC11/11
14 Duchess of York to Lady Strathmore, n.d. [30 November 1924], Glamis Archives (RA)
15 Duchess of York to Lady Strathmore, 29 December 1924, Glamis Archives (RA)
16 Duchess of York to D'Arcy Osborne, 31 January 1925, RA QEQM/OUT/OSBORNE
17 Captain Roy Salmon to his mother, 19 February 1925, private collection
18 Duchess of York to D'Arcy Osborne, 4 May 1925, RA QEQM/OUT/OSBORNE
19 Conversations with Eric Anderson, 1994–5, RA QEQM/ADD/MISC
20 Kenneth Rose, King George V, Weidenfeld & Nicolson, 1983, p. 343
21 Harold Nicolson, King George V: His Life and Reign, Pan Books, 1967,p. 543
22 Wheeler-Bennett, King George VI, p. 213
23 Duchess of York to Mrs Beevers, 5 October 1926, Beevers Papers
24 Duchess of York to Queen Mary, 30 December 1926, RA QM/PRIV/CC11/93
25 Duchess of York, diary, 6 January 1927, RA QEQM/PRIV/DIARY/6
26 King George V to Queen Mary, 29 August 1927, RA QM/PRIV/CC4/277
27 Duchess of York to Most Rev. Cosmo Lang, 10 September 1930, Lambeth Palace Library, Lang 318 f. 186
28 Duchess of York to Princess Elizabeth, 29 December 1935, RA QEII/PRIV/RF

29 Queen Elizabeth to Duke of Windsor, 11 December 1936, RA EDW/PRIV/MAIN/A/
    3068
30 Queen Elizabeth to Most Rev. Cosmo Lang, 12 December 1936, Lambeth Palace
    Library, Lang 318ff. 177–80

LETTERS/DIARIES

undated [9 January 1920]: Glamis Archives (CH)
11 June 1920: Glamis Archives (CH)
13 July 1920: Glamis Archives (CH)
undated [14 September 1920]: Glamis Archives (CH)
undated [23 September 1920]: Glamis Archives (CH)
undated [?November 1920]: Glamis Archives (CH)
undated [13 December 1920]: RA GVI/PRIV/RF/26/01
23 December 1920: RA GVI/PRIV/RF/26/02
10 January 1921: RA GVI/PRIV/RF/26/04
28 February 1921: RA GVI/PRIV/RF/26/07
6 March 1921: RA QEQM/OUT/SHAKERLEY
12 April 1921: Glamis Archives (CH)
undated [18 May 1921]: Glamis Archives (CH)
28 May 1921: RA GVI/PRIV/RF/26/10
9 June 1921: RA GVI/PRIV/RF/26/11
undated [18 July 1921]: RA GVI/PRIV/RF/26/12
6 August 1921: RA GVI/PRIV/RF/26/13
4 October 1921: RA GVI/PRIV/RF/26/15
11 October 1921: RA GVI/PRIV/RF/26/16
16 December 1921: RA GVI/PRIV/RF/26/21
undated [December 1921]: RA GVI/PRIV/RF/26/22
undated [8 March 1922]: RA GVI/PRIV/RF/26/26
undated [12 March 1922]: RA GVI/PRIV/RF/26/27
18 March 1922: RA GVI/PRIV/RF/26/28
3 October 1922: RA GVI/PRIV/RF/26/34
[26] October 1922: RA QEQM/OUT/OSBORNE
undated Friday [1922]: RA QEQM/OUT/OSBORNE
undated Friday [1922]: RA QEQM/OUT/OSBORNE
4 January 1923: RA GVI/PRIV/RF/26/49
4 January 1923: RA QEQM/PRIV/DIARY/3
5 January 1923: RA QEQM/PRIV/DIARY/3
6 January 1923: RA QEQM/PRIV/DIARY/3
7 January 1923: RA QEQM/PRIV/DIARY/3
undated [8 January 1923]: RA GVI/PRIV/RF/26/50
8 January 1923: RA QEQM/PRIV/DIARY/3
11 January 1923: RA QEQM/PRIV/DIARY/3
12 January 1923: RA QEQM/PRIV/DIARY/3
13 January 1923: RA QEQM/PRIV/DIARY/3
14 January 1923: RA QEQM/PRIV/DIARY/3
15 January 1923: RA QEQM/PRIV/DIARY/3
16 January 1923: Penn Papers
16 January 1923: RA QEQM/PRIV/DIARY/3
17 January 1923: RA GV/PRIV/AA61/342

17 January 1923: RA/QM/PRIV/CC11/34
17 January 1923: RA QEQM/OUT/OSBORNE
17 January 1923: RA QEQM/PRIV/DIARY/3
19 January 1923: Penn Papers
19 January 1923: RA QEQM/PRIV/DIARY/3
21 January 1923: Glamis Archives (CH)
25 January 1923: Glamis Archives (CH)
undated [25 January 1923]: RA GVI/PRIV/RF/26/51
4 February 1923: Glamis Archives (CH)
13 February 1923: RA QEQM/PRIV/DIARY/3
undated [February 1923]: RA GVI/PRIV/RF/26/53
undated [13 March 1923]: RA GVI/PRIV/RF/26/54
undated [14 March 1923]: RA GVI/PRIV/RF/26/55
19 March 1923: RA QEQM/PRIV/DIARY/3
undated [31 March 1923]: RA GVI/PRIV/RF/26/58
5 April 1923: RA QEQM/PRIV/DIARY/3
12 April 1923: RA QEQM/OUT/OSBORNE
24 April 1923: RA QEQM/PRIV/DIARY/3
25 April 1923: RA QEQM/PRIV/DIARY/3
26 April 1923: RA QEQM/PRIV/DIARY/3
undated [27 April 1923]: Glamis Archives (RA)
28 June 1923: RA QEQM/OUT/OSBORNE
19 September 1923: RA QM/PRIV/CC11/47
undated [27 September 1923]: RA GVI/PRIV/RF/26/60
17 October 1923: RA QEQM/OUT/OSBORNE
21 [22] October [1923]: Glamis Archives (Box 270)
26 October [1923]: Glamis Archives (CH)
8 January 1924: RA QEQM/PRIV/DIARY/4
14 January 1924: RA QEQM/PRIV/DIARY/4
14 January 1924 [misdated 1923]: RA GV/PRIV/AA61/343
17 March 1924: RA QEQM/OUT/OSBORNE
22 March 1924: RA QEQM/OUT/OSBORNE
26 April 1924: RA QEQM/PRIV/DIARY/4
3 June 1924: RA QEQM/PRIV/DIARY/4
2 October 1924: RA GV/PRIV/AA61/344
1 November 1924: RA QEQM/PRIV/DIARY/4
4 December 1924: RA QEQM/OUT/OSBORNE
11 December 1924: RA QEQM/PRIV/DIARY/4
12 December 1924: Glamis Archives (RA)
16 December 1924: RA QEQM/PRIV/DIARY/4
29 December 1924: Glamis Archives (RA)
13 January 1925: RA EDW/PRIV/MAIN/B/76
31 January 1925: RA QEQM/OUT/OSBORNE
undated [March 1925]: Glamis Archives (RA)
30 March 1925: Glamis Archives (270/II)
6 April 1925: RA QEQM/PRIV/DIARY/5
9 April 1925: RA QEQM/PRIV/DIARY/5
10 April 1925: RA QEQM/PRIV/DIARY/5
4 May 1925: RA QEQM/OUT/OSBORNE
9 May 1925: RA QEQM/PRIV/DIARY/5

10 September 1925: RA GVI/PRIV/RF/26/65

28 October 1925: RA QM/PRIV/CC11/82

8 January 1926: Beevers Papers

13 March 1926: RA QEQM/OUT/GRAHAM/1

12 April 1926: RA QM/PRIV/CC11/86

9 August 1926: Glamis Archives (CH)

5 October 1926: Beevers Papers

20 October 1926: RA QEQM/OUT/WALSH

28 October 1926: Glamis Archives (RA)

6 January 1927: RA QEQM/PRIV/DIARY/6

9 January 1927: RA QM/PRIV/CC11/95

9 January 1927: Bowes Lyon Papers (SPW)

11 January 1927: RA QEQM/PRIV/DIARY/6

5 February 1927: RA QEQM/PRIV/DIARY/6

9 February 1927: RA QM/PRIV/CC11/101

8 March 1927: RA QM/PRIV/CC11/104

15 March 1927: RA GVI/PRIV/RF/26/67

17 March 1927: RA QEQM/OUT/ELPHINSTONE

10 April 1927: Glamis Archives (RA)

20 April 1927: RA QM/PRIV/CC11/109

12 June 1927: RA GV/PRIV/AA61/32

22 September 1927: RA QM/PRIV/CC11/119

9 April 1928: RA QM/PRIV/CC11/122

13 July 1928: RA QEQM/OUT/OSBORNE

24 December 1928: RA QEQM/OUT/ELPHINSTONE

15 March 1929: RA QM/PRIV/CC11/135

16 March 1929: RA QEQM/OUT/OSBORNE

21 August 1929: RA GV/PRIV/AA61/86

11 November 1929: Sitwell Papers (Weston)

17 November 1929: RA QEQM/OUT/OSBORNE

31 December 1929: Beevers Papers

11 February 1930: RA QM/PRIV/CC11/153

11 March 1930: RA QEQM/OUT/OSBORNE

14 April 1930: RA QM/PRIV/CC11/154

undated Thursday [June 1930] RA QEQM/OUT/GRAHAM/47

31 July 1930: RA QM/PRIV/CC11/159

5 August 1930: RA QM/PRIV/CC11/161

27 August 1930: RA QM/PRIV/CC11/163

undated [27 August 1930]: RA GVI/PRIV/RF/26/69

6 September 1930: RA QM/PRIV/CC11/16

9 September 1930: RA GVI/PRIV/RF/26/70

10 September 1930: Lambeth Palace Library, Lang 318 f. 186

undated [12 September 1930]: RA GVI/PRIV/RF/26/72

1 October 1930: RA QEQM/OUT/GRAHAM/53

24 October 1930: Glamis Archives (CH)

17 December 1930: RA/GVI/OUT

26 January 1931: RA QM/PRIV/CC11/175

16 March 1931: Beevers Papers

20 March 1931: CAC, DUFC 11/2

19 June 1931: RA QEQM/OUT/MOLYNEUX/46

24 July 1931: RA GV/PRIV/AA 62/136

3 August 1931: RA QEQM/OUT/OSBORNE

16 September 1931: RA QM/PRIV/CC11/184

undated [January 1932]: RA QEQM/OUT/OSBORNE

30 April 1932: Beevers Papers

14 June 1932: RA QEQM/OUT/MOLYNEUX/59

5 August 1932: RA GV/PRIV/AA61/158

10 October 1932: RA QEQM/OUT/OSBORNE

30 November and 20 December 1932: RA QEQM/OUT/
    OSBORNE

20 February 1933: RA QEQM/OUT/GRAHAM/72

31 July 1933: Glamis Archives (CH)

1 August 1933: RA QM/PRIV/CC11/214

24 October 1933: Glamis Archives (Box 242, Bundle 7)

undated [1930–6]: RA QEQM/PRIV/PERS

12 January 1934: Lambeth Palace Library, Lang 318 f. 174

31 January 1934: CAC, DUFC 11/2

28 July 1934: RA QEQM/OUT/OSBORNE

6 August 1934: RA GV/PRIV/AA61/188

18 August 1934: RA QEQM/OUT/MOLYNEUX/71

23 February 1935: CAC, DUFC 11/2

1 April 1935: Vyner Papers

27 June 1935: CAC, DUFC 11/2

5 August 1935: RA QM/PRIV/CC 12/12

1 October 1935: CAC, DUFC 11/2

29 December 1935: RA QEII/PRIV/RF

29 December 1935: RA QEQM/OUT/MOLYNEUX/74

30 December 1935: RA GV/PRIV/AA61/241

3 January 1936: RA QEII/PRIV/RF

10 January 1936: RA QEQM/OUT/OSBORNE

18 January 1936: RA QM/PRIV/CC12/22

11 March 1936: RA QM/PRIV/CC12/24

3 August 1936: CAC, DUFC 11/2

27 August 1936: Glamis Archives (RA)

19 September 1936: RA QM/PRIV/CC12/32

11 October 1936: RA QM/PRIV/CC12/34

21 October 1936: RA QM/PRIV/CC12/36

23 October 1936: Glamis Archives (RA)

29 October 1936: RA EDW/MAIN/A/3024

undated [17 November 1936]: RA EDW/ADD/ABD/1

20 November 1936: RA EDW/ADD/ABD/1

23 November 1936: RA EDW/PRIV/MAIN/B/111

23 November 1936: Lady Murray Papers

3 December 1936: RA QEQM/OUT/MOLYNEUX/83

6 December 1936: RA QEQM/OUT/ELPHINSTONE

7 December 1936: Sitwell Papers (Weston)

7 December 1936: RA QEQM/OUT/MISC

10 December 1936: RA EDW/ADD/ABD/1

11 December 1936: RA EDW/PRIV/MAIN/A/3068

12 December 1936: Lambeth Palace Library, Lang 318 ff. 177–80

14 December 1936: RA QM/PRIV/CC12/40

16 December 1936: RA QEQM/OUT/OSBORNE

17 December 1936: Sitwell Papers (Weston)

14 January 1937: Lambeth Palace Library, Lang 318 ff. 181–3

2 February 1937: RA QM/PRIV/CC12/42

19 February 1937: RA QEQM/OUT/SITWELL

16 April 1937: Clark Papers

15 May 1937: Lambeth Palace Library, Lang 318 ff. 184–6

PART THREE: QUEEN

INTRODUCTION

1   Lord Wigram to Most Rev. Cosmo Lang, 5 April 1937, Lambeth Palace Library, Lang 318 ff. 136–7

2   Queen Mary to Queen Elizabeth, 21 May 1937, RA QEQM/PRIV/RF

3   Queen Elizabeth, notes, 4 September 1939, RA QEQM/PRIV/PERS

4   Queen Elizabeth to Queen Mary, 13 September 1940, RA QM/PRIV/CC12/135

5   Winston Churchill, *The Second World War*, Vol 3, p. 539 and Hansard 15 May 1945

6   Malcolm MacDonald to Queen Elizabeth, 27 December 1977, RA QEQM/PRIV/PAL

7   Queen Elizabeth to Princess Elizabeth, 24 November 1947, RA QEII/PRIV/RF

8   Sir Alan Lascelles to Queen Elizabeth, 23 September 1951, RA QEQM/PRIV/MISCOFF

9   Queen Elizabeth to Queen Mary, 6 February 1952, RA QM/PRIV/CC14/44

10   Queen Elizabeth to Sir Alan Lascelles, 15 February 1952, RA PS/PSO/AL/Box B

LETTERS/DIARIES

3 June 1937: RA QM/PRIV/CC14/74

18 August 1937: RA QM/PRIV/CC12/54

21 September 1937: RA GVI/OUT/MONCKTON

26 October 1937: RA QM/PRIV/CC12/61

7 December 1937: RA QEQM/OUT/MOLYNEUX/91

18 December 1937: Sitwell Papers (Weston)

5 January 1938: RA QEII/PRIV/RF

5 January 1938: RA QEQM/OUT/OSBORNE

15 January 1938: RA EDW/PRIV/MAIN/B/129

19 March 1938: Clark Papers

23 June 1938: Lambeth Palace Library, Lang 318 ff. 188–9

30 June 1938: Penn Papers

2 July 1938: BUA NC7/4/8

30 September 1938: BUA NC13/11/656

11 October 1938: Sitwell Papers (Weston)

13 December 1938: Clark Papers

9 February 1939: Clark Papers

5 May 1939: Lambeth Palace Library, Lang 318 ff. 193–4

6 May 1939: RA QEII/PRIV/RF

8 May 1939: RA QM/PRIV/CC12/93

13 May 1939: RA QEII/PRIV/RF

23 May 1939: RA QEII/PRIV/RF

27 May 1939: RA QEII/PRIV/RF

1 June 1939: RA QM/PRIV/CC12/99

5 June 1939: RA QEII/PRIV/RF

11 June 1939: RA QM/PRIV/CC12/101

11 June 1939: RA QEII/PRIV/RF

28 June 1939: RA QEQM/OUT/MISC

31 August 1939: RA QM/PRIV/CC12/110

4 September 1939: RA QEQM/PRIV/PERS

8 September 1939: Lambeth Palace Library, Lang 318 ff. 196–8

26 September 1939: RA QM/PRIV/CC12/113

2 October 1939: RA QEQM/OUT/PAUY (copy of original in
      The Prince Paul of Yugoslavia Papers, Box 2, Bakhmeteff
      Archive of Russian and East European History and Culture,
      Columbia University)

6 November 1939: Lambeth Palace Library, Lang 318 ff. 199–200

11 November 1939: RA QEQMH/SPE

12 November 1939: RA QEQM/OUT/GRAHAM/98

15 November 1939: BIUY Hickleton Papers, A2/278/26A 1

6 December 1939: RA QEQM/OUT/PAUY

1 February 1940: BIUY Hickleton Papers, A2/278/26A 3

1 February 1940: Sitwell Papers (Weston)

26 February 1940: RA QEQM/OUT/ELPHINSTONE

1 April 1940: Lady Murray Papers

1 April 1940: BIUY Hickleton Papers, A2/278/26A 4

17 May 1940: BUA NC1/23/81A Cadbury Research Library:
      Special Collections, University of Birmingham

11 June 1940: Franklin D. Roosevelt Presidential Library and
      Museum, Hyde Park, NY

24 July 1940: RA QM/PRIV/CC12/131

20 August 1940: RA QM/PRIV/CC12/132

13 September 1940: RA QM/PRIV/CC12/135

5 October 1940: RA AEC/GG/012

19 October 1940: RAQM/PRIV/CC12/139

25 October 1940: RA QEQM/OUT/ELPHINSTONE

31 October 1940: RA QM/PRIV/CC12/141

7 January 1941: RA QM/PRIV/CC12/147

14 January 1941: RA QEQM/OUT/GDK

7 February 1941: RA QEQM/OUT/ELPHINSTONE

5 March 1941: Linley/Chatto Papers

8 March 1941: RA QEII/PRIV/RF

21 March 1941: RA QM/PRIV/CC12/158

23 [22] March 1941: RA QEQMH/GEN/1990/W-Z (copy of
      MS 1416/1/4/8, Special Collections, Reading University)

23 April 1941: BIUY Hickleton Papers, A2/278/26A 1–6

12 May 1941: Martin Gilbert, *The Churchill War Papers*, vol 3,
      The Ever-Widening War. 1941, Heinemann 2000, p. 651

29 July 1941: Sitwell Papers (Weston)

10 August 1941: RA QEQMH/GEN/1941/America

28 August 1941: RA QM/PRIV/CC12/173

9 December 1941: RA QM/PRIV/CC12/179

28 December 1941: RA QM/PRIV/CC12/182

19 January 1942: RA QEQM/OUT/MISC (incomplete draft)

27 February 1942: Margaret Rhodes Papers

5 March 1942: Penn Papers

10 April 1942: RA QM/PRIV/CC13/10

5 June 1942: Vyner Papers

9 July 1942: RA QEQM/OUT/MOLYNEUX/107

31 August 1942: Bowes Lyon Papers (SPW)

13 September 1942: Sitwell Papers (Weston)

27 September 1942: Sitwell Papers (Weston)

30 September 1942: Penn Papers

30 September 1942: RA GVI/PRIV/RF/26/74

7 October 1942: Penn Papers

10 October 1942: RA GVI/PRIV/RF/26/76

12 October 1942: Penn Papers

13 October 1942: RA QM/PRIV/CC13/24

16 October 1942: Sitwell Papers (Weston)

19 October 1942: RA QM/PRIV/CC13/26

2 November 1942: RA QM/PRIV/CC13/28

2 December 1942: RA QEQM/OUT/ELPHINSTONE

21 December 1942: Clark Papers

3 January 1943: Sitwell Papers (Weston)

25 January 1943: Woods Papers

14 February 1943: Bowes Lyon Papers (SPW)

19 February 1943: RA QM/PRIV/CC13/39

5 March 1943: Sitwell Papers (Weston)

19 March 1943: Lady Murray Papers

21 March 1943: RA GVI/PRIV/RF/26/77

1 April 1943: RA QEQM/OUT/GRAHAM/107

6 April 1943: CAC, CHAR 20/98 A/54

11 April 1943: RA PS/PSO/AL/Box B

11 April 1943: RA QEQMH/PS/SPE

13 April 1943: CAC, CHAR 20/98A/56

15 April 1943: RA QEQM/OUT/ELPHINSTONE

18 April 1943: RA PS/PSO/AL/Box B

11 June 1943: RA QM/PRIV/CC13/54

14 June 1943: RA GVI/PRIV/RF/26/78

17 June 1943: RA GVI/PRIV/RF/26/79

24 June 1943: RA QM/PRIV/CC13/55

17 October 1943: Bowes Lyon Papers (SPW)

23 October 1943: RA QM/PRIV/CC13/69

20 November 1943: RA QM/PRIV/CC 13/74

30 November 1943: Sitwell Papers (Weston)

11 February 1944: Clark Papers

27 February 1944: Sitwell Papers (Weston)

7 March 1944: Bodleian Library, MS Bonham Carter 169/122–3

11 April 1944: RA QM/PRIV/CC13/85

4 May 1944: RA QEQM/OUT/ELPHINSTONE

4 May 1944: Sitwell Papers (Weston)

18 June 1944: Penn Papers

21 June 1944: Sitwell Papers (Weston)

26 June 1944: Clark Papers
27 June 1944: RA QEQM/OUT/CHILD
8 July 1944: RA QM/PRIV/CC13/93
17 July 1944: RA QM/PRIV/CC13/95
26 July 1944: RA GVI/PRIV/RF/26/80
26 July 1944: RA QM/PRIV/CC13/96
10 August 1944: Sitwell Papers (Weston)
19 August 1944: RA QM/PRIV/CC13/98
4 October 1944: RA PS/PSO/AL/Box B
9 October 1944: Penn Papers
6 November 1944: RA QM/PRIV/CC13/109
7 November 1944: Bowes Lyon Papers, (SPW)
13 November 1944: RA QM/PRIV/CC13/111
14 November 1944: Bowes Lyon Papers (SPW)
14 November 1944: CAC, CHAR 1/380/52
1 January 1945: By courtesy of Diana Way
26 January 1945: RA QM/PRIV/CC13/117
14 February 1945: RA QEQM/OUT/OSBORNE
20 March 1945: RA QEQM/OUT/MOLYNEUX/113
10 April 1945: RA QM/PRIV/CC13/121
12 May 1945: Vyner Papers
14 May 1945: Sitwell Papers (Weston)
11 June 1945: RA QM/PRIV/CC13/126
26 July 1945: RA QM/PRIV/CC13/128
15 August 1945: RA QEQM/OUT/GRAHAM/117
22 August 1945: Sitwell Papers (Weston)
18 September 1945: RA QM/PRIV/CC13/133
8 October 1945: Penn Papers
19 December 1945: RA QEQM/OUT/MOLYNEUX/115
31 December 1945: Beevers Papers
1 January [1946]: RA QEQM/OUT/OSBORNE
6 January 1946: Frankin D. Roosevelt Presidential Library and
        Museum, Hyde Park, NY
15 May 1946: RA QM/PRIV/CC13/148
25 September 1946: Hatfield House, Papers of Elizabeth,
        Marchioness of Salisbury
8 October 1946: RA GVI/PRIV/RF/26/82
9 October 1946: RA QEQM/OUT/ELPHINSTONE
12 November 1946: Sitwell Papers (Weston)
1 February 1947: RA QM/PRIV/CC13/162
21 February 1947: RA QM/PRIV/CC13/169
9 March 1947: RA QM/PRIV/CC13/172
16 April 1947: RA QM/PRIV/CC13/176
26 April 1947: RA QEQM/OUT/ELPHINSTONE
7 July 1947: RA QEQM/OUT/ELPHINSTONE
9 July 1947: The Duke of Edinburgh, Personal Archives,
        Buckingham Palace
10 July 1947: Sitwell Papers (Weston)
24 November 1947: RA QEII/PRIV/RF
30 November 1947: RA QEII/PRIV/RF

1 December 1947: The Duke of Edinburgh, Personal Archives, Buckingham Palace

26 April 1948: Penn Papers

27 July 1948: RA PS/PSO/AL/Box B

6 August 1948: Sitwell Papers (Weston)

14 November 1948: RA QM/PRIV/CC13/211

20 November 1948: RA QM/PRIV/CC13/212

8 December 1948: RA QM/PRIV/CC13/214

12 December 1948: RA QM/PRIV/CC13/216

27 December 1948: RA QEQM/PRIV/OUT/MISC

5 January 1949: RA QEQM/OUT/PAUY

13 February 1949: RA QM/PRIV/CC13/219

5 March 1949: RA QEQM/OUT/OSBORNE

8 May 1949: Linley/Chatto Papers

15 July 1949: The Duke of Edinburgh, Personal Archives, Buckingham Palace

21 July 1949: Franklin D. Roosevelt Presidential Library and Museum, Hyde Park, NY

29 November 1949: RA QEII/PRIV/RF

21 December 1949: RA QEII/PRIV/RF

21 December 1949: The Duke of Edinburgh, Personal Archives, Buckingham Palace

25 January 1950: RA QEQM/OUT/SITWELL

3 March 1950: The Duke of Edinburgh, Personal Archives, Buckingham Palace

27 March 1950: Cazalet Papers

24 April 1950: RA QEII/PRIV/RF

14 May 1950: Spencer Archives (Althorp)

24 May 1950: Cazalet Papers

21 June 1950: Sitwell Papers (Weston)

21 July 1950: The Duke of Edinburgh, Personal Archives, Buckingham Palace

15 October 1950: RA QM/PRIV/CC14/15

7 December 1950: Cazalet Papers

12 December 1950: RA QEII/PRIV/RF

29 December 1950: RA QEII/PRIV/RF

31 January 1951: RA QEII/PRIV/RF

7 April 1951: RA QEII/PRIV/RF

17 September 1951: RA QM/PRIV/CC14/36

23 September 1951: RA QM/PRIV/CC14/38

23 September 1951: RA PS/PSO/AL/Box B

15 October 1951: RA QEII/PRIV/RF

26 December 1951: Penn Papers

2 February 1952: RA QEII/PRIV/RF

6 February 1952: RA QM/PRIV/CC14/44

undated [9 February 1952]: The Duke of Edinburgh, Personal Archives, Buckingham Palace

11 February 1952: Penn Papers

11 February 1952: Spencer Archives (Althorp)

12 February 1952: RA PS/PSO/AL/Box B

15 February 1952: RA PS/PSO/AL/Box B
18 February 1952: RA QEQMH/PS/RF/DEATH/GVI
18 February 1952: CAC, CHUR 2/197

PART FOUR: QUEEN MOTHER

Introduction

1 Queen Elizabeth to Sir Alan Lascelles, 25 February 1952, RA PS/PSO/AL/Box B
2 Queen Elizabeth to D'Arcy Osborne, 29 November 1952, RA QEQM/OUT/OSBORNE
3 Queen Elizabeth to Rachel Bowes Lyon, 1 October 1961, Bowes Lyon Papers (SPW)
4 Frank Prochaska, *Royal Bounty: The Making of a Welfare Monarchy,* Yale University Press, 1995, p. 235
5 Queen Elizabeth's speech, January 1993, RA QEQMH/PS/PAT/Sandringham

Letters/Diaries

28 February 1952: Logue Papers
13 March 1952: Cazalet Papers
undated [?late February–March 1952]: RA QEII/PRIV/RF
31 March 1952: RA GVI/ADD/MISC/COPY
28 April 1952: Hatfield House, Papers of Elizabeth, Marchioness of Salisbury
3 May 1952: Sitwell Papers (Weston)
21 July 1952: RA QEII/PRIV/RF
6 August 1952: Penn Papers
undated [?early August 1952]: RA QEII/PRIV/RF
6 August 1952: Hatfield House, Papers of Elizabeth, Marchioness of Salisbury
31 August 1952: RA QM/PRIV/CC14/59
15 September 1952: Edith Sitwell Papers, Harry Ransom Centre, University of Austin, Texas
3 October 1952: Hatfield House, Papers of fifth Marquess of Salisbury
29 November 1952: CAC, LASL 2/3/5
29 November 1952: RA QEQM/OUT/OSBORNE
5 January 1953: The Prince Paul of Yugoslavia Papers, Box 2, Bakhmeteff Archive of Russian and East European History and Culture, Columbia University
3 February 1953: RA QEII/PRIV/RF
2 March 1953: RA QM/PRIV/CC14/62
13 April 1953: Vyner Papers
27 May 1953: RA QEII/PRIV/RF
12 June 1953: CAC, LASL/2/3/7
7 July 1953: RA QEII/PRIV/RF
9 July 1953: RA QEQM/OUT/SITWELL
23 August 1953: RA QEII/PRIV/RF
7 November 1953: RA QEII/PRIV/RF
11 November 1953: CAC, LASL 2/2/15
23 November 1953: RA QEII/PRIV/RF

14 December 1953: RA QEII/PRIV/RF

28 December 1953: RA QEII/PRIV/RF

10 January 1954: RA QEII/PRIV/RF

10 March 1954: RA QEII/PRIV/RF

28 March 1954: RA QEII/PRIV/RF

26 August 1954: RA QEII/PRIV/RF

13 September 1954: Penn Papers

26 September 1954: Hatfield House, Papers of Elizabeth,
    Marchioness of Salisbury

5 November 1954: RA QEII/PRIV/RF

13 November 1954: Linley/Chatto Papers

17 January 1955: CAC, LASL 2/2/20

9 September 1955: Linley/Chatto Papers

11 October 1955: Linley/Chatto Papers

29 October 1955: Bowes Lyon Papers (SPW)

23 January 1956: RA QEII/PRIV/RF

7 February 1956: RA QEII/PRIV/RF

28 March 1956: Cazalet Papers

12 April 1956: RA QEII/PRIV/RF

14 October 1956: RA QEQM/OUT/OSBORNE

14 January 1957: Sitwell Archives (Renishaw)

28 January 1957: RA QEII/PRIV/RF

1 July 1957: Clark Papers

9 February 1958: RA QEII/PRIV/RF

18 February 1958: RA QEII/PRIV/RF

18 February 1958: RA QEQM/OUT/BOYD-ROCHFORT

22 February 1958: Linley/Chatto Papers

1 March 1958: RA QEII/PRIV/RF

3 June 1958: RA QEQM/OUT/OSBORNE

5 June 1958: RA QEQM/OUT/BOYD-ROCHFORT

24 July 1958: Linley/Chatto Papers

30 January 1959: RA QEQM/OUT/OSBORNE

21 February 1959: Linley/Chatto Papers

14 April 1959: RA QEQM/OUT/BOYD-ROCHFORT

12 October 1959: Cazalet Papers

23 March 1960: Hatfield House, Papers of Elizabeth, Marchioness
    of Salisbury

7 May 1960: The Duke of Edinburgh, Personal Archives,
    Buckingham Palace

22 May 1960: Linley/Chatto Papers

25 August 1960: RA QEII/PRIV/RF

17 February 1961: RA QEII/PRIV/RF

7 April 1961: Penn Papers

23 May 1961: RA QEII/PRIV/RF

20 June 1961: RA QEQM/OUT/OSBORNE

20 August 1961: RA QEQM/OUT/BOYD-ROCHFORT

19 September 1961: RA QEII/PRIV/RF

20 September 1961: RA QEQM/OUT/MISC

10 November 1961: RA QEII/PRIV/RF

13 February 1962: RA QEQM/OUT/OSBORNE

1 August 1962: Bowes Lyon Papers (SPW)

7 February 1963: RA QEQM/OUT/OSBORNE

27 October 1963: Beaton Papers, by permission of the Masters and
Fellows of John's College, Cambridge

27 December 1963: RA QEQM/OUT/OSBORNE

31 December 1963: Sitwell Archives (Renishaw)

11 February 1964: Clarence House Archives

19 February 1964: The Duke of Edinburgh, Personal Archives,
Buckingham Palace

20 February 1964: Beaton Papers, by permission of the Masters and
Fellows of St John's College, Cambridge

28 March 1964: Linley/Chatto Papers

16 August 1964: Linley/Chatto Papers

11 January 1965: RA QEQMH/GEN/1971/P

29 June 1965: the letters of noël coward, edited by barry day,
methuen/drama 2007, p. 726

26 February 1966: Clarence House Archives

10 April 1966: Cazalet Papers

21 April 1966: Snowdon Papers

9 May 1966: Ballantrae Papers, NLS Acc 9259/109

10 July 1966: Clarence House Archives

15 August 1966: Red House Archives, Aldeburgh

15 December 1966: Clarence House Archives

7 August 1967: Clarence House Archives

3 April 1968: RA QEQM/OUT/BOYD-ROCHFORT

6 June 1968: RA QEQMH/GEN/1968/H–K

26 December 1968: RA QEQM/OUT/SITWELL

11 May 1969: Clarence House Archives

8 July 1969: Snowdon Papers

4 December 1969: The Duke of Edinburgh, Personal Archives,
Buckingham Palace

12 February 1970: Eton College Library, Diana Cooper Papers

10 August 1970: Red House Archives, Aldeburgh

14 August 1970: Clarence House Archives

7 February 1971: Harbottle Papers

18 June 1971: Penn Papers

3 October 1971: Clarence House Archives

3 December 1971: Clarence House Archives

16 December 1971: Snowdon Papers

undated [29 April 1972]: RA QEQMH/GEN/1972/N–Q

20 May 1972: Clarence House Archives

5 July 1972: Ballantrae Papers, NLS Acc 9259/109

17 July 1972: Bowes Lyon Papers (SPW)

17 August 1972: The Duke of Edinburgh, Personal Archives,
Buckingham Palace

6 March 1973: Snowdon Papers

27 June 1973: Cazalet Papers

29 June 1973: Clarence House Archives

14 December 1973: Red House Archives, Aldeburgh

20 February 1974: Red House Archives, Aldeburgh

4 June 1974: RA QEQM/OUT/BETJEMAN

14 July 1974: Clark Papers

18 August 1974: RA QEQM/OUT/ANST

4 Mar 1975: RA QEQM/OUT/BOYD-ROCHFORT

23 May 1975: Clarence House Archives

1 July 1975: Red House Archives, Aldeburgh

14 August 1975: RA QEII/PRIV/RF

18 August 1975: Red House Archives, Aldeburgh

1 September 1975: RA QEII/PRIV/RF

19 September 1975: The Duke of Edinburgh, Personal Archives,
    Buckingham Palace

24 November 1975: RA QEQM/OUT/PAUY

25 November 1975: Clarence House Archives

19 February 1976: Walwyn Papers

25 April 1976: RA QEII/PRIV/RF

23 September 1976: Stark Papers, John Murray Archive,
    Albemarle Street

2 November 1976: Clarence House Archives

11 June 1977: The Duke of Edinburgh, Personal Archives,
    Buckingham Palace

29 August 1977: RA QEII/PRIV/RF

2 November 1977: Collection of Anthony Russell-Roberts

26 August 1978: Clarence House Archives

23 September 1978: Farrell Papers

30 December 1978: Hugo Vickers Collection

4 February 1979: RA QEII/PRIV/RF

24 February 1979: RA QEQM/PRIV/RF

25 February 1979: Linley/Chatto Papers

15 August 1979: Farrell Papers

26 April 1980: RA QEII/PRIV/RF

22 May 1980: Clarence House Archives

5 August 1980: RA QEII/PRIV/RF

5 August 1980: Linley/Chatto Papers

22 October 1980: RA QEII/PRIV/RF

28 March 1981: Eton College Library, Diana Cooper Papers

17 May 1981: RA QEQM/OUT/ANST

21 May 1981: Farrell Papers

20 October 1981: Snowdon Papers

23 July 1982: Parker Bowles Papers

5 August 1982: Clarence House Archives

18 October 1982: RA QEII/PRIV/RF

3 December 1982: Walwyn Papers

8 January 1983: Cazalet Papers

17 February 1983: Hugo Vickers Collection

28 February 1983: RA QEII/PRIV/RF

19 April 1983: Clarence House Archives

18 September 1983: Walwyn Papers

19 November 1983: RA QEII/PRIV/RF

1 March 1984: The Duke of Edinburgh, Personal Archives,
    Buckingham Palace

6 August 1984: Clarence House Archives

3 October 1984: RA QEII/PRIV/RF

6 February 1985: RA QEII/PRIV/RF

22 March 1986: H. C. Knight Letters

10 April 1986: RA QEII/PRIV/RF

28 June 1986: Woods Papers

2 May 1988: RA QEII/PRIV/RF

3 June 1988: RA QEQMH/PS/SPE

19 July 1988: Bowes Lyon Papers (SPW)

10 September 1988: Cazalet Papers

24 September 1988: Clarence House Archives

26 December 1988: Clarence House Archives

11 February 1989: Windham Papers

11 February 1989: Stark Papers, John Murray Archive,
    Albemarle Street

24 June 1989: Acland Papers

5 September 1989: RA QEII/PRIV/RF

30 December 1989: Sir John Johnston Collection

13 April 1990: The Duke of Edinburgh, Personal Archives,
    Buckingham Palace

4 August 1990: Clarence House Archives

18 August 1990: RA QEII/OUT/HUGHES

27 April 1991: Snowdon Papers

12 July 1991: Wyatt Papers

25 January 1992: RA QEII/OUT/HUGHES

5 February 1992: RA QEII/PRIV/RF

22 February 1992: RA QEQM/OUT/MISC

5 June 1992: RA QEII/OUT/HUGHES

3 February 1993: RA QEII/PRIV/RF

21 April 1993: The Duke of Edinburgh, Personal Archives,
    Buckingham Palace

21 June 1993: RA QEII/PRIV/RF

18 July 1993: RA QEII/OUT/HUGHES

14 August 1994: Wyatt Papers

10 October 1994: RA CPW/OUT/HUGHES

19 October 1994: Crawford/Phipps Papers

10 June 1995: RA CPW/OUT/HUGHES

18 August 1995: RA CPW/OUT/HUGHES

29 January 1996: Bowes Lyon Papers (SPW)

9 February 1996: French Papers

10 June 1996: The Duke of Edinburgh, Personal Archives,
    Buckingham Palace

2 September 1996: RA QEII/PRIV/RF

7 January 1997: Slater Papers

15 February 1997: RA CPW/OUT/HUGHES

3 May 1997: RA QEII/PRIV/RF

26 June 1997: Acland Papers

7 February 1999: Harbottle Papers

29 August 2000: RA QEQM/OUT/SHAKERLEY

21 October 2000: Crawford/Phipps Papers

December 2000: Courtesy of Sir Michael Peat
4 June 2001: Farrell Papers
5 July 2001: Ogilvy Papers
August 2001: Clarence House Archives

INDEX